Modern Web Development with ASP.NET Core 3
Second Edition

An end to end guide covering the latest features of Visual Studio 2019, Blazor and Entity Framework

Ricardo Peres

BIRMINGHAM - MUMBAI

Modern Web Development with ASP.NET Core 3
Second Edition

Commissioning Editor: Richa Tripathi
Acquisition Editor: Alok Dhuri
Content Development Editor: Tiksha Lad
Senior Editor: Afshaan Khan
Technical Editor: Gaurav Gala
Copy Editor: Safis Editing
Project Coordinator: Deeksha Thakkar
Proofreader: Safis Editing
Indexer: Pratik Shirodkar
Production Designer: Alishon Mendonca

First published: November 2017
Second edition: June 2020

Production reference: 2130720

Published by Packt Publishing Ltd.
Livery Place
35 Livery Street
Birmingham
B3 2PB, UK.

ISBN 978-1-78961-976-8

www.packt.com

I would like to thank my son, Francisco, and daughter, Madalena, for all their love; they are the reason why I wrote this book.

Big thanks to Guilherme Castela and Pedro Januário: the best of friends. I couldn't have done it without you guys!

In memory of my parents, Irene and Jorge Peres, with love and "saudades."

`Packt.com`

Subscribe to our online digital library for full access to over 7,000 books and videos, as well as industry leading tools to help you plan your personal development and advance your career. For more information, please visit our website.

Why subscribe?

- Spend less time learning and more time coding with practical eBooks and Videos from over 4,000 industry professionals

- Improve your learning with Skill Plans built especially for you

- Get a free eBook or video every month

- Fully searchable for easy access to vital information

- Copy and paste, print, and bookmark content

Did you know that Packt offers eBook versions of every book published, with PDF and ePub files available? You can upgrade to the eBook version at `www.packt.com` and as a print book customer, you are entitled to a discount on the eBook copy. Get in touch with us at `customercare@packtpub.com` for more details.

At `www.packt.com`, you can also read a collection of free technical articles, sign up for a range of free newsletters, and receive exclusive discounts and offers on Packt books and eBooks.

Contributors

About the author

Ricardo Peres is a Portuguese developer, blogger, and book author and is currently a team leader at Dixons Carphone. He has over 20 years of experience in software development and his interests include distributed systems, architectures, design patterns, and .NET development. He won the Microsoft MVP award in 2015 and has held this title up to 2020.

He also authored *Entity Framework Core Cookbook – Second Edition* and *Mastering ASP.NET Core 2.0*, and was a technical reviewer for *Learning NHibernate 4* for Packt. He also contributed to Syncfusion's *Succinctly* collection, with titles on .NET development.

Ricardo maintains a blog—*Development With A Dot*—where he writes about technical issues. You can catch up with him on Twitter at `@rjperes75`.

About the reviewers

Alvin Ashcraft is a developer who lives near Philadelphia. He has spent his 25-year career building software with C#, Visual Studio, WPF, ASP.NET, and more. He has been awarded the Microsoft MVP title nine times. You can find his daily links for .NET developers on his blog, *Morning Dew*. He works as a principal software engineer for Allscripts, building healthcare software. He was previously employed by software companies, including Oracle. He has reviewed other titles for Packt Publishing, including *C# 8 and .NET Core 3 Projects Using Azure*, *Mastering Entity Framework Core 2.0*, and *Learn ASP.NET Core 3*.

Prakash Tripathi is a technical manager by profession and a speaker and author by passion. He has extensive experience in the design, development, maintenance, and support of enterprise applications, primarily using Microsoft technologies and platforms. He is active in technical communities and has been awarded the Microsoft MVP title four times in a row since 2016. He holds a master's degree in computer applications from MANIT Bhopal, India.

Packt is searching for authors like you

If you're interested in becoming an author for Packt, please visit `authors.packtpub.com` and apply today. We have worked with thousands of developers and tech professionals, just like you, to help them share their insight with the global tech community. You can make a general application, apply for a specific hot topic that we are recruiting an author for, or submit your own idea.

Table of Contents

Section 2: Improving Productivity

Section 3: Advanced Topics

Preface

In this book, we will discuss the new and latest features that have been added by Microsoft to ASP.NET Core 3.

We will delve deep into the applications and understand how to apply them for the various new tools that have been introduced. We will be looking at Blazor, gRPC, the `dotnet` tools, error handling methods, and Razor Pages. We have so many new topics to look at this time, so it is going to be one hell of a joyride. Sit back and enjoy!

Who this book is for

If you are a developer with basic knowledge of the ASP.NET MVC framework and want to build powerful applications, then this book is for you. Developers who want to explore the latest changes in ASP.NET Core 3.0 to build professional-level applications will also find this book useful. Familiarity with C#, ASP.NET Core, HTML, and CSS is expected in order to get the most out of this book.

What this book covers

Chapter 1, *Getting Started with ASP.NET Core*, explains the very basics of .NET and ASP.NET Core, including the MVC pattern, which is the typical usage pattern of ASP.NET Core.

Chapter 2, *Configuration*, presents you with the configuration options available to .NET/ASP.NET Core developers.

Chapter 3, *Routing*, explains how an HTTP request is mapped to controller actions by means of routes, how they are selected, and how the parameters are matched.

Chapter 4, *Controllers and Actions*, explains how controllers and actions work, what API and OData controllers are, what the life cycle of a controller is, and how controllers are found.

Chapter 5, *Views*, explains how to work with views, which make up the user interface of ASP.NET Core.

Chapter 6, *Using Forms and Models*, shows us how to work with user-submitted data in forms.

Chapter 7, *Implementing Razor Pages,* describes what Razor Pages are—an alternative development model for ASP.NET Core.

Chapter 8, *API Controllers,* shows us how to work with API (non-visual) controllers.

Chapter 9, *Reusable Components,* talks about reusability in ASP.NET Core.

Chapter 10, *Understanding Filters,* talks about the different kinds of filters available to ASP.NET Core developers.

Chapter 11, *Security,* shows us how to implement authentication and authorization. Here, we will also cover how to enforce HTTPS security and how to prevent tampering.

Chapter 12, *Logging, Tracing, and Diagnostics,* explains how we can get a glimpse of what is going on with our ASP.NET Core application.

Chapter 13, *Understanding How Testing Works,* explains how to add unit and functional/integration tests to our solutions.

Chapter 14, *Client-Side Development,* covers how to integrate ASP.NET Core with common client-side frameworks.

Chapter 15, *Improving the Performance and Scalability,* covers how to improve the performance of our web application.

Chapter 16, *Real-Time Communication,* will help us learn how to apply real-time communication techniques to code.

Chapter 17, *Introducing Blazor,* is a new addition to this version and will explain Blazer for interoperability, dependency injections, HTTP calls, and more.

Chapter 18, *gRPC and Other Topics,* is a collection of topics and framework details that an ASP.NET Core developer ought to know but that didn't fit into the rest of the chapters of this book.

Chapter 19, *Application Deployment,* will help us learn how to deploy an ASP.NET Core application to different targets, such as on-premises and the cloud.

Chapter 20, *Appendix A: The dotnet Tool,* provides a short description of the basics and other useful topics relating to ASP.NET Core, including a description of its tools and features.

To get the most out of this book

It is good to be familiar with C#, ASP.NET Core, HTML, and CSS to get the most out of this book. It does go without saying that reading the first edition of this book will prove helpful.

Software/hardware covered in this book	OS requirements
Docker	Windows or Linux
Visual Studio 2019 Community edition	Windows, Linux

Download the example code files

You can download the example code files for this book from your account at www.packt.com. If you purchased this book elsewhere, you can visit www.packtpub.com/support and register to have the files emailed directly to you.

You can download the code files by following these steps:

1. Log in or register at www.packt.com.
2. Select the **Support** tab.
3. Click on **Code Downloads**.
4. Enter the name of the book in the **Search** box and follow the onscreen instructions.

Once the file is downloaded, please make sure that you unzip or extract the folder using the latest version of:

- WinRAR/7-Zip for Windows
- Zipeg/iZip/UnRarX for Mac
- 7-Zip/PeaZip for Linux

The code bundle for the book is also hosted on GitHub at https://github.com/PacktPublishing/Modern-Web-Development-with-ASP.NET-Core-3-Second-Edition. In case there's an update to the code, it will be updated on the existing GitHub repository.

We also have other code bundles from our rich catalog of books and videos available at https://github.com/PacktPublishing/. Check them out!

Download the color images

We also provide a PDF file that has color images of the screenshots/diagrams used in this book. You can download it here: https://static.packt-cdn.com/downloads/9781789619768_ColorImages.pdf.

Conventions used

There are a number of text conventions used throughout this book.

CodeInText: Indicates code words in text, database table names, folder names, filenames, file extensions, pathnames, dummy URLs, user input, and Twitter handles. Here is an example: "Keep in mind that, in general, claims do not mean anything, but, there are a few exceptions: Name and Role can be used for security checks, as we will see in a moment..."

A block of code is set as follows:

```
var principal = new WindowsPrincipal(identity);
var isAdmin = principal.IsInRole(WindowsBuiltInRole.Administrator);
```

When we wish to draw your attention to a particular part of a code block, the relevant lines or items are set in bold:

```
"iisSettings": {
  "windowsAuthentication": true,
  "anonymousAuthentication": false,
  "iisExpress": {
    "applicationUrl": "http://localhost:5000/",
    "sslPort": 0
  }
}
```

Any command-line input or output is written as follows:

```
Add-Migration "Initial"
Update-Database
```

Bold: Indicates a new term, an important word, or words that you see onscreen. For example, words in menus or dialog boxes appear in the text like this. Here is an example: "Right-click on the web project and select **New Scaffolded Item...**"

Warnings or important notes appear like this.

 Tips and tricks appear like this.

Get in touch

Feedback from our readers is always welcome.

General feedback: If you have questions about any aspect of this book, mention the book title in the subject of your message and email us at customercare@packtpub.com.

Errata: Although we have taken every care to ensure the accuracy of our content, mistakes do happen. If you have found a mistake in this book, we would be grateful if you would report this to us. Please visit www.packtpub.com/support/errata, selecting your book, clicking on the Errata Submission Form link, and entering the details.

Piracy: If you come across any illegal copies of our works in any form on the Internet, we would be grateful if you would provide us with the location address or website name. Please contact us at copyright@packt.com with a link to the material.

If you are interested in becoming an author: If there is a topic that you have expertise in and you are interested in either writing or contributing to a book, please visit authors.packtpub.com.

Reviews

Please leave a review. Once you have read and used this book, why not leave a review on the site that you purchased it from? Potential readers can then see and use your unbiased opinion to make purchase decisions, we at Packt can understand what you think about our products, and our authors can see your feedback on their book. Thank you!

For more information about Packt, please visit packt.com.

Section 1: The Fundamentals of ASP.NET Core 3

This first section will cover the fundamentals of ASP.NET Core and the **Model-View-Controller** (**MVC**) pattern and how the two meet, and .NET Core and its concepts will be explored.

This section has the following chapters:

Getting Started with ASP.NET Core

Welcome to my new book on ASP.NET Core 3!

.NET and ASP.NET Core are relatively new in the technological landscape, as they were only officially released in August 2017. Given that .NET is in the name, you would think that these would probably only be new versions of the highly popular .NET Framework, but that is not the case: we are talking about something that is truly new!

It's not just multiplatform support (howdy, Linux!), but it's so much more. It's the new modularity in everything: the transparent way by which we can now change things—the source code in front of our eyes teasing us to contribute to it, to make it better—is indeed a lot different from previous versions of .NET Core!

In this first chapter, we are going to talk a bit about what changed in ASP.NET and .NET in the core versions, and also about the new underlying concepts, such as OWIN, runtime environments, and **dependency injection** (**DI**).

In this chapter, we will cover the following topics:

- History of ASP.NET Core
- Introduction to .NET Core
- Inversion of control and DI
- OWIN
- The MVC pattern
- Hosting
- Environments
- How the bootstrap process works for ASP.NET Core apps
- The generic host

- What's new since ASP.NET Core 2
- The NuGet and `dotnet` tools

Technical requirements

This chapter does not require any particular software component, as it deals more with concepts.

You can find the GitHub link at `https://github.com/PacktPublishing/Modern-Web-Development-with-ASP.NET-Core-3-Second-Edition`.

Getting started

Microsoft ASP.NET was released 15 years ago, in 2002, as part of the then shiny new .NET Framework. It inherited the name **ASP** (short for **Active Server Pages**) from its predecessor, with which it barely shared anything else, other than being a technology for developing dynamic server-side content for the internet, which ran on Windows platforms only.

ASP.NET gained tremendous popularity, it has to be said, and competed hand to hand with other popular web frameworks, such as **Java Enterprise Edition (JEE)** and PHP. In fact, it still does, with sites such as **BuiltWith** giving it a share of 21% (ASP.NET and ASP.NET MVC combined), way ahead of Java (`https://trends.builtwith.com/framework`). ASP.NET was not just for writing dynamic web pages. It could also be used for XML (SOAP) web services, which, in early 2000, were quite popular. It benefited from the .NET Framework and its big library of classes and reusable components, which made enterprise development almost seem easy!

Its first version, ASP.NET 1, introduced web forms, an attempt to bring to the web the event and component model of desktop-style applications, shielding users from some of the less friendly aspects of HTML, HTTP, and state maintenance. To a degree, it was highly successful; using Visual Studio, you could easily create a data-driven dynamic site in just a few minutes! A great deal of stuff could be accomplished merely through markup, with no code changes (read or compile) needed.

Version 2 came along a few years afterward, and among all the other goodies, it brought with it extensibility in the form of a provider model. A lot of its functionality could be adapted by the means of custom providers. Later on, it received the addition of the AJAX Extensions, which made AJAX-style effects astonishingly easy. It set the standard for years to come, leaving only room for more components.

To be honest, the following versions, 3.5, 4, and 4.5, only offered more of the same, with new specialized controls for displaying data and charts for retrieving and manipulating data and a few security improvements. A big change was that some of the framework libraries were released as open source.

Between versions 3.5 and 4, Microsoft released a totally new framework, based on the **model-view-controller** (**MVC**) pattern, and it was mostly open source. Although it sits on top of the infrastructure laid out by ASP.NET, it offered a whole new development paradigm, which this time fully embraced HTTP and HTML. It seemed to be the current trend for web development across technologies, and the likes of PHP, Ruby, and Java, and .NET developers were generally pleased with it. ASP.NET developers now had two choices—Web Forms and MVC, both sharing the ASP.NET pipeline and .NET libraries, but offering two radically different approaches to getting content to the browser.

In the meantime, the now venerable .NET Framework had grown up in an ever-changing world. In the modern enterprise, the needs have changed, and sentences such as *runs on Windows only* or *we need to wait XX years for the next version* became barely acceptable. Acknowledging this, Microsoft started working on something new, something different that would set the agenda for years to come. Enter .NET Core!

In late 2014, Microsoft announced .NET Core. It was meant to be a platform-independent, language-agnostic, free, and open source full rewrite of the .NET Framework. Its main characteristics were as follows:

- The base class libraries of .NET were to be rewritten from scratch while keeping the same (simplified) public APIs, which meant that not all of them would be initially available.
- It was also able to run on non-Windows operating systems, specifically several Linux and macOS flavors, and in mobile devices, so all Windows-specific code (and APIs) would be discarded.
- All of its components were to be delivered as NuGet packages, meaning that only a small bootstrap binary would need to be installed in the host machine.

- There was no longer a dependency (or, let's say, a very close relationship) with IIS, so it was able to be autohosted or run inside a hosting process, like, well, IIS.
- It would be open source and developers would be able to influence it, either by creating issues or by submitting pull requests.

This eventually took place in July 2016, when version 1.0 of .NET Core was released. The .NET developers could now write once and deploy (almost) everywhere and they finally had a say on the direction the framework was taking!

Rewriting the whole .NET Framework from scratch is a task of epic proportions, so Microsoft had to make decisions and define priorities. One of them was to ditch ASP.NET Web Forms and to only include MVC. So gone were the days when ASP.NET and Web Forms were synonyms, and the same happened with ASP.NET Core and MVC: it's now just ASP.NET Core! And it's not just that the ASP.NET Web API, which used to be a different project type, was now merged with ASP.NET Core as well (a wise decision from Microsoft, as basically the two technologies, MVC and Web API, had a lot of overlap and even had classes with the same name for pretty much the same purpose).

So, what does this mean for developers? Here are my personal thoughts about how the tech has fared:

- C#, Visual Basic, and F#; F# has gained a lot of momentum among the developer communities, and they have built templates for Visual Studio as well as lots of useful libraries.
- Open source is great! If you want to change anything, you can just grab the code from GitHub and make the changes yourself! If they're good enough, then chances are that others may be interested in them too, so why not submit a pull request to have them integrated?
- We don't need to decide upfront if we want to use MVC or the web API. It's just a matter of adding one or two NuGet packages anytime and adding a couple of lines to the `Startup.cs` file; the same controller can serve both API and web requests seamlessly.
- Attribute routing is built in, so there's no need for any explicit configuration.
- ASP.NET Core now uses **Open Web Interface for .NET (OWIN)** based middleware and configuration, so you will need to (significantly) change your modules and handlers so that they fit into this model; MVC/web API filters are basically the same.

- There is no dependency on IIS or Windows, meaning that we can easily write our apps in good old Windows/Visual Studio and then just deploy them to Azure/AWS/Docker/Linux/macOS. It's actually pretty cool to debug our app in Docker/Linux from Visual Studio! It can run self-hosted in a console application too.
- A consequence of the latter is that there are no more **IIS Manager** or `web.config/machine.config` files.
- Not all libraries are already available for .NET Core, meaning that you will either need to find replacements or implement the features yourself. The website `https://icanhasdot.net/Stats` has a good list of whatever is/is not available for .NET Core, and there is also a list in the project's roadmap at `https://github.com/dotnet/core/blob/master/roadmap.md`.
- Even the core (pun intended) .NET Core classes are still lacking some methods that used to be there; take, for example, some methods in the `System.Environment` class.
- You need to handpick the NuGet packages for the libraries you want to use, including for classes that you took for granted in the old days. For .NET; this includes, for example, `System.Collections` (`https://www.nuget.org/packages/System.Collections`), as they are not automatically referenced. Sometimes it's hard to find out which NuGet package contains the classes you want; when this happens, `http://packagesearch.azurewebsites.net` may come in handy.
- There is no more Web Forms (and the visual designer in Visual Studio); now it's MVC all the way, or Blazor, which offers some resemblance to Web Forms, and has some advantages too! Yay!

Let's see begin by looking at what .NET Core is all about.

Beginning with .NET Core

Talking about ASP.NET Core without explaining .NET Core is somewhat cumbersome. .NET Core is the framework everyone is talking about, and for good reasons. ASP.NET Core is probably the most interesting API right now, as it seems that everything is moving to the web.

And why is that? Well, all these APIs relied heavily on Windows-native features; in fact, Windows Forms was merely a wrapper around the Win32 API that has accompanied Windows since its early days. Because .NET Core is multiplatform, it would be a tremendous effort to have versions of these APIs for all supported platforms. But of course, in no way does this mean that it won't happen; it's just that it hasn't happened yet.

With .NET Core, a host machine only needs a relatively small bootstrap code to run an application; the app itself needs to include all the reference libraries that it needs to operate. Interestingly, it is possible to compile a .NET Core application to native format, thereby producing a machine-specific executable that includes in it all the dependencies, and can even be run in a machine without the .NET Core bootstrapper.

As I said previously, .NET Core was written from scratch, which unfortunately means that not all the APIs that we were used to have been ported. Specifically, as of version 3, the following features are still missing:

- ASP.NET Web Forms (`System.Web.UI`)
- XML Web Services (`System.Web.Services`)
- LINQ to SQL (`System.Data.Linq`)
- Windows Communication Foundation server-side classes (`System.ServiceModel`)
- Windows Workflow Foundation (`System.Workflow` and `System.Activities`)
- .NET Remoting (`System.Runtime.Remoting`)
- Active Directory/LDAP (`System.DirectoryServices`)
- Enterprise Services (`System.EnterpriseServices`)
- Email (`System.Net.Mail`)
- XML and XSD (`System.Xml.Xsl` and `System.Xml.Schema`)
- I/O ports (`System.IO.Ports`)
- Managed Addin Framework (`System.Addin`)
- Speech (`System.Speech`)
- Configuration (`System.Configuration`); this one was replaced with a new configuration API (`Microsoft.Extensions.Configuration`)
- Windows Management Instrumentation (`System.Management`)
- Windows Registry (`Microsoft.Win32`) in operating systems other than Windows

This is by no means an exhaustive list. As you can see, there are a lot of features missing. Still, it is quite possible to achieve pretty much whatever we need to, provided we do things in a different way and handle the extra burden! Mind you, Windows Forms and WPF are already supported on all platforms.

The following APIs are new or still around, and are safe to use:

- MVC and Web API (`Microsoft.AspNetCore.Mvc`)
- Entity Framework Core (`Microsoft.EntityFrameworkCore`)
- Roslyn for code generation and analysis (`Microsoft.CodeAnalysis`)
- All Azure APIs
- Managed Extensibility Framework (`System.Composition`)
- Text encoding/decoding and regular expression processing (`System.Text`)
- JSON serialization (`System.Runtime.Serialization.Json`)
- Low-level code generation (`System.Reflection.Emit`)
- Most of ADO.NET (`System.Data`, `System.Data.Common`, `System.Data.SqlClient`, and `System.Data.SqlTypes`)
- LINQ and Parallel LINQ (`System.Linq`)
- Collections, including concurrent (`System.Collections`, `System.Collections.Generic`, `System.Collections.ObjectModel`, `System.Collections.Specialized`, and `System.Collections.Concurrent`)
- Threading, inter-process communication, and task primitives (`System.Threading`)
- Input/output, compression, isolated storage, memory-mapped files, pipes (`System.IO`)
- XML (`System.Xml`)
- Windows Communication Foundation client-side classes (`System.ServiceModel`)
- Cryptography (`System.Security.Cryptography`)
- Platform Invoke and COM Interop (`System.Runtime.InteropServices`)
- Universal Windows Platform (`Windows`)
- Event Tracing for Windows (`System.Diagnostics.Tracing`)
- Data Annotations (`System.ComponentModel.DataAnnotations`)
- Networking, including HTTP (`System.Net`)
- Reflection (`System.Reflection`)
- Maths and numerics (`System.Numerics`)

- Reactive Extensions (`System.Reactive`)
- Globalization and localization (`System.Globalization`, `System.Resources`)
- Caching (including in-memory and Redis) (`Microsoft.Extensions.Caching`)
- Logging (`Microsoft.Extensions.Logging`)
- Configuration (`Microsoft.Extensions.Configuration`)

Again, this is not the full list, but you get the picture. These are just Microsoft APIs that are made available for .NET Core; there are obviously thousands of others from different vendors.

 And why are these APIs supported? Well, because they are specified in **.NET Standard**, and .NET Core implements this standard! More on this in a moment.

In .NET Core, there is no longer a **Global Assembly Cache** (**GAC**), but there is a centralized location (per user) for storing NuGet packages, called `%HOMEPATH%.nugetpackages`, which prevents you from having duplicated packages locally for all of your projects. .NET Core 2.0 introduced the **runtime store**, which is somewhat similar to GAC. Essentially, it is a folder on a local machine where some packages are made available and compiled for the machine's architecture. Packages stored there are never downloaded from NuGet; they are instead referenced locally and do not need to be included with your app. A welcome addition, I have to say! You can read more about metapackages and the runtime store at `https://docs.microsoft.com/en-us/aspnet/core/fundamentals/metapackage`.

As of ASP.NET Core 2.1, a change was made from the previous version: whereas before there was a dependency on the `Microsoft.AspNetCore.All` metapackage, now the dependency is on `Microsoft.AspNetCore.App`. To cut a long story short, this one has far fewer dependencies. Specifically, the following dependencies have been removed:

- `Microsoft.Data.Sqlite`
- `Microsoft.Data.Sqlite.Core`
- `Microsoft.EntityFrameworkCore.Sqlite`
- `Microsoft.EntityFrameworkCore.Sqlite.Core`
- `Microsoft.Extensions.Caching.Redis`
- `Microsoft.AspNetCore.DataProtection.AzureStorage`

- Microsoft.Extensions.Configuration.AzureKeyVault
- Microsoft.AspNetCore.DataProtection.AzureKeyVault
- Microsoft.AspNetCore.Identity.Service.AzureKeyVault
- Microsoft.AspNetCore.AzureKeyVault.HostingStartup
- Microsoft.AspNetCore.ApplicationInsights.HostingStartup

Visual Studio templates for .NET Core since version 3.0 already reference this new metapackage, and in general, things should just work; you may need to add explicit references to one of these missing packages, if you use it.

Interestingly, since version 3, you no longer need to reference this metapackage in your .csproj file; it is referenced by default when you reference the .NET Core 3 framework. The following is a minimum .NET Core 3 .csproj file:

```
<Project Sdk="Microsoft.NET.Sdk.Web">
  <PropertyGroup>
    <TargetFramework>netcoreapp3.1</TargetFramework>
  </PropertyGroup>
</Project>
```

For .NET Core 3.1, you should replace netcoreapp3.0 with netcoreapp3.1. In a moment, we will learn more about this.

NuGet packages are at the heart of .NET Core, and mostly everything needs to be obtained from NuGet. Even projects in the same Visual Studio solution are referenced from one another as NuGet packages. When using .NET Core, you will need to explicitly add the NuGet packages that contain the functionality that you wish to use. It is likely that you may come across some of the following packages in some of your projects:

Package	Purpose
Microsoft.AspNetCore.Authentication.JwtBearer	JWT authentication
Microsoft.AspNetCore.Mvc.TagHelpers	Tag helpers
Microsoft.EntityFrameworkCore	Entity Framework Core
Microsoft.Extensions.Caching.Memory	In-memory caching
Microsoft.Extensions.Caching.Redis	Redis caching
Microsoft.Extensions.Configuration	General configuration classes

`Microsoft.Extensions.Configuration.EnvironmentVariables`	Configuration from environment variables
`Microsoft.Extensions.Configuration.Json`	Configuration from JSON files
`Microsoft.Extensions.Configuration.UserSecrets`	Configuration from user secrets (`https://docs.microsoft.com/en-us/aspnet/core/security/app-secrets`)
`Microsoft.Extensions.Configuration.Xml`	Configuration in XML
`Microsoft.Extensions.DependencyInjection`	Built-in DI framework
`Microsoft.Extensions.Logging`	Logging base classes
`Microsoft.Extensions.Logging.Console`	Logging to the console
`Microsoft.Extensions.Logging.Debug`	Logging to debug
`System.Collections`	Collections
`System.ComponentModel`	Classes and interfaces used in the definition of components and data sources
`System.ComponentModel.Annotations`	Data annotations for validation and metadata
`System.Data.Common`	ADO.NET
`System.Globalization`	Globalization and localization APIs
`System.IO`	Input/output APIs

`System.Linq.Parallel`	Parallel LINQ
`System.Net`	Networking APIs
`System.Reflection`	Reflection
`System.Security.Claims`	Security based upon claims
`System.Threading.Tasks`	Tasks implementation
`System.Xml.XDocument`	XML APIs
`System.Transactions`	Ambient transactions

Again, this not an exhaustive list, but you get the picture. You may not see references to all of these packages, because adding one package that has dependencies will bring all these dependencies along, and big packages have a lot of dependencies.

There are no more `.exe` files; now, all assemblies are `.dll`, which means that they need to be run using the `dotnet` command-line utility. All .NET Core applications start with a static `Main` method, as the .NET Framework Console and Windows Forms did, but now we need the `dotnet` utility to run them. The `dotnet` tool is a very versatile tool, and can be used to build, run, deploy, and restore NuGet packages, execute unit tests, and create NuGet packages from a project. As I said, it is also possible to compile an assembly to the native format, but we won't be covering that here.

.NET Core ships with built-in DI, logging, and a flexible configuration framework, which allows you to plug in your own providers if you so wish. All of the new APIs (such as Entity Framework Core and ASP.NET Core) use these services uniformly. For the very first time, we can see a coherent behavior across APIs.

Also, most productivity APIs, such as ASP.NET and Entity Framework, allow you to replace the services they're built upon with customized versions, allowing you to make them work exactly the way you want them to—provided, of course, that you know what you are doing—and these services are generally based upon interfaces. Everything is much more modular and transparent.

Unit testing got first-class citizenship in .NET Core. Most new APIs were designed with testability in mind (think, for example, of the new in-memory provider for Entity Framework Core), and the tooling (`dotnet`) has an explicit option for executing unit tests, which can be written in any framework (currently, **xUnit**, **NUnit**, **MbUnit**, and **MSTest**, among others, have released unit test frameworks compatible with .NET Core). We will cover unit testing in `Chapter 13`, *Understanding How Testing Works*.

Next, let's look at the platforms that support .NET Core.

Supported platforms

.NET Core works on the following platforms:

- Windows 7 SP1 or higher
- Windows Server 2008 R2 SP1 or higher
- Red Hat Enterprise Linux 7.2 or higher
- Fedora 23 or higher
- Debian 8.2 or higher
- Ubuntu 14.04 LTS/16.04 LTS, or higher
- Linux Mint 17 or higher
- openSUSE 13.2 or higher
- CentOS 7.1 or higher
- Oracle Linux 7.1 or higher
- macOS X 10.11 or higher

This covers all modern Windows, Linux, and macOS distributions (Windows 7 SP1 was released in 2010). It may well work in other distributions, but these are the ones that have been thoroughly tested by Microsoft.

So, how does this work? It turns out that whenever you request a NuGet package that needs native libraries that are not included in the operating system, these are also included in the .nupkg archive. .NET Core uses **Platform Invoke** (**P/Invoke**) to call the operating-system-specific libraries. This means that you do not have to worry about the process to be located—adding a NuGet package and publishing the project is the same no matter what the target operating system will be.

Keep in mind that platform independence is transparent to you, the developer—unless, of course, you also happen to be a library author, in which case you may need to care about it.

Let's now see how the different frameworks that used to make up .NET are now supported.

Dependencies and frameworks

Inside a .NET Core project, you specify the frameworks that you wish to target. What are these frameworks? Well, .NET Core itself, but the classic .NET Framework as well, Xamarin, **Universal Windows Platform** (**UWP**), **Portable Class Libraries** (**PCL**), Mono, Windows Phone, and more.

In the early days of .NET Core, you would either target .NET Core itself, or/as well as one of these other frameworks. Now it is advisable to target standards instead. Now we have .NET Standard, and the differences between the two are as follows:

- .NET Standard is a specification (a contract) that covers which APIs a .NET platform has to implement.
- .NET Core is a concrete .NET platform and implements the .NET Standard.
- The latest .NET Standard will always cover the highest .NET full framework released.

David Fowler (https://twitter.com/davidfowl) of Microsoft came up with the following analogy:

```
interface INetStandard10
{
    void Primitives();
    void Reflection();
    void Tasks();
    void Collections();
    void Linq();
}


interface INetStandard11 : INetStandard10
{
    void ConcurrentCollections();
    void InteropServices();
}

interface INetFramework45 : INetStandard11
{
    // Platform specific APIs
    void AppDomain();
    void Xml();
    void Drawing();
    void SystemWeb();
    void WPF();
    void WindowsForms();
```

```
        void WCF();
    }
```

This should make it very easy to understand. As you can see, all .NET APIs that need Windows (WPF, Windows Forms, Drawing) are only available in a specific platform (.NET 4.5), not a standard. Standards are for cross-platform functionality.

 For more information, please refer to `https://docs.microsoft.com/en-us/dotnet/articles/standard/library`.

So instead of targeting a specific version, such as .NET 4.5.1, .NET Core 1.0, Mono, Universal Windows Platform 10, you should target a .NET Standard. Your project is guaranteed to work on all platforms that support that standard (or a higher one), either existing or waiting to be created. You should try to keep your dependency to the lowest standard possible to increase the number of platforms that your app will work on, if that is important to you.

The current mapping between the different .NET frameworks and the .NET Standard they implement at the time this book was written is always available at `https://github.com/dotnet/standard/blob/master/docs/versions.md`.
.NET Core 2.0 and .NET Standard 2.0 were made available in August 2017, and now four frameworks target .NET Standard 2.0:

- .NET Framework full
- .NET Core 2.x
- Xamarin
- Mono

.NET Core 3.0 was made available on September 2019 and with it .NET Standard 2.1.

You can have your dependencies specified per target or for all targets. In the former case, all of the dependencies need to support all of the targets, and in the latter, we can have different dependencies for each target. You'll probably want a mix of the two, with common libraries as global dependencies and more specialized libraries specified only where available. If you target more than one standard (or framework), then pay attention, because you may have to resort to conditional definitions (`#if`) to target those features that only exist in one of them. Let's see how.

The .NET Standard FAQ is available in GitHub at `https://github.com/dotnet/standard/blob/master/docs/faq.md`.

Targeting .NET Core or the full .NET framework

It is important that you know that you can target the full .NET framework in an ASP.NET Core application! However, if you do this, you will lose the platform independence—that is, you will only be able to run it on Windows.

By default, an ASP.NET Core project targets `netcoreapp1.x`, `netcoreapp2.x`, or `netcoreapp3.x`, depending on whether you are targeting ASP.NET Core 1.x, 2.x, or 3.x, but you can change it in the `.csproj` file. If you just want to target one framework, then modify the `TargetFramework` element like this:

```
<TargetFramework>net461</TargetFramework>
```

Or, if you want to target more than one, replace `TargetFramework` with `TargetFrameworks`:

```
<TargetFrameworks>netcoreapp3.0;net461</TargetFrameworks>
```

For more information, please refer to the Microsoft documentation at `https://docs.microsoft.com/en-us/dotnet/core/tools/csproj`.

For .NET Core and .NET Standard, you should use the following names in `TargetFramework` or `TargetFrameworks`:

.NET Core/Standard Version	Moniker
.NET Core 1	`netcoreapp1.0`
.NET Core 1.1	`netcoreapp1.1`
.NET Core 2	`netcoreapp2.0`
.NET Core 2.1	`netcoreapp2.1`
.NET Core 2.2	`netcoreapp2.2`
.NET Core 3.0	`netcoreapp3.0`
.NET Core 3.1	`netcoreapp3.1`
.NET Standard 1.0	`netstandard1.0`
.NET Standard 1.1	`netstandard1.1`

.NET Standard 1.2	`netstandard1.2`
.NET Standard 1.3	`netstandard1.3`
.NET Standard 1.4	`netstandard1.4`
.NET Standard 1.5	`netstandard1.5`
.NET Standard 1.6	`netstandard1.6`
.NET Standard 2.0	`netstandard2.0`
.NET Standard 2.1	`netstandard2.1`

Please see `https://docs.microsoft.com/en-us/dotnet/standard/frameworks` for the up-to-date list. Next, let's see how generic hosting works.

Understanding the generic host

Starting with version 3.0, ASP.NET Core is now bootstrapped using a generic host. This means that it is not tied specifically to HTTP or any other web protocol, but it potentially supports any kind of protocol, including low-level TCP. The templates have changed and now the bootstrap looks something like this:

```
Host
  .CreateDefaultBuilder(args)
  .ConfigureWebHostDefaults(webBuilder =>
  {
      webBuilder.UseStartup<Startup>();
  });
```

We are now using the `Host` class to create an instance of a class that implements `IHostBuilder`, not `IWebHostBuilder`, although the result is the same.

We can interfere in the bootstrap process by means of extension methods. Specifically, we can configure the following:

- Services registration
- Logging
- Configuration
- Web hosting defaults (host, startup class)

Here is a full example of changing the configuration:

```
Host
    .CreateDefaultBuilder(args)
    .ConfigureHostConfiguration(builder =>
```

```
{
    //host configuration (Kestrel or HTTP.sys)
    builder.Properties["key"] = "value";
})
.ConfigureAppConfiguration(builder =>
{
    //app configuration
    builder.Add(new JsonConfigurationSource { Path =
    "./configuration.json", Optional = true });
    builder.Properties["key"] = "value";
})
.ConfigureLogging(builder =>
{
    //add logging providers
    builder.AddConsole();
})
.ConfigureServices(services =>
{
    //register services
    services.AddSingleton<IMyService, MyService>();
})
.ConfigureWebHostDefaults(webBuilder =>
{
    builder.ConfigureKestrel(options =>
    {
        //set Kestrel options
    });

    //set the startup class
    webBuilder.UseStartup<Startup>();
})
```

It normally doesn't make sense to change the IHostLifetime of the application, because this is tied to the type of the application we're building. The options we have are as follows:

- ConsoleLifetime: The default, cross-platform host; listens to CTRL-C and SIGINT, SIGTERM signals for stops
- SystemdLifetime: For operating systems that use systemd, such as MacOS and Linux; listens to SIGTERM signals
- WindowsServiceLifetime: Only for Windows; listens to Windows service events

It is the host's responsibility to call the IHostApplicationLifetime events when the application has finished loading, is about to stop, or has stopped. You can read about it in Chapter 18, *gRPC and Other Topics*.

Services registered in `ConfigureServices` will be available to be injected into the `Startup` class's constructor, and will also be present in the `services` parameter passed to its `ConfigureServices` method. The same goes for the logging providers and to the app configuration. Next, let's move on to the MVC pattern.

Understanding the MVC pattern

Let's go back to ASP.NET now. For those of you that are still working with Web Forms, what is this MVC thing anyway, and where did it come from?

Let's face it: it was pretty easy to do terrible things in Web Forms, such as add lots of sensitive code in the page (which wouldn't be compiled until the page was accessed by the browser), adding complex business logic to a page class, having several megabytes of code in View State going back and forth on every request, and so on. There was no mechanism at all, other than the developer's discretion, to do things the right way. Plus, it was terrible to unit test it, because it relied on browser submission (`POST`) and JavaScript to have things working properly, such as binding actions to event handlers and submitted values to controls. There had to be a different solution, and in fact, there was.

The **model-view-controller (MVC)** design pattern was defined in the late 1970s and early 1980s of the past century (scary, isn't it?). It was conceived as a way to properly separate things that shouldn't conceptually be together, such as the code to render a **user interface** (UI) and the code that contains the business logic and data access that will feed and control that UI. In the MVC paradigm (and its offspring), we have controllers that expose public actions. Inside each action, the controller applies any business logic it needs to and then decides which view it should render, passing it enough information (the model) so that it can do its job. A controller knows nothing about UI elements—it just takes the data and execution context it needs to operate inside the action and goes from there. Likewise, a view will not know anything about databases, web services, connection strings, SQL, and the like—it just renders data, possibly making simple decisions about the way to do it. As for the model, it's basically anything you want that contains the information required by the view, including lists of records, static user information, and more. This strict separation makes things much easier to manage, test, and implement. Of course, the MVC pattern is not specific to the web—it can be used whenever this separation of concerns is useful, such as when we have a UI and some code to control it.

The following diagram presents the relationship between views, controllers, and models:

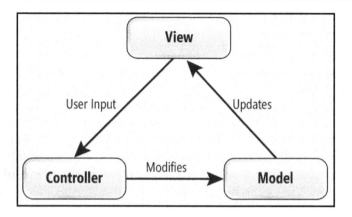

Image taken
from https://docs.microsoft.com/en-us/archive/msdn-magazine/2013/november/asp-net-single-page-applications-build-modern-responsive-web-apps-with-asp-net

MVC is normally associated with **object-oriented programming (OOP)**, but there are implementations in a myriad of languages, including JavaScript and PHP. The .NET MVC implementation has the following basic characteristics:

- **Controller** classes are either **Plain Old CLR Objects (POCOs)** or inherit from a base class, `Controller`. Inheriting from `Controller` is not required (unlike in previous versions), but it does make things slightly easier. Controller classes are instantiated by the ASP.NET Core DI framework, which means they can have the services they depend upon passed into them.

- **Actions** are public methods in a controller; they can take parameters, both simple types as well as complex ones (POCOs). MVC uses what is called model binding to translate information sent from the browser (the query string, headers, cookies, forms, DI, and other locations) into method parameters. The choice of which method to invoke from which controller from the request URLs and submitted parameters is achieved by a mix of a routing table, convention, and helper attributes.

- The **model** is sent from the controller to the view in the return of an action method, and it can be basically anything (or nothing). Of course, action methods for API calls do not return views, but can return a model together with an HTTP status code. There are other ways to pass data to the view, such as the view bag, which is essentially an untyped dictionary of data (a big bag); the difference between the two is that the model is normally typed. A model is automatically validated and bound to the action method parameters.

- **Views** consist of **domain-specific language** (DSL) files that are interpreted by a view engine and turned into something that the browser can interpret, such as HTML. ASP.NET Core features an extensible view engine framework, but includes a single implementation, **Razor**. Razor offers a simple syntax that allows developers to mix HTML and C# to get hold of the model passed in and make decisions as to what to do with it. Views can be constrained by layouts (Web Forms developers can think of layouts as master pages) and they can include other partial views (similar to web user controls in Web Forms). A view for the Razor view engine has the `.cshtml` extension, and cannot be accessed directly—only as the result of an action invocation. Views can be precompiled so that syntax errors are detected sooner.
- **Filters** are used to intercept, modify, or fully replace the request; built-in filters enable you to, for example, prevent access to unauthenticated users or redirect to an error page in the event of an exception occurring.

Now, there are other patterns similar in purpose to MVC, such as **model-view-presenter** (**MVP**) or **model-view-ViewModel** (**MVVM**). We will only focus on Microsoft's implementation of MVC and its specifics. In particular, the version of MVC that ships with ASP.NET Core is version 6, because it builds on version 5, which was previously available for the .NET full framework, but both add and drop a couple of features. Because it now sits on the new .NET Core framework, it is fully based on OWIN, so there's no more `Global.asax.cs` file. More on this later on.

The way in which MVC is implemented in ASP.NET focuses on the following:

- **URLs**: They are now more meaningful and **Search Engine Optimization** (**SEO**) friendly.
- **HTTP verbs**: Verbs now exactly state what the operation is supposed to do—for example, `GET` is used for idempotent operations, `POST` for new contents, `PUT` for full content updates, `PATCH` for partial content updates, and `DELETE` for removals, among others.
- **HTTP status codes**: These are used for returning operation result codes, which is more important in the case of Web APIs.

For example, issuing a `GET` request to `http://somehost/Product/120` is likely to return a view for a product with an ID of `120`, and a `DELETE` request for the same URL will probably delete this product and return either an HTTP status code or a nice view informing us of the fact.

URLs and their binding to controllers and actions are configurable through routes, and it is likely that this URL will be handled by a controller called `ProductController` and an action method that is configured to handle GET or DELETE requests. Views cannot be extracted from the URL because they are determined inside the action method.

We will cover Microsoft's implementation of MVC in depth in the following chapters. Of course, being a .NET Core feature, all of its components are available as NuGet packages. Some of the ones you will likely find are as follows:

Package	Purpose
`Microsoft.AspNetCore.Antiforgery`	Antiforgery APIs
`Microsoft.AspNetCore.Authentication`	Authentication base classes
`Microsoft.AspNetCore.Authentication.Cookies`	Authentication through cookies
`Microsoft.AspNetCore.Authentication.JwtBearer`	JWT authentication
`Microsoft.AspNetCore.Authorization`	Authorization APIs
`Microsoft.AspNetCore.Diagnostics`	Diagnostics APIs
`Microsoft.AspNetCore.Hosting`	Hosting base classes
`Microsoft.AspNetCore.Identity`	Identity authentication
`Microsoft.AspNetCore.Identity.EntityFrameworkCore`	Identity with Entity Framework Core as the store
`Microsoft.AspNetCore.Localization.Routing`	Localization through routing
`Microsoft.AspNetCore.Mvc`	The core MVC features
`Microsoft.AspNetCore.Mvc.Cors`	Support for **Cross-Origin Request Scripting** (**CORS**)
`Microsoft.AspNetCore.Mvc.DataAnnotations`	Validation through data annotations
`Microsoft.AspNetCore.Mvc.Localization`	Localization-based APIs

`Microsoft.AspNetCore.Mvc.TagHelpers`	Tag helpers functionality
`Microsoft.AspNetCore.Mvc.Versioning`	Web API versioning
`Microsoft.AspNetCore.ResponseCaching`	Response caching
`Microsoft.AspNetCore.Routing`	Routing
`Microsoft.AspNetCore.Server.IISIntegration`	IIS integration
`Microsoft.AspNetCore.Server.Kestrel`	Kestrel server
`Microsoft.AspNetCore.Server.WebListener` (`Microsoft.AspNetCore.Server.HttpSys` in ASP.NET Core 2)	WebListener server (now called `HTTP.sys`). See `https://docs.microsoft.com/en-us/aspnet/core/fundamentals/servers/httpsys`.
`Microsoft.AspNetCore.Session`	Session functionality
`Microsoft.AspNetCore.StaticFiles`	Ability to serve static files

You may or may not need all these packages, but you should make yourself familiar with them.

 In ASP.NET Core 2.0, there was the `Microsoft.AspNetCore.All` NuGet metapackage, and since 2.1 there is `Microsoft.AspNetCore.App`. The former included lots of packages, so a decision was made to have another metapackage with far fewer dependencies. Since version 2.1, all projects will include `Microsoft.AspNetCore.App`, and you may need to add other dependencies, such as SQLite, Redis, Azure Storage, and ApplicationInsights. You can read a discussion about it at `https://github.com/aspnet/Announcements/issues/287`.

Next, let's see how context execution works.

Getting your context

You will probably remember the `HttpContext` class from ASP.NET. The current instance of this class would represent the current context of execution, which included both the request information and the response channel. It was ubiquitous, and even though in Web Forms it was sometimes hidden, it was the way by which the web application communicated with the client.

Of course, ASP.NET Core also has an `HttpContext` class, but there is a big difference: there is no longer a `Current` static property that lets us get hold of the current context—instead, the process is a bit more convoluted. Anyway, all of the **infrastructure** classes—middleware, controllers, views, Razor pages, view components, tag helpers, and filters—allow easy access to the current context. Those who don't can leverage the `IHttpContextAccessor` interface through DI and get a pointer to the current context:

```
//this is required to register the IHttpContextAccessor
//services.AddHttpContextAccessor();

...

public MyType(IHttpContextAccessor httpContextAccessor)
{
    var httpContext = httpContextAccessor.HttpContext;
}
```

So, besides `User`, `Request`, and `Response` properties, which are mostly similar to their pre-Core counterparts, we also have the following:

- A `Features` collection, which exposes all of the features implemented by the current hosting server (Kestrel, WebListener/`HTTP.sys`, and more).
- A `RequestServices` property, which gives us access to the built-in DI framework (more on this in the following chapters).
- A `TraceIdentifier` property, which uniquely identifies a request in ASP.NET Core 2.x; in earlier versions, we had to access this through a feature.

- A `Connection` object, from which we can obtain relevant information about the client connection, such as the client certificates, for example:
  - The `Authentication` object, giving easy access to security primitives, such as sign in, sign out, deny, and more.
  - The `Session` object, which is implemented by the `ISessionFeature` feature, and is exposed directly by the `HttpContext`.
  - The `ClientCertificate` property contains any SSL certificate sent by the client as part of the handshake protocol.

The context is a vital part of an ASP.NET Core application, as we will see.

Working with the context

The main operations we will likely be doing with the context are as follows:

- Reading values from the request
- Writing to the response
- Reading and writing cookies
- Getting the current user
- Getting the address of the remote user
- Accessing the session
- Accessing services from the DI framework

Here are some examples:

```
//writing to the response
HttpContext.Response.StatusCode = 200;
HttpContext.Response.ContentType = "text/plain";
HttpContext.Response.WriteAsync("Hello, World!");

//getting values from the request
var id = HttpContext.Request.Query["id"].Single();
var host = HttpContext.Request.Host;
var payload = HttpContext.Request.Form["payload"].SingleOrDefault();

//reading and writing cookies
var isAuthenticated = HttpContext.Request.Cookies["id"].Any();
HttpContext.Response.Cookies.Append("id", email);

//getting the current user
```

```
var user = HttpContext.User;

//getting the address of the remote user
var ip = HttpContext.Connection.RemoteIpAddress;

//accessing the session
HttpContext.Session.SetString("id", email);
var id = HttpContext.Session.GetString("id");

//getting services from DI
var myService = HttpContext.RequestServices.Get<IMyService>();
```

Essentially, everything we will be doing through constructs, such as MVC's controllers and actions, are built around these and other simple `HttpContext` operations. The next topic we will look at is the OWIN pipeline.

Understanding the OWIN pipeline

Previous versions of ASP.NET had a very close relationship with **Internet Information Services** (**IIS**), Microsoft's flagship web server that ships with Windows. In fact, IIS was the only supported way to host ASP.NET.

Wanting to change this, Microsoft defined the **Open Web Interface for .NET** (**OWIN**) specification, which you can read about at `http://owin.org`. In a nutshell, it is the standard for decoupling server and application code, and for the execution pipeline for web requests. Because it is just a standard and knows nothing about the web server (if any), it can be used to extract its features.

.NET Core borrowed heavily from the OWIN specification. There are no more `Global.asax`, `web.config`, or `machine.config` configuration files, modules, or handlers. What we have is the following:

- The bootstrap code in `Program.Main` declares a class that contains a convention-defined method (`Startup` will be used if no class is declared).
- This conventional method, which should be called `Configure`, receives a reference to an `IApplicationBuilder` instance (it can take other services to be injected from the service provider).
- You then start adding middleware to the `IApplicationBuilder`; this middleware is what will handle your web requests.

A simple example is in order. First, the bootstrap class, which is by default named `Program`:

```
public class Program
{
    public static void Main(string [] args) =>
        CreateWebHostBuilder(args).Build().Run();

    public static IHostBuilder CreateHostBuilder(string [] args) =>
        Host
            .CreateDefaultBuilder(args)
            .ConfigureWebHostDefaults(builder =>
                {
                    builder.UseStartup<Startup>();
                });
}
```

Things can get more complicated, but don't worry too much about it now. Later on, I will explain what this all means. For the time being, it's enough to know that we are leveraging a `Host` to host Kestrel (the default host), and passing a conventional class called `Startup`. This `Startup` class looks like this (in a simplified way):

```
public class Startup
{
    public IConfiguration Configuration { get; }

        {
        this.Configuration = configuration;
    }

    public void Configure(IApplicationBuilder app)
    {
        app.Run(async (context) => {
            await context.Response.WriteAsync("Hello, OWIN World!");
        }
    }
}
```

There are a couple of things here that deserve an explanation. First, you will notice that the `Startup` class does not implement any interface or inherit from an explicit base class. This is because the `Configure` method does not have a predefined signature, other than its name, taking as its first parameter an `IApplicationBuilder`. For example, the following is also allowed:

```
public void Configure(IApplicationBuilder app, IWebHostEnvironment
env) { ... }
```

This version even gives you more than what you asked for. But I digress. The `IApplicationBuilder` interface defines a `Run` method. This method takes a `RequestDelegate` parameter, which is a delegate definition that accepts an `HttpContext` (remember that?) as its sole parameter and returns a `Task`. In my example, we made it asynchronous by adding `async` and `await` keywords to it, but it need not be so. All you have to do is make sure you extract whatever you want from the `HttpContext` and write whatever you want to it—this is your web pipeline. It wraps both the HTTP request and response objects, and we call it `middleware`.

The `Run` method is a full-blown pipeline on its own, but we can plug other steps (middleware) into the pipeline by using the (pun intended) `Use` method:

```
app.Use(async (context, next) =>
{
    await context.Response.WriteAsync("Hello from a middleware!");
    await next();
});
```

This way, we can add multiple steps, and they all will be executed in the order they were defined:

```
app.Use(async (context, next) =>
{
    await context.Response.WriteAsync("step 1!");
    await next();
});

app.Use(async (context, next) =>
{
    await context.Response.WriteAsync("step 2!");
});
```

Just keep in mind that the order does matter here; the next example shows this:

```
app.Use(async (context, next) =>
{
    try
    {
        //step 1
        await next();
    }
    catch (Exception ex)
    {
        await context.Response.WriteAsync($"Exception {ex.Message} was
        caught!");
    }
```

```
});

app.Use(async (context, next) =>
{
    //step 2
    throw new Exception();
});
```

Because the first step was added before the second, it wraps it, so any exceptions thrown by step two will be caught by step one; if they were added in a different order, this wouldn't happen.

The Use method takes an HttpContext instance as its parameter and returns a Func<Task>, which is normally a call to the next handler, so that the pipeline proceeds.

We could extract the lambda to its own method, like this:

```
async Task Process(HttpContext context, Func<Task> next)
{
    await context.Response.WriteAsync("Step 1");
    await next();
}

app.Use(Process);
```

It is even possible to extract the middleware to its own class and apply it using the generic UseMiddleware method:

```
public class Middleware
{
    private readonly RequestDelegate _next;

    public Middleware(RequestDelegate next)
    {
        this._next = next;
    }
    public async Task InvokeAsync(HttpContext context)
    {
        await context.Response.WriteAsync("This is a middleware
class!");
    }
}

//in Startup.Configure
app.UseMiddleWare<Middleware>();
```

In this case, the constructor needs to take as its first parameter a pointer to the next middleware in the pipeline, as a `RequestDelegate` instance.

I think by now you've got the picture: OWIN defines a pipeline to which you can add handlers which are then called in sequence. The difference between `Run` and `Use` is that the former ends the pipeline—that is, it won't call anything after itself.

The following diagram (from Microsoft) clearly shows this:

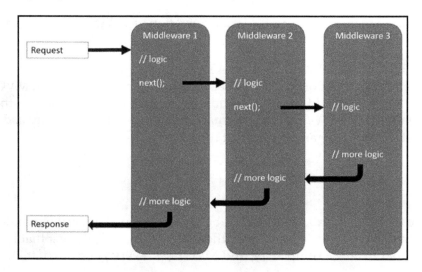

Image taken from https://docs.microsoft.com/en-us/dotnet/architecture/blazor-for-web-forms-developers/middleware

The first middleware, in a way, wraps all of the next ones. For example, imagine that you want to add exception handling to all the steps in the pipeline. You could do something like this:

```
app.Use(async (context, next) =>
{
    try
    {
        //log call
        await next(context);
    }
    catch (Exception ex)
    {
        //do something with the exception
    }
    await context.Response.WriteAsync("outside an exception handler");
});
```

The call to `next()` is wrapped in a `try...catch` block, so any exception that may be thrown by another middleware in the pipeline, as long as it was added after this one, will be caught.

 You can set the status code of a response, but be aware that, if an exception is thrown, it will be reset to **500 Server Error**!

You can read more about Microsoft's implementation of OWIN at `https://docs.` `microsoft.com/en-us/aspnet/core/fundamentals/owin`.

Why is OWIN important? Well, because ASP.NET Core (and its MVC implementation) are built on it. We will see later that in order to have an MVC application, we need to add the MVC middleware to the OWIN pipeline in the `Startup` class's `Configure` method, normally as shown in the following code, using the new endpoint routing and the default route:

```
    {
    endpoints.MapDefaultControllerRoute();
});
```

As you know, this book talks essentially about the MVC pattern, but we could go equally with this kind of middleware, without any MVC stuff; it's just that it would be much harder to tackle complexity, and MVC does a very good job of that.

OWIN is essentially ASP.NET Core middleware. Everything that we add in a `UseXXX` extension is middleware. Let's look at how we can host an ASP.NET Core project next.

Hosting ASP.NET Core

You probably noticed, when we talked about OWIN, that I mentioned that the sample app was hosted in Kestrel. Kestrel is the name of a platform-independent web server fully written in .NET Core (of course, using the native libraries of your operating system). You need to host your web application somewhere, and .NET Core offers the following options:

- **Kestrel**: Platform independent, your host of choice if you want to have your code run on any platform.

- **WebListener**: A Windows-only host, offering significant performance advantages over Kestrel, but also has the disadvantage of needing Windows; starting with ASP.NET Core 2, it is now called `HTTP.sys`.
- **IIS**: As in the past, you can continue to host your web app in IIS, on Windows, benefiting from the *old* pipeline and configuration tools.

A server in this context is merely an implementation of `IServer`, an interface defined in the `Microsoft.AspNetCore.Hosting` NuGet package. This defines the base contract that a server offers, which can be described as follows:

- A `Start` method, where all the fun begins. It is responsible for creating the `HttpContext`, setting up the `Request` and `Response` properties, and calling the conventional `Configure` method.
- A collection of `Features` that are supported by the implementation. There are dozens of features, but at the very least, a server needs to support `IHttpRequestFeature` and `IHttpResponseFeature`.

Each of these server implementations is provided in NuGet packages:

Server	Package
Kestrel	`Microsoft.AspNetCore.Server.Kestrel`
WebListener/`HTTP.sys`	`Microsoft.AspNetCore.Server.WebListener` (`Microsoft.AspNetCore.Server.HttpSys` from ASP.NET Core 2)
IIS	`Microsoft.AspNetCore.Server.IISIntegration`

IIS cannot be used on its own. IIS is, of course, a Windows-native application and is therefore not available through NuGet, but the `Microsoft.AspNetCore.Server.IISIntegration` package includes the IIS **ASP.NET Core module**, which needs to be installed in IIS so that it can run ASP.NET Core apps with Kestrel (WebListener is not compatible with IIS). There are, of course, other server implementations by third-party providers (take, as an example, **Nowin**, available at `https://github.com/Bobris/Nowin`). The ASP.NET Core module acts as a reverse proxy, receiving requests through IIS and then calling ASP.NET Core, in the same process space. Other reverse proxies are **Apache** and **NGINX**. Reverse proxies are useful because they provide additional features that are not part of ASP.NET Core; they accept requests, do their magic, and forward the requests to ASP.NET Core so that it too can do its magic.

So, what is there to know about these, and how can we select one of these hosting servers?

Kestrel

Kestrel is the *default*, multiplatform, web server. It offers acceptable performance, but lacks lots of features that are expected in real life:

- No support for Windows authentication (as time passes, this becomes less of a problem)
- No direct file transmission
- No strong security protection (large requests, and more)

From this, it should be clear that Kestrel is not meant to be used in production unless it is sitting behind a reverse proxy (such as NGINX, Apache, or IIS). It is configured at bootstrap through the `UseKestrel` extension method, and if you need to configure its options, you will need to supply an additional lambda:

```
Host.CreateDefaultBuilder(args)
    .ConfigureWebHostDefaults(webBuilder =>
    {
        webBuilder
            .UseStartup<Startup>()
            .UseKestrel(opt => { opt.Limits.MaxConcurrentConnections =
            10; })
    });
```

You can read more about it at `https://docs.microsoft.com/en-us/aspnet/core/fundamentals/servers/kestrel`.

WebListener/HTTP.sys

This one is for Windows only, as it is a wrapper around `HTTP.sys`, the Windows subsystem that handles web requests. It offers by far the best performance, supports HTTP/2, WebSockets, Windows Authentication, direct file transmission, port sharing, response caching, and mostly anything that you can think of. The disadvantage, of course, is that it requires Windows 7 or Windows Server 2008 R2 and later. At bootstrap, use the `UseWebListener` extension method to add it to the host builder, possibly with a configuration parameter:

```
.UseWebListener(opt =>
{
    opt.ListenerSettings.Authentication.AllowAnonymous = false;
})
```

Since ASP.NET Core 2.0, `WebListener` is called `HTTP.sys`.

IIS

We already know about IIS. IIS can be used as a reverse proxy for Kestrel, or to add features that the host does not support, such as Windows Authentication. For that, we should include support for IIS by calling `UseIISIntegration`. Here, the configuration should be done through the `Web.config` file, which in this case is a requirement (the Visual Studio template will add this file to the root of your project).

NGINX

NGINX (pronounced *EngineX*) is a UNIX and Linux reverse proxy that can be used with ASP.NET Core. We will talk a bit more about NGINX in `Chapter 19`, *Application Deployment*.

Apache

Apache, the popular UNIX and Linux server (which actually also runs in Windows) can also act as a reverse proxy. You can find more information in `Chapter 17`, *Deployment*.

Configuration

As we've seen, usually, the server is chosen using a `Host` instance. As a minimum, you need to tell it which server to use and what the root directory is:

```
Host.CreateDefaultBuilder(args)
    .ConfigureWebHostDefaults(webBuilder =>
    {
        webBuilder
            .UseStartup<Startup>()
            .UseKestrel()
            .UseContentRoot(Directory.GetCurrentDirectory());
    });
```

Actually, the calls to `UseKestrel` and `UseContentRoot(Directory.GetCurrentDirectory())` are already done by `ConfigureWebHostDefaults`, so you can skip them.

Features

Different servers will offer different features. Essentially, a feature in this context is just a configuration that is available per request and offers properties that can be inspected and changed. Here are some of the features that are included out of the box:

Interface	Feature
`IExceptionHandlerPathFeature`	Access the last error that occurred and the request path, if we are using centralized exception handling.
`IEndpointFeature`	Access to endpoint routing.
`IHttpRequestFeature`	Access to the request object and collections (form, headers, cookies, query strings, and more).
`IHttpResponseFeature`	Access to the response object and collections (headers, cookies, content, and more).
`IHttpAuthenticationFeature`	Authentication based on claims and principals.
`IHttpUpgradeFeature`	Support for HTTP upgrades (see `https://tools.ietf.org/html/rfc2616.html#section-14.42`).
`IHttpBufferingFeature`	Response buffering.
`IHttpConnectionFeature`	Properties for local host calls.
`IHttpRequestLifetimeFeature`	Detecting whether a client has disconnected, and the ability to actually disconnect it.
`IHttpResetFeature`	Used to send reset messages to protocols that support it (HTTP/2).
`IHttpSendFileFeature`	The ability to directly send a file as a response.
`IHttpWebSocketFeature`	WebSockets.
`IHttpRequestIdentifierFeature`	Uniquely identifying requests.
`IHttpsCompressionFeature`	Access to request and response compression.
`IFormFeature`	Access to request form data.
`ISessionFeature`	Supplies the session functionality. Needs to be added by the session middleware; not available otherwise.
`IQueryFeature`	Access query string.
`ITlsConnectionFeature`	Retrieving client certificates.
`ITlsTokenBindingFeature`	Working with TLS tokens.
`IStatusCodePagesFeature`	Redirecting to errors based on the HTTP status code.

This is by no means the full list, as it may change, depending on your exact configuration (your choice of host, and so on). There is no base interface for features. All of these features can be obtained through the `Features` property of the `Server` or from the `HttpContext` by requesting its interface:

```
var con = HttpContext.Features.Get<IHttpConnectionFeature>();
```

This is one way to obtain access to the functionality that the feature supplies, but for some features, there are workarounds. For example, the ASP.NET `Session` object can be obtained directly from the `HttpContext`. Features are essentially how the `HttpContext` class gets the behavior it exposes; for example, request and response objects, sessions, and more. Middleware classes can provide their own features so that they are available downstream by adding them directly to the `Features` collection:

```
HttpContext.Features.Set(new MyFeature());
```

There can be only one feature per type—for example, one per `IMyFeature1`, one per `IMyFeature2`, and so on.

Launch configuration

Visual Studio can have more than one configuration per project, meaning that it can launch your project in several ways, and there's a toolbar button that shows just this fact:

In particular, we can choose whether to launch our web application using IIS (or IIS Express) as the host, or use whatever is specified in the code (Kestrel or `HTTP.sys`). The launch settings are stored in the `PropertieslaunchSettings.json` file, which is created by default by Visual Studio. This file has the following (or similar) contents:

```
{
    "iisSettings": {
      "windowsAuthentication": true,
      "anonymousAuthentication": true,
      "iisExpress": {
        "applicationUrl": "http://localhost:24896/",
        "sslPort": 0
      }
    },
    "profiles": {
      "IIS Express": {
        "commandName": "IISExpress",
        "launchBrowser": true,
        "environmentVariables": {
          "ASPNETCORE_ENVIRONMENT": "Development"
        }
      },
      "Web": {
        "commandName": "Project",
        "launchBrowser": true,
        "launchUrl": "http://localhost:5000",
        "environmentVariables": {
          "ASPNETCORE_ENVIRONMENT": "Development"
        }
      }
    }
}
```

 Where I have `"Web"`, you should have the name of your application.

Here, we can see the default ports plus the environment name to be used (to be discussed shortly). This file does not need to be changed by hand (although it can be); you can see it in visual form using the project properties:

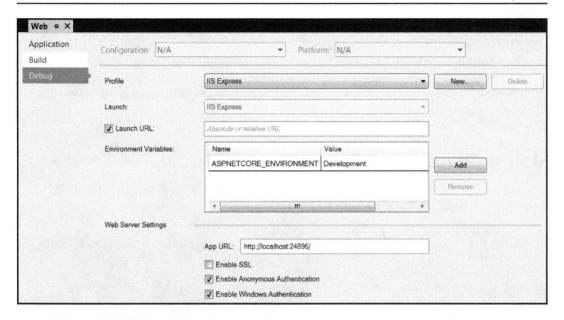

Let's now look at a special case in which the port needs to be set dynamically.

Setting the listen port and address

There may be a need for setting the listen port—for example, you already have one or more servers running on the same machine. When this happens, you can either pick one port that you are sure is not being used or you can let ASP.NET Core pick one for you. Setting the listen address is also relevant if you want to restrict where you want to accept requests from. There are many ways to achieve this; let's go through them one by one.

By default, ASP.NET Core accepts requests at the following locations:

- `http://localhost:5000`
- `https://localhost:5001` (when using a local certificate)

Using the command line

When you start your application using `dotnet`, you can pass the `--urls` parameter to specify the URLs to which it should listen:

```
dotnet run --urls "http://localhost:5000;https://localhost:5001"
```

This, of course, is static. Here you specify that you are binding HTTP to `localhost` only, on port `5000` and `HTTPS` to `localhost` too, on port `5001`. If you want to bind to any host, you should use `0.0.0.0` instead of `localhost`.

This approach is a good one for Docker deployments. Let's now see how to do this, using environment variables.

Using environment variables

Another alternative is to use the `ASPNETCORE_URLS` environment variables. It is basically the same as the previous approach:

```
//Linux, MacOS
export ASPNETCORE_URLS="http://localhost:5000;https://localhost:5001"

//Windows
set ASPNETCORE_URLS="http://localhost:5000;https://localhost:5001"
```

This is also OK for Docker.

Next, let's look at how to use the configuration file for Visual Studio.

Using launchSettings.json

The `launchSettings.json` is where Visual Studio keeps the configuration details for running a web solution. Its structure looks like this:

```
{
  "iisSettings": {
    "windowsAuthentication": false,
    "anonymousAuthentication": true,
    "iisExpress": {
      "applicationUrl": "http://localhost:7788",
      "sslPort": 44399
    }
  },
  "profiles": {
    "IIS Express": {
      "commandName": "IISExpress",
      "launchBrowser": true,
      "environmentVariables": {
        "ASPNETCORE_ENVIRONMENT": "Development"
      }
    },
    "Web": {
```

```
    "commandName": "Project",
    "launchBrowser": true,
    "environmentVariables": {
      "ASPNETCORE_ENVIRONMENT": "Development"
    },
    "applicationUrl": "https://localhost:5001;http://localhost:5000"
  }
 }
}
```

You can see where the URLs, address, and port are specified in bold, and where you can change them. For IIS Express, you need to edit the .vs\config\applicationhost.config, located inside the root solution folder.

This approach is, of course, only for local development.

Using code

We can also specify the listen addresses in code, which is more useful for dynamic cases, where we want to build the address dynamically:

```
public static IHostBuilder CreateHostBuilder(string[] args) =>
    Host
        .CreateDefaultBuilder(args)
        .ConfigureWebHostDefaults(webBuilder =>
        {
            webBuilder
                .UseStartup<Startup>()
                .UseUrls("http://localhost:5000",
                "https://localhost.5001");
        });
```

Setting ports dynamically

What if we need to use a dynamically assigned port? This may occur when the port that we'd like to use is already taken. ASP.NET Core fully supports this by setting the port to 0, but this needs to be done at the actual host level. This only works with Kestrel; HTTP.sys does not support this. Let's see how we can do this:

```
public static IHostBuilder CreateHostBuilder(string[] args) =>
    Host
        .CreateDefaultBuilder(args)
        .ConfigureWebHostDefaults(webBuilder =>
        {
            webBuilder
```

```
                          .UseStartup<Startup>()
                          .UseKestrel(options =>
                          {
                              options.ListenAnyIP(0);
                          });
                });
```

If you want to find out which addresses we are using, you must make use of a feature called `IServerAddressesFeature`. One way to do this is to have a look at it in the `Configure` method, but only after the application starts:

```
public void Configure(IApplicationBuilder app, IWebHostEnvironment
env, IHostApplicationLifetime events)
{
    events.ApplicationStarted.Register(() =>
    {
        var feature =
app.ServerFeatures.Get<IServerAddressesFeature>();
        var addresses = feature.Addresses;
    });

    //rest goes here
}
```

This example illustrates two concepts: server features and host application events. I register a handler to the `ApplicationStarted` event, and when it is raised, I ask for a server feature, `IServerAddressesFeature`, that contains all the addresses, including ports, that my application is currently bound to. From here, I can see the port that was chosen.

 We read about server features in this chapter. Application events are discussed in `Chapter 18`, *gRPC and Other Topics*.

Now that we've learned the basics of hosting, let's now focus on another key aspect of ASP.NET Core: the inversion of control and the DI framework pattern.

Inversion of control and dependency injection

Inversion of control (**IoC**) and **dependency injection** (**DI**) are two related but different patterns. The first tells us that we should not depend on actual, concrete classes, but instead on abstract base classes or interfaces that specify the functionality we're interested in.

Depending on its registrations, the IoC framework will return a concrete class that matches our desired interface or abstract base class. DI, on the other hand, is the process by which, when a concrete class is built, the dependencies it needs are then passed to its constructor (constructor injection, although there are other options). These two patterns go very well together, and throughout the book, I will use the terms IoC or DI container/framework to mean the same thing.

.NET always had support for a limited form of IoC; Windows Forms designers used it at design time to get access to the current designer's services, for example, and Windows Workflow Foundation also used it to get registered extensions at runtime. But in .NET Core, Microsoft centralized it and made it a first-class citizen of the ecosystem. Now, virtually everything is dependent on the IoC and DI framework. It is made available in the `Microsoft.Extensions.DependencyInjection` NuGet package.

An IoC and DI container allow services (classes) to be registered and accessed by their abstract base class or an interface that they implement. Application code does not need to care about the actual class that implements the contract, and this makes it very easy to switch the actual dependencies in the configuration or at runtime. Other than that, it also injects dependencies into the actual classes that it is building. Say, for example, you have this scenario:

```
public interface IMyService
{
    void MyOperation();
}

public interface IMyOtherService
{
    void MyOtherOperation();
}

public class MyService : IMyService
{
    private readonly IMyOtherService _other;
```

```
public MyService(IMyOtherService other)
{
    this._other = other;
}
public void Operation()
{
    //do something
}
}
```

If you register a `MyService` class with the DI container, then when it builds an actual instance, it will know that it will also need to build an instance of `IMyOtherService` to pass to the `MyService` constructor, and this will cascade for every dependency in the actual `IMyOtherService` implementation.

The `Host`, when it is building the host, initializes an `IServiceCollection` instance, which is then passed to the `Startup` class's `ConfigureServices` method. This is a conventional method that should be used for our own registrations.

Now, a service registration has three components:

- The type under which it will be registered (the unique key of the registration)
- Its lifetime
- The actual instance factory

A lifetime can be one of the following:

- `Scoped`: A new instance of the service will be created for each web request (or scope), and the same instance will always be returned for the same request (scope) whenever we ask the DI framework for it.
- `Singleton`: The instance to be created will be kept in memory, and it will always be returned.
- `Transient`: A new instance will be created whenever it is requested.

The instance factory can be one of the following:

- An actual instance, which is always regarded as a `Singleton`; of course, this cannot be used with the `Transient` or `Scoped` lifetimes
- A concrete `Type`, which will then be instantiated as needed
- A `Func<IServiceProvider, object>` delegate that knows how to create instances of the concrete type after receiving a reference to the DI container

You register services and their implementations through
the ConfigureServices method's services parameter, which is an
IServiceCollection implementation:

```
//for a scoped registration
services.Add(new ServiceDescriptor(typeof(IMyService),
typeof(MyService), ServiceLifetime.Scoped);

//for singleton, both work
services.Add(new ServiceDescriptor(typeof(IMyService),
typeof(MyService),
    ServiceLifetime.Singleton);
services.Add(new ServiceDescriptor(typeof(IMyService),
newMyService());

//with a factory that provides the service provider as a parameter,
from //which you can retrieve //other services
services.Add(new ServiceDescriptor(typeof(IMyService),
(serviceProvider) =>
    new MyService(), ServiceLifetime.Transient);
```

There are several extension methods that allow us to do registrations; all of the
following are identical:

```
services.AddScoped<IMyService, MyService>();
services.AddScoped<IMyService>(sp =>
    new MyService((IMyOtherService) sp.GetService
    (typeof(IMyOtherService)))));
services.AddScoped(typeof(IMyService), typeof(MyService));
services.Add(new ServiceDescriptor(typeof(IMyService),
typeof(MyService), ServiceLifetime.Scoped));
```

The same goes for all other lifetimes.

The DI container also supports generic types—for example, if you register an open
generic type, such as MyGenericService<T>, you can ask for a specific instance,
such as MyGenericService<ServiceProviderOptions>:

```
//register an open generic type
services.AddScoped(typeof(MyGenericService<>));

//build the service provider
var serviceProvider = services.BuildServiceProvider();

//retrieve a constructed generic type
var myGenericService = serviceProvider.GetService
<MyGenericService<string>>();
```

It is possible to traverse an `IServiceCollection` object to see what's already registered. It is nothing but a collection of `ServiceDescriptor` instances. If we want, we can access individual registrations and even replace one for another.

It is also possible to remove all registrations for a certain base type or interface:

```
services.RemoveAll<IMyService>();
```

The `RemoveAll` extension method is available on the `Microsoft.Extensions.DependencyInjection.Extensions` namespace.

 One very important thing to bear in mind is that any services that implement `IDisposable` and are registered for either the `Scoped` or the `Transient` lifetimes will be disposed of at the end of the request.

The DI framework has the concept of scopes, to which scoped registrations are bound. We can create new scopes and have our services associated with them. We can use the `IServiceScopeFactory` interface, which is automatically registered and it allows us to do things like this:

```
var serviceProvider = services.BuildServiceProvider();
var factory = serviceProvider.GetService<IServiceScopeFactory>();

using (var scope = factory.CreateScope())
{
    var svc = scope.ServiceProvider.GetService<IMyService>();
}
```

Any scope-bound service returned from the service provider inside the `CreateScope` inner scope is destroyed with the scope. Interestingly, if any scope-registered service implements `IDisposable`, then its `Dispose` method will be called at the end of the scope.

You need to keep a few things in mind:

- The same `Type` can be registered multiple times, but only for the same lifetime.
- You can have several implementations registered for the same `Type`, and they will be returned in a call to `GetServices`.
- Only the last registered implementation for a given `Type` is returned by `GetService`.

- You cannot register a `Singleton` service that takes a dependency that is `Scoped`, as it wouldn't make sense; by definition `Scoped` changes every time.
- You cannot pass a concrete instance to a `Scoped` or `Transient` registration.
- You can only resolve, from the factory delegate, services that have themselves been registered; the factory delegate, however, will only be called after all services have been registered, so you do not need to worry about the registration order.
- The resolution will return `null` if no service from the given `Type` is registered; no exception will be thrown.
- An exception will be thrown if a registered type has on its constructor a nonresolvable type—that is, a type that is not registered on the DI provider.

Several .NET Core APIs supply extension methods that perform their registrations—for example, `AddMvc` , `AddDbContext` or `AddSession`. By default, ASP.NET Core's bootstrap automatically registers the following services:

Service Type
`Microsoft.AspNetCore.Hosting.Builder.IApplicationBuilderFactory`
`Microsoft.AspNetCore.Hosting.IWebHostEnvironment`
`Microsoft.AspNetCore.Hosting.IStartup`
`Microsoft.AspNetCore.Hosting.IStartupFilter`
`Microsoft.AspNetCore.Hosting.Server.IServer`
`Microsoft.AspNetCore.Http.IHttpContextFactory`
`Microsoft.Extensions.Configuration.IConfiguration`
`Microsoft.Extensions.Hosting.IHostApplicationLifetime`
`Microsoft.Extensions.Logging.ILogger<T>`
`Microsoft.Extensions.Logging.ILoggerFactory`
`Microsoft.Extensions.Logging.ILoggerFactory`
`Microsoft.Extensions.ObjectPool.ObjectPoolProvider`
`Microsoft.Extensions.Options.IConfigureOptions<T>`
`Microsoft.Extensions.Options.IOptions<T>`
`Microsoft.Extensions.Options.IConfigureOptions<T>`
`Microsoft.Extensions.Options.IOptionsSnapshot<T>`
`Microsoft.Extensions.Options.IOptionsMonitor<T>`
`Microsoft.Extensions.Options.IOptionsChangeTokenSource<T>`
`Microsoft.Extensions.Options.IOptionsFactory<T>`

`System.Diagnostics.DiagnosticListener`
`System.Diagnostics.DiagnosticListener`
`System.Diagnostics.DiagnosticSource`

After all the registrations are done, eventually, the actual dependency framework will be built from the `IServiceCollection` instance. Its public interface is none other than the *venerable* `IServiceProvider`, which has been around since .NET 1.0. It exposes a single method, `GetService`, which takes a `Type` as its single parameter to resolve.

There are, however, a few useful generic extension methods available in the `Microsoft.Extensions.DependencyInjection` package and namespace:

- `GetService<T>()`: Returns an instance of the service type that has already been cast appropriately, if one is registered, or `null` otherwise
- `GetRequiredService<T>()`: Tries to retrieve a registration for the given service type, and throws an exception if none is found
- `GetServices<T>()`: Returns all of the services whose registration keys match (is identical, implements, or is a subclass) to the given service key

You can register multiple services for the same `Type`, but only the last that is registered will be retrievable using `GetService()`. Interestingly, all of them will be returned using `GetServices()`!

Keep in mind that the latest registration for a `Type` overrides any previous one, meaning that you will get the latest item when you use a `GetService`, but all of the registrations are returnable by `GetServices`.

Although the most common usage will probably be constructor injection, where the DI framework creates a concrete type passing it all of its dependencies in the constructor, it is also possible to request at any given time an instance of the service we want, by using a reference to a `IServiceProvider`, like the one available in the following context:

```
var urlFactory = this.HttpContext.RequestServices.
GetService<IUrlHelperFactory>();
```

This is called the service locator pattern and some people consider it an antipattern. I won't go over it here, as I believe this discussion is pointless.

The `IServiceProvider` instance itself is registered on the DI provider, making it a possible candidate for injection!

If, by any chance, you want to build an instance of a type that takes on its constructor services that should come from the DI provider, you can use the `ActivatorUtilities.CreateInstance` method:

```
var instance =
ActivatorUtilities.CreateInstance<MyType>(serviceProvider);
```

Or, if we have a reference to a `Type`, you can use the following:

```
MyType instance = (MyType)
ActivatorUtilities.CreateInstance(serviceProvider, typeof(MyType));
```

Finally, I need to talk about something else. People have been using third-party DI and IoC frameworks for ages. .NET Core, being as flexible as it is, certainly allows us to use our own, which may offer additional features to what the built-in one provides. All we need is for our DI provider of choice to also expose an `IServiceProvider` implementation; if it does, we just need to return it from the `ConfigureServices` method:

```
public IServiceProvider ConfigureServices(IServiceCollection services)
{
    //AutoFac
    var builder = new ContainerBuilder();
    //add registrations from services
    builder.Populate(services);
    return new AutofacServiceProvider(builder.Build());
}
```

`AutofacServiceProvider` also implements `IServiceProvider`, and therefore we can return it from `ConfigureServices` and have it as replacement for the out-of-the-box DI container.

All in all, it's very good to see IoC and DI. This is just the basics; we will talk about DI in pretty much all of the rest of this book.

Validating dependencies

Normally, you inject dependencies to controllers (and other components) through their constructors. The problem is, we may not know that a service that we depend upon is missing its registration until it's too late—we try to access a controller that depends upon it and it crashes.

When running in the `Development` environment, this is checked for us. We register all controllers as services:

```
services
    .AddControllers()
    .AddControllersAsServices();
```

Then, when accessing a controller, the web app—any web app, not one that has a specific dependency—ASP.NET Core will try to validate all of the dependencies that it has registered, and, if it finds one for which a dependency is not found, an exception is thrown. This exception will tell you exactly what service is missing. ASP.NET Core also checks the validity of scoped services—for example, you cannot have a service registered as `Scoped` be retrieved from outside of a scope (usually a web request).

You can actually control this behavior for environments other than `Development` by adding the following to the bootstrap code in `Program`:

```
public static IHostBuilder CreateHostBuilder(string[] args) =>
    Host
        .CreateDefaultBuilder(args)
        .ConfigureWebHostDefaults(builder =>
        {
            builder.UseStartup<Startup>();
            builder.UseDefaultServiceProvider(options =>
            {
                options.ValidateOnBuild = true;
                options.ValidateScopes = true;
            });
        });
```

Note the `ValidateOnBuild` and `ValidateScopes` properties. `ValidateOnBuild` is for doing what we just saw—testing that the dependency graph is valid—and `ValidateScopes` is for testing that services that require a scope are retrieved from inside one. By default, both are `false`, except in the `Development` environment.

So next, let's move on to understand the environments in which we work.

Knowing the environments

.NET Core has the concept of the environment. An environment is basically a runtime setting in the form of an environment variable called ASPNETCORE_ENVIRONMENT. This variable can take one of the following values (note that these are case sensitive):

- Development: A development environment, which probably does not need much explaining
- Staging: A preproduction environment used for testing
- Production: An environment (or as similar as possible) in which the application will live once it is released

To be specific, you can pass any value, but these have particular significance to .NET Core. There are several ways by which you can access the current environment, but you're most likely to use one of the following methods, extension methods and properties of the IWebHostEnvironment interface (add a using reference to the Microsoft.Extensions.Hosting namespace):

- IsDevelopment()
- IsProduction()
- IsStaging()
- IsEnvironment("SomeEnvironment")
- EnvironmentName

The IsDevelopment, IsProduction, and IsStaging extension methods are just convenience methods using the IsEnvironment method. Based on the actual environment, you can make decisions about the code, such as picking a different connection string, web service URL, and so on. It is important to point out that this has nothing to do with **debug** or **release** compiler configurations.

You normally get an instance of IWebHostEnvironment from the arguments to the Configure method of the Startup class:

```
public void Configure(IApplicationBuilder app, IWebHostEnvironment
env) { ... }
```

But you also get it from the DI container, which is available from the HttpContext class, among other places, as the RequestServices property:

```
var env =
HttpContext.RequestServices.GetService<IWebHostEnvironment>();
```

Or you can just inject `IWebHostEnvironment` into your controller as the following:

```
public IActionResult Index([FromServices] IWebHostEnvironment env) {
... }
```

This allows you to check your current environment any time, so that you have conditional logic.

 The `IWebHostEnvironment` replaces the old `IHostingEnvironment` interface available in pre-3 .NET Core, now deprecated.

A final note: service configuration plays well with environments. Instead of a single `ConfigureServices` method, we can have multiple methods, named `ConfigureDevelopmentServices`, `ConfigureStagingServices`, and `ConfigureProductionServices`. To be clear, any environment name can be added after the `Configure` prefix and before `Services`. The environment-specific method (for example, `ConfigureDevelopmentServices`) will be called instead of the generic one (`ConfigureServices`):

```
public void ConfigureDevelopmentServices(IServiceCollection services)
{
    //WILL be called for environment Development
}

public void ConfigureServices(IServiceCollection services)
{
    //will NOT be called for environment Development
}
```

And, if we want to take it a bit further, we can even do the same for the `Startup` class: we can create one class per environment, with it as the suffix:

```
public class StartupDevelopment
{
    public StartupDevelopment(IConfiguration configuration) { ... }

    public void ConfigureServices(IServiceCollection services) { ... }

    public void Configure(IApplicationBuilder app, IWebHostEnvironment
env) { ... }
}
```

Or, if we want to dynamically specify a class that resides in a different assembly, we'll have to slightly change the code in the `Program` class, so as to bootstrap from an assembly:

```
public static IHostBuilder CreateHostBuilder(string[] args) =>
    Host
        .CreateDefaultBuilder(args)
        .ConfigureWebHostDefaults(builder =>
        {
            builder.UseStartup(typeof(Startup).Assembly.FullName);
        });
```

We can do it from an assembly instead of from a specific class:

```
public static IHostBuilder CreateHostBuilder(string[] args) =>
    Host
        .CreateDefaultBuilder(args)
        .ConfigureWebHostDefaults(builder =>
        {
            builder.UseStartup<Startup>();
        });
```

A nice feature that can help us better organize our code! Let's now have a look at the standard project templates that we can use to start creating our projects.

Understanding the project templates

The Visual Studio template for creating an ASP.NET Core project, since version 3.x, adds the following (or very similar) contents to the `Program` class:

```
public static void Main(string[] args)
{
    CreateHostBuilder(args).Build().Run();
}

public static IHostBuilder CreateHostBuilder(string[] args) =>
    Host
        .CreateDefaultBuilder(args)
        .ConfigureWebHostDefaults(builder =>
        {
            builder.UseStartup<Startup>();
        });
```

This has changed a bit since previous versions and is now more opinionated; I already showed this when talking about OWIN earlier in this chapter.

The `Host` class exposes the static `CreateDefaultBuilder`, which returns a fully built `IHostBuilder` instance. The `CreateDefaultBuilder` method is actually doing a lot of things behind our backs:

- Creates a `ConfigurationBuilder` and adds the environment variables provider to it (see `Chapter 2`, Configuration, for more details)
- Adds the `appsettings.json` (mandatory) and `appsettings.<environment>.json` (optional) JSON files and provider to the configuration builder
- Configures the user secrets configuration, if running in development mode
- Configures command-line configuration, if command-line arguments were passed
- Sets Kestrel as the host to use and loads Kestrel-related configurations
- Sets the content root to be the current directory
- Sets the host to use the URLs passed as the `ASPNETCORE_SERVER.URLS` environment variable, if it exists
- Configures logging to the console, debug, EventSource, and EventLog (if in Windows)
- Adds IIS integration
- Sets the default host lifetime as `ConsoleHostLifetime`
- Configures service provider parameters to validate the scope of registered services and lifetimes if running in the `Development` environment
- Registers some services, such as `IConfiguration`

These are the defaults you get, but you can override any of them by using some extension methods over the `IHostBuilder` interface:

```
Host
    .CreateDefaultBuilder(args)
    .ConfigureAppConfiguration((context, builder) =>
    {
        //add or remove from the configuration builder
    })
    .ConfigureContainer<MyContainer>((context, container) =>
    {
        //configure container
    })
    .ConfigureLogging((context, builder) =>
    {
        //add or remove from the logging builder
    });
    .ConfigureServices(services =>
```

```
{
    //register services
})
.ConfigureWebHostDefaults(builder =>
{
    builder.UseStartup<Startup>();
});
```

After the default builder is instantiated, we ask it to use the `Startup` class, which is where we can configure the exact stuff we want, such as registered services, middleware components, and so on

`IHostBuilder` then builds an `IHost` and then we ask it to run. This is what actually gets our application working.

We have talked about the `Startup` class before. Basically, it exposes two methods, named `ConfigureServices` and `Configure` by convention; the first is used to register services and their implementations with the default DI provider (and possibly use a different one), and the second one is used to add middleware components to the ASP.NET Core pipeline.

The main things you need to remember here are as follows:

- Kestrel is the default host server.
- Configuration providers for JSON and the environment are added automatically; user secrets are added if running in `Development` environment. There should be one `appsettings.json` file and possibly one `appsettings.<environment>.json` file, with overrides per environment.
- Logging is enabled for the console and debug pane of Visual Studio.

Now that we have looked at these templates, let's see what has changed since version 2.0 and how the different tools, templates, features, and so on are affected by it.

What's new since version 2.0?

Let's see what is new in version 2.0 by going through the following sections.

ASP.NET Core 2.1

ASP.NET Core 2.1 was released on the web on May 30 2018. It doesn't contain a large number of breaking changes or fantastic new features, but I would highlight the following ones.

SignalR

SignalR, the real-time communication library for ASP.NET Core, finally made it out of prerelease. It has lots of goodies that didn't exist in pre-Core versions, and we will cover it in its own chapter.

Razor class libraries

It is now possible to package Razor UI files (`.cshtml`) as NuGet packages. This opens the door to lots of interesting possibilities. There will be more on this in the chapter about component reuse.

Razor pages improvements

Razor pages, introduced in ASP.NET Core 2.0, now also support areas and have a couple of additional features. We will go through them in the chapter on views.

New partial tag helper

There's a new `<partial>` tag helper that provides a somewhat cleaner alternative to `RenderPartial`. Again, it will be discussed in the chapter about component reuse.

Top-level parameter validation

In previous versions of ASP.NET Core, you had to explicitly check the validation status of your model, usually through a call to `ModelState.IsValid`. Now, this is no longer the case, and the validation of parameters using any validator is configured is done automatically. We'll talk more about this in the chapter dedicated to forms and models.

Identity UI library and scaffolding

Together with the new Razor UI class libraries, Visual Studio now has support for scaffolding, and ASP.NET Core Identity is a good candidate for this. What this means is that if we select ASP.NET Core Identity as the authentication provider, we can cherry pick the UI components we're interested in (login page, login status, and so on) and provide the rest. This will be covered in the chapter dedicated to security.

Virtual authentication schemes

There's a new mechanism by which we can abstract (and possibly combine) different authentication providers: it's called virtual authentication schemes, and we will talk about it in the chapter on security.

HTTPS by default

What else can I say? HTTPS is now the default, but configurable through the Visual Studio wizard. Hopefully, it will both make your applications more secure and prevent some subtle problems that only arise when deploying to production. It will be covered in the chapter on security.

GDPR-related template changes

The **Global Data Protection Regulation (GDPR)** imposed a number of constraints when it comes to tracking users and storing their data. The new Visual Studio templates and the ASP.NET Core 2.1 APIs introduced some changes related to cookie tracking and explicit user consent. We will talk about all these in the security chapter.

If you want to know more about GDPR, please visit `https://eugdpr.org`.

MVC functional test improvements

Functional (or integration) tests are now easier to set up because .NET Core 2.1 makes some assumptions that are generally ok. There will be more on this in the chapter on testing.

API conventions and supporting types

There have been some improvements in regards to providing metadata and discoverability for API endpoints, all of which will be covered in a new chapter about API controllers and actions.

Generic host builder

This may not be too important for ASP.NET Core developers, but there's a new host builder that can be used to build non-HTTP endpoints. Because this is too specific, we won't talk about it in this book.

Updated SPA templates

There are new templates for **single-page applications** (**SPAs**) available for some of the most popular JavaScript frameworks: Angular, React, and React with Redux. I will (briefly) cover these in the chapter about client-side development.

ASP.NET Core 2.2

ASP.NET Core 2.2 was released in December 2018. Some of the changes are outlined in the following sections.

API code analyzers

Visual Studio can now automatically add attributes that describe the return types and codes for API actions based on conventions.

Health check API

Health check APIs were previously available as prerelease code, but are now available as stable and fully supported checks for multiple conditions.

Endpoint routing

There is now a faster routing mechanism that also allows the inferring of the current route much earlier in the pipeline. It also includes parameter transformers.

Problem details (RFC 7807) support

There is new support for the implementation of RFC 7807 problem details for representing API errors.

ASP.NET Core 3.0

ASP.NET Core 3.0 was released in September 2019. Here are some of its biggest changes.

C# 8.0

Together with .NET Core 3.0, Visual Studio 2019 was updated to support the new language features of C# 8.0.

.NET Standard 2.1

The new .NET Standard was also released, with a much greater API surface.

Blazor

Blazor (server hosting model) is now included with .NET Core 3.

Built-in JSON support

.NET now features its own JSON library, `System.Text.Json`.

HTTP/2 support

`HttpClient` now supports HTTP/2 and is enabled by default in Kestrel.

gRPC

gRPC for .NET has been released. Visual Studio and `dotnet` now have templates for gRPC.

IdentityServer integration

Authentication is now capable of integrating with `IdentityServer` out of the box.

Endpoint routing

Endpoint routing is now the default.

Migrating to ASP.NET Core 3.x

Updating a project to version 3 should be as simple as updating the `TargetFramework` property of the `.csproj` files to contain `netcoreapp3.0` (or `netcoreapp3.1`, for .NET Core 3.1) instead of `netcoreapp2.0` and removing any references to `Microsoft.AspNetCore.App`. It is also mandatory to remove `DotNetCliToolReference`, as it is deprecated and its purpose replaced by global tools. Of course, when Visual Studio asks you to update the NuGet packages of your solution, you should do it to use the latest features.

 For a detailed, step-by-step tutorial, please go to `https://docs.microsoft.com/en-us/aspnet/core/migration/20_21`.

Version set

Some features of ASP.NET Core will only be available if you explicitly ask for them. This is done by calling the `SetCompatibilityVersion` extension method:

```
services  .AddMvc() .SetCompatibilityVersion
(CompatibilityVersion.Version_3_0);
```

The values you can pass to the `SetCompatibilityVersion` method are as follows:

- `Latest`: Use the latest features (at the time of the writing of this book, version **3**)
- `Version_2_0`: Use only the subset supported as of ASP.NET Core **2.0**
- `Version_2_1`: Use the features introduced in version **2.1**
- `Version_3_0`: Use the features of version **3**

Because we want to explore all features available to ASP.NET Core, let's call it with either `Latest` or `Version_3_0`. If you don't specify a value, it will default to the latest major version: **3**.

 There is no flag for version **3.1** because this release does not contain breaking changes from version **3**.

Let's now move on to look at some tools that will be covered in more depth in the two appendices at the end of the book.

The NuGet and dotnet tools

There are two tools that are closely related to the .NET Core SDK:

- `dotnet`
- `nuget`

These tools are must-haves for .NET development: the first, `dotnet`, is what, NuGet ecosystem of libraries and installs, publishes, and otherwise manages sets of NuGet packages. This one is

`dotnet` always executes with the most recent .NET Core version available on the system. In *Appendix 1*, you will find a good description of this tool and its usages.

You can get the `nuget` tool from `https://www.nuget.org/packages/NuGet.CommandLine`.

Summary

In this first chapter, we went through some of the biggest changes in ASP.NET Core and .NET Core. You are introduced to some of the key concepts in .NET Core: the NuGet distribution mode, the OWIN pipeline, the hosting model, environments, the improved context, and the built-in dependency framework, which are new in ASP.NET Core 3. We also had a look at the `nuget` and `dotnet` tools, the Swiss army knife of command-line .NET development, which will be covered in more detail in *Appendix 1*.

In the next chapter, we will start our .NET Core journey by exploring the configuration of an application.

Questions

By now you should be able to answer the following questions:

1. What are the benefits of DI?
2. What are environments?
3. What does MVC mean?
4. What are the supported lifetimes in the built-in DI container?
5. What is the difference between .NET Core and the .NET Standard?
6. What is a metapackage?
7. What is OWIN?

Configuration 2

This chapter covers the configuration of an ASP.NET Core application. Every application needs configuration in one form or another because it makes it much easier to change the underlying behavior should anything happen—think about connection strings, credentials, **Internet Protocol** (**IP**) addresses, or any other kind of data that can change over time and is therefore not appropriate to be hardcoded.

Configuration can be done in many ways, some of which don't even require redeploying your application, which is a huge benefit. Luckily, .NET Core was conceived with this in mind and is also very extensible, so it can cover most scenarios, basic and advanced. It also plays nicely with other aspects, such as security and dependency injection.

Also, a very typical configuration just features switching or toggling: something is either enabled or not. .NET Core 3 introduced a new feature toggling library that is outside the main configuration framework, but it will be covered here.

After reading this chapter, you should be able to understand the following:

- How the configuration works on the .NET Core framework
- Which configuration sources we have available
- How to extend it to be more helpful and match your necessities
- Runtime host configuration
- The new feature toggle mechanism introduced in .NET Core 3

Technical requirements

In order to implement the examples introduced in this chapter, you will need the .NET Core 3 **software development kit (SDK)** and some kind of text editor. Of course, Visual Studio 2019 (any edition) meets all the requirements, but you can also use Visual Studio Code, for example.

The source code can be retrieved from GitHub here: `https://github.com/ PacktPublishing/Modern-Web-Development-with-ASP.NET-Core-3-Second-Edition`.

Getting started

Previous versions of .NET had a relatively simple configuration system, where all settings went into **Extensible Markup Language (XML)** files with the `.config` extension. There was a basic schema that could handle both system settings and untyped key-value pairs, but they were all strings. There was also some degree of inheritance, as some of the settings could be defined machine-wide and then overridden per application, and even in virtual applications underneath an **Internet Information Services (IIS)** application. It was possible to define custom sections with typed settings and complex structures by writing and registering .NET classes.

However, as convenient as this would seem, it turns out it had its limitations—namely, the following:

- Only XML files were supported; it was not possible to have other configuration sources out of the box.
- It was difficult to have different configuration files/configuration sections per environment (staging, **quality assurance (QA)**, production, and more).
- It was not possible to receive notifications when the configuration changed.
- It was tricky to save changes.

Moreover, as dependency injection was not part of the core .NET infrastructure, there was no way to have configuration values injected into its services automatically. Let's see how .NET Core 3 helps us overcome these limitations.

Configurations in .NET Core

Realizing this, Microsoft made configuration a first-order concept in .NET Core and did so in quite a flexible, extensible way. It all starts with a builder instance; we add providers to it, and when we've finished, we just ask it to build a configuration object that will hold all the values loaded from each provider in memory.

This configuration object will be capable of returning configuration settings from any of the added providers transparently, which means that regardless of the source, we use the same syntax for querying configuration options. It will hold an in-memory representation of all the values loaded from all registered providers, and will allow you to change them, or add new entries.

The base class model for the configuration **application programming interface (API)** in .NET Core looks like this:

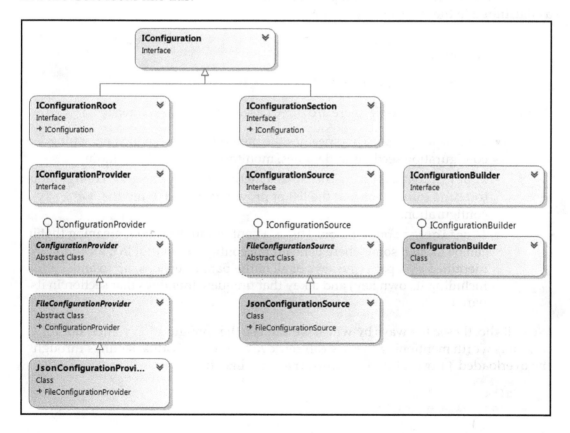

So, the provider mechanism is split into two base interfaces and their implementations, as follows:

- `IConfigurationSource` is responsible for creating a concrete instance of an `IConfigurationProvider`; each of the available providers (coming next) implements this interface.
- `IConfigurationProvider` specifies the contract for actually retrieving values, reloading, and more; the root class that implements this is `ConfigurationProvider`, and there's also a particular implementation that serves as the root for all file-based providers, `FileConfigurationProvider`.

`ConfigurationBuilder` itself is just a specific implementation of the `IConfigurationBuilder` interface, and there are no other implementations. Its contract specifies how we can add providers and build the configuration from them, as illustrated in the following code block:

```
var builder = new ConfigurationBuilder()    .Add(source1)
    .Add(source2);

var cfg = builder.Build();
```

As for the configuration itself, there are three base interfaces, as follows:

- `IConfiguration`: This specifies the methods for retrieving and setting configuration sections and values, monitoring changes, and more.
- `IConfigurationRoot`: This adds a method for reloading the configuration to `IConfiguration` and the list of providers used to build the configuration.
- `IConfigurationSection`: This is a configuration section, meaning that it can be located somewhere beneath the configuration root in a location identified by a path (the keys of all of the parent sections, up to and including its own key) and a key that uniquely identifies that section in its parent.

We will shortly see the ways by which we can use the configuration values, but for now, it is worth mentioning that we can retrieve and set individual settings through the overloaded `[]` operator in `IConfiguration`, like this:

```
cfg["key"] = "value";
string value = cfg["key"];
```

This takes a string as `key` and returns a string as the `value`, and in the next sections, we will see how we can circumvent this limitation. If no entry for the given key exists, it returns `null`.

> All keys are case-insensitive. A path is composed of a colon (`:`)-combined set of keys and subkeys that can be used to get to a specific value.

The .NET Core configuration has the concept of sections. We can get hold of a particular section, or even check whether it exists altogether, by running the following code:

```
var section = cfg.GetSection("ConnectionStrings");
var exists = section.Exists();
```

By convention, sections are separated by `:`. Getting a value from a section with a section-specific key is the same as retrieving it from the configuration root with a fully qualified key. For example, if you have a key of `A:B:C`, this is the same as having a key of `C` inside section `B` of section `A`, as illustrated in the following screenshot:

```
var valueFromRoot = cfg["A:B:C"];
var aSection = cfg.GetSection("A");
var bSection = aSection.GetSection("B");
var valueFromSection = bSection["C"];
```

For the record, the core configuration API is implemented in the `Microsoft.Extensions.Configuration` and `Microsoft.Extensions.Configuration.Binder` NuGet packages, which are automatically included by other packages, such as those of the specific providers. Let's now have a look at the available providers.

> ASP.NET Core 2 and later automatically registers the `IConfiguration` instance in the dependency injection framework; for previous versions, you need to do this manually.

Providers

The available Microsoft configuration providers (and their NuGet packages) are as follows:

- **JavaScript Object Notation (JSON)** files: `Microsoft.Extensions.Configuration.Json`
- XML files: `Microsoft.Extensions.Configuration.Xml`
- **Initialization (INI)** files: `Microsoft.Extensions.Configuration.Ini`
- User secrets: `Microsoft.Extensions.Configuration.UserSecrets`
- Azure Key Vault: `Microsoft.Extensions.Configuration.AzureKeyVault`
- Environment variables: `Microsoft.Extensions.Configuration.EnvironmentVariables`
- Command line: `Microsoft.Extensions.Configuration.CommandLine`
- Memory: `Microsoft.Extensions.Configuration`
- Docker secrets: `Microsoft.Extensions.Configuration.DockerSecrets`

 Some of these are based upon the `FileConfigurationProvider` class: JSON, XML, and INI.

When you reference these packages, you automatically make their extensions available. So, for example, if you want to add the JSON provider, you have two options, detailed next.

You can add a `JsonConfigurationSource` directly, like this:

```
var jsonSource = new JsonConfigurationSource {
  Path = "appsettings.json" };
builder.Add(jsonSource);
```

Alternatively, you can use the `AddJsonFile` extension method, like this:

```
builder.AddJsonFile("appsettings.json");
```

Most likely, the extension methods are what you need. As I said, you can have any number of providers at the same time, as illustrated in the following code snippet:

```
builder
    .AddJsonFile("appsettings.json")
```

```
    .AddEnvironmentVariables()
    .AddXmlFile("web.config");
```

You just need to keep in mind that if two providers return the same configuration setting, the order by which they were added matters; the result you get will come from the last provider added, as it will override the previous ones. So, for example, imagine you are adding two JSON configuration files, one that is common across all environments (development, staging, and production), and another for a specific environment; in this case, you would likely have the following:

```
builder
    .AddJsonFile("appsettings.json")
    .AddJsonFile($"appsettings.{env.EnvironmentName}.json");
```

 This is so the environment-specific configuration file takes precedence.

Each provider will, of course, feature different properties for setting up; all file-based providers will require, for instance, a file path, but that doesn't make sense when we're talking about environment variables.

File-based providers

Both JSON, XML, and INI configuration sources are based on files. Therefore, their classes inherit from the `FileConfigurationSource` abstract base class. This class offers the following configuration properties:

- `Path`: The actual, fully qualified physical path where the file is to be found; this is a required setting.
- `Optional`: A Boolean flag for specifying whether the absence of the file causes a runtime error (`false`) or not (`true`); the default is `false`.
- `ReloadOnChange`: Here, you decide whether to automatically detect changes to the source file (`true`) or not (`false`); the default is `false`.
- `ReloadDelay`: The delay, in milliseconds, before reloading the file in the event that a change was detected (`ReloadOnChange` set to `true`); the default is 250 milliseconds.

- `OnLoadException`: A delegate to be called should an error occur while parsing the source file; this is empty by default.
- `FileProvider`: The file provider that actually retrieves the file; the default is an instance of `PhysicalFileProvider`, set with the folder of the `Path` property.

All of the extension methods allow you to supply values for each of these properties, except `OnLoadException`. You are also free to specify your own concrete implementation of `IFileProvider`, which you should do if you have specific needs, such as getting files from inside a ZIP file. `ConfigurationBuilder` has an extension method, `SetBasePath`, that sets a default `PhysicalFileProvider` pointing to a folder on your filesystem so that you can pass relative file paths to the configuration source's `Path` property.

If you set `ReloadOnChange` to `true`, .NET Core will start an operating system-specific file that monitors a watch on the source file; because these things come with a cost, try not to have many watches.

A typical example would be as follows:

```
builder
    .SetBasePath(@"C:\Configuration")
    .AddJsonFile(path: "appsettings.json", optional: false,
      reloadOnChange: true)
    .AddJsonFile(path: $"appsettings.{env.EnvironmentName}.json",
      optional: true, reloadOnChange: true);
```

This would result in the `appsettings.json` file being loaded from the `C:\Configuration` folder (and throwing an exception if it is not present), and then loading `appsettings.Development.json` (this time, ignoring it if the file doesn't exist). Whenever there's a change in either file, they are reloaded and the configuration is updated.

 Very important: in operating systems or filesystems where the case matters, such as Linux, make sure that the name of the file that takes the environment name (for example, `appsettings.Development.json`) is in the right case—otherwise, it won't be found!

If, however, we wanted to add an error handler, we need to add the configuration source manually, as follows:

```
var jsonSource = new JsonConfigurationSource { Path = "filename.json"
};
jsonSource.OnLoadException = (x) =>
{
    if (x.Exception is FileNotFoundException ex)
    {
        Console.Out.WriteLine($"File {ex.FileName} not found");
        x.Ignore = true;
    }
};
builder.Add(jsonSource);
```

This way, we can prevent certain errors from crashing our application.

All file-based providers are added by an extension method with the name `AddxxxFile`, where `xxx` is the actual type—`Json`, `Xml`, or `Ini`—and always takes the same parameters (`path`, `optional`, and `reloadOnChange`).

JSON provider

We typically add a JSON configuration file using the `AddJsonFile` extension method. The JSON provider will load a file containing JSON contents and make its structure available for configuration, using dotted notation. A typical example is shown in the following code snippet:

```
{
    "ConnectionStrings": {
        "DefaultConnection": "Server=(localdb)mssqllocaldb;
          Database=aspnetcore"
    }
}
```

Any valid JSON content will work. As of now, it is not possible to specify a schema. Sections are just sub-elements of the JSON content.

An example of code used to load a configuration value would be as follows:

```
var defaultConnection = cfg["ConnectionStrings:DefaultConnection"];
```

XML provider

XML is becoming less and less common, with JSON, inversely, becoming increasingly popular; however, there are still good reasons to use XML. So, we add an XML file using the `AddXmlFile` extension method, and as far as configuration is concerned, we need to wrap our XML contents in a `settings` node; the XML declaration is optional. Refer to the following example:

```
<settings Flag="2">
    <MySettings>
        <Option>10</Option>
    </MySettings>
</settings>
```

Again, as of now, it is not possible to specify a validating schema. With this provider, sections are implemented as sub-elements.

Two examples of this are as follows:

```
var flag = cfg["Flag"];
var option = cfg["MySettings:Option"];
```

INI provider

INI files are a thing of the past, but, for historical reasons, Microsoft is still supporting them (actually, Linux also makes use of INI files too). In case you're not familiar with its syntax, this is what it looks like:

```
[SectionA]
Option1=Value1
Option2=Value2

[SectionB]
Option1=Value3
```

You add INI files to the configuration through the `AddIniFile` extension method.

One word of advice: both XML and JSON file formats support anything that INI files do, so unless you have a very specific requirement, you're better off with either JSON or XML.

Sections in INI files just map to the intrinsic sections provided by the INI file specification.

A single example is as follows:

```
var optionB2 = cfg["SectionB:Option1"];
```

Other providers

Besides file-based providers, there are other ways to store and retrieve configuration information. Here, we list the currently available options in .NET Core.

User secrets

.NET Core introduced **user secrets** as a means of storing sensitive information per user. The benefit of this is that it is kept in a secure manner, out of configuration files, and is not visible by other users. A user secrets store is identified (for a given user) by `userSecretsId`, which the Visual Studio template initializes as a mix of a string and a **globally unique identifier** (**GUID**), such as `aspnet-Web-f22b64ea-be5e-432d-abc6-0275a9c00377`.

Secrets in a store can be listed, added, or removed through the `dotnet` executable, as illustrated in the following code snippet:

```
dotnet user-secrets list                 --lists all the values in the
                                                           store
dotnet user-secrets set "key" "value"    --set "key" to be "value"
dotnet user-secrets remove "key"         --remove entry for "key"
dotnet user-secrets clear                --remove all entries
```

You will need the `Microsoft.Extensions.SecretManager.Tools` package. The `dotnet user-secrets` command will only work when in the presence of a project file that specifies the `userSecretsId` store ID. The `AddUserSecrets` extension method is what we use to add user secrets to the configuration, and it will either pick up this `userSecretsId` setting automatically, or you can provide your own at runtime, as follows:

```
builder.AddUserSecrets(userSecretdId: "[User Secrets Id]");
```

Another option is to get the user secrets ID from an assembly, in which case this needs to be decorated with the `UserSecretsIdAttribute` attribute, as follows:

```
[assembly: UserSecretsId("aspnet-Web-f22b64ea-be5e-432d-
abc6-0275a9c00377")
```

In this case, the way to load it is demonstrated in the following code snippet:

```
builder.AddUserSecrets<Startup>();
```

 Be warned: if you have more than one assembly with the same user secret ID (by mistake), the application will throw an exception when loading them.

Yet another way to specify user secrets (in ASP.NET Core 2.x) is through the `.csproj` file, by using a `UserSecretsId` element, as illustrated in the following code snippet:

```
<PropertyGroup>
    <TargetFramework>netcoreapp2.1</TargetFramework>
    <UserSecretsId>9094c8e7-0000-0000-0000-
c26798dc18d2</UserSecretsId>
</PropertyGroup>
```

Regardless of how you specify the user secrets ID, as with all the other providers, the way to load a value is as follows:

```
var value = cfg["key"];
```

In case you are interested, you can read more about .NET Core user secrets here: https://docs.microsoft.com/en-us/aspnet/core/security/app-secrets

Azure Key Vault

Azure Key Vault is an Azure service that you can leverage for enterprise-level secure key-value storage. The full description is outside the scope of this book, but you can read about it here: https://azure.microsoft.com/en-us/services/key-vault. Suffice to say that you add the Azure Key Vault provider through the `AddAzureKeyVault` extension method, as depicted in this line of code:

```
builder.AddAzureKeyVault(vault: "https://[Vault].vault.azure.net/",
    clientId: "[Client ID]", clientSecret: "[Client Secret]");
```

After this, all are added to the configuration object, and you can retrieve them in the usual way.

Command line

Another very popular way to get configuration settings is the command line. Executables regularly expect information to be passed in the command line, so as to dictate what should be done or to control how it should happen.

The extension method to use is `AddCommandLine`, and it expects a required and an optional parameter, as follows:

```
builder.AddCommandLine(args:
Environment.GetCommandLineArgs().Skip(1).ToArray());
```

The `args` parameter will typically come from `Environment.GetCommandLineArgs()`, and we take the first parameter out, as this is the entry assembly's name. If we are building our configuration object in `Program.Main`, we can use its `args` parameter too.

Now, there are several ways to specify parameters. One way is illustrated in the following code snippet:

```
Key1=Value1
--Key2=Value2
/Key3=Value3
--Key4 Value4
/Key5 Value5
```

Here is another example:

```
dotnet run MyProject Key1=Value1 --Key2=Value2 /Key3=Value3 --Key4
Value4 /Key5 Value5
```

If the value has spaces in it, you need to wrap it in quotes ("). You can't use – (single dash), as this would be interpreted as a parameter to `dotnet` instead.

The optional parameter to `AddCommandLine`, `switchMappings`, is a dictionary that can be used to create new keys that will duplicate those from the command line, as follows:

```
var switchMappings = new Dictionary<string,
string>(StringComparer.OrdinalIgnoreCase)
    { { "--Key1", "AnotherKey" } };

builder.AddCommandLine(
    args: Environment.GetCommandLineArgs().Skip(1).ToArray(),
    switchMappings: switchMappings);
```

These keys can even have special characters in them—for example, `--a:key` and `/some.key` are valid keys.

Again, use the same syntax to retrieve their values.

Environment variables

Environment variables exist in all operating systems and can also be regarded as a source of configuration. Many tools out there, such as Docker, rely on environment variables for getting their operating context.

Adding environment variables to a .NET Core configuration is straightforward; you just need to call `AddEnvironmentVariables`. By default, this will bring all the existing environment variables into the configuration, but we can also specify a prefix, and filter out all variables that do not start with it, as follows:

```
builder.AddEnvironmentVariables(prefix: "ASPNET_");
```

So, this will add both `ASPNET_TargetHost` and `ASPNET_TargetPort`, but not `PATH` or `COMPUTERNAME`.

Sections are supported if you separate names with double underscores (for example, __). For example, say you have this environment variable:

```
ASPNETCORE__ADMINGROUP__USERS=rjperes,pm
```

You could access the `ADMINGROUP` section like this:

```
var group = cfg
    .GetSection("ASPNETCORE")
    .GetSection("ADMINGROUP");
var users = group["USERS"];
```

Memory

The memory provider is a convenient way of specifying values dynamically at runtime and for using dictionary objects. We add the provider with the `AddInMemoryCollection` extension method, as follows:

```
var properties = new Dictionary<string, string> { { "key", "value" }
};
builder.AddInMemoryCollection(properties);
```

The advantage of this approach is that it is easy to populate a dictionary with whatever values we want, particularly in unit tests.

Docker

The ability to have secrets coming from Docker-stored files is relatively new in .NET Core. Basically, it will try to load text files in a specific directory inside a Docker instance as the values where the key is the filename itself. This is an actual feature of Docker, about which you can read more here: `https://docs.docker.com/engine/swarm/secrets`

The `AddDockerSecrets` extension method takes two optional parameters—the user secrets directory and whether or not this directory itself is optional; in other words, just ignore it if it's not there. This is illustrated in the following code snippet:

```
builder.AddDockerSecrets(secretsPath: "/var/lib/secrets", optional:
true);
```

It is possible to specify these two parameters plus an `ignore` prefix and a delegate for filtering out files by their names if we use the overload that takes a configuration object, as illustrated in the following code block:

```
builder.AddDockerSecrets(opt =>
{
    opt.SecretsDirectory = "/var/lib/secrets";
    opt.Optional = true;
    opt.IgnorePrefix = "ignore.";
    opt.IgnoreCondition = (filename) =>
!filename.Contains($".{env.EnvironmentName}.");
});
```

Here, we are filtering out both files starting with `ignore.`, as well as those that do not contain the current environment name (for example, `.Development.`). Pretty cool!

Default providers

The ASP.NET Core code included in the default application templates (`WebHostBuilder.CreateDefaultBuilder`) registers the following providers:

- JSON
- Environment

- Command line
- User secrets

Of course, you can add new providers to the configuration builder to match your needs. Next, we will see how we can create a custom provider for specific configuration needs.

Creating a custom provider

Although we have several options for storing configuration values, you may have your own specific needs. For example, if you are using Windows, you might want to store your configuration settings in the Registry. For that, you need a custom provider. Let's see how we can build one.

First, you need to add the `Microsoft.Win32.Registry` NuGet package to your project. Then, we start by implementing `IConfigurationSource`, as follows:

```
public sealed class RegistryConfigurationSource : IConfigurationSource
{
    public RegistryHive Hive { get; set; } = RegistryHive.CurrentUser;

    public IConfigurationProvider Build(IConfigurationBuilder builder)
    {
        return new RegistryConfigurationProvider(this);
    }
}
```

As you can see from the preceding code block, the only configurable property is `Hive`, by means of which you can specify a specific Registry hive, with `CurrentUser` (`HKEY_CURRENT_USER`) being the default.

Next, we need an `IConfigurationProvider` implementation. Let's inherit from the `ConfigurationProvider` class, as this takes care of some of the basic implementations, such as reloading (which we do not support as we go directly to the source). The code can be seen here:

```
public sealed class RegistryConfigurationProvider :
ConfigurationProvider
{
    private readonly RegistryConfigurationSource _configurationSource;

    public RegistryConfigurationProvider(
     RegistryConfigurationSource configurationSource)
    {
```

```
        _configurationSource = configurationSource;
    }

    private RegistryKey GetRegistryKey(string key)
    {
        RegistryKey regKey;
        switch (_configurationSource.Hive)
        {
            case RegistryHive.ClassesRoot:
                regKey = Registry.ClassesRoot;
                break;

            case RegistryHive.CurrentConfig:
                regKey = Registry.CurrentConfig;
                break;

            case RegistryHive.CurrentUser:
                regKey = Registry.CurrentUser;
                break;

            case RegistryHive.LocalMachine:
                regKey = Registry.LocalMachine;
                break;

            case RegistryHive.PerformanceData:
                regKey = Registry.PerformanceData;
                break;

            case RegistryHive.Users:
                regKey = Registry.Users;
                break;

            default:
              throw new InvalidOperationException($"Supplied hive
                {_configurationSource.Hive} is invalid.");
        }

        var parts = key.Split('\\');
        var subKey = string.Join("", parts.Where(
          (x, i) => i < parts.Length - 1));

        return regKey.OpenSubKey(subKey);
    }

    public override bool TryGet(string key, out string value)
    {
        var regKey = this.GetRegistryKey(key);
        var parts = key.Split('\\');
```

```
        var name = parts.Last();
        var regValue = regKey.GetValue(name);

        value = regValue?.ToString();

        return regValue != null;
    }

    public override void Set(string key, string value)
    {
        var regKey = this.GetRegistryKey(key);
        var parts = key.Split('');
        var name = parts.Last();

        regKey.SetValue(name, value);
    }
}
```

This provider class leverages the `Registry` API to retrieve values from the Windows Registry, which, of course, will not work on non-Windows machines. The `TryGet` and `Set` methods, defined in the `ConfigurationProvider` class, both delegate to the private `GetRegistryKey` method, which retrieves a key-value pair from the Registry.

Finally, let's add a friendly extension method to make registration simpler, as follows:

```
public static class RegistryConfigurationExtensions
{
    public static IConfigurationBuilder AddRegistry(
        this IConfigurationBuilder builder,
        RegistryHive hive = RegistryHive.CurrentUser)
    {
        return builder.Add(new RegistryConfigurationSource { Hive =
hive });
    }
}
```

Now, you can use this provider, as follows:

```
builder
    .AddJsonFile("appsettings.json")
    .AddRegistry(RegistryHive.LocalMachine);
```

Nice and easy, don't you think? Now, let's see how we can use the configuration files for the providers that we registered.

Using configuration values

So, we've now seen how to set up configuration providers, but how exactly can we use these configuration values? Let's see in the following sections.

Getting and setting values explicitly

Remember that the .NET configuration allows you to set both reading and writing, both using the [] notation, as illustrated in the following code snippet:

```
var value = cfg["key"];
cfg["another.key"] = "another value";
```

Of course, setting a value in the configuration object does not mean that it will get persisted into any provider; the configuration is kept in memory only.

It is also possible to try to have the value converted to a specific type, as follows:

```
cfg["count"] = "0";
var count = cfg.GetValue<int>("count");
```

 Don't forget that the value that you want to convert needs to be convertible from a string; in particular, it needs to have TypeConverter defined for that purpose, which all .NET Core primitive types do. The conversion will take place using the current culture.

Configuration sections

It is also possible to use **configuration sections**. A configuration section is specified through a colon (:), as in section:subsection. An infinite nesting of sections can be specified. But—I hear you ask—what is a configuration section, and how do we define one? Well, that depends on the configuration source you're using.

In the case of JSON, a configuration section will basically map to a complex property. Have a look at the following code snippet to view an example of this:

```
{
    "section-1": {
        "section-2": {
            "section-3": {
                "a-key": "value"
```

```
            }
        }
      }
    }
```

 Not all providers are capable of handling configuration sections or handle them in the same way. In XML, each section corresponds to a node; for INI files, there is a direct mapping; and for the Azure Key Vault, user secrets, memory (dictionaries), and providers, sections are specified as keys separated by colons (for example, `ASPNET:Variable`, `MyApp:Variable`, `Data:Blog:ConnectionString`, and more). For environment variables, they are separated by double underscores (__). The example Registry provider I showed earlier does not, however, support them.

We have a couple of sections here, as follows:

- The root section
- `section-1`
- `section-2`
- `section-3`

So, if we wanted to access a value for the `a-key` key, we would do so using the following syntax:

```
var aKey = cfg["section-1:section-2:section-3:a-key"];
```

Alternatively, we could ask for the `section-3` section and get the `a-key` value directly from it, as illustrated in the following code snippet:

```
var section3 = cfg.GetSection("section-1:section-2:section-3");
var aKey = section3["a-key"];
var key = section3.Key;    //section-3
var path = section3.Path;  //section-1:section-2:section-3
```

A section will contain the path from where it was obtained. This is defined in the `IConfigurationSection` interface, which inherits from `IConfiguration`, thus making all of its extension methods available too.

By the way, you can ask for any configuration section and a value will always be returned, but this doesn't mean that it exists. You can use the `Exists` extension method to check for that possibility, as follows:

```
var fairyLandSection = cfg.GetSection("fairy:land");
var exists = fairyLandSection.Exists();  //false
```

A configuration section may have children, and we can list them using `GetChildren`, like this:

```
var section1 = cfg.GetSection("section-1");
var subSections = section1.GetChildren();  //section-2
```

.NET Core includes a shorthand for a typical configuration section and connection strings. This is the `GetConnectionString` extension method, and it basically looks for a connection string named `ConnectionStrings` and returns a named value from it. You can use the JSON schema introduced when we discussed the JSON provider as a reference, as follows:

```
var blogConnectionString =
cfg.GetConnectionString("DefaultConnection");
```

Getting all values

It may not be that useful, but it is possible to get a list of all configuration values (together with their keys) present in a configuration object. We do this using the `AsEnumerable` extension method, illustrated in the following code snippet:

```
var keysAndValues = cfg.AsEnumerable().ToDictionary(kv => kv.Key, kv
=> kv.Value);
```

There's also a `makePathsRelative` parameter, which, by default, is `false` and can be used in a configuration section to strip out the section's key from the returned entries' keys. Say, for example, that you are working on the `section-3` section. If you call `AsEnumerable` with `makePathsRelative` set to `true`, then the entry for `a-key` will appear as `a-key` instead of `section-1:section-2:section-3:a-key`.

Binding to classes

Another interesting option is to bind the current configuration to a class. The binding process will pick up any sections and their properties present in the configuration and try to map them to a .NET class. Let's say we have the following JSON configuration:

```
{
    "Logging": {
        "IncludeScopes": false,
        "LogLevel": {
          "Default": "Debug",
          "System": "Information",
          "Microsoft": "Information"
        }
    }
}
```

We also have a couple of classes, such as these ones:

```
public class LoggingSettings
{
    public bool IncludeScopes { get; set; }
    public LogLevelSettings LogLevel { get; set; }
}

public class LogLevelSettings
{
    public LogLevel Default { get; set; }
    public LogLevel System { get; set; }
    public LogLevel Microsoft { get; set; }
}
```

 LogLevel **comes from the** Microsoft.Extensions.Logging **namespace.**

You can bind the two together, like this:

```
var settings = new LoggingSettings { LogLevel = new LogLevelSettings()
};
cfg.GetSection("Logging").Bind(settings);
```

The values of LoggingSettings will be automatically populated from the current configuration, leaving untouched any properties of the target instance for which there are no values in the configuration. Of course, this can be done for any configuration section, so if your settings are not stored at the root level, it will still work.

Mind you, these won't be automatically refreshed whenever the underlying data changes. We will see in a moment how we can do that.

Another option is to have the configuration build and return a self-instantiated instance, as follows:

```
var settings = cfg.GetSection("Logging").Get<LoggingSettings>();
```

For this to work, the template class cannot be abstract and needs to have a public parameterless constructor defined.

 Don't forget that an error will occur if—and only if—a configuration value cannot be bound, either directly as a string or through `TypeConverter` to the target property in the **Plain Old CLR Object (POCO)** class. If no such property exists, it will be silently ignored. The `TypeConverter` class comes from the `System.ComponentModel` NuGet package and namespace.

Since when using a file-based configuration, all properties are stored as strings, the providers need to know how to convert these into the target types. Fortunately, the included providers know how to do this for most types, such as the following:

- Strings
- Integers
- Floating points (provided the decimal character is the same as per the current culture)
- Booleans (`true` or `false` in any casing)
- Dates (the format must match the current culture or be compliant **Request for Comments (RFC)** 3339/**International Organization for Standardization (ISO)** 8601)
- Time (*hh:mm:ss* or RFC 3339/ISO 8601)
- GUIDs
- Enumerations

Injecting values

OK—so, we now know how to load configuration values from several sources, and we also know a couple of ways to ask for them explicitly. However, .NET Core relies heavily on dependency injection, so we might want to use that for configuration settings as well.

First, it should be fairly obvious that we can register the configuration object itself with the dependency injection framework, as follows:

```
var cfg = builder.Build();
services.AddSingleton(cfg);
```

Wherever we ask for an `IConfigurationRoot` object, we will get this one. We can also register it as the base `IConfiguration`, which is safe as well, although we miss the ability to reload the configuration (we will cover this in more detail later on). This is illustrated here:

```
services.AddSingleton<IConfiguration>(cfg);
```

 Since version 2.0, ASP.NET Core automatically registers the configuration object (`IConfiguration`) with the dependency injection framework.

We might also be interested in injecting a POCO class with configuration settings. In that case, we use `Configure`, as follows:

```
services.Configure<LoggingSettings>(settings =>
{
    settings.IncludeScopes = true;
    settings.Default = LogLevel.Debug;
});
```

Here, we are using the `Configure` extension method, which allows us to specify values for a POCO class to be created at runtime whenever it is requested. Rather than doing this manually, we can ask the configuration object to do it, as follows:

```
services.Configure<LoggingSettings>(settings =>
{
    cfg.GetSection("Logging").Bind(settings);
});
```

Even better, we can pass named configuration options, as follows:

```
services.Configure<LoggingSettings>("Elasticsearch", settings =>
{
this.Configuration.GetSection("Logging:Elasticsearch").Bind(settings);
});

services.Configure<LoggingSettings>("Console", settings =>
{
    this.Configuration.GetSection("Logging:Console").Bind(settings);
});
```

In a minute, we will see how we can use these named configuration options.

We can even pass in the configuration root itself, or a sub-section of it, which is way simpler, as illustrated in the following code snippet:

```
services.Configure<LoggingSettings>(cfg.GetSection("Logging"));
```

Of course, we might as well register our POCO class with the dependency injection framework, as follows:

```
var cfg = builder.Build();
var settings = builder.GetSection("Logging").Get<LoggingSettings>();
services.AddSingleton(settings);
```

If we use the `Configure` method, the configuration instances will be available from the dependency injection framework as instances of `IOptions<T>`, where `T` is a template parameter of the type passed to `Configure`— as per this example, `IOptions<LoggingSettings>`.

The `IOptions<T>` interface specifies a `Value` property by which we can access the underlying instance that was passed or set in `Configure`. The good thing is that this is dynamically executed at runtime if—and only if—it is actually requested, meaning no binding from configuration to the POCO class will occur unless we explicitly want it.

A final note: before using `Configure`, we need to add support for it to the `services` collection as follows:

```
services.AddOptions();
```

For this, the `Microsoft.Extensions.Options` NuGet package will need to be added first, which will ensure that all required services are properly registered.

Retrieving named configuration options

When we register a POCO configuration by means of the `Configure` family of methods, essentially we are registering it to the dependency injection container as `IOption<T>`. This means that whenever we want to have it injected, we can just declare `IOption<T>`, such as `IOption<LoggingSettings>`. But if we want to use named configuration values, we need to use `IOptionsSnapshot<T>` instead. This interface exposes a nice `Get` method that takes as its sole parameter the named configuration setting, as follows:

```
public HomeController(IOptionsSnapshot<LoggingSettings> settings)
{
    var elasticsearchSettings = settings.Get("Elasticsearch");
    var consoleSettings = settings.Get("Console");
}
```

You must remember that we registered the `LoggingSettings` class through a call to the `Configure` method, which takes a name parameter.

Reloading and handling change notifications

You may remember that when we talked about the file-based providers, we mentioned the `reloadOnChange` parameter. This sets up a file-monitoring operation by which the operating system notifies .NET when the file's contents have changed. Even if we don't enable that, it is possible to ask the providers to reload their configuration. The `IConfigurationRoot` interface exposes a `Reload` method for just that purpose, as illustrated in the following code snippet:

```
var cfg = builder.Build();
cfg.Reload();
```

So, if we reload explicitly the configuration, we're pretty confident that when we ask for a configuration key, we will get the updated value in case the configuration has changed in the meantime. If we don't, however, the APIs we've already seen don't ensure that we get the updated version every time. For that, we can do either of the following:

- Register a change notification callback, so as to be notified whenever the underlying file content changes
- Inject a live snapshot of the data, whose value changes whenever the source changes too

For the first option, we need to get a handle to the reload token, and then register our callback actions in it, as follows:

```
var token = cfg.GetReloadToken();
token.RegisterChangeCallback(callback: (state) =>
{
    //state will be someData
    //push the changes to whoever needs it
}, state: "SomeData");
```

For the latter option, instead of injecting IOptions<T>, we need to use IOptionsSnapshot<T>. Just by changing this, we can be sure that the injected value will come from the current, up-to-date configuration source, and not the one that was there when the configuration object was created. Have a look at the following code snippet for an example of this:

```
public class HomeController : Controller
{
    private readonly LoggingSettings _settings;

    public HomeController(IOptionsSnapshot<LoggingSettings> settings)
    {
        _settings = settings.Value;
    }
}
```

It is safe to always use IOptionsSnapshot<T> instead of IOptions<T> as the overhead is minimal.

Running pre- and post-configuration actions

There's a new feature since ASP.NET Core 2.0: running pre- and post-configuration actions for configured types. What this means is, after all the configuration is done, and before a configured type is retrieved from dependency injection, all instances of registered classes are given a chance to execute and make modifications to the configuration. This is true for both unnamed as well as named configuration options.

For unnamed configuration options (Configure with no name parameter), there is an interface called IConfigureOptions<T>, illustrated in the following code snippet:

```
public class PreConfigureLoggingSettings :
IConfigureOptions<LoggingSettings>
{
```

```
    public void Configure(LoggingSettings options)
    {
        //act upon the configured instance
    }
}
```

And, for named configuration options (`Configure` with the name parameter), we have `IConfigureNamedOptions<T>`, as illustrated in the following code snippet:

```
public class PreConfigureNamedLoggingSettings :
IConfigureNamedOptions<LoggingSettings>
{
    public void Configure(string name, LoggingSettings options)
    {
        //act upon the configured instance
    }

    public void Configure(LoggingSettings options)
    {
    }
}
```

These classes, when registered, will be fired before the delegate passed to the `Configure` method. The configuration is simple, as can be seen in the following code snippet:

```
services.ConfigureOptions<PreConfigureLoggingSettings>();
services.ConfigureOptions<PreConfigureNamedLoggingSettings>();
```

But there's more: besides running actions before the configuration delegate, we can also run afterward. Enter `IPostConfigureOptions<T>`—this time, there are no different interfaces for named versus unnamed configuration options' registrations, as illustrated in the following code snippet:

```
public class PostConfigureLoggingSettings :
IPostConfigureOptions<LoggingSettings>
{
    public void PostConfigure(string name, LoggingSettings options) {
... }
}
```

To finalize, each of these classes is instantiated by the dependency injection container, which means that we can use constructor injection! This works like a charm, and can be seen in the following code snippet:

```
public PreConfigureLoggingSettings(IConfiguration configuration) { ...
}
```

This is true for `IConfigureOptions<T>`, `IConfigureNamedOptions<T>`, and `IPostConfigureOptions<T>` as well.

And now, let's see some of the changes from previous versions.

Changes from version 2.x

The big change from version 2.0 was that, as of 2.1, the configuration is done by convention—that is, the process of adding `appsettings.json` JSON files (generic and optional per environment) and all that is hidden from the users.

This is defined in the `WebHost.CreateDefaultBuilder` method. You can, however, still build your own `ConfigurationBuilder` and add whatever you like to it. To do this, you call the `ConfigureAppConfiguration` method, as described in Chapter 1, *Getting Started with ASP.NET Core*, and illustrated in the following code block:

```
Host
    .CreateDefaultBuilder(args)
    .ConfigureAppConfiguration(builder =>
    {
        var jsonSource = new JsonConfigurationSource { Path =
            "appsettings.json" };
        builder.Add(jsonSource);
    })
    .ConfigureWebHostDefaults(builder =>
    {
        builder.UseStartup<Startup>();
    });
```

Or, if you just want to add a single entry to the configuration that is built by default (or, to the one you're modifying), you call the `UseSettings` extension method, as follows:

```
Host
    .CreateDefaultBuilder(args)
    .ConfigureWebHostDefaults(builder =>
    {
        builder.UseSetting("key", "value");
        builder.UseStartup<Startup>();
    });
```

So, when the `Startup` class is instantiated, it will get passed an `IConfiguration` object that is built from the code that you put in here.

Warning: when using `UseSetting`, the value will be written to all registered configuration providers.

After seeing how the application configuration is done, let's see how we can do the same for the host.

Configuring the runtime host

.NET Core 3 introduced a not-so-well-known configuration mechanism that still has some use: a runtime host configuration. The idea here is that you provide configuration settings, as key-value pairs, in the `.csproj` file. You can retrieve them programmatically from the `AppContext` class. Here is an example project file:

```
<Project Sdk="Microsoft.NET.Sdk.Web">
    <PropertyGroup>
        <TargetFramework>netcoreapp3.0</TargetFramework>
    </PropertyGroup>
    <ItemGroup>
        <RuntimeHostConfigurationOption Include="Foo" Value="Bar" />
    </ItemGroup>
</Project>
```

The `"Foo"` setting is retrievable through a call to the `GetData` method of the `AppContext` class, as illustrated in the following code snippet:

```
var bar = AppContext.GetData("Foo");
```

If the named entry does not exist, `GetData` just returns `null`. Mind you, `GetData` is prototyped as returning an `object`, but in this case, it will return a `string`.

Normally, you wouldn't want to do that, but should you ever want to create or modify one entry of a runtime host configuration setting, you can do that through the application domain, as follows:

```
AppDomain.CurrentDomain.SetData("Foo", "ReBar");
```

Mind you, this is not a replacement for a well-structured and properly defined configuration. What .NET Core does is, at run and deployment time, it copies the contents of the `RuntimeHostConfigurationOption` sections (and some more) to a generated `${project}.runtimeconfig.json` file that is placed together with the generated binary.

We'll now see a new feature of ASP.NET Core: feature toggles.

Understanding feature toggling

.NET Core 3 introduced the `Microsoft.FeatureManagement.AspNetCore` library, which is very handy for doing feature toggling. In a nutshell, a feature is either enabled or not, and this is configured through the configuration (any source) by a Boolean switch.

For more complex scenarios, you can define a configuration to be made available for a particular feature; this can be taken into consideration to determine whether or not it is enabled.

Feature toggling can be applied to an action method by applying the `[FeatureGate]` attribute with any number of feature names, as follows:

```
[FeatureGate("MyFeature1", "MyFeature2")]
public IActionResult FeactureEnabledAction() { ... }
```

When the `[FeatureGate]` attribute is applied to an action method and the feature is disabled, any attempts to access it will result in an **HTTP 404 Not Found** result. It can take any number of feature names and as well as an optional requirement type, which can be either `All` or `Any`, meaning that either all features need to be enabled or at least one has to be enabled. This is illustrated in the following code snippet:

```
[FeatureGate(RequirementType.All, "MyFeature1", "MyFeature2")]
public IActionResult FeactureEnabledAction() { ... }
```

Alternatively, this can be asked for explicitly, through an instance of an injected `IFeatureManager`, as follows:

```
public HomeController(IFeatureManager featureManager)
{
    _featureManager = featureManager;
}

public async Task<IActionResult> Index()
```

```
{
    var isEnabled = await _featureManager.IsEnabledAsync("MyFeature");
}
```

Of course, you can inject `IFeatureManager` anywhere. An example of this can be seen in the following code snippet:

```
@inject IFeatureManager FeatureManager

@if (await FeatureManager.IsEnabledAsync("MyFeature")) {
    <p>MyFeature is enabled!</p>
}
```

But another option, on a view, would be to use the `<feature>` tag helper, like this:

```
<feature name="MyFeature">
    <p>MyFeature is enabled!</p>
</feature>
```

Similar to the `[FeatureGate]` attribute, you can specify multiple feature names in the `name` attribute, and you can also specify one of `Any` or `All` in `requirement`. You can also `negate` the value, as follows:

```
<feature name="MyFeature">
    <p>MyFeature is enabled!</p>
</feature>
<feature name="MyFeature" negate="true">
    <p>MyFeature is disabled!</p>
</feature>
```

This is useful—as you can see—because you can provide content for both when the feature is enabled and when it is not.

Tag helpers need to be registered—this normally happens on the `_ViewImports.cshtml` file, as follows:

```
@addTagHelper *, Microsoft.AspNetCore.Mvc.TagHelpers
```

At the very least, we need to have the following configuration—for example—on an `appsettings.json` file, for a feature named `MyFeature`:

```
{
    "FeatureManagement": {
        "MyFeature": true
    }
}
```

The default is always `false`, meaning that the feature is disabled. Any changes done at runtime to the configuration file are detected by the feature management library.

Setup is pretty straightforward—in the `ConfigureServices` method, just call the `AddFeatureManagement` extension method. This is what registers the `IFeatureManager` interface (plus a few others that we will see later), as follows:

```
services
    .AddFeatureManagement()
    .AddFeatureFilter<MyFeatureFilter>();
```

And there is another overload of `AddFeatureManagement` that takes as a parameter an `IConfiguration` object, should you wish to build your own. Next, you need to register as many feature filters as you want to use, with consecutive calls to `AddFeatureFilter`.

Included feature filters

The feature filters package includes the following filters:

- `PercentageFilter`: This allows a certain defined percentage of items to pass.
- `TimeWindowFilter`: A feature is enabled only during the defined date-and-time window.

Each of these filters has its own configuration schema—let's have a look at each.

Percentage filter

The percentage filter takes as its sole parameter—well, the percentage we're interested in. Every time it is invoked, it will return enabled approximately that percentage of times. The configuration in the `appsettings.json` file should look like this:

```
"FeatureManagement": {
  "HalfTime": {
    "EnabledFor": [
      {
        "Name": "Microsoft.Percentage",
        "Parameters": {
          "Value": 50
        }
```

```
            }
        ]
    }
}
```

You can see that you declare the name of the feature gate, `"HalfTime"`, and the percentage parameter—50, in this example.

You also declare the attribute, as follows:

```
[FeatureGate("HalfTime")]
public IActionResult Action() { ... }
```

Time window filter

This one allows a feature to be made available automatically when a certain date and time comes. A configuration for Christmas Day looks like this:

```
"FeatureManagement": {
  "Christmas": {
    "EnabledFor": [
      {
        "Name": "Microsoft.TimeWindow",
        "Parameters": {
          "Start": "25 Dec 2019 00:00:00 +00:00",
          "End": "26 Dec 2019 00:00:00 +00:00"
        }
      }
    ]
  }
}
```

Notice the format of the date and time—this is culture-agnostic. You need to declare both the start and end time, together with the name of the feature gate: `"Christmas"`.

The feature gate declaration is illustrated in the following code snippet:

```
[FeatureGate("Christmas")]
public IActionResult Action() { ... }
```

Custom feature filters

Building a simple feature filter is straightforward—just implement IFeatureFilter, which only has a single method, as follows:

```
[FilterAlias("MyFeature")]
public class MyFeatureFilter : IFeatureFilter
{
    public bool Evaluate(FeatureFilterEvaluationContext context)
    {
        //return true or false
    }
}
```

Then, register it on ConfigureServices, like this:

```
services
    .AddFeatureManagement()
    .AddFeatureFilter<MyFeatureFilter>();
```

The FeatureFilterEvaluationContext class provides only two properties, as follows:

- FeatureName (string): The name of the current feature
- Parameters (IConfiguration): The configuration object that is used to feed the feature filter

However, we can leverage the built-in dependency injection mechanism of .NET Core and have it inject into our feature filter something such as IHttpContextAccessor, from which we can gain access to the current HTTP context, and from it to pretty much anything you need. This can be achieved as follows:

```
private readonly HttpContext _httpContext;

public MyFeatureFilter(IHttpContextAccessor httpContextAccessor)
{
    this._httpContext = httpContextAccessor.HttpContext;
}
```

You are also not limited to a yes/no value from the configuration—you can have rich configuration settings. For example, let's see how we can have our own model in the configuration file— although, for the sake of simplicity, we will make this a simple one. Imagine the following simple class:

```
public class MySettings
{
    public string A { get; set; }
    public int B { get; set; }
}
```

We want to persist this class in a configuration file, like this:

```
{
  "FeatureManagement": {
    "MyFeature": {
      "EnabledFor": [
        {
          "Name": "MyFeature",
          "Parameters": {
            "A": "AAAAA",
            "B": 10
          }
        }
      ]
    }
  }
}
```

This configuration can be read from a custom feature inside the `Evaluate` method, like this:

```
var settings = context.Parameters.Get<MySettings>();
```

The `MySettings` class is automatically deserialized from the configuration setting and made available to a .NET class.

Consistency between checks

You may notice that for some features—such as the percentage feature—if you call it twice during the same request, you may get different values, as illustrated in the following code snippet:

```
var isEnabled1 = await _featureManager.IsEnabledAsync("HalfTime");
var isEnabled2 = await _featureManager.IsEnabledAsync("Halftime");
```

In general, you want to avoid this whenever your feature either does complex calculations or some random operations, and you want to get consistent results for the duration of a request. In this case, you want to use IFeatureManagerSnapshot instead of IFeatureManager. IFeatureManagerSnapshot inherits from IFeatureManager but its implementations cache the results in the request, which means that you always get the same result. And IFeatureManagerSnapshot is also registered on the dependency injection framework, so you can use it whenever you would use IFeatureManager.

Disabled features handler

When you try to access an action method that is decorated with a feature gate that targets a feature (or features) that is disabled, then the action method is not reachable and, by default, we will get an **HTTP 403 Forbidden** error. However, this can be changed by applying a custom disabled features handler.

A disabled features handler is a concrete class that implements IDisabledFeaturesHandler, such as this one:

```
public sealed class RedirectDisabledFeatureHandler :
IDisabledFeaturesHandler
{
    public RedirectDisabledFeatureHandler(string url)
    {
       this.Url = url;
    }

    public string Url { get; }

    public Task HandleDisabledFeatures(IEnumerable<string> features,
    ActionExecutingContext context)
    {
        context.Result = new RedirectResult(this.Url);
        return Task.CompletedTask;
    }
}
```

This class redirects to a **Uniform Resource Locator** (**URL**) that is passed as a parameter. You register it through a call to UseDisabledFeaturesHandler, as follows:

```
services
    .AddFeatureManagement()
    .AddFeatureFilter<MyFeatureFilter>()
```

```
.UseDisabledFeaturesHandler(new
RedirectDisabledFeatureHandler("/Home/FeatureDisabled"));
```

You can only register one handler, and that's all it takes. Whenever we try to access an action method for which there is a feature gate defined that evaluates to `false`, it will be called, and the most obvious response will be to redirect to some page, as we can see in the example I gave.

In this section, we learned about a new feature of ASP.NET Core: feature toggling. This is a streamlined version of configuration that is more suitable for on/off switches and has some nice functionality associated. May you find it useful!

Summary

Because JSON is the standard nowadays, we should stick with the JSON provider and enable the reloading of the configuration upon changes. We should add the common file first, and then optional overrides for each of the different environments (beware the order in which you add each source). We learned how the default configuration of ASP.NET Core already loads JSON files, including different ones for the different environments.

We then saw how to use configuration sections to better organize the settings, and we also looked at using POCO wrappers for them.

So, this made us ponder whether we should use `IOptions<T>` or our own POCO classes to inject configuration values. Well, if you don't want to pollute your classes or assemblies with references to .NET Core configuration packages, you should stick to your POCO classes. We're not too worried about this, so we recommend keeping the interface wrappers.

We will use `IOptionsSnapshot<T>` instead of `IOptions<T>` so that we always get the latest version of the configuration settings.

After this, we looked at feature toggling, to quickly enable or disable features that are just on or off.

In this chapter, we saw the many ways in which we can provide configuration to an ASP.NET Core application. We learned how to build a simple provider that takes configuration from the Windows Registry. We then discussed the many ways in which we can inject configuration settings using the built-in dependency injection framework, and how to be notified of changes in the configuration sources.

Questions

After reading the chapter, you should now be able to answer the following questions:

1. What is the root interface for retrieving configuration values?
2. What are the built-in file-based configuration providers in .NET Core?
3. Is it possible to bind configurations to POCO classes out of the box?
4. What is the difference between the `IOptions<T>` and `IOptionsSnapshot<T>` interfaces?
5. Do we need to register the configuration object explicitly in the dependency injection container?
6. How can we have optional configuration files?
7. Is it possible to get notifications whenever a configuration changes?

3
Routing

This chapter talks about routing, that is, the process by which ASP.NET Core translates a user request into an MVC controller and action. This can be a complex process because subtle changes in a request can lead to different endpoints (controller/action pairs) being called. Several aspects need to be taken into account: the protocol (HTTP or HTTPS), whether the user issuing the request is authenticated or not, the HTTP verbs, the path of the request, the query string, and the actual types of the path and query string parameter values.

Routing also defines what happens when a route is *not* matched, that is, the catch-all route, and it can be used for complex situations where we need to define custom route constraints.

ASP.NET Core offers different ways by which we can configure routing, which can be divided into convention-based and explicit configuration.

By the end of this chapter, you will be able to define routing tables and apply routing configuration in all of the different ways made available by ASP.NET Core for MVC applications.

The objectives of this chapter are listed here:

- Understanding endpoint routing
- Configuring routing
- Understanding routing tables
- Using route templates
- Matching route parameters
- Using dynamic routing
- Learning route selection through attributes
- Forcing host selection from attributes
- Setting route defaults
- Routing to inline handlers

- Applying route constraints
- Using route data tokens
- Routing to areas
- Using attributes for routing
- Using routes for error handling

Technical requirements

In order to implement the examples introduced in this chapter, you will need the .NET Core 3 SDK and a text editor. Of course, Visual Studio 2019 (any edition) meets all the requirements, but you can also use Visual Studio Code, for example.

The source code can be retrieved from GitHub here: `https://github.com/ PacktPublishing/Modern-Web-Development-with-ASP.NET-Core-3-Second-Edition`

Getting started

In the old days of web applications, things were simple—if you wanted a page, you had to have a physical one. However, things have since evolved and ASP.NET Core is now an MVC framework. What does that mean? Well, in MVC, there are no such thing as physical pages (although this is not exactly true); instead, it uses routing to direct **requests** to **route handlers**. The most common route handlers in MVC are **controller actions**. After this chapter, you will learn how to use routing to access your controller actions.

A request is just some relative URL, such as this:

```
/Search/Mastering%ASP.NET%Core
/Admin/Books
/Book/1
```

This results in more readable URLs, and is also advantageous for search engines such as Google. The subject of optimizing a site—including its public URLs—for search engines is called **Search Engine Optimization (SEO)**.

When ASP.NET Core receives a request, one of the following two things can happen:

- There is a physical file that matches the request.
- There is a route that accepts the request.

In order for ASP.NET Core to serve physical files, it needs to be configured—for that, we use the `UseStaticFiles` extension method in `Configure`, which adds the static files, processing middleware to the pipeline; the call to `UseStaticFiles` is included in the Visual Studio template for ASP.NET Core web applications. If we don't enable static file serving, or if no file exists, the requests need to be handled by a **route handler**. The most common route handler in MVC is a **controller action**.

A **controller** is a class that exposes an **action** that knows how to process a request. An **action** is a method that may take parameters and returns an **action result**. A **routing table** is what we use to direct **requests** to **controller actions**.

There are two APIs that we can use to register routes:

- Fluent API (code)
- Attributes

In previous versions, we had to explicitly add support for routing attributes, but they are now first-class citizens of .NET Core. Let's go through them, starting with the routing table concept.

Endpoint routing

Endpoint routing was introduced in ASP.NET Core 2.2 and is now the default mechanism as of 3.0. The main advantage is that it supports many different mechanisms that, although leveraging routing and middleware, are very different—MVC, Razor Pages, gRPC, Blazor, SignalR, and whatnot. You still register the services you want in `ConfigureServices` and then add the middleware to the pipeline using extension methods in the `Configure` method. Endpoint routing makes the framework more flexible because it decouples route matching and resolution from endpoint dispatching, which used to be all part of the MVC functionality.

There are three required method calls:

- `AddRouting`: Where we register the required services and optionally configure some of its options (`ConfigureServices`)
- `UseRouting`: Where we actually add the routing middleware (`Configure`); this matches requests to an endpoint
- `UseEndpoints`: Where we configure the endpoints to be made available (`Configure`); this executes the matched endpoint

Now, on a Razor view (or page), if you want to generate a hyperlink on the fly that points to an addressable resource, regardless of what it is (an action method, a Razor page, or whatever else), you can just use the `Url.RouteUrl` overloaded method:

```
<!-- a Razor page -->
<a href="@Url.RouteUrl(new { page = "Admin" })">Admin</a>

<!-- an action method on a controller -->
<a href="@Url.RouteUrl(new { action = "Contact", controller = "Home"
})">Contact</a>
```

If, for any reason, you need to generate a link on a middleware component, you can inject a `LinkGenerator` class. It exposes discrete methods that allow you to retrieve many different types of URL information:

- `Get{Path,Uri}ByAction`: Returns the full path (URL) to a controller's action method
- `Get{Path,Uri}ByAddress`: Returns the full path (URL) from a base path and specified route values
- `Get{Path,Uri}ByName`: Returns the full path (URL) from an endpoint name and specified route values
- `Get{Path,Uri}ByPage`: Returns the full path (URL) from a Razor page name
- `Get{Path,Uri}ByRouteValues`: Returns the full path (URL) from a named endpoint route and route values

The difference between the `*Path` and `*Uri` versions is that the former returns absolute paths (for example, `/controller/action`) and the latter returns protocol-qualified full paths (for example, `http://host:8080/controller/action`).

If you need to get the current endpoint, there is a new extension method, `GetEndpoint` over `HttpContext`, which you can use for just that:

```
var endpoint = this.HttpContext.GetEndpoint();
var displayName = endpoint.DisplayName;
var metadata = endpoint.Metadata.ToArray();
```

The endpoint does not offer much, other than `DisplayName` and the `Metadata` collection. `DisplayName` is the fully qualified name of the action method, including the class and the assembly, unless a display name was set, and the `Metadata` collection contains all of the metadata, including attributes and conventions, that was applied to the current action method.

You can ask for a specific metadata interface using the `Get<T>` generic method; the metadata-specific interfaces are as follows:

- `IDataTokensMetadata`: This is used to get access for the data tokens (see the next section for more on this).
- `IEndpointNameMetadata`: This is used to get the optional endpoint name.
- `IHostMetadata`: This is used to get host restrictions for the endpoint.
- `IHttpMethodMetadata`: This is used to get method restrictions for the endpoint.
- `IRouteNameMetadata`: This is used to get the route name specified when the route table was defined.
- `ISuppressLinkGenerationMetadata`: If this interface's `SuppressLinkGeneration` property is set to `true`, then this endpoint will not be considered when generating links, using the `LinkGenerator` class.
- `ISuppressMatchingMetadata`: If this interface's `SuppressMatching` property is `true`, then the URL for this endpoint will not be considered for URL matching.

For example, say we want to get the current route name:

```
var routeName =
HttpContext.GetEndpoint().Metadata.Get<IRouteNameMetadata>();
```

 Keep in mind that `Get<>` returns the first occurrence of any registered metadata that implements the passed type.

We can add custom metadata and set the display name on an endpoint upon construction like this:

```
app.UseEndpoints(endpoints =>
{
    endpoints
        .MapControllerRoute
        (
            name: "Default",
            pattern: "{controller=Home}/{action=Index}/{id?}",
        )
        .WithDisplayName("Foo")
        .WithMetadata(new MyMetadata1(), new MyMetadata2());
});
```

This example shows a typical controller route with a display name set (`WithDisplayName`) and also custom metadata (`MyMetadata1` and `MyMetadata2`); these classes are just for demo purposes.

Having seen how endpoint routing works, let's now see how we can configure the routing table.

Route configuration

There are a few options we can configure for route generation, all of which are configured through the `AddRouting` extension method over the services definition:

```
services.AddRouting(options =>
{
    options.LowercaseUrls = true;
    options.AppendTrailingSlash = true;
    options.ConstraintMap.Add("evenint",
typeof(EvenIntRouteConstraint));
});
```

The `RouteOptions` class supports the following properties:

- `AppendTrailingSlash`: Determines whether or not a trailing slash (/) should be appended to all generated URLs; the default is `false` (meaning it shouldn't)
- `LowercaseUrls`: Determines whether or not the generated URLs should be lowercase; the default is `false`
- `ConstraintMap`: Determines where constraints are mapped; more on this when we talk about route constraints

But route configuration does not end here—the next section is actually the most important one: *Creating routing tables*.

Creating routing tables

In Chapter 1, *Getting Started with ASP.NET Core*, we talked about the OWIN pipeline, explaining that we use middleware to build this pipeline. It turns out that there is an MVC middleware that is responsible for interpreting requests and translating them into controller actions. To do this, we need a **routing table**.

There is only one routing table, as can be seen in this example from the default Visual Studio template:

```
app.UseRouting();
app.UseEndpoints(endpoints =>
{
    endpoints.MapControllerRoute(
        name: "default",
        pattern: "{controller=Home}/{action=Index}/{id?}");
});
```

What do we see here? The `UseEndpoints` extension method of `IApplicationBuilder` has a parameter that is an instance of `IEndpointRouteBuilder`, which lets us add routes to it. A route essentially comprises the following components:

- A name (`default`)
- A template pattern (`{controller=Home}/{action=Index}/{id?}`)
- Optional default values for each routing parameter (`Home`, `Index`)

Also, we have some defaults:

- If no controller is supplied for the URL, then `Home` is used as the default.
- If no action is supplied, for any controller, then `Index` is used as the default.

There are some optional parameters that weren't shown in this example:

- Optional routing parameter constraints
- Optional data tokens
- A route handler
- A route constraints resolver

We will go through all of these in this chapter. This is the default MVC template, and this call is identical to having this:

```
endpoints.MapDefaultControllerRoute();
```

As for the actual route, the name is just something that has meaning for us, and it is not used in any way. More interesting is the template, which we will see in a moment.

For the record, if you wish to map only controllers, you should include the following call:

```
endpoints.MapControllers();
```

This will not include support for Razor Pages; for that, you need this:

```
endpoints.MapRazorPages();
```

Having said this, we can have multiple routes defined:

```
app.UseEndpoints(endpoints =>
{
    endpoints.MapControllerRoute(
        name: "default",
        pattern: "{controller=Home}/{action=Index}/{id?}");

    endpoints.MapControllerRoute(
        name: "admin",
        pattern: "admin/{controller}/{action=Index}");
});
```

In this example, we have two routes: the second maps a request starting with `admin`, and it requires an explicit controller name, as it does not have a default. The action does have one (`Index`).

 Routes are searched in order; the first one that matches the request is used.

Here we've seen how to map requests to resources that do exist. The following section explains what to do when the requested resource does *not* exist!

Fallback endpoints

To define a fallback route—a route that is matched if no other route matches—we can have a fallback to a page (any relative URL), with or without an area:

```
endpoints.MapFallbackToPage("/Admin");
endpoints.MapFallbackToAreaPage("/", "Admin");
```

Alternatively, we can have a fallback page with a file:

```
endpoints.MapFallbackToFile("index.html");
```

We can have a controller action, with or without an area:

```
endpoints.MapFallbackToController("Index", "Home");
endpoints.MapFallbackToAreaController("Index", "Home", "Admin");
```

Or, finally, we can have a delegate, which receives as its sole parameter the request context (HttpContext), from which you can make a decision:

```
endpoints.MapFallback(ctx =>
{
    ctx.Response.Redirect("/Login");
    return Task.CompletedTask;
});
```

Each of these MapFallback* extension methods has an overload that has the first parameter of type string that is called pattern. If this overload is used, the pattern parameter can be used to restrict the fallback to requests that match this pattern. See this, for example:

```
endpoints.MapFallbackToPage("/spa/{**path:nonfile}", "/Missing");
```

A fallback route should be the last entry on the endpoints routing table.

Let's now see how we can enhance the route by using special tokens in the route templates.

Using route templates

A template is a relative URL, so it mustn't start with a slash (/). In it, you define the structure of your site, or, more accurately, the structure that you intend to make available. As ASP.NET Core is an MVC framework, the template should describe how to map the request to an action method in a controller. The following is the template:

```
{controller=Home}/{action=Index}/{id?}
```

It consists of sections separated by slashes, where each section has some tokens (inside curly braces).

Another example would be this:

```
sample/page
```

Here it is not clear what we want, as there are no mentions of `controller` or `action`. However, this is a perfectly valid template, and the required information needs to come from elsewhere.

A template can have the following elements:

- Alphanumeric literals
- String fragments inside curly braces (`{ }`), which are named tokens and can be mapped to action method parameters
- Named tokens with equal assignments (=) have default values, in case the token is not supplied in the URL; it doesn't make sense to have a token with a default value followed by a required token without
- Tokens that end with a question mark (?), which are optional, meaning they are not required; optional tokens cannot be followed by required tokens
- Tokens that start with a star (*), which are entirely optional and match anything; they need to be the last element in the template

Tokens are always alphanumeric character segments and can be separated by separator symbols (/, ?, -, (,), and so on). However, you don't need to use separators; the following is perfectly valid—notice the lack of a slash between the `action` and `id` tokens:

```
{controller=Admin}/{action=Process}{id}
```

Another slightly more complex example follows, which involves adding a catch-all token `querystring`:

```
{controller=Admin}/{action=Process}/{?id}?{*querystring}
```

This template will match the following URLs:

URL	Parameters
/	controller: Admin action: Process id: N/A querystring: N/A
/Account	controller: Account action: Process id: N/A querystring: N/A

/Admin/Process	controller: `Admin` action: `Process` id: N/A querystring: N/A
/Admin/Process/1212	controller: `Admin` action: `Process` id: `1212`
/Admin/Process/1212?force=true	controller: `Admin` action: `Process` id: `1212` querystring: `force=true`

Yet another perfectly valid example would be this:

```
api/{controller=Search}/{action=Query}?term={term}
```

That would match the following:

```
api?term=.net+core
api/Search?term=java
api/Search/Query?term=php
```

Note that any literals must be present exactly the same way as shown, in the URL, regardless of the casing.

Now, let's see how the route parameters specified in templates are matched.

Matching route parameters

Remember that a template needs to have a `controller` token and an `action` token; these are the only required tokens and have special meaning. A controller will match a controller class and an action will match one of its public methods. Any other template parameter will match the parameter of the same name in the action method. For example, take a route with the following template:

```
{controller=Search}/{action=Query}/{phrase}
```

That route will map to this `Query` method in a class called `SearchController`:

```
public IActionResult Query(string phrase) { ... }
```

By convention, the name of the controller in a template does not take the `Controller` suffix.

If a route token is optional, then it must map to a parameter that has a default value:

```
{controller=Account}/{action=List}/{page?}
```

A matching method would have the following signature:

```
public IActionResult List(int page = 0)
```

Notice that the `page` parameter is an `int` instance that has a default value of `0`. This might be used, for example, for paging, where the default page is the first one (zero-based). This would be the same as having a token with a default of `0` and mapping it to a parameter without a default value.

So far, we've only seen how we can map simple values of strings or basic types; we will soon see how we can use other types.

We've mentioned that the `action` parameter is required, but, although this is true in a way, its value may be skipped. In this case, ASP.NET Core will use a value from the HTTP action header, such as `GET`, `POST`, `PUT`, `DELETE`, and so on. This is particularly useful in the case of web APIs and is often very intuitive. So, for example, take a route with a template such as this:

```
api/{controller}/{id}
```

Say it has a request of this:

```
GET /api/Values/12
```

It can be mapped to a method such as this, in a controller named `ValuesController`:

```
public IActionResult Get(int id) { ... }
```

So, we just learned how template parameters are matched from templates to controller classes' methods. Now we will learn about dynamic routing, where the mapping is not pre-defined.

Using dynamic routing

Up until now, we've seen routing tables that statically map route templates to controller actions, but there is another kind: dynamic routes. In this case, we are still using route templates, but the thing is, we can change them dynamically.

A dynamic route handler is registered through a call to `MapDynamicControllerRoute`. I will provide an example that uses a translation service to translate the controller and action names supplied by the user, in any language to plain English, as they exist in the project.

Let's start from the beginning. We define the interface for the translation service:

```
public interface ITranslator
{
    Task<string> Translate(string sourceLanguage, string term);
}
```

As you can see, this has a single asynchronous method, `Translate`, that takes two parameters: the source language and the term to translate. Let's not waste much time with this.

The core dynamic routing functionality is implemented as a class inheriting from `DynamicRouteValueTransformer`. Here is an example of one such class, followed by its explanation:

```
public sealed class TranslateRouteValueTransformer :
DynamicRouteValueTransformer
{
    private const string _languageKey = "language";
    private const string _actionKey = "action";
    private const string _controllerKey = "controller";

    private readonly ITranslator _translator;

    public TranslateRouteValueTransformer(ITranslator translator)
    {
        this._translator = translator;
    }

    public override async ValueTask<RouteValueDictionary>
TransformAsync(
        HttpContext httpContext, RouteValueDictionary values)
    {
        var language = values[_languageKey] as string;
        var controller = values[_controllerKey] as string;
```

```
        var action = values[_actionKey] as string;

        controller = await this._translator.Translate(
          language, controller) ?? controller;
        action = await this._translator.Translate(language, action)
          ?? action;

        values[_controllerKey] = controller;
        values[_actionKey] = action;

        return values;
    }
}
```

The `TranslateRouteValueTransformer` class receives on its constructor an instance of `ITranslator`, which it saves as a local field. On the `TransformAsync` method, it retrieves the values for the route template values, `language`, `controller`, and `action`; for `controller` and `action`, it has them translated by `ITranslator`. The resulting values are then stored again in the route values dictionary, which is returned in the end.

To make this work, we need three things:

1. We need to register `ITranslator` as a service in `ConfigureServices`:

   ```
   services.AddSingleton<ITranslator, MyTranslator>();
   //MyTranslator is just for demo purposes, you need to roll out
   your own dictionary implementation
   ```

2. We need to register `TranslateRouteValueTransformer` as a service too:

   ```
   services.AddSingleton<TranslateRouteValueTransformer>();
   ```

3. And finally, we need to register a dynamic route:

   ```
   app.UseEndpoints(endpoints =>
   {
   endpoints.MapDynamicControllerRoute<TranslateRouteValueTransfo
   rmer>(
           pattern: "{language}/{controller}/{action}/{id?}");
       //now adding the default route
       endpoints.MapDefaultControllerRoute();
   });
   ```

As you can see, our dynamic route looks for a pattern of `language/controller/action/id`, where the `id` part is optional. Any request that can be mapped to this pattern will fall into this dynamic route.

Keep in mind that the purpose of dynamic routes is not to change the route pattern, but just to change the route template tokens. This will not cause any redirect, but will actually determine how the request is to be processed, the action method and the controller, and any other route parameters.

To bring this section to a close, this example allows the resolution of these routes, provided that the dictionary supports French (fr), German (de), and Portuguese (pt):

- /fr/Maison/Index to /Home/Index
- /pt/Casa/Indice to /Home/Index
- /de/Zuhause/Index to /Home/Index

 You can have multiple dynamic routes with different patterns; this is perfectly OK.

Having learned about dynamic routes, let's go back to static routes, this time using attributes in classes and methods to define the routes.

Selecting routes from attributes

ASP.NET Core, or rather, the routing middleware, will take the request URL and check for all the routes it knows about, to see whether any match the request. It will do so while respecting the route insertion order, so be aware that your request may accidentally fall into a route that isn't the one you were expecting. Always add the most specific ones first, and then the generic ones.

After a template is found that matches the request, ASP.NET Core will check whether there is an available action method on the target controller that does not have a NonActionAttribute instance that forbids a method to be used as an action, or has an attribute inheriting from HttpMethodAttribute that matches the current HTTP verb. These are listed here:

- HttpGetAttribute
- HttpPostAttribute
- HttpPutAttribute
- HttpDeleteAttribute
- HttpOptionsAttribute

- `HttpPatchAttribute`
- `HttpHeadAttribute`

All of them inherit from `HttpMethodAttribute`: this is the root class to use for filtering based on the HTTP verb.

If any of these is found, then the route will only be selected if the HTTP verb matches one of the verbs specified. There can be many attributes, meaning the action method will be callable using any of the HTTP verbs specified.

 There are other HTTP verbs, but ASP.NET Core only supports these out of the box. If you wish to support others, you need to subclass `HttpMethodAttribute` and supply your list or use `ActionVerbsAttribute`. Interestingly, ASP.NET Core—as before in the ASP.NET web API—offers an alternative way of locating an action method: if the action token is not supplied, it will look for an action method whose name matches the current HTTP verb, regardless of the casing.

You can use these attributes to supply different action names, which allows you to use method overloading. For example, if you have two methods with the same name that take different parameters, the only way to differentiate between them is by using different action names:

```
public class CalculatorController
{
    //Calculator/CalculateDirectly
    [HttpGet(Name = "CalculateDirectly")]
    public IActionResult Calculate(int a, int b) { ... }

    //Calculator/CalculateByKey
    [HttpGet(Name = "CalculateById")]
    public IActionResult Calculate(Guid calculationId) { ... }
}
```

If that's not possible, then you can use different target HTTP verbs:

```
//GET Calculator/Calculate
[HttpGet]
public IActionResult Calculate(int a, int b) { ... }

//POST Calculator/Calculate
[HttpPost]
public IActionResult Calculate([FromBody] Calculation calculation) {
... }
```

Of course, you can limit an action method—or the whole controller—so that it can only be accessed if the request is authenticated by using `AuthorizeAttribute`. We won't go over that here, as it will be discussed in `Chapter 11`, *Security*.

It is worth noting, however, that even if the whole controller is marked with `AuthorizeAttribute`, individual actions can still be accessible if they bear `AllowAnonymousAttribute`:

```
[Authorize]
public class PrivateController
{
    [AllowAnonymous]
    public IActionResult Backdoor() { ... }
}
```

Another option is to constrain an action based on the content type of the request. You use `ConsumesAttribute` for that purpose, and you can apply it as follows:

```
[HttpPost]
[Consumes("application/json")]
public IActionResult Process(string payload) { ... }
```

> For an explanation of what content types are, please see `https://www.w3.org/Protocols/rfc1341/4_Content-Type.html`.

Another attribute that contributes to the route selection is `RequireHttpsAttribute`. If it's present in a method or controller class, a request is only accepted if it comes through HTTPS.

Finally, there are route constraints. These are generally used to validate the tokens passed in the request, but they can be used to validate the request as a whole. We will discuss them shortly.

So, the sequence is as follows:

1. Find the first template that matches the request.
2. Check that a valid controller exists.
3. Check that a valid action method exists in the controller, either by action name or by verb matching.

4. Check that any constraints present are valid.

5. Check that any attributes that contribute to the route selection (`AuthorizeAttribute`, `NonActionAttribute`, `ConsumesAttribute`, `ActionVerbsAttribute`, `RequireHttpsAttribute`, and `HttpMethodAttribute`) all are valid.

We will see how constraints can affect route selection shortly.

Using special routes

The following routes are special because they have a particular meaning to ASP.NET Core:

- `[HttpGet("")]`: This is the controller's default action; only one can be defined. If applied on a method without required parameters, it will be the default action for the whole app.
- `[HttpGet("~/")]`: This is the application's default action for the default controller: it maps to the root of the application (for example, **/**).

So, if you set `[HttpGet("")]` on a controller's action method and do not define any other route, then it will be the default action for that controller, and if you set `[HttpGet("~/")]` with no routing table, then it will be the default action and the default controller.

The next section explains how to restrict a route based on the calling host and/or the server's port.

Host selection from attributes

Starting in ASP.NET 3, it is also possible to restrict a route based on the host header and port. You can either do that through attributes or by using fluent (code-based) configuration.

Here's an example of using attributes:

```
[Host("localhost", "127.0.0.1")]
public IActionResult Local() { ... }

[Host("localhost:80")]
public IActionResult LocalPort80() { ... }
```

```
[Host(":8080")]
public IActionResult Port8080() { ... }
```

We have three examples of using the `[Host]` attribute here:

1. The first one makes the `Local` action method reachable only if the local header is `localhost` or `127.0.0.1`; any number of host headers can be provided.
2. The second example demands a combination of host header and port, in this case, `80`.
3. The final one just expects port `8080`.

The `[Host]` attribute can, of course, be combined with any `[Http*]` or `[Route]` ones.

Here's how to do this through code:

```
endpoints.MapControllerRoute("Local",
"Home/Local").RequireHost("localhost", "127.0.0.1");
```

This example only accepts requests from either `"localhost"` or `"127.0.0.1"` (generally these are synonyms) for the given route.

Now, the next topic will be how to specify defaults for route template parameters.

Setting route defaults

We've seen how we can specify default values for route parameters in the template, but there's also another way: by overloading the `MapControllerRoute` extension method that takes an object containing default values. Instead of supplying these defaults as strings, you can have this:

```
app.UseEndpoints(endpoints =>
{
    endpoints.MapControllerRoute(
        name: "default",
        pattern: "{controller}/{action}/{id?}",
        defaults: new { controller = "Home", action = "Index" });
});
```

This is valid even if you don't have the tokens in the route, as follows:

```
app.UseEndpoints(endpoints =>
{
```

```
endpoints.MapControllerRoute(
    name: "default",
    pattern: "My/Route",
    defaults: new { controller = "My", action = "Route" });
});
```

Remember that you do have to supply `controller` and `action`; if they are not present in the template, they need to be supplied as defaults.

The next section delves into the inner workings of routes and how we can work around with requests.

Routing to inline handlers

It is possible in ASP.NET Core to handle a request directly, that is, to not route to a controller action. We define inline handlers by using an extension method that specifies the HTTP verb and the template to match, as follows:

- `MapGet`: HTTP `Get`
- `MapPost`: HTTP `Post`
- `MapPut`: HTTP `Put`
- `MapDelete`: HTTP `Delete`
- `MapVerb`: Any named HTTP verb; for example, `Get` is the same as using `MapGet`

There are actually two extension methods, `MapXXX` and `MapXXXMiddleware`, the first taking a delegate and the second a middleware class. An example follows.

These methods offer two possible signatures (except for `Map<verb>`, which takes the HTTP verb) and take the following parameters:

- `pattern`: This is a route template.
- `requestHandler`: This is a handler that takes the current context (`HttpContext`) and returns a task.

Here are two examples. In the first, we are merely setting the response content type and writing some text to the output:

```
endpoints.MapGet(
    pattern: "DirectRoute",
    requestDelegate: async ctx =>
    {
```

```
        ctx.Response.ContentType = "text/plain";
        await ctx.Response.WriteAsync("Here's your response!");
    });
```

Here, we are adding a middleware to the response:

```
var newAppBuilder = endpoints.CreateApplicationBuilder();
newAppBuilder.UseMiddleware<ResponseMiddleware>();

endpoints.MapGet(
    pattern: "DirectMiddlewareRoute", newAppBuilder.Build());
```

`ResponseMiddleware` could be something like this:

```
public class ResponseMiddleware
{
    private readonly RequestDelegate _next;

    public ResponseMiddleware(RequestDelegate next)
    {
        this._next = next;
    }

    public async Task InvokeAsync(HttpContext ctx)
    {
        await ctx.Response.WriteAsync("Hello, from a middleware!");
    }
}
```

 When using `MapMiddlewareXXX`, you can't return the next delegate, as it is meant to be the only response.

The two approaches, using a handler or the application builder, are similar, as the former gives us direct access to the request context, while the latter allows us to add steps to the request pipeline for a particular route template. It all depends on what you want to do.

 You cannot mix direct handlers with controllers: the first handler that is picked up in the routing table will be processed, and no other. So, for example, if you have `MapGet` followed by `MapControllerRoute` for the same template, the handler or action specified in `MapGet` will be processed, but not the controller in `MapControllerRoute`.

Now that we understand how to handle routing requests, next we'll learn how to constrain the applicability of a route.

Applying route constraints

When we define a route template or pattern, we may also want to specify how that route shall be matched, which is *constraining* it. We can constrain a route in a number of ways, such as these:

- The request needs to match a given HTTP method.
- The request needs to match a given content type.
- Its parameters need to match certain rules.

A constraint can be expressed in the route template or as a discrete object, using the `MapControllerRoute` method. If you choose to use the route template, you need to specify its name next to the token to which it applies:

```
{controller=Home}/{action=Index}/{id:int}
```

Notice `{id:int}`: this constrains the `id` parameter to an integer, and is one of the provided constraints that we will talk about in a moment. Another option is to make use of the `defaults` parameter:

```
app.UseEndpoints(endpoints =>
{
    endpoints.MapControllerRoute(
        name: "default",
        pattern: "{controller}/{action}/{id?}",
        defaults: new { controller = "Home", action = "Index" },
        constraints: new { id = new IntRouteConstraint() });
});
```

You should be able to guess that the anonymous class that is passed in the `constraints` parameter must have properties that match the route parameters.

Following on from this example, you can also pass constraints that are not bound to any route parameter, but instead perform some kind of bespoke validation, as follows:

```
endpoints.MapControllerRoute(
    name: "default",
    pattern: "{controller}/{action}/{id?}",
    defaults: new { controller = "Home", action = "Index" },
    constraints: new { foo = new BarRouteConstraint() });
```

In this case, the `BarRouteConstraint` constraint class will still be called and can be used to invalidate a route selection.

HTTP methods

As we said earlier, in order to make an action method available to only some HTTP verbs or a specific content type, you can use one of the following:

- `HttpGetAttribute`
- `HttpPostAttribute`
- `HttpPutAttribute`
- `HttpDeleteAttribute`
- `HttpOptionsAttribute`
- `HttpPatchAttribute`
- `HttpHeadAttribute`
- `ActionVerbsAttribute`
- `ConsumesAttribute`

The names should be self-explanatory. You can add attributes for different verbs, and if any of them is present, the route will only match if its verb matches one of these attributes. `ActionVerbsAttribute` lets you pass a single method, or a list of methods, that you wish to support. `ConsumesAttribute` takes a valid content type.

Default constraints

ASP.NET Core includes the following constraints:

Constraint	Purpose	Example
alpha (`AlphaRouteConstraint`)	Limits the text to alphanumeric characters, that is, excluding symbols	`{term:alpha}`
bool (`BoolRouteConstraint`)	Is only `true` or `false`	`{force:bool}`
datetime (`DateTimeRouteConstraint`)	Gives a date or date and time pattern	`{lower:datetime}`
decimal (`DecimalRouteConstraint`)	Includes decimal values	`{lat:decimal}`
double (`DoubleRouteConstraint`)	Includes double precision floating point values	`{precision:double}`

exists (KnownValueRouteConstraint)	Forces a route token to be present	{action:exists}
float (FloatRouteConstraint)	Includes single precision floating point values	{accuracy:float}
guid (GuidRouteConstraint)	Includes GUIDs	{id:guid}
int (IntRouteConstraint)	Includes integer values	{id:int}
length (LengthRouteConstraint)	Includes a constrained string	{term:length(5,10)
long (LongRouteConstraint)	Includes a long integer	{id:long}
max (MaxRouteConstraint)	This is the maximum value for an integer	{page:max(100)}
min (MinRouteConstraint)	This is the minimum value for an integer	{page:min(1)}
maxlength (MaxLengthRouteConstraint)	Includes any alphanumeric string up to a maximum length	{term:maxlength(10)}
minlength (MinLengthRouteConstraint)	Includes any alphanumeric string with a minimum length	{term:minlength(10)}
range (RangeRouteConstraint)	Includes an integer range	{page:range(1,100)}
regex (RegexRouteConstraint)	A regular expression	{isbn:regex(^d{9}[d|X]$)}
required (RequiredRouteConstraint)	Includes a required value, that must physically exist	{term:required}

A route parameter can take many constraints at once, separated by :, as here:

```
Calculator/Calculate({a:int:max(10)},{b:int:max(10)})
```

In this example, the a and b parameters need to be integers and have a maximum value of 10, at the same time. Another example follows:

```
Book/Find({isbn:regex(^d{9}[d|X]$)})
```

This will match an ISBN string starting with nine digits and followed by either a trailing digit or the X character.

It is also possible to provide your own custom constraints, which we will see next.

Creating custom constraints

A constraint is any class that implements IRouteConstraint. If it is meant to be used inline in a route template, then it must be registered. Here's an example of a route constraint for validating even numbers:

```
public class EvenIntRouteConstraint : IRouteConstraint
{
    public bool Match(
        HttpContext httpContext,
        IRouter route,
        string routeKey,
        RouteValueDictionary values,
        RouteDirection routeDirection)
    {
        if ((!values.ContainsKey(routeKey)) || (values[routeKey] ==
null))
        {
            return false;
        }

        var value = values[routeKey].ToString();

        if (!int.TryParse(value, out var intValue))
        {
            return false;
        }

        return (intValue % 2) == 0;
    }
}
```

You should be able to tell that all route parameters are provided in the values collection and that the route parameter name is in routeKey. If no route parameter is actually supplied, it will just return false, as it will if the parameter cannot be parsed into an integer. Now, to register your constraint, you need to use the AddRouting method shown earlier this chapter:

```
services.AddRouting(options =>
{
    options.ConstraintMap.Add("evenint",
typeof(EvenIntRouteConstraint));
});
```

This is actually the same as retrieving `RouteOptions` from the registered configuration:

```
services.Configure<RouteOptions>(options =>
{
    //do the same
});
```

That's all there is to it.

If you wish to use a route constraint to validate a URL—or any of the request parameters—you can use a route constraint not bound to a route key:

```
public class IsAuthenticatedRouteConstraint : IRouteConstraint
{
    public bool Match(
        HttpContext httpContext,
        IRouter route,
        string routeKey,
        RouteValueDictionary values,
        RouteDirection routeDirection)
    {
        return httpContext.Request.Cookies.ContainsKey("auth");
    }
}
```

Granted, there are other (even better) ways to do this; this was only included as an example.

Now we can use it like this, in a route:

```
Calculator/Calculate({a:evenint},{b:evenint})
```

If, on the other hand, you prefer to use the constraint classes directly in your `MapControllerRoute` calls, you do not need to register them. Regardless, the route constraint collection is available as the `IInlineConstraintResolver` service:

```
var inlineConstraintResolver = routes
    .ServiceProvider
    .GetRequiredService<IInlineConstraintResolver>();
```

 If you wish to specify custom route constraints in routing attributes, you will need to register them.

In this chapter, we've seen how to define constraints for route tokens, including creating our own, which can be very useful for validating URLs upfront. The next section explains what data tokens are.

Route data tokens

A **route data token**, as opposed to a **route token** or **route parameter**, is just some arbitrary data that you supply in a routing table entry and is available for use in the route handling pipeline, including the MVC action method. Unlike route tokens, route data tokens can be any kind of object, not just strings. They have absolutely no meaning for MVC, and will just be ignored, but they can be useful, because you can have multiple routes pointing to the same action method, and you may want to use data tokens to find out which route triggered the call.

You can pass a data token as follows:

```
app.UseEndpoints(endpoints =>
{
    endpoints.MapControllerRoute(
        name: "default",
        pattern: "{controller}/{action}/{id?}",
        defaults: new { controller = "Home", action = "Index" },
        constraints: null,
        dataTokens: new { foo = "bar" });
});
```

You can also retrieve them from the IDataTokensMetatata metadata item, as from inside a controller action:

```
public class HomeController : Controller
{
    public IActionResult Index()
    {
        var metadata = this.HttpContext.GetEndpoint().Metadata.
          GetMetadata<IDataTokensMetadata>();
        var foo = metadata?.DataTokens["foo"] as string;
        return this.View();
    }
}
```

Because the DataTokens values are prototyped as object, you need to know what you will be retrieving. Also, be aware, the GetMetadata<IDataTokensMetadata>() method may return null if no data tokens were set!

There is no way to change the values of data tokens. Plus, the old `RouteData` property of the `ControllerBase` class and the `GetRouteData` extension method over `HttpContext` are now obsolete and may be removed in a future version of ASP.NET Core.

Finally, let's move on and see how we can configure routing to areas.

Routing to areas

MVC has supported the concept of areas for a long time. Essentially, areas are for segregating and organizing controllers and views, so that, for example, you can have identically named controllers in different areas.

Visual Studio lets you create folders in a project and then add controllers and views to them. You can mark these folders as areas.

Where routing is concerned, areas add another route token, appropriately named `area`, to `controller` and `action`. If you are to use areas, you will likely have another segment in your template, such as this:

```
Products/Phones/Index
Reporting/Sales/Index
```

Here, `Products` and `Reporting` are areas. You need to map them to routes so that they are recognized by MVC. You can use the `MapControllerRoute` extension method, but you will need to supply the `area` token as follows:

```
app.UseEndpoints(endpoints =>
{
    endpoints.MapControllerRoute(
        name: "default",
        pattern: "{area:exists}/{controller}/{action}/{id?}",
        defaults: new { controller = "Home", action = "Index" });
});
```

You can also use the `MapAreaControllerRoute` extension method, which takes care of adding the `area` parameter:

```
endpoints.MapAreaControllerRoute(
    name: "default",
    areaName: "Products",
    pattern: "List/{controller}/{action}/{id?}",
    defaults: new { controller = "Phones", action = "Index" });
```

This route will map a request of `List/Phones/Index` to an `Index` action method of a `PhonesController` controller inside the `Products` area.

That's it for areas. Let's now have a look at routing attributes.

Using routing attributes

An alternative to adding routes to a routing table is using **routing attributes**. Routing attributes existed before ASP.NET Core and were even around in ASP.NET MVC and Web API. If we want to have routing attributes automatically recognized by ASP.NET Core, we need to do this:

```
app.UseEndpoints(endpoints =>
{
    endpoints.MapControllers();
});
```

In the following sections, we will learn about a few routing attributes and see how to apply them.

Let's see how we can define routes with attributes.

Defining routes

These attributes are used to define routes and can be composed together; if we add a routing attribute to a class and another to one of its methods, the actual route will result from both of them.

The most obvious use of routing attributes would be to decorate an action method, as follows:

```
[Route("Home/Index")]
public IActionResult Index() { ... }
```

If, for example, you have many actions in the same controller and you wish to map them all using the same prefix (`Home`), you can do the following:

```
[Route("Home")]
public class HomeController
{
    [Route("Index")]
    public IActionResult Index() { ... }
```

```
[Route("About")]
public IActionResult About() { ... }
}
```

 In previous (non-Core) versions of MVC and Web API, you could use `RoutePrefixAttribute` for this purpose. Now, `RouteAttribute` takes care of both cases.

Routes are additive, which means if you specify a route in a controller and then on an action method, you will get both, as in `Home/Index` or `Home/About`.

As you can see, the route parameter in the `HomeController` class matches the conventional name for the controller (`Home`). Because of this, we can also use the `[controller]` special token:

```
[Route("[controller]")]
public class HomeController { ... }
```

For an API controller, we can use this:

```
[Route("api/[controller]")]
public class ServicesController { ... }
```

In addition, each of the actions is mapped with a name that exactly matches the method's name. Likewise, we can use `[action]`:

```
[Route("[action]")]
public IActionResult Index() { ... }

[Route("[action]")]
public IActionResult About() { ... }
```

Multiple route attributes can be passed, so that the action method will respond to different requests:

```
[Route("[action]")]
[Route("")]
[Route("Default")]
public IActionResult Index() { ... }
```

The `Index` method will be callable by any one of the following requests:

```
/Home
/Home/Index
/Home/Default
```

Notice that the `Home` part comes from the route attribute applied at the class level. If, on the other hand, you specify a slash in the template, you make the template absolute; this template will look as follows:

```
[Route("Default/Index")]
public IActionResult Index() { ... }
```

This can only be accessed as follows:

```
/Default/Index
```

If you want to take the controller into consideration, you should either name it explicitly in the template or use the `[controller]` special token:

```
[Route("[controller]/Default/Index")]
public IActionResult Index() { ... }
```

This will be accessible as follows:

```
/Home/Default/Index
```

> The `[controller]` and `[action]` tokens are for when we want to use constants for routes. These constants have the potential to be used in lots of places, as they are not stuck to specific actions and controllers. They were not available in previous versions of ASP.NET MVC or Web API.

Default routes

With routing attributes, you can specify the default controller by applying `RouteAttribute` with a blank template:

```
[Route("")]
public class HomeController { ... }
```

The default action in a controller will also be the one with an empty template, as follows:

```
[Route("")]
public IActionResult Index() { ... }
```

If there is no method with an empty route template, ASP.NET Core will try to find one with a name matching the current HTTP method.

Constraining routes

You can also specify route constraints, and the syntax is identical to what we've seen before:

```
[Route("Calculate({a:int},{b:int})")]
public IActionResult Calculate(int a, int b) { ... }
```

Defining areas

You can define routes that include areas too, by applying `AreaAttribute` to a controller:

```
[Area("Products")]
[Route("[controller]")]
public class ReportingController { ... }
```

Similar to `[controller]` and `[action]`, there is also the special `[area]` token that you can use in your templates to indicate the current area, as inferred from the filesystem:

```
[Route("[area]/Default")]
public IActionResult Index() { ... }
```

Specifying action names

You can specify an action name for a controller method, through `ActionNameAttribute`, as follows:

```
[ActionName("Default")]
public IActionResult Index() { ... }
```

You can also do this through any one of the HTTP verb selection attributes (`HttpGetAttribute`, `HttpPostAttribute`, `HttpPutAttribute`, `HttpOptionsAttribute`, `HttpPatchAttribute`, `HttpDeleteAttribute` or `HttpHeadAttribute`):

```
[HttpGet(Name = "Default")]
public IActionResult Index() { ... }
```

Please do remember that you cannot specify a route template and an action name at the same time, as this will result in an exception being thrown at startup time when ASP.NET Core scans the routing attributes. Also, do not specify ActionNameAttribute and a verb selection attribute at the same time as specifying the action name.

Defining non-actions

If you want to prevent a public method in a controller class from being used as an action, you can decorate it with NonActionAttribute:

```
[NonAction]
public IActionResult Process() { ... }
```

Restricting routes

When we talked about route constraints, we saw that we can restrict an action method so that it is only callable if one or more the following conditions are met:

- It matches a given HTTP verb (ActionVerbsAttribute, Http*Attribute).
- It is called using HTTPS (RequireHttpsAttribute).
- It is called with a given content type (ConsumesAttribute).

We won't go into this in any further detail, as this has been explained before.

Setting route values

It is possible to supply arbitrary route values in an action method. This is the purpose of the RouteValueAttribute abstract class. You need to inherit from it:

```
public class CustomRouteValueAttribute : RouteValueAttribute
{
    public CustomRouteValueAttribute(string value) : base("custom",
value) { }
}
```

Then, apply and use it as follows:

```
[CustomRouteValue("foo")]
public IActionResult Index()
```

```
{
    var foo = this.ControllerContext.RouteData.Values["foo"];
    return this.View();
}
```

 `AreaAttribute` is an example of a class inheriting from `RouteValueAttribute`. There is no way to pass arbitrary route data tokens through attributes.

As you can see, quite a lot can be achieved through attributes. That also includes error handling; let's see more about that now.

Error handling in routing

What do we do with errors—exceptions caught during the processing of a request, for example, when a resource is not found? You can use routing for this. Here, we will present a few strategies:

- Routing
- Adding a catch-all route
- Showing developer error pages
- Using the status code pages middleware

We will learn about these in the following sections.

Routing errors to controller routes

You can force a specific controller's action to be called when an error occurs by calling `UseExceptionHandler`:

```
app.UseExceptionHandler("/Home/Error");
```

What you put in this view (`Error`) is entirely up to you, mind you.

You can even do something more interesting, that is, register middleware to execute upon the occurrence of an error, as follows:

```
app.UseExceptionHandler(errorApp =>
{
    errorApp.Run(async context =>
    {
```

```
            var errorFeature = context.Features.Get<IException
             HandlerPathFeature>();
            var exception = errorFeature.Error;   //you may want to check
   what
                                               //the exception is
            var path = errorFeature.Path;
            await context.Response.WriteAsync("Error: " +
   exception.Message);
        });
   });
```

 You will need to add a `using` reference for
the `Microsoft.AspNetCore.Http` namespace in order to use the
`WriteAsync` method.

The `IExceptionHandlerPathFeature` feature allows you to retrieve the exception
that occurred and the request path. Using this approach, you have to generate the
output yourself; that is, you do not have the benefit of having an MVC view.

Next, we will how we can show user-friendly error pages.

Using developer exception pages

For running in development mode, you are likely to want a page that shows
developer-related information, in which case, you should
call `UseDeveloperExceptionPage` instead:

```
   app.UseDeveloperExceptionPage();
```

This will show the exception message, including all request properties and the stack
trace, based on a default template that also contains environment variables. It is
normally only used for the `Development` environment, as it may contain sensitive
information that could potentially be used by an attacker.

Since .NET Core 3, it is possible to tweak the output of this, by means of
an `IDeveloperPageExceptionFilter` implementation. We register one in the
Dependency Injection container and either provide our own output in the
`HandleExceptionAsync` method or just return the default implementation:

```
   services.AddSingleton<IDeveloperPageExceptionFilter,
   CustomDeveloperPageExceptionFilter>();
```

This method is very simple: it receives an error context and a delegate that points to the next exception filter in the pipeline, which is normally the one that produces the default error page:

```
class CustomDeveloperPageExceptionFilter :
IDeveloperPageExceptionFilter
{
    public async Task HandleExceptionAsync(ErrorContext
     errorContext, Func<ErrorContext, Task> next)
    {
        if (errorContext.Exception is DbException)
        {
            await errorContext.HttpContext.Response.WriteAsync("Error
             connecting to the DB");
        }
        else
        {
            await next(errorContext);
        }
    }
}
```

This simple example has conditional logic that depends on the exception and either sends a custom text or just delegates to the default handler.

Using a catch-all route

You can add a catch-all route by adding an action method with a route that will always match if no other does (like the fallback page in the *Fallback endpoints section*). For example, we can use routing attributes as follows:

```
[HttpGet("{*url}", Order = int.MaxValue)]
public IActionResult CatchAll()
{
    this.Response.StatusCode = StatusCodes.Status404NotFound;
    return this.View();
}
```

The same, of course, can be achieved with fluent configuration, in the `Configure` method:

```
app.UseEndpoints(endpoints =>
{
    //default routes go here
    endpoints.MapControllerRoute(
        name: "CatchAll",
```

```
        pattern: "{*url}",
        defaults: new { controller = "CatchAll", action = "CatchAll" }
    );
});
```

Here, all you need to do is add a nice view with a friendly error message! Be aware that the other actions in the same controller also need to have routes specified; otherwise, the default route will become `CatchAll`!

 Fallback pages are a simpler alternative to catch-all routes.

Using status code pages middleware

Let's see now how we can respond to errors with HTTP status codes, the standard way of returning high-level responses to the client.

Status code pages

A different option is to add code in response to a particular HTTP status code between **400 Bad Request** and **599 Network Connect Time Out** that does not have a body (has not been handled), and we do that through `UseStatusCodePages`:

```
app.UseStatusCodePages(async context => {
context.HttpContext.Response.ContentType = "text/plain";
 var statusCode = context.HttpContext.Response.StatusCode;
 await context.HttpContext.Response.WriteAsync("HTTP status code: " +
statusCode); });
```

The method adds a middleware component to the pipeline that is responsible for, after an exception occurs, doing two things:

- Filling the `Error` property on the `IStatusCodePagesFeature` feature
- Handling the execution from there

Here's a different overload, doing essentially the same as the last one:

```
app.UseStatusCodePages("text/plain", "Error status code: {0}");
```

Here's something for automatically redirecting to a route (with an HTTP code of **302 Found**) with a particular status code as a route value:

```
app.UseStatusCodePagesWithRedirects("/error/{0}");
```

This one, instead, re-executes the pipeline without issuing a redirect, thus making it faster:

```
app.UseStatusCodePagesWithReExecute("/error/{0}");
```

All of the execution associated with specific status codes can be disabled through the `IStatusCodePagesFeature` feature:

```
var statusCodePagesFeature =
HttpContext.Features.Get<IStatusCodePagesFeature>();
statusCodePagesFeature.Enabled = false;
```

Routing to specific status code pages

You can add an action such as this to a controller to have it respond to a request of `"error/404"` (just replace the error code with whatever you want):

```
[Route("error/404")]
public IActionResult Error404()
{
    this.Response.StatusCode = StatusCodes.Status404NotFound;
    return this.View();
}
```

Now, either add an `Error404` view or instead call a generic view, passing it the `404` status code, perhaps through the view bag. Again, this route can be configured fluently, as follows:

```
endpoints.MapControllerRoute(
    name: "Error404",
    pattern: "error/404",
    defaults: new { controller = "CatchAll", action = "Error404" }
);
```

This, of course, needs to be used either with `UseStatusCodePagesWithRedirects` or `UseStatusCodePagesWithReExecute`.

Any status code

To catch all errors in a single method, do the following:

```
[Route("error/{statusCode:int}")]
public IActionResult Error(int statusCode)
{
    this.Response.StatusCode = statusCode;
    this.ViewBag.StatusCode = statusCode;
    return this.View();
}
```

Here, we are calling a generic view called `Error` (inferred from the action name), so we need to pass it the originating status code, which we do through the view bag, as follows:

```
endpoints.MapControllerRoute(
    name: "Error",
    pattern: "error/{statusCode:int}",
    defaults: new { controller = "CatchAll", action = "Error" }
);
```

For a request of `/error/<statusCode>`, we are directed to the `CatchAllController` controller and `Error` action. Again, this requires `UseStatusCodePagesWithRedirects` or `UseStatusCodePagesWithReExecute`.

Here we presented different ways to handle errors, either based on an exception or on a status code. Pick the one that suits you best!

Summary

In real life, chances are you will mix code-based routing configuration and attributes. In our example, we will be using localization features, which require a lot of configuration, typically code-based configuration. Attribute routing also has its place, because we can directly define accessible endpoints that do not need to be restricted by general routing templates. Route constraints are very powerful and should be used.

It is always good to start with the included default route template and go from there. It should be sufficient for around 80% of your needs. Others will either be defined through a custom route or routing attributes.

We saw in this chapter that security is something that needs to be taken into account, and using routing attributes for this purpose seems ideal, as we can immediately see what the security restrictions are by looking at controller methods.

We've seen the different ways in which we can configure routing, in other words, turning browser requests into actions. We looked at code-based and attribute-based routing and learned about some of their strengths and limitations. We found out how we can restrict URL parameters to be of certain types or match certain requirements, as well as how to prevent an action method from being called unless it matches a specific verb, HTTPS requirement, or request content type. Finally, we looked at how to use routes to direct to status code or error specific actions so as to return friendly error pages.

Quite a few of the topics covered in this chapter will surface again in later chapters. In the next chapter, we will be talking about probably the most important pieces of MVC, which were also the main subject of this chapter: controllers and actions.

Questions

So, now that you're at the end of this chapter, you should be able to answer the following questions:

1. What are the special route tokens?
2. How can we prevent a route from being selected depending on the request's HTTP verb?
3. How can we prevent a route from being selected unless the request uses HTTPS?
4. How can we serve different views depending on the occurred HTTP error code?
5. How can we prevent methods in controllers from being called?
6. How can we force a route value to be of a particular type (for example, a number)?
7. What is a route handler?

4
Controllers and Actions

This chapter talks about arguably the most important feature of MVC: where the logic is stored. This is where you implement the stuff that your application does, where a substantial part of your business logic is.

Controllers and actions are found by convention and are called as the result of routing rules, which were introduced in the previous chapter. But things can get very complex—there are many ways by which an action can retrieve data from the request; it can be asynchronous or synchronous and it can return many different kinds of data. This data can be cached so that essentially there is no performance penalty in repeating the request.

As we know, HTTP is stateless, but that does not really play well with modern applications like the ones we're interested in, so we need to maintain the state between requests. We would also like to return data, numbers, and text according to the culture and language of the person that is issuing the request. We will look at all of these topics in the course of this chapter.

In this chapter, we will learn about the following topics:

- How to use controllers
- How controllers are found
- What is the controller life cycle?
- What are controller actions?
- How to do error handling
- How to cache responses
- How to maintain the state between requests
- Using dependency injection
- Applying globalization and localization

Technical requirements

In order to implement the examples introduced in this chapter, you will need the .NET Core 3 SDK and a text editor. Of course, Visual Studio 2019 (any edition) meets all the requirements, but you can also use Visual Studio Code, for example.

The source code can be retrieved from GitHub at `https://github.com/PacktPublishing/Modern-Web-Development-with-ASP.NET-Core-3-Second-Edition`.

Getting started

We will be working where the actual code is, where you get things done and where you process the requests from the browser. We will talk about MVC controllers returning views, but also about persisting data across requests, injecting dependencies into our controllers and actions, and how to add localization support to the code. All in all, it's a very important chapter, so I ask for your full attention.

In this chapter, we will be talking about the most important aspects of an MVC application:

- Controllers
- Actions

We will study each of these in the coming sections.

Using controllers

In MVC, a controller is responsible for handling requests. It is where the business logic is located, where data is retrieved, request parameters validated, and so on. In object-oriented languages, such as those that support .NET Framework, this is implemented in classes. Keep in mind that the MVC pattern advocates a strong separation of responsibilities, which makes all of its components particularly important; even given this fact, a controller is really the only required part of ASP.NET Core, as you can live without views. Just think of web services that do not return any user interface or models. This is a very important aspect of ASP.NET Core.

Controller base classes

ASP.NET Core (as with its predecessors) offers a base class called `ControllerBase` that you can inherit from, although it is not strictly necessary. We will discuss this in more detail later on in this chapter. However, inheriting from `ControllerBase` has a few advantages:

- Easy access to model validation

- Helper methods to return different results (redirect, JSON, views, text, and more)

- Direct access to the request and response infrastructure objects, including headers, cookies, and more

- Ability to intercept/override action events

In reality, there is another class, `Controller`, that in turn inherits from `ControllerBase`, which you should inherit from in case you want to work with views. A case where you wouldn't need to work with views would be if you are writing a web service (web API).

The templates in Visual Studio always generate controllers that inherit from the `Controller` class, but you can change them to POCOs if you like. The only real requirement, unless you want to change the convention, is to add the `Controller` suffix to all your controllers. The namespace or physical location is irrelevant—for example, you can create controllers in different folders or namespaces.

The `ControllerBase` class, among others, makes the following properties available:

- `ControllerContext` (`ControllerContext`): The execution context for the current controller and request, which includes the action descriptor (used to guess which action should be called) and value provider factories, from which the action parameters are obtained; it's an instance of the class.

- `HttpContext` (`HttpContext`): The HTTP context, which includes the request and response objects, from which we can obtain and set all headers, cookies, status codes, authentication information, certificates, and more; also provides access to the dependency injection (DI) framework, framework features, the session state (if it's enabled), and the underlying connection properties.

- `MetadataProvider` (`IModelMetadataProvider`): This is used to extract metadata—validators, textual descriptors, and editing information—for the class model.
- `ModelBinderFactory` (`IModelBinderFactory`): This is an object that is used to create the binders that, in turn, are used to bind submitted request properties to a given class model.
- `ModelState` (`ModelStateDictionary`): This is the submitted model's values and validation results.
- `ObjectValidator` (`IObjectModelValidator`): This is an instance that is used to validate the submitted model.
- `Request` (`HttpRequest`): This handles the convenience pointer to the same object inside the `HttpContext`.
- `Response` (`HttpResponse`): This handles the convenience pointer to the same object inside the `HttpContext`.
- `Url` (`IUrlHelper`): This is an instance that enables convenience methods to generate URL links to specific controller actions.
- `User` (`ClaimsPrincipal`): This holds a reference to the current ASP.NET Core user; depending on the actual authentication mechanism in use, it will hold different values and claims, and even if it is not authenticated, this will never be `null`.

The `Controller` class offers all of the preceding properties plus view-specific properties:

- `RouteData` (`RouteData`): This contains the MVC route data parameters.
- `ViewBag` (dynamic): This is a dynamic collection of data to be made available in a view.
- `ViewData` (`ViewDataDictionary`): This is identical to `ViewBag`, but is strongly typed in the form of a key–value dictionary.
- `TempData` (`ITempDataDictionary`): This is a strongly typed dictionary for data to maintain until the next form submission.

It's safe and convenient to inherit from `Controller`, even if you do not use views; it won't cause any problems.

Of course, your controller needs to offer at least one action method that can be used to perform an action and return something meaningful to the caller, be it an HTML view, some JSON content, or just an HTTP status code.

You also have a number of virtual methods that you can override so as to perform actions before, after, or instead of an action method being called. These are defined in the interfaces `IActionFilter` and `IAsyncActionFilter`, which are implemented by `Controller`:

- `OnActionExecuted` is called after an action is called.
- `OnActionExecuting` is called synchronously just before an action is called.
- `OnActionExecutingAsync` is called asynchronously before an action is called.

These interfaces are the bases of filters, which we will discuss in more detail later on.

> I almost forgot: if a controller class has the `[NonController]` attribute applied to it, then it is not considered and cannot be used as a controller.

POCO controllers

In ASP.NET Core, your controllers do not need to inherit from any base class or implement a particular interface. As we mentioned earlier, all they need is the `Controller` suffix, by convention, and to avoid the `[NonController]` attribute. The problem with this approach is that you lose all helper methods and context properties (`HttpContext`, `ControllerContext`, `ViewBag`, and `Url`), but you can have them injected. Let's see how this works.

> If you add the `[Controller]` attribute to any POCO class, you can turn it into a controller, regardless of its name.

Adding context to POCO controllers

Say for example, that you have a POCO controller, `HomeController`. You don't have the various context and view bag-related properties, but with a couple of attributes applied to appropriately typed properties, you can have the infrastructure inject them, as shown in the following example:

```
public class HomeController
{
    private readonly IUrlHelperFactory _url;

    public HomeController(IHttpContextAccessor ctx, IUrlHelperFactory
url)
    {
        this.HttpContext = ctx.HttpContext;
        this._url = url;
    }

    [ControllerContext]
    public ControllerContext { get; set; }

    public HttpContext HttpContext { get; set; }

    [ActionContext]
    public ActionContext ActionContext { get; set; }

    [ViewDataDictionary]
    public ViewDataDictionary ViewBag { get; set; }

    public IUrlHelper Url { get; set; }

    public string Index()
    {
        this.Url = this.Url ??
this._url.GetUrlHelper(this.ActionContext);
        return "Hello, World!";
    }
}
```

You will notice a few interesting things here:

- `ActionContext`, `ControllerContext`, and `ViewBag` are automatically injected just by adding the `[ActionContext]`, `[ControllerContext]`, and `[ViewDataDictionary]` attributes to properties of any name, and with the `ActionContext`, `ControllerContext` and `ViewDataDictionary` types, respectively.

- When the controller is instantiated by the ASP.NET Core infrastructure, the dependency injection framework injects the `IHttpContextAccessor` and `IUrlHelperFactory` objects.
- The `HttpContext` object needs to be obtained from the passed `IHttpContextAccessor` instance.
- In order to build an `IUrlHelper`, the `IUrlHelperFactory` needs an instance of `ActionContext`; because we don't have that at constructor time, we need to build it later on, for example, in an action method (in this example, `Index`).

However, to make this work, we need to tell ASP.NET Core to register the default implementations of `IHttpContextAccessor` and `IUrlHelperFactory`. This is normally done in the `ConfigureServices` method of the `Startup` class:

```
services.AddScoped<IHttpContextAccessor, HttpContextAccessor>();
//or, since version 2.1:
services.AddHttpContextAccessor();
services.AddScoped<IUrlHelperFactory, UrlHelperFactory>();
```

These properties will behave in exactly the same way as their non-POCO counterparts that are inherited from `ControllerBase` and `Controller`.

Intercepting actions in POCO controllers

If you want, you can also implement one of the filter interfaces so that you can interact with the request before or after an action is called, such as `IActionFilter`:

```
public class HomeController : IActionFilter
{
    public void OnActionExecuting(ActionExecutingContext context)
    {
        //before the action is called
    }

    public void OnActionExecuted(ActionExecutedContext context)
    {
        //after the action is called
    }
}
```

If you prefer to have an asynchronous handler, implement the asynchronous version (`IAsyncXXXFilter`) instead. We will talk more about filters in `Chapter 10`, *Understanding Filters*.

Let's now see how controllers are discovered by the framework.

Finding controllers

Regardless of whether you go for POCO or non-POCO controllers, ASP.NET Core will apply the same rules for discovering controllers, which are as follows:

- They need to have the `Controller` suffix (strictly speaking, this can be changed, but we will leave this for now).
- They need to be instantiable classes (nonabstract, nongeneric, and nonstatic).
- They cannot have the `[NonController]` attribute applied to them.
- If they are POCO and do not have the `Controller` suffix, you can decorate them with the `[Controller]` attribute.

 By convention, the files that contain the controller classes are stored in a folder called `Controllers`, and also in a `Controllers` namespace, but this is just ignored.

Controller classes are looked up by the name in the route—the controller parameter—and they are searched in the assemblies registered for that purpose. By default, the currently executing assembly is included in the search, but all assemblies registered as *application parts* are too. You can register additional application parts when you add the MVC features to the dependency injection framework (`ConfigureServices` method) as follows:

```
services.AddMvc()
.AddApplicationPart(typeof(MyCustomComponent).GetTypeInfo().Assembly);
```

Here, we are adding a reference to the assembly that contains a hypothetical class, `MyCustomComponent`. After we do this, any controllers that are located in it are available for use. In order to get the full list of found controllers, we can use `ControllerFeature` and populate it through `ApplicationPartManager`:

```
services.AddMvc()
.AddApplicationPart(typeof(MyCustomComponent).GetTypeInfo().Assembly)
    .ConfigureApplicationPartManager(parts =>
    {
        var controllerFeature = new ControllerFeature();
        parts.PopulateFeature(controllerFeature);
        //controllerFeature.Controllers contains the list of
discovered
        //controllers' types
    });
```

Controllers are only discovered once, at startup time, which is a good thing performance-wise.

If there are two controllers with the same name but that are in different namespaces, and they both expose an action method that matches the current request, then ASP.NET won't know which one to pick and will throw an exception. If this happens, we need to give one of the classes a new controller name by applying a `[ControllerName]` attribute, as shown in the following code:

```
namespace Controllers
{
    public class HomeController
    {
    }

    namespace Admin
    {
        [ControllerName("AdminHome")]
        public class HomeController
        {
        }
    }
}
```

We could also change the action name, as we will see in a moment. Now, let's see what happens once the controller type has been found.

Controller life cycle

After a controller's type is located, ASP.NET Core starts a process to instantiate it. The process is as follows:

1. The default controller factory (`IControllerFactory`) is obtained from the **dependency injection (DI)** framework and its `CreateController` method is called.

2. The controller factory uses the registered controller activator (`IControllerActivator`), also obtained from the DI, to obtain an instance to the controller (`IControllerActivator.Create`).

3. The action method is located using the `IActionSelector` from the DI.

4. If the controller implements any filter interfaces (`IActionFilter`, `IResourceFilter`, and more), or if the action has any filter attributes, then the appropriate methods are called upon it and on global filters.

5. The action method is called by the `IActionInvoker` from the `IActionInvokerProvider`, also obtained from the DI.

6. Any filter methods are called upon the controller, the action method's filter attributes, and the global filters.

7. The controller factory releases the controller (`IControllerFactory.ReleaseController`).

8. The controller activator releases the controller (`IControllerActivator.Release`).

9. If the controller implements `IDisposable`, then the `Dispose` method is called upon it.

Most of these components can be registered through the built-in DI framework—for example, if you want to replace the default `IControllerFactory` implementation, then you could do this in the `ConfigureServices` method:

```
services.AddSingleton<IControllerFactory, CustomControllerFactory>();
```

Now, imagine that you wanted to write an action selector that would redirect all calls to a specific method of a class. You could write a redirect action selector as follows:

```
public class RedirectActionSelector : IActionSelector
{
    public ActionDescriptor SelectBestCandidate(
        RouteContext context,
        IReadOnlyList<ActionDescriptor> candidates)
    {
```

```
        var descriptor = new ControllerActionDescriptor();
        descriptor.ControllerName = typeof(MyController).Name;
        descriptor.MethodInfo = typeof(MyController).
        GetMethod("MyAction");
        descriptor.ActionName = descriptor.MethodInfo.Name;
        return descriptor;
    }

    public IReadOnlyList<ActionDescriptor> SelectCandidates(
    RouteContext context)
    {
        return new List<ActionDescriptor>();
    }
}
```

This will redirect any request to the `MyAction` method of the `MyController` class. Hey, it's just for fun, remember?

Now let's have a look at actions.

Actions

The action method is where all the action happens (pun intended). It is the entry point to the code that handles your request. The found action method is called from the `IActionInvoker` implementation; it must be a **physical**, nongeneric, public instance method of a controller class. The action selection mechanism is quite complex and relies on the route **action** parameter.

The name of the action method should be the same as this parameter, but that doesn't mean that it is the physical method name; you can also apply the `[ActionName]` attribute to set it to something different, and this is of particular use if we have overloaded methods:

```
[ActionName("BinaryOperation")]
public IActionResult Operation(int a, int b) { ... }

[ActionName("UnaryOperation")]
public IActionResult Operation(int a) { ... }
```

In the following sections, we will see how actions work and how they work in the context of the controller.

Finding actions

After discovering a set of candidate controllers for handling the request, ASP.NET Core will check them all to see if they offer a method that matches the current route (see `Chapter 3`, *Routing*):

- It must be public, nonstatic, and nongeneric.
- Its name must match the route's action (the physical name may be different as long as it has an `[ActionName]` attribute).
- Its parameters must match the nonoptional parameters specified in the route (those not marked as optional and without default values); if the route specifies an `id` value, then there must be an `id` parameter and type, and if the `id` has a route constraint of `int`, like in `{id:int}`, then it must be of the `int` type.
- The action method can have a parameter of the `IFormCollection`, `IFormFile`, or `IFormFileCollection` type, as these are always accepted.
- It cannot have a `[NonAction]` attribute applied to it.

The actual rules for getting the applicable action are as follows:

- If the action name was supplied in the URL, then it is tentatively used.
- If there is a default action specified in a route—based on fluent configuration or attributes—then it is tentatively used.

When I mean tentatively, I mean to say that there may be constraint attributes (more on this in a minute) or mandatory attributes that need to be checked—for example, if an action method requires a mandatory parameter and it cannot be found in the request or in any of the sources, then the action cannot be used to serve the current request.

Synchronous and asynchronous actions

An action method can be synchronous or asynchronous. For the asynchronous version, it should be prototyped as follows:

```
public async Task<IActionResult> Index() { ... }
```

Of course, you can add any number of parameters you like, as with a synchronous action method. The key here, however, is to mark the method as `async` and to return `Task<IActionResult>` instead of just `IActionResult` (or another inherited type).

Why should you use asynchronous actions? Well, you need to understand the following facts:

- Web servers have a number of threads that they use to handle incoming requests.
- When a request is accepted, one of these threads is blocked while it is waiting to process it.
- If the request takes too long, then this thread is unavailable to answer other requests.

Enter asynchronous actions. With asynchronous actions, as soon as a thread accepts an incoming request, it immediately passes it along to a background thread that will take care of it, releasing the main thread. This is very handy, because it will be available to accept other requests. This is not related to performance, but scalability; using asynchronous actions allows your application to always be responsive, even if it is still processing requests in the background.

Getting the context

We've seen how you can access the context in both POCO and controller-based controllers. By context, we're talking about three things concerning action methods:

- The HTTP context, represented by the `HttpContext` class, from which you can gain access to the current user, the low-level request and response properties, such as cookies, headers, and so on.
- The controller context, an instance of `ControllerContext`, which gives you access to the current model state, route data, action descriptor, and so on.
- The action context, of the `ActionContext` type, which gives you pretty much the same information that you get from `ControllerContext`, but used in different places; so if, in the future, a new feature is added to only one, it will not show up on the other.

Having access to the context is important because you may need to make decisions based on the information you can obtain from it, or, for example, set response headers or cookies directly. You can see that ASP.NET Core has dropped the `HttpContext.Current` property that had been around since the beginning of ASP.NET, so you don't have immediate access to it; however, you can get it from either `ControllerContext` or `ActionContext`, or have it injected into your dependency-injection-build component by having your constructor take an instance of `IHttpContextAccessor`.

Action constraints

The following attributes and interfaces, when implemented in an attribute applied to the action method, will possibly prevent it from being called:

- `[NonAction]`: The action is never called.
- `[Consumes]`: If there are many candidate methods—for example, in the case of method overloading—then this attribute is used to check whether any of the methods accept the currently requested content type.
- `[RequireHttps]`: If present, the action method will only be called if the request protocol is HTTPS.
- `IActionConstraint`: If an attribute applied to an action method implements this interface, then its `Accept` method is called to see whether the action should be called.
- `IActionHttpMethodProvider`: This is implemented by `[AcceptVerbs]`, `[HttpGet]`, `[HttpPost]`, and other HTTP method selector attributes; if present, the action method will only be called if the current request's HTTP verb matches one of the values returned by the `HttpMethods` property.
- `IAuthorizeData`: Any attribute that implements this interface, the most notorious of all being `[Authorize]`, will be checked to see whether the current identity (as specified by `ClaimsPrincipal` assigned to the `HttpContext`'s `User` property) has the right policy and roles.
- `Filters`: If a filter attribute, such as `IActionFilter`, is applied to the action or if `IAuthorizationFilter`, for example, is invoked and possibly either throws an exception or returns an `IActionResult`, which prevents the action from being called (`NotFoundObjectResult`, `UnauthorizedResult`, and more).

This implementation of `IActionConstraint` will apply custom logic to decide whether a method can be called in its `Accept` method:

```
public class CustomAuthorizationAttribute: Attribute,
IActionConstraint
{
    public int Order { get; } = int.MaxValue;

    public bool Accept(ActionConstraintContext context)
    {
        return
         context.CurrentCandidate.Action.DisplayName
         .Contains("Authorized");
    }
}
```

The `context` parameter grants access to the route context, and from there, to the HTTP context and the current candidate method. These should be more than enough to make a decision.

The order by which a constraint is applied might be relevant, as the `Order` property of the `IActionConstraint` interface, when used in an attribute, will determine the relative order of execution of all the attributes applied to the same method.

Action parameters

An action method can take parameters. These parameters can be, for example, submitted form values or query string parameters. There are essentially three ways by which we can get all submitted values:

- `IFormCollection`, `IFormFile`, and `IFormFileCollection`: A parameter of any of these types will contain the list of values submitted by an HTML form; they won't be used in a `GET` request as it is not possible to upload files with `GET`.
- `HttpContext`: Directly accessing the context and retrieving values from either the `Request.Form` or `Request.QueryString` collections.
- Adding named parameters that match values in the request that we want to access individually.

The latter can either be of basic types, such as `string`, `int`, and more, or they can be of a complex type. The way their values are injected is configurable and based on a provider model. `IValueProviderFactory` and `IValueProvider` are used to obtain the values for these attributes. ASP.NET Core offers developers a chance to inspect the collection of value provider factories through the `AddMvc` method:

```
services.AddMvc(options =>
{
    options.ValueProviderFactories.Add(new
CustomValueProviderFactory());
});
```

Out of the box, the following value provider factories are available and registered in the following order:

- `FormValueProviderFactory`: Injects values from a submitted form, such as `<input type="text" name="myParam"/>`.
- `RouteValueProviderFactory`: Route parameters—for example, `[controller]/[action]/{id?}`.
- `QueryStringValueProviderFactory`: Query string values—for example, `?id=100`.
- `JQueryFormValueProviderFactory`: jQuery form values.

The order, however, is important, because it determines the order in which the value providers are added to the collection that ASP.NET Core uses to actually get the values. Each value provider factory will have its `CreateValueProviderAsync` method called and will typically populate a collection of value providers (for example, `QueryStringValueProviderFactory` will add an instance of `QueryStringValueProvider`, and so on).

This means that, for example, if you submitted a form value with the name `myField` and you are passing another value for `myField` via a query string, then the first one is going to be used; however, many providers can be used at once—for example, if you have a route that expects an `id` parameter but can also accept query string parameters:

```
[Route("[controller]/[action]/{id}?{*querystring}")]
public IActionResult ProcessOrder(int id, bool processed) { ... }
```

This will happily access a request of `/Home/Process/120?processed=true`, where the `id` comes from the route and is processed from the query string provider.

Some methods of sending values allow them to be optional—for example, route parameters. With that being the case, you need to make sure that the parameters in the action method also permit the following:

- Reference types, including those that can have a `null` value
- Value types, which should have a default value, such as `int a = 0`

For example, if you want to have a value from a route injected into an action method parameter, you could do it like this, if the value is mandatory:

```
[Route("[controller]/[action]/{id}")]
public IActionResult Process(int id) { ... }
```

If it is optional, you could do it like this :

```
[Route("[controller]/[action]/{id?}")]
public IActionResult Process(int? id = null) { ... }
```

Value providers are more interesting because they are the ones that actually return the values for the action method parameters. They try to find a value from its name—the action method parameter name. ASP.NET will iterate the list of supplied value providers, call its `ContainsPrefix` method for each parameter, and if the result is `true`, it will then call the `GetValue` method.

Even if the supplied value providers are convenient, you might want to obtain values from other sources—for example, I can think of the following:

- Cookies
- Headers
- Session values

Say that you would like to have cookie values injected automatically into an action method's parameters. For this, you would write a `CookieValueProviderFactory`, which might well look like this:

```
public class CookieValueProviderFactory : IValueProviderFactory
{
    public Task CreateValueProviderAsync(
     ValueProviderFactoryContext context)
    {
        context.ValueProviders.Add(new
         CookieValueProvider(context.ActionContext));
        return Task.CompletedTask;
    }
}
```

Then you could write a `CookieValueProvider` to go along with it:

```
public class CookieValueProvider : IValueProvider
{
    private readonly ActionContext _actionContext;

    public CookieValueProvider(ActionContext actionContext)
    {
        this._actionContext = actionContext;
    }

    public bool ContainsPrefix(string prefix)
    {
        return this._actionContext.HttpContext.Request.Cookies
        .ContainsKey(prefix);
    }

    public ValueProviderResult GetValue(string key)
    {
        return new ValueProviderResult(this._actionContext.HttpContext
        .Request.Cookies[key]);
    }
}
```

After which, you would register it in the `AddMvc` method, in the `ValueProviders` collection of `MvcOptions`:

```
services.AddMvc(options =>
{
    options.ValueProviderFactories.Add(new
CookieValueProviderFactory());
}):
```

Now you can have cookie values injected transparently into your actions without any additional effort.

 Don't forget that, because of C# limitations, you cannot have variables or parameters that contain – or other special characters, so you cannot inject values for parameters that have these in their names out of the box. In this cookie example, you won't be able to have a parameter for a cookie with a name like `AUTH-COOKIE`.

You can, however, in the same action method, have parameters that come from different sources, as follows:

```
[HttpGet("{id}")]
public IActionResult Process(string id, Model model) { ... }
```

But what if the target action method parameter is not of the string type? The answer lies in **model binding**.

Model binding

Model binding is the process by which ASP.NET Core translates parts of the request, including route values, query strings, submitted forms, and more into strongly typed parameters. As is the case in most APIs of ASP.NET Core, this is an extensible mechanism. Do not get confused with model value providers; the responsibility of model binders is not to supply the values, but merely to make them fit into whatever class we tell them to!

Out of the box, ASP.NET can translate to the following:

- `IFormCollection`, `IFormFile`, and `IFormFileCollection` parameters
- Primitive/base types (which handle conversion to and from strings)
- Enumerations
- POCO classes
- Dictionaries
- Collections
- Cancelation tokens (more on this later on)

The model binder providers are configured in the `MvcOptions` class, which is normally accessible through the `AddMvc` call:

```
services.AddMvc(options =>
{
    options.ModelBinderProviders.Add(new CustomModelBinderProvider());
});
```

Most scenarios that you will be interested in should already be supported. What you can also do is specify the source from which a parameter is to be obtained. So, let's see how we can use this ability.

Body

In the case where you are calling an action using an HTTP verb that lets you pass a payload (POST, PUT, and PATCH), you can ask for your parameter to receive a value from this payload by applying a [FromBody] attribute:

```
[HttpPost]
public IActionResult Submit([FromBody] string payload) { ... }
```

Besides using a string value, you can provide your own POCO class, which will be populated from the payload, if the format is supported by one of the input formatters configured (more on this in a second).

Form

Another option is to have a parameter coming from a specific named field in a submitted form, and for that, we use the [FromForm] attribute:

```
[HttpPost]
public IActionResult Submit([FromForm] string email) { ... }
```

There is a Name property that, if supplied, will get the value from the specified named form field (for example, [FromForm(Name = "UserEmail")]).

Header

A header is also a good candidate for retrieving values, hence the [FromHeader] attribute:

```
public IActionResult Get([FromHeader] string accept) { ... }
```

The [FromHeader] attribute allows us to specify the actual header name (for example, [FromHeader(Name = "Content-Type")]), and if this is not specified, it will look for the name of the parameter that it is applied to.

By default, it can only bind to strings or collections of strings, but you can force it to accept other target types (provided the input is valid for that type). Just set the `AllowBindingHeaderValuesToNonStringModelTypes` property to `true` when configuring MVC:

```
services.AddMvc(options =>
{
    options.AllowBindingHeaderValuesToNonStringModelTypes = true;
});
```

Query string

We can also retrieve values via the query string, using the `[FromQuery]` attribute:

```
public IActionResult Get([FromQuery] string id) { ... }
```

You can also specify the query string parameter name using the `Name` property, `[FromQuery(Name = "Id")]`. Mind you, by convention, if you don't specify this attribute, you can still pass values from the query string and they will be passed along to the action method parameters.

Route

The route parameters can also be a source of data—enter `[FromRoute]`:

```
[HttpGet("{id}")]
public IActionResult Get([FromRoute] string id) { ... }
```

Similar to most other binding attributes, you can specify a name to indicate the route parameter that the value should come from (for example, `[FromRoute(Name = "Id")]`).

Dependency injection

You can also use a dependency injection, such as (`[FromServices]`):

```
public IActionResult Get([FromServices] IHttpContextAccessor accessor)
{ ... }
```

Of course, the service you are injecting needs to be registered in the DI framework in advance.

Custom binders

It is also possible to specify your own binder. To do this, you can use the [ModelBinder] attribute, which takes an optional Type as its parameter. What's funny about this is that it can be used in different scenarios, such as the following:

- If you apply it to a property or field on your controller class, then it will be bound to a request parameter coming from any of the supported value providers (query string, route, form, and more):

```
[ModelBinder]
public string Id { get; set; }
```

- If you pass a type of a class that implements IModelBinder, then you can use this class for the actual binding process, but only for the parameter, property, or field you are applying it to:

```
public IActionResult
Process([ModelBinder(typeof(CustomModelBinder))] Model model) {
... }
```

A simple model binder that does HTML formatting could be written as follows:

```
public class HtmlEncodeModelBinder : IModelBinder
{
    private readonly IModelBinder _fallbackBinder;

    public HtmlEncodeModelBinder(IModelBinder fallbackBinder)
    {
        if (fallbackBinder == null)
            throw new ArgumentNullException(nameof(fallbackBinder));

        _fallbackBinder = fallbackBinder;
    }
    public Task BindModelAsync(ModelBindingContext bindingContext)
    {
        if (bindingContext == null)
            throw new ArgumentNullException(nameof(bindingContext));

        var valueProviderResult = bindingContext.ValueProvider.
        GetValue(bindingContext.ModelName);
        if (valueProviderResult == ValueProviderResult.None)
        {
            return _fallbackBinder.BindModelAsync(bindingContext);
        }

        var valueAsString = valueProviderResult.FirstValue;
```

```
        if (string.IsNullOrEmpty(valueAsString))
        {
            return _fallbackBinder.BindModelAsync(bindingContext);
        }

        var result = HtmlEncoder.Default.Encode(valueAsString);

        bindingContext.Result = ModelBindingResult.Success(result);
        return Task.CompletedTask;
    }
}
```

 The code for this was written by Steve Gordon and is available at `https://www.stevejgordon.co.uk/html-encode-string-aspnet-core-model-binding`.

The code doesn't do much: it takes a fallback binder in its constructor and uses it if there is no value to bind or if the value is a `null` or empty string; otherwise, it HTML-encodes it.

You can also add a model-binding provider to the global list. The first one that handles the target type will be picked up. The interface for a model-binding provider is defined by the `IModelBinderProvider` (who knew?), and it only specifies a single method, `GetBinder`. If it returns non-null, then the binder will be used.

Let's look at a model binder provider that would apply this model binder to string parameters that have a custom attribute:

```
public class HtmlEncodeAttribute : Attribute { }

public class HtmlEncodeModelBinderProvider : IModelBinderProvider
{
    public IModelBinder GetBinder(ModelBinderProviderContext context)
    {
        if (context == null) throw new
        ArgumentNullException(nameof(context));

        if ((context.Metadata.ModelType == typeof(string)) &&
            (context.Metadata.ModelType.GetTypeInfo().
             IsDefined(typeof(HtmlEncodeAttribute))))
        {
            return new HtmlEncodeModelBinder(new
SimpleTypeModelBinder(
            context.Metadata.ModelType));
        }
```

```
        return null;
    }
}
```

After this, we register it in `AddMvc` to the `ValueProviderFactories` collection; this collection is iterated until a proper model binder is returned from `GetBinder`, in which case, it is used as follows:

```
services.AddMvc(options =>
{
    options.ValueProviderFactories.Add(new
    HtmlEncodeModelBinderProvider());
});
```

We have created a simple marker attribute, `HtmlEncodeAttribute` (as well as a model-binder provider), that checks whether the target model is of the string type and has the `[HtmlEncode]` attribute applied to it. If so, it applies the `HtmlEncodeModelBinder`. It's as simple as that:

```
public IActionResult Process([HtmlEncode] string html) { ... }
```

We will be revisiting model binding later on in this chapter when we talk about HTML forms.

Property binding

Any properties in your controller that are decorated with the `[BindProperty]` attribute are also bound from the request data. You can also apply the same binding source attributes (`[FromQuery]`, `[FromBody]`, and so on), but to have them populated on `GET` requests, you need to tell the framework to do this explicitly:

```
[BindProperty(SupportsGet = true)]
public string Id { get; set; }
```

You can also apply this to controller-level property-validation attributes (for example, `[Required]`, `[MaxLength]`, and so on), and they will be used to validate the value of each property. `[BindRequired]` also works, meaning that if a value for a property is not provided, it results in an error.

Input formatters

When you are binding a POCO class from the payload by applying the `[FromBody]` attribute, ASP.NET Core will try to deserialize the POCO type from the payload as a string. For this, it uses an **input formatter**. Similar to **output formatters**, these are used to convert to and from common formats, such as JSON or XML. Support for JSON comes out of the box, but you will need to explicitly add support for XML. You can do so by including the NuGet package `Microsoft.AspNetCore.Mvc.Formatters.Xml` and explicitly add support to the pipeline:

```
services
    .AddMvc()
    .AddXmlSerializerFormatters();
```

If you are curious, what this does is add an instance of `XmlSerializerInputFormatter` to the `MvcOptions'` `InputFormatters` collection. The list is iterated until one formatter is capable of processing the data. The included formatters are as follows:

- `JsonInputFormatter`, which can import from any JSON content (`application/json`)
- `JsonPatchInputFormatter`, which can import from JSON patch contents (`application/json-patch+json`)

Explicit binding

You can also fine-tune which parts of your model class are bound, and how they are bound, by applying attributes—for example, if you want to exclude a property from being bound, you can apply the `[BindNever]` attribute:

```
public class Model
{
    [BindNever]
    public int Id { get; set; }
}
```

Alternatively, if you want to explicitly define which properties should be bound, you can apply `[Bind]` to a `Model` class:

```
[Bind("Name, Email")]
public class Model
{
```

```
    public int Id { get; set; }
    public string Name { get; set; }
    public string Email { get; set; }
}
```

If you pass a value to the `Prefix` property, you can instruct ASP.NET Core to retrieve the value to bind from a property with that prefix—for example, if you have several form values with the same name (for example, `option`), then you can bind them all to a collection:

```
[Bind(Prefix = "Option")]
public string[] Option { get; set; }
```

Normally, if a value for a property is not supplied in the source medium, such as the `POST` payload or the query string, the property doesn't get a value. However, you can force this, as follows:

```
[BindRequired]
public string Email { get; set; }
```

If the `Email` parameter is not passed, then `ModelState.IsValid` will be `false` and an exception will be thrown.

You can also specify the default binding behavior at class level and then override it on a property-by-property basis with a `[BindingBehavior]`:

```
[BindingBehavior(BindingBehavior.Required)]
public class Model
{
    [BindNever]
    public int Id { get; set; }
    public string Name { get; set; }
    public string Email { get; set; }
}
```

So, we have three situations:

- If a value is present in the request, bind it to the model (`[Bind]`).
- Ignore any value passed in the model (`[BindNever]`).
- Demand that a value is passed in the request (`[BindRequired]`).

We should also mention that these attributes can be applied to action method parameters as follows:

```
public IActionResult Process(string id, [BindRequired] int state) {
... }
```

Canceling requests

Sometimes, a request is canceled by the client, such as when someone closes the browser, navigates to another page, or refreshes the page. The problem is, you don't know that it happened, and you continue to execute your action method not knowing that the answer will be discarded. To help in these scenarios, ASP.NET Core lets you add a parameter of the `CancelationToken` type. This is the standard way to allow the cancelation of asynchronous tasks in .NET and .NET Core. It works as follows:

```
public async Task<IActionResult> Index(CancelationToken cancel) { ...
}
```

If, for whatever reason, the ASP.NET Core host (Kestrel, WebListener) detects that the client has disconnected, it fires the cancelation token (its `IsCancelationRequested` is set to `true`, the same for `HttpContext.RequestAborted`). A benefit is that you can pass this `CancelationToken` instance to any asynchronous methods you may be using (for example, `HttpClient.SendAsync()`, `DbSet<T>.ToListAsync()`, and more) and they will also be canceled along with the client request!

Model validation

Once your model (the parameters that are passed to the action method) are properly built and their properties have had their values set, they can be validated. Validation itself is configurable.

All values obtained from all value providers are available in the `ModelState` property, defined in the `ControllerBase` class. For any given type, the `IsValid` property will say whether ASP.NET considers the model valid as per its configured validators.

By default, the registered implementation relies on the registered model metadata and model validator providers, which include the `DataAnnotationsModelValidatorProvider`. This performs validation against the `System.ComponentModel.DataAnnotations` API, namely, all classes derived from `ValidationAttribute` (`RequiredAttribute`, `RegularExpressionAttribute`, `MaxLengthAttribute`, and more), but also `IValidatableObject` implementations. This is the *de facto* validation standard in .NET, and it is capable of handling most cases.

When the model is populated, it is also automatically validated, but you can also explicitly ask for model validation by calling the `TryValidateModel` method in your action—for example, if you change anything in it:

```
public IActionResult Process(Model model)
{
    if (this.TryValidateModel(model))
    {
        return this.Ok();
    }
    else
    {
        return this.Error();
    }
}
```

Since ASP.NET Core 2.1, you can apply validation attributes to action parameters themselves, and you get validation for them too:

```
public IActionResult Process([Required, EmailAddress] string email) {
... }
```

As we have mentioned, `ModelState` will have the `IsValid` property set according to the validation result, but we can also force revalidation. If you want to check a specific property, you can use the overload of `TryValidateModel` that takes an additional string parameter:

```
if (this.TryValidateModel(model, "Email")) { ... }
```

Behind the scenes, all registered validators are called and the method will return a Boolean flag with the result of all validations.

We will revisit model validation in an upcoming chapter. For now, let's see how we can plug in a custom model validator. We do this in `ConfigureServices` using the `AddMvc` method:

```
services.AddMvc(options =>
{
    options.ModelValidatorProviders.Add(new
      CustomModelValidatorProvider());
});
```

The `CustomModelValidatorProvider` looks as follows:

```
public class CustomModelValidatorProvider : IModelValidatorProvider
{
    public void CreateValidators(ModelValidatorProviderContext
```

```
context)
    {
        context.Results.Add(new ValidatorItem { Validator =
        new CustomModelValidator() });
    }
}
```

The main logic simply goes in `CustomModelValidator`:

```
public class CustomObjectModelValidator : IModelValidator
{
    public IEnumerable<ModelValidationResult>
     Validate(ModelValidationContext context)
    {
        if (context.Model is ICustomValidatable)
        {
            //supply custom validation logic here and return a
collection
            //of ModelValidationResult
        }

        return Enumerable.Empty<ModelValidationResult>();
    }
}
```

The `ICustomValidatable` interface (and implementation) is left to you, dear reader, as an exercise. Hopefully, it won't be too difficult to understand.

This `ICustomValidatable` implementation should look at the state of its class and return one or more `ModelValidationResults` for any problems it finds.

Since ASP.NET Core 2.1, the `[ApiController]` attribute adds a convention to controllers—typically API controllers—which triggers model validation automatically when an action method is called. You can use it, but what it does is return a 400 HTTP status code (`https://developer.mozilla.org/en-US/docs/Web/HTTP/Status/400`) and a description of the validation errors in JSON format, which is probably not what you want when working with views. You can use an action filter for the same purpose; let's look at one example:

```
[Serializable]
[AttributeUsage(AttributeTargets.Class | AttributeTargets.Method,
    AllowMultiple = false,
    Inherited = true)]
public sealed class ValidateModelStateAttribute :
ActionFilterAttribute
{
    public ValidateModelStateAttribute(string redirectUrl)
```

```csharp
        {
            this.RedirectUrl = redirectUrl;
        }

        public ValidateModelStateAttribute(
            string actionName,
            string controllerName = null,
            object routeValues = null)
        {
            this.ControllerName = controllerName;
            this.ActionName = actionName;
            this.RouteValues = routeValues;
        }

        public string RedirectUrl { get; }
        public string ActionName { get; }
        public string ControllerName { get; }
        public object RouteValues { get; }

        public override Task OnResultExecutionAsync(ResultExecutingContext
         context, ResultExecutionDelegate next)
        {
            if (!context.ModelState.IsValid)
            {
                if (!string.IsNullOrWhiteSpace(this.RedirectUrl))
                {
                    context.Result = new RedirectResult(this.RedirectUrl);
                }
                else if (!string.IsNullOrWhiteSpace(this.ActionName))
                {
                    context.Result = new RedirectToActionResult

                    (this.ActionName, this.ControllerName,
                        this.RouteValues);
                }
                else
                {
                    context.Result = new BadRequestObjectResult
                     (context.ModelState);
                }
            }

            return base.OnResultExecutionAsync(context, next);
        }
    }
```

This is an action filter and it is also an attribute, which means that it can be registered globally:

```
services.AddMvc(options =>
{
    options.AllowValidatingTopLevelNodes = true;
    options.Filters.Add(new
ValidateModelStateAttribute("/Home/Error"));
});
```

It can also be registered by adding the attribute to a controller class or action method. This class offers two controllers:

- One for specifying the redirection as a full URL
- Another for using a controller name, action method, and possibly route parameters

It inherits from `ActionFilterAttribute`, which in turn implements `IActionFilter` and `IAsyncActionFilter`. Here, we are interested in the asynchronous version—a good practice—which means that we override `OnResultExecutionAsync`. This method is called before the control is passed to the action method, and here we check whether the model is valid. If it is not, then redirect it to the proper location, depending on how the class was instantiated.

By the way, controller properties are only validated if the `AllowValidatingTopLevelNodes` property is set to `true`, as in this example; otherwise, any errors will be ignored.

Action results

Actions process requests and typically either return content or an HTTP status code to the calling client. In ASP.NET Core, broadly speaking, there are two possible return types:

- An implementation of `IActionResult`
- Any .NET POCO class

Implementations of `IActionResult` wrap the actual response, plus a content type header and HTTP status code, and are generally useful. This interface defines only a single method, `ExecuteResultAsync`, which takes a single parameter of the `ActionContext`type that wraps all properties that describe the current request:

- `ActionDescriptor`: Describes the action method to call
- `HttpContext`: Describes the request context
- `ModelState`: Describes the submitted model properties and its validation state
- `RouteData`: Describes the route parameters

So you can see that `IActionResult` is actually an implementation of the command design pattern (`https://sourcemaking.com/design_patterns/command`) in the sense that it actually executes, and doesn't just store data. A very simple implementation of `IActionResult` that returns a string and the HTTP status code `200` might be as follows:

```
public class HelloWorldResult : IActionResult
{
    public async Task ExecuteResultAsync(ActionContext actionContext)
    {
        actionContext.HttpContext.Response.StatusCode = StatusCodes
         .Status200OK;
        await actionContext.HttpContext.Response.WriteAsync("Hello,
         World!");
    }
}
```

As we will see shortly, `IActionResult` is now the interface that describes HTML results as well as API-style results. The `ControllerBase` and `Controller` classes offer the following convenient methods for returning `IActionResult` implementations:

- `BadRequest` (`BadRequestResult`, HTTP code `400`): The request was not valid.
- `Challenge` (`ChallengeResult`, HTTP code `401`): A challenge for authentication.
- `Content` (`ContentResult`, HTTP code `200`): Any content.
- `Created` (`CreatedResult`, HTTP code `201`): A result that indicates that a resource was created.
- `CreatedAtAction` (`CreatedAtActionResult`, HTTP code `201`): A result that indicates that a resource was created by an action.

- `CreatedAtRoute` (`CreatedAtRouteResult`, HTTP code 201): A result that indicates that a resource was created in a named route.
- `File` (`VirtualFileResult`, `FileStreamResult`, `FileContentResult`, HTTP code 200).
- `Forbid` (`ForbidResult`, HTTP code 403).
- `LocalRedirect` (`LocalRedirectResult`, HTTP code 302): Redirects to a local resource.
- `LocalRedirectPermanent` (`LocalRedirectResult`, HTTP code 301): A permanent redirect to a local resource.
- `NoContent` (`NoContentResult`, HTTP code 204): No content to deploy.
- `NotFound` (`NotFoundObjectResult`, HTTP code 404): Resource not found.
- `Ok` (`OkResult`, HTTP code 200): OK.
- No method (`PartialViewResult`, HTTP code 200): Requested HTTP method not supported.
- `PhysicalFile` (`PhysicalFileResult`, HTTP code 200): A physical file's content.
- `Redirect` (`RedirectResult`, HTTP code 302): Redirect to an absolute URL.
- `RedirectPermanent` (`RedirectResult`, HTTP code 301): Permanent redirect to an absolute URL.
- `RedirectToAction` (`RedirectToActionResult`, HTTP code 302): A redirect to an action of a local controller.
- `RedirectToActionPermanent` (`RedirectToActionResult`, HTTP code 301): A permanent redirect to an action of a local controller.
- `RedirectToPage` (`RedirectToPageResult`, HTTP code 302, from ASP.NET Core 2): A redirect to a local Razor page.
- `RedirectToPagePermanent` (`RedirectToPageResult`, HTTP code 301): A permanent redirect to a local Razor page.
- `RedirectToPagePermanentPreserveMethod` (`RedirectToPageResult`, HTTP code 301): A permanent redirect to a local page preserving the original requested HTTP method.
- `RedirectToPagePreserveMethod` (`RedirectToPageResult`, HTTP code 302): A redirect to a local page.
- `RedirectToRoute` (`RedirectToRouteResult`, HTTP code 302): A redirect to a named route.

- `RedirectToRoutePermanent` (`RedirectToRouteResult`, HTTP code 301): A permanent redirect to a named route.
- `SignIn` (`SignInResult`): Signs in.
- `SignOut` (`SignOutResult`): Signs out.
- `StatusCode` (`StatusCodeResult`, `ObjectResult`, any HTTP code).
- No method (`UnsupportedMediaTypeResult`, HTTP code 415): Accepted content type does not match what can be returned.
- `Unauthorized` (`UnauthorizedResult`, HTTP code 401): Not allowed to request the resource.
- `View` (`ViewResult`, HTTP code 200, declared in `Controller` class): A view.
- `ViewComponent` (`ViewComponentResult`, HTTP code 200): The result of invoking a view component.

Some of these results also assign a content type—for example, `ContentResult` will return `text/plain` by default (this can be changed), `JsonResult` will return `application/json`, and so on. Some of the names are self-explanatory; others may require some clarification:

- There are always four versions of the `Redirect` methods—the regular one for temporary redirects, one for permanent redirects, and two additional versions that also preserve the original request HTTP method. It is possible to redirect to an arbitrary URL, the URL for a specific controller action, a Razor page URL, and a local (relative) URL.
- The preserve method in a redirect means that the new request to be issued by the browser will keep the original HTTP verb.
- The `File` and `Physical` file methods offer several ways to return file contents, either through a URL, a `Stream`, a byte array, or a physical file location. The `Physical` method allows you to directly send a file from a filesystem location, which may result in better performance. You also have the option to set an `ETag` or a `LastModified` date on the content you wish to transmit.
- `ViewResult` and `PartialViewResult` differ in that the latter only looks for partial views.
- Some methods may return different results, depending on the overload used (and its parameters, of course).

- `SignIn`, `SignOut`, and `Challenge` are related to authentication and are pointless if not configured. `SignIn` will redirect to the configured login URL and `SignOut` will clear the authentication cookie.

- Not all of these results return contents; some of them only return a status code and some headers (for example, `SignInResult`, `SignOutResult`, `StatusCodeResult`, `UnauthorizedResult`, `NoContentResult`, `NotFoundObjectResult`, `ChallengeResult`, `BadRequestResult`, `ForbidResult`, `OkResult`, `CreatedResult`, `CreatedAtActionResult`, `CreatedAtRouteResult`, and all the `Redirect*` results). On the other hand, `JsonResult`, `ContentResult`, `VirtualFileResult`, `FileStreamResult`, `FileContentResult`, and `ViewResult` all return contents.

All the action result classes that return views (`ViewResult`) or parts of views (`PartialViewResult`) take a `Model` property, which is prototyped as an `object`. You can use it to pass any arbitrary data to the view, but remember that the view must declare a model of a compatible type. Alas, you cannot pass anonymous types, as the view will have no way to locate its properties. In `Chapter 6`, *Using Forms and Models*, I will present a solution for this.

Returning an action result is probably the most typical use of a controller, but you can also certainly return any .NET object. To do this, you must declare your method to return whatever type you want:

```
public string SayHello()
{
    return "Hello, World!";
}
```

This is a perfectly valid action method; however, there are a few things you need to know:

- The returned object is wrapped in an `ObjectResult` before any filters are called (`IActionFilter`, `IResultFilter`, for example).

- The object is formatted (serialized) by one of the configured *output formatters*, the first that says it can handle it.

- If you want to change either the status code or the content type of the response, you will need to resort to the `HttpContext.Response` object.

Why return a POCO class or an `ObjectResult`? Well, `ObjectResult` gives you a couple of extra advantages:

- You can supply a collection of output formatters (`Formatters` collection).
- You can tell it to use a selection of content types (`ContentTypes`).
- You can specify the status code to return (`StatusCode`).

Let's look at output formatters in more detail with regard to API actions. For now, let's look at an example action result, one that returns contents as an XML:

```
public class XmlResult : ActionResult
{
    public XmlResult(object value)
    {
        this.Value = value;
    }

    public object Value { get; }

    public override Task ExecuteResultAsync(ActionContext context)
    {
        if (this.Value != null)
        {
            var serializer = new XmlSerializer(this.Value.GetType());
            using (var stream = new MemoryStream())
            {
                serializer.Serialize(stream, this.Value);
                var data = stream.ToArray();
                context.HttpContext.Response.ContentType =
                 "application/xml";
                context.HttpContext.Response.ContentLength =
data.Length;
                context.HttpContext.Response.Body.Write(data, 0,
                 data.Length);
            }
        }

        return base.ExecuteResultAsync(context);
    }
}
```

In this code, we instantiate an `XmlSerializer` instance bound to the type of the value that we want to return and use it to serialize this value into a string, which we then write to the response. You will need to add a reference to the `System.Xml.XmlSerializer` NuGet package for the `XmlSerializer` class. This further results in the redirecting and streaming of the actions. Let's see what these are.

Redirecting

A redirect occurs when the server instructs the client (the browser) to go to another location after receiving a request from it:

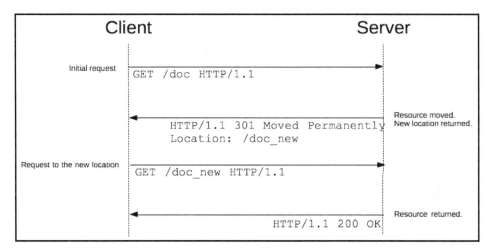

There are at least 10 methods for implementing redirects. What changes here is the HTTP status code that is returned to the client and how the redirection URL is generated. We have redirects for the following:

- **A specific URL, either full or local**: `Redirect`
- **A local URL**: `LocalRedirect`
- **A named route**: `RedirectToRoute`
- **A specific controller and action**: `RedirectToAction`
- **A Razor page (more on this in** Chapter 7, *Implementing Razor Pages***)**: `RedirectToPage`

All of these methods return HTTP status code 302 (see `https://developer.mozilla.org/en-US/docs/Web/HTTP/Status/302`), which is a temporary redirection. Then we have alternative versions that send HTTP 301 (`https://developer.mozilla.org/en-US/docs/Web/HTTP/Status/301`), a permanent redirect, which means that browsers are instructed to cache responses and learn that when asked to go to the original URL, they should instead access the new one. These methods are similar to the previous ones, but end in `Permanent`:

- **A specific URL**: `RedirectPermanent`
- **A local URL**: `LocalRedirectPermanent`

- **A named route**: RedirectToRoutePermanent
- **A specific controller and action**: RedirectToActionPermanent
- **A Razor page (more on this in** Chapter 7, *Implementing Razor Pages*): RedirectToPagePermanent

Then there's still another variation, one that keeps the original HTTP verb and is based on the HTTP 308 (https://developer.mozilla.org/en-US/docs/Web/HTTP/Status/308). For example, it may be the case that the browser was trying to access a resource using HTTP POST, the server returns an HTTP status 308, and redirects to another URL; the client must then request this URL again using POST instead of GET, which is what happens with the other codes. For this situation, we have other variations:

- **A specific URL**: RedirectPermanentPreserveMethod
- **A local URL**: LocalRedirectPreserveMethod
- **A named route**: RedirectToRoutePermanentPreserveMethod
- **A specific controller and action**: RedirectToActionPermanentPreserveMethod
- **A Razor page (more on this in** Chapter 7, *Implementing Razor pages*): RedirectToPagePermanentPreserveMethod

Streaming

If you ever need to stream content to the client, you should use the FileStreamResult class. In the following example code, we are streaming an MP4 file:

```
[HttpGet("[action]/{name}")]
public async Task<FileStreamResult> Stream(string name)
{
    var stream = await System.IO.File.OpenRead($"{name}.mp4");
    return new FileStreamResult(stream, "video/mp4");
}
```

Note that there is no method in the ControllerBase or Controller class for returning a FileStreamResult, so you need to build it yourself, passing it a stream and the desired content type. This will keep the client connected until the transmission ends or the browser navigates to another URL.

Now let's see what we can do to handle errors.

Error handling

In the previous chapter, we saw how to redirect to specific actions when an error occurs. Another option could be to leverage the `IExceptionFilter` and `IAsyncExceptionFilter` interfaces, one of the filter classes, to have the controller itself—or some other class—implement error handling directly.

In our controller, it's just a matter of implementing the `IExceptionFilter` class, which only has one method, `OnException`:

```
public void OnException(ExceptionContext context)
{
    var ex = context.Exception;

    //do something with the exception

    //mark it as handled, so that it does not propagate
    context.ExceptionHandled = true;
}
```

In the asynchronous version, `IAsyncExceptionFilter`, the `OnExceptionAsync` method takes the same parameter but must return a `Task`.

In `Chapter 10`, *Understanding Filters*, we will learn more about the concept of filters. For now, it is enough to say that should any exception be thrown from an action in a controller implementing `IExceptionFilter`, its `OnException` method will be called.

 Don't forget to set `ExceptionHandled` to `true` if you don't want the exception to propagate!

The next topic is related to performance: response caching.

Response caching

An action response of any type (HTML or JSON, for example) may be cached in the client in order to improve performance. Needless to say, this should only happen if the result that it is returning rarely changes. This is specified in **RFC 7234, HTTP/1.1 Caching** (`https://tools.ietf.org/html/rfc7234`).

Essentially, response caching is a mechanism by which the server notifies the client (the browser or a client API) to keep the response returned (including headers) for a URL for a certain amount of time and to use it, during that time, for all subsequent invocations of the URL. Only the GET HTTP verb can be cached, as it is designed to be idempotent: PUT, POST, PATCH, or DELETE cannot be cached.

We add support for resource caching in ConfigureServices as follows:

```
services.AddResponseCaching();
```

We use it in Configure, which basically adds the response caching middleware to the ASP.NET Core pipeline:

```
app.UseResponseCaching();
```

We can also set a couple of options in the call to AddResponseCaching, such as the following:

- MaximumBodySize (int): This is the maximum size of the response that can be stored in the client response cache; the default is 64 KB.
- UseCaseSensitivePaths (bool): This enables you to configure the request URL for the caching key as case-sensitive or not; the default is false.

These can be used using an overload of the AddResponseCaching method:

```
services.AddResponseCaching(options =>
{
    options.MaximumBodySize *= 2;
    options.UseCaseSensitivePaths = true;
});
```

We can also have an action result cached by applying the [ResponseCache] attribute to either the action or the whole controller class. Following this, we have a couple of options—we can either specify each of the cache parameters directly in the attribute or we can tell it to use a **cache profile**.

The options are as follows:

- Duration (int): The number of seconds to cache; the default is 0
- Location (ResponseCacheDuration): The location of the cache (Client, None, Any); the default is Any
- NoStore (bool): Whether to prevent the storing of the result; the default is false

- VaryByHeader (`string`): The comma-separated list of headers for which an instance of the result is cached; the default is `null`
- VaryByQueryKeys (`string []`): A list of query string parameters for which an instance of the result is cached; the default is `null`
- CacheProfileName (`string`): The cache profile name, which is incompatible with the other options; the default is null

As we have mentioned, you either specify all of the individual options (or at least those that you need) or you specify a cache profile name. Cache profiles are defined at `Startup` in the `ConfigureServices` method through the `AddMvc` extension method, as follows:

```
services.AddMvc(options =>
{
    options.CacheProfiles.Add("5minutes", new CacheProfile
    {
        Duration = 5 * 60,
        Location = ResponseCacheLocation.Any,
        VaryByHeader = "Accept-Language"
    });
});
```

This cache profile specifies that results are kept for five minutes, with different instances for different values of the `Accept-Language` header. After this, you only need to specify the name `5minutes`:

```
[ResponseCache(CacheProfileName = "5minutes")]
public IActionResult Cache() { ... }
```

The `VaryByHeader` and `VaryByQueryKeys` properties, if they have values, will keep different instances of the same cached response for each value of either the request header or the query string parameter (or both). For example, if your application supports multiple languages and you use the `Accept-Language` HTTP header to indicate which language should be served, the results are kept in cache for each of the requested languages—one for `pt-PT`, one for `en-GB`, and so on.

It's generally preferable to use cache profiles, rather than providing all parameters in the attribute.

Let's now see how we can maintain the state between subsequent requests.

Maintaining the state

What if you need to maintain a state, either from one component to the other in the same request, or across requests? Web applications have traditionally offered solutions for this. Let's explore the options we have.

Using the request

Any object that you store in the request (in memory) will be available throughout its duration. Items are a strongly typed dictionary in the `HttpContext` class:

```
this.HttpContext.Items["timestamp"] = DateTime.UtcNow;
```

You can check for the existence of the item before accessing it; it is worth noting that the following is case sensitive:

```
if (this.HttpContext.Items.ContainsKey("timestamp")) { ... }
```

Of course, you can also remove an item:

```
this.HttpContext.Items.Remove("timestamp");
```

Using form data

The `Form` collection keeps track of all values submitted by an HTML FORM, normally after a POST request. To access it, you use the `Form` property of the `Request` object of `HttpContext`:

```
var isChecked =
this.HttpContext.Request.Form["isChecked"].Equals("on");
```

You can program defensively by first checking for the existence of the value (case insensitive):

```
if (this.HttpContext.Request.Form.ContainsKey("isChecked")) { ... }
```

It is possible to obtain multiple values, and in this case, you can count them and get all their values:

```
var count = this.HttpContext.Request.Form["isChecked"].Count;
var values = this.HttpContext.Request.Form["isChecked"].ToArray();
```

Using the query string

Usually, you won't store data in the query string, but will instead get data from it—for example, `http://servername.com?isChecked=true`. The `Query` collection keeps track of all parameters that are sent in the URL as strings:

```
var isChecked =
this.HttpContext.Request.Query["isChecked"].Equals("true");
```

To check for the presence of a value, we use the following:

```
if (this.HttpContext.Request.Query.ContainsKey("isChecked")) { ... }
```

This also supports multiple values:

```
var count = this.HttpContext.Request.Query["isChecked"].Count;
var values = this.HttpContext.Request.Query["isChecked"].ToArray();
```

Using the route

As with the query string approach, you typically only get values from the route and do not write to them; however, you do have methods in the `IUrlHelper` interface—which is normally accessible through the `Url` property of the `ControllerBase` class—that generate action URLs, from which you can pack arbitrary values.

Route parameters look like `http://servername.com/admin/user/121`, and use a route template of `[controller]/[action]/{id}`.

To get a route parameter (a string), you do the following:

```
var id = this.RouteData.Values["id"];
```

To check that it's there, use the following:

```
if (this.RouteData.ContainsKey("id")) { ... }
```

Using cookies

Cookies have been around for a long time and are the basis of a lot of functionality on the web, such as authentication and sessions. They are specified in RFC 6265 (`https://tools.ietf.org/html/rfc6265`). Essentially, they are a way of storing small amounts of text in the client.

You can both read and write cookies. To read a cookie value, you only need to know its name; its value will come as a string:

```
var username = this.HttpContext.Request.Cookies["username"];
```

Of course, you can also check that the cookie exists with the following:

```
if (this.HttpContext.Request.Cookies.ContainsKey("username")) { ... }
```

To send a cookie to the client as part of the response, you need a bit more information, namely the following:

- `Name` (`string`): A name (what else?)
- `Value` (`string`): A string value
- `Expires` (`DateTime`): An optional expiration timestamp (the default is for the cookie to be session-based, meaning that it will vanish once the browser closes)
- `Path` (`string`): An optional path from which the cookie is to be made available (the default is `/`)
- `Domain` (`string`): An optional domain (the default is the current fully qualified hostname)
- `Secure` (`bool`): An optional secure flag that, if present, will cause the cookie to only be available if the request is being served using HTTPS (the default is `false`)
- `HttpOnly` (`bool`): Another optional flag that indicates whether the cookie will be readable by JavaScript on the client browser (the default is also `false`)

We add a cookie to the request object as follows:

```
this.HttpContext.Response.Cookies.Append("username", "rjperes", new
CookieOptions
    {
        Domain = "packtpub.com",
        Expires = DateTimeOffset.Now.AddDays(1),
        HttpOnly = true,
        Secure = true,
        Path = "/"
    });
```

The third parameter, of the `CookieOptions` type is optional, in which case the cookie assumes the default values.

The only way you can revoke a cookie is by adding one with the same name and an expiration date in the past.

 You mustn't forget that there is a limit to the number of cookies you can store per domain, as well as a limit to the actual size of an individual cookie value; these shouldn't be used for large amounts of data. For more information, please consult RFC 6265.

Using sessions

Sessions are a way to persist data per client. Typically, sessions rely on cookies, but it's possible (yet error prone) to use query string parameters, and ASP.NET Core does not support this out of the box. In ASP.NET Core, sessions are opt-in; in other words, they need to be explicitly added. We need to add the NuGet package `Microsoft.AspNetCore.Session` and explicitly add support in the `Configure` and `ConfigureServices` methods of the `Startup` class:

```
public void ConfigureServices(IServiceCollection services)
{
    services.AddSession();
    //rest goes here
}

public void Configure(IApplicationBuilder app, IWebHostEnvironment env)
{
    app.UseSession();
    //rest goes here
}
```

After that, the `Session` object is made available in the `HttpContext` instance:

```
var value = this.HttpContext.Session.Get("key");  //byte[]
```

A better approach is to use the `GetString` extension method and serialize/deserialize to JSON:

```
var json = this.HttpContext.Session.GetString("key");
var model = JsonSerializer.Deserialize<Model>(json);
```

Here, `Model` is just a POCO class and `JsonSerializer` is a class from `System.Text.Json` that has static methods for serializing and deserializing to and from JSON strings.

To store a value in the session, we use the `Set` or `SetString` methods:

```
this.HttpContext.Session.Set("key", value); //value is byte[]
```

The JSON approach is as follows:

```
var json = JsonSerializer.Serialize(model);
this.HttpContext.Session.SetString("key", json);
```

Removal is achieved by either setting the value to `null` or calling `Remove`. Similar to `GetString` and `SetString`, there are also the `GetInt32` and `SetInt32` extension methods. Use what best suits your needs, but never forget that the data is always stored as a byte array.

If you want to check for the existence of a value in the session, you should use the `TryGetValue` method:

```
byte[] data;
if (this.HttpContext.Session.TryGetValue("key", out data)) { ... }
```

That's pretty much it for using the session as a general-purpose dictionary. Now it's, configuration time! You can set some values, mostly around the cookie that is used to store the session, plus the idle interval, in a `SessionOptions` object:

```
services.AddSession(options =>
{
    options.CookieDomain = "packtpub.com";
    options.CookieHttpOnly = true;
    options.CookieName = ".SeSsIoN";
    options.CookiePath = "/";
    options.CookieSecure = true;
    options.IdleTimeout = TimeSpan.FromMinutes(30);
});
```

These can also be configured in the `UseSession` method in `Configure`:

```
app.UseSession(new SessionOptions { ... });
```

One final thing to note is that a session, by default, will use in-memory storage, which won't make it overly resilient or useful in real-life apps; however, if a distributed cache provider is registered before the call to `AddSession`, the session will use that instead! So, let's take a look at the next topic to see how we can configure it.

Before moving on, we need to keep in mind the following:

- There's a bit of a performance penalty in storing objects in the session.
- An object may be evicted from the session if the idle timeout is reached.
- Accessing an object in the session prolongs its lifetime—that is, its idle timeout is reset.

Using the cache

Unlike previous versions of ASP.NET, there is no longer built-in support for the cache; like most things in .NET Core, it is still available but as a pluggable service. There are essentially two kinds of cache in .NET Core:

- In-memory cache, which is represented by the `IMemoryCache` interface
- Distributed cache, which uses the `IDistributedCache` interface

ASP .NET Core includes a default implementation of `IMemoryCache` as well as one for `IDistributedCache`. The caveat for the distributed implementation is that it is also in-memory—it is only meant to be used in testing, but the good thing is that there are several implementations available, such as Redis (`https://redis.io/`) or SQL Server.

 In-memory and distributed caches can be used simultaneously, as they are unaware of each other.

Both the distributed and in-memory cache store instances as byte arrays (`byte[]`) but a good workaround is to first convert your objects to JSON and then use the method extensions that work with strings as follows:

```
var json = JsonSerializer.Serialize(model);
var model = JsonSerializer.Deserialize<Model>(json);
```

In-memory cache

In order to use the in-memory cache, you need to register its service in `ConfigureServices` using the following default options:

```
services.AddMemoryCache();
```

If you prefer, you can also fine-tune them by using the overloaded extension method that takes a `MemoryCacheOptions` instance:

```
services.AddMemoryCache(options =>
{
    options.Clock = new SystemClock();
    options.CompactOnMemoryPressure = true;
    options.ExpirationScanFrequency = TimeSpan.FromSeconds(5 * 60);
});
```

The purposes of these properties are as follows:

- `Clock` (`ISystemClock`): This is an implementation of `ISystemClock` that will be used for the expiration calculation. It is useful for unit testing and mocking; there is no default.
- `CompactOnMemoryPressure` (`bool`): This is used to remove the oldest objects from the cache when the available memory gets too low; the default is `true`.
- `ExpirationScanFrequency` (`TimeSpan`): This sets the interval that .NET Core uses to determine whether to remove objects from the cache; the default is one minute.

In order to use the in-memory cache, we need to retrieve an instance of `IMemoryCache` from the dependency injection:

```
public IActionResult StoreInCache(Model model, [FromServices]
IMemoryCache cache)
{
    cache.Set("model", model);
    return this.Ok();
}
```

We will look at `[FromServices]` in more detail in the *Dependency injection section*.

`IMemoryCache`supports all the operations that you might expect, plus a few others:

- `CreateEntry`: Creates an entry in the cache and gives you access to expiration
- `Get`/`GetAsync`: Retrieves an item from the cache, synchronously or asynchronously
- `GetOrCreate`/`GetOrCreateAsync`: Returns an item from the cache if it exists, or creates one, synchronously or asynchronously
- `Set`/`SetAsync`: Adds or modifies an item in the cache, synchronously or asynchronously

- `Remove`: Removes an item from the cache
- `TryGetValue`: Tentatively tries to get an item from the cache, synchronously

That's pretty much it! The memory cache will be available for all requests in the same application and will go away once the application is restarted or stopped.

Distributed cache

The default out-of-the-box implementation of the distributed cache is pretty much useless in real-life scenarios, but it might be a good starting point. Here's how to add support for it in `ConfigureServices`:

```
services.AddDistributedMemoryCache();
```

There are no other options—it's just that. In order to use it, ask the Dependency Injection container for an instance of `IDistributedCache`:

```
private readonly IDistributedCache _cache;

public CacheController(IDistributedCache cache)
{
    this._cache = cache;
}

public IActionResult Get(int id)
{
    return this.Content(this._cache.GetString(id.ToString()));
}
```

The included implementation will behave in exactly the same ways as the in-memory cache, but there are also some good alternatives for a more serious use case. The API it offers does the following:

- `Get`/`GetAsync`: Returns an item from the cache
- `Refresh`/`RefreshAsync`: Refreshes an item in the cache, prolonging its lifetime
- `Remove`/`RemoveAsync`: Removes an item from the cache
- `Set`/`SetAsync`: Adds an item to the cache or modifies its current value

Be warned that because the cache is now distributed and may take some time to synchronize, an item that you store in it may not be immediately available to all clients.

Redis

Redis is an open source distributed cache system. Its description is beyond the scope of this book, but it's sufficient to say that Microsoft has made a client implementation available for it in the form of the `Microsoft.Extensions.Caching.Redis` NuGet package. After you add this package, you get a couple of extension methods that you need to use to register a couple of services in `ConfigureServices`, which replaces the `Configuration` and `InstanceName` properties with the proper values:

```
services.AddDistributedRedisCache(options =>
{
    options.Configuration = "servername";
    options.InstanceName = "Shopping";
});
```

And that's it! Now, whenever you ask for an instance of `IDistributedCache`, you will get one that uses Redis underneath.

 There is a good introduction to Redis available at `https://redis.io/topics/quickstart`.

SQL Server

Another option is to use the SQL Server as a distributed cache. `Microsoft.Extensions.Caching.SqlServer` is the NuGet package that adds support for it. You can add support for it in `ConfigureServices` as follows:

```
services.AddDistributedSqlServerCache(options =>
{
    options.ConnectionString = @"Server=.; Database=DistCache;
     Integrated Security=SSPI;";
    options.SchemaName = "dbo";
    options.TableName = "Cache";
});
```

The rest is identical, so just get hold of `IDistributedCache` from the DI and off you go.

 ASP.NET Core no longer includes the `HttpApplication` and `HttpApplicationState` classes, which is where you could keep state applications. This mechanism had its problems, and it's better if you rely on either an in-memory or distributed cache instead.

Using temporary data

The `Controller` class offers a `TempData` property of the `ITempDataDictionary` type. Temporary data is a way of storing an item in a request so that it is still available in the next request. It's provider based, and there are currently two providers available:

- Cookie (`CookieTempDataProvider`)
- Session (`SessionStateTempDataProvider`)

For the latter, you need to enable session state support. To do this, you pick one of the providers and register it using the dependency injection framework, normally in the `ConfigureServices` method:

```
//only pick one of these
//for cookies
services.AddSingleton<ITempDataProvider, CookieTempDataProvider>();
//for session
services.AddSingleton<ITempDataProvider,
SessionStateTempDataProvider>();
```

Since ASP.NET Core 2, the `CookieTempDataProvider` is already registered. If you use `SessionStateTempDataProvider`, you also need to enable sessions.

After you have selected one of the providers, you can add data to the `TempData` collection:

```
this.TempData["key"] = "value";
```

Retrieving and checking the existence is trivial, as you can see in the following code:

```
if (this.TempData.ContainsKey("key"))
{
    var value = this.TempData["key"];
}
```

After you have enabled temporary data by registering one of the providers, you can use the `[SaveTempData]` attribute. When applied to a class that is returned by an action result, it will automatically be kept in temporary data.

The `[TempData]` attribute, if applied to a property in the `model` class, will automatically persist the value for that property in temporary data:

```
[TempData]
public OrderModel Order { get; set; }
```

Comparing state maintenance techniques

The following table provides a simple comparison of all the different techniques that can be used to maintain the state among requests:

Technique	Storable objects	Is secure	Is shared	In process	Expiration
Request	`object`	Yes	No	Yes	No
Form	`string`	Yes (if using HTTPS)	No	Yes	No
Query string	`string`	No	Yes	Yes	No
Route	`string`	No	Yes	Yes	No
Cookies	`string`	Yes (if set to HTTPS only)	No	No	Yes
Session	`byte[]`	Yes	No	Maybe	Yes
Cache	`object`	Yes	Yes	Maybe	Yes
Temporary data	`string`	Yes	No	No	Yes

Needless to say, not all of these techniques serve the same purpose; instead, they are used in different scenarios.

In the next section, we will learn how to use dependency injection inside controllers.

Dependency injection

ASP.NET Core instantiates the controllers through its built-in **DI** framework. Since it fully supports constructor injection, you can have any registered services injected as parameters to your constructor:

```
//ConfigureServices
services.AddSingleton<IHttpContextAccessor, HttpContextAccessor>();

//HomeController
public HomeController(IHttpContextAccessor accessor) { ... }
```

However, you can also request a service from the DI in a service locator way by leveraging the `HttpContext.RequestServices` property as follows:

```
var accessor =
this.HttpContext.RequestServices.GetService<IHttpContextAccessor>();
```

For the strongly typed `GetService<T>` extension method, you need to add a reference to the `Microsoft.Extensions.DependencyInjection` namespace.

In action methods, you can also inject a service by decorating its typed parameter with the `[FromServices]` attribute, as follows:

```
public IActionResult Index([FromServices] IHttpContextAccessor
accessor) { ... }
```

The next topic covers a very important topic, especially for those that wish to implement multilingual sites.

Globalization and localization

If you need to build an application that will be used by people in different countries, you may want to have all of it, or at least parts of it, translated. It's not just that, though: you may also want to have decimal numbers and currency symbols presented in a way that users would expect. The process by which an application is made to support different cultures is called **globalization**, and **localization** is the process of adapting it to a specific culture—for example, by presenting it with text in a specific language.

ASP.NET Core, like previous versions, fully supports these two entwined concepts by applying a specific culture to a request and letting it flow, and by having the ability to serve string resources according to the language of the requester.

We first need to add support for globalization and localization, and we do this by adding the `Microsoft.AspNetCore.Localization.Routing` package to the project. As far as this chapter is concerned, we want to be able to do the following:

- Set the culture for the current request
- Hand resource strings that match the current culture

Let's configure localization in the `ConfigureServices` method with a call to `AddLocalization`. We'll pick the `Resources` folder as the source for resource files, as we'll see in a minute:

```
services.AddLocalization(options =>
{
    options.ResourcesPath = "Resources";
});
```

We create this `Resources` folder and inside it, we create a `Controllers` folder. Using Visual Studio, let's also create two resource files, one called `HomeController.en.resx` and the other called `HomeController.pt.resx`. The `resx` extension is a standard extension for resource files that are basically XML files containing key–value pairs. On each of these files, add an entry with the key `Hello` and the following value:

Portuguese	English
Olá!	Hello!

It should look like the following screenshot. Note that each file has the name of the controller class plus a two-letter culture identifier:

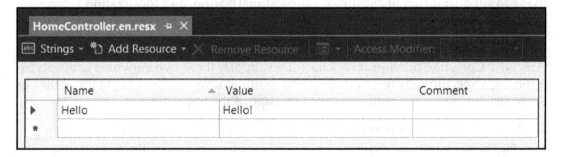

Now, let's define a range of cultures and languages to support. To make it simple, let's say that we will support **Portuguese (pt)** and **English (en)**:

```
var supportedCultures = new List<CultureInfo>
{
    new CultureInfo("pt"),
    new CultureInfo("en")
};
```

We are using `pt` and `en`, generic culture descriptors, but we could have also used `pt-pt` and `en-gb` for specific cultures. Feel free to add these if you want.

We then configure `RequestLocalizationOptions` in order to have a default language:

```
services.Configure<RequestLocalizationOptions>(options =>
{
    options.DefaultRequestCulture =
        new RequestCulture(supportedCultures.First().Name,
        supportedCultures.First().Name);
    options.SupportedCultures = supportedCultures;
    options.SupportedUICultures = supportedCultures;
    options.RequestCultureProviders = new[] {
        new AcceptLanguageHeaderRequestCultureProvider { Options =
        options } };
});
```

The process by which a culture is obtained from the browser is based upon a provider model. The following providers are available:

- `AcceptLanguageHeaderRequestCultureProvider` gets the culture from the `Accept-Language` header.
- `CookieRequestCultureProvider` gets the culture from a cookie.
- `QueryStringRequestCultureProvider` gets the culture from a query string parameter.
- `RouteDataRequestCultureProvider` gets the culture from a route parameter.

Just replace the `RequestCultureProviders` assignments in the previous code with the ones you want. As you can see, there are many options available, each featuring the different features that you need to set, such as the cookie name, the query string parameter, the route parameter name, and so on:

```
new CookieRequestCultureProvider { CookieName = "culture" }
new QueryStringRequestCultureProvider { QueryStringKey = "culture" }
new RouteDataRequestCultureProvider { RouteDataStringKey = "culture" }
```

In the second chapter, we looked at route constraints, so here we will introduce the culture route constraint:

```
public sealed class CultureRouteConstraint : IRouteConstraint
{
```

```csharp
public const string CultureKey = "culture";

public bool Match(
    HttpContext httpContext,
    IRouter route,
    string routeKey,
    RouteValueDictionary values,
    RouteDirection routeDirection)
{
    if ((!values.ContainsKey(CultureKey)) || (values
    [CultureKey] == null))
    {
        return false;
    }

    var lang = values[CultureKey].ToString();

    var requestLocalizationOptions = httpContext
        .RequestServices
        .GetRequiredService<IOptions<RequestLocalization
        Options>>();

    if ((requestLocalizationOptions.Value.SupportedCultures
     == null)
        || (requestLocalizationOptions.Value.SupportedCultures.
          Count == 0))
    {
        try
        {
            new System.Globalization.CultureInfo(lang);
          //if invalid, throws an exception
            return true;
        }
        catch
        {
            //an invalid culture was supplied
            return false;
        }
    }

    //checks if any of the configured supported cultures matches
the
    //one requested
    return requestLocalizationOptions.Value.SupportedCultures
        .Any(culture => culture.Name.Equals(lang, StringComparison
        .CurrentCultureIgnoreCase));
    }
}
```

The `Match` method only operates if there is a value specified for the culture key; if so, it extracts its value and checks the `RequestLocalizationOptions` to see if it is a supported culture or if it is a valid one. Essentially, what this does is allow the verification of route values, such as `{language:culture}`, and if the value is not a valid culture, you will get an exception. This route constraint needs to be registered before it can be used, as follows:

```
services.Configure<RouteOptions>(options =>
{
    options.ConstraintMap.Add(CultureRouteConstraint.CultureKey,
typeof
    (CultureRouteConstraint));
});
```

Now, we want our controller to respond to the browser's language settings. For example, in Chrome, we will configure this in **Settings** | **Languages** | **Language and input settings**:

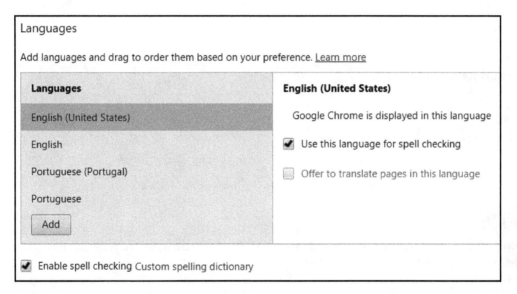

What this setting does is configure the `Accept-Language` HTTP header that the browser will send upon each request. We are going to take advantage of this to decide what language we will present.

Each controller that we wish to make localization-aware needs to be changed as follows:

- Add a middleware filter attribute in order to inject a middleware component.
- Inject a string localizer that we can use to fetch appropriately translated resources.

Here is what that should look like:

```
[MiddlewareFilter(typeof(LocalizationPipeline))]
public class HomeController
{
    private readonly IStringLocalizer<HomeController> _localizer;

    public HomeController(IStringLocalizer<HomeController> localizer)
    {
        this._localizer = localizer;
    }
}
```

The `LocalizationPipeline` is actually an OWIN middleware component, and should look as follows:

```
public class LocalizationPipeline
{
    public static void Configure(
        IApplicationBuilder app,
        IOptions<RequestLocalizationOptions> options)
    {
        app.UseRequestLocalization(options.Value);
    }
}
```

Now, if we want to access a specific resource in a culture-specific way, all we need to do is the following:

```
var hello = this._localizer["Hello"];
```

The returned string will come from the right resource file, based on the current culture, as originated from the browser. You can check this by looking at the `CultureInfo.CurrentCulture` and `CultureInfo.CurrentUICulture` properties.

There are a couple of final things to note:

- You can have several resource files per language, or more accurately, per specific (for example, en, pt) and generic language (for example, en-gb, en-us); if the browser requests a specific language (for example, en-gb, en-us), then the localizer will try to find a resource file with that as a suffix, and if it cannot find one, it will try the generic language (for example, en). If this also fails, it will return the resource key provided (for example, Hello)

- The localizer never returns an error or a null value, but you can check whether the value exists for the current language with the following:

```
var exists = this._localizer["Hello"].ResourceNotFound;
```

The topics discussed here are very important if you are going to implement sites that need to support multiple cultures or languages, but you should also consider using it if you would like to have the text in your site in files, such as resources, so that they can be easily edited and replaced.

Summary

In this chapter, we saw that using POCO controllers is not really needed, and it requires more work than whatever benefit we can take out of it, so we should have our controllers inherit from `Controller`.

Then we saw that using asynchronous actions is good for improved scalability as it won't affect performance much, but your app will be more responsive.

You can forget about XML formatting, as JSON works perfectly, and is the standard way to send and process data on the web.

We learned that we should use POCO classes as the model for our actions. The built-in model binders work well, as we'll see in upcoming chapters, but you can add the cookie value provider as it may come in handy.

As far as model validation is concerned, we saw that it is better to stick to the good old data annotations API. If necessary, you should implement `IValidatableObject` in your model.

The Redis distributed cache system is very popular and is supported by both Azure and AWS. Redis should be your choice for a distributed cache to keep reference data; in other words, stuff that isn't changed often.

Performance-wise, response caching is also useful. The products page shouldn't change that much, so at least we can keep it in the cache for a few hours.

This was a long chapter where we covered controllers and actions, arguably the most important aspects of ASP.NET Core. We also covered parts of the model concept, such as binding, injection, and validation. We saw how we can maintain the state and the possible values that we can return from an action. We also learned how to use resources for translation purposes. Some of these concepts will be revisited in future chapters; in the next one, we will be talking about views.

Questions

You should now be able to answer the following questions:

1. What is the default validation provider for the model state?
2. What is an action?
3. What is globalization and how does it differ from localization?
4. What is temporary data used for?
5. What is a cache good for?
6. What is a session?
7. What are the benefits of a controller inheriting from the `Controller` base class?

5
Views

After we've talked about how the application works from the server side, it's time to look at the client side. In this chapter, we will cover the visual side of a **Model-View-Controller** (**MVC**) app: the views.

A view in this context is a combination of **HyperText Markup Language** (**HTML**) and code that executes on the server side and whose output is combined and sent to the client at the end of the request.

To help achieve consistency and reusability, ASP.NET Core offers a couple of mechanisms, page layouts, and partial views that can be very handy. Also, because we may want to support different languages and cultures, we have built-in localization support, which helps provide a better user experience.

In this chapter, we will learn the following:

- What are Razor views
- What are partial views
- What are view layouts
- What are the base Razor view classes
- How Razor finds view files
- How to inject services into a view
- What is a location expander
- How to perform view localization
- How to mix code and markup on a view
- How to enable view compilation upon publishing

Technical requirements

In order to implement the examples introduced in this chapter, you will need the .NET Core 3 **software development kit** (**SDK**) and some form of text editor. Of course, Visual Studio 2019 (any edition) meets all the requirements, but you can also use Visual Studio Code, for example, or Visual Studio for Mac.

The source code can be retrieved from GitHub at `https://github.com/ PacktPublishing/Modern-Web-Development-with-ASP.NET-Core-3-Second-Edition`.

Getting started

Views are the **V** in **MVC**. They are the visual part of the application. Typically, a web app renders HTML pages, meaning HTML views. A view is a template that consists of a mix of HTML and possibly some server-side content.

ASP.NET Core uses view engines to actually render the views, an extensible mechanism. Before the time of Core, there were several view engines available; although their purpose was always to generate HTML, they offered subtle differences in terms of syntax and the features they supported. Currently, ASP.NET Core only includes one view engine, called **Razor**, as the other one that used to be available, Web Forms, was dropped. Razor has been around for quite some time and has been improved in the process of adding it to ASP.NET Core.

Razor files have the `cshtml` extension (for C# HTML) and, by convention, are kept in a folder called `Views` underneath the application, and under a folder with the name of the controller to which they apply, such as `Home`. There may be global and local views, and we will learn the distinction in a moment.

The typical way to have a controller action returning a view is by returning the result of executing the `View` method of the `Controller` class. This creates `ViewResult`, and it can take a number of options, as follows:

- `ContentType` (`string`): An optional content type to return to the client; `text/html` is the default
- `Model` (`object`): Just any object that we want to make available to the view
- `StatusCode` (`int`): An optional status code to return; if none is provided, it will be `200`
- `TempData` (`ITempDataDictionary`): Strongly typed temporary data to make available until the next request

- ViewData (ViewDataDictionary): A key-value collection of arbitrary data to pass to the view
- ViewName (string): The name of the view to render

The only required parameter is ViewName, and, if it's not supplied, the current action name will be used; that is to say, if we are executing in an action method named Index, and we want to return a view but don't supply its name, Index will be used, as illustrated in the following code snippet:

```
public IActionResult Index()
{
    return this.View();   //ViewName = Index
}
```

There are some overloads to the View method that basically take either the viewName, the model, or both, as illustrated in the following code snippet:

```
return this.View(
    viewName: "SomeView",
    model: new Model()
);
```

> Beware—if your model is of the string type, .NET may mistakenly choose the View overload that takes a view name!

Now, imagine you want to return a view with a specific content type or status code. You can get the ViewResult object from the View method call and then change it, like this:

```
var view = this.View(new Model());
view.ContentType = "text/plain";
view.StatusCode = StatusCodes.Status201Created;
return view;
```

Or, if we want to set some view data, we can run the following code:

```
view.ViewData["result"] = "success";
```

One thing that you must not forget upfront is, if you have not registered your MVC services with AddMvc, you will need to do so with AddControllersWithViews, like this:

```
services.AddControllersWithViews();
```

This will result in slightly less memory pressure than `AddMvc` because it will not, for example, register the services that are needed for Razor pages (do not confuse them with Razor views, the scope of this chapter!).

 Razor Pages and Razor views are not the same thing: Razor Pages are callable on their own, whereas Razor views are returned by controller action methods. Razor Pages will be discussed in their own chapter.

Let's carry on by exploring the view class.

Understanding views

A Razor view is actually a template that is transformed into a class that inherits from `RazorPage<T>`. The generic parameter is actually the type of model, as we will see in a moment. This class inherits from `RazorPage`, which exposes a few useful properties, as follows:

- `IsLayoutBeingRendered` (`bool`): Whether a layout page is currently being rendered or not
- `BodyContent` (`IHtmlContent`): The resulting page's body contents; will only be available at a later time
- `TempData` (`ITempDataDictionary`): The temporary data dictionary
- `ViewBag` (`dynamic`): Access to the view bag, which holds arbitrary data prototyped as `dynamic`
- `User` (`ClaimsPrincipal`): The current user, as in `HttpContext.User`
- `Output` (`TextWriter`): The output writer, to which the HTML results are sent once the page is processed
- `DiagnosticSource` (`DiagnosticSource`): Allows the logging of diagnostic messages, covered here
- `HtmlEncoder` (`HtmlEncoder`): The HTML encoder used for encoding the results as they are sent in the response
- `Layout` (`string`): The current layout file
- `ViewContext` (`ViewContext`): The view context
- `Path` (`string`): The current view file path
- `Context` (`HttpContext`): The HTTP context

All of these properties can be used in a view.

We can, of course, define our own class that derives from `RazorPage<T>` and have our view use it, by using `@inherits`, like this:

```
public class MyPage : RazorPage<dynamic>
{
    public override Task ExecuteAsync()
    {
        return Task.CompletedTask;
    }
}
```

The only required method is `ExecuteAsync`, but you don't need to worry about that. If we now inherit from this class, we will see the following:

```
@inherits MyPage
```

Or, if we want the generated class to implement some interface, we can use the `@implements` keyword instead—like, for example, for `IDisposable`, as illustrated in the following code snippet:

```
@implements IDisposable

@public void Dispose()
{
    //do something
}
```

In this case, we must, of course, implement all interface members ourselves.

Understanding the view life cycle

When an action signals that a view should be rendered, the following occurs (in a simplified way):

- The action returns a `ViewResult` object because `ViewResult` implements `IActionResult`, and its `ExecuteResultAsync` method is called asynchronously.
- The default implementation attempts to find `ViewResultExecutor` from the **dependency injection** (**DI**) framework.
- The `FindView` method is called on `ViewResultExecutor`, which uses an injected `ICompositeViewEngine`, also obtained from the DI framework, to obtain `IView` from the list of registered view engines.

- The view engine chosen will be an implementation of `IRazorViewEngine` (which, in turn, extends `IViewEngine`).
- The `IView` implementation uses the registered `IFileProviders` to load the view file.
- `ViewResultExecutor` is then asked to invoke the view, through its `ExecuteAsync` method, which ends up invoking the `ExecuteAsync` methods of the base `ViewExecutor`.
- `ViewExecutor` builds and initializes some infrastructure objects such as `ViewContext` and ends up invoking `IView` `RenderAsync` method.
- Another service (`ICompilationService`) is used to compile the C# code.
- The registered `IRazorPageFactoryProvider` creates a factory method for creating a .NET class that inherits from `IRazorPage`.
- `IRazorPageActivator` is passed an instance of the new `IRazorPage`.
- The `ExecuteAsync` method of `IRazorPage` is called.

Here, I didn't mention the filters, but they are here as well, except action filters, as I said.

Why is this important? Well, you may need to implement your own version of—say—`IRazorPageActivator` so that you can perform some custom initialization or DI in the Razor view, as illustrated in the following code block:

```
public class CustomRazorPageActivator : IRazorPageActivator
{
    private readonly IRazorPageActivator _activator;

    public CustomRazorPageActivator(
        IModelMetadataProvider metadataProvider,
        IUrlHelperFactory urlHelperFactory,
        IJsonHelper jsonHelper,
        DiagnosticSource diagnosticSource,
        HtmlEncoder htmlEncoder,
        IModelExpressionProvider modelExpressionProvider)
    {
        this._activator = new RazorPageActivator(
            metadataProvider,
            urlHelperFactory,
            jsonHelper,
            diagnosticSource, htmlEncoder,
            modelExpressionProvider);
    }

    public void Activate(IRazorPage page, ViewContext context)
```

```
        {
            if (page is ICustomInitializable)
            {
                (page as ICustomInitializable).Init(context);
            }

            this._activator.Activate(page, context);
        }
    }
```

All you need to do is register this implementation in `ConfigureServices`, for the `IRazorPageActivator` service, like this:

```
services.AddSingleton<IRazorPageActivator,
CustomRazorPageActivator>();
```

Now, how are views located?

Locating views

When asked to return a view (`ViewResult`), the framework needs first to locate the view file (`.cshtml`).

The built-in conventions around locating view files are as follows:

- View files end with the `cshtml` extension.
- View filenames should be identical to the view names, minus the extension (for example, a view of `Index` will be stored in a file named `Index.cshtml`).
- View files are stored in a `Views` folder and inside a folder named after the controller they are returned from—for example, `Views\Home`.
- Global or shared views are stored in either the `Views` folder directly or inside a `Shared` folder inside of it—for example, `Views\Shared`.

Actually, this is controlled by the `ViewLocationFormats` collection of the `RazorViewEngineOptions` class (Razor is the only included view engine). This has the following entries, by default:

- `/Views/{1}/{0}.cshtml`
- `/Views/Shared/{0}.cshtml`

The {1} token is replaced by the current controller name and {0} is replaced by the view name. The / location is relative to the ASP.NET Core application folder, not `wwwroot`.

If you want the Razor engine to look in different locations, all you need to do is tell it; so, through the `AddRazorOptions` method, that is usually called in sequence to `AddMvc`, in the `ConfigureServices` method, like this:

```
services
    .AddMvc()
    .AddRazorOptions(options =>
    {
options.ViewLocationFormats.Add("/AdditionalViews/{0}.cshtml");
    });
```

The view locations are searched sequentially in the `ViewLocationFormats` collection until one file is found.

The actual view file contents are loaded through `IFileProviders`. By default, only one file provider is registered (`PhysicalFileProvider`), but more can be added through the configuration. The code can be seen in the following snippet:

```
services
    .AddMvc()
    .AddRazorOptions(options =>
    {
        options.FileProviders.Add(new CustomFileProvider());
    });
```

Adding custom file providers may prove useful—for example, if you want to load contents from non-orthodox locations, such as databases, ZIP files, assembly resources, and so on. There are multiple ways to do this. Let's try them in the following subsections.

Using view location expanders

There is an advanced feature by which we can control, per request, the locations to search the view files: it's called **view location expanders**. View location expanders are a Razor thing, and thus are also configured through `AddRazorOptions`, as illustrated in the following code snippet:

```
services
    .AddMvc()
```

```
      .AddRazorOptions(options =>
  {
    options.ViewLocationExpanders.Add(new ThemesViewLocationExpander
    ("Mastering"));
  });
```

A view location expander is just some class that implements the `IViewExpander` contract. For example, imagine you want to have a theme framework that would add a couple of folders to the `views` search path. You could write it like this:

```
public class ThemesViewLocationExpander : IViewLocationExpander
{
    public ThemesViewLocationExpander(string theme)
    {
        this.Theme = theme;
    }

    public string Theme { get; }

    public IEnumerable<string> ExpandViewLocations(
        ViewLocationExpanderContext context,
        IEnumerable<string> viewLocations)
    {
        var theme = context.Values["theme"];

        return viewLocations
            .Select(x => x.Replace("/Views/", "/Views/" + theme +
"/"))
            .Concat(viewLocations);
    }

    public void PopulateValues(ViewLocationExpanderContext context)
    {
        context.Values["theme"] = this.Theme;
    }
}
```

The default search locations, as we've seen, are the following:

- `/Views/{1}/{0}.cshtml`
- `/Views/Shared/{0}.cshtml`

By adding this view location expander, for a theme called `Mastering`, these will become the following:

- `/Views/{1}/{0}.cshtml`
- `/Views/Mastering/{1}/{0}.cshtml`
- `/Views/Shared/Mastering/{0}.cshtml`
- `/Views/Shared/{0}.cshtml`

The `IViewLocationExpander` interface defines only two methods, as follows:

- `PopulateValues`: Used to initialize the view location expander; in this example, I used it to pass some value in the context.
- `ExpandViewLocations`: This will be called to retrieve the desired view locations.

View location expanders are queued, so they will be called in sequence, from the registration order; each `ExpandViewLocations` method will be called with all the locations returned from the previous one.

Both methods, through the `context` parameter, have access to all the request parameters (`HttpContext`, `RouteData`, and so on), so you can be as creative as you like, and define the search locations for the views according to whatever rationale you can think of.

Using view engines

It was mentioned at the start of the chapter that ASP.NET Core only includes one view engine, Razor, but nothing prevents us from adding more. This can be achieved through the `ViewEngines` collection of `MvcViewOptions`, as illustrated in the following code snippet:

```
services
    .AddMvc()
    .AddViewOptions(options =>
    {
        options.ViewEngines.Add(new CustomViewEngine());
    });
```

A view engine is an implementation of `IViewEngine`, and the only included implementation is `RazorViewEngine`.

Again, view engines are searched sequentially when ASP.NET Core is asked to render a view and the first one that returns one is the one that is used. The only two methods defined by `IViewEngine` are as follows:

- `FindView` (`ViewEngineResult`): Tries to find a view from `ActionContext`
- `GetView` (`ViewEngineResult`): Tries to find a view from a path

Both methods return `null` if no view is found.

A view is an implementation of `IView`, and the ones returned by `RazorViewEngine` are all `RazorView`. The only notable method in the `IView` contract is `RenderAsync`, which is the one responsible for actually rendering a view from `ViewContext`.

 A view engine is not an easy task. You can find a sample implementation written by Dave Paquette in a blog post at: `http://www.davepaquette.com/archive/2016/11/22/creating-a-new-view-engine-in-asp-net-core.aspx`.

A Razor view is a template composed essentially of HTML, but it also accepts fragments—which can be quite large, actually—of server-side C# code. Consider the requirements for it, as follows:

- First, you may need to define the type of model that your view receives from the controller. By default, it is dynamic, but you can change it with a `@model` directive, like this:

```
@model MyNamespace.MyCustomModel
```

- Doing this is exactly the same as specifying the base class of your view. This is accomplished by using `@inherits`, like this:

```
@inherits RazorPage<MyNamespace.MyCustomModel>
```

 Remember: the default is `RazorPage<dynamic>`. Don't forget: you cannot have `@inherits` and `@model` at the same time with different types!

- If you don't want to write the full type name, you can add as many `@using` declarations as you want, as illustrated in the following code snippet:

```
@using My.Namespace
@using My.Other.Namespace
```

- You can intermix HTML with Razor expressions, which are processed on the server side. Razor expressions always start with the @ character. For example, if you want to output the currently logged-in user, you could write this:

```
User: @User.Identity.Name
```

- You can output any method that returns either a `string` or an `IHtmlContent` directly, like this:

```
@Html.Raw(ViewBag.Message)
```

- If you need to evaluate some simple code, you will need to include it inside parentheses, like this:

```
Last week: @(DateTime.Today - TimeSpan.FromDays(7))
```

Remember—if your expression has a space, you need to include it inside parentheses, the only exception being the `await` keyword, as illustrated in the following code snippet:

```
@await Component.InvokeAsync("Process");
```

- You can encode HTML (implicitly using the `HtmlEncoder` instance supplied in the `HtmlEncoder` property), like this:

```
@("<span>Hello, World</span>")
```

This will output an HTML-encoded string, as illustrated in the following code snippet:

```
&lt;span&gt;Hello, World&lt;/span&gt;
```

More complex expressions, such as the definition of variables, setting values to properties, or calling of methods that do not return a **stringy** result (`string`, `IHtmlContent`) need to go in a special block, in which you can put pretty much anything you would like in a .NET method, as illustrated in the following code snippet:

```
@{
    var user = @User.Identity.Name;
    OutputUser(user);
    Layout = "Master";
}
```

Sentences inside @{} blocks need to be separated by semicolons.

A variable defined in this way can be used in any other place in the view—after the declaration, of course.

Let's look at conditionals (`if`, `else if`, `else` and `switch`) now, which are nothing special. Have a look at the following code snippet:

```
//check if the user issuing the current request is authenticated
somehow
@if (this.User.Identity.IsAuthenticated)
{
    <p>Logged in</p>
}
else
{
    <p>Not logged in</p>
}

//check the authentication type for the current user
@switch (this.User.Identity.AuthenticationType)
{
    case "Claims":
        <p>Logged in</p>
        break;

    case null:
        <p>Not logged in</p>
        break;
}
```

The first condition checks whether the current user is authenticated, and displays an HTML block accordingly. On the second, we have a `switch` instruction, on which we can specify multiple possible values; in this case, we are only looking at two, `"Claims"` and `null`, which essentially yields the same result as the first condition.

Loops use a special syntax, where you can mix together HTML (any valid **Extensible Markup Language** (**XML**) element) and code, as illustrated in the following code snippet:

```
@for (var i = 0; i < 10; i++)
{
```

```
    <p>Number: @i</p>
}
```

Note that this will not work because `Number` is not included inside an XML element, as illustrated in the following code snippet:

```
@for (var i = 0; i < 10; i++)
{
    Number: @i
}
```

But the following syntax (`@:`) would work:

```
@:Number: @i
```

This makes the rest of the line be treated as an HTML chunk.

The same syntax can be used in `foreach` and `while`.

Now, let's have a look at `try/catch` blocks, shown in the following code snippet:

```
@try
{
    SomeMethodCall();
}
catch (Exception ex)
{
    <p class="error">An error occurred: @ex.Message</p>
    Log(ex);
}
```

Consider the `@using` and `@lock` blocks shown in the following code snippet:

```
@using (Html.BeginForm())
{
    //the result is disposed at the end of the block
}

@lock (SyncRoot)
{
    //synchronized block
}
```

Now, what if you want to output the @ character? You need to escape it with another @, like this:

```
<p>Please enter your username @@domain.com</p>
```

But Razor views recognize emails and do not force them to be encoded, as illustrated in the following code snippet:

```
<input type="email" name="email" value="nobody@domain.com"/>
```

Finally, comments—single or multiline—are also supported, as illustrated in the following code snippet:

```
@*this is a single-line Razor comment*@
@*
  this
  is a multi-line
  Razor comment
*@
```

Inside a @{ } block, you can add C# comments too, as illustrated in the following code snippet:

```
@{
    //this is a single-line C# comment
    /*
    this
    is a multi-line
    C# comment
    */
}
```

Of course, because a view is essentially HTML, you can also use HTML comments, as illustrated in the following code snippet:

```
<!-- this is an HTML comment -->
```

The difference between C#, Razor, and HTML comments is that only HTML comments are left by the Razor compilation process; the others are discarded.

We can add functions (which are actually, in object-oriented terminology, methods) to our Razor views; these are just .NET methods that are only visible in the scope of a view. To create them, we need to group them inside a @functions directive, like this:

```
@functions
{
    int Count(int a, int b) { return a + b; }

    public T GetValueOrDefault<T>(T item) where T : class, new()
    {
```

```
                    return item ?? new T();
        }
    }
```

It is possible to specify visibility. By default, this happens inside a class, which is called a private class. It is probably pointless to specify visibility since the generated class is only known at runtime, and there is no easy way to access it.

The @functions name is actually slightly misleading, as you can declare fields and properties inside of it, as can be seen in the following code block:

```
@functions
{
    int? _state;
    int State
    {
        get
        {
            if (_state == null)
            {
                _state = 10;
            }
            return _state;
        }
    }
}
```

This example shows a simple private field that is encapsulated behind a property that has some logic behind it: the first time it is accessed, it sets the field to a default value; otherwise, it just returns what the current value is.

Logging and diagnostics

As usual, you can obtain a reference to ILogger<T> from the DI framework and use it in your views, like this:

```
@inject ILogger<MyView> Logger
```

But there is also another built-in mechanism, the `DiagnosticSource` class, and property, which is declared in the `RazorPage` base class. By calling its `Write` method, you can write custom messages to a diagnostics framework. These messages can be any .NET object, even an anonymous one, and there is no need to worry about its serialization. Have a look at the following code snippet:

```
@{
    DiagnosticSource.Write("MyDiagnostic", new { data = "A diagnostic"
});
}
```

What happens with this diagnostic message is actually somewhat configurable. First, let's add the `Microsoft.Extensions.DiagnosticAdapter` NuGet package, and then create a custom listener for the events generated for this diagnostic source, like this:

```
public class DiagnosticListener
{
    [DiagnosticName("MyDiagnostic")]
    public virtual void OnDiagnostic(string data)
    {
        //do something with data
    }
}
```

We can add as many listeners as we want, targeting different event names. The actual method name does not matter, as long as it has a `[DiagnosticName]` attribute applied to it that matches an event name. We need to register and hook it to the .NET Core framework, in the `Configure` method, by adding a reference to the `DiagnosticListener` service so that we can interact with it, like this:

```
public void Configure(IApplicationBuilder app, DiagnosticListener
diagnosticListener)
{
    var listener = new DiagnosticListener();
    diagnosticListener.SubscribeWithAdapter(listener);

    //rest goes here
}
```

Notice that the name in the [DiagnosticName] attribute and
DiagnosticSource.Write call match, and also, the name, data, of the anonymous
type in the Write call matches the parameter name (and type) of the OnDiagnostic
method.

Built-in .NET Core classes produce diagnostics for the following:

- Microsoft.AspNetCore.Diagnostics.HandledException
- Microsoft.AspNetCore.Diagnostics.UnhandledException
- Microsoft.AspNetCore.Hosting.BeginRequest
- Microsoft.AspNetCore.Hosting.EndRequest
- Microsoft.AspNetCore.Hosting.UnhandledException
- Microsoft.AspNetCore.Mvc.AfterAction
- Microsoft.AspNetCore.Mvc.AfterActionMethod
- Microsoft.AspNetCore.Mvc.AfterActionResult
- Microsoft.AspNetCore.Mvc.AfterView
- Microsoft.AspNetCore.Mvc.AfterViewComponent
- Microsoft.AspNetCore.Mvc.BeforeAction
- Microsoft.AspNetCore.Mvc.BeforeActionMethod
- Microsoft.AspNetCore.Mvc.BeforeActionResult
- Microsoft.AspNetCore.Mvc.BeforeView
- Microsoft.AspNetCore.Mvc.BeforeViewComponent
- Microsoft.AspNetCore.Mvc.Razor.AfterViewPage
- Microsoft.AspNetCore.Mvc.Razor.BeforeViewPage
- Microsoft.AspNetCore.Mvc.Razor.BeginInstrumentationContext
- Microsoft.AspNetCore.Mvc.Razor.EndInstrumentationContext
- Microsoft.AspNetCore.Mvc.ViewComponentAfterViewExecute
- Microsoft.AspNetCore.Mvc.ViewComponentBeforeViewExecute
- Microsoft.AspNetCore.Mvc.ViewFound
- Microsoft.AspNetCore.Mvc.ViewNotFound

Hopefully, the names should be self-explanatory. Why would you use this mechanism over the `ILogger`-based one? This one makes it very easy to add listeners to a diagnostic source, with strongly typed methods. I will talk more about the differences between the two in `Chapter 12`, *Logging, Tracing, and Diagnostics*.

View compilation

Normally, a view is only compiled when it is first used—that is, a controller action returns `ViewResult`. What this means is that any eventual syntax errors will only be caught at runtime when the framework is rendering the page; plus, even if there are no errors, ASP.NET Core takes some time (in the order of milliseconds, mind you) to compile the view. This does not need to be the case, however.

Unlike previous versions, ASP.NET Core 3 does not recompile a view when the Razor file changes, by default. For that, you have to restart your server. If you want to have this behavior back, you need to add a reference to the `Microsoft.AspNetCore.Mvc.Razor.RuntimeCompilation` NuGet package and add the following line to the `services` configuration:

```
services
    .AddMvc()
    .AddRazorRuntimeCompilation();
```

Or, you may prefer to enable this only for the debug version of your app, which excludes it from production builds. In that case, you can do it like this:

```
var mvc = services.AddMvc();

#if DEBUG
mvc.AddRazorRuntimeCompilation();
#endif
```

Or, for a specific environment, you can inject `IWebHostEnvironment` into your `Startup` class, store it, and check the current environment before making the call to `AddRazorRuntimeCompilation`, as follows:

```
public IConfiguration Configuration { get; }
public IWebHostEnvironment Environment { get; }

public Startup(IConfiguration configuration, IWebHostEnvironment
environment)
{
    this.Configuration = configuration;
```

```
    this.Environment = environment;
}

var mvc = services.AddMvc();

if (this.Environment.IsDevelopment())
{
    mvc.AddRazorRuntimeCompilation();
}
```

Microsoft makes available a NuGet package, which is
`Microsoft.AspNetCore.Mvc.Razor.ViewCompilation`, that you can add as a
reference to your project. After this, you can enable view compilation at publishing
time, and currently, the only way to do this is by manually editing the `.csproj` file.
Look for the first `<PropertyGroup>` instance declared in it, the one that contains the
`<TargetFramework>` element, and add a `<MvcRazorCompileOnPublish>` and a
`<PreserveCompilationContext>` element. The result should look like this:

```
<PropertyGroup>
  <TargetFramework>netcoreapp3</TargetFramework>
  <MvcRazorCompileOnPublish>true</MvcRazorCompileOnPublish>
  <PreserveCompilationContext>true</PreserveCompilationContext>
</PropertyGroup>
```

Now, whenever you publish your project, either using Visual Studio or the `dotnet`
`publish` command, you will get errors.

Do not forget that the precompilation only occurs at **publish**, not
build, time!

The class that is generated for each view exposes a property called `Html` that is of
type `IHtmlHelper<T>`, T being the type of your model. This property has some
interesting methods that can be used for rendering HTML, as follows:

- Generating links (`ActionLink`, `RouteLink`)

- Generating forms for a given model or model property (`BeginForm`, `BeginRouteForm`, `CheckBox`, `CheckBoxFor`, `Display`, `DisplayFor`, `DisplayForModel`, `DisplayName`, `DisplayNameFor`, `DisplayNameForInnerType`, `DisplayNameForModel`, `DisplayText`, `DisplayTextFor`, `DropDownList`, `DropDownListFor`, `Editor`, `EditorFor`, `EditorForModel`, `EndForm`, `Hidden`, `HiddenFor`, `Id`, `IdFor`, `IdForModel`, `Label`, `LabelFor`, `LabelForModel`, `ListBox`, `ListBoxFor`, `Name`, `NameFor`, `NameForModel`, `Password`, `PasswordFor`, `RadioButton`, `RadioButtonFor`, `TextArea`, `TextAreaFor`, `TextBox`, `TextBoxFor`, `Value`, `ValueFor`, `ValueForModel`)
- Displaying validation messages (`ValidationMessage`, `ValidationMessageFor`, `ValidationSummary`)
- Rendering anti-forgery tokens (`AntiForgeryToken`)
- Outputting raw HTML (`Raw`)
- Including partial views (`Partial`, `PartialAsync`, `RenderPartial`, `RenderPartialAsync`)
- Getting access to the context properties (`ViewContext`, `ViewBag`, `ViewData`, `TempData`) and also the base classes' (`RazorPage`, `RazorPage<T>`) properties (`UrlEncoder`, `MetadataProvider`)
- A couple of configuration properties (`Html5DateRenderingMode`, `IdAttributeDotReplacement`)

We will look into these methods in more detail in `Chapter 13`, *Understanding How Testing Works*. For now, let's see how we can add our own extension (helper) methods. The easiest way is to add an extension method over `IHtmlHelper<T>`, as illustrated in the following code snippet:

```
public static HtmlString CurrentUser(this IHtmlHelper<T> html)
{
    return new HtmlString(html.ViewContext.HttpContext.
    User.Identity.Name);
}
```

Now, you can use it in every view, like this:

```
@Html.CurrentUser()
```

Make sure that you either return `string` or `IHtmlContent` from it; otherwise, you won't be able to use this syntax.

We've seen that the `ViewResult` class offers the following three properties that can be used to pass data from an action into a view:

- **The model** (`Model`): In the early days of ASP.NET MVC, this was the only mechanism that could be used; we needed to define a possibly quite complex class with all the data that we would like to make available.
- **The view data** (`ViewData`): Now that we have a strongly typed collection of random values, this has gained in popularity against the model.
- **The temporary data** (`TempData`): Data that will only be available until the next request.

These properties are eventually passed along to identically named ones in the `RazorPage<T>` class.

It is even possible, but not too common, to specify the view engine (an instance of `IViewEngine`) that should be used by the view rendering process, by setting a value to the `ViewEngine` property. Normally, this is looked after automatically.

Passing data to views

Next we will be talking about different ways to pass data to a view.

Using the model

By default, a Razor view inherits from `RazorPage<dynamic>`, which means that the model is prototyped as `dynamic`.

This will be the type for the `Model` property. This is a flexible solution because you can pass whatever you want in the model, but you won't get IntelliSense—Visual Studio support in completion—for it.

You could, however, specify a strongly typed model through `inherits`, like this:

```
@inherits RazorPage<ProcessModel>
```

This could also be achieved by using the `model` directive, like this:

```
@model ProcessModel
```

These are essentially the same. Visual Studio helps you find its properties and methods, as illustrated in the following screenshot:

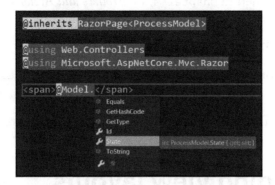

One thing to keep in mind is that you cannot pass an anonymous type on your controller, as the view won't be able to access its properties. See the next chapter for a solution to this.

Using the ViewBag property

The view bag (`ViewBag` property) came as a complement for the model, but, in my perspective, has long taken over it. Why is that? Well, I guess the problem is that you need to change the model class whenever you need more properties, and it's much easier to just stick new items in the view bag.

There are two options for using the view bag, as follows:

- Through the `ViewBag` dynamic property, which is not runtime-safe, like this:

  ```
  <script>alert('@ViewBag.Message');</script>
  ```

- Through the `ViewData` strongly typed dictionary, like this:

  ```
  <script>alert('@ViewData["Message"]');</script>
  ```

`ViewBag` is just a wrapper around `ViewData`—anything that is added to one can be retrieved from the other, and vice versa. A good reason for picking `ViewData` is if the stored data's name contains a space or other special character such as –, /, @, and so on.

Using temporary data

Temporary data, explained in Chapter 4, *Controllers and Actions*, can be retrieved in a similar way to ViewData, should we need to, as follows:

```
<script>alert('@TempData["Message"]');</script>
```

Remember that temporary data only exists in the scope of the next request, as its name implies.

Next, we will explore the mechanism for defining a common structure for our views.

Understanding view layouts

View layouts are similar to master pages in good old ASP.NET Web Forms. They define a base layout and, possibly, default contents that several views can use, so as to maximize, reuse, and offer a consistent structure. An example view layout can be seen in the following screenshot:

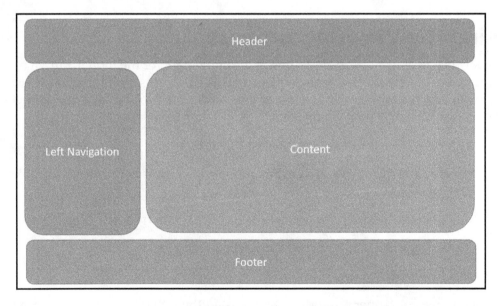

Image taken from https://docs.microsoft.com/en-us/aspnet/core/mvc/views/layout

View layouts themselves are also Razor views, and they can be controlled by setting the Layout property in a view, which is defined in the RazorPage base class, as follows:

```
@{ Layout = "_Layout"; }
```

The Layout property is just the name of a view, one that can be discovered in the usual way.

The only thing that is required in a layout view is a call to the RenderBody method; this causes the actual view that is using it to be rendered. It is also possible to define section placeholders, which may be used by actual views to provide content. A section is defined by a RenderSection call, as illustrated in the following code block:

```
<!DOCTYPE html>
<html>
  <head><title></title>
    @RenderSection("Head", required: false)
  </head>
  <body>
    @RenderSection("Header", required: false)
    <div style="float:left">
        @RenderSection("LeftNavigation", required: false)
    </div>
    @RenderBody
    <div style="float:right">
        @RenderSection("Content", required: true)
    </div>
    @RenderSection("Footer", required: false)
  </body>
</html>
```

As you can see, RenderSection takes the following two parameters:

- A name, which must be unique among the layout
- Depending on whether the section is required, the required parameter (the default is true)

There are also asynchronous versions of RenderSection, appropriately named RenderSectionAsync.

> Unlike ASP.NET Web Forms content placeholders, it is not possible to supply default content on a view layout.

If a section is defined as required, a view page that uses the layout view must declare a `section` for it, as follows:

```
@section Content
{
    <h1>Hello, World!</h1>
}
```

If no sections are defined, the Razor compilation system just takes the compiled view and inserts its contents in the location where `RenderBody` is called.

You can check whether a section is defined or not by executing the following code:

```
@if (IsSectionDefined("Content")) { ... }
```

The `IsLayoutBeingRendered` property tells us whether a layout view is defined, found, and is currently being rendered.

If you know that a section is defined as required in the view layout but you still do not wish to render it, you can call `IgnoreSection`, like this:

```
@IgnoreSection(sectionName: "Content")
```

And if for whatever reason you decide not to include any contents of your actual view in a view layout, you can call `IgnoreBody`.

 Layouts can be nested—that is, a top-level view can define one layout that also has its own layout, and so on.

Next, let's explore the view types and how they are used.

Understanding partial views

A partial view is similar to a regular view, but it is intended to be included in the middle of one. The syntax and feature set are exactly the same. The concept is similar to that of user controls in ASP.NET Web Forms, and the idea is basically **DRY** (short for **Don't Repeat Yourself**). By wrapping common content in a partial view, we can reference it in different places.

There are three ways in which you can include a partial view in the middle of a view, both in a synchronous and an asynchronous manner. The first way involves the `Partial` and `PartialAsync` methods, as illustrated in the following code snippet:

```
@Html.Partial("LoginStatus")
@await Html.PartialAsync("LoginStatus")
```

You would use the asynchronous version if the view has any code that needs to run asynchronously.

Another way to include partial contents is through `RenderPartial` and `RenderPartialAsync`, as illustrated in the following code snippet:

```
@{ Html.RenderPartial("LoginStatus"); }
@{ await Html.RenderPartialAsync("LoginStatus"); }
```

What is the difference between the two?, I hear you ask. Well, `Partial/PartialAsync` returns `IHtmlContent`, which is essentially an encoded string, and `RenderPartial/RenderPartialAsync` directly writes to the underlying output writer, possibly resulting in a (slightly) better performance.

The third one is to use the `<partial>` tag helper that came out in ASP.NET Core 2.1, as illustrated in the following code snippet:

```
<partial name="Shared/_ProductPartial.cshtml" />
```

Partial views and view layouts are two different, complementary, mechanisms to allow reuse. They should be used together, not one instead of the other.

Let's see how partial views work.

Passing data to partial views

Both `Partial` and `RenderPartial` offer overloads that allow us to pass a model object, as illustrated in the following code snippet:

```
@Html.Partial("OrderStatus", new { Id = 100 })
@{ Html.RenderPartial("OrderStatus", new { Id = 100 }); }
```

Of course, the model declared in the `OrderStatus` view must be compatible with the passed model, which will always happen if it is declared as dynamic (the default); if it's not, then it will throw an exception, so beware!

For `Partial/PartialAsync`, we can also pass values for its `ViewBag`, like this:

```
@Html.Partial("OrderStatus", new { Id = 100 }, ViewData)
@await Html.PartialAsync("OrderStatus", new { Id = 100 }, ViewData)
```

Here, we are just passing along the current view bag, but it need not be the case.

 Partial views can be nested, meaning that a partial view can include other partial views.

Finding partial views

The discovery of partial views is slightly different, for the following reasons:

- If only a name is supplied (for example, `LoginStatus`), view files are discovered using the same rules as with global views.
- If the view name ends with `.cshtml` (for example, `LoginStatus.cshtml`), then the view file is only looked up in the same folder as the containing view.
- If the view name starts with either `~/` or `/` (for example, `~/Views/Status/LoginStatus.cshtml`), then the view file is looked up in a folder relative to the web application root (not the `wwwroot` folder, mind you).
- If the view name starts with `../` (for example, `../Status/LoginStatus.cshtml`), then the view engine tries to find it in a folder relative to one of the calling views.

Multiple partial views with the same name can exist if located in different folders.

Understanding the special view files

ASP.NET Core recognizes two special view files, which, if present, are treated specially, as follows:

- `_ViewImports.cshtml`: Used to specify Razor directives that should apply to all views (`@addTagHelper`, `@removeTagHelper`, `@tagHelperPrefix`, `@using`, `@model`, `@inherits`, and `@inject`), as illustrated in the following code snippet:

  ```
  @using Microsoft.AspNetCore.Mvc.Razor
  @using My.Custom.Namespace
  @inject IMyService Service
  ```

- `_ViewStart.cshtml`: Any code that is placed here will be executed for all views; for this reason, it is a good place for setting the global common layout (which, of course, can be overridden by each view), a common model, or base view page, as follows:

  ```
  @{ Layout = "_Layout"; }
  ```

But there are other uses too, such as the following:

- Adding `@using` directives so that all views have access to the same namespaces
- Adding `@inject` directives
- Registering tag helpers through `@addTagHelper`
- Defining static methods (most useful for Razor Pages)

The Visual Studio template adds these files to the `Views` folder of the application. This means that they cannot be normally referenced, as this folder is outside the default search locations for views.

 Special files are aware of areas, meaning that if you are using areas and you add one of these files to an area, it will be executed after the global one.

Let's see some of the options we can configure for views.

Understanding the view options

As developers, we get to influence some of the ways views—and, in particular, Razor views—work. Normally, this is done through configuration, through `AddViewOptions` and `AddRazorOptions` extension methods, which are commonly called in sequence to `AddMvc`, in the `ConfigureServices` method, as illustrated in the following code snippet:

```
services
    .AddMvc()
    .AddViewOptions(options =>
    {
        //global view options
    })
    .AddRazorOptions(options =>
    {
        //razor-specific options
    });
```

Through `AddViewOptions`, we can configure the following properties of the `MvcViewOptions` class:

- `ClientModelValidatorProviders`
  (`IList<IClientModelValidatorProvider>`): A collection of client-model validator providers, to be used when the model is to be validated on the client side; this will be discussed in Chapter 11, *Security*, but by default, it includes `DefaultClientModelValidatorProvider`, `DataAnnotationsClientModelValidatorProvider`, and `NumericClientModelValidatorProvider`.
- `HtmlHelperOptions` (`HtmlHelperOptions`): Several options related to the generation of HTML; this is discussed next.
- `ViewEngines` (`IList<IViewEngine>`): The registered view engines; by default, this only contains an instance of `RazorViewEngine`.

`HtmlHelperOptions` features the following properties:

- `ClientValidationEnabled` (`bool`): Whether client validation should be enabled or not; the default is `true`.
- `Html5DateRenderingMode` (`Html5DateRenderingMode`): The format for rendering `DateTime` values as strings in HTML5 form fields; the default is `Rfc3339`, which renders `DateTime` as `2017-08-19T12:00:00-01:00`.

- `IdAttributeDotReplacement` (`string`): The string to be used instead of dots (`.`) when MVC renders input fields for a model; the default is `_`.
- `ValidationMessageElement` (`string`): The HTML element that will be used to render its specific validation message; the default is `span`.
- `ValidationSummaryMessageElement` (`string`): The HTML element for rendering the global validation summary; the default is `span`.

The `AddRazorOptions` method provides features that are more specific to Razor views, as follows:

- `AdditionalCompilationReferences` (`IList<MetadataReference>`): A collection of assembly references from where ASP.NET Core elements (controllers, view components, tag helpers, and more) can be loaded; empty by default
- `AreaViewLocationFormats` (`IList<string>`): The list of folders to be searched, inside an area folder, for views; similar to `ViewLocationFormats`, but applies to areas
- `CompilationCallback` (`Action<RoslynCompilationContext>`): A callback method that is called after each element is compiled; safe to ignore, as it should only be used by advanced developers
- `CompilationOptions` (`CSharpCompilationOptions`): A set of C# compilation options
- `FileProviders` (`IList<IFileProvider>`): The collection of file providers; by default, only contains an instance of `PhysicalFileProvider`
- `ParseOptions` (`CSharpParseOptions`): A set of C# parsing options
- `ViewLocationExpanders` (`IList<IViewLocationExpander>`): The collection of view location expanders
- `ViewLocationFormats` (`IList<string>`): The locations to be searched for view files, discussed earlier

Normally, `MetadataReference` is obtained using one of the static methods of the `MetadataReference` class, as follows:

```
var asm =
MetadataReference.CreateFromFile("\Some\Folder\MyAssembly.dll");
```

The `CSharpCompilationOptions` and `CSharpParseOptions` classes are quite extensive and include, mostly, every setting that the compiler supports, even some that are not easily found in Visual Studio. Explaining all of them would be tedious and really off-topic, but I'm going to give you just two examples here:

```
services
    .AddMvc()
    .AddRazorOptions(options =>
    {
        //enable C# 7 syntax
options.ParseOptions.WithLanguageVersion(LanguageVersion.CSharp7);

        //add a using declaration for the System.Linq namespace
        options.CompilationOptions.Usings.Add("System.Linq");
    });
```

This code runs as part of the bootstrap process and it sets an option for Razor Pages to use C# version 7. It is also adding an implicit `using` statement for the `System.Linq` namespace.

Now, we will see how to logically (and physically) organize our site functionality: areas.

Referencing the base path of the application

The base path was described in `Chapter 2`, *Configuration*, as a means to host our application in a path other than `/`. Should you need to get the base path for your app in a view, you can use this:

```
<script>
var basePath = '@Url.Content("~/")';
</script>
```

In this example, we are storing the configured base path (which maps to the special ~ folder) to a JavaScript variable.

Now that we understand how layouts work, let's see how to use areas on a website.

Using areas

Areas are a way for you to segregate functionality within your website. For example, anything related to the **admin** area goes in one place—for example, a physical folder, including its own controllers, views, and so on. In terms of views, the only thing worth mentioning is how we can configure the paths where view files can be found. This is controlled through the `AreaViewLocationFormats` collection of the `RazorViewEngineOptions` class, as illustrated in the following code snippet:

```
services
    .AddMvc()
    .AddRazorOptions(options =>
    {
        options.AreaViewLocationFormats.Add("/SharedGlobal
        /Areas/{2}.cshtml");
    });
```

The included values are the following ones:

- `/Areas/{2}/Views/{1}/{0}.cshtml`
- `/Areas/{2}/Views/Shared/{0}.cshtml`
- `/Views/Shared/{0}.cshtml`

Here, the `{2}` token stands for the area name, whereas `{0}` is for the view name, and `{1}` stands for the controller name, as seen previously. Essentially, you have a similar structure as for non-area views, but you now have views that are shared globally or per area.

As stated previously, you can add special files to areas. Now, let's see how DI works in views.

Dependency injection

View classes (`RazorPage<T>`) support services being injected in their constructors, as illustrated in the following code snippet:

```
public class MyPage : RazorPage<dynamic>
{
    public MyPage(IMyService svc)
    {
        //constructor injection
    }
}
```

Views also support having services injected into them. Just declare an `@inject` element in the `.cshtml` file with the service type to retrieve and the local variable to hold it, probably at the beginning of the view, like this:

```
@inject IHelloService Service
```

After this, you can use the injected `Service` variable, like this:

```
@Service.SayHello()
```

 There may be the need to either fully qualify the type name or add a `@using` declaration for its namespace.

Let's see now how to have our application respond in different languages.

Using translations

We've seen in the previous chapter that ASP.NET Core includes built-in mechanisms for displaying resources in different languages; this definitely includes views. Actually, there are two ways to display translated texts, as follows:

- Resources
- Translated views

Let's start with resources.

Using resources

So, let's assume we have a couple of resource files (`.resx`), for languages **PT** and **EN**. Let's store them under the `Resources` folder (this can be configured, as we'll see in a moment), underneath a folder called `Views`, and inside a folder named after the controller the views are to be served from (say, `Home`, for example). The filenames themselves must match the action names—so, for example, we might have the following:

- `Resources\Views\Home\Index.en.resx`
- `Resources\Views\Home\Index.pt.resx`

Before we can use them, we need to configure the localization services, in
`ConfigureServices`, like this:

```
services
    .AddMvc()
    .AddMvcLocalization(
        format: LanguageViewLocationExpanderFormat.Suffix,
        localizationOptionsSetupAction: options =>
        {
            options.ResourcesPath = "Resources";
        });
```

The two parameters to `AddMvcLocalization` represent the following:

- `format` (`LanguageViewLocalizationExpanderFormat`): The format to
  use for stating the culture of the resource file
- `localizationOptionsSetupAction`
  (`Action<LocalizationOptions>`): The action to be taken for configuring
  the location mechanism, such as specifying the path of the resource
  (currently only the `ResourcesPath` property)

The two possible values of `LanguageViewLocalizationExpanderFormat` are as
follows:

- `SubFolder`: This means that every resource file should be stored under a
  folder named after the culture (for example, `Resources\Views\Home\en`,
  `Resources\Views\Home\en-gb`, `Resources\Views\Home\pt`,
  `Resources\Views\Home\pt-pt`, and so on).
- `Suffix`: The culture is part of the filename (for example, `Index.en.resx`,
  `Index.pt.resx`, and so on).

As for the `LocalizationOptions` structure, its `ResourcePath` property already has
a default of `Resources`.

After we register this, we need to actually add the middleware that is responsible for setting the culture and the UI culture:

```
var supportedCultures = new[] { "en", "pt" };

var localizationOptions = new RequestLocalizationOptions()
    .SetDefaultCulture(supportedCultures[0])
    .AddSupportedCultures(supportedCultures)
    .AddSupportedUICultures(supportedCultures);

app.UseRequestLocalization(localizationOptions);
```

This should go in the `Configure` method. Here is a little explanation for this:

1. We must define the cultures that will be made available for selecting; these should map to the resource files that we have.
2. One of them will be the default (**fallback**) culture if no specific culture is set by the browser.
3. Here we are setting both the current culture (`CultureInfo.CurrentCulture`) as well as the current UI culture (`CultureInfo.CurrentUICulture`); they are useful because we may want to format a string value on the server before sending it to a view, and in this case we want the server code to be using the appropriate culture.

As for resource providers, ASP.NET Core includes three of them, and all are included in the `RequestLocalizationOptions` class by default, in this order:

- `QueryStringRequestCultureProvider`: Looks for the `culture` query string key
- `CookieRequestCultureProvider`: Gets the culture to use from the `.AspNetCore.Culture` cookie
- `AcceptLanguageHeaderRequestCultureProvider`: Looks for the `Accept-Language` HTTP header

The list of providers (classes that implement `IRequestCultureProvider`) is stored in the `RequestLocalizationOptions`.

`RequestCultureProviders` and this list is crossed until it finds one provider that returns a value.

When it comes to actually using the values from the resource files, we need to inject into the views an instance of IViewLocalizer and retrieve values from it, like this:

```
@inject IViewLocalizer Localizer
<h1>@Localizer["Hello"]</h1>
```

The IViewLocalizer interface extends IHtmlLocalizer, so it inherits all its properties and methods.

You can also use **shared resources**. A shared resource is a set of .resx files, plus an empty class, and they are not tied to a specific action or controller. These should be stored in the Resources folder, but the namespace of this class should be set to the assembly default namespace, as illustrated in the following code snippet:

```
namespace chapter05
{
    public class SharedResources { }
}
```

For this example, the resource files should be called SharedResources.en.resx, or the name of any other culture.

Then, in your view, inject a reference to IHtmlLocalizer<SharedResources>, like this:

```
@inject IHtmlLocalizer<SharedResources> SharedLocalizer
<h1>@SharedLocalizer["Hello"]</h1>
```

Next, we have translated views.

Using translated views

Another option is to have an entire view translated; by translated, I mean that ASP.NET Core will look for a view that matches the current language before falling back to a general one.

In order to activate this feature, you need to call AddViewLocalization, as follows:

```
services
    .AddMvc()
    .AddViewLocalization();
```

What this does is add a **view location expander** (remember this?) called `LanguageViewLocationExpander`. This duplicates the registered view locations so as to include ones with the current language as the file suffix. For example, we may have the following initial view location formats:

- `/Views/{1}/{0}.cshtml`
- `/Views/Shared/{0}.cshtml`

For the `pt` language, these will become the following:

- `/Views/{1}/{0}.pt.cshtml`
- `/Views/{1}/{0}.cshtml`
- `/Views/Shared/{0}.pt.cshtml`
- `/Views/Shared/{0}.cshtml`

Because the order matters, this effectively means that ASP.NET Core will first try to find a view ending with `.pt` (such as `Index.pt.cshtml`), and only after that, if not found, will it resort to locating the generic one (for example, `Index.cshtml`). Cool, don't you think? Of course, a translated view can be totally different than a generic one, even though this was mostly designed with translation in mind.

Summary

View layouts are a must-have; try to avoid nested (or too nested) view layouts, as it may be difficult to understand the final result. Partial views are also very handy, but make sure you use them to avoid repeating code.

We should also avoid having code in views—for example, by specifying custom view classes; use filters for that purpose. We saw that we should consider the localization needs of your app upfront; it's very difficult and error-prone to refactor an existing app that does not use localization to introduce it.

Then, next, we saw that for security, you can use code or tag helpers to keep sensitive parts of your views secure.

Stick to the conventions in terms of folder names and the like. This will make things easier for everyone, currently and in the future, in your team.

We learned that `_ViewImports.cshtml` and `_ViewStart.cshtml` are your friends—use them for common code that you want to be applied to all your pages.

Consider view compilation—it really helps in detecting some problems before they bite you.

In this chapter, we covered the views feature of ASP.NET Core, using the built-in Razor engine. We saw how we can use view layouts to introduce a coherent layout and partial views for encapsulation and reuse. We learned the ways in which we can pass data from a controller to a view.

In the next chapter, we will continue working with views, and, in particular, with HTML forms. We will go deeper into some of the topics that were introduced here.

Questions

You should now be able to answer these questions:

1. What is the base class for a view?
2. How can you inject services into a view?
3. What is a view location expander?
4. What is a view layout?
5. What are partial views?
6. Which functionality can replace partial views?
7. What does the `_ViewStart.cshtml` special file do?

2
Section 2: Improving Productivity

This section will show us how to get productive by enforcing reuse, process forms, and effective security measures.

This section has the following chapters:

Using Forms and Models

6

In this chapter, we will learn how to build forms for displaying and capturing data for use in our application, how to bind controls to models, and how to use validation techniques to exclude invalid data. We will cover client-submitted data—namely, HTML forms and their server-side counterpart, models, and files. With these, we will learn how to deal with user-submitted data.

Specifically, we will talk about the following:

- Using the form context
- Working with the model
- Understanding the model metadata and using metadata to influence form generation
- How can we use HTML helpers to generate HTML
- Working with templates
- Binding forms to object models
- Validating the model
- Using AJAX
- Uploading files

Technical requirements

In order to implement the examples introduced in this chapter, you will need the .NET Core 3 SDK and a text editor. Of course, Visual Studio 2019 (any edition) meets all of our requirements, but you can also use Visual Studio Code, for example.

The source code for this chapter can be retrieved from GitHub at `https://github.com/PacktPublishing/Modern-Web-Development-with-ASP.NET-Core-3-Second-Edition`.

Getting started

Because views are essentially HTML, nothing prevents you from manually adding your markup to them, which can include values obtained from the controller either through the model, view bag, or temporary data. ASP.NET Core, however, like previous versions, has built-in methods to assist you in generating HTML that matches your model (structure and content) and displaying model validation errors and other useful model metadata.

Because all of this works on top of the model, for the framework to be able to extract any relevant information, we need to use strongly typed views, not dynamic views; this means adding either an @model or @inherits directive to the views with the appropriate model type. To be clear, the model is the object that you pass to the ViewResult object returned from your controller, possibly returned from the View method, and it must either match the declared @model directive in the view or its @inherit declaration.

Let's begin by looking at the form context and then we will see how we can get information about the model.

Using the form context

The view context object (ViewContext) is available in the view components (which will be discussed in Chapter 9, *Reusable Components*) and as a property of Razor Pages (IRazorPage), meaning you can access it in views. In it, besides the usual context properties (such as HttpContext, ModelStateDictionary, RouteData, and ActionDescriptor), you also have access to the **form context** (FormContext) object. This object offers the following properties:

- CanRenderAtEndOfForm (bool): Indicates whether the form can render additional content (EndOfFormContent) at the end.
- EndOfFormContent (IList<IHtmlContent>): A collection of content to add at the end of the form (before the </form> tag).
- FormData (IDictionary<string, object>): The submitted form data.
- HasAntiforgeryToken (bool): Indicates whether the form is rendering the anti-forgery token, which depends on how the BeginForm method was called. The default is true.

- `HasEndOfFormContent` (`bool`): Indicates whether any end-of-form content has been added.
- `HasFormData` (`bool`): Indicates whether the `FormData` dictionary has been used and contains data.

Additionally, it offers a single method, `RenderedField`, with two overloads:

- One that returns an indication of whether a form field has been rendered in the current view
- Another that sets this flag for a specific field (typically called by the infrastructure)

Developers can leverage the form context to render additional data with the form, such as validation scripts or extra fields.

Now that we've seen what the global context looks like, let's see how we can extract information about the model.

Working with the model

The ASP.NET Core framework uses a **model metadata provider** to extract information from the model. This metadata provider can be accessed through `MetadataProperty` of `Html` and is exposed as `IModelMetadataProvider`. By default, it is set to an instance of `DefaultModelMetadataProvider`, which can be changed through the dependency injection framework, and its contract defines only two relevant methods:

- `GetMetadataForType` (`ModelMetadata`): Returns metadata for the model type itself
- `GetMetadataForProperties` (`IEnumerable<ModelMetadata>`): Metadata for all of the public model properties

You never normally call these methods; they are called internally by the framework. The `ModelMetadata` class they return (which may actually be of a derived class, such as `DefaultModelMetadata`) is what should interest us more. This metadata returns the following:

- The display name and description of the type or property (`DisplayName`)
- The data type (`DataType`)
- The text placeholder (`Placeholder`)

- The text to display in case of a null value (`NullDisplayText`)
- The display format (`DisplayFormatString`)
- Whether the property is required (`IsRequired`)
- Whether the property is read-only (`IsReadOnly`)
- Whether the property is required for binding (`IsBindingRequired`)
- The model binder (`BinderType`)
- The binder model's name (`BinderModelName`)
- The model's binding source (`BindingSource`)
- The property's containing class (`ContainerType`)

These properties are used by the HTML helpers when generating HTML for the model and they affect how it is produced.

By default, if no model metadata provider is supplied and no attributes are present, safe or empty values are assumed for the metadata properties. It is, however, possible to override them. Let's understand how each of these attributes is used.

We will start by looking at the display name (`DisplayName`) and description (`Description`). These can be controlled by the `[Display]` attribute from the `System.ComponentModel.DataAnnotations` namespace. This attribute also sets the placeholder/watermark for the property (`Placeholder`):

```
[Display(Name = "Work Email", Description = "The work email",
    Prompt = "Please enter the work email")]
public string WorkEmail { get; set; }
```

Marking a property as required (`IsRequired`) is achieved through `[Required]`. All of the other validation attributes, which are inherited from `ValidationAttribute` (such as `Required` and `MaxLength`), can also be supplied, as follows:

```
[Required]
[Range(1, 100)]
public int Quantity { get; set; }
```

Whether the property can be edited (`IsReadOnly`) is controlled by whether the property has a setter and whether it has an `[Editable]` attribute applied (the default value is `true`):

```
[Editable(true)]
public string Email { get; set; }
```

The data type (`DataType`) contained in a string can be defined by applying a `[DataType]` attribute, or one inherited from it:

```
[DataType(DataType.Email)]
public string Email { get; set; }
```

There are a few attribute classes that inherit from `DataTypeAttribute` and can be used instead of it:

- `[EmailAddress]`: Same as `DataType.EmailAddress`
- `[CreditCard]`: `DataType.CreditCard`
- `[Phone]`: `DataType.PhoneNumber`
- `[Url]`: `DataType.Url`
- `[EnumDataType]`: `DataType.Custom`
- `[FileExtensions]`: `DataType.Upload`

 `DataType` has several other possible values; I advise you to have a look into it.

The text to display whether a value is `null` (`NullDisplayText`) and the display format (`DisplayFormatString`) can both be set through the `[DisplayFormat]` attribute:

```
[DisplayFormat(NullDisplayText = "No birthday supplied",
DataFormatString = "{0:yyyyMMdd}")]
public DateTime? Birthday { get; set; }
```

When it comes to binding form fields to class properties, `[ModelBinder]` can be used to specify a custom model binder type (the `BinderType` property) and the name in the model to bind to (`ModelBinderName`); typically, you do not supply the name of the model as it is assumed to be the same as the property name:

```
[ModelBinder(typeof(GenderModelBinder), Name = "Gender")]
public string Gender { get; set; }
```

Here, we are specifying a custom model binder that will try to retrieve a value from the request and convert it into the appropriate type. Here is a possible implementation:

```
public enum Gender
{
    Unspecified = 0,
```

```
        Male,
        Female
    }

    public class GenderModelBinder : IModelBinder
    {
        public Task BindModelAsync(ModelBindingContext bindingContext)
        {
            var modelName = bindingContext.ModelName;
            var valueProviderResult = bindingContext.
            ValueProvider.GetValue(modelName);

            if (valueProviderResult != ValueProviderResult.None)
            {
                bindingContext.ModelState.SetModelValue(modelName,
                valueProviderResult);

                var value = valueProviderResult.FirstValue;

                if (!string.IsNullOrWhiteSpace(value))
                {
                    if (Enum.TryParse<Gender>(value, out var gender))
                    {
                        bindingContext.Result = ModelBindingResult.
                        Success(gender);
                    }
                    else
                    {
                        bindingContext.ModelState.TryAddModelError
                        (modelName, "Invalid gender.");
                    }
                }
            }

            return Task.CompletedTask;
        }
    }
```

What this does is it looks up the passed form name using the current value provider and then, if it is set, checks whether it matches the Gender enumeration. If so, then it sets it as the return value (bindingContext.Result); otherwise, it adds a model error.

If a property is required by setting `[Bind]`, `[BindRequired]`, `[BindingBehavior]`, or `[BindNever]`, then `IsBindingRequired` will be `true`:

```
[BindNever]  //same as [BindingBehavior(BindingBehavior.Never)]
public int Id { get; set; }
[BindRequired]  //same as [BindingBehavior(BindingBehavior.Required)]
public string Email { get; set; }
[BindingBehavior(BindingBehavior.Optional)]  //default, try to bind if
a
                                    //value is provided
public DateTime? Birthday { get; set; }
```

`[Bind]` is applied to the class itself or to a parameter to specify which properties should be bound or otherwise excluded from the binding. Here, we are mentioning which should be bound:

```
[Bind(Include = "Email")]
public class ContactModel
{
    public int Id { get; set; }
    public string Email { get; set; }
}
```

The `BindingSource` property is set if we use one of the `IBindingSourceMetadata` attributes:

- `[FromBody]`
- `[FromForm]`
- `[FromHeader]`
- `[FromQuery]`
- `[FromRoute]`
- `[FromServices]`

The default model metadata provider recognizes these attributes, but you can certainly roll out your own provider and supply properties in any other way.

There are times when you should not apply attributes to model properties—for example, when the model class is generated automatically. In that case, you can apply a `[ModelMetadataType]` attribute, usually in another file where you specify the class that will be used to retrieve metadata attributes from:

```
public partial class ContactModel
{
    public int Id { get; set; }
```

```
    public string Email { get; set; }
}
```

You can add an attribute to this same class from another file:

```
[ModelMetadataType(typeof(ContactModelMetadata))]
public partial class ContactModel
{
}
```

In the following example, we specified the individual properties we want to bind:

```
public sealed class ContactModelMetadata
{
    [BindNever]
    public int Id { get; set; }
    [BindRequired]
    [EmailAddress]
    public string Email { get; set; }
}
```

 Besides using the model, it is also possible to bind properties on the controller itself. All that is said also applies, but these properties need to take the [BindProperty] attribute. See Chapter 4, *Controllers and Actions*, for more information.

Let's now see how we can work with anonymous types.

Using models of anonymous types

As in previous versions of ASP.NET MVC, you cannot pass an anonymous type as the model to your view. Even if you can, the view won't have access to its properties, even if the view is set to use dynamic as the model type. What you can do is use an extension method such as this one to turn your anonymous type into ExpandoObject, a common implementation of dynamic:

```
public static ExpandoObject ToExpando(this object anonymousObject)
{
    var anonymousDictionary = HtmlHelper.
    AnonymousObjectToHtmlAttributes(anonymousObject);
    IDictionary<string, object> expando = new ExpandoObject();

    foreach (var item in anonymousDictionary)
    {
        expando.Add(item);
```

```
    }

    return expando as ExpandoObject;
}
```

You can use this in your controller:

```
return this.View(new { Foo = "bar" }.ToExpando());
```

In your view file, you use it as follows:

```
@model dynamic

<p>@Model.Foo</p>
```

We're done with model binding for now, so let's proceed with HTML helpers.

Using HTML helpers

HTML helpers are methods of the view's `Html` object (`IHtmlHelper`) and exist to aid in generating HTML. We may not know the exact syntax and URLs to routes can be tricky to generate, but there are two more important reasons why we use them. HTML helpers generate the appropriate code for display and editing purposes based on the model metadata, and they also include error and description placeholders. It is important to keep in mind that they are always based on the model.

In general, the built-in HTML helpers have two overloads:

- One that takes a strongly typed model (for example, `EditorFor(x => x.FirstName)`)
- Another that takes dynamic parameters in the form of strings (for example, `EditorFor("FirstName")`)

Also, they all take an optional parameter, `htmlAttributes`, that can be used to add any attribute to the rendered HTML element (for example, `TextBoxFor(x => x.FirstName, htmlAttributes: new { @class = "first-name" })`). For this reason, as we go through the different HTML helpers, I will skip the `htmlAttributes` parameter.

Forms

In order to submit values, we first need a form; the HTML `form` element can be used for this. The `BeginForm` helper generates one for us:

```
@using (Html.BeginForm())
{
 <p>Form goes here</p>
}
```

It returns an `IDisposable` instance; therefore, it should be used in a `using` block. This way, we ensure it is properly terminated.

This method has several overloads and among them all, it can take the following parameters:

- `actionName` (`string`): An optional name of a controller action. If present, the `controllerName` parameter must also be supplied.
- `controllerName` (`string`): An optional name of a controller; it must go along with `actionName`.
- `method` (`FormMethod`): An optional HTML form method (`GET` or `POST`); if not supplied, it defaults to `POST`.
- `routeName` (`string`): An optional route name (the name of a route registered through fluent configuration).
- `routeValues` (`object`): An optional object instance containing route values specific to `routeName`.
- `antiForgery` (`bool?`): Indicates whether or not the form should include an anti-forgery token (more on this later on); if not supplied, it is included by default.

There is another form generation method, `BeginRouteForm`, that is more focused on routes, so it always takes a `routeName` parameter. Anything that it does can also be achieved with `BeginForm`.

There are two alternatives for defining the target for the form submittal:

- `actionName` and `controllerName`: An action and an optional controller name to where the form will be submitted. If the controller name is omitted, it will default to the current one.
- `routeName`: A route name, as defined in the routing table, which will, in turn, consist of a controller and an action.

One of these must be chosen.

Single-line text boxes

All of the primitive .NET types can be edited through a text box. By text box, I mean an <input> element with an appropriate `type` attribute. For that, we have the `TextBoxFor` and `TextBox` methods, the former for the strongly typed version (the one that uses LINQ expressions based on the model) and the other for the string-based version. These methods can be used as follows:

```
@Html.TextBoxFor(x => x.FirstName)
@Html.TextBox("FirstName")
```

These methods have several overloads that take the `format` parameter.

`format` (`string`): An optional format string for cases where the type to render implements `IFormattable`

For example, if the value to be rendered represents money, we could have a line such as the following:

```
@Html.TextBoxFor(model => model.Balance, "{0:c}");
```

Here, `c` is used to format currency.

The `TextBox` and `TextBoxFor` HTML helpers render an <input> tag with a value of `type` that depends on the actual type of the property and its data type metadata (`DefaultModelMetadata.DataTypeName`):

- `text`: For string properties without any particular `DataType` attribute
- `date` and `datetime`: For `DateTime` properties, depending on the presence of `DataType` with a value of either `Date` or `DateTime`
- `number`: For numeric properties
- `email`: For string properties when associated with a `DataType` attribute of `EmailAddress`
- `url`: String properties with a `DataType` attribute of `Url`
- `time`: The `TimeSpan` properties or string properties with a `DataType` attribute of `Time`
- `tel`: String properties with a `DataType` attribute of `PhoneNumber`

The type of the `<input>` tag is one of the HTML5-supported values. You can read more about it at `https://developer.mozilla.org/en-US/docs/Web/HTML/Element/input`.

Multi-line text boxes

If we instead want to render multi-line text boxes, we must use the `TextArea` and `TextAreaFor` methods. These render HTML `textarea` elements and their parameters:

- `rows` (`int`): The rows to generate (the `textarea rows` attribute)
- `columns` (`int`): The `cols` attribute

After this, we move on to see how passwords work.

Passwords

Passwords (`<input type="password">`) are produced by one of the `Password` and `PasswordFor` methods. The only optional value they can take is the initial password which is `value` (`string`), the initial password.

Next, come the dropdowns.

Dropdowns

The `DropDownList` and `DropDownListFor` methods render a `<select>` element with values specified in the form of a collection of `SelectListItem` items. The parameters are as follows:

- `selectList` (`IEnumerable<SelectListItem>`): The list of items to display
- `optionLabel` (`string`): The default empty item

The `SelectListItem` class exposes the following properties:

- `Disabled` (`bool`): Indicates whether the item is available. The default is `false`.
- `Group` (`SelectListGroup`): An optional group.

- `Selected` (`bool`): Indicates whether the item is selected. There can only be one item marked as selected; therefore, the default is `false`.
- `Text` (`string`): The textual value to display.
- `Value` (`string`): The value to use.

The `SelectListGroup` class offers two properties:

- `Name` (`string`): The mandatory group name, used to group together multiple list items.
- `Disabled` (`bool`): Indicates whether the group is disabled. It is `false` by default.

There are two helper methods, `GetEnumSelectList` and `GetEnumSelectList<>`, that return, in the form of `IEnumerable<SelectListItem>`, the names and values of enumeration fields. This can be useful if we wish to use them to feed a drop-down list.

List boxes

The `ListBox` and `ListBoxFor` methods are similar to their drop-down list counterparts. The only difference is that the generated `<select>` element has its `multiple` attributes set to `true`. It only takes a single parameter, which is `selectList` (`IEnumerable<SelectListItem>`), for the items to show.

Radio buttons

As for radio buttons, we have the `RadioButton` and `RadioButtonFor` methods, which render `<input>` with a type of `radio`:

- `value` (`object`): The value to use for the radio button
- `isChecked` (`bool?`): Indicates whether the radio button is checked (which is default)

The radio button group name will be the name of the property that it is being generated to—for example, the following:

```
@Html.RadioButtonFor(m => m.Gender, "M" ) %> Male
@Html.RadioButtonFor(m => m.Gender, "F" ) %> Female
```

Checkboxes

Checkboxes are contemplated, too, by means of the `CheckBox`, `CheckBoxFor`, and `CheckBoxForModel` methods. This time, they render a `<input>` tag with a type of `checkbox`. The sole parameter is the following:

- `isChecked` (`bool?`): Indicates whether the checkbox is checked. The default is `false`.

Again, the group name will come from the property, as is the case for radio buttons.

One thing to keep in mind when working with checkboxes is that we would normally bind a checkbox value to a `bool` parameter. In that case, we must not forget to supply a value of `true` for the checkbox; otherwise, the form will contain no data for its field.

Hidden values

`Hidden`, `HiddenFor`, and `HiddenForModel` render an `<input type="hidden">` element. The model or its properties can be explicitly overridden with the following parameter:

- `value` (`object`): A value to include in the hidden field

Another option is to decorate your model class property with the `[HiddenInput]` attribute, as in the following example:

```
[HiddenInput(DisplayValue = false)]
public bool IsActive { get; set; } = true;
```

The `DisplayValue` parameter causes the property to not be output as a label when using automatic model editors.

Links

If we want to generate hyperlinks (`<a>`) to specific controller actions, we can use the `ActionLink` method. It has several overloads that accept the following parameters:

- `linkText` (`string`): The link text
- `actionName` (`string`): The action name
- `controllerName` (`string`): The controller name, which must be supplied together with `actionName`

- routeValues (object): An optional value (a POCO class or a dictionary) containing route values
- protocol (string): The optional URL protocol (for example, http, https, and so on)
- hostname (string): The optional URL hostname
- fragment (string): The optional URL anchor (for example, #anchorname)
- port (int): The optional URL port

As we can see, this method can generate links for either the same host as the web app or a different one.

Another option is to use a route name and for that purpose, there is the RouteLink method; the only difference is that instead of the actionName and controllerName parameters, it takes a routeName parameter, asrouteName (string), the name of a route for which to generate the link.

Next, we have labels.

Labels

Label, LabelFor, and LabelForModel render a <label> element with either a textual representation of the model or optional text:

- labelText (string): The text to add to the label

After labels, we have raw HTML.

Raw HTML

This renders HTML-encoded content. Its sole parameter is as follows:

- value (string, object): Content to display after HTML encoding

The next features we are about to learn are IDs, names, and values.

IDs, names, and values

These are often useful to extract some properties from the generated HTML elements, the generated ID, and the name. This is commonly required for JavaScript:

- `Id`, `IdFor`, and `IdForModel`: Return the value for the `id` attribute
- `Name`, `NameFor`, and `NameForModel`: The value for the `name` attribute
- `DisplayName`, `DisplayNameFor`, and `DisplayNameForModel`: The display name for the given property
- `DisplayText` and `DisplayTextFor`: The display text for the property or model
- `Value`, `ValueFor`, and `ValueForModel`: The first non-null value from the view bag

Generic editor and display

We've seen that we can use templates for individual model properties or for the model itself. To render display templates, we have the `Display`, `DisplayFor`, and `DisplayForModel` methods. All of them accept the following optional parameters:

- `templateName` (`string`): The name of a template that will override the one in the model metadata (`DefaultModelMetadata.TemplateHint`)
- `additionalViewData` (`object`): An object or `IDictionary` that is merged into the view bag
- `htmlFieldName` (`string`): The name of the generated HTML `<input>` field

A property is only rendered in display mode if its metadata states it as such (`DefaultModelMetadata.ShowForDisplay`).

As for edit templates, the methods are similar: `Editor`, `EditorFor`, and `EditorForModel`. These take exactly the same parameters as their display counterparts. It is important to mention that editors will only be generated for properties that are defined—as per their metadata—to be editable (`DefaultModelMetadata.ShowForEdit`).

Utility methods and properties

The `IHtmlHelper` class also exposes a few other utility methods:

- `Encode`: HTML-encodes a string using the configured HTML encoder
- `FormatValue`: Renders a formatted version of the passed value

Also, it exposes the following context properties:

- `IdAttributeDotReplacement`: This is the dot replacement string used for generating ID values
  (from `MvcViewOptions.HtmlHelperOptions.IdAttributeDotReplacement`)
- `Html5DateRenderingMode`: The HTML5 date rendering mode (from `MvcViewOptions.HtmlHelperOptions.Html5DateRenderingMode`)
- `MetadataProvider`: The model metadata provider
- `TempData`: Temporary data
- `ViewData` or `ViewBag`: The strongly/loosely typed view bag
- `ViewContext`: All of the view's context, including the HTTP context (`HttpContext`), the route data (`RouteData`), the form context (`FormContext`), and the parsed model (`ModelStateDictionary`)

Next are the validation messages.

Validation messages

Validation messages can be displayed for individual validated properties or as a summary for all the models. For displaying individual messages, we use the `ValidationMessage` and `ValidationMessageFor` methods, which accept the following optional attribute:

- `message` (`string`): An error message that overrides the one from the validation framework

For the validation summary, we have `ValidationSummary` and it accepts the following parameters:

- `excludePropertyErrors` (`bool`): If set, displays only model-level (top) errors, not errors for individual properties
- `message` (`string`): A message that is displayed with the individual errors
- `tag` (`string`): The HTML tag to use that overrides `MvcViewOptions.HtmlHelperOptions.ValidationSummaryMessageElement`)

After the validations, we move on to the next feature, which is the custom helpers.

Custom helpers

Some HTML elements have no corresponding HTML helper—for example, `button`. It is easy to add one, though. So, let's create an extension method over `IHtmlHelper`:

```
public static class HtmlHelperExtensions
{
    public static IHtmlContent Button(this IHtmlHelper html, string
text)
    {
        return html.Button(text, null);
    }

    public static IHtmlContent Button(this IHtmlHelper html, string
text, object htmlAttributes)
    {
        return html.Button(text, null, null, htmlAttributes);
    }

    public static IHtmlContent Button(
        this IHtmlHelper html,
        string text,
        string action,
        object htmlAttributes)
    {
        return html.Button(text, action, null, htmlAttributes);
    }

    public static IHtmlContent Button(this IHtmlHelper html, string
text, string action)
    {
        return html.Button(text, action, null, null);
```

```
}

public static IHtmlContent Button(
    this IHtmlHelper html,
    string text,
    string action,
    string controller)
{
    return html.Button(text, action, controller, null);
}

public static IHtmlContent Button(
    this IHtmlHelper html,
    string text,
    string action,
    string controller,
    object htmlAttributes)
{
    if (html == null)
    {
        throw new ArgumentNullException(nameof(html));
    }

    if (string.IsNullOrWhiteSpace(text))
    {
        throw new ArgumentNullException(nameof(text));
    }

    var builder = new TagBuilder("button");
    builder.InnerHtml.Append(text);

    if (htmlAttributes != null)
    {
        foreach (var prop in htmlAttributes.GetType()
        .GetTypeInfo().GetProperties())
        {
            builder.MergeAttribute(prop.Name,
                prop.GetValue(htmlAttributes)?.ToString() ??
                string.Empty);
        }
    }

    var url = new UrlHelper(new ActionContext(
        html.ViewContext.HttpContext,
        html.ViewContext.RouteData,
        html.ViewContext.ActionDescriptor));

    if (!string.IsNullOrWhiteSpace(action))
```

```
        {
            if (!string.IsNullOrEmpty(controller))
            {
                builder.Attributes["formaction"] = url.Action(
                action, controller);
            }
            else
            {
                builder.Attributes["formaction"] = url.Action(action);
            }
        }

        return builder;
    }
}
```

This extension method uses the common guidelines for all the other HTML helpers:

- Several overloads for each of the possible parameters
- Has a parameter of the `object` type called `htmlAttributes`, which is used for any custom HTML attributes that we wish to add
- Uses the `UrlHelper` class to generate correct route links for the controller action, if supplied
- Returns an instance of `IHtmlContent`

Using it is simple:

```
@Html.Button("Submit")
```

It can also be used with a specific action and controller:

```
@Html.Button("Submit", action: "Validate", controller: "Validation")
```

It can even be used with some custom attributes:

```
@Html.Button("Submit", new { @class = "save" })
```

Since ASP.NET Core does not offer any HTML helpers for submitting the form, I hope you find this useful!

This concludes our study of custom helpers. Let's focus now on writing templates for commonly used pieces of markup.

Using templates

When the `Display`, `DisplayFor<T>`, or `DisplayForModel` HTML helper methods are called, the ASP.NET Core framework renders the target property (or model) value in a way that is specific to that property (or model class) and can be affected by its metadata. For example, `ModelMetadata.DisplayFormatString` is used for rendering the property in the desired format. However, suppose we want a slightly more complex HTML—for example, in the case of composite properties. Enter display templates!

Display templates are a Razor feature; basically, they are partial views that are stored in a folder called `DisplayTemplates` under `Views\Shared` and their model is set to target a .NET class. Let's imagine, for a moment, that we have a `Location` class that stores the `Latitude` and `Longitude` values:

```
public class Location
{
    public decimal Latitude { get; set; }
    public decimal Longitude { get; set; }
}
```

If we want to have a custom display template for this, we could have a partial view, as follows:

```
@model Location
<div><span>Latitude: @Model.Latitude</span> - <span>Longitude:
@Model.Longitude</span></div>
```

So, this file is stored in `Views/Shared/DisplayTemplates/Location.cshtml`, but now you need to associate the `Location` class to it, which you can do by applying `[UIHint]` to a property of that type:

```
[UIHint("Location")]
public Location Location { get; set; }
```

> The `[UIHint]` attribute accepts a view name. It is searched in the `Views\Shared\DisplayTemplates` folder.

Similar to display templates, we have **editor templates**. Editor templates are rendered by `Editor`, `EditorFor`, or `EditorForModel` and their main difference from display templates is that the partial view files are stored in `Views\Shared\EditorTemplates`. Of course, in these templates, you would probably add HTML editor elements, even with custom JavaScript. For the case of the `Location` class, we could have the following:

```
@model Location
<div>
    <span>Latitude: @Html.TextBoxFor(x => x.Latitude)</span>
    <span>Longitude: @Html.TextBoxFor(x => x.Longitude)</span>
</div>
```

There can be only one `[UIHint]` attribute specified, which means that both templates—display and editor—must use the same name. Also, custom templates are not rendered by `EditorForModel` or `DisplayForModel`; you need to explicitly render them using `EditorFor` and `DisplayFor`.

OK, we've seen how to use templates for commonly used markup elements, which is very useful from a reusing perspective. Let's have a look now at model binding.

Enforcing model binding

ASP.NET Core tries to automatically populate (set values of their properties and fields) any parameters of an action method. This happens because it has a built-in (although configurable) **model binder provider**, which creates a **model binder**. These model binders know how to bind data from the many binding sources (discussed previously) to POCO classes in many formats.

Model binders

The model binder provider interface is `IModelBinderProvider` and the model binder, unsurprisingly, is `IModelBinder`. The model binder providers are registered in the `ModelBinderProviders` collection of `MvcOptions`:

```
services.AddMvc(options =>
{
    options.ModelBinderProviders.Add(new CustomModelBinderProvider());
});
```

The included providers are as follows:

- `BinderTypeModelBinderProvider`: Custom model binder (`IModelBinder`)
- `ServicesModelBinderProvider`: `[FromServices]`
- `BodyModelBinderProvider`: `[FromBody]`
- `HeaderModelBinderProvider`: `[FromHeader]`
- `SimpleTypeModelBinderProvider`: Basic types using a type converter
- `CancellationTokenModelBinderProvider`: `CancellationToken`
- `ByteArrayModelBinderProvider`: Deserializes from Base64 strings into byte arrays
- `FormFileModelBinderProvider`: `[FromForm]`
- `FormCollectionModelBinderProvider`: `IFormCollection`
- `KeyValuePairModelBinderProvider`: `KeyValuePair<TKey, TValue>`
- `DictionaryModelBinderProvider`: `IDictionary<TKey, TValue>`
- `ArrayModelBinderProvider`: Arrays of objects
- `CollectionModelBinderProvider`: Collections of objects (`ICollection<TElement>`, `IEnumerable<TElement>`, or `IList<TElement>`)
- `ComplexTypeModelBinderProvider`: Nested properties (for example, `TopProperty.MidProperty.BottomProperty`)

These providers help assign values to the following types:

- Simple properties using type converters
- POCO classes
- Nested POCO classes
- Arrays of POCO classes
- Dictionaries
- Collections of POCO classes

For example, take a model of the following class:

```
public class Order
{
    public int Id { get; set; }
    public int CustomerId { get; set; }
    public OrderState State { get; set; }
    public DateTime Timestamp { get; set; }
```

```
        public List<OrderDetail> Details { get; set; }
    }

    public enum OrderState
    {
        Received,
        InProcess,
        Sent,
        Delivered,
        Cancelled,
        Returned
    }

    public class OrderDetail
    {
        public int ProductId { get; set; }
        public int Quantity { get; set; }
    }

    public class Location
    {
        public int X { get; set; }
        public int Y { get; set; }
    }
```

Here, we have properties of different types, including primitive types, enumerations, and collections of POCO classes. When we generate a form for a model such as this, perhaps using the HTML helpers that were described previously, you will get HTML form elements containing values such as the following:

```
Id=43434
CustomerId=100
State=InProcess
Timestamp=2017-06-15T20:00:00
Details[0]_ProductId=45
Details[0]_Quantity=1
Details[1]_ProductId=47
Details[1]_Quantity=3
X=10
Y=20
```

Notice the _ character separating the child property names—it is configured by default to replace dots (.) in the MvcViewOptions.HtmlHelper.IdAttributeDotReplacement property. As you can see, ASP.NET Core can bind even somewhat complex cases.

Model binding sources

So, we declare a model (or individual base type parameters) as a parameter to an action method and we can apply model binding source attributes to instruct ASP.NET Core to get the values from a specific location. Again, these are as follows:

- [FromServices]: The object will be inserted from the dependency injection container.
- [FromBody]: The value will come from the payload of a POST request, normally either as JSON or XML.
- [FromForm]: The value will come from the posted form.
- [FromQuery]: The value will be obtained from the query string.
- [FromHeader]: The value will be read from the request headers.
- [FromRoute]: The value will come from the route as a named template item.

You can mix different model binding source attributes on the same method, as follows:

```
public IActionResult Process(
    [FromQuery] int id,
    [FromHeader] string contentType,
    [FromBody] Complex complex) { ... }
```

[FromPost] will take key-value pairs in either a multipart/form-data or application/x-www-form-urlencoded format.

One thing that you need to keep in mind is that there can only be one parameter with a [FromBody] attribute, which makes sense as the body is unique and it doesn't make sense to have it bound to two different objects. It only makes sense to apply it to POCO classes too. [FromBody] works with the registered **input formatters**; it tries to deserialize whatever payload is sent (normally by POST or PUT) by going through each input formatter. The first one to respond with a non-null value yields the result. Input formatters look at the request's Content-Type header (for example, application/xml or application/json) to determine whether they can process the request and deserialize it into the target type. We will look at input formatters in more detail in Chapter 8, *API Controllers*.

You can construct POCO objects from the query string using `[FromQuery]`. ASP.NET Core is smart enough to do that, provided you supply a value for each of the properties of the POCO on the query string, as follows:

```
//call this with: SetLocation?X=10&Y=20
public IActionResult SetLocation([FromQuery] Location location) { ...
}
```

Some of these attributes take an optional `Name` parameter, which can be used to explicitly state the source name, as follows:

```
[FromHeader(Name = "User-Agent")]
[FromQuery(Name = "Id")]
[FromRoute(Name = "controller")]
[FromForm(Name = "form_field")]
```

If you don't specify the source name, it will use the name of the parameter.

If you don't specify any attributes, ASP.NET Core will take the following logic when trying to bind values:

1. If the request is a `POST` value, it will try to bind values from the form (as with `[FromForm]`).
2. Then, it will route the values (`[FromRoute]`).
3. Then, it will query the string (`[FromQuery]`).

So, `[FromBody]`, `[FromServices]`, and `[FromHeader]` are never used automatically. You always need to apply attributes (or define a convention).

If no value can be found for a parameter in your action method using either the default logic or any attributes, that value will receive a default value:

- The default value for value types (`0` for integers, `false` for Boolean values, and so on)
- An instantiated object for classes

If you want to force the model state to be invalid if a value cannot be found for a parameter, apply the `[BindRequired]` attribute to it:

```
public IActionResult SetLocation(
    [BindRequired] [FromQuery] int x,
    [BindRequired] [FromQuery] int y) { ... }
```

In this case, you will get an error when trying to call this action without providing the X and Y parameters. You can also apply it to model classes, in which case, all of its properties will need to be supplied, as follows:

```
[BindRequired]
public class Location
{
    public int X { get; set; }
    public int Y { get; set; }
}
```

This also has some limitations as you cannot bind to an abstract class, a value type (struct), or a class without a public parameterless constructor. If you want to bind to an abstract class or one without a public, parameterless constructor, you need to roll out your own model binder and return an instance yourself.

Dynamic binding

What if you don't know upfront what the request will contain—for example, if you want to accept anything that is posted? You essentially have three ways of accepting it:

- Use a string parameter, if the payload can be represented as a string.
- Use a custom model binder.
- Use one of the JSON-aware parameter types.

If you use a string parameter, it will just contain the payload as is, but ASP.NET Core also supports binding JSON payloads to either a dynamic or System.Text.Json.JsonElement parameter. JsonElement, in case you're not familiar, is part of the new System.Text.Json API, which replaces **JSON.NET** (Newtonsoft.Json) as the included JSON serializer. ASP.NET Core can bind POST with a content type of application/json to one of these parameter types without any additional configuration, as follows:

```
[HttpPost]
public IActionResult Process([FromBody] dynamic payload) { ... }
```

The dynamic parameter will actually be an instance of JsonElement. You can't declare the parameter to be of an interface or abstract base class unless you use your own model binder and return a constructed instance from it.

Now, let's move on to validating the model post that binds it.

JSON.NET is still available as an open source project from GitHub at `https://github.com/JamesNK/Newtonsoft.Json`. You can use it instead of the built-in JSON serializer. To do this, have a look at `https://docs.microsoft.com/en-us/aspnet/core/migration/22-to-30?view=aspnetcore-3.1`.

Model validation

We all know that client-side validation by validating a page without having to post its content is what we expect from a web app these days. However, this may not be sufficient—for example for the (granted, few) cases where JavaScript is disabled. In this case, we need to ensure we validate our data on the server-side before actually doing anything with it. ASP.NET Core supports both scenarios; let's see how.

Server-side validation

The result of validating a submitted model (normally through `POST`) is always available in the `ModelState` property of the `ControllerBase` class, and it is also present in the `ActionContext` class. Consider the following code snippet:

```
if (!this.ModelState.IsValid)
{
    if (this.ModelState["Email"].Errors.Any())
    {
        var emailErrors = string.
            Join(Environment.NewLine, this.ModelState
            ["Email"].Errors.Select(e => e.ErrorMessage));
    }
}
```

As you can see, we have both the global validation state (`IsValid`) and the individual property error messages (for example, `["Email"].Errors`).

Using the built-in validators, all based on the `System.ComponentModel.DataAnnotations` API, the following validations are performed:

- Validation based on attributes (`ValidationAttribute`-derived)
- Validation based on the `IValidatableObject` interface

Validation is executed when a form is posted or when it is explicitly invoked by a call to `TryValidateModel` if you happened to change the model. The `ModelState` property is of the `ModelStateDictionary` type, which exposes the following properties:

- `Item` (`ModelStateEntry`): Access to individual model properties' states
- `Keys` (`KeyEnumerable`): The collection of model properties' names
- `Values` (`ValueEnumerable`): The model properties' values
- `Count` (`int`): The count of model properties
- `ErrorCount` (`int`): The error count
- `HasReachedMaxErrors` (`bool`): Whether or not the found errors have reached the configured maximum
- `MaxAllowedErrors` (`int`): The configured maximum number of errors (see the *Configuration* section)
- `Root` (`ModelStateEntry`): The root object's model state
- `IsValid` (`bool`): Whether or not the model is valid
- `ValidationState` (`ModelValidationState`): The validation state for the model (`Unvalidated`, `Invalid`, `Valid`, or `Skipped`)

Validation based on attributes is associated with the property to which the validation attribute is located (some validation attributes can also be applied to classes). The property's name will be the key and the property's value will be the value in the `ModelStateDictionary`. For each property, once a validator fails, any other eventual validators will not be fired and the model state will be immediately invalid. Each property exposes a collection of one or more `ModelError` objects:

```
IEnumerable<ModelError> errors = this.ModelState["email"];
```

This class has two properties:

- `ErrorMessage` (`string`): The message produced by the property validator(s), if any
- `Exception` (`Exception`): Any exception produced while validating this particular property

After this, we move to the configuration for it.

Configuration

There are a couple of configuration options available through the AddMvc method as part of the MvcOptions class:

- MaxModelValidationErrors (int): The maximum number of validation errors before no more validation is performed (the default is 200).
- ModelValidatorProviders (IList<IModelValidatorProvider>): The registered model validation providers. By default, it contains an instance of DefaultModelValidatorProvider and one of DataAnnotationsModelValidatorProvider.

These built-in providers basically do the following:

- DefaultModelValidatorProvider: If a property has an attribute that implements IModelValidator, it uses it for validation.
- DataAnnotationsModelValidatorProvider: Hooks any ValidatorAttribute instances that the property to validate may have.

Data annotation validation

System.ComponentModel.DataAnnotations offers the following validation attributes:

- [Compare]: Compares two properties to see whether they have the same value.
- [CreditCard]: The string property must have a valid credit card format.
- [CustomValidation]: Custom validation through an external method.
- [DataType]: Validates a property against a specific data type (DateTime, Date, Time, Duration, PhoneNumber, Currency, Text, Html, MultilineText, EmailAddress, Password, Url, ImageUrl, CreditCard, PostalCode, or Upload).
- [EmailAddress]: Checks whether the string property is a valid email address.
- [MaxLength]: The maximum length of a string property.
- [MinLength]: The minimum length of a string property.
- [Phone]: Checks that the string property has a phone-like structure (US only).
- [Range]: The maximum and minimum values of a property.

- [RegularExpression]: Uses a regular expression to validate a string property.
- [Remote]: Uses a controller action to validate a model.
- [Required]: Checks whether the property has a value set.
- [StringLength]: Checks the maximum and minimum lengths of a string; same as one [MinLength] value and one [MaxLength] value, but using this, you only need one attribute.
- [Url]: Checks that the string property is a valid URL.

All of these attributes are hooked automatically by the registered DataAnnotationsModelValidatorProvider.

For custom validation, we have two options:

- Inherit from ValidationAttribute and implement its IsValid method:

```
[AttributeUsage(AttributeTargets.Property, AllowMultiple =
false, Inherited = true)]
public sealed class IsEvenAttribute : ValidationAttribute
{
    protected override ValidationResult IsValid(object value,
    ValidationContext validationContext)
    {
        if (value != null)
        {
            try
            {
                var convertedValue = Convert.ToDouble(value);
                var isValid = (convertedValue % 2) == 0;

                if (!isValid)
                {
                    return new
ValidationResult(this.ErrorMessage,
                        new[] { validationContext.MemberName });
                }
            }
            catch { }
        }

        return ValidationResult.Success;
    }
}
```

- Implement a validation method:

```
[CustomValidation(typeof(ValidationMethods), "ValidateEmail")]
public string Email { get; set; }
```

In this `ValidationMethods` class, add the following method:

```
public static ValidationResult ValidateEmail(string email,
ValidationContext context)
{
    if (!string.IsNullOrWhiteSpace(email))
    {
        if (!Regex.IsMatch(email, @"^([\w\.\-]+)@([\w\-]+
        )((\.(\w){2,3})+)$"))
        {
            return new ValidationResult("Invalid email",
            new[] { context.MemberName });
        }
    }

    return ValidationResult.Success;
}
```

A few things to note:

- This validation attribute *only* checks for valid emails; it *does not* check for required values.
- The `ValidationContext` attribute has some useful properties, such as the current member name being validated (`MemberName`), its display name (`DisplayName`), and the root validating object (`ObjectInstance`).
- `ValidationResult.Success` is `null`.

The signature of the validation method can vary:

- The first parameter can either be strongly typed (for example, `string`) or loosely typed (for example, `object`), but it must be compatible with the property to be validated.
- It can be `static` or instance.
- It can take the `ValidationContext` parameter or not.

Why choose one or the other? The `[CustomValidation]` attribute potentially promotes reuse by having a set of shared methods that can be used in different contexts. We also have an error message in this attribute.

[CustomValidation] can be applied to either a property or the whole class.

Error messages

There are three ways by which you can set an error message to display in the case of a validation error:

- ErrorMessage: A plain old error message string, with no magic attached.
- ErrorMessageString: A format string that can take tokens (for example, {0}, {1}) that depend on the actual validation attribute; token {0} is usually the name of the property being validated.
- ErrorMessageResourceType and ErrorMessageResourceName: It is possible to ask for the error message to come from a string property (ErrorMessageResourceName) declared in an external type (ErrorMessageResourceType); this is a common approach if you would like to localize your error messages.

After this, we move on to the next feature.

Self-validation

You would implement IValidatableObject (also supported by DataAnnotationsValidatorProvider) if the validation you need involves several properties of a class, similar to what you would achieve with applying [CustomValidation] to the whole class. We say that this class is self-validatable. The IValidatableObject interface specifies a single method, Validate, and the following is a possible implementation:

```
public class ProductOrder : IValidatableObject
{
    public int Id { get; set; }
    public DateTime Timestamp { get; set; }
    public int ProductId { get; set; }
    public int Quantity { get; set; }
    public decimal Price { get; set; }

    public IEnumerable<ValidationResult> Validate(ValidationContext
    context)
    {
```

```
        if (this.Id <= 0)
        {
            yield return new ValidationResult("Missing id", new []
            { "Id" });
        }

        if (this.ProductId <= 0)
        {
            yield return new ValidationResult("Invalid product",
            new [] { "ProductId" });
        }

        if (this.Quantity <= 0)
        {
            yield return new ValidationResult("Invalid quantity",
            new [] { "Quantity" });
        }

        if (this.Timestamp > DateTime.Now)
        {
            yield return new ValidationResult("Order date
            is in the future",  new [] { "Timestamp" });
        }
    }
}
```

After self-validation, let us move on to custom validation.

Custom validation

Yet another option for custom validation involves hooking a new model validator provider and a bespoke model validator. Model validator providers are instances of `IModelValidatorProvider`, such as this one:

```
public sealed class IsEvenModelValidatorProvider :
IModelValidatorProvider
{
    public void CreateValidators(ModelValidatorProviderContext
context)
    {
        if (context.ModelMetadata.ModelType == typeof(string)
            || context.ModelMetadata.ModelType == typeof(int)
            || context.ModelMetadata.ModelType == typeof(uint)
            || context.ModelMetadata.ModelType == typeof(long)
            || context.ModelMetadata.ModelType == typeof(ulong)
            || context.ModelMetadata.ModelType == typeof(short)
            || context.ModelMetadata.ModelType == typeof(ushort)
```

```
                || context.ModelMetadata.ModelType == typeof(float)
                || context.ModelMetadata.ModelType == typeof(double))
        {
            if (!context.Results.Any(x => x.Validator is
            IsEvenModelValidator))
            {
                context.Results.Add(new ValidatorItem
                {
                    Validator = new IsEvenModelValidator(),
                    IsReusable = true
                });
            }
        }
    }
}
```

This checks whether the target property (`context.ModelMetadata`) is one of the expected types (numbers or strings) and then it adds an `IsEvenModelValidator` attribute. When validation is triggered, this validator will be called.

For the sake of completion, here is its code:

```
public sealed class IsEvenModelValidator : IModelValidator
{
    public IEnumerable<ModelValidationResult>
    Validate(ModelValidationContext context)
    {
        if (context.Model != null)
        {
            try
            {
                var value = Convert.ToDouble(context.Model);
                if ((value % 2) == 0)
                {
                    yield break;
                }
            }
            catch { }
        }

        yield return new ModelValidationResult(
            context.ModelMetadata.PropertyName,
            $"{context.ModelMetadata.PropertyName} is not even.");
    }
}
```

This validator code tries to convert a number to a `double` value (because it's more generic) and then checks whether the number is even. If the value is `null` or not convertible, it just returns an empty result.

Preventing validation

If you don't wish for your model—either the whole class or one or more properties—to be validated, you can apply the `[ValidateNever]` attribute to it. This implements the `IPropertyValidationFilter` interface, which can be used to selectively include or exclude properties from the validation process. I find that the way the `[ValidateNever]` attribute is implemented, however, doesn't make much sense as it forces you to include it in the model class, not on the model parameter, which in my opinion would make more sense.

Automatic validation

In `Chapter 4`, *Controllers and Actions*, we saw how we can register a filter that can be used to trigger automatic model validation—which is already the case when you use `POST`—and perform actions accordingly. Please do take a look at this chapter for more information.

Client-side model validation

Because server-side validation requires a post, sometimes it's more useful and provides a better user experience to perform the validation on the client side. Let's see how we can do this.

All of the built-in validators also include client-side behavior; what this means is that, if you are using jQuery's unobtrusive validation—included by default in the ASP.NET Core templates—you get it automatically. Unobtrusive validation requires the following JavaScript modules:

- jQuery itself (`jquery-xxx.js`): https://jquery.com/
- jQuery validation (`jquery.validate.js`): https://jqueryvalidation.org/
- `jquery.validate.unobtrusive.js`: https://github.com/aspnet/jquery-validation-unobtrusive

The actual filenames may vary slightly (minimized versus normal version or including a version number), but that is all. They are installed by default to `wwwroot\lib\jquery`, `wwwroot\lib\jquery-validation`, and `wwwroot\lib\jquery-validation-unobtrusive`.

Behind the scenes, the included validators add HTML5 attributes (`data-*`) to each property to validate the HTML form elements and, when the form is about to be submitted, force validation to occur. Client-side validation is only performed if it is enabled (more on this in the next topic).

Configuration

Client validation providers are configured through the `AddViewOptions` method, which takes a lambda function that exposes `MvcViewOptions`:

- `ClientModelValidatorProviders` (`IList<IClientModelValidatorProvider>`): The registered client model validators; by default, it contains one `DefaultClientModelValidatorProvider` attribute, one `DataAnnotationsClientModelValidatorProvider` attribute, and one `NumericClientModelValidatorProvider` attribute.
- `HtmlHelperOptions.ClientValidationEnabled` (`bool`): Whether or not client-side validation is enabled. The default is `true`, meaning it is enabled.
- `ValidationMessageElement` (`string`): The HTML element used for inserting the validation error messages for each validated property. The default is `span`.
- `ValidationSummaryMessageElement` (`string`): The HTML element used for inserting the validation error messages summary for the model. The default is `span`.

The included `IClientModelValidatorProvider` attributes have the following purposes:

- `DefaultClientModelValidatorProvider`: If the validation attribute implements `IClientModelValidator`, it uses it for the validation, regardless of having a specific client model validator provider.
- `NumericClientModelValidatorProvider`: Restricts text boxes to only contain numeric values.

- `DataAnnotationsClientModelValidatorProvider`: **Adds support for** all the included data annotations validators.

Custom validation

You can certainly roll out your own client-side validator; the core of it is the `IClientModelValidator` and `IClientModelValidatorProvider` interfaces. Picking up on the `IsEvenAttribute` attribute that we saw earlier, let's see how we can achieve the same validation on the client-side.

First, let's register a **client model validator provider**:

```
services
    .AddMvc()
    .AddViewOptions(options =>
    {
        options.ClientModelValidatorProviders.Add(new
        IsEvenClientModelValidatorProvider());
    });
```

The code for the `IsEvenClientModelValidatorProvider` attribute is as follows:

```
public sealed class IsEvenClientModelValidatorProvider :
IClientModelValidatorProvider
{
    public void CreateValidators(ClientValidatorProviderContext
context)
    {
        if (context.ModelMetadata.ModelType == typeof(string)
            || context.ModelMetadata.ModelType == typeof(int)
            || context.ModelMetadata.ModelType == typeof(uint)
            || context.ModelMetadata.ModelType == typeof(long)
            || context.ModelMetadata.ModelType == typeof(ulong)
            || context.ModelMetadata.ModelType == typeof(short)
            || context.ModelMetadata.ModelType == typeof(ushort)
            || context.ModelMetadata.ModelType == typeof(float)
            || context.ModelMetadata.ModelType == typeof(double))
        {
            if (context.ModelMetadata.ValidatorMetadata.
            OfType<IsEvenAttribute>().Any())
            {
                if (!context.Results.Any(x => x.Validator is
                IsEvenClientModelValidator))
                {
                    context.Results.Add(new ClientValidatorItem
                    {
```

```
                    Validator = new IsEvenClientModelValidator(),
                    IsReusable = true
                });
        }
      }
    }
  }
}
```

This requires some explanation. The `CreateValidators` infrastructure method is called to give the client model validator provider a chance to add custom validators. If the property currently being inspected (`context.ModelMetadata`) is of one of the supported types (`context.ModelMetadata.ModelType`), numbers, or strings—and simultaneously contains an `IsEvenAttribute` attribute and does not contain any `IsEvenClientModelValidator` attributes—we add one to the validators collection (`context.Results`) in the form of `ClientValidatorItem` that contains an `IsEvenClientModelValidator` attribute, which is safe to reuse (`IsReusable`) as it doesn't keep any state.

Now, let's see what the `IsEvenClientModelValidator` attribute looks like:

```
public sealed class IsEvenClientModelValidator : IClientModelValidator
{
    public void AddValidation(ClientModelValidationContext context)
    {
        context.Attributes["data-val"] = true.ToString().
        ToLowerInvariant();
        context.Attributes["data-val-iseven"] = this.GetErrorMessage
        (context);
    }

    private string GetErrorMessage(ClientModelValidationContext
context)
    {
        var attr = context
            .ModelMetadata
            .ValidatorMetadata
            .OfType<IsEvenAttribute>()
            .SingleOrDefault();

        var msg = attr.FormatErrorMessage(context.
        ModelMetadata.PropertyName);

        return msg;
    }
}
```

It works like this:

1. Two attributes are added to the HTML element that is used to edit the model property:
    *   `data-val`: This means the element should be validated.
    *   `data-val-iseven`: The error message to use for the `iseven` rule in case the element is invalid.
2. The error message is retrieved from the `IsEvenAttribute` attribute's `FormatErrorMessage` method. We know there is `IsEvenAttribute`; otherwise, we wouldn't be here.

Finally, we need to add somehow a JavaScript validation code, perhaps in a separate `.js` file:

```javascript
(function ($) {
  var $jQval = $.validator;
  $jQval.addMethod('iseven', function (value, element, params) {
    if (!value) {
      return true;
    }

    value = parseFloat($.trim(value));

    if (!value) {
      return true;
    }

    var isEven = (value % 2) === 0;
      return isEven;
    });

    var adapters = $jQval.unobtrusive.adapters;
    adapters.addBool('iseven');
}) (jQuery);
```

What we are doing here is registering a custom jQuery validation function under the `iseven` name, which, when fired, checks whether the value is empty and tries to convert it into a floating-point number (this works for both integers and floating-point numbers). Finally, it checks whether this value is even or not and returns appropriately. It goes without saying that this validation function is hooked automatically by the unobtrusive validation framework, so you do not need to be worried about it not validating.

The error message is displayed in both the element-specific error message label and in the error message summary if it is present in the view.

You may find the process a bit convoluted, in which case, you will be happy to know that you can add together the validation attribute and the `IClientModelValidator` implementation; it will work just the same and this is possible because of the included `DefaultClientModelValidatorProvider` attribute. It is, however, advisable to separate them because of the **Single Responsibility Principle (SRP)** and the **Separation of Concerns (SoC)**.

In this section, we've seen how to write a custom validator that works on the client side or on the server side. Now, let's see how we can implement an AJAX experience.

Using AJAX for validation

AJAX is a term coined long ago to represent a feature of modern browsers by which asynchronous HTTP requests can be done, via JavaScript or by the browser, without a full page reload.

ASP.NET Core does not offer any support for AJAX, which doesn't mean that you can't use it—it is just the case that you need to do it manually.

The following example uses jQuery to retrieve values in a form and send them to an action method. Make sure the jQuery library is included in either the view file or the layout:

```
<form>
  <fieldset>
    <div><label for="name">Name: </label></div>
    <div><input type="text" name="name" id="name" />
    <div><label for="email">Email: </label></div>
    <div><input type="email" name="email" id="email" />
    <div><label for="gender">Gender: </label></div>
    <div><select name="gender" id="gender">
    <option>Female</option>
    <option>Male</option>
    </select></div>
  </fieldset>
</form>
<script>
```

```
$('#submit').click(function(evt) {
  evt.preventDefault();

  var payload = $('form').serialize();

  $.ajax({
    url: '@Url.Action("Save", "Repository")',
    type: 'POST',
    data: payload,
    success: function (result) {
      //success
    },
    error: function (error) {
      //error
    }
  });
});

</script>
```

This section of JavaScript code does the following things:

- Binds a click event handler to an HTML element with an ID of `submit`.
- Serializes all the `form` elements.
- Creates a `POST` AJAX request to a controller action named `Save` in a controller called `RepositoryController`.
- If the AJAX call succeeds, the `success` function is called; otherwise, an `error` function is called instead.

 The URL to the controller action is generated by the `Action` method. It is important not to have it hardcoded but to instead rely on this HTML helper to return the proper URL.

Let's now see how we can perform validation AJAX-style using a built-in mechanism.

Validation

One of the included validation attributes, `[Remote]`, uses AJAX to perform validation on the server-side transparently. When applied to a property of the model, it takes a controller and an `action` parameter that must refer to an existing controller action:

```
[Remote(action: "CheckEmailExists", controller: "Validation")]
public string Email { get; set; }
```

This controller action must have a structure similar to this one, minus—of course—the parameters to the action:

```
[AcceptVerbs("Get", "Post")]
public IActionResult CheckEmailExists(string email)
{
    if (this._repository.CheckEmailExists(email))
    {
        return this.Json(false);
    }

    return this.Json(true);
}
```

Essentially, it must return a JSON-formatted value of `true` if the validation succeeds or `false`, otherwise.

 This validation can not only be used for a simple property of a primitive type (such as `string`) but also for any POCO class.

Enforcing restrictions

In previous (pre-Core) versions of ASP.NET MVC, there was an attribute, `[AjaxOnly]`, that could be used to restrict an action to only be callable by AJAX. While it is no longer present, it is very easy to bring it back by writing a **resource filter**, as follows:

```
[AttributeUsage(AttributeTargets.Method, AllowMultiple = false,
Inherited = true)]
public sealed class AjaxOnlyAttribute : Attribute, IResourceFilter
{
    public void OnResourceExecuted(ResourceExecutedContext context)
```

```
    {
    }

    public void OnResourceExecuting(ResourceExecutingContext context)
    {
        if (context.HttpContext.Request.Headers["X-Requested-With"]
        != "XMLHttpRequest")
        {
            context.Result = new StatusCodeResult
            ((int)HttpStatusCode.NotFound);
        }
    }
}
```

This attribute implements the **resource filter** interface, IResourceFilter, which will be discussed in Chapter 10, *Understanding Filters*, and basically, what it does is check for the presence of a specific header (X-Requested-With), which is an indication that the current request is being carried out by AJAX if its value is XMLHttpRequest. If not, it sets the response result, thereby short-circuiting any other possible filters. To apply it, just place it next to an action that you want to restrict:

```
[AjaxOnly]
public IActionResult AjaxOnly(Model model) { ... }
```

For an overview of AJAX and the XMLHttpRequest object, please see https://developer.mozilla.org/en/docs/Web/API/XMLHttpRequest.

After this, we move on learning how to return content from AJAX.

Returning content from AJAX

According to the best practices, your AJAX endpoints should return data; in the modern world, when it comes to web apps, this data is normally in the form of JSON. So, you will most likely use the JsonResult class to return contents to the client code. As for sending data to the server, if you use jQuery, it will take care of everything for you and it works. Otherwise, you will need to serialize data to a proper format—perhaps JSON, too. Set the appropriate content-type header and off you go.

Uploading files

File uploading is a process where we send files from our computer to a server—in this case, running ASP.NET Core. File uploading in HTTP requires two things:

- You must use the POST verb.
- The multipart/form-data encoding must be set on the form.

Where ASP.NET Core is concerned, the included model binders know how to bind any posted files to an IFormFile object (or collection of objects). For example, take a form such as the following:

```
@using (Html.BeginForm("SaveForm", "Repository", FormMethod.Post,
    new { enctype = "multipart/form-data" }))
{
    <input type="file" name="file" />
    <input type="submit" value="Save"/>
}
```

You can retrieve the file in an action method such as this one:

```
[HttpPost("[controller]/[action]")]
public IActionResult SaveForm(IFormFile file)
{
  var length = file.Length;
  var name = file.Name;
  //do something with the file
  return this.View();
}
```

However, the HTML file upload specification (https://www.w3.org/TR/2010/WD-html-markup-20101019/input.file.html) also mentions the possibility to submit multiple files at once with the multiple attribute. In that case, you can just declare your parameter as an array of IFormFile instances (a collection will also work):

```
public IActionResult SaveForm(IFormFile[] file) { ... }
```

The IFormFile interface gives you everything you need to manipulate these files:

- ContentType (string): The content type of the posted file
- ContentDisposition (string): The inner content-disposition header containing the HTML input name and selected filename
- Headers (IHeaderDictionary): Any headers sent with the file
- Length (long): The length, in bytes, of the posted file

- `Name` (`string`): The HTML name of the input element that originated the file upload
- `FileName` (`string`): The temporary filename in the filesystem where the posted file was saved

By using `CopyTo` and `CopyToAsync`, you can easily copy the contents of the posted file as arrays of bytes from the `Stream` source to another. `OpenReadStream` allows you to peek into the actual file contents.

The default file upload mechanism makes uses of a temporary file in the filesystem, but you can roll out your mechanism. For additional information, please refer to the following post by Microsoft:

`https://docs.microsoft.com/en-us/aspnet/core/mvc/models/file-uploads`.

Direct access to submitted files

There is also the possibility of directly accessing the `HttpContext.Request.Form.Files` collection. This collection is prototyped as `IFormFileCollection` and it exposes a collection of `IFormFile`.

This concludes this chapter on how to work with files. Most complex applications will need this somewhere, so it's useful to have this knowledge.

Summary

This chapter dealt with data coming from the user and data that, because of that, needs to be validated; otherwise, it would be possible to submit invalid information, even if improperly formatted. After reading through this chapter, you should be able to design a form to receive complex data structures as well as validate them.

For validation, you should probably stick to data annotations attributes and `IValidatableObject` implementations, if need be. These are used in a plethora of other .NET APIs and are pretty much the standard for validation.

It would be good to implement client-side validation and AJAX as it provides a much better user experience, but never forget to also validate on the server side!

There is probably no need for custom model binders as the included ones seem to cover most cases.

Display and editor templates are very handy, so you should try to use them as it may reduce the code you need to add every time, especially if you want to reuse it.

In this chapter, we've seen how we can work with models, produce HTML for them—including with templates—validate it on the frontend and backend, see the validation error messages, and bind your model to and from HTML form elements.

In the next chapter, we will talk about a whole different subject—Razor Pages!

Questions

You should be able to answer these questions, with the answers in the *Assessments* section:

1. What is the default validation provider?
2. What do we call the methods used to render HTML fields?
3. What is model metadata?
4. Does ASP.NET Core support client-side validation?
5. What is the base interface that can be bound to an uploaded file?
6. What is unobtrusive validation?
7. How can we perform server-side validation?

7
Implementing Razor Pages

This chapter covers Razor Pages, a functionality introduced in ASP.NET Core 2.0, which provides a simplified development model that does not use controllers.

By studying this chapter, we will be able to develop dynamic websites that are driven by data.

We will talk about the following:

- Assets search order
- Working with the page model
- The commonality in Razor views
- Enforcing security

Technical requirements

To implement the examples introduced in this chapter, you will need the .NET Core 3 SDK and a text editor. Of course, Visual Studio 2019 (any edition) meets all of the requirements, but you can also use Visual Studio Code, for example.

The source code can be retrieved from GitHub
here: `https://github.com/PacktPublishing/Modern-Web-Development-with-ASP.NET-Core-3-Second-Edition`

Getting started

Razor Pages was introduced in ASP.NET Core 2.0, and they follow a totally different approach from the rest of ASP.NET Core. Instead of the MVC pattern, Razor pages are self-contained files, similar to XAML controls or ASP.NET Web Forms, because they can also have a code-behind file. There is no longer a controller/view separation, as Razor pages have all they need in a single file although we can also specify a class for them.

To use Razor Pages, you need a compatible Visual Studio version, starting from 2017 Update 3, plus you need to have ASP.NET Core 2.0 or higher installed:

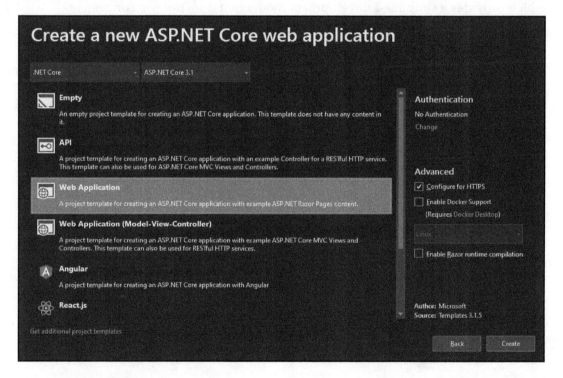

Razor Pages is physically stored in the filesystem, underneath a `Pages` folder (this is by convention), and the pages should have the same `.cshtml` extension as regular Razor views. What differentiates them is the new `@page` directive. This is shown with the following code:

```
@page
@model HelloWorldModel
<!DOCTYPE html>
```

```
<html>
  <head><title>Hello World</title></head>
  <body>
    <h1>@Html.Raw("Hello, World!")</h1>
  </body>
</html>
```

Adding an @page directive (preferably as the first line) automatically turns the .cshtml file into a Razor page. There is no need to reference any specific NuGet package or perform any configuration because it is enabled by default.

Accessing a Razor page is straightforward; as no routing is involved, they can be called directly, without the .cshtml extension:

- /HelloWorld
- /Admin/Settings

The only requirement is that the pages are located somewhere inside the Pages root folder. The Index.cshtml file is served by default, meaning if one such file is located inside a Pages\Admin folder, it is served without having to be explicitly requested; /Admin will serve the \Pages\Admin\Index.cshtml file.

For routing to a Razor page, you need to explicitly enable it using the new endpoint routing mechanism:

```
app.UseEndpoints(endpoints =>
{
    endpoints.MapRazorPages();
});
```

You can even use the new RequireHost extension method to ensure that Razor pages are only accessible when using certain host headers or ports. Don't forget to also register the services needed for it:

```
services.AddRazorPages();
```

 Leave the Pages prefix and the .cshtml extension out; they cannot be used in the request. Also, Razor pages cannot start with an underscore (_).

Let's begin with the assets search order to understand how Razor pages are located.

Assets search order

Razor Pages assets (`.cshtml` files) will be searched in the following folders and order:

- Current folder inside `Pages`
- `/Pages/Shared/`
- `/Views/Shared/`

This means that the view name, as requested by the user, or layout, will be looked for first in the current folder (as per the request's path), then in the `/Pages/Shared` folder, and lastly in `/Views/Shared`—all relative to the root folder of the application.

So, after learning the basics, let's jump into the page model, a very important concept.

Working with the page model

You can use the exact same syntax as you would with a Razor view, but there's something more; a Razor page inherently has a `PageModel` class associated with it—notice the `@model` directive pointing to `HelloWorldModel`. This class must inherit from `PageModel`, and in it, you can define methods for handling HTTP methods, such as `GET` or `POST`. The file containing the definition of the page model class must have the same physical name as the Razor page with a `.cs` extension, be located in the same folder, and inherit from `PageModel`. So, for example, if the previous file was named `HelloWorld.cshtml`, then its page model would go in a `HelloWorld.cshtml.cs` file:

```
public class HelloWorldModel : PageModel
{
}
```

If you do not wish to specify a custom page model class, one is provided for you automatically, and you can still specify handler methods directly in the `.cshtml` file:

```
@functions
{
    public async Task<IActionResult> OnGetAsync()
    {
        if (!this.User.Identity.IsAuthenticated)
        {
```

```
            return this.RedirectToAction(actionName: "Login",
            controllerName: "Account");
        }

        return this.Page();
    }
}
```

Consider the following properties that, for example, you might declare in the `PageModel`-derived class:

```
public string Message { get; set; }

public void OnGet()
{
    this.Message = "Hello, World!";
}
```

These can then be used in the `.cshtml` file:

```
<p>Message: @Model.Message</p>
```

You can even have the class declared there:

```
@page
@model IndexModel
@functions
{
    public class IndexModel : PageModel
    {
        public async Task<IActionResult> OnGetAsync()
        {
            //whatever
        }
    }
}
```

The `PageModel` class offers the following properties:

- `HttpContext` (`HttpContext`): The usual context
- `ModelState` (`ModelStateDictionary`): The model state, filled from all of the value providers
- `PageContext` (`PageContext`): Offers access to the current handler method (if any), plus the value provider and view start factory collections
- `Request` (`HttpRequest`): The same value as `HttpContext.Request`, the request object

- Response (HttpResponse from HttpContext.Response): The response object
- RouteData (RouteData): The route data, not normally needed
- TempData (ITempDataDictionary): Temporary data
- Url (IUrlHelper): Used for generating URLs that point to route actions, for exampleUser (ClaimsPrincipal coming from HttpContext.User): The current user, as determined by the authentication mechanism in use
- ViewData (ViewDataDictionary): The view bag, as introduced in Chapter 4, *Controllers and Actions*

This is the general information about the page model—let's now see each of these features in detail; so, first, let's see how to implement a page handler.

Understanding page handlers

The HTTP method handlers can have several signatures:

- The name must start with On and be followed by the HTTP method name (Get, Post, Put, Delete, and so on).
- The return type must either be void or IActionResult.
- If we are to use the asynchronous version, the method must either return Task or Task<IActionResult> and optionally have the async keyword applied to it, and it should end with the Async suffix.
- They can either take parameters (basic types with default values or complex types), no parameters at all, or an IFormCollection parameter.

You can now add methods for handling requests, either synchronously, as shown here:

```
public IActionResult OnGet()
{
    if (this.HttpContext.Request.Headers["HTTP-
    Referer"].SingleOrDefault().Contains("google.com") == true)
    {
        //hey, someone found us through Google!
    }

    return this.Page();
}
```

Or these can handle requests asynchronously:

```
public async Task<IActionResult> OnGetAsync()
{
    //...
    return this.Page();
}
```

 You cannot have both a synchronous and an asynchronous handler method or multiple overloads for the same HTTP verb, as it will result in a runtime error.

You can even have custom handlers, which do not follow these patterns. A few ways to achieve that are as follows:

- Pass a `handler` parameter in the query string, for example, `?handler=MyHandler`.
- Pass the `handler` parameter in the route instead, for example, `@page "{handler?}"`.
- In the `<form>`, `<input>`, or `<button>` tags, set an `asp-page-handler` attribute, for example, `asp-page-handler="MyHandler"` (this uses the tag handler functionality).

This way, you can have a method such as the following:

```
public async Task<IActionResult> OnPostMyHandlerAsync() { ... }
```

Regardless of the name you give it, you will always have the `On` prefix and the `Async` suffix, if it is an asynchronous handler.

If you want to have your page post to multiple handlers, depending on what is clicked, it's easy:

```
<form method="post">
    <input type="submit" value="One Handler" asp-page-handler="One" />
    <input type="submit" value="Another Handler" asp-page-handler="Two" />
</form>
```

For this to work, both buttons must be inside a form with a `POST` method and the default tag helpers must be registered in `_ViewImports.cshtml`:

```
@addTagHelper *, Microsoft.AspNetCore.Mvc.TagHelpers
```

The handler's names must follow the convention. For this example, you can have them as the following:

```
public void OnPostOne() { ... }

public async Task<IActionResult> OnPostTwoAsync() { ... }
```

This is just an example—they can be asynchronous or not, and return values or not too. Inside they can perform tasks such as redirection by returning `IActionResult`:

```
public async Task<IActionResult> OnPostTwoAsync()
{
    return this.RedirectToPage("/Pages/Success");
}
```

Not all action results make sense though; for example, it doesn't make sense to return `ViewResult`, as Razor Pages does not execute in the context of a controller. If this is not required, you do not even need to return `IActionResult`:

```
public void OnGet()
{
    //initialize everything
}
```

And these can be used as helpers for returning `IActionResults`, in pretty much the same way as the `ControllerBase` and `Controller` classes:

- Challenge (`ChallengeResult`)
- Content (`ContentResult`)
- File (`FileContentResult`, `FileStreamResult`, `VirtualFileResult`)
- Forbid (`ForbidResult`)
- LocalRedirect (`LocalRedirectResult`)
- LocalRedirectPermanent (`LocalRedirectResult`)
- LocalRedirectPermanentPreserveMethod (`LocalRedirectResult`)
- LocalRedirectPreserveMethod (`LocalRedirectResult`)
- NotFound (`NotFoundResult`, `NotFoundObjectResult`)
- Page (`PageResult`)
- PhysicalFile (`PhysicalFileResult`)
- Redirect (`RedirectResult`)
- RedirectPermanent (`RedirectResult`)
- RedirectPermanentPreserveMethod (`RedirectResult`)

- RedirectPreserveMethod (RedirectResult)
- RedirectToAction (RedirectToActionResult)
- RedirectToActionPermanent (RedirectToActionResult)
- RedirectToActionPermanentPreserveMethod (RedirectToActionResult)
- RedirectToActionPreserveMethod (RedirectToActionResult)
- RedirectToPage (RedirectToPageResult)
- RedirectToPagePermanent (RedirectToPageResult)
- RedirectToPagePermanentPreserveMethod (RedirectToPageResult)
- RedirectToPagePreserveMethod (RedirectToPageResult)
- RedirectToRoute (RedirectToRouteResult)
- RedirectToRoutePermanent (RedirectToRouteResult)
- RedirectToRoutePermanentPreserveMethod (RedirectToRouteResult)
- RedirectToRoutePreserveMethod (RedirectToRouteResult)
- SignIn (SignInResult)
- SignOut (SignOutResult)
- StatusCode (StatusCodeResult, ObjectResult)
- Unauthorized (UnauthorizedResult)

Some of these methods offer overloads, and each of these can return different result types.

Finally, if you want, you can pass parameters to your handlers:

```
<input type="submit" value="Third Handler" asp-page-handler="Three"
asp-route-foo="bar" />
```

Just declare a parameter on the handler:

```
public void OnPostThree(string foo)
{
    //do something with the value of foo
}
```

Having seen how a page handler can be implemented, let's see now how we can bind a request to a class model.

Doing model binding

If you declare a property in the page model class (or in a @functions block, for that matter) and decorate it with a [BindProperty] attribute, it will be bound automatically, using the same rules (binding source providers and binding attributes) as described in the previous chapter:

```
[BindProperty]
public Order Order { get; set; }
```

You will then be able to access and change any of its properties, perhaps in an HTTP handler method. You can also supply your own binder through the BinderType property. BindProperty can also bind on GET calls if its SupportsGet property is set to true.

If you prefer, you can also apply the [BindProperties] attribute to the whole class, and all of its properties will be automatically bound:

```
[BindProperties]
public class Model
{
    public int OneProperty { get; set; }
    public string AnotherProperty { get; set; }
}
```

 Do notice that properties bound this way will only be so for non-GET calls (typically POST) unless you set its SupportsGet property (both [BindProperty] and [BindProperties] have SupportsGet). It works pretty much the same as [ModelBinder], but the latter never binds on GET requests.

Also, similarly to controller actions, parameters in HTTP handler methods are automatically bound:

```
public void OnGet(int? id = null)
{
    //?id=1212
}
```

You can opt for not declaring a model as part of the handler method signature but instead update it dynamically:

```
public void OnPost()
{
    var model = new OrderModel();
    this.TryUpdateModel(model);
}
```

A possible reason for this would be that the same page handles different requests and, consequently, different models.

Now that we've seen how to turn a request into a class, it's time to learn how to validate it!

Doing model validation

Model validation also works in pretty much the same way as in controllers:

```
public IActionResult OnPost()
{
    var model = new OrderModel();

    this.TryUpdateModel(model);

    if (this.TryValidateModel(model))
    {
        return this.RedirectToPage("/Pages/Error");
    }

    return this.Page();
}
```

Similarly to controllers, the `ModelState` property also keeps track of all injected values and their validation state.

Maintaining state

All of the usual ways to persist data apply also to Razor Pages, so there is nothing specific worth mentioning here.

Using view layouts

Razor Pages can use the same layout functionality as views, but you are advised to keep your layout pages outside the `Views\Shared` folder, as this is reserved for views.

Using partial views

Like view layouts, partial views are also supported in exactly the same way.

Let's see now how areas are supported.

Using areas

As of ASP.NET Core 2.1, Razor Pages also supports areas. Areas are a way to physically separate modules inside our application, in folders. This just means that Razor Pages can be addressed inside these folders, as in these examples:

- `/Admin/Index`
- `/HR/Index`
- `/Orders/Index`

Notice that these folders must be created below an `Areas` folder on the root of the project, like this:

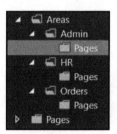

And inside each named area, we must create a `Pages` folder. Inside of it, you can put whatever you like, such as `.cshtml` files, `_ViewStart.cshml`, and many others. Areas are enabled by default.

It's time to mention the special files that exist for Razor views and Razor Pages.

Special files

The _ViewStart.cshtml and _ViewImports.cshtml files are respected by Razor Pages and treated in the same way as for regular Razor views, that is, they are called before the actual page. They also work in areas too, meaning you can have different files, one per each area.

Next, let's discuss filters.

Using filters

Razor Pages works with any filters except action filters—these will not be triggered, as you don't have actions. There is also a new filter, IPageFilter, with an asynchronous version as well, IAsyncPageFilter. I already talked about them in the Using filters section, so I won't repeat myself here.

Dependency injection, as we will see next, is also supported.

Using dependency injection

You can have dependencies injected in the constructor of your page model class in the usual way:

```
public class HelloWorldModel : PageModel
{
    public HelloWorldModel(IMyService svc)
    {
        //yes, dependency injection in the constructor also works!
    }
}
```

If you decorate a property in your custom page model with [FromServices], it will be honored, and the property will have its value set from the dependency injection framework, from its declared type.

You can also use the @inject directive, in the same way as you would in a Razor view.

Now, we will see how we can configure Razor Pages specific options.

Configuring options

The `AddRazorPagesOptions` extension method can be called subsequently to `AddMvc` so that we can configure some of the options of Razor Pages:

```
services
    .AddMvc()
    .AddRazorPagesOptions(options =>
    {
        options.RootDirectory = "/Pages";
    });
```

The `RazorPagesOptions` class offers the following properties:

- `AllowAreas` (`bool`): Whether or not areas should be allowed—the default is `false`
- `AllowMappingHeadRequestsToGetHandler` (`bool`): Whether or not `HEAD` requests will be turned into `GET` requests if the Razor page (or it's model) does not provide a handler for `HEAD`—the default is `false`
- `Conventions` (`IList<IApplicationModelConvention>`): The conventions to use—this will be discussed in a future chapter
- `RootDirectory` (`string`): The root directory, relative to the application root, which is normally set to `/Pages`

In addition, there are a few extension methods that are configured through `RazorPagesOptions`, and basically, add one or more conventions:

- `AllowAnonymousToFolder`: Allows anonymous requests to all pages under a specific folder
- `AllowAnonymousToPage`: Allows anonymous requests for a given page
- `AuthorizeFolder`: Defines an authorization policy for all pages under a specific folder (this will be discussed in more depth in `Chapter 11`, *Security*)
- `AuthorizePage`: Defines an authorization policy for a specific page
- `ConfigureFilter`: Allows the configuration (adding and removing) of global filters

Check out the following example:

```
services
    .AddMvc()
    .AddRazorPagesOptions(options =>
```

```
    {
        options.Conventions.AllowAnonymousToPage("/Pages/HelloWorld");
    });
```

Page routes are a specific kind of configuration that we will see next.

Understanding page routes

Besides calling Razor pages directly, you can also have them answer to routes. There is a new `AddPageRoute` extension method for `RazorPagesOptions` that you can leverage to add friendly routes to your pages:

```
services
    .AddMvc()
    .AddRazorPagesOptions(options =>
    {
        options.Conventions.AddPageRoute("/Order",
"My/Order/{id:int}");
    });
```

Interestingly, we can see that Razor Pages depends on the MVC framework somehow.

The parameters to `AddPageRoute` are as follows:

- pageName (`string`): The name of a page to direct to, starting with /, and without the `.cshtml` suffix
- route (`string`): A regular route, with possible some route or query string parameters

In the view, you can then access any route or query string parameters using `HttpContext.RouteData` or `HttpContext.Request.Query`.

Interestingly, here's how you set a page (`/HelloWorld`) to be your default one:

```
.AddRazorPagesOptions(options =>
{
    options.Conventions.AddPageRoute("/HelloWorld", "");
});
```

Moreover, you can have your Razor page to listen to a specific route, by adding a route template parameter to the `page` directive:

```
@page "{id:int}"
```

In this case, if the Razor page is called without the id parameter, which must also be of the int type, it will not be found and an HTTP **404** error will be returned instead.

Next up, how to enforce security rules in Razor Pages.

Enforcing security

There are essentially two ways by which we can enforce security rules over Razor Pages:

- By applying the [Authorize] attribute to page models or page handlers
- By defining conventions

Let's start with the attribute approach.

Using the [Authorize] attribute

It's simple for a whole page:

```
[Authorize]
public class AdminIndexModel: PageModel
{
}
```

Or you can also use it for a single handler:

```
public class AdminIndexModel: PageModel
{
    [Authorize]
    public void OnGet() { ... }
}
```

And now, let's move on to conventions.

Conventions

Using the `AddRazorPagesOptions` extension method, we can control how security can be applied to one or more pages or folders. The available methods are the following:

- `AllowAnonymousToPage`: Grants anonymous access to a single page
- `AllowAnonymousToFolder`: Grants anonymous access to all pages underneath a given folder
- `AuthorizePage`: Defines an authorization policy for a page
- `AuthorizeFolder`: Defines an authorization policy for all pages underneath a folder

Here's an example:

```
services
    .AddMvc()
    .AddRazorPagesOptions(options =>
    {
        //adds an AuthorizeAttribute with a named Policy property
        options.Conventions.AuthorizePage("/ShoppingBag",
        "Authenticated");
        //adds an AuthorizeAttribute
        options.Conventions.AuthorizeFolder("/Products");
        //adds an AllowAnonymousAttribute
        options.Conventions.AllowAnonymousToPage("/Login");
        options.Conventions.AllowAnonymousToFolder("/Images");
    });
```

Here, we are making sure the `"/ShoppingBag"` endpoint is only available for the `"Authenticated"` policy and ensuring that whoever tries to access `"/Products"` needs to be authorized. Lastly, both `"/Login"` and `"/Images"` URLs are available for anyone, including anonymous users.

And now, what can we learn about XSS attacks?

Cross-site request scripting

Razor Pages on the server, by default, checks for **Cross-Site Request Scripting (XSS)** attacks. If you want to use AJAX with Razor Pages, make sure you include the anti-forgery token in your page and send the header in each AJAX request, as described in `Chapter 11`, *Security*, in the *Anti-forgery protection* section.

Summary

First, choosing between regular views and Razor Pages is a decision that should be made upfront—they're just too different. Having controllers and views may be more appealing to people who have worked with MVC before, and I'd say it can result in better coupling and organization, but Razor Pages is just so easy to use—no server-side code and no recompilation (if the page model is not used) are required.

Keep on using partial views and view layouts as they are a good mechanism to improve reusability.

The same security concerns apply to Razor Pages as they do to controller actions. It might be better to prefer conventions over attributes, as we have a central location where the security information is stored.

In this chapter, we were introduced to the new Razor Pages feature of ASP.NET Core 2, which, although different from the ordinary views, shares quite a bit of functionality. It can be used for simpler solutions, without all of the hassle of controllers and actions.

In the next chapter, we shall see how we can extract information about what is happening inside ASP.NET Core.

Questions

You should now be able to answer the following questions:

1. Do Razor pages use code-behind?
2. What is the purpose of the page model?
3. What are page handlers?
4. How can we restrict a Razor page from being called by anonymous users?
5. What are the two ways by which we can inject services into a Razor page?
6. Do Razor pages use page layouts?
7. Where are Razor pages served by default?

8
API Controllers

This chapter introduces API controllers. An API controller is just an MVC controller that doesn't return a UI but instead works with requests and payloads and returns responses in machine-readable formats, such as JSON or XML. We will cover a number of aspects related to API controllers, from security to versioning.

The following topics will be covered in this chapter:

- Introduction to REST
- Model binding
- Authorizing access to resources
- Applying OpenAPI conventions
- Returning validation results
- Performing content negotiation
- Handling errors
- Understanding API versioning
- Generating API documentation
- Serving OData

By the end of this chapter, we will be able to work with authentication and validation overall, without much human interaction.

Technical requirements

In order to implement the examples introduced in this chapter, you will need the .NET Core 3 SDK and a text editor. Of course, Visual Studio 2019 (any edition) meets all the requirements, but you can also use Visual Studio Code, for example.

The source code for this chapter can be retrieved from GitHub from `https://github.com/PacktPublishing/Modern-Web-Development-with-ASP.NET-Core-3-Second-Edition`.

Getting started with web APIs

Not all actions are meant to return HTML (such as views). Some return content is only suitable for non-human processing, such as some client APIs. In this case, other content is more suitable than HTML—namely, a **presentation** language, such as JSON or XML. Sometimes, it is only necessary to return an HTTP status code or some response headers. In the past, this was done with APIs outside the ASP.NET MVC, such as with Microsoft's **ASP.NET Web API** (https://www.asp.net/web-api), **Nancy** (http://nancyfx.org), or **ServiceStack** (https://servicestack.net).

Let's look at the ASP.NET web API. It shared quite a few concepts and similarly named (and purposed) APIs with MVC, but it was an entirely different project that used different assemblies and a different bootstrap mechanism such as **Open Web Interface for .NET (OWIN)**. Unsurprisingly, Microsoft made the decision with ASP.NET Core to unify the MVC and web API; now, there is no more web API, just the MVC. All of the API's features can be found on the MVC, however.

There is a concept called **Representational State Transfer (REST)**, which is the *de facto* standard for writing web services and APIs that embrace HTTP in its entirety, including its verbs, headers, and URLs. ASP.NET Core allows us to write web services that comply with what REST proposes.

API controllers differ from non-API controllers because the former does not return a UI—HTML or otherwise—but rather, consumes and returns data. This data is essentially machine-readable and uses enterprise-standard formats, such as XML and JSON. Sometimes, it is possible to negotiate what the acceptable and returned protocols are. In any case, whenever data is received, it should be validated.

The API features of ASP.NET Core build on the MVC functionality, but it does not need all of the functionality. it. So, you may need to add the MVC functionality, as follows:

```
services.AddMvc();
```

Alternatively, you could use just the bare minimum for the API, which may be enough for your needs and uses less memory:

```
services.AddControllers();
```

Now that we've learned a bit about the basics, let's delve further into REST.

Understanding REST

REST is a style—rather than an architectural pattern—that prescribes the use of meaningful URLs and HTTP verbs.

Verbs represent operations. Take the following, for example:

HTTP verb	Meaning
GET	Reads
PUT	Updates or replaces
POST	Creates
PATCH	Partially updates
DELETE	Deletes

As you can see, this resembles what we have in the ASP.NET MVC, but HTML forms only use POST and GET.

URLs, on the other hand, expose entities and identifiers. Take the following examples:

- http://store.com/products/1
- http://profile.net/users/rjperes
- http://search.pt/term/rest+api

All of these URLs have a different meaning; if, for example, each URL is called using a GET verb, it should return results and cause no side effects. For POST, new records should be created. PUT updates an existing record and DELETE removes the underlying record.

As you can imagine, the actual content that is required for POST, PUT, and PATCH cannot always be sent through the URL; if the content is complex, they need to be sent as payloads. GET and DELETE normally do not take complex parameters.

REST is particularly useful for creating **Create, Retrieve, Update, and Delete (CRUD)**-style applications. These are applications used for the addition of records, such as blog posts.

Finally, HTTP status codes represent the outcome of operations, such as the following:

- 200 OK: An entity/entities was/were successfully retrieved.
- 201 Created: An entity was successfully created.

- 202 `Accepted`: An entity was accepted to be deleted or updated.
- 204 `No Content`: A request was processed successfully but did not return any content.
- 404 `Not Found`: The requested entity does not exist.
- 409 `Conflict`: The entity to save conflicts with the persisted version.
- 422 `Unprocessable Entity`: The entity failed to validate.
- 501 `Bad Request`: A bad request was issued.

 For more information about the REST and RESTful APIs, please read `https://searchmicroservices.techtarget.com/definition/RESTful-API`.

In this section, we've learned about REST, which is essentially a consent mechanism. Let's now look at ASP.NET Core—specifically, how we turn a request into a .NET class.

Model binding

Normally, when using a REST API, we use either `POST`, `PUT`, or sometimes even `PATCH` verbs to send content as payloads. This content is then translated into POCO classes, which are defined as parameters to action methods.

It turns out that ASP.NET Core can bind payloads to POCOs if you bind from the body of the request or from the query string, but you cannot exclude (or include) specific properties using the `[Bind]`, `[BindNever]`, and `[BindRequired]` attributes. A typical example is as follows:

```
[ApiController]
public class PetController : ControllerBase
{
    [HttpPost]
    public IActionResult Post([FromBody] Pet pet) { ... }
}
```

This is because ASP.NET Core uses input formatters to bind requests to models, and since these can change, it's up to them to decide what properties should be skipped or not—for example, a certain JSON serializer might use some attributes to configure property serialization, which would be ignored by others.

Authorizing access to resources

While forms normally use username and password pairs to enforce authentication, that is not normally the case with APIs. However, the concepts of both authentication and authorization apply, too; authorization is ensured by means of roles, claims, or custom rules, but authentication is usually achieved through **JSON Web Tokens (JWTs)**. JWTs are similar to cookies, but cookies are stored in the browser and web APIs are not usually called by a browser but by an API client. ASP.NET Core offers a mechanism for checking both the authentication of a request and for checking that the requester is entitled to do what it wants to do. Explaining how to do this is the purpose of this chapter.

Using JWTs

JWTs are open-standard—defined in RFC 7519—securely representing claims between two connecting parties using HTTP for communication. The spec is available at `https://tools.ietf.org/html/rfc7519`.

Using JWTs is similar to using cookies for authentication, but cookies are usually associated with human interaction, whereas JWTs are more common in machine-to-machine scenarios, such as web services. Using cookies requires a cookie container that can hold them and send them upon each request—normally, the browser does this for us. However, with web APIs, the request is not often made by a browser.

Let's have a look at a full example. Before we delve into the code, make sure you add the `Microsoft.AspNetCore.Authentication.JwtBearer` NuGet package to the code.

Let's see how we can generate a token by looking at a simple `GenerateToken` method that, for example, generates a token for a given username:

```
private string GenerateToken(string username)
{
    var claims = new Claim[]
        {
            new Claim(ClaimTypes.Name, username),
            new Claim(JwtRegisteredClaimNames.Nbf,
                new
DateTimeOffset(DateTime.UtcNow).ToUnixTimeSeconds()
                .ToString()),
            new Claim(JwtRegisteredClaimNames.Exp,
                new DateTimeOffset(DateTime.UtcNow.AddDays(1))
```

```
                .ToUnixTimeSeconds().ToString()),
        };

    var token = new JwtSecurityToken(
        new JwtHeader(new SigningCredentials(
            new SymmetricSecurityKey(Encoding.UTF8.GetBytes("<at-
least-16-
            character-secret-key>")),
            SecurityAlgorithms.HmacSha256)),
        new JwtPayload(claims));

    return new JwtSecurityTokenHandler().WriteToken(token);
}
```

This code allows anyone with a valid username/password pair to request a JWT that lasts for 1 day (`DateTime.UtcNow.AddDays(1)`). The secret key (`<at-least-16-character-secret-key>`), of course, can be generate from configuration and should not really be hardcoded.

Now, to set up the authentication, we need to go to `ConfigureServices`; this is how it looks in ASP.NET Core 2.x and higher:

```
services
    .AddAuthentication(options =>
    {
        options.DefaultAuthenticateScheme = JwtBearerDefaults.
        AuthenticationScheme;
        options.DefaultChallengeScheme = JwtBearerDefaults.
        AuthenticationScheme;
    })
    .AddJwtBearer(JwtBearerDefaults.AuthenticationScheme, options =>
    {
        options.TokenValidationParameters = new
TokenValidationParameters
        {
            ValidateAudience = false,
            ValidateIssuer = false,
            ValidateIssuerSigningKey = true,
            IssuerSigningKey = new SymmetricSecurityKey(
                Encoding.UTF8.GetBytes("<at-least-16-character
                -secret-key>")),
            ValidateLifetime = true,
            ClockSkew = TimeSpan.FromMinutes(5)
        };
    });
```

`ClockSkew` allows differences in clock synchronization between the server and any clients connected to it. In this case, we are allowing a 5-minute tolerance, which means clients whose token has expired by less than 5 minutes will still be accepted. This needs to go in `Configure` to add the authentication middleware to the pipeline:

```
app.UseAuthentication();
```

Now, any requests for action methods with the `[Authorize]` attribute will be checked for the JWT and will only be accepted if it is valid. To make sure this happens, you need to send the authorization token with all requests (including AJAX calls); this is the `Authorization` header and it looks like this:

```
Authorization: Bearer <my-long-jwt-authorization-token>
```

The `<my-long-jwt-authorization-token>` value is the one produced from the `GenerateToken` method shown earlier.

You can play around with and generate valid JWT tokens using a number of public sites, such as `https://jwt.io`. Of course, you need to find a way to store the token for the duration of the request (HTML local storage, for example—see `https://developer.mozilla.org/en-US/docs/Web/API/Window/localStorage` for more information). If the token is tampered with or its timeout is reached, you will get an authorization error.

If you wish, you can instruct ASP.NET Core to use a different authentication validation provider—for example, you can have both cookie- and JWT-based authorization providers. You only need to use the `AuthenticationSchemes` property of the `[Authorize]` attribute, as follows, for JWT:

```
[Authorize(AuthenticationSchemes =
JwtBearerDefaults.AuthenticationScheme)]
```

The following can be used to use cookies:

```
[Authorize(AuthenticationSchemes =
CookieAuthenticationDefaults.AuthenticationScheme)]
```

You can mix different authentication schemes on the same ASP.NET Core app.

Now that we've finished with authentication, let's look at the mechanism that Visual Studio offers for enforcing REST conventions.

Applying OpenAPI REST conventions

ASP.NET Core 2.2 introduced API web analyzers to Visual Studio. These analyzers are used to enforce REST conventions. Simply put, we state that an assembly or class should follow some convention; Visual Studio then checks whether its methods declare—for the purpose of OpenAPI (Swagger)—the proper response types and status codes and offers to fix this by adding the correct attributes if needed. This is purely a design-time feature, not something that you code, for a change.

The `Microsoft.AspNetCore.Mvc.Api.Analyzers` NuGet package includes some standard conventions for REST APIs in the form of the `DefaultApiConventions` class. If we want to ensure that all types in the current assembly follow these conventions, we apply the following attribute at the assembly level:

```
[assembly: ApiConventionType(typeof(DefaultApiConventions))]
```

If we only want to do this at a class level, we take out the `assembly` modifier and instead apply it to a class, usually a controller, as follows:

```
[ApiConventionType(typeof(DefaultApiConventions))]
public class PerController : ControllerBase { }
```

Alternatively, we can do so at a method level:

```
[ApiConventionMethod(typeof(DefaultApiConventions),
nameof(DefaultApiConventions.Put))]
[HttpPut("{id}")]
public async Task<ActionResult<Pet>> PutPet(int id, Pet pet) { ... }
```

Note that in this case, we are specifying the name of the method (`Put`) that holds the conventions that we want to use for this method. In all the other cases, Visual Studio looks for hints at the convention methods, specified as attributes, which it uses to match the methods in the current context.

The `DefaultApiConventions` class has conventions for the following kinds of methods (same as the HTTP verbs):

- `Get` or `Find`
- `Post` or `Create`
- `Put`, `Edit`, or `Update`
- `Delete`

For each of these, Visual Studio offers to add appropriate status code (`[ProducesResponseType]`) attributes. So, it goes like this:

Method	Commands
GET	200 OK: Content was found and is returned with success. 404 Not Found: Content was not found.
POST	201 Created: Content was created successfully. 400 Bad Request: Bad or invalid request issued.
PUT	204 No Content: No content issued. 404 Not Found: The content to be updated was not found.400 Bad Request: Bad or invalid request issued.
DELETE	200 OK: Content deleted successfully. 404 Not Found: Content was not found.400 Bad Request: Bad or invalid request issued.

The following is an example of using Visual Studio to add response types that are missing for a method that matches the GET convention:

It is possible to roll out our own conventions, but these are the default ones for REST APIs, so we should probably stick to them. If you wish to learn more about this, please have a look at https://docs.microsoft.com/en-us/aspnet/core/web-api/advanced/conventions.

Returning validation results

Before ASP.NET 2.1, you would need to explicitly look at the model validation result—for example, by inspecting ModelState.IsValid—and act accordingly, returning, for example, BadRequestResult. Since then, for any controllers that feature the [ApiController] attribute, ASP.NET Core will add an action filter called ModelStateInvalidFilter, which, before an action method is actually run, inspects the model for validity and returns BadRequestResult for us. The pseudocode looks as follows:

```
public void OnActionExecuting(ActionExecutingContext context)
{
    if (!context.ModelState.IsValid)
    {
        context.Result = new
BadRequestObjectResult(context.ModelState);
    }
}
```

The response sent to the client includes the model validation errors and, by default, a special content type of `application/problem+json`. We will discuss this in greater detail when we talk about error handling later in this chapter.

You can disable this behavior completely by setting a value of `false` to the `ApiBehaviorOptions.SuppressModelStateInvalidFilter` property:

```
services.Configure<ApiBehaviorOptions>(options =>
{
    options.SuppressModelStateInvalidFilter = true;
});
```

You can just hide the validation details, which can be useful from a security point of view:

```
options.SuppressUseValidationProblemDetailsForInvalidModelStateRespons
es = true;
```

Yet another option is to explicitly state how a model validation error will be translated to a response. The `ApiBehaviorOptions` class offers a property called `InvalidModelStateResponseFactory`, delegated just for this purpose. This takes `ActionContext` as its sole parameter, from which we can inspect `ModelState`, as well as other possibly useful properties. The following code sample shows how we can return a different result depending on the number of model validation errors:

```
options.InvalidModelStateResponseFactory = (ctx) =>
{
    if (ctx.ModelState.ErrorCount > 1)
    {
        return new JsonResult(new { Errors = ctx.ModelState.ErrorCount
});
    }
    return new BadRequestObjectResult(ctx.ModelState);
};
```

In this example, if the error count is greater than 1, we return a JSON result; otherwise, we fall back to the default bad request.

Now, let's see how content negotiation works when requested by a client.

Performing content negotiation

Content negotiation is the process by which the application returns data in a format that is requested by the client. This is usually done for API-style invocations, not requests that serve HTML. For example, a certain client might want data returned in JSON format, while others might prefer XML. ASP.NET Core supports this.

There are essentially two ways to achieve this:

- Through a route or query string parameter
- Through the `Accept` request header

The first approach lets you specify the format that you're interested in on the URL. Let's see how this works first:

1. Say you have the following action method:

```
public Model Process() { ... }
```

2. Let's forget what `Model` actually is as it's just a POCO class that contains the properties you're interested in. It could be as simple as this:

```
public class Model
{
    public int A { get; set; }
    public string B { get; set; }
}
```

3. Out of the box, ASP.NET Core includes a formatter for JSON, but you can also add a NuGet package, also from Microsoft, that adds support for XML—`Microsoft.AspNetCore.Mvc.Formatters.Xml`. As well as adding it to the services, you also need to tell ASP.NET what mapping to use; in this case, the `.xml` format to the `application/xml` content type:

```
services
    .AddMvc(options =>
    {
options.FormatterMappings.SetMediaTypeMappingForFormat("xml",
        "application/xml");
    })
    .AddXmlSerializerFormatters();
```

Calling `AddXmlSerializerFormatters` already does this:

```
services
    .AddMvc()
    .AddXmlSerializerFormatters();
```

4. There is already a mapping from `json` to `application/json`, so there is no need to add this as it will be the default. Then, you need to decorate your action method with a route that specifies the `format` parameter:

```
[Route("[controller]/[action]/{format}")]
public Model Process() { ... }
```

5. You also need to decorate your controller class with the `[FormatFilter]` attribute, as follows:

```
[FormatFilter]
public class HomeController { }
```

6. Now, if you call your action with `json` or `xml` as the `format` route value, you will get an answer properly formatted according to the format you specified, such as this for XML:

```
<Model xmlns:xsi="http://www.w3.org/2001/XMLSchema-instance"
xmlns:xsd="http://www.w3.org/2001/XMLSchema">
    <A>1</A>
    <B>two</B>
</Model>
```

7. You will get the following for JSON:

```
{"a":1,"b":"two"}
```

8. The other way is to use the request's `Accept` header, which is a standard way of specifying the content we're interested in receiving. API clients don't typically use this, but browsers do. In the `AddMvc` call, you need to activate the `RespectBrowserAcceptHeader` property:

```
services
    .AddMvc(options =>
    {
        options.RespectBrowserAcceptHeader = true;
    })
    .AddXmlSerializerFormatters();
```

Now, if you send an `Accept` header of
either `application/xml` or `application/json` (this is the default), you will get the
result in the desired format.

 For more information about the `Accept` header, please
consult `https://developer.mozilla.org/en-US/docs/Web/HTTP/`
`Headers/Accept`.

For the sake of completeness, the JSON formatter allows us to specify additional
options through the use of the `AddJsonOptions` extension method:

```
services
    .AddMvc()
    .AddJsonOptions(options =>
    {
        options.JsonSerializerOptions.PropertyNamingPolicy =
        JsonNamingPolicy.CamelCase;
    });
```

This configures the resolver to use `camelCasing` instead of the default option. There
are too many options to discuss here and since they're not really that relevant, we
won't cover them.

Now that we've looked at request acceptance, let's now look at response formatting.

Output formatters

What does returning an object in an HTTP response mean? Well, the object needs to
be turned into something that can be transmitted over the wire. Some typical
response types are as follows:

- `text/html`: For HTML content
- `text/plain`: For generic text content
- `application/json`: For JSON content
- `application/xml`: For XML content
- `binary/octet-stream`: For any binary content

Therefore, the object you return needs to be turned into something that can be sent
using one of these content types. For this, ASP.NET Core uses the concept of an
output formatter. An output formatter is essentially an implementation
of `IOutputFormatter`.

Out of the box, ASP.NET Core includes the following output formatters:

- `HttpNoContentOutputFormatter` doesn't write any content at all; only returns a `204` HTTP status code.
- `StringOutputFormatter` outputs strings as is.
- `StreamOutputFormatter` writes a stream as a series of bytes.
- `JsonOutputFormatter` serializes the object to JSON.

There are also a couple of types of XML formatters that can be installed using the `Microsoft.AspNetCore.Mvc.Formatters.Xml` NuGet package and registered either through `AddXmlDataContractSerializerFormatters` (for `DataContractSerializer`) or `AddXmlSerializerFormatters` (for `XmlSerializer`).

 Data contracts and XML serializers use different approaches; for example, different attributes to control the output.

Output formatters can be configured using the `AddMvc` extension method overload, which takes a parameter, as follows:

```
services.AddMvc(options =>
{
    options.OutputFormatters.Insert(0, new MyOutputFormatter());
});
```

So, how is an output formatter selected? ASP.NET Core iterates the list of configured formatters and calls its `IOutputFormatter.CanWriteResult` method. The first formatter that returns `true` is the one that is used to serialize the object to the output stream (the `WriteAsync` method).

Handling null values

When an ASP.NET Core API controller returns a `null` value that is normally wrapped in `IActionResult` and takes a value, ASP.NET Core automatically switches the return value to `NoContentResult` (HTTP 204 No Content). This behavior is probably OK most of the time, but it may be undesirable at other points. Fortunately, it can be controlled by us; this is actually done through the `HttpNoContentOutputFormatter` output formatter, which is registered by default.

So, if we want to disable it, all we need to do is remove this formatter:

```
services.AddMvc(options =>
{
options.OutputFormatters.RemoveType<HttpNoContentOutputFormatter>();
});
```

In this case, be warned that you may end up returning, for example, a response of 200 OK with a null response if you don't validate the response being returned. If you wish, you can implement a result filter that returns something else—for example, NotFoundResult—in the event of the response being null. This would look something as follows:

```
public sealed class NoResultToNotFoundFilterAttribute : Attribute,
IAlwaysRunResultFilter
{
    public void OnResultExecuting(ResultExecutingContext context)
    {
        if ((context.Result is ObjectResult result) && (result.Value
        == null))
        {
            context.Result = new NotFoundResult();
        }
    }

    public void OnResultExecuted(ResultExecutedContext context) { }
}
```

Notice that we implemented this as an always run result filter, described in Chapter 10, *Understanding Filters*. You just need to register this filter as a global filter and you're good to go.

This concludes the section on content negotiation. In the next section, we will be looking at error handling.

Handling errors

Error handling, when we are talking about APIs, means returning information that can possibly be consumed by a non-human endpoint in the event of an error that can provide useful information. The W3C (which is World Wide Web Consortium) this, on RFC 7807 (https://tools.ietf.org/html/rfc7807), as "*a way to carry machine-readable details of errors in an HTTP response*".

The idea here is that when an error occurs, we gather all the useful information and return a response that describes what happened with the appropriate level of detail.

One way to intercept any exceptions that occur on a web request is through an exception handler—a middleware that is added through a call to `UseExceptionHandler`. Let's look at an example:

```
app.UseExceptionHandler(errorApp =>
{
    errorApp.Run(async context =>
    {
        var errorFeature = context.Features.Get
        <IExceptionHandlerPathFeature>();
        var exception = errorFeature.Error;
        var path = errorFeature.Path;
        var problemDetails = new ProblemDetails
        {
            Instance = $"urn:my:error:{Guid.NewGuid()}",
            Detail = exception.Message
        };

        if (exception is BadHttpRequestException
badHttpRequestException)
        {
            problemDetails.Title = "Invalid request!";
            problemDetails.Status = StatusCodes.Status400BadRequest;
        }
        else
        {
            problemDetails.Title = "An unexpected error occurred!";
            problemDetails.Status = StatusCodes
            .Status500InternalServerError;
        }

        context.Response.ContentType = "application/problem+json";
        context.Response.StatusCode = problemDetails.Status.Value;

        await context.Response.WriteAsync(JsonSerializer.
        Serialize(problemDetails));
    });
});
```

What we have here is a handler that is called in the event of an exception; we retrieve the current exception through `IExceptionHandlerPathFeature` and check what it is. There is another feature class, `IExceptionHandlerFeature`, but `IExceptionHandlerPathFeature` extends it and adds a `Path` property to the already existing `Error` property.

We then build an instance of a `ProblemDetails` class (provided by .NET Core; you can inherit from it should you wish to provide your own properties) and fill in the appropriate properties. We then set the response content type to `application/problem+json`, as defined by the RFC interface, and serialize this instance as JSON to the response stream.

The properties of the `ProblemDetails` class have the following meanings (from the RFC):

- `Type` (`string`): A URI reference (`RFC3986`) that identifies the problem type. If not supplied, it defaults to `about:blank`.
- `Title` (`string`): A short, human-readable summary of the problem type. This should not change from occurrence to occurrence of the problem, except for the purposes of localization.
- `Detail` (`string`): A human-readable explanation specific to this occurrence of the problem.
- `Instance` (`string`): A URI reference that identifies the specific occurrence of the problem. It may or may not yield further information if dereferenced.
- `Status` (`int`): The HTTP status code.

Of course, the exact level of detail depends on the message that occurred and on what you want to expose to the client, so you must consider this carefully by inspecting the exception, the request URL, and any other possible parameters.

Since ASP.NET Core 3, we can also create a `ProblemDetails` object such as this within a controller action method:

```
var problemDetails =
ProblemDetailsFactory.CreateProblemDetails(HttpContext);
```

This includes general information about the exception that occurred and, in the case of a more specific model validation error, which is not a server-side error and normally does not throw any exception, we can do this instead:

```
var validationProblemDetails = ProblemDetailsFactory.
 CreateValidationProblemDetails(HttpContext, ModelState);
```

This includes all of the validation errors in the generated object. You could have code such as this in a controller:

```
if (!this.ModelState.IsValid)
{
    var validationProblemDetails = ProblemDetailsFactory
      .CreateValidationProblemDetails(HttpContext,
        ModelState);

    return BadRequest(validationProblemDetails);
}
```

That's all for error handling; the next section explains how we can have multiple versions of an API and have our customers select the one that they're interested in.

Understanding API versioning

Also related to API (web service)-style method invocations is versioning. By versioning your API, you can have multiple simultaneous versions of it by possibly taking different payloads and returning different results. ASP.NET Core supports API versioning through the `Microsoft.AspNetCore.Mvc.Versioning` library.

Out of the box, you can apply the following techniques to specify the version that you're interested in:

- A URL query string parameter
- A header
- Any of the previous options—either the query string or a header

Let's say you have two controller classes of the same name in two different namespaces:

```
namespace Controllers.V1
{
    [ApiVersion("1.0")]
    public class ApiController
    {
        [ApiVersion("1.0", Deprecated = true)]
        [HttpGet("[controller]/[action]/{version:apiversion}")]
        public Model Get() { ... }

        [ApiVersion("2.0")]
        [ApiVersion("3.0")]
```

```
          public Model GetV2() { ... }
    ]
}
```

Here, you can see that we applied a couple of [ApiVersion] attributes to each, with each one specifying an API version that the controller supports. Let's see how we can implement versioning, starting with the route approach.

Using header values

We will configure API versioning to infer the desired version from a header field. We configure versioning in the ConfigureServices method. Notice the HeaderApiVersionReader class:

```
services.AddApiVersioning(options =>
{
    options.ApiVersionReader = new HeaderApiVersionReader("api-
version");
});
```

Here, we're saying that the version should come from the header string called api-version. This is not a standard value; it's just some string we picked up.

Now, when calling your API at /Api/Get, while passing an api-version header with a value of 1.0, the request will be handled by the Controllers.V1.ApiController class. If you pass a value of 2.0 or 3.0, however, it will be picked up by the Controllers.V2.ApiController class.

Using a header is the most transparent technique, but it is also one that you can't easily force, for example, using a browser. Let's look at another technique.

Using the query string

In order to infer the version from the URL, we need to use the QueryStringApiVersionReader class, as follows:

```
services.AddApiVersioning(options =>
{
    options.ApiVersionReader = new QueryStringApiVersionReader("api-
version");
});
```

We also need to configure a route that takes this into account:

```
[Route("[controller]/{version:apiversion}")]
public Model Get() { ... }
```

Now, if we make a request to /api/1.0, we get version 1.0, and the same goes for 2.0 and 3.0.

 If we want to be more flexible, we can use the QueryStringOrHeaderApiVersionReader class as ApiVersionReader; both approaches will work.

We've seen how to specify a version using either the query string or a header. Let's now see how to mark a version as deprecated.

Deprecating versions

You can say that one version is obsolete by setting a flag to the Deprecated property:

```
[ApiVersion("1.0", Deprecated = true)]
```

Now, if you set the ReportApiVersions flag to true, you will receive the versions that are supported and those that aren't as part of the response:

```
services.AddApiVersioning(options =>
{
    options.ReportApiVersions = true;
    options.ApiVersionReader = new QueryStringApiVersionReader("
     api-version");
});
```

This yields the following response headers:

```
api-deprecated-versions: 1.0
api-supported-versions: 2.0, 3.0
```

Now, let's move on to see how default versions work.

Default versions

You can also specify a default version:

```
services.AddApiVersioning(options =>
{
    options.AssumeDefaultVersionWhenUnspecified = true;
    options.DefaultApiVersion = new ApiVersion(2, 0);
    options.ApiVersionReader = new QueryStringApiVersionReader("
     api-version");
});
```

In this case, if you don't specify a version, it will assume that you want version 2.0.

Version mapping

As we've seen, the `Controllers.V2.ApiController` class is mapped to two versions—2.0 and 3.0. But what happens if you want to handle version 3.0 separately? Well, you simply add a `[MapToApiVersion]` attribute to a new method:

```
[MapToApiVersion("3.0")]
public Model GetV3() { ... }
```

Henceforth, all requests for version 3.0 will be handled by this method.

Invalid versions

If an unsupported version is requested, not a deprecated one, an exception will be thrown and returned to the client, as follows:

```
{
  "error":
  {
    "code": "ApiVersionUnspecified",
    "message":"An API version is required, but was not specified."
  }
}
```

That's about it for versioning ASP.NET Core web APIs. As you can see, you have several options, from using the URL to using headers, and you can have multiple, simultaneous versions of your API. This will hopefully help you migrate clients running an old version to the new one.

Next, we'll see how to generate documentation for an API and even create a UI for calling it from the browser.

Generating API documentation

Web APIs have a specification that was initially called **Swagger** but now goes by the name **OpenAPI** (`https://github.com/OAI/OpenAPI-Specification`). It is used to describe the endpoints and versions offered by some APIs. The Swagger v3.0 specification contributed to the OpenAPI Initiative, and so Swagger is merged with OpenAPI.

It is still colloquially called Swagger in several places, and there is also an open source implementation for .NET called **Swashbuckle**, which is available on NuGet as `Swashbuckle.AspNetCore` (`https://github.com/domaindrivendev/Swashbuckle.AspNetCore`). What this package does is inspect the action methods of your controllers and generate a JSON document that describes them. It also offers a simple web interface for invoking each of these action methods—how cool is that?

In order to use `Swashbuckle.AspNetCore`, we need to add a few NuGet packages—`Swashbuckle.AspNetCore`, `.SwaggerGen`, `Swashbuckle.AspNetCore.SwaggerUI`, and `Microsoft.OpenApi`. The latter is added automatically by the former. To use Swashbuckle, as with most ASP.NET Core APIs, we first need to register the required services to the dependency injection framework (`ConfigureServices`). This is done as follows:

```
services.AddSwaggerGen(c =>
{
    c.SwaggerDoc("v1", new OpenApiInfo {
        Title = "My API V1",
        Version = "v1",
        OpenApiContact = new Contact {
            Email = "rjperes@hotmail.com",
            Name = "Ricardo Peres",
            Url = "http://weblogs.asp.net/ricardoperes"
        }
    });
});
```

We add the Swagger middleware to the pipeline in the `Configure` method:

```
app.UseSwagger();
app.UseSwaggerUI(options =>
{
```

```
        options.SwaggerEndpoint("/swagger/v1/swagger.json", "My API V1");
});
```

The two calls, `UseSwagger` and `UseSwaggerUI`, refer to two different functionalities; the first is for the actual API documentation and the second is the UI for invoking controller actions.

You can add as many calls to `AddSwaggerGen` as you like, with different API names or versions. Each version will generate a different API version document.

Swashbuckle works by introspecting all the controllers and their action methods, but it will only find those that you explicitly want it to find, such as the following:

- Controllers marked with a `[Route]` attribute
- Action methods marked with `[Route]`, `[HttpGet]`, `[HttpPost]`, `[HttpPut]`, `[HttpDelete]`, `[HttpOptions]`, `[HttpPatch]`, or `[HttpMethod]` and with an explicit route template

Swashbuckle will also look at the following:

- `[Produces]`: The content type(s) and contract of the POCO class(es) that may be produced by an action method.
- `[ProducesResponseType]`: The contract and status code that may be returned by an action method. You can have as many as you like for different status codes.
- `[ProducesDefaultResponseType]`: The contract that is returned for any status code not explicitly mentioned by a `[ProducesResponseType]` attribute.
- `[ProducesErrorResponseType]`: The contract to be returned in the event of an error.
- `[Consumes]`: The content type(s) that will be accepted by an action method

These attributes can be applied at the class (controller) or method (action) level; so, for example, if all actions in a controller consume and produce JSON, you could have this:

```
[Produces("application/json")]
[Consumes("application/json")]
public class HomeController : Controller { }
```

When you access the /swagger/v1/swagger.json URL, you get something like this:

```
{
    "swagger": "2.0",
    "info": {
      "version": "v1",
      "title": "My API V1",
      "contact": {
          "name": "Ricardo Peres",
          "url": "http://weblogs.asp.net/ricardoperes",
          "email": "rjperes@hotmail.com"
      }
    },
    "basePath": "/",
    "paths": {
      "/Home": {
        "get": {
          "tags": [ "Home" ],
          "operationId": "HomeIndexGet",
          "consumes": ["application/json"],
          "produces": ["application/json"],
          "responses": {
            "200": {
              "description": "Success"
            }
          }
        }
      }
    },
    "definitions": {},
    "securityDefinitions": {}
}
```

Due to space constraints, we have only included one action method, Index, of the Home controller in this sample output. However, you can see a single document, named My API V1 version V1. For each action method, Swashbuckle describes the HTTP methods it accepts, any content types that it accepts (these can be specified through the use of the [Consumes] attribute) and returns (as set by [Produces]), and the return status codes (the [ProducesResponseType] attribute). If these are not specified, the defaults are used, which is 200 for the status code, no accept, or return content types.

This version has nothing to do with the versioning schema discussed in the previous topic.

If a single method can return more than one document type or status code, you can apply as many [Produces] and [ProducesResponseType] attributes as you wish:

```
[ProducesResponseType(typeof(Model), StatusCodes.Status201Created)]
[ProducesResponseType(typeof(Model), StatusCodes.Status202Accepted)]
[ProducesResponseType(typeof(Model),
StatusCodes.Status304NotModified)]
[ProducesDefaultResponseType]
public IActionResult AddOrUpdate(Model model) { ... }
```

In this case, we mean the following:

- If the model already exists somewhere, then we return HTTP 303 Not Modified.
- If the model was changed, we return HTTP 202 Accepted.
- If the model was added, we then return HTTP 201 Created.

All of this is inferred from the REST conventions, mind you!

A word of caution—the difference between [Produces] and [ProducesResponseType] is that the former is a result filter that sets the response type to be of a specific value and the latter only declares it! This may be relevant if you wish to use content negotiation, so it's something that you must keep in mind!

For each document you add with AddSwaggerGen, you get a different URL, such as /swagger/v1/swagger.json, /swagger/v2/swagger.json, and more.

Of greater interest is the generated UI, which can be accessed through the /swagger endpoint:

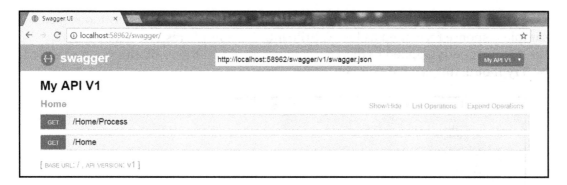

Here, we can see two actions (known as **operations**)—/Home and /Home/Process.
They are two action methods in the Home controller, and these are the routes
to access each one. For the sake of clarity, let's consider the Process action method to
have the following signature:

```
[HttpGet("Process")]
[ProducesResponseType(typeof(Model), StatusCodes.Status200OK)]
public IActionResult Process(string id, int state) { ... }
```

Now, expanding the operations yields the following:

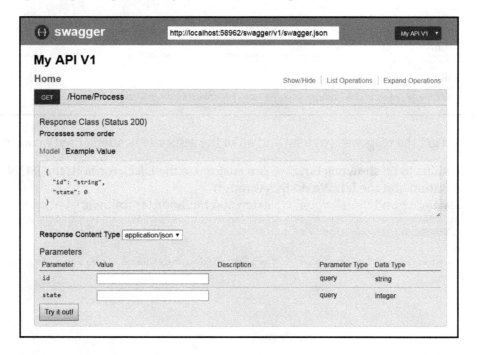

Here, you get a form that asks for the parameters to `Process` and even shows you a sample response formatted as JSON. Brilliant! This sample response comes from the `Type` property applied to the `[Produces]` attribute. If you fill this out and click on **Try it out!**, this is what you get:

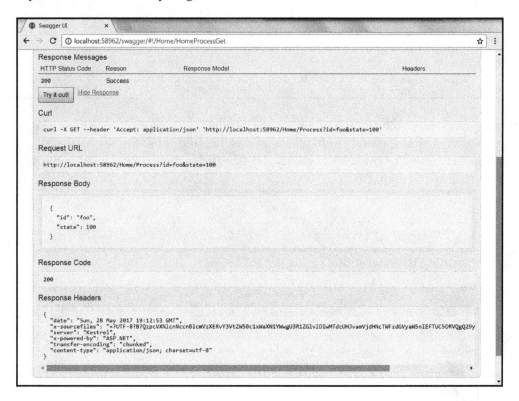

Here, you get the response payload and all of the response headers. Pretty cool, right?

What remains to be shown is how we can customize the URLs for both the JSON documentation and the UI. We do this through the `UseSwagger` and `UseSwaggerUI` extension methods, as follows:

```
app.UseSwagger(options =>
{
    options.RouteTemplate = "api-doc/{documentName}/swagger.json";
});
```

The `RouteTemplate` property only needs to take a `{documentName}` token, the default being `swagger/{documentName}/swagger.json`. This token is replaced by whatever you add as the first parameter to the `SwaggerDoc` call in the `AddSwaggerGen` lambda. Don't forget that if you change one, you need to change both, as shown:

```
app.UseSwaggerUI(options =>
{
    options.SwaggerEndpoint("/api-doc/v1/swagger.json", "My API V1");
});
```

 There are lots of other configuration options, so we advise you to take a look at the documentation available at `https://github.com/domaindrivendev/Swashbuckle.AspNetCore`.

After the generation, let us see how to add the documentation.

Adding API documentation

Swashbuckle can add the documentation that is provided with the code, as long as we make MSBuild generate an XML file for it. Using Visual Studio, this is just a matter of setting a property on the `.csproj` file:

```
<PropertyGroup>
    <GenerateDocumentationFile>true</GenerateDocumentationFile>
    <NoWarn>$(NoWarn);1591</NoWarn>
</PropertyGroup>
```

This results in every documentation comment in the code to be included in an XML file that is suitable to be fed into Swashbuckle. In order to load this file, we need to do the following:

```
services.AddSwaggerGen(options =>
{
    options.SwaggerDoc("v1", new OpenApiInfo {
        Title = "My API V1",
        Version = "v1",
        Contact = new OpenApiContact {
            Email = "rjperes@hotmail.com",
            Name = "Ricardo Peres",
            Url = "http://weblogs.asp.net/ricardoperes"
        }
    });
    //assume that the XML file will have the same name as the current
```

```
        //assembly
        var xmlFile =
$"{Assembly.GetExecutingAssembly().GetName().Name}.xml";
        var xmlPath = Path.Combine(AppContext.BaseDirectory, xmlFile);
        options.IncludeXmlComments(xmlPath);
});
```

Now, all comments for public types and their public members and parameters will be shown on the Swashbuckle user interface.

Serving OData

OData is an open standard for querying data over the web. It allows us to expose metadata about a domain model and to query it using nothing more than HTTP verbs and the query string. It can be used, for example, to expose any data model as a REST API.

Previous versions of ASP.NET already supported it, and since version 2.0, it is also supported in ASP.NET Core through the `Microsoft.AspNetCore.OData` NuGet package.

 For additional information about the OData spec, please check out `https://www.odata.org`.

In the case of ASP.NET Core, OData allows us to query, through the URL, any collection that implements `IQueryable<T>` or `IEnumerable<T>`; in the first case, this means that the query will not be executed in memory, but it will be translated to the data source-specific dialect. In the case of an object-relational mapper, such as **Entity Framework (EF)** Core or NHibernate, this is SQL.

Throughout the course of the following sections, we will see how OData can be used to expose an object model to the web so that it can be queried easily using nothing but the browser. Let's start at the beginning with the setup.

Setting up OData

So, after adding the `Microsoft.AspNetCore.OData` NuGet package, we need to register the required services and declare the model that we will be exposing. Let's take a look at some code:

```
private static IEdmModel GetEdmModel()
{
    var builder = new ODataConventionModelBuilder();
    //register an entity set of type Order and call it Orders
    builder.EntitySet<Order>("Orders");
    //same for products
    builder.EntitySet<Product>("Products");
    //add other entity sets here
    return builder.GetEdmModel();
}

public void ConfigureServices(IServiceCollection services)
{
    //rest goes here
    services.AddOData();
    services
        .AddControllers()
        .SetCompatibilityVersion(CompatibilityVersion.Latest);
}

public void Configure(IApplicationBuilder app)
{
    //rest goes here
    app.UseRouting();
    app.UseEndpoints(endpoints =>
    {
        endpoints.MapControllers();
        //add a route named odata for an endpoint /odata using the EDM
        //model
        endpoints.MapODataRoute("odata", "odata", GetEdmModel());
    });
}
```

Notice that the `GetEdmModel` method returns the entity sets that will be made available to the OData endpoint—in this case, `Products` and `Orders`, as an **Entity Data Model (EDM)**. There are more advanced capabilities, such as declaring functions, but we won't cover them here.

We must register the services by calling the `AddOData` extension method in `ConfigureServices` and then, in `Configure`, when we include the MVC middleware, we need to declare a route where the OData endpoint will listen—in this example, this is `odata`.

The `MapODataRoute` extension method takes the name of the route as the first parameter, the actual URL path as the second parameter, and, lastly, the EDM model.

Now, we need to add a controller to actually return collections or single items; this controller must inherit from `ODataController`, a class that inherits from `ControllerBase` and, therefore, inherits its methods (no need for the `Controller` class because this one basically adds view-related methods):

```
[ODataRoutePrefix("Products")]
public class ProductsController : ODataController
{
    private readonly ProductContext _ctx;

    public ProductsController(ProductContext ctx)
    {
        this._ctx = ctx;
    }

    [EnableQuery]
    public IQueryable<Product> Get() => _ctx.Products;

    public async Task<Product> Get(int id) => await _ctx.Products.
     FindAsync(id);
}
```

The `[ORouteDataPrefix]` attribute indicates the prefix to be used for this controller if we do not wish to use the default convention of the controller name minus the `Controller` suffix. It can be safely omitted, otherwise.

Notice the `[EnableQuery]` attribute in the method that returns the collection; this is the attribute that does the actual magic by allowing it to be queried over the URL. Also, the two methods named `Get` also have an attribute of `ODataRoute`, but the overload that takes the `id` parameter also mentions it in its constructor; this is so that it can be mapped to the parameter.

This setup allows the following HTTP calls:

- `GET /odata/$metadata#Product`: For retrieving the metadata—a set of public properties—of the `Product` entity
- `GET /odata/Products` to `ProductController.Get()`: Returns all of the products, allowing querying over them
- `GET/ odata/Products(1)` to `ProductController.Get(1)`: Returns a single product

Now that we've seen how to prepare ASP.NET Core for OData, let's look at how we can query our model.

Getting metadata

There is no need to declare a return type of `IQueryable<T>`, as long as the actual return value is of this type—for example, `IActionResult, ActionResult<IQueryable<T>>`, or even `Task<IQueryable<T>>`, where `T` is an actual type. If you don't return an `IQueryable<T>` type, but instead, for example, something that implements `IEnumerable<T>`, querying is also possible, but just not on the server side (as in the database server), but in memory instead.

Listing collections

Calling the OData endpoint (`odata`, as specified earlier), we get to see the list of entities that are exposed. In our example, this is the `Products` and `Orders` collections:

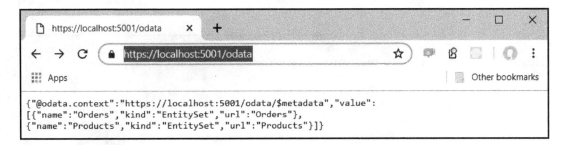

The preceding screenshot shows the collections exposed by our model in the endpoint that we defined. Let's now look at the metadata for each of these entities.

Entity metadata

The metadata for an entity shows all of the entity's properties and is available at the following endpoint:

```
/odata/$metadata
```

The following is the output we get when we run this:

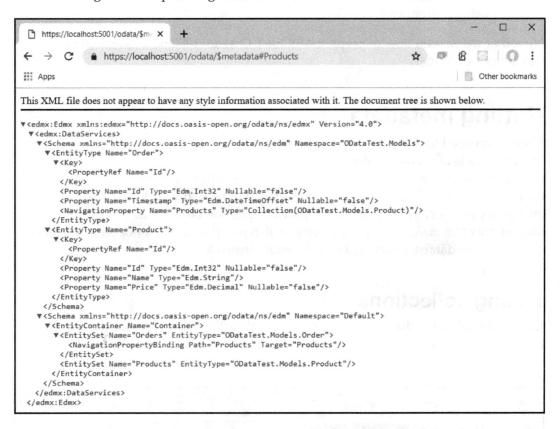

This shows all of the entity properties as well as all of its collections.

Let's now see how we can filter the metadata.

Querying

Querying an entity is just a matter of accessing the endpoint for that entity:

```
/odata/Products
```

This will return all the records for that entity, but what if we just want a few of them?

Filtering an entity

Querying over the URL can be achieved by adding a query parameter named `$filter`, as follows:

```
/odata/Products?$filter=Price gt 100
```

The following is the output we get on running the query:

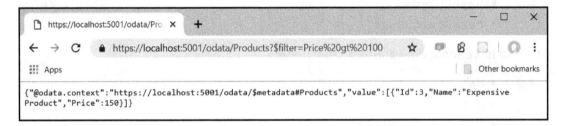

You can expect the usual operators for the different property types, such as the following:

- Greater than/less than: `gt` or `lt`
- Greater or equal to/less or equal to: `gte` or `lte`
- Equals/does not equal: `eq` or `ne`
- And/or/not: `and`, `or`, or `not`
- Enumeration flags: `has`

As you can see, we can combine expressions using `and`, `or`, and `not`, even including parentheses to group conditions.

For string properties, we can use other operators:

- `concat`
- `contains`
- `endswith`

- indexof
- length
- startswith
- substring
- tolower
- toupper
- trim

When working with string literals, make sure you enclose them with `'`, as follows:

```
/odata/Products?$filter=Name eq 'Expensive Product'
```

For collections, we have the following:

- in
- hassubset
- hassubsequence

We also have some date and time functions:

- date
- day
- fractionalseconds
- hour
- maxdatetime
- mindatetime
- minute
- month
- now
- second
- time
- totaloffsetminutes
- totalseconds
- year

Some math functions that are available are as follows:

- `ceiling`
- `floor`
- `round`

Some type functions are as follows:

- `cast`
- `isof`

Some geo functions (where the underlying data access layer supports the function) are as follows:

- `geo.distance`
- `geo.intersects`
- `geo.length`

Some lambda operators are as follows:

- `any`
- `all`

I won't try to explain all of these. For a detailed explanation of each function, please have a look at the OData specification reference documentation, available at `https://www.odata.org/documentation`.

Projections

A projection allows you to retrieve just the properties that you're interested. For example, for `Products`, you may want just the `Name` and the `Price` properties. You can get this by including a `$select` parameter on the query string:

```
/odata/Products?$select=Price
```

The following is the output of the query:

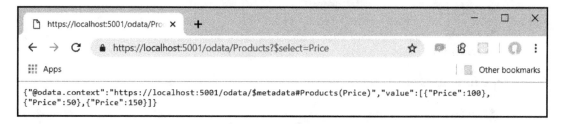

You can specify many fields for projection, each separated by commas.

Paging

We can specify a page size and an optional starting position by adding `$top` and `$skip`:

```
/odata/Products?$top=2&$skip=2
```

The following is the output:

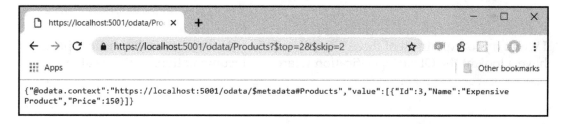

This returns up to 10 records, starting from the 21st. Never forget, however, that you shouldn't apply paging without an explicit sort order, otherwise the results may not be what you expect.

Sorting

Sorting is achieved through `$orderby`:

```
/odata/Products?$orderby=Price
```

The following is the output:

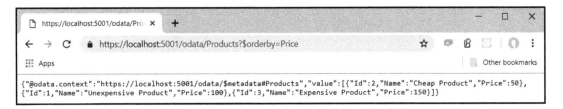

To see these results in descending order, use `desc`:

```
/odata/Products?$orderby=Price desc
```

The following is the output for the descending order results:

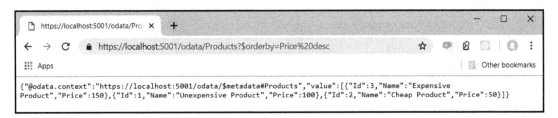

It is also possible to order by several properties:

```
/odata/Products?$orderby=Price desc,Name asc
```

The `asc` value is the default and can be omitted.

Expansion

Using an expansion we can force the traversal of a related entity through a navigation property. It is the `$expand` parameter that we want to use in this case:

```
/odata/Orders?$expand=Products
```

Mind you, this is the same as calling the `Include` extension method in an EF Core LINQ query for a child collection, forcing EF Core to include it in the query and instantiate all its records as entities.

Counting

Even when using filters, we can return the total number of records by including a $count keyword with a value of true:

```
/odata/Products?$count=true
```

After this, let us look at the configuring options.

Configuring options

The OData options are configured in the UseMVC extension method. By default, no option is allowed, and so they must be explicitly set. The available actions that can be allowed are as follows:

- Selection of entities (Select)
- Expansion of child properties and collections (Expand)
- Filtering (Filter)
- Sorting (OrderBy)
- Counting (Count)

Multiple options can be chained together, as follows:

```
public void Configure(IApplicationBuilder app)
{
    //rest goes here
    app.UseMvc(options =>
    {
        options.Select().Expand().Filter().OrderBy().Count();
        options.MapODataServiceRoute("odata", "odata", GetEdmModel());
    });
}
```

This tells OData that selection, expansion, filtering, ordering, and counts are allowed.

Limits

It is usually advised that you set some limits to queries, so as to minimize resource consumption.

Maximum returnable records

It is possible—and recommended—to set the maximum number of records to be returned by a query. This is done to save resources. We can do this when configuring the OData options using the `MaxTop` extension method:

```
app.UseMvc(options =>
{
    options.MaxTop(10);
    options.MapODataServiceRoute("odata", "odata", GetEdmModel());
});
```

This defines the maximum number of entities to retrieve as 10.

Expansion

You can also configure whether or not to allow expansion for the `$expand` command:

```
options.Expand();
```

If this is supplied, queries can be more complex and can return substantially more results as they can bring child entities together with the master ones.

> If you wish to play with OData with a complex model, please go to `https://www.odata.org/odata-services`.

Summary

In the chapter, we saw how we can make use of JWTs to authenticate our endpoints without the need for human interaction.

We now know how to use the Data Validation API to perform automatic model validation. Then, we learned that content negotiation can be useful if you wish to return data in different formats; but, in reality, JSON is the *de facto* standard for data exchange over the web these days.

The OpenAPI specification is also helpful in development mode to inspect your endpoints and issue requests against them.

Next, we saw that OData is a great addition to ASP.NET Core, especially when integrated with EF Core or any other data provider that exposes data as `IQueryable<T>`.

In this chapter, we also learned how REST is implemented in ASP.NET Core to expose APIs. We looked at how to carry out model binding and validate data before this. We were also introduced to the JWT mechanism for authorizing endpoints and how to carry out versioning and content negotiation. Finally, we looked at how we can leverage OData to expose a data model to the web.

In the next chapter, we will cover the ways in which we can create reusable components.

Questions

You should now be able to answer the following questions:

1. What is OData?
2. What is content negotiation?
3. Why is it not suitable to use cookies for authentication in web APIs?
4. What are the different ways that we can ask for a specific version of our API?
5. What is the purpose of conventions with regard to action methods?
6. What are the problem details?
7. What is REST?

9
Reusable Components

This chapter covers ASP.NET Core's reusable components. By reusable, I mean that they can potentially be used across different projects—or in the same project in different places—with different parameters, yielding possibly distinct results. In this chapter, we will cover **view components** and **tag helpers** (which are new to ASP.NET Core), tag helper components (new to ASP.NET Core 2), and our old friend, partial views.

In this chapter, we will cover the following topics:

- View components
- Tag helpers
- Tag helper components
- Partial views
- Razor class libraries
- Adding external contents

Technical requirements

In order to implement the examples introduced in this chapter, you will need the .NET Core 3 SDK and a text editor. Of course, Visual Studio 2019 (any edition) meets all the requirements, but you can also use Visual Studio Code.

The source code can be retrieved from GitHub at `https://github.com/PacktPublishing/Modern-Web-Development-with-ASP.NET-Core-3-Second-Edition`.

All of the techniques introduced in this chapter help structure the code and minimize the size of the global code base.

Diving into the view components

View components are new to ASP.NET Core—they didn't exist in ASP.NET pre-Core. You can think of them as replacements for partial views (which are still around) and the `RenderAction` method for returning child actions (which is no longer available). No more being tied to controllers; they are reusable because they can be loaded from external assemblies (that is, not the assembly of the web app) and they are better suited than partial views to render complex HTML. In the following sections, we will understand what view components are, how they work, and where we use them, as well as compare them to partial views.

Discovering view components

View components can be discovered in one of the following ways:

- By inheriting from the `ViewComponent` class
- By adding a `[ViewComponent]` attribute
- By adding the `ViewComponent` suffix to a class

You will most likely inherit the components from the `ViewComponent` class as this class offers a couple of useful methods. View components can be loaded from external assemblies if the web app references them or they are registered as application parts:

```
services
    .AddMvc()
    .ConfigureApplicationPartManager(options =>
    {
        options.ApplicationParts.Add(new AssemblyPart(Assembly.Load
        ("ClassLibrary")));
    })
```

For POCO view components, you won't get easy access to the ambient context of your request. If you have to choose between the preceding options, opt for inheriting from `ViewComponent` because otherwise, you will need to put in extra work to get all the references (such as `HttpContext` and so on) that you need. We will describe this in more detail in the *Dependency injection* section later.

View components need only declare a single method, `InvokeAsync`:

```
public class MyViewComponent : ViewComponent
{
    public async Task<IViewComponentResult> InvokeAsync()
    {
        return this.Content("This is a view component");
    }
}
```

You can also use parameters, as we will see.

The `[ViewComponent]` attribute can be used to change the name of the view component, but you should be aware that doing it implies that you need to use this name when loading it:

```
[ViewComponent(Name = "MyView")]
public class SomeViewComponent : ViewComponent { ... }
```

Do not give it a name that has hyphens ("-"), as it will affect the usage! We will see this in the next section.

Using view components

View components are called from views and there are two different syntaxes:

- A **code syntax** lets you pass parameters of complex types, but the code must be syntactically valid:

  ```
  @await Component.InvokeAsync("MyViewComponent", new {
  Parameter
   = 4, OtherParameter = true })
  ```

  The `InvokeAsync` method takes a view component name - by default, the name of the class minus the `ViewComponent` suffix - and an optional parameter containing the parameters to be passed to the view component's `InvokeAsync` method; this method can take any number of parameters and return an instance of `IViewComponentResult`.

- **Markup** uses the tag helpers syntax (more on this shortly); notice the `vc` namespace:

  ```
  <vc:my-view-component parameter="4" otherParameter="true"/>
  ```

Again, this is the name of the class without the `ViewComponent` suffix, but using hyphen casing. Here you also need to use the `Name` specified in the `[ViewComponent]` attribute, if any. Do not use hyphens in the naming.

 Pascal-cased class and method parameters for tag helpers are translated into lower-kebab case, which you can read about at `http://stackoverflow.com/questions/11273282/whats-the-name-for-dash-separated-case/12273101#12273101`.

If you have complex parameters that cannot be represented easily by attributes, you should choose the code syntax. Also, the namespace is configurable.

Another option is to return a view component from a controller action in the form of `ViewComponentResult`:

```
public IActionResult MyAction()
{
    return this.ViewComponent("MyViewComponent");
}
```

This is very similar to returning a partial view, only in view components, all of the contents need to be generated by code. That is, if you want to return custom HTML, you will likely need to build by concatenating strings.

View component results

View components return an instance of `IViewComponentResult`, which has three implementations in ASP.NET Core, each returned by a method of the `ViewComponent` class:

- `Content` (`ContentViewComponentResult`): Returns string content.
- `View` (`ViewViewComponentResult`): Returns a partial view.
- `HtmlViewComponentResult`: Similar to `ContentViewComponentResult`, but returns encoded HTML instead. There is no method that creates an instance of this class, but you can instantiate one yourself.

 The rules for discovering partial view files are identical to the ones described earlier in `Chapter 5`, *Views*.

The `IViewComponentResult` interface only specifies a single method in both the asynchronous (`ExecuteAsync`) and synchronous (`Execute`) versions. It takes an instance of `ViewComponentContext` as its sole parameter, which has the following properties:

- `Arguments` (`IDictionary<string, object>`): The named properties of the object passed to the `InvokeAsync` method
- `HtmlEncoder` (`HtmlEncoder`): The HTML output encoder
- `ViewComponentDescriptor` (`ViewComponentDescriptor`): Describes the current view component
- `ViewContext` (`ViewContext`): All of the view context, including the current view object, the HTTP context, the route data, the model, the form context, and the action descriptor
- `ViewData` (`ViewDataDictionary`): The view data from the controller
- `Writer` (`TextWriter`): Used to write directly to the output stream

Since you have access to all of these contexts, you can do pretty much what you want—such as access headers, cookies, and request parameters—but you wouldn't use the view component results for redirection, only for rendering HTML.

Dependency injection

You can register view components as services by calling the `AddViewComponentsAsServices` extension method on top of the `AddMvc` method in `ConfigureServices`:

```
services
    .AddMvc()
    .AddViewComponentsAsServices();
```

View components support constructor injection, so you can declare any registered types in the constructor:

```
public class MyViewComponent : ViewComponent
{
    private readonly ILoggerFactory loggerFactory;

    public MyViewComponent(ILoggerFactory loggerFactory)
    {
        this._loggerFactory = loggerFactory;
    }
}
```

A common need is to get hold of the current `HttpContext`; if you need it in a POCO controller, you need to inject an `IHttpContextAccessor` instance:

```
public class MyViewComponent : ViewComponent
{
    public MyViewComponent(IHttpContextAccessor httpAccessor)
    {
        this.HttpContext = httpAccessor.HttpContext;
    }

    public HttpContext HttpContext { get; }
}
```

In this example, we inject the `IHttpContextAccessor` interface, from which we can extract the current `HttpContext` instance of the request. Don't forget that, for this to work, the following line must be present in `ConfigureServices`:

```
services.AddHttpContextAccessor();
```

View components versus partial views

As you can see, view components and partial views share some similarities; they are both reusable mechanisms to generate markup. The difference between the two is that partial views inherit a big part of the context of the containing view, such as the model and the view data collection, so the two views—views and partial views—must be compatible. For example, they must have a compatible model. This is not the case for view components, which you invoke with whatever data you like.

Next, we will talk about a very similar topic that uses a different syntax that is closer to HTML—tag helpers.

Exploring the tag helpers

Tag helpers are also new to ASP.NET Core. A tag helper is a mechanism for adding server-side processing to a regular HTML/XML tag; you can think of them as similar to ASP.NET Web Forms' server-side controls, although there are several differences. Tag helpers are registered on Razor views and when any tag on the view matches a tag helper, it is fired. They are an alternative (and, arguably, simpler) to HTML helpers as they result in much cleaner markup without code blocks.

A tag helper's functionality is specified through the `ITagHelper` interface, in which the `TagHelper` abstract base class offers a base implementation. Its life cycle includes two methods:

- `Init`: Called when the tag helper is initialized, prior to any possible child
- `ProcessAsync`: The actual processing of a tag helper

A tag helper, on the view side, is nothing more than a regular tag and, as such, it can contain other tags, which themselves may also be tag helpers. Let's look at an example:

```
<time></time>
```

As you can see, it is nothing more than a plain XML tag—not HTML because there is no tag such as this on any version of HTML.

In order to add custom server-side behavior, we define a tag helper class as follows:

```
public class TimeTagHelper : TagHelper
{
    public override Task ProcessAsync(TagHelperContext context,
    TagHelperOutput output)
    {
        var time = DateTime.Now.ToString();

        output.Content.Append(time);

        return base.ProcessAsync(context, output);
    }
}
```

Tag helpers are recursive, meaning tag helpers declared inside other tag helpers are all processed.

We'll shortly look at what we need to do for ASP.NET Core to recognize this, but for now, let's have a look at the parameters of the `ProcessAsync` method.

`TagHelperContext` contains the context, as seen in the tag helper. It includes the following properties:

- `AllAttributes` (`ReadOnlyTagHelperAttributeList`): All of the attributes declared in the view for this tag helper
- `Items` (`IDictionary<string, object>`): A freeform collection of items used to pass context to other tag helpers on the current request
- `UniqueId` (`string`): A unique identifier for the current tag helper

As for `TagHelperOutput`, it not only allows the return of content to the view, but also the return of any content that is declared inside the tag. It exposes the following properties:

- `IsContentModified` (`bool`): A read-only flag that says whether the contents have been modified
- `Order` (`int`): The order that the tag helper is processed
- `PostElement` (`TagHelperContent`): The following tag element
- `PostContent` (`TagHelperContent`): The content following the current tag
- `Content` (`TagHelperContent`): The current tag's content
- `PreContent` (`TagHelperContent`): The content prior to the current tag
- `PreElement` (`TagHelperContent`): The previous tag element
- `TagMode` (`TagMode`): The tag mode (`SelfClosing`, `StartTagAndEndTag`, and `StartTagOnly`), which is used to define how the tag should be validated in the markup (allowing inner content is `SelfClosing`, just a tag with no self-content is `StartTagOnly`)
- `TagName` (`string`): The name of the tag in the view
- `Attributes` (`TagHelperAttributeList`): The original list of attributes of the tag, which can be modified

For example, imagine you had this tag, instead:

```
<time format="yyyy-MM-dd">Current date is: {0}</time>
```

Here, you need to access both an attribute (`format`) and the contents of the `<time>` tag. Let's see how we can achieve this:

```
public class TimeTagHelper : TagHelper
{
    public string Format { get; set; }

    public override async Task ProcessAsync(TagHelperContext
      context, TagHelperOutput output)
    {
        var content = await output.GetChildContentAsync();
        var stringContent = content.GetContent();
        var time = DateTime.Now.ToString(this.Format);

        output.TagName = "span";
        output.Content.Append(string.Format(CultureInfo.Invariant
        Culture, stringContent, time));

        return base.ProcessAsync(context, output);
```

```
        }
    }
```

Here, we can see that we are doing a couple of things:

- Getting the value of the `Format` attribute
- Getting all the tag's content
- Setting the target tag's name to `span`
- Using the content and the format to output a string with the formatted timestamp

This is essentially the way to go to get content and attributes. You can also add attributes to the output (by adding values to `output.Attributes`), change the output tag name (`output.TagName`), or prevent any content from being generated at all (by using the `output.SuppressOutput` method).

When outputting contents, we can either return plain strings, which are encoded as per the view's `HtmlEncoder` instance, or return already encoded contents—in which case, instead of `Append`, we would call `AppendHtml`:

```
output.Content.Append("<p>hello, world!</p>");
```

Besides appending, we can also replace all of the content; for that, we call `\t` or `SetHtmlContent`, or even clear everything (`Clear` or `SuppressOutput`).

An `[OutputElementHint]` attribute can be used to provide a hint as to what tag will output—this is useful so that Visual Studio knows to give hints about attributes of some other elements, such as `img`:

```
[OutputElementHint("img")]
```

This way, when you add your custom tag in markup, Visual Studio will suggest all of the `img` element's attributes, such as `SRC`.

We can use the `context.Items` collection to pass data from one tag helper to another—remember that the `Order` property defines which will be processed first.

Let's look at the properties exposed by tag helpers now.

Understanding the properties of a tag helper

Any public properties in the tag helper class can be set through the view. By default, the same name in either lowercase or the same case is used, but we can give a property a different name to be used in the view by applying an `[HtmlAttributeName]` attribute:

```
[HtmlAttributeName("time-format")]
public string Format { get; set; }
```

In this case, the attribute must now be declared as `time-format`.

If, on the other hand, we do not want to allow a property's value to be set through the view's markup, we can apply the `[HtmlAttributeNotBound]` attribute to it.

Properties of basic types can be specified in the markup, as well as a couple of others that can be converted from strings (such as `Guid`, `TimeSpan`, and `DateTime`) and any enumerations.

We can use Razor expressions to pass code-generated values to tag attributes:

```
<time format="GetTimeFormat()">Time is {0}</format>
```

Finally, it is worth mentioning that we can get Visual Studio's IntelliSense for the view's model if we use a property of the `ModelExpression` type:

```
public ModelExpression FormatFrom { get; set; }
```

This is what it would look like:

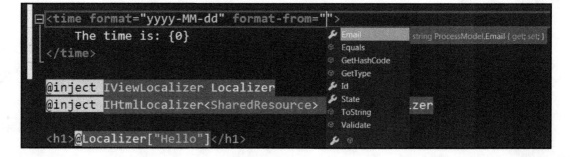

To actually retrieve the value of the property, we need to analyze the `Name` and `Metadata` properties of `ModelExpression`.

Restricting the applicability of a tag helper

A tag helper can be restricted in its applicability in a few ways:

- It can target a specific element—either a known HTML tag or a custom XML tag.
- Its target tag must be contained inside another tag.
- Its target tag must have certain attributes, possibly with a specific format.
- Its tag must have a specific structure.

A number of restrictions can be specified in terms of several [HtmlTargetElement] attributes:

```
//matches any a elements
[HtmlTargetElement("a")]
//matches any a elements contained inside a div tag
[HtmlTargetElement("a", ParentTag = "div")]
//matches any a elements that target a JavaScript file ending in .js
[HtmlTargetElement("a", Attributes = "[href$='.js']")]
//matches any a elements that target a link starting with ~
[HtmlTargetElement("a", Attributes = "[href^='~']")]
//matches any a elements with a value for the name attribute
[HtmlTargetElement("a", Attributes = "name")]
//matches any a elements with a specific id
[HtmlTargetElement("a", Attributes = "id='link'")]
//matches any a elements that do not have any inner contents (for
example, <a/>)
[HtmlTargetElement("a", TagStructure = TagStructure.WithoutEndTag)]
```

So, we have the following properties:

- ParentTag (string): The name of a parent tag
- Attributes (string): A comma-separated list of attributes and optional values
- TagStructure (TagStructure): The format of the tag, with the default being Unspecified

TagStructure specifies whether the tag is self-closing (WithoutEndTag) or may have contents (NormalOrSelfClosing).

If a tag helper is found that does not match its applicability rules, an exception is thrown at runtime. Multiple rules can be specified at the same time and different tag helpers can match the same rules.

If you target *, it will apply to any element.

Discovering tag helpers

A tag helper needs to implement the `ITagHelper` interface. Tag helpers need to be explicitly added, and a good place to do so is the `_ViewImports.cshtml` file. Anything placed here will apply to all views. Let's see how each one works:

- The `addTagHelper` directive adds a specific assembly and tag helpers:

  ```
  @addTagHelper *, Microsoft.AspNetCore.Mvc.TagHelpers
  ```

 The syntax is `@addTagHelper <types>, <assembly>`, where * stands for all types.

- If we want to prevent a specific tag helper from being used, we apply one or more `removeTagHelper` directives:

  ```
  @removeTagHelper
  Microsoft.AspNetCore.Mvc.TagHelpers.AnchorTagHelper,
  Microsoft.AspNetCore.Mvc.TagHelpers
  ```

- If we want to make the use of tag helpers explicit, we can force them to have a prefix by using a `tagHelperPrefix` directive:

  ```
  @tagHelperPrefix asp:
  ```

- Finally, we also have the option to disable any possible tag helpers that target a certain tag. We just prefix it with the `!` character:

  ```
  <!a href="...">link</a>
  ```

Dependency injection

Tag helpers are instantiated by the dependency injection mechanism, which means that they can take registered services in the constructor.

Neither the `Init`, `Process`, or `ProcessAsync` methods offer access to the execution context, but—similar to POCO controllers and view components—we can inject `ViewContext`:

```
[ViewContext]
public ViewContext ViewContext { get; set; }
```

From here, we have access to `HttpContext` and `ActionDescriptor`, as well as the route data, the view data, and so on.

Studying the included tag helpers

The following tag helpers are included in the `Microsoft.AspNetCore.Mvc.TagHelpers` assembly:

- `AnchorTagHelper` (`<a>`): Renders an anchor
- `CacheTagHelper` (`<cache>`): Defines an in-memory cached area
- `ComponentTagHelper` (`<component>`): Renders a Blazor component
- `DistributedCacheTagHelper` (`<distributed-cache>`): Renders a distributed cached area
- `EnvironmentTagHelper` (`<environment>`): Decides whether to render depending on the current environment
- `FormActionTagHelper` (`<form>`): Renders a form that renders to a controller action
- `FormTagHelper` (`<form>`): Renders a form
- `ImageTagHelper` (`<img>`): Renders an image
- `InputTagHelper` (`<input>`): Renders an input element
- `LabelTagHelper` (`<label>`): Renders a label
- `LinkTagHelper` (`<link>`): Renders an internal link
- `OptionTagHelper` (`<option>`): Renders a select option
- `PartialTagHelper` (`<partial>`): Renders a Razor partial view
- `RenderAtEndOfFormTagHelper` (`<form>`): Renders content at the end of a form
- `ScriptTagHelper` (`<script>`): Renders a script
- `SelectTagHelper` (`<select>`): Renders a `select` element
- `TextAreaTagHelper` (`<textarea>`): Renders a text area

- `ValidationMessageTagHelper` (`<span>`): Renders a validation message placeholder
- `ValidationSummaryTagHelper` (`<div>`): Renders a validation summary placeholder

Some of these translate URLs that start with ~ to the server-specific address or add controller and action attributes, which are in turn translated to controller action URLs:

```
<a href="~">Root</a>
<a asp-controller="Account" asp-action="Logout">Logout</a>
<form asp-controller="Account" asp-action="Login">
</form>
```

For example, you can have your application deployed under / or under virtual path, such as /admin. If you do not know this upfront, you can't just hardcode your links to point to /, but instead, you can use ~ and the ASP.NET Core framework will make sure it is set to the right path.

However, some other tags are quite powerful and offer very interesting features.

The `<a>` tag

The `<a>` tag helper offers some properties for anchors that allow you to target specific actions of specific controllers, Razor pages, or named routes:

```
<a
  asp-action="ActionName"
  asp-controller="ControllerName"
  asp-page="RazorPageName"
  asp-route="RouteName"
  asp-area="AreaName">...</a>
```

Notice how we can always specify the area name, regardless of whether we are targeting a controller's action, a Razor page, or a particular route by name.

If you add `asp-action` but not the `asp-controller` attribute, it will default to the current controller.

The properties are as follows:

- `asp-action` (`string`): The name of an action of a controller.
- `asp-area` (`string`): The name of an area.

- `asp-controller` (`string`): The name of a controller, which should be used with `asp-action`. If not supplied, it defaults to the current controller.
- `asp-page` (`string`): The name of a Razor page.
- `asp-route` (`string`): The name of a route, as specified in the endpoints definition.

You can start the hyperlink with a `"~/"` instead of `"/"`, which means that local paths with be mapped according to the base path of the application - for example, if the application is deployed to `"/app"`, then a URL of `"~/file"` will be turned to `"/app/file"`.

The <cache> tag

This tag helper caches the contents declared in it in the memory cache (any instance of `IMemoryCache` registered in the dependency injection framework). The only options we have are the duration to keep the cache and whether it is relative, absolute, or sliding. Let's look at the most basic example of this:

```
<cache expires-after="TimeSpan.FromMinutes(5)">
@DateTime.Now
</cache>
```

This will keep the string in the `<cache>` tag in the memory cache for a certain amount of time. We also have the following properties:

- `enabled` (`bool`): Whether it is enabled (which is the default)
- `expires-after` (`TimeSpan`): A value for relative expiration
- `expires-on` (`DateTime`): Absolute expiration
- `expires-sliding` (`TimeSpan`): Sliding expiration, which is almost identical to relative expiration, except it restarts every time the cache is hit
- `priority` (`CacheItemPriority`): A priority for the cache, with the default being `Normal`
- `vary-by` (`string`): An arbitrary (and possibly dynamic) string value to vary the cache by
- `vary-by-cookie` (`string`): A comma-separated list of cookie names to vary the cache by
- `vary-by-header` (`string`): A comma-separated list of header names to vary the cache by

- `vary-by-query` (`string`): A comma-separated list of `query` string parameter names to vary the cache by
- `vary-by-route` (`string`): A comma-separated list of route data parameters to vary the cache by
- `vary-by-user` (`bool`): Whether to vary the cache as per the logged-in username (the default is `false`)

Either `expires-after`, `expires-on`, or `expires-sliding` must be supplied, but the default value is 20 minutes. For `vary-by`, it is common to set a model value, such as an order or product ID, as follows:

```
<cache vary-by="@ProductId">
...
</cache>
```

The <component> tag

This tag helper was only introduced to .NET Core 3.0 and is related to Blazor, which we will talk about in more detail in `Chapter 17`, *Introducing Blazor*. Essentially, it renders a Blazor component (a `.razor` file). It accepts the following parameters:

- `type` (`string`): The name of the `.razor` file.
- `render-mode` (`RenderMode`): One of the possible rendering modes that are discussed in `Chapter 17`, *Introducing Blazor*.
- `param-XXX` (`string`): Optional parameters to be passed to the Blazor component; XXX should match the names of the properties on the component.

The tag is as follows:

```
<component type="typeof(SomeComponent)" render-mode="ServerPrerendered" param-Text="Hello, World"/>
```

The <distributed-cache> tag

The `<distributed-cache>` tag is identical to the `<cache>` tag helper, except it uses distributed cache (`IDistributedCache`). It adds another property to the ones supplied by `<cache>`—name (`string`), which is a unique name for the distributed cache entry. Each entry should have its own tag:

```
<distributed-cache name="redis" />
```

The <environment> tag

The `<environment>` tag is also very handy—it provides the ability to add content depending on the environment that is running (for example, `Development`, `Staging`, and `Production`):

```
<environment names="Development,Staging">
    <script src="development/file.js"></script>
</environment>
<environment names="Production">
    <script src="production/file.js"></script>
</environment>
```

From ASP.NET Core 2 onward, besides `names`, we also have two new attributes—`include` and `exclude`. `include` is exactly the same as `names`, whereas `exclude` does what you would expect—it shows the contents for all the environments except those listed after the command (comma-separated).

The properties for these attributes are as follows:

- `include`: Provides a list of environments to include for the rendering
- `exclude`: Provides a list of environments to exclude from the rendering

`exclude` always takes precedence.

The <form> tag

The form tag helper can be used instead of `IHtmlHelper.BeginForm()`. Both offer the same features, including posting to specific controller actions and adding anti-forgery tokens as hidden fields (refer to `Chapter 11`, *Security*, for more information). Let's look at the following example:

```
<form asp-controller="Home" asp-antiforgery="false" asp-
action="Process">
```

Anti-forgery is turned on by default. Its properties are as follows:

- `asp-controller`: The controller name—if not supplied, it defaults to the current one (if using MVC).
- `asp-action`: The controller's action method
- `asp-area`: The name of an area where the target controller is located
- `asp-page`: A Razor Page that will handle the form

- asp-page-hander: The name of a page handler method in an Razor Page that will handle the form
- asp-route: A named route
- asp-antiforgery: Decides whether to detect a request forgery—turned on by default

Notice that asp-controller, asp-area and asp-action can be used together, but it doesn't make any sense to combine them with asp-route or asp-page, as these are different ways to specify a destination.

The <script> tag

The <script> tag helper allows test, default, and fallback values to be specified for the source property. The test is a JavaScript expression; let's look at an example:

```
<!-- if the current browser does not have the window.Promise property
load a polyfill -->
<script asp-fallback-test="window.Promise" src="file.js" asp-fallback-
src="polyfill.js"></script>
```

It can also be used to load all the files into a folder at once (with some possible exceptions):

```
<script asp-src-include="~/app/**/*.js" asp-src-
exclude="~/app/services/**/*.js"></script>
```

Finally, it can also be used to bust caching by adding a version number to local scripts; this version reflects the file's timestamp:

```
<script src="~/file.js" asp-append-version="true"></script>
```

You might have noticed the leading ~ symbol in the src attribute; it is automatically replaced by the root folder of your application. For example, if your app is deployed in /, it will use /, but if it is deployed in /virtualPath, then ~ is replaced by /virtualPath. This is the base path that is described in Chapter 2, *Configuration*.

The <link> tag

The <link> tag helper can suffix a local URL with a version to make it cache-friendly:

```
<link rel="stylesheet" href="~/css/site.min.css" asp-append-
version="true"/>
```

Similar to the `<script>` tag helper, it includes content conditionally:

```
<link rel="stylesheet" href="file.css" asp-fallback-
href="otherfile.css"
    asp-fallback-test-class="hidden" asp-fallback-test-property
    ="visibility"
    asp-fallback-test-value="hidden" />
```

The <select> tag

The `<select>` tag helper knows how to retrieve items from a model property of an enumerable type or from a collection of `SelectListItem` objects:

```
@functions
{
    IEnumerable<SelectListItem> GetItems()
    {
        yield return new SelectListItem { Text = "Red", Value =
"#FF0000" };
        yield return new SelectListItem { Text = "Green",
        Value = "#00FF00" };
        yield return new SelectListItem { Text = "Blue",
        Value = "#0000FF",
         Selected = true };
    }
}
<select asp-items="GetItems()"/>
```

There are two important properties:

- `asp-for`: The property or method to retrieve the currently selected item (or list of items) from
- `asp-items`: The property or method to retrieve the items to fill the list from

The <partial> tag

This tag was introduced to ASP.NET 2.1; it renders a partial view, which is pretty much what the `RenderPartial(Async)` and `Partial(Async)` methods do.

```
<partial name="_PartialFile" for="ModelProperty" model="Model" view-
data="ViewData"></partial>
```

Besides the `name` partial view (which is the only required property), we can also pass it a view data object (`view-data`) and a model (a `for` property or `model`). The `for` property can be used to pass an expression relative to the model of the containing view; for example, a property of the model. If you prefer, you can pass a whole new model to the partial view by assigning a value to the `model` property. Mind you, `for` and `model` are mutually exclusive; you can only use one of them. If you don't use either, the current model is passed to the partial view.

The properties are as follows:

- `for` (`Expression`): An optional expression, relative to the current model, to pass to the partial view. It cannot be used with `model`.
- `model` (`object`): An optional model to pass to the partial view. If set, it must match its declared model type. It cannot be used with `for`.
- `name` (`string`): Required. This is the name of the partial view to render.

Validation message and summary

The `ValidationMessageTagHelper` and `ValidationSummaryTagHelper` tag helpers merely add a validation message for any model properties in a `<span>` tag and in a `<div>` tag for the whole model. For example, say you want to get the current validation message for the `Email` model property. You would do the following:

```
<span asp-validation-for="Email"/>
```

For the whole model, do the following:

```
<div asp-validation-summary/>
```

The next topic introduces the concept of tag helpers to a higher level. We will see how the tag helper components work.

Tag helper components

Tag helper components were introduced to ASP.NET Core 2.0. They are a way of using DI to insert markup in the output. Imagine, for example, inserting JavaScript or CSS files at specific locations in your views.

Tag helper components must implement `ITagHelperComponent` and are registered in the DI framework (the `ConfigureServices` method):

```
services.AddSingleton<ITagHelperComponent,
HelloWorldTagHelperComponent>();
```

The `ITagHelperComponent` interface only specifies one method, `ProcessAsync`. Each registered tag helper component has its `ProcessAsync` method called for every tag found on the current view, including layouts, giving it a chance to inject custom tag helpers:

```
public class HelloWorldTagHelperComponent : TagHelperComponent
{
    public override Task ProcessAsync(TagHelperContext context,
    TagHelperOutput output)
    {
        if (context.TagName.ToLowerInvariant() == "head")
        {
            output.Content.AppendHtml("<script>window.alert('Hello,
            World!')</script>");
        }

        return Task.CompletedTask;
    }
}
```

This example inserts custom JavaScript at the end of the current tag's content, if this tag is `head`.

The `TagHelperComponent` class implements `ITagHelperComponent` and offers virtual methods that we can override as we please. We have the same two methods as with the `ITagHelper` interface—`Init` and `ProcessAsync`—and they are used in the same way.

`ProcessAsync` takes two parameters, which are the same as the ones the `ITagHelper` interface's `ProcessAsync` method takes.

 Tag helper components, as they are instantiated by the DI framework, fully support constructor injection.

Let's now talk a bit about partial views, which are one of the building blocks of Razor MVC.

Partial views

We already covered partial views in `Chapter 8`, *API Controllers*. Although they are a very interesting mechanism for reusing content, they historically have a problem—they could not be reused across assemblies. There has always been a way around this; the idea is to mark the view's `.cshtml` file as an embedded resource:

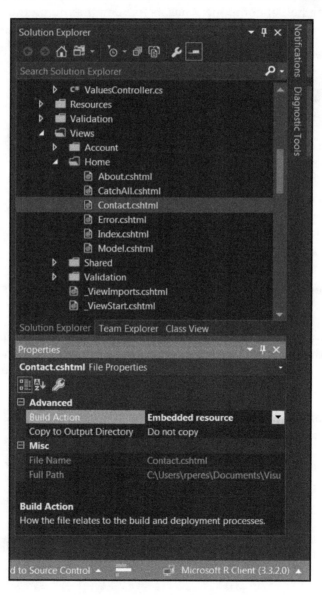

Then, we just need to use a file provider that knows how to retrieve the file contents from assembly-embedded resources. Add the `Microsoft.Extensions.FileProviders.Embedded` NuGet package for this example.

When registering the MVC services in `ConfigureServices`, we need to register another file provider, `EmbeddedFileProvider`, passing it to the assembly that contains the embedded resource:

```
services
    .AddMvc()
    .AddRazorOptions(options =>
    {
        var assembly = typeof(MyViewComponent).GetTypeInfo().Assembly;
        var embeddedFileProvider = new EmbeddedFileProvider(assembly,
        "ReusableComponents");
        options.FileProviders.Add(embeddedFileProvider);
    });
```

In this case, the `MyViewComponent` class is hosted on the same assembly where the view is embedded and its default namespace is `ReusableComponents`. When trying to load a file, ASP.NET Core will go through all the registered file providers until one returns a non-null result.

Fortunately, we now have **Razor class libraries**, which we will cover shortly.

Partial views versus view components

These two mechanisms are similar, but you would choose to use partial views if you have a somewhat large chunk of HTML that you want to render in view components, as you would need to manipulate strings and return them by code. On the other hand, partial views are external files, which can have advantages.

Next, we will talk about something totally different—libraries of code that you can reuse in projects.

Understanding Razor class libraries

Razor class libraries were introduced to ASP.NET Core 2.2. What it means is that all components—code- or file-based—can be added to an assembly and then referenced by an application. If, for example, this class library contains multiple .cshtml files, we can refer to them in our controllers or provide overrides for them in the application, provided that the same path is respected. Think, for example, of the authentication and registration views provided by Identity; if you don't like any of them, you can provide an alternative one while keeping the others.

Razor class libraries can be created using Visual Studio:

It essentially produces a `.csproj` file that uses
the `Microsoft.NET.Sdk.Razor` SDK (Razor class libraries) instead
of `Microsoft.NET.Sdk.Web` (for web applications) or `Microsoft.NET.Sdk` (for
.NET Core assemblies):

```
<Project Sdk="Microsoft.NET.Sdk.Razor">
    <PropertyGroup>
        <TargetFramework>netstandard3.0</TargetFramework>
    </PropertyGroup>
    <ItemGroup>
        <PackageReference Include="Microsoft.AspNetCore.Mvc" />
    </ItemGroup>
</Project>
```

When referencing a Razor class library assembly, ASP.NET Core knows just what to
do, and you can reference its components without any other effort.

Referencing static content

If you create a `wwwroot` folder in a Razor class library project, you can access any
static content (such as `.js`, `.css`, and images) stored in it in a project that references
it. Just create links by using the following format:

```
<script src="_content/<ClassLib>/<File>"></script>
```

Here, `<ClassLib>` is the name of the referenced Razor class library and `<File>` is the
name of the static file. One thing to keep in mind is that you need to have support for
loading static files, e.g., in `Configure`, add this:

```
app.UseStaticFiles();
```

Referencing external components

View components and tag helpers can be added by referencing assemblies that
contain them, which is done when a project is created or is being worked on.
However, we can add references at runtime, too. These are called application parts.

In order to register an application part for a Razor class library, here's what we do:

```
services
    .AddMvc()
    .ConfigureApplicationManager(options =>
    {
```

```
        var path = "<path-to-razor-class-library-dll>";
        var asm = Assembly.LoadFrom(path);
        options.ApplicationParts.Add(new
CompiledRazorAssemblyPart(asm));
    });
```

`CompiledRazorAssemblyPart` should be used for Razor class libraries, which also includes static (file-based) resources. We can also do this for types, in which case the class to use is `AssemblyPart`.

Here, we've seen how we can reference parts from external assemblies, which can include any reusable components. This is the last topic of this chapter. In the next chapter, we will cover filters.

Summary

In this chapter, we saw that we always use the supplied base classes for view components, tag helpers, and tag helper components, as they make our life much easier.

It is preferred to use tag helpers over HTML helpers wherever possible and to write our own tag helpers as they are much easier to read than code. Tag helper components are very useful for inserting code automatically in specific locations. The `<cache>`, `<distributed-cache>`, and `<environment>` tag helpers are very interesting and will help you out a lot.

Then, we saw that partial views are preferable to view components when you have a template that you wish to render that is easier to code in HTML. View components are all about code and it's harder to implement HTML by string concatenation. On the other hand, view components let you pass parameters much more easily.

Razor class libraries are a new way of distributing static assets between projects. Make sure you use them!

We also learned that tag helper components are a very nice way of injecting HTML elements anywhere from a centralized location. Use them for common CSS and JavaScript.

In this chapter, we looked at techniques for reusing components across projects. Code reuse is almost always a good idea and you can use view components with parameters to help achieve this. In the next chapter, we will cover filters, which are a process for intercepting, and possibly modifying requests and responses.

Questions

You should now be able to answer the following questions:

1. How can we load partial views from a different assembly?
2. What are the two ways of rendering partial views?
3. What is the difference between tag helpers and tag helper components?
4. How can we restrict what is displayed on a view depending on the environment?
5. What is the difference between Razor class libraries and class libraries?
6. What are embedded resources?
7. What are the two syntaxes for executing view components?

10
Understanding Filters

Filters are a mechanism that ASP.NET Core makes available to apply cross-cutting concerns, such as logging, exception handling, enforcing authorization and authentication, and more. They have been around since the early days of the ASP.NET MVC, but have been augmented in Core.

Filters in ASP.NET Core are an interception mechanism by which we can execute code before, instead of after, a request is processed. Think of them as a way to add custom steps to a pipeline without actually doing so; it remains unchanged but instead, we have finer-grained control over what we are intercepting. They are useful for implementing cross-cutting operations, such as access control, caching, or logging. Here, we will discuss the following:

- Learning about the different filter types
- Understanding authorization filters
- Understanding resource filters
- Understanding action filters
- Understanding result filters
- Understanding exception filters
- Understanding page filters
- Understanding always-run-result filters

Technical requirements

In order to implement the examples introduced in this chapter, you will need the .NET Core 3 SDK and a text editor. Of course, Visual Studio 2019 (any edition) meets all the requirements, but you can also use Visual Studio Code, for example.

The source code can be retrieved from GitHub at `https://github.com/PacktPublishing/Modern-Web-Development-with-ASP.NET-Core-3-Second-Edition`.

Filters in the pipeline

Filters are part of the pipeline. They execute after ASP.NET Core selects the controller (or Razor page) to run. This is illustrated in the following diagram:

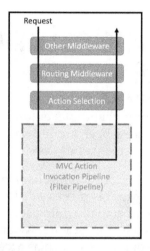

Image obtained from https://docs.microsoft.com/en-us/aspnet/core/mvc/controllers/filters

Filters are an interception mechanism. A filter does something before, after, or instead of a controller (or Razor page) action. The next section explains what the different filter types are.

Understanding the filter types

In ASP.NET Core 3 (and version 2, for that matter), we have the following filters:

- **Authorization**
  (`IAuthorizationFilter` and `IAsyncAuthorizationFilter`): These control whether the user performing the current request has permission to access the specified resource; if not, then the rest of the pipeline is short-circuited and an error message is returned.
- **Resource** (`IResourceFilter` and `IAsyncResourceFilter`): These execute after a request is authorized but before action selection and model binding. These are new to ASP.NET Core.
- **Action** (`IActionFilter` and `IAsyncActionFilter`): These are executed before and after the action method is called.

- **Result** (`IResultFilter` and `IAsyncResultFilter`): These occur before and after the actual execution of an action result (the `IActionResult.ExecuteResultAsync` method).

- **Exception** (`IExceptionFilter` and `IAsyncExceptionFilter`): These are called when an exception is thrown during the course of the action being processed.

- **Page** (`IPageFilter` and `IAsyncPageFilter`): These occur before and after a Razor page handler method is called and are new to ASP.NET Core 2.

- **Always run result** (`IAlwaysRunResultFilter` and `IAsyncAlwaysRunResultFilter`): These are new to ASP.NET Core 2.1 and are similar to an **action** filter, but unlike this, the always run result, always runs, even when there is an exception:

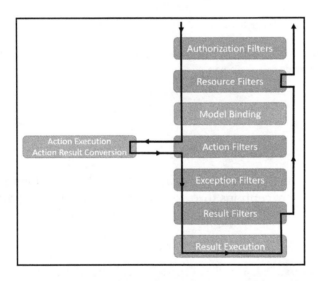

Image obtained from https://docs.microsoft.com/en-us/aspnet/core/mvc/controllers/filters

Filters of these kinds have pre-methods and post-methods that are called before and after the target event, respectively—authorization, resource, action, result, and page. The pre-method version always ends in executing and the post-method version ends in execution. For example, for action filters, the methods are called `OnActionExecuting` and& `OnActionExecuted`. Authorization and exception filters, of course, only offer a single method—`OnAuthorization` and `OnException`, respectively—but you can think of them as post-event methods.

The only base class for all filters is `IFilterMetadata`, which offers no methods or properties and is just meant as a marker interface. Because of this, the ASP.NET Core framework must check the concrete type of a filter to try to identify the known interfaces that it implements.

Let's start with the two cross-cutting types of filters, which have types.

Synchronous versus asynchronous

Each filter type offers both a synchronous and an asynchronous version, the latter having an `Async` prefix. The difference between the two is that in the asynchronous version, only the pre-method is defined and it is called asynchronously; for action filters, the synchronous version offers `OnActionExecuting`/`OnActionExecuted` and the asynchronous version offers a single `OnActionExecutionAsync` method. Only exception filters do not offer an asynchronous version.

Choose either asynchronous or synchronous filters, but not both! Now, let's have a look at the filter applicability scope.

Filter scope

Filters can be applied at different levels:

- **Global**: Global filters apply to all controllers and actions and so they also capture any exceptions thrown. Global filters are added through the `AddMvc` method to the `Filters` collection of the `MvcOptions` class:

  ```
  services.AddMvc(options =>
  {
      options.Filters.Add(new AuthorizeAttribute());
  });
  ```

- **Controller**: Controller-level filters are generally added through resources applied to the controller class and apply to any actions called on them:

  ```
  [Authorize]
  public class HomeController : Controller { ... }
  ```

- **Action**: These filters only apply to the action method where they are declared:

```
public class HomeController
{
    [Authorize]
    public IActionResult Index() { ... }
}
```

The `Filters` collection of `MvcOptions` can take either a filter type or an instance of a filter. Use the filter type if you want the filter to be built using the DI framework.

Let's now look at the execution order of filters.

Execution order

Filters are called in the following order:

- Authorization
- Resource
- Action
- Page (for Razor Pages only)
- Result
- Always run result

Exception and page filters, of course, are special, so they are only called on the occurrence of an exception or when calling a Razor page, respectively.

Because most filters have a pre-method and a post-method, the actual order looks like this:

- IAuthorizationFilter.OnAuthorization
- IResourceFilter.OnResourceExecuting
- IActionFilter.OnActionExecuting
- <controller action>
- IActionFilter.OnActionExecuted
- IResultFilter.OnResultExecuting
- IAlwaysRunResultFilter.OnResultExecuting
- IAlwaysRunResultFilter.OnResultExecuted

- `IResultFilter.OnResultExecuted`
- `IResourceFilter.OnResourceExecuted`

`<Controller action>` is, of course, the action method on the controller, in case we are using the MVC (for Razor Pages, refer to `Chapter 7`, *Implementing Razor Pages*).

It is possible to short-circuit some of the filters; for example, if on a resource or authorization filter we return a result, by setting a value to the `Result` property of the context, the action filter or any other filter set to execute after it will not be called. However, any registered always-run-result filter will always run.

Depending on how the filters are applied, we can influence this order; for example, for global filters, filters of the same type are ordered according to the index in the `MvcOptions.Filters` collection, as follows:

```
options.Filters.Insert(0, new AuthorizeAttribute());  //first one
```

For attribute filters, the `IOrderedFilter` interface provides an `Order` property, which can be used to order attributes of the same scope (global, controller, or action):

```
[Cache(Order = 1)]
[Authorize(Order = 0)]
[Log(Order = 2)]
public IActionResult Index() { ... }
```

Let's now see how we can apply and order filters through attributes.

Applying filters through attributes

Filter interfaces can be implemented by a regular attribute (the `Attribute` class) and it will then act as a filter; there are some abstract base attribute classes`ActionFilterAttribute` (action and result filters), `ResultFilterAttribute` (result filters), and `ExceptionFilterAttribute` (exception filters) that can be subclassed to implement this behavior. These classes implement both the synchronous and asynchronous versions and also support ordering the order by which they will be called—by implementing `IOrderedFilter`. So, if you want to have a filter attribute that handles actions and results, you can inherit from `ActionFilterAttribute` and implement just one or more of its virtual methods:

- `OnActionExecuting`
- `OnActionExecuted`

- OnActionExecutionAsync
- OnResultExecuting
- OnResultExecuted
- OnResultExecutionAsync

For example, if you wish to override some behavior on the abstract `ActionFilterAttribute` filter attribute to do something before an action is invoked, you can try the following:

```
public class LogActionAttribute : ActionFilterAttribute
{
    public override void OnActionExecuting(ActionExecutingContext
    context)
    {
        var loggerFactory = context.HttpContext.RequestServices.
        GetRequiredService<ILoggerFactory>();
        var logger = _loggerFactory.CreateLogger
        (context.Controller.GetType());
        logger.LogTrace($"Before {context.ActionDescriptor.
        DisplayName}");
    }
}
```

Here, we are injecting the logger factory through the attribute's constructor, which inherits from `ActionFilterAttribute`, and getting a logger from it.

Filter ordering

Filters of the same kind will be ordered according to either of the following:

- The order in which they were inserted into the `MvcOptions.Filters` collection
- If the filter implements `IOrderedFilter`, its `Order` property

For example, all global filters of the authorization type will be sorted according to these rules, then all controller-level filters being applied to a controller, then all action-level filters.

All of the `ActionFilterAttribute`, `MiddlewareFilterAttribute`, `ServiceFilterAttribute`, and `TypeFilterAttribute` classes implement `IOrderedFilter`; these are the most common ways by which you can inject filters into controllers and actions.

Let's now see how filters can be created.

Factories and providers

A filter factory is just an instance of a class that creates filters; the only requisite is that it implements `IFilterFactory`, which, because it inherits from `IFilterMetadata`, can also be used as a global filter or in a custom attribute. Why would you do that? Well, because when the filter factory runs, you will probably learn something more from the current execution context. Let's see an example:

```
public class CustomFilterFactory : IFilterFactory
{
    public bool IsReusable => true;

    public IFilterMetadata CreateInstance(IServiceProvider
    serviceProvider)
    {
        //get some service from the DI framework
        var svc = serviceProvider.GetRequiredService<IMyService>();
        //create our filter passing it the service
        return new CustomFilter(svc);
    }
}
```

This filter factory depends on a very specific service that is required to be registered. For registering this custom filter factory globally, we use the following:

```
services.AddMvc(options =>
{
    options.Filters.Insert(0, new CustomFilterFactory());
});
```

Implementing `IFilterFactory` in an attribute is equally simple, so I won't show it here.

The contract for a filter factory is simple:

- `IsReusable` (`bool`): Tells the framework if it is safe to reuse the filter factory across requests.
- `CreateInstance`: This method returns a filter.

The `CreateInstance` method takes an `IServiceProvider` instance as its sole parameter and returns an `IFilterMetadata` object, meaning you can return any kind of filter you want (or even another filter factory).

A filter provider (`IFilterProvider`) is the actual implementation that is registered in the DI framework as part of the MVC configuration and is the one that fires all the different filter behaviors. The default implementation is `DefaultFilterProvider`. The `IFilterProvider` interface has a single property:

- `Order` (`int`): The order by which the provider will be executed. This offers the following two methods:

  - `OnProvidersExecuting`: Called to inject filters in its context parameter
  - `OnProvidersExecuted`: Called after all filters have been executed

What about the DI—is there any way to use it with filters? Oh yes, there is, and we'll see how just now!

DI

The ways to add filters that we've seen so far—globally through the `Filters` collection or by means of attributes—are not DI-friendly; in the first case, you add an already instantiated object, and for attributes, they are static data that is not instantiated by the DI framework. However, we have the `[ServiceFilter]` attribute—it accepts the type of a filter class (of any kind) as its sole required parameter and it uses the DI framework to instantiate it; what's more, it even allows ordering:

```
[ServiceFilter(typeof(CacheFilter), Order = 2)]
[ServiceFilter(typeof(LogFilter), Order = 1)]
public class HomeController : Controller { ... }
```

The `LogFilter` class, for example, might look like this:

```
public class LogFilter : IAsyncActionFilter
{
    private readonly ILoggerFactory _loggerFactory;

    public LogFilter(ILoggerFactory loggerFactory)
    {
        this._loggerFactory = loggerFactory;
    }

    public Task OnActionExecutionAsync(ActionExecutingContext
    context, ActionExecutionDelegate next)
    {
        var logger = this._loggerFactory.CreateLogger
        (context.Controller.GetType());
        logger.LogTrace($"{context.ActionDescriptor.DisplayName}
        action called");
        return next();
    }
}
```

`ILoggerFactory` is passed in the controller by the DI framework, as usual, and the `LogFilter` class itself must be registered:

```
services.AddSingleton<LogFilter>();
```

There is another special attribute, `[TypeFilter]`, which, given a certain type and some optional arguments, tries to instantiate it:

```
[TypeFilter(typeof(CacheFilter), Arguments = new object[] { 60 * 1000
* 60 })]
```

These arguments are passed as parameters to the constructor of the filter type. This time, no DI is used; it will just pass along any values it receives when attempting to build the concrete type, in the same way as `Activator.CreateInstance` does.

If you want, you can change the default filter provider by supplying your own implementation for the `IFilterProvider` service:

```
services.AddSingleton<IFilterProvider, CustomFilterProvider>();
```

This process is complex because you need to return filters coming from the global repository (`MvcOptions`), attributes applied to the class, the method, and more, so you'd better know what you're doing. If in doubt, keep the existing implementation.

The other way is to use the `RequestServices` service locator:

```
var svc =
context.HttpContext.RequestServices.GetService<IMyService>();
```

This is available in every filter that exposes the `HttpContext` object.

Accessing the context

You can pass the context from one filter to another by using the `HttpContext.Items` collection, as follows:

```
public class FirstFilter : IActionFilter
{
    public void OnActionExecuting(ActionExecutingContext context) { }

    public void OnActionExecuted(ActionExecutedContext context)
    {
        context.HttpContext.Items["WasFirstFilterExecuted"] = true;
    }
}

public class SecondFilter : IActionFilter
{
    public void OnActionExecuted(ActionExecutedContext context) { }

    public void OnActionExecuting(ActionExecutingContext context)
    {
        if (context.HttpContext.Items["WasFirstFilterExecuted"]
        is bool parameter && parameter)
        {
            //proceed accordingly
        }
    }
}
```

The first filter that is called sets a flag in the current request items, and the second checks for its presence and carries out an action accordingly. We just need to be certain of the order by which filters will be applied, and this can be achieved through the `IOrderedFilter.Order` property, as mentioned previously, exposed by `ActionFilterAttribute`, `ServiceFilterAttribute`, and `TypeFilterAttribute`.

Now, let's see how filters actually work.

Applying authorization filters

This kind of filter is used to authorize the current user. The most notorious authorization attribute is [Authorize] and it can be used for common checks, such as being authenticated, belonging to a given role, or fulfilling a given policy.

This attribute does not implement either IAuthorizationFilter or IAsyncAuthorizationFilter, but instead, it implements IAuthorizeData, which lets us specify either role names (the Roles property), a custom policy name (Policy), or authentication schemes (AuthenticationSchemes). This attribute is handled by a built-in filter called AuthorizeFilter, which is added by default when we add the authorization middleware (AddAuthorization).

Other things that you can check in an authorization attribute include, for example, the following:

- Validating the source IP or domain of the client
- Verifying whether a given cookie is present
- Validating the client certificate

So, for custom authorization, we either need to implement IAuthorizationFilter or IAsyncAuthorizationFilter; the first one exposes a single method, OnAuthorization. The context object passed to the OnAuthorization method exposes HttpContext, ModelState, RouteData, and ActionDescriptor for the current request and the MVC action; you can use any of these to perform your own custom authorization. If you do not wish to authorize access, you can return UnauthorizedResult in the context's Result property, as follows:

```
public void OnAuthorization(AuthorizationFilterContext context)
{
    var entry = Dns.GetHostEntryAsync(context.HttpContext.
    Connection.RemoteIpAddress)
        .GetAwaiter()
        .GetResult();

    if (!entry.HostName.EndsWith(".MyDomain",
    StringComparison.OrdinalIgnoreCase))
    {
        context.Result = new UnauthorizedResult();
    }
}
```

In this case, if the request does not come from a known domain, it is denied access.

The `AuthorizationFilterContext` class has the following properties:

- `ActionDescriptor` (`ActionDescriptor`): The descriptor of the action to be called
- `Filters` (`IList<IFilterMetadata>`): The filters bound to this request
- `HttpContext` (`HttpContext`): The HTTP context
- `ModelState` (`ModelStateDictionary`): The model state (not used for authorization filters)
- `Result` (`IActionResult`): An optional result to return to the client, bypassing the request pipeline
- `RouteData` (`RouteData`): Route data of the request

You may be tempted to add a global filter that requires users to be authenticated everywhere; in this case, keep in mind that at least the entry page and the action that takes the credentials need to allow anonymous access.

As for `IAsyncAuthorizationFilter`, its `OnAuthorizationAsync` method also takes an `AuthorizationFilterContext` parameter, the only difference being that it is called asynchronously.

So now, let's look at a few authorization policies that need to be followed.

Authorization policies

In Chapter 9, *Reusable Components*, we talked about authorization handlers. They can be added as global filters, too, through the `AuthorizeFilter` class, which is a filter factory. Here's one example:

```
services.AddMvc(options =>
{
    var policy = new AuthorizationPolicyBuilder()
        .RequireAssertion(ctx => true) //let everything pass
        .Build();

    options.Filters.Add(new AuthorizeFilter(policy));
});
```

Here, we are building a policy with a specific assertion (in this case, we are allowing everything to be `true`), and we are adding a global `AuthorizeFilter` parameter that is built from this policy. This will then apply to all requests.

OK, we're done with authorization filters, so now let's look at resource filters.

Resource filters

In resource filters, you can apply similar logic as authorization filters but it executes slightly after the authorization filters, and you have more information. For example, when resource filters execute, the user has already logged in (if using authentication). Some common uses for resource filters are the following:

- Logging
- Caching
- Throttling
- Modifying model binding

The `IResourceFilter` interface defines two methods:

- `OnResourceExecuting`: Called before the request reaches the action
- `OnResourceExecuted`: Called after the action is executed

Each of these methods takes a single parameter of the `ResourceExecutingContext` and `ResourceExecutedContext` types for pre-events and post-events, respectively. `ResourceExecutingContext` offers the following properties, which reflect the context prior to the resource being processed:

- `Result` (`IActionResult`): If you wish to short-circuit the request pipeline, you can set a value here, and all the other filters and middleware will be bypassed (except the `OnResourceExecuted` method), returning this result; if you want to return a POCO value, wrap it in `ObjectResult`.
- `ValueProviderFactories` (`IList<IValueProviderFactory>`): Here, you can inspect, add, or modify the collection of value provider factories to be used when providing values to the target action's parameters.

As for `ResourceExecutedContext`, we have the following:

- `Canceled` (`bool`): Whether or not a result was set in `OnResourceExecuting`.
- `Exception` (`Exception`): Any exception thrown during the processing of the resource.

- `ExceptionDispatchInfo` (`ExceptionDispatchInfo`): The exception dispatch object, used for capturing the stack trace of an exception and, optionally, re-throwing it, while preserving this context.
- `ExceptionHandled` (`bool`): Whether the exception was handled or not (if there was one), the default being `false`; if not handled, then the framework will re-throw it.
- `Result` (`IActionResult`): The action set by the `OnExecuting` method, which can also be set here.

If an exception is thrown during the processing of the resource (in the action method or in another filter) and it is not explicitly marked as handled (`ExceptionHandled`) by the resource filter, it will be thrown by the framework, resulting in an error. If you want to know more, consult the documentation for `ExceptionDispatchInfo` at `https://msdn.microsoft.com/en-us/library/system.runtime.exceptionservices.exceptiondispatchinfo.aspx`.

The asynchronous alternative, `IAsyncResourceFilter`, only declares a single method, `OnResourceExecutionAsync`, taking two parameters—`ResourceExecutingContext` (the same as for the `OnResourceExecuting` method) and `ResourceExecutionDelegate`; this one is interesting, as you can use it to inject other middleware at runtime to the pipeline.

Here is an example of a caching filter:

```
[AttributeUsage(AttributeTargets.Method, Inherited = true,
AllowMultiple = false)]
public sealed class CacheResourceFilter : Attribute, IResourceFilter
{
    public TimeSpan Duration { get; }

    public CacheResourceFilter(TimeSpan duration)
    {
        this.Duration = duration;
    }

    public void OnResourceExecuted(ResourceExecutedContext context)
    {
        var cacheKey = context.HttpContext.Request.Path.ToString()
        .ToLowerInvariant();
        var memoryCache = context.HttpContext.RequestServices.
        GetRequiredService<IMemoryCache>();

        var result = context.Result as ContentResult;
```

```
        if (result != null)
        {
            memoryCache.Set(cacheKey, result.Content, this.Duration);
        }
    }

    public void OnResourceExecuting(ResourceExecutingContext context)
    {
        var cacheKey = context.HttpContext.Request.Path.ToString()
        .ToLowerInvariant();
        var memoryCache = context.HttpContext.RequestServices.
        GetRequiredService<IMemoryCache>();

        if (memoryCache.TryGetValue(cacheKey, out var cachedValue))
        {
            if (cachedValue != null && cachedValue
            is string cachedValueString)
            {
                context.Result = new ContentResult() {
                Content = cachedValueString };
            }
        }
    }
}
```

This filter takes the request path and checks that the `IMemoryCache` service, which it retrieves from the current context, has a value for it, and if it does, it sets the content from it. This is before the request is executed (`OnResourceExecuting`). After the resource is executed, the filter just stores the content in the memory cache. To make this work, we need to have the `IMemoryCache` service registered.

Again, do not implement the synchronous and asynchronous interfaces at the same time as only the asynchronous interface will be used.

That is it for resource filters; let's move on to action filters.

Understanding action filters

Action filters are invoked before and after an action method is called, so they can be used, for example, to do the following:

- Cache results
- Modify parameters
- Modify results

Now, we already have the parameters to the action method, which come from the value providers. Here, the filter interfaces are `IActionFilter` and `IAsyncActionFilter`. The synchronous one offers two methods, `OnActionExecuting` and `OnActionExecuted`. They are for pre-event and post-event notifications. `OnActionExecuting` takes a single parameter of the `ActionExecutingContext` type, offering the following properties:

- `Result` (`IActionResult`): Set a value here to short-circuit the request processing pipeline and return a value to the client, without actually executing the action.
- `ActionArguments` (`IDictionary<string, object>`): The parameters of the action method.
- `Controller` (`object`): The target controller instance.

You may be wondering why the `Controller` property is not prototyped as `ControllerBase` or `Controller`: do not forget that we can have POCO controllers!

The `ActionArguments` parameter has entries for each parameter of the target action method, and its values have been provided by the registered value providers.

The post-event method, `OnActionExecuted`, takes a parameter of the `ActionExecutedContext` type, which exposes the following properties:

- `Canceled` (`bool`): Whether or not a result was set in `OnActionExecuting`.
- `Controller` (`object`): The controller instance.
- `Exception` (`Exception`): Any exception thrown during the processing of the resource.
- `ExceptionDispatchInfo` (`ExceptionDispatchInfo`): The exception dispatch object, used for capturing the stack trace of an exception and, optionally, re-throwing it, while preserving this context.
- `ExceptionHandled` (`bool`): Whether the exception was handled or not (if there was one), the default being `false`; if not handled, then the framework will re-throw it.
- `Result` (`IActionResult`): The action set by the `OnExecuting` method, which can also be set here.

As for `IAsyncActionFilter`, it offers a single method, which is, `OnActionExecutionAsync`. It takes two parameters in the same fashion as `OnResourceExecutionAsync`: `ActionExecutingContext` and `ActionExecutionDelegate`. The `ActionExecutionDelegate` instance points to the next action filter method in the pipeline.

Now, we will move on to understanding result filters and how they are used in code.

Result filters

Result filters let you execute custom actions before and after the result is processed if an action executes with success. Action results are represented by `IActionResult`, and we can have code run before and after `ExecuteResultAsync` is called. Some common uses for result filters include the following:

- Caching (as before)
- Interception (modification of the response)
- Adding response headers
- Result formatting

The `IResultFilter` interface defines the `OnResultExecuting` and `OnResultExecuted` methods. The first takes an instance of `ResultExecutingContext` as its sole parameter, which offers the following properties:

- `Cancel` (bool): Whether or not to cancel the processing of the result
- `Result` (IActionResult): The result to process in case we want to bypass the returned result's execution
- `Controller` (object): The controller instance

As for the post-event method, `OnResultExecuted`, we have the following properties in `ResultExecutedContext`:

- `Canceled` (bool): Whether or not a result was set in `OnResultExecuting`.
- `Controller` (object): The controller instance.
- `Exception` (Exception): Any exception thrown during the processing of the resource.

- ExceptionDispatchInfo (ExceptionDispatchInfo): The exception dispatch object, used for capturing the stack trace of an exception and, optionally, re-throwing it, while preserving this context.
- ExceptionHandled (bool): Whether the exception was handled or not (if there was one), the default being false; if not handled, then the framework will re-throw it.
- Result (IActionResult): The action set by the OnResultExecuting method, which can also be set here.

These are exactly the same as for ResourceExecutedContext. As usual, we also have an asynchronous version of the result filters, IAsyncResultFilter, which, following the same pattern, offers a single method called OnResultExecutionAsync that has two parameters—one of the ResultExecutingContext type, which has the following properties:

- Cancel (bool): Whether or not to cancel the processing of the result
- Result (IActionResult): The result to process in case we want to bypass the returned result's execution
- Controller (object): The controller instance

The other parameter is ResultExecutionDelegate, which will point to the next delegate of the IAsyncResultFilter type in the pipeline. Here is a simple example of a result filter:

```
public class CacheFilter : IResultFilter
{
    private readonly IMemoryCache _cache;

    public CacheFilter(IMemoryCache cache)
    {
        this._cache = cache;
    }

    private object GetKey(ActionDescriptor action)
    {
        //generate a key and return it, for now, just return the id
        return action.Id;
    }

    public void OnResultExecuted(ResultExecutedContext context)
    {
    }

    public void OnResultExecuting(ResultExecutingContext context)
```

```
        {
            var key = this.GetKey(context.ActionDescriptor);
            string html;

            if (this._cache.TryGetValue<string>(key, out html))
            {
                context.Result = new ContentResult { Content = html,
                ContentType = "text/html" };
            }
            else
            {
                if (context.Result is ViewResult)
                {
                    //get the rendered view, maybe using a TextWriter, and
                    //store it in the cache
                }
            }
        }
    }
}
```

When this filter runs, it checks whether there is an entry in the cache for the current action and parameters and if so, it just returns it as the result.

Let's have a look now at filters that deal with exceptions.

Exception filters

These are the easiest to understand; whenever there's an exception under the scope of an exception filter (action, controller, or global), its `OnException` method is called. This is pretty useful for logging errors, as you can imagine.

The `OnException` method takes a parameter of the `ExceptionContext` type:

- `Exception` (`Exception`): Any exception thrown during the processing of the resource.
- `ExceptionDispatchInfo` (`ExceptionDispatchInfo`): The exception dispatch object, used for capturing the stack trace of an exception and, optionally, re-throwing it while preserving this context.
- `ExceptionHandled` (`bool`): Whether the exception was handled or not (if there was one), the default being `false`; if not handled, then the framework will re-throw it.
- `Result` (`IActionResult`): Possibly an action result (if one was set) which can also be set here.

There is no `Controller` property because the exception may have been thrown outside of a controller.

The asynchronous interface, `IAsyncExceptionFilter`, has a single method declared, `OnExceptionAsync`, and it also receives a parameter of the `ExceptionContext` type. The behavior is exactly the same as its synchronous counterpart, but it is called in another thread.

Caught exceptions are propagated unless the `ExceptionHandled` property is set to `true`. If you do handle the exception, it is your responsibility to return a result (the `Result` property) or write something to the output, as in this example:

```
public sealed class ErrorFilter : IAsyncExceptionFilter
{
    public async Task OnExceptionAsync(ExceptionContext context)
    {
        context.ExceptionHandled = true;
        await context.HttpContext.Response.WriteAsync($"An
        error occurred: {context.Exception.Message}");
    }
}
```

This filter should be registered as a global one:

```
services.AddMvc(options =>
{
    options.Filters.Insert(0, new ErrorFilter());
});
```

This concludes the section on exception filters. Let's now look at the Razor Pages-specific filters.

Razor page filters

This is a new filter for Razor Pages. Basically, we can have custom actions that are fired before or after a Razor Pages model method. As for the other filters, the filter is available in synchronous (`IPageFilter`) and asynchronous flavors (`IAsyncPageFilter`).

Starting with the synchronous version, it declares the following three methods:

- `OnPageHandlerSelected`: Called after the framework selects a target handler method for the processing of the request, giving developers a chance to change this
- `OnPageHandlerExecuting`: Called before the handler is invoked
- `OnPageHandlerExecuted`: Called after the handler is invoked

`OnPageHandlerSelected` takes a parameter of the `PageHandlerSelectedContext` type, and this class offers the following properties:

- `ActionDescriptor` (`CompiledPageActionDescriptor`): Describes the handler and model classes
- `HandlerMethod` (`HandlerMethodDescriptor`): The method that will be called, which can be changed
- `HandlerInstance` (`object`): The instance that will handle the request

The pre-event handler, `OnPageHandlerExecuting`, takes a single parameter of the `PageHandlerExecutingContext` type with the following properties:

- `ActionDescriptor` (`CompiledPageActionDescriptor`): The handler and model classes
- `Result` (`IActionResult`): The result to return if we want to override the default processing of the page
- `HandlerArguments` (`IDictionary<string, object>`): The arguments to be passed to the handler method
- `HandlerMethod` (`HandlerMethodDescriptor`): The method that will be called on the handler instance
- `HandlerInstance` (`object`): The instance that will handle the request

As for the post-event, `OnPageHandlerExecuted`, we have a parameter of the `PageHandlerExecutedContext` type, which has similar properties to `PageHandlerExecutingContext`:

- `ActionDescriptor` (`CompiledPageActionDescriptor`): The handler and model classes.
- `Canceled` (`bool`): Whether or not the current processing has been canceled by setting a result in the pre-event.

- `HandlerMethod` (`HandlerMethodDescriptor`): The method that will be called on the handler instance.
- `HandlerInstance` (`object`): The instance that will handle the request.
- `Exception` (`Exception`): Any exception thrown during the processing of the resource.
- `ExceptionDispatchInfo` (`ExceptionDispatchInfo`): The exception dispatch object, used for capturing the stack trace of an exception and, optionally, re-throwing it.
- `ExceptionHandled` (`bool`): Whether the exception was handled or not; the default is false, meaning the framework will re-throw it.
- `Result` (`IActionResult`): The result to return if we want to override the default processing of the page.

Finally, the asynchronous interface offers two asynchronous methods, which are the counterparts to `OnPageHandlerSelected` (now called `OnPageHandlerSelectionAsync`) and `OnPageHandlerExecuted` (now called `OnPageHandlerExecutionAsync`) `OnPageHandlerSelectionAsync` has an instance of `PageHandlerSelectedContext` as its single parameter and `OnPageHandlerExecutionAsync` takes two parameters—`PageHandlerExecutingContext` and `PageHandlerExecutionDelegate`. `PageHandlerExecutionDelegate` is, again, a delegate that points to the next method of the same type in the pipeline, if one exists.

That is all there is to Razor Pages filters, so let's have a look now at a different, peculiar kind of filter.

Always-run-result filters

An always-run-result filter (`IAlwaysRunResultFilter` and `IAsyncAlwaysRunResultFilter`) is an interesting filter that was only introduced recently (to ASP.NET Core 2.1). Its purpose is to always have something run, even when an action does not run, such as when there is an exception or when an authorization or resource filter short-circuits the pipeline and returns something directly. It offers two methods—one that is called before the result is processed and the other after it (or after its short-circuiting at the end of the request). These methods take one `ResultExecutingContext` or `ResultExecutedContext` parameter, respectively, which we discussed when we addressed result filters.

One possible usage for an always-run-result filter could be, for example, to check whether a `null` value was returned by the controller and if so, replace it with `NotFoundResult`. We can achieve this with the following code:

```
[AttributeUsage(AttributeTargets.Class, Inherited = true,
AllowMultiple = false)]
public sealed class NotFoundAttribute : Attribute,
IAlwaysRunResultFilter
{
    public void OnResultExecuted(ResultExecutedContext context)
    {
        if (context.Result is ObjectResult objectResult &&
        objectResult.Value == null)
        {
            objectResult.Value = new {}; //anonymous method,
            //add whatever properties you like
        }
    }

    public void OnResultExecuting(ResultExecutingContext context)
    {
    }
}
```

This attribute, when applied to a class (which only makes sense in a controller) checks whether the result is `null`, in which case it sets it as `NotFoundResult`.

Summary

In this chapter, we saw that in general, the asynchronous versions of each filter method are preferred because they are inherently more scalable—a thread does not block while filters are being invoked—and also that on the same class, threads do not mix the synchronous and asynchronous versions of a filter interface because only the asynchronous version is called. It is best not to mix synchronous and asynchronous filters at all! In this section, we also saw what the filter types are based on.

An important observation is that we can use the DI through the `[ServiceFilter]` attribute if we need to inject dependencies into our filters. For global filters, add the filter type to the `MvcOptions.Filters` collection in `AddMvc`, rather than a filter instance.

Then, we saw that we need to be aware of each filter's intended purpose and not use a resource filter for authorization. Use action filters if you need to intercept action parameters or carry out caching, and result filters for modifying the output or the format of a result. Then, we saw that exception filters are crucial for logging failures; these are safe to have at a global level. We also learned that we need to apply authorization filters to protect any sensitive resources and choose the best possible authorization (roles, policies, or merely being authenticated).

Next, we understood that it is crucial to pay attention to the scope of the filter—carefully opt for a global, controller, or action, whatever best suits your needs.

Overall, in this chapter, we looked at the interception mechanisms of ASP.NET Core, and in the next chapter, we will talk about securing access and using views and forms.

Questions

You should now be able to answer these questions:

1. What are the two interfaces used to control authorization to a resource?
2. Why are there two versions of each kind of filter?
3. How can we apply a filter by specifying its type on an action method?
4. How can we apply ordering to the application of filters?
5. What are the different levels to which we can apply filters?
6. How can we pass the context from one filter to another?
7. How can filters make use of a DI?

11
Security

Security is a very hot topic nowadays; no company can afford to have their customers' data exposed as seen in recent times, which is very unfortunate. Security is not just about data; it covers a lot of aspects. It's not just about restricting access to a website or to specific parts of it; it is about preventing the upload of malicious content, storing configuration (and other) data, allowing access to scripts for specific origins, and, most importantly, creating a secure channel for communicating between clients and the server.

After reading this chapter, you will have a very good understanding of the many aspects of security surrounding an ASP.NET Core application.

We will cover the following topics in this chapter:

- Authenticating users
- Authorizing requests
- Checking requests for forgery
- Applying **HyperText Markup Language (HTML)** encoding
- Working with **HyperText Transfer Protocol Secure (HTTPS)**
- Understanding **cross-origin resource sharing (CORS)**
- Using data protection
- Protecting static files
- Applying **HTTP Strict Transfer Security (HSTS)**
- Learning about the **General Data Protection Regulation (GDPR)**
- Binding security

We will begin with two topics: **authentication**—who is who; and **authorization**—who can do what. These are the building blocks for any secure web application. Let's study each in the following sections.

Technical requirements

In order to implement the examples introduced in this chapter, you will need the .NET Core 3 **software development kit (SDK)** and some form of text editor. Of course, Visual Studio 2019 (any edition) meets all the requirements, but you can also use Visual Studio Code, for example.

The source code can be retrieved from GitHub here: `https://github.com/PacktPublishing/Modern-Web-Development-with-ASP.NET-Core-3-Second-Edition`.

Authenticating users

Authentication is the process by which you tell your application who you are; from this moment on, the application will know you—for a certain period of time, at least.

Authentication is not the same as—although it is related to—authorization. You probably need authentication if you have resources that require authorization to access them.

The general authorization flow is as follows:

1. Someone requests access to a protected resource.
2. The framework checks that the user is not authorized and redirects them to a login page, issuing a `302` code. This is the challenge stage.
3. The user supplies their credentials.
4. The credentials are checked and, if they are valid, the user is directed to the requested resource (`HTTP 302`) with a cookie (usually) that identifies them as being logged in.
5. Otherwise, the framework redirects to the failed login page.
6. Access to the protected resource is now granted.

The following screenshot describes the HTTP flow between the client browser and the application:

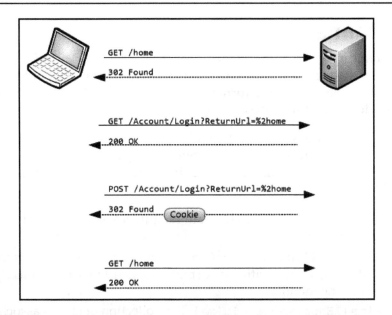

Image taken from https://docs.microsoft.com/en-us/aspnet/web-api/overview/security/basic-authentication

In ASP.NET Core, we use the `[Authorize]` attribute or some form of filter to restrict access to a resource, either through a controller as a whole or through some specific action methods, as shown in the following code snippet:

```
//whole controller is protected
[Authorize]
public class AdminController { }

public class SearchController
{
    //only this method is restricted
    [Authorize]
    public IActionResult Admin() { ... }
}
```

Beyond this, when we try to access one of these resources, we will end up with a `401 Unauthorized` error code. What we need is some form of middleware that is capable of intercepting this error code and proceeding accordingly.

The next section is only relevant to Windows developers. We will see how authorization works for Windows first.

Using claims

Modern authentication and authorization uses the concept of claims for storing information that the logged-in user will have access to. This will include roles, for example, but it can be any other information, as dictated by the authentication provider (Windows or a third party).

In .NET Core, the root class, where all identity information is made available, is `ClaimsPrincipal`. A reference to the current identity is available in the `HttpContext` class, as `HttpContext.User`. In it, we can find three important properties, detailed as follows:

- `Identity` (`IIdentity`): The main identity associated with the currently logged-in user
- `Identities` (`IEnumerable<ClaimsIdentity>`): The collection of identities associated with the currently logged-in user; it typically only contains one identity
- `Claims` (`IEnumerable<Claim>`): The collection of claims associated with the currently logged-in user

The `Identity` property contains the following:

- `Name` (`string`): The name of the logged-in user, if any
- `IsAuthenticated` (`bool`): Whether or not the current user is authenticated
- `AuthenticationType` (`string`): The current authentication type, if in use

Don't forget that, as we will see, we can use multiple authentication types on the same application, each with a different name, and a user will be authenticated against one of them.

As for the `Claims` class, a typical collection of claims might contain the following claim types, which will map to the `Type` property of the `Claim` class:

- `ClaimTypes.Authentication`
- `ClaimTypes.Country`
- `ClaimTypes.DateOfBirth`
- `ClaimTypes.Email`
- `ClaimTypes.Gender`
- `ClaimTypes.GivenName`

- `ClaimTypes.HomePhone`
- `ClaimTypes.MobilePhone`
- `ClaimTypes.Name`
- `ClaimTypes.Role`
- `ClaimTypes.Surname`
- `ClaimTypes.WindowsAccountName`

This will, however, depend on the authentication provider. There are actually a lot more standardized claims, as you can see from the `ClaimTypes` class, but nothing prevents anyone from adding their own claims. Keep in mind that, in general, claims do not mean anything, but there are a few exceptions: `Name` and `Role` can be used for security checks, as we will see in a moment.

So, the `Claim` class features the following main properties:

- `Issuer` (`string`): The claim issuer
- `Type` (`string`): The type of the claim—typically, one from `ClaimTypes`, but might be something else
- `Value` (`string`): The value for the claim

Let's start our discussion of authentication by talking about Windows authentication.

Windows authentication

ASP.NET Core, because it is platform-agnostic, does not natively support Windows authentication. Probably the best way to achieve this, if we do need it, is to use **Internet Information Server (IIS)**/IIS Express as a **reverse proxy**, handling all the requests and directing them to ASP.NET Core.

For IIS Express, we need to configure the launch settings in the project's `Properties\launchSettings.json` file as follows, with the changes in **bold**:

```
"iisSettings": {
  "windowsAuthentication": true,
  "anonymousAuthentication": false,
  "iisExpress": {
    "applicationUrl": "http://localhost:5000/",
    "sslPort": 0
  }
}
```

For IIS, we need to make sure that `AspNetCoreModule` is enabled for our website.

In any case, we need to configure Windows authentication in the `ConfigureServices` method, like this:

```
services.AddAuthentication(IISDefaults.AuthenticationScheme);
```

Finally, the `AspNetCoreModule` makes use of a `Web.config` file that is not needed or used by ASP.NET Core itself; it is used for deployment and includes the following content:

```xml
<?xml version="1.0" encoding="utf-8"?>
  <configuration>
      <system.webServer>
          <aspNetCore forwardWindowsAuthToken="true"
           processPath="%LAUNCHER_PATH%"
              arguments="%LAUNCHER_ARGS%" />
          <handlers>
              <add name="aspNetCore" path="*" verb="*"
                modules="AspNetCoreModule"
                   resourceType="Unspecified" />
          </handlers>
      </system.webServer>
  </configuration>
```

And that's it. The `[Authorize]` attribute will require authenticated users and will be happy with Windows authentication. `HttpContext.User` will be set to an instance of `WindowsPrincipal`, a subset of `ClaimsPrincipal`, and any Windows groups will be available as roles and also as claims (`ClaimTypes.Role`). The Windows name will be set in `ClaimsIdentity.Name` in the form of `domain\user`.

In any place where you want to get the current Windows authentication, you can use the following code:

```
var identity = WindowsIdentity.GetCurrent();
```

Additionally, for example, if you want to know whether the current user belongs to a specific role, such as the built-in administrators, you can use the following code:

```
var principal = new WindowsPrincipal(identity);
var isAdmin = principal.IsInRole(WindowsBuiltInRole.Administrator);
```

This code will return `true` if the current user is part of the Windows built-in administrators' group.

Don't forget that, although this code will compile on any platform, you can only use Windows authentication on Windows. You can check that by using `System.Runtime.InteropServices.RuntimeInformatio n.IsOSPlatform(System.Runtime.InteropServices.OSPlatf orm.Windows)`.

Next, let's now see how to bake our own authentication mechanism for all non-Windows developers.

Custom authentication

ASP.NET Core does not include any authentication provider, unlike previous versions of ASP.NET that shipped with support for Windows and **Structured Query Language** (**SQL**)-based authentication—the membership provider. This means that we have to implement everything manually—or not quite, as we will see in a moment.

The method used to register the services is `AddAuthentication`, which can be followed by `AddCookie`, as shown in the following code:

```
services
.AddAuthentication(CookieAuthenticationDefaults.AuthenticationScheme)
    .AddCookie(CookieAuthenticationDefaults.AuthenticationScheme,
options
=>
    {
        options.LoginPath = "/Account/Login/";
        options.AccessDeniedPath = "/Account/Forbidden/";
        options.LogoutPath = "/Account/Logout";
        options.ReturnUrlParameter = "ReturnUrl";
    });
```

We add the `UseAuthentication` method in `Configure`, like this:

```
app.UseAuthentication();
```

The changes in `AccountController` are minor—we must call the `SignInAsync` and `SignOutAsync` extension methods over the `HttpContext` instance instead of calling the **old** versions in `HttpContext.Authorization`, as illustrated in the following code block:

```
[HttpPost]
[AllowAnonymous]
```

```
public async Task<IActionResult> PerformLogin(string username, string
password, string returnUrl,
    bool isPersistent)
{
    //...check validity of credentials
    await this.HttpContext.SignInAsync(CookieAuthenticationDefaults.
    AuthenticationScheme, new ClaimsPrincipal(user), new
    AuthenticationProperties { IsPersistent = isPersistent });
    return this.LocalRedirect(returnUrl);
}

[HttpGet]
public async Task<IActionResult> Logout()
{
    await this.HttpContext.SignOutAsync(CookieAuthenticationDefaults
    .AuthenticationScheme);
    //...
}
```

Before using these new methods, add a `using` statement for the
`Microsoft.AspNetCore.Authentication` namespace.

A minimum login page (`Views/Account/Login`) could look like this:

```
using (Html.BeginForm(nameof(AccountController.PerformLogin),
"Account", FormMethod.Post))
{
    <fieldset>
        <p>Username:</p>
        <p><input type="text" name="username" /></p>
        <p>Password:</p>
        <p><input type="password" name="password" /></p>
        <p>Remember me: <input type="checkbox" name="isPersistent"
        value="true" /></p>
        <input type="hidden" name="ReturnUrl" value="@Context.Request.
        Query["ReturnUrl"]"/>
        <button>Login</button>
    </fieldset>
}
```

Instead of implementing our own authentication mechanism, it is quite often more
convenient to use an existing and well-established one, and that's exactly what we
will talk about next.

Identity

Because you shouldn't have to deal with low-level authentication yourself, there are a number of packages that can assist you in that task. The one that Microsoft recommends is **Microsoft Identity** (`http://github.com/aspnet/identity`).

Identity is an extensible library for doing username-password authentication and storing user properties. It is modular and, by default, it uses **Entity Framework (EF)** Core for the data store persistence. Of course, because EF itself is quite extensible, it can use any of its data providers (SQL Server, SQLite, Redis, and so on). The NuGet packages for Identity with EF Core are `Microsoft.AspNetCore.Identity.EntityFrameworkCore`, `Microsoft.EntityFrameworkCore.Tools`, and `Microsoft.AspNetCore.Diagnostics.EntityFramework`, and you should also know that Identity is installed by default with the Visual Studio templates for *ASP.NET Core Web Applications* if we choose to use authentication through **Individual User Accounts**. The following screenshot shows the Visual Studio screen, where we can select the authentication method:

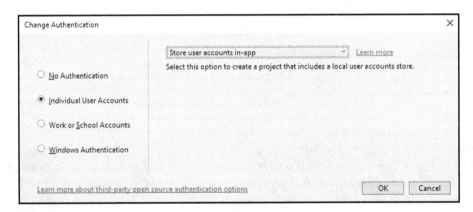

Identity supports both user properties and roles. In order to use Identity, we first need to register its services, as follows:

```
services
    .AddDbContext<ApplicationDbContext>(options =>
        options.UseSqlServer(this.Configuration.
        GetConnectionString("DefaultConnection")))
    .AddDefaultIdentity<IdentityUser>(options => options.SignIn.
    RequireConfirmedAccount = false)
    .AddEntityFrameworkStores<ApplicationDbContext>();
```

By all means, do replace the connection string key
(Data:DefaultConnection:ConnectionString) in the configuration to whatever
suits you best, and make sure it points to a valid configuration value.

It will be something like this:

```
"ConnectionStrings": {
    "DefaultConnection": "Server=(localdb)\\mssqllocaldb;
    Database=aspnet-chapter07-2AF3F755-0DFD-4E20-BBA4-9B9C3F56378B;
    Trusted_Connection=True;MultipleActiveResultSets=true"
},
```

Identity supports a large number of options when it comes to security; these can be
configured on the call to AddDefaultIdentity, as follows:

```
services.AddDefaultIdentity<IdentityUser>(options =>
{
    options.SignIn.RequireConfirmedAccount = false;
    options.Password.RequireDigit = false;
    options.Password.RequireLowercase = false;
    options.Password.RequiredUniqueChars = 0;
    options.Password.RequiredLength = 0;
    options.Password.RequireNonAlphanumeric = false;
    options.Password.RequireUppercase = false;

    options.Lockout.DefaultLockoutTimeSpan = TimeSpan.FromMinutes(30);
    options.Lockout.MaxFailedAccessAttempts = 10;
});
```

This example sets numerous options for login, such as disabling the confirmation of
the email, simplifying the password requirements, and setting the timeout and
number of failed login attempts. I won't go through all of the available options; please
refer to the Identity site for the full picture: https://docs.microsoft.com/en-us/
aspnet/core/security/authentication/identity

And, if you need to change the path and cookie options, you need to use
ConfigureApplicationCookie, as per this example:

```
services.ConfigureApplicationCookie(options =>
{
    options.Cookie.HttpOnly = true;
    options.ExpireTimeSpan = TimeSpan.FromMinutes(20);
    options.SlidingExpiration = true;

    options.LoginPath = "/Account/Login";
    options.AccessDeniedPath = "/Account/Forbidden";
    options.LogoutPath = "/Account/Logout";
```

```
        options.ReturnUrlParameter = "ReturnUrl";
});
```

This simple example sets the paths to be the same as the ones provided earlier, in the custom authentication topic, and sets a few cookie properties too, listed as follows:

- `HttpOnly`: Requires that the cookies be sent with the `HttpOnly` flag set (see https://owasp.org/www-community/HttpOnly)
- `ExpireTimeSpan`: The duration of the authentication cookie
- `SlidingExpiration`: Sets the cookie expiration to be sliding—that is, it is renewed for an equal amount of time for each time the application is accessed

The Identity registration code (the first code listing in this subsection) mentioned the `ApplicationDbContext` and `IdentityUser` classes. A skeleton of these classes is added automatically when we create a project using the Visual Studio template that uses custom authentication, but I'm adding them here for your reference, as follows:

```
public class ApplicationDbContext : IdentityDbContext
{
    public ApplicationDbContext(DbContextOptions options) :
base(options) { }
}
```

Now, this is very important, you need to create the database before using Identity. To do that, open `Package Manager Console` and run these commands:

```
Add-Migration "Initial"
Update-Database
```

After this, we can add some additional properties to the model.

Adding custom properties

Nothing fancy here, as you can see. The only thing worth mentioning is that you can add your own custom properties to the `IdentityUser` and `IdentityRole` classes, and these will be persisted and retrieved as part of the login process. Why would you want to do that? Well, because these base classes do not contain any useful properties—only username, email, and phone (for the user), and the role name. These classes map, respectively, a user and a role, where a user can have a single role and each role can have multiple users associated with it. You just need to create new classes and have the context use them, as illustrated in the following code block:

```
public class ApplicationUser : IdentityUser
{
    public ApplicationUser() {}
    public ApplicationUser(string userName) : base(userName) {}

    //add other properties here, with public getters and setters
    [PersonalData]
    [MaxLength(50)]
    public string FullName { get; set; }
    [PersonalData]
    public DateTime? Birthday { get; set; }
}

public class ApplicationRole : IdentityRole
{
    public ApplicationRole() {}
    public ApplicationRole(string roleName) : base(roleName) {}

    //add other properties here, with public getters and setters
}
```

Notice the `[PersonalData]` attribute to mark the new properties being added: this is a requirement so that so it's automatically available for download and deletion. This is a requirement for **GDPR**, discussed later on in this chapter. If you don't care about it, you can leave it out.

 You can add validation attributes to this model.

You also need to modify your context to use the new properties, like this:

```
public class ApplicationDbContext : IdentityDbContext<ApplicationUser,
ApplicationRole, string>
```

```
{
    public ApplicationDbContext(DbContextOptions options) :
base(options) {}
}
```

The names `ApplicationUser` and `ApplicationRole` are typical names for custom classes for identity and role data. Notice the three generic arguments to `ApplicationDbContext`: these are the types of Identity user and role, and the type of the primary key, which is `string`.

You must also change the registration code in the `Startup` class to refer to the new Identity user class, as follows:

```
services
    .AddDefaultIdentity<ApplicationUser>(options =>
    {
        //...
    });
```

Finally, we must create a migration and update the database to reflect the changes, from inside Visual Studio (`Package Manager Console`), as follows:

```
Add-Migration "PersonalData"
Update-Database
```

Or, we can do this from the command line, like this:

```
dotnet ef migrations add PersonalData
dotnet ef database update
```

Of course, if we have custom data, we also need to update the registration forms so that they include the new properties.

Updating the user interface

Fortunately, ASP.NET Core Identity fully supports this: it is possible to supply all or some forms, and they will replace the ones provided!

Right-click on the web project and select **New Scaffolded Item...**, as illustrated in the following screenshot:

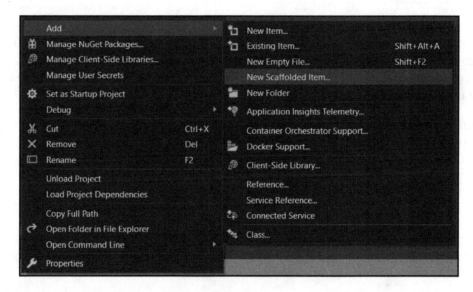

Then, after it, select **Identity**, as illustrated in the following screenshot:

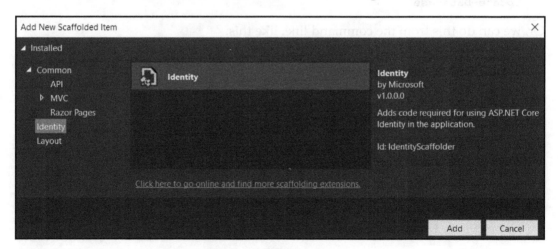

Then, we have the choice to pick which pages we want to override in the current project, as illustrated in the following screenshot:

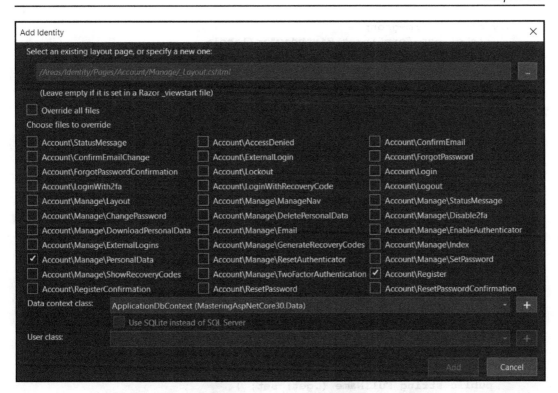

Notice that you must select the context (DbContext—derived class) to use. The files will then, by default, be created under a new folder, Areas/Identity, which will correspond to a **Model-View-Controller** (**MVC**) area. The pages themselves are Razor pages, meaning that they do not use controllers, but they do use a code-behind file (both a .cshtml and a .cshtml.cs file).

So, if you followed my example and added FullName and Birthday properties to the ApplicationUser class and generated pages for the account registration, we need to add them, in the Areas/Identity/Pages/Account/Manage/Register.cshtml file (changes in bold), like this:

```
...
<div asp-validation-summary="All" class="text-danger"></div>
<div class="form-group">
    <label asp-for="Input.FullName"></label>
    <input asp-for="Input.FullName" class="form-control" />
    <span asp-validation-for="Input.FullName" class="text-
danger"></span>
</div>
```

```html
<div class="form-group">
    <label asp-for="Input.Birthday"></label>
    <input type="date" asp-for="Input.Birthday" class="form-control"
/>
    <span asp-validation-for="Input.Birthday" class="text-
danger"></span>
</div>
<div class="form-group">
  <label asp-for="Input.Email"></label>
    <input asp-for="Input.Email" class="form-control" />
    <span asp-validation-for="Input.Email" class="text-danger"></span>
</div>
...
```

And in, `Register.cshtml.cs`, we need to add the code to persist the data, like this:

```csharp
...
[BindProperty]
public InputModel Input { get; set; }

public class InputModel
{
    [Display(Name = "Full Name")]
    [DataType(DataType.Text)]
    [MaxLength(50)]
    public string FullName { get; set; }

    [Display(Name = "Birthday")]
    [DataType(DataType.Date)]
    public DateTime? Birthday { get; set; }

    [Required]
    [EmailAddress]
    [Display(Name = "Email")]
    public string Email { get; set; }
    ...
}

public async Task<IActionResult> OnPostAsync(string returnUrl = null)
{
    returnUrl = returnUrl ?? Url.Content("~/");

    if (ModelState.IsValid)
    {
        var user = new ApplicationUser { UserName = Input.Email,
            Email = Input.Email,
            Birthday = Input.Birthday, FullName = Input.FullName };
        var result = await _userManager.CreateAsync(user,
```

```
Input.Password);
    ...
}
...
```

Essentially, we're just adding the new properties to `InputModel`, which is just a **Plain Old CLR Object** (**POCO**) class used to bind the form data, and from there to the `ApplicationUser` class, which is then passed to the `CreateAsync` method.

Using the Identity provider

Now, picking up on the previous authentication example, let's see how it goes with Identity:

```
public class AccountController : Controller
{
    private readonly IOptions<IdentityOptions> _options;
    private readonly UserManager<ApplicationUser> _userManager;
    private readonly RoleManager<ApplicationRole> _roleManager;
    private readonly SignInManager<ApplicationUser> _signInManager;

    public AccountController(
        IOptions<IdentityOptions> options,
        UserManager<ApplicationUser> userManager,
        RoleManager<ApplicationRole> roleManager,
        SignInManager<ApplicationUser> signInManager)
    {
        this._options = options;
        this._signInManager = signInManager;
        this._userManager = userManager;
        this._roleManager = roleManager;
    }

    [HttpPost]
    [AllowAnonymous]
    public async Task<IActionResult> PerformLogin(string username,
    string password, string returnUrl)
    {
        var result = await this._signInManager.PasswordSignInAsync
        (username, password,
            isPersistent: true,
            lockoutOnFailure: false);

        if (result.Succeeded)
        {
            return this.LocalRedirect(returnUrl);
        }
```

```
                    else if (result.IsLockedOut)
                    {
                        this.ModelState.AddModelError("User", "User is locked
out");
                        return this.View("Login");
                    }

                    return this.Redirect(this._options.Value.Cookies.
                    ApplicationCookie.AccessDeniedPath);
                }

                [HttpGet]
                public async Task<IActionResult> Logout()
                {
                    await this._signInManager.SignOutAsync();
                    return this.RedirectToRoute("Default");
                }

                private async Task<ApplicationUser> GetCurrentUserAsync()
                {
                    //the current user properties
                    return await this._userManager.GetUserAsync
                    (this.HttpContext.User);
                }

                private async Task<ApplicationRole> GetUserRoleAsync(string id)
                {
                    //the role for the given user
                    return await this._roleManager.FindByIdAsync(id);
                }
        }
```

The classes used to manage the authentication process are UserManager<T>, SignInManager<T>, and RoleManager<T>, all of which are generic and take as parameters either the concrete identity user or the identity role class. These classes are registered to the **dependency injection (DI)** framework by the call to AddDefaultIdentity and are, therefore, available to be injected anywhere you need them. For the record, calling AddDefaultIdentity is the same as adding the following services:

```
services
    .AddIdentity()              //adds core functionality
    .AddDefaultUI()            //adds self-contained Razor Pages UI
in
                                // an area called /Identity
    .AddDefaultTokenProviders(); //for generating tokens for new
                                // passwords, resetting operations
```

We are calling the following three methods of the `UserManager<T>` class:

- `PasswordSignInAsync`: This is the method that actually validates the username and password, returning the status of the user; optionally, it sets the cookie as persistent (`isPersistent`), meaning that the user will remain authenticated for a certain period of time, as specified in the configuration settings, and also indicating whether or not to lock the user in the case of a number of failed attempts (`lockoutOnFailure`)—again, configurable.
- `SignOutAsync`: Signs out the current user by setting an expiration for the authentication cookie
- `RefreshSignInAsync`: Refreshes the authentication cookie by extending its expiration (not shown here)

The `UserManager<T>` class exposes a few useful methods, as follows:

- `GetUserAsync`: Retrieves the data (either `IdentityUser` or a subclass) for the current user
- `CreateAsync`: Creates a user (not shown here)
- `UpdateAsync`: Updates a user (not shown here)
- `DeleteAsync`: Deletes a user (not shown here)
- `AddClaimAsync/RemoveClaimAsync`: Adds/removes a claim to/from a user (not shown here)
- `AddToRoleAsync/RemoveFromRoleAsync`: Adds/removes a user to/from a role (not shown here)
- `ConfirmEmailAsync`: Confirms an email for a recently created user (not shown here)
- `FindByEmailAsync/FindByIdAsync/FindByNameAsync`: Tries to find users by email/ID/name (not shown here)

As for `RoleManager<T>`, its only use here is to retrieve the role (`IdentityRole`—derived) for the current user by means of its `FindByIdAsync`method (not shown here).

As you can see, the code is pretty similar to the previous code, but this is just a teaser as Identity supports lots of other features, including the following:

- User registration, including email activation codes
- Assigning roles to users
- Account locking after a number of failed login attempts
- Two-factor authentication
- Password retrieval
- External authentication providers

Please consult the Identity site for more information: `https://www.asp.net/identity`

Now, let's see a very popular server for integrating data sources and serving authentication requests to multiple clients.

Using IdentityServer

IdentityServer is an open source implementation of the **OpenID Connect** and **OAuth 2.0** protocols for ASP.NET. The version we are interested in, **IdentityServer4**, was designed specifically for ASP.NET Core; its source code is made available at `https://github.com/IdentityServer/IdentityServer4` and its documentation at `http://docs.identityserver.io/`. It is so popular that it is, in fact, Microsoft's recommended implementation for service federation and **single sign-on** (**SSO**).

This is the OAuth 2.0 flow for granting access to a resource:

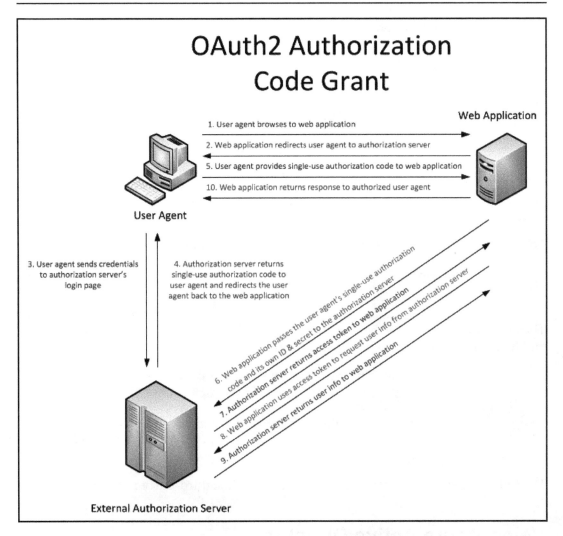

OAuth2 Authorization Code Grant

Web Application

1. User agent browses to web application

2. Web application redirects user agent to authorization server

5. User agent provides single-use authorization code to web application

10. Web application returns response to authorized user agent

User Agent

3. User agent sends credentials to authorization server's login page

4. Authorization server returns single-use authorization code to user agent and redirects the user agent back to the web application

6. Web application passes the user agent's single-use authorization code and its own ID & secret to the authorization server

7. Authorization server returns access token to web application

8. Web application uses access token to request user info from authorization server

9. Authorization server returns user info to web application

External Authorization Server

Image taken from https://docs.microsoft.com/en-us/aspnet/web-api/overview/security/external-authentication-services

IdentityServer, loosely speaking, can be used for authentication as a service, meaning it can accept requests for authentication, validate them against any number of data stores, and grant access tokens.

We won't go into the details of setting up IdentityServer as it can be quite complex and has a huge number of features. What we are interested in is how we can use it to authenticate users. For this, we will need the
`Microsoft.AspNetCore.Authentication.OpenIdConnect` and
`IdentityServer4.AccessTokenValidation` NuGet packages.

We set all the configuration in the `ConfigureServices` method, as illustrated in the following code block:

```
services.AddCookieAuthentication(CookieAuthenticationDefaults.Authenti
cationScheme);

services.AddOpenIdConnectAuthentication(options =>
{
    options.ClientId = "MasteringAspNetCore";
    //change the IdentityServer4 URL
    options.Authority = "https://servername:5000";
    //uncomment the next line if not using HTTPS
    //options.RequireHttpsMetadata = false;
});
```

Then, add the authentication middleware, in `Configure`, like this:

```
JwtSecurityTokenHandler.DefaultInboundClaimTypeMap.Clear();

app.UseAuthentication();
```

These two lines will first erase the mapping of claims for **JSON Web Token (JWT)** and then add the authentication middleware.

> For additional information, consult the wiki article at `https://social.technet.microsoft.com/wiki/contents/articles/37169.secure-your-netcore-web-applications-using-identityserver-4.aspx` and the IdentityServer Identity documentation at `http://docs.identityserver.io/en/release/quickstarts/6_aspnet_identity.html`.

The following sections describe authentication against third-party providers.

Using Azure Active Directory

With everything moving to the cloud, it should come as no surprise that ASP.NET Core also supports authentication with **Azure Active Directory (Azure AD)**. When you create a new project, you have the option to select **Work or School Accounts** for authentication and then enter the details of your Azure cloud, as illustrated in the following screenshot:

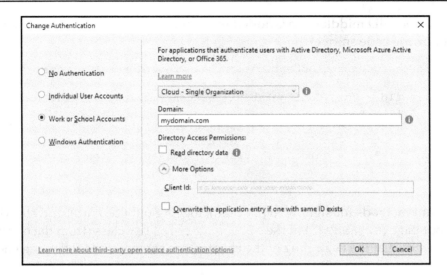

You must enter a valid domain!

Essentially, the wizard adds the following two NuGet packages to the project Microsoft.AspNetCore.Authentication.Cookies and Microsoft.AspNetCore.Authentication.OpenIdConnect (Azure authentication is based on OpenID). It also adds the following entry to the appsettings.json configuration file:

```
"Authentication": {
  "AzureAd": {
    "AADInstance": "https://login.microsoftonline.com/",
    "CallbackPath": "/signin-oidc",
    "ClientId": "<client id>",
    "Domain": "mydomain.com",
    "TenantId": "<tenant id>"
  }
}
```

The authentication uses cookies, so a similar entry is added to the ConfigureServices method, as illustrated in the following code snippet:

```
services.AddAuthentication(options =>
    options.SignInScheme = CookieAuthenticationDefaults
    .AuthenticationScheme
);
```

Finally, the OpenID middleware is added to the pipeline in `Configure`, as illustrated in the following code snippet:

```
app.UseOpenIdConnectAuthentication(new OpenIdConnectOptions
{
    ClientId = this.Configuration["Authentication:AzureAd:ClientId"],
    Authority =
this.Configuration["Authentication:AzureAd:AADInstance"] +
            this.Configuration["Authentication:AzureAd:TenantId"],
    CallbackPath = this.Configuration["Authentication:AzureAd:
    CallbackPath"]
});
```

The relevant methods for signing in (`SignIn`), logging out (`Logout`), and showing the logged-out page (`SignedOut`) in the `AccountController` class (from the original listing presented at the beginning of the chapter) are shown in the following code block:

```
[HttpGet]
public async Task<IActionResult> Logout()
{
    var callbackUrl = this.Url.Action("SignedOut", "Account",
        values: null,
        protocol: this.Request.Scheme);
    return this.SignOut(new AuthenticationProperties {
    RedirectUri = callbackUrl },
        CookieAuthenticationDefaults.AuthenticationScheme,
        OpenIdConnectDefaults.AuthenticationScheme);
}

[HttpGet]
public IActionResult SignedOut()
{
    return this.View();
}

[HttpGet]
public IActionResult SignIn()
{
    return this.Challenge(new AuthenticationProperties { RedirectUri =
"/" },
        OpenIdConnectDefaults.AuthenticationScheme);
    });
}
```

Now, we will see how we can use well-known social networking applications as authentication providers for our application.

Using social logins

Another option for keeping and maintaining user credentials yourself is to use authentication information from third parties, such as social networking apps. This is an interesting option because you don't require users to go through the account creation process; you just trust the external authentication provider for that.

All external authentication providers follow this flow:

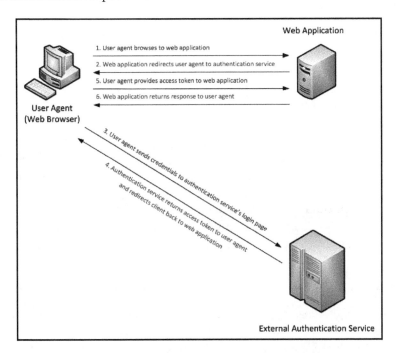

Image taken from https://docs.microsoft.com/en-us/aspnet/web-api/overview/security/external-authentication-services

 For more information, please consult https://docs.microsoft. com/en-us/aspnet/core/security/authentication/social/

This mechanism is based on providers, and there are a number of them made available by Microsoft; you must be aware that all of these rely on Identity, so you need to configure it first (UseIdentity). When you create your project, make sure you choose to use authentication and select individual accounts. This will ensure that the proper template is used and the required files are present in the project. Let's study a few in the coming sections.

Facebook

Facebook doesn't really need an introduction. Its provider is available as a `Microsoft.AspNetCore.Authentication.Facebook` NuGet package. You will need to create a developer account with Facebook first, and then use the application ID and user secret when registering the provider in the `Configure` method, as follows:

```
app.UseFacebookAuthentication(new FacebookOptions()
{
    AppId = Configuration["Authentication:Facebook:AppId"],
    AppSecret = Configuration["Authentication:Facebook:AppSecret"]
});
```

Facebook login details are available here: `https://docs.microsoft.com/en-us/aspnet/core/security/authentication/social/facebook-logins`

Twitter

Twitter is another popular social networking site, and the provider for it is available as a `Microsoft.AspNetCore.Authentication.Twitter` NuGet package. You will also need to register your application in the Twitter developer site. Its configuration goes like this:

```
app.UseTwitterAuthentication(new TwitterOptions()
{
    ConsumerKey = Configuration["Authentication:Twitter:ConsumerKey"],
    ConsumerSecret = Configuration["Authentication:Twitter:ConsumerSecret"]
});
```

Twitter login details are available here: `https://docs.microsoft.com/en-us/aspnet/core/security/authentication/social/twitter-logins`.

Google

The **Google** provider is contained in the
`Microsoft.AspNetCore.Authentication.Google` NuGet package. Again, you will need to create a developer account and register your app beforehand. The Google provider is configured like this:

```
app.UseGoogleAuthentication(new GoogleOptions()
{
    ClientId = Configuration["Authentication:Google:ClientId"],
    ClientSecret = Configuration["Authentication:Google:ClientSecret"]
});
```

For more information about the Google provider, please consult `https://docs.microsoft.com/en-us/aspnet/core/security/authentication/social/google-logins`.

Microsoft

Of course, **Microsoft** makes available a provider for its own authentication service; this is included in the
`Microsoft.AspNetCore.Authentication.MicrosoftAccount` NuGet package, and the configuration goes like this:

```
app.UseMicrosoftAccountAuthentication(new MicrosoftAccountOptions()
{
    ClientId = Configuration["Authentication:Microsoft:ClientId"],
    ClientSecret =
Configuration["Authentication:Microsoft:ClientSecret"]
});
```

Go to `https://docs.microsoft.com/en-us/aspnet/core/security/authentication/social/microsoft-logins` for more information.

All of these mechanisms rely on cookies for persisting authentication, so it makes sense that we talk a bit about cookie security.

Cookie security

The `CookieAuthenticationOptions` class has a few properties that can be used for configuring extra security, listed as follows:

- `Cookie.HttpOnly` (`bool`): Whether the cookie should be HTTP-only or not (see https://www.owasp.org/index.php/HttpOnly); the default is `false`. If not set, then the `HttpOnly` flag is not sent.
- `Cookie.Secure` (`CookieSecurePolicy`): Whether the cookie should be sent only over HTTPS (`Always`), always (`None`), or according to the request (`SameAsRequest`), which is the default; if not set, the `Secure` flag is not sent.
- `Cookie.Path` (`string`): An optional path to which the cookie applies; if not set, it defaults to the current application path.
- `Cookie.Domain` (`string`): An optional domain for the cookie; if not set, the site's domain will be used.
- `DataProtectionProvider` (`IDataProtectionProvider`): An optional data protection provider, used to encrypt and decrypt the cookie value; by default, it is `null`.
- `CookieManager` (`ICookieManager`): An optional storage for cookies; it might be useful, for example, to share cookies between applications (see https://docs.microsoft.com/en-us/aspnet/core/security/data-protection/compatibility/cookie-sharing).
- `IsEssential` (`bool`): Whether or not the cookie is essential, in terms of where GDPR is concerned (ss).
- `ClaimsIssuer` (`string`): Who issued the cookie's claims.
- `ExpireTimeSpan` (`TimeSpan`): The authentication cookie's validity.
- `SlidingExpiration` (`bool`): Whether or not the cookie's validity specified in `ExpireTimeSpan` should be renewed on every request(default).
- `AccessDeniedPath` (`string`): The path to which the browser is redirected if the authentication fails, after the challenge stage.
- `LoginPath` (`string`): The login path to which the browser will be redirected should there be a need to authenticate (challenge phase).
- `LogoutPath` (`string`): The logout path, where authentication cookies (and what-not) are cleaned.
- `ReturnUrlParameter` (`string`): The query string parameter where, in the challenge stage, the original **Uniform Resource Locator** (**URL**) will be kept; it defaults to `ReturnURL`.

Sliding expiration means that the period of time specified in the expiration will be extended every time the server receives a request: a cookie with the same name is returned with the same expiration that overrides the previous one.

All these properties are available in Identity. In order to set values, you can either build a `CookieAuthenticationOptions` instance or use the delegate available as the `AddCookie` extension method after calling `AddAuthentication`, in `ConfigureServices`, like this:

```
services
    .AddAuthentication()
    .AddCookie(options =>
    {
        //set global properties
        options.LoginPath = "/Account/Login";
        options.AccessDeniedPath = "/Account/Forbidden";
        options.LogoutPath = "/Account/Logout";
        options.ReturnUrlParameter = "ReturnUrl";
    });
```

The HTTP cookie specification is available at `https://tools.ietf.org/html/rfc6265`.

Supporting SameSite cookies

SameSite is an extension to **Request for Comments** (**RFC**) 6265, known as RFC 6265bis, which defines HTTP cookies, and its purpose is to mitigate **Cross-Site Request Forgery** (**CSRF**) attacks by optionally only allowing cookies to be set from the same site context. For example, imagine your site is located at `www.abc.com`; then, `dev.abc.com` is also considered to be the **same site**, whereas `xpto.com` is considered **cross-site**.

SameSite is sent by the browser together with the rest of the cookie parameters and it has three options, as listed here:

- `Strict`: A cookie will only be sent if the site for the cookie matches the site currently viewed on the browser.
- `Lax`: Cookies are only set when the domain in the URL of the browser matches the domain of the cookie.
- `None`: Must be sent through HTTPS

For Edge, FireFox, and Chrome, the default is now `Lax`, which means third-party cookies are now blocked.

SameSite security can be set on the `CookieOptions` class, which means that it can be set together when we set a cookie explicitly, or on the cookie builder available on `CookieAuthenticationOptions` when using cookie-based authentication mechanisms, as illustrated in the following code:

```
services
    .AddAuthentication()
    .AddCookie(options =>
    {
        options.Cookie.SameSite = SameSiteMode.Strict;
    });
```

The possible values that we can pass to `SameSite` are the following ones:

- `Lax`: The client browser should send cookies with same-site and cross-site top-level requests.
- `None`: No same-site validation is performed on the client.
- `Strict`: The client browser should only send the cookie with same-site requests.
- `Unspecified`: This is the default, and it will be dictated by the client browser.

We must not forget to add the cookie middleware to the pipeline, before adding the authentication, like this:

```
public void Configure(IApplicationBuilder app, IWebHostEnvironment
env)
{
    app.UseCookiePolicy();
    app.UseAuthentication();
    //rest goes here
}
```

Now that we've talked about authentication—namely, building a custom authentication provider and using `IdentityServer` or social sites for authentication—and some cookie security, let's talk a bit about authorization.

Authorizing requests

Here, we will see how we can control access to parts of the application, be it controllers or more fine-grained.

So, let's say you want to mark either a whole controller or specific actions as requiring authentication. The easiest way is to add an `[Authorize]` attribute to the controller class, just like that. If you try to access the protected controller or resource, a `401 authorization Required` error will be returned.

In order to add authorization support, we must add the required middleware to the `Configure` method, after the `UseAuthentication` call, like this:

```
app.UseRouting();

app.UseCookiePolicy();
app.UseAuthentication();
app.UseAuthorization();

app.UseEndpoints(endpoints =>
{
    //...
});
```

Do not forget about this order—`UseAuthentication` before `UseAuthorization`—this is mandatory!

The following sections describe different ways to declare authorization rules for resources on our web application. Let's start with roles, which are a common way to define groups of users.

Authorization based on roles

If we want to go a little further in the authorization process, we can request that a protected resource controller, or action only be accessible when the authenticated user is in a given role. Roles are just claims and are supported by any authentication mechanism, shown as follows:

```
[Authorize(Roles = "Admin")]
public IActionResult Admin() { ... }
```

It is possible to specify multiple roles, separated by commas. In the following case, access will be granted if the current user is in at least one of these roles:

```
[Authorize(Roles = "Admin,Supervisor")]
```

If you ever want to know by code whether the current user belongs to a specific role, you can use the `ClaimsPrincipal` instance's `IsInRole` method, as illustrated in the following code snippet:

```
var isAdmin = this.HttpContext.User.IsInRole("Admin");
```

This will return `true` if the current user is a member of the `Admin` group.

Another way to define authorization is through policies, which allow a more fine-grained control over the permissions. Let's now see what this is all about.

Policy-based authorization

Policies are a far more flexible way to grant authorization; here, we can use whatever rule we want, not just the rule belonging to a certain role or being authenticated.

To use policies, we need to decorate the resources to protect (controllers, actions) with the `[Authorize]` attribute and the `Policy` property, as illustrated in the following code snippet:

```
[Authorize(Policy = "EmployeeOnly")]
```

Policies are configured through the `AddAuthorization` method, in an `AuthorizationOptions` class, as illustrated in the following code snippet

```
services.AddAuthorization(options =>
{
    options.AddPolicy("EmployeeOnly", policy => policy.RequireClaim
    ("EmployeeNumber"));
});
```

This code is requiring that the current user has a specific claim, but we can think of other examples, such as only allowing local requests. `RequireAssertion` allows us to specify arbitrary conditions, as illustrated in the following code block:

```
options.AddPolicy("LocalOnly", builder =>
{
    builder.RequireAssertion(ctx =>
    {
        var success = false;
```

```
            if (ctx.Resource is AuthorizationFilterContext mvcContext)
            {
                success = IPAddress.IsLoopback(mvcContext.HttpContext.
                Connection.RemoteIpAddress);
            }
            return success;
        });
    });
```

Notice that here, we are assuming that the Resource property is AuthorizationFilterContext. Remember that this will only be true if we are in the context of an [Authorize] filter; otherwise, it won't be the case.

You can also use policies for specific claims (RequireClaim) or roles (RequireRole), for being authenticated (RequireAuthenticatedUser), or even for having a specific username (RequireUserName), and even combine all of them, as follows:

```
options.AddPolicy("Complex", builder =>
{
    //a specific username
    builder.RequireUserName("admin");
    //being authenticated
    builder.RequireAuthenticatedUser();
    //a claim (Claim) with any one of three options (A, B or C)
    builder.RequireClaim("Claim", "A", "B", "C");
    //any of of two roles
    builder.RequireRole("Admin", "Supervisor");
});
```

The sky is the limit—you can use whatever logic you want to grant access. The Resource property is prototyped as object, which means it can take any value; if called as part of the MVC authorization filter, it will always be an instance of AuthorizationFilterContext.

Let's now see a way to encapsulate these policies in reusable classes.

Authorization handlers

Authorization handlers are a way to encapsulate business validations in classes. There is an Authorization API composed of the following:

- IAuthorizationService: The entry point for all the authorization checks
- IAuthorizationHandler: An implementation of an authorization rule

- IAuthorizationRequirement: The contract for a single authorization requirement, to be passed to an authorization handler
- AuthorizationHandler<TRequirement>: An abstract base implementation of IAuthorizationHandler that is bound to a specific IAuthorizationRequirement

We implement an IAuthorizationHandler (perhaps subclassing from AuthorizationHandler<TRequirement>) and we define our rules in there, like this:

```
public sealed class DayOfWeekAuthorizationHandler :
AuthorizationHandler<DayOfWeekRequirement>
{
    protected override Task HandleRequirementAsync(
        AuthorizationHandlerContext context,
        DayOfWeekRequirement requirement)
    {
        if ((context.Resource is DayOfWeek requestedRequirement) &&
        (requestedRequirement == requirement.DayOfWeek))
        {
            context.Succeed(requirement);
        }
        else
        {
            context.Fail();
        }

        return Task.CompletedTask;
    }
}

public sealed class DayOfWeekRequirement : IAuthorizationRequirement
{
    public DayOfWeekRequirement(DayOfWeek dow)
    {
        this.DayOfWeek = dow;
    }

    public DayOfWeek DayOfWeek { get; }
}
```

This handler responds to a requirement of DayOfWeekRequirement type. It is bound automatically to it when one such requirement is passed to the AuthorizeAsync method.

An authorization pipeline can take a number of requirements, and for the authorization to succeed, all of the requirements must succeed too. This is a very simple example by which we have a requirement for a specific day of the week, and the authorization handler either succeeds or fails, depending on whether the current day of the week matches the given requirement.

The `IAuthorizationService` class is registered with the DI framework; the default instance is `DefaultAuthorizationService`. We would fire a check for permission using the following code:

```
IAuthorizationService authSvc = ...;

if (await (authSvc.AuthorizeAsync(
    user: this.User,
    resource: DateTime.Today.DayOfWeek,
    requirement: new
DayOfWeekRequirement(DayOfWeek.Monday))).Succeeded)
) { ... }
```

An authorization handler can also be bound to a policy name, as illustrated in the following code snippet:

```
services.AddAuthorization(options =>
{
    options.AddPolicy("DayOfWeek", builder =>
    {
        builder.AddRequirements(new DayOfWeekRequirement
        (DayOfWeek.Friday));
    });
});
```

In this case, the previous call would be the following instead:

```
if ((await (authSvc.AuthorizeAsync(
    user: this.User,
    resource: DateTime.Today.DayOfWeek,
    policyName: "DayOfWeek"))).Succeeded)
) { ... }
```

The parameters of these two overloads are the following:

- user (`ClaimsPrincipal`): The currently logged-in user
- policyName (`string`): A registered policy name

- resource (`object`): Any object that will be passed to the authorization pipeline
- requirement (`IAuthorizationRequirement`): One or more requirements that will be passed along to the authorization handler

If we ever want to override the default authorization handler, we can do so very easily in `ConfigureServices`, like this:

```
services.AddSingleton<IAuthorizationHandler,
DayOfWeekAuthorizationHandler>();
```

This will register a custom authorization handler on which we need to perform our own checks. Beware when replacing the default handler because this can be tricky and it's easy to forget something!

Now, if we need to use the context for more complex validations, we need to inject it into the handler. The following example will allow access to requests coming from just the localhost:

```
public sealed class LocalIpRequirement : IAuthorizationRequirement
{
 public const string Name = "LocalIp";
}

public sealed class LocalIpHandler :
AuthorizationHandler<LocalIpRequirement>
{
    public LocalIpHandler(IHttpContextAccessor httpContextAccessor)
    {
        this.HttpContext = httpContextAccessor.HttpContext;
    }

    public HttpContext HttpContext { get; }

    protected override Task HandleRequirementAsync(
        AuthorizationHandlerContext context,
        LocalIpRequirement requirement)
    {
        var success = IPAddress.IsLoopback(this.HttpContext.Connection
        .RemoteIpAddress);

        if (success)
        {
            context.Succeed(requirement);
        }
        else
```

```
    {
        context.Fail();
    }

    return Task.CompletedTask;
    }
}
```

For this to work, we need to do the following:

1. Register the `IHttpContextAccessor` service, like this:

   ```
   services.AddHttpContextAccessor();
   ```

2. Register `LocalIpHandler` as a scoped service, like this:

   ```
   services.AddScoped<IAuthorizationHandler, LocalIpHandler>();
   ```

3. When we want to check whether the current request matches the policy, we do it like this:

   ```
   var result = await authSvc.AuthorizeAsync(
       user: this.User,
       requirement: new LocalIpRequirement(),
       policyName: LocalIpRequirement.Name
   );

   if (result.Succeeded) { ... }
   ```

And we should be fine.

Now, let's look at a way of querying current permissions defined as policies.

Resource-based authorization

We can leverage the authorization handlers to have resource-based authorization. Basically, we ask the authorization service to check for permission to access a given resource and policy. We call one of the `AuthorizeAsync` methods of the `IAuthorizationService` instance, as illustrated in the following code snippet:

```
IAuthorizationService authSvc = ...;

if ((await authSvc.AuthorizeAsync(this.User, resource,
"Policy")).Succeeded) { ... }
```

The IAuthorizationService instance is normally obtained from the DI framework. The AuthorizeAsync method takes the following parameters:

- user (ClaimsPrincipal): The current user
- resource (object): A resource to check for permission against policyName
- policyName (string): The name of the policy for which to check permission for resource

This method can be called in both the controller and a view to check for fine-grained permissions. What it will do is execute AuthorizationPolicy registered under the policy name passing it the resource, which, in turn, will call all the registered authorization handlers.

A typical example of a fine-grained authorization check would be to ask for edit permission on a given record—for example, in a view, like this:

```
@inject IAuthorizationService authSvc
@model Order

@{
    var order = Model;
}

@if ((await (authSvc.AuthorizeAsync(User, order,
"Order.Edit"))).Succeeded)
{
    @Html.EditorForModel()
}
else
{
    @Html.DisplayForModel()
}
```

Here, we are checking a policy named Order.Edit, which is expecting a resource of the Ordertype. All of its requirements are run, and, if they all succeed, then we are entitled to edit the order; otherwise, we just display it.

And what if we need to allow any user to access a protected resource-controller action or Razor page?

Allowing anonymous access

If, for any reason when using access control, you want to allow access to specific controllers or a specific action in a controller, you can apply to it the `[AllowAnonymous]` attribute. This will bypass any security handlers and execute the action. Of course, in the action or view, you can still perform explicit security checks by checking the `HttpContext.User.Identity` property.

Authorization is one of the two building blocks, and we talked about the different ways in which we can define rules for web resources or named policies. In the next sections, we will talk about other aspects of security, starting with request forgery.

Checking requests for forgery

CSRF (or **XSRF**) attacks are one of the most common hacks by which a user is tricked into performing some action in one of the sites to which they are logged in. For example, imagine you have just visited your e-banking site and then you go to a malicious site, without having logged out; some JavaScript on the malicious site could have the browser post to the e-banking site an instruction to transfer some amount of money to another account. Realizing that this is a serious problem, Microsoft has long supported an anti-forgery package, `Microsoft.AspNetCore.Antiforgery`, which implements a mixture of the *Double Submit Cookie* and *Encrypted Token* pattern described in the **Open Web Application Security Project (OWASP)** cheat sheet: `https://www.owasp.org/index.php/Cross-Site_Request_Forgery_(CSRF)_Prevention_Cheat_Sheet#CSRF_Specific_Defense`

OWASP aims to provide a not-for-profit repository of best practices related to security on the web. It lists common security problems and explains how to address them.

The anti-forgery framework does the following:

- Generates a hidden field with an anti-forgery token on every form (this could also be a header)
- Sends a cookie with the same token
- Upon postback, checks that it received an anti-forgery token as part of the payload, and that it is identical to the anti-forgery cookie

The `BeginForm` method, by default, outputs an anti-forgery token when it produces a `<form>` tag, unless called with the `antiforgery` parameter set to `false`.

You will need to register the required services by calling `AddAntiforgery`, as illustrated in the following code snippet:

```
services.AddAntiforgery(options =>
{
    options.FormFieldName = "__RequestVerificationToken";
});
```

The possible options are as follows:

- `CookieName` (`string`): The name of the cookie to replace the default one; this is automatically generated with a prefix of `.AspNetCore.Antiforgery`.
- `CookiePath` (`PathString?`): An optional path to restrict the applicability of the cookie; the default is `null`, meaning that no path setting will be sent with the cookie
- `CookieDomain` (`string`): An optional domain to restrict (or augment) the applicability of the cookie; the default is `null`, so no domain setting will be set
- `FormFieldName` (`string`): The name of the hidden form field where the anti-forgery token is to be stored; the default is `__RequestVerificationToken`, and this is required
- `HeaderName` (`string`): The header name that will store the token; the default is `RequestVerificationToken`
- `RequireSsl` (`bool`): `True` if the anti-forgery cookie is to be sent only using HTTPS; the default is `false`
- `SuppressXFrameOptionsHeader` (`bool`): Whether or not the `X-Frame-Options` header should be sent; the default is `false`, which means that a value of `SAMEORIGIN` will be sent

The anti-forgery service is registered under the `IAntiforgery` interface.

There are a number of attributes that can be used to control the default behavior, listed as follows:

- `[ValidateAntiforgeryToken]`: Adds anti-forgery validation to a specific controller or action
- `[IgnoreAntiforgeryToken]`: Disables anti-forgery validation on a specific controller or action, if it has been globally enabled
- `[AutoValidateAntiforgeryToken]`: Adds anti-forgery validation to any unsafe requests (`POST`, `PUT`, `DELETE`, `PATCH`)

All of these can be added as global filters beside attributes, as illustrated in the following code snippet:

```
services.AddMvc(options =>
{
    options.Filters.Add(new AutoValidateAntiforgeryTokenAttribute());
});
```

The difference between `[ValidateAntiforgeryToken]` and `[AutoValidateAntiforgeryToken]` is that the latter is designed to be used as a global filter; there is no need to apply it everywhere explicitly.

 Check out `https://docs.microsoft.com/en-us/aspnet/core/security/anti-request-forgery` for a more in-depth explanation of the anti-forgery options available.

What if you want to use it with AJAX, to also protect these kinds of requests? Well, first, you need to get a token from the server and the name of the header to use so that you can add it to each AJAX request. You can inject the token into a view and then add it to the AJAX headers—for example, using jQuery, as illustrated in the following code block:

```
@using Microsoft.AspNetCore.Antiforgery
@inject IAntiforgery AntiForgery;

var headers = {};
headers['RequestVerificationToken'] = '@AntiForgery.GetAndStoreTokens
(HttpContext).RequestToken';

$.ajax({
    type: 'POST',
    url: url,
    headers: headers}
)
.done(function(data) { ... });
```

Here, we are sending the anti-forgery token with every AJAX request seamlessly, so the ASP.NET Core framework catches it and is happy with it.

Next, we will see how to prevent script injection by using HTML coding.

Applying HTML encoding

The views engine in ASP.NET Core uses HTML encoders to render HTML, in an effort to prevent script injection attacks. The `RazorPage` class, the base for all Razor views, features an `HtmlEncoder` property of `HtmlEncoder` type. By default, it is obtained from DI as `DefaultHtmlEncoder` , but you can set it to a different instance, although it is probably not needed. We ask for content to be encoded explicitly by using the `@("...")` Razor syntax, like this:

```
@("<div>encoded string</div>")
```

This will render the following HTML-encoded string:

```
&lt;div&gt;encoded string&lt;/div&gt;
```

You can also explicitly do it using the `Encode` method of the `IHtmHelper` object, like this:

```
@Html.Encode("<div>encoded string</div>")
```

Lastly, if you have a helper method that returns a value of `IHtmlContent`, it will automatically be rendered using the registered `HtmlEncoder`.

 If you want to learn more about script injection, please consult `https://www.owasp.org/index.php/Code_Injection`.

So much for script injection protection. Now, let's move on to HTTPS.

Working with HTTPS

The usage of HTTPS is becoming more and more common these days—not only is the performance penalty that existed in the early days now gone, but it is also significantly cheaper to get a certificate; in some cases, it may even be free—for example, **Let's Encrypt** (`https://letsencrypt.org`) offers such certificates. Plus, search engines such as Google boost results for sites served through HTTPS. Of course, ASP.NET Core fully supports HTTPS. We will now see how to add certificates so that we can serve our sites using HTTPS, and how to restrict access to HTTPS only.

Let's begin with certificates.

Certificates

In order to use HTTPS, we need a valid certificate—one that browsers accept as valid. We can either acquire one from a root certificate provider or we can generate one, for development purposes. This won't be recognized as coming from a trusted source.

In order to generate a certificate and install it on the machine's store (on Windows and macOS), we run the following code:

```
dotnet dev-certs https --clean
dotnet dev-certs https --trust
```

If we need to, we can export the certificate file to the filesystem, like this:

`dotnet dev-certs https --trust -ep .\certificate.pfx`

Keep in mind that the certificate serves the following two purposes:

- Encrypting the communication
- Ensuring that the web server is trustworthy

A development certificate such as the one generated by the `dotnet` tool only serves the first purpose.

After we have obtained a certificate, we must now use it, and this depends on our hosting choice. This is covered next.

Hosting our app

The way to proceed depends on whether we are connecting to the ASP.NET Core host (such as Kestrel) directly or through a reverse proxy such as IIS Express. IIS Express is the light version of IIS that you can run locally for development purposes. It offers all the features of full-blown IIS, but not quite the same performance and scalability. Let's see what IIS Express is.

IIS Express

If we are to use IIS Express, we just need to configure its settings to enable **Secure Sockets Layer** (**SSL**), shown as follows:

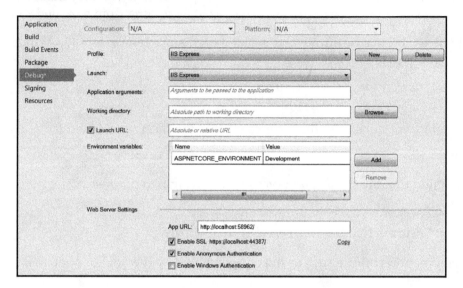

Kestrel

If, on the other hand, we are going with Kestrel, things are a bit different. First, we will need the `Microsoft.AspNetCore.Server.Kestrel.Https` NuGet package and a certificate file. In the bootstrap code, it is used implicitly. We need to run the following code:

```
Host
    .CreateDefaultBuilder(args)
    .ConfigureWebHostDefaults(builder =>
    {
        builder.ConfigureKestrel(options =>
        {
            options.ListenAnyIP(443, listenOptions =>
            {
                listenOptions.UseHttps("certificate.pfx",
"<password>");
            });
        });
        builder.UseStartup<Startup>();
    });
```

You will observe the following:

- A certificate is loaded from a file called `certificate.pfx`, protected by a password of `<password>`.
- We listen on port `443` for any of the local IP addresses.

If we just want to change the default port and hosting server (Kestrel) but not use a certificate, it's easy to do by code, as follows:

```
builder.UseSetting("https_port", "4430");
```

This can also happen through the `ASPNETCORE_HTTPS_PORT` environment variable.

HTTP.sys

For `HTTP.sys`, we will need the `Microsoft.AspNetCore.Server.HttpSys` package, and instead of `ConfigureKestrel`, we call `UseHttpSys`, like this:

```
.UseHttpSys(options =>
{
    options.UrlPrefixes.Add("https://*:443");
});
```

A certificate for use with `HTTP.sys` needs to be configured on Windows, for the specific port and host header that you wish to serve.

In the modern web, we are likely to want to use HTTPS only, so let's see how we can enforce this.

Forcing HTTPS

Sometimes, we may require that all calls are made through HTTPS, and all other requests are rejected. For that we can use a global filter, `RequireHttpsAttribute`, as illustrated in the following code block:

```
services.Configure<MvcOptions>(options =>
{
    options.SslPort = 443; //this is the default and can be omitted
    options.Filters.Add(new RequireHttpsAttribute());
});
```

We also need to tell MVC which port we are using for HTTPS, just for cases where we use a non-standard one (`443` is the standard).

Another option is to do it controller by controller, like this:

```
[RequireHttps]
public class SecureController : Controller
{
}
```

Or, this can happen action by action, like this:

```
public class SecureController : Controller
{
    [HttpPost]
    [RequireHttps]
    public IActionResult ReceiveSensitiveData(SensitiveData data) {
... }
}
```

 Mind you, using `[RequireHttps]` in web APIs might not be a good idea—if your API client is not expecting it, it will fail and you may not know what the problem is.

What if we have the two versions, HTTP and HTTPS, and want to silently direct our clients to using HTTPS?

Redirecting to HTTPS

ASP.NET Core includes a redirection middleware. It is similar in functionality to the ASP.NET IIS Rewrite module (see https://www.iis.net/learn/extensions/url-rewrite-module). Its description is beyond the scope of this chapter, but it is sufficient to explain how we can force a redirect from HTTP to HTTPS. Have a look at the following code snippet:

```
var options = new RewriteOptions()
    .AddRedirectToHttps();

app.UseRewriter(options);
```

This simple code in `Configure` registers the redirection middleware and instructs it to redirect all traffic coming to HTTP to the HTTPS protocol. It's as simple as that, but it can even be simpler: since version 2.1 of ASP.NET Core, all we need to do is call `UseHttpsRedirection` in the `Configure` method, like this:

```
app.UseHttpsRedirection();
```

And should we want to specify additional information, we call
`AddHttpsRedirection` with options in `ConfigureServices`, like this:

```
services.AddHttpsRedirection(options =>
{
    options.RedirectStatusCode =
StatusCodes.Status307TemporaryRedirect;
    options.HttpsPort = 4430;
});
```

> Again, redirecting to HTTPS with web APIs might not be a good
> idea because API clients may be configured to not follow redirects.

Still on the HTTPS track, let's now study another mechanism for directing users to
HTTPS.

Using HSTS

HSTS is a web security policy mechanism that helps protect websites against protocol
downgrade attacks (HTTPS -> HTTP) and cookie hijacking. It allows web servers to
declare that web browsers should only interact with it using secure HTTPS
connections, and never via the insecure HTTP protocol. Browsers memorize this
definition.

> To learn more about HSTS, please consult `https://developer.`
> `mozilla.org/en-US/docs/Web/HTTP/Headers/Strict-Transport-`
> `Security.`

HSTS is added to the `Configure` method, like this:

```
app.UseHsts();
```

It adds a header to the response, like this:

```
Strict-Transport-Security: max-age=31536000
```

As you can see, it has a `max-age` parameter. We configure it through a call to
`AddHsts`, in `ConfigureServices`, like this:

```
services.AddHsts(options =>
{
```

```
        options.MaxAge = TimeSpan.FromDays(7);
        options.IncludeSubDomains = true;
        options.ExcludedHosts.Add("test");
        options.Preload = true;
    });
```

HSTS preload

If a site sends the `preload` directive in an HSTS header, it is considered to be requesting inclusion in the preload list and may be submitted via the form on the `https://hstspreload.org` site.

So, in this section, we've seen how to use HTTPS, from building a certificate, to using it, and forcing redirection from HTTP to HTTPS. Now, let's move on to other aspects of security, starting with CORS.

Understanding CORS

CORS is essentially the ability to request a resource from one domain from a page being served by a different domain: think, for example, of a page at `http://mysite.com` requesting a JavaScript file from `http://javascriptdepository.com`. This is done in all big portals—for example, for including visitor tracking or ad scripts. Modern browsers forbid this by default, but it is possible to enable it on a case-by-case basis.

 If you want to learn more about CORS, please consult `https://developer.mozilla.org/en/docs/Web/HTTP/Access_control_CORS`.

ASP.NET Core supports CORS servicing. You first need to register the required services (in `ConfigureServices`), like this:

```
services.AddCors();
```

Or, a slightly more complex example involves defining a policy, like this:

```
services.AddCors(options =>
{
    options.AddPolicy("CorsPolicy", builder =>
        builder
            .AllowAnyOrigin()
```

```
                    .AllowAnyMethod()
                    .AllowAnyHeader()
                    .AllowCredentials()
        );
    });
```

A policy can take specific URLs; there is no need to support any origin. Have a look at the following code example:

```
builder
    .WithOrigins("http://mysite.com", "http://myothersite.com")
```

A more complete example, with headers, methods, and origins, would be this:

```
var policy = new CorsPolicy();
policy.Headers.Add("*");
policy.Methods.Add("*");
policy.Origins.Add("*");
policy.SupportsCredentials = true;

services.AddCors(options =>
{
    options.AddPolicy("CorsPolicy", policy);
});
```

The `Headers`, `Methods`, and `Origins` collections contain all the values that should be allowed explicitly; adding * to them is the same as calling `AllowAnyHeader`, `AllowAnyMethod`, and `AllowAnyOrigin`. Setting `SupportsCredentials` to `true` means that an `Access-Control-Allow-Credentials` header will be returned, meaning that the application allows login credentials to be sent from a different domain. Beware of this setting because it means that a user in a different domain can try to log in to your app, probably even as the result of malicious code. Use this judiciously.

And then, add the CORS middleware in `Configure`, which will result in globally allowing CORS requests. The code can be seen in the following snippet:

```
app.UseCors(builder => builder.WithOrigins("http://mysite.com"));
```

Or, do this with a specific policy, like this:

```
app.UseCors("CorsPolicy");
```

All of this requires the `Microsoft.AspNetCore.Cors` NuGet package, mind you. You can add as many URLs as you like, using the `WithOrigins` method, and it can be called sequentially with all the addresses that are to be granted access. You can restrict it to specific headers and methods too, as follows:

```
app.UseCors(builder =>
    builder
        .WithOrigins("http://mysite.com", "http://myothersite.com")
        .WithMethods("GET")
);
```

One thing to keep in mind is that `UseCors` must be called before `UseMvc`!

If, on the other hand, you want to enable CORS on a controller by controller or action by action basis, you can use the `[EnableCors]` attribute, as illustrated in the following code snippet:

```
[EnableCors("CorsPolicy")]
public class HomeController : Controller { ... }
```

Here, you need to specify a policy name and not individual URLs. Likewise, you can disable CORS for a specific controller or action by applying the `[DisableCors]` attribute. This one does not take a policy name; it just disables CORS completely.

Now for something completely different. Let's study the providers available to ASP.NET Core for encrypting and decrypting data on the fly.

Using data protection

ASP.NET Core uses **data protection providers** to protect data that is exposed to third parties, such as cookies. The `IDataProtectionProvider` interface defines its contract and ASP.NET Core ships with a default instance registered in the DI framework of `KeyRingBasedDataProtector`, as illustrated in the following code snippet:

```
services.AddDataProtection();
```

The data protection provider is used by the cookies' authentication and also the cookie temp data provider APIs. A data protection provider exposes a method, `CreateProtector`, that is used to retrieve a protector instance, which can then be used to protect a string, as illustrated in the following code snippet:

```
var protector = provider.CreateProtector("MasteringAspNetCore");
var input = "Hello, World";
var output = protector.Protect(input);
//CfDJ8AAAAAAAAAAAAAAAAAAAA...uGoxWLjGKtm1SkNACQ
```

You can certainly use it for other purposes, but for the two presented previously, you just need to pass a provider instance to the `CookiesAuthenticationOptions` instance, in the `ConfigureServices` method, as illustrated in the following code snippet:

```
services.AddCookieAuthentication(CookieAuthenticationDefaults.Authenti
cationScheme, options =>
{
    options.DataProtectionProvider = instance;
});
```

The `CookieTempDataProvider` class already receives an instance of `IDataProtectionProvider` in its constructor, so when the DI framework builds it, it passes in the registered instance.

A data protection provider is very useful if you are using a clustered solution and you want to share a state among the different machines of the cluster in a secure way. In that case, you should use both a data protection and a distributed cache provider (`IDistributedCache` implementation), such as Redis, where you will store the shared key. If, for some reason, you need to go without a distributed provider, you can store the shared key file locally. It goes like this:

```
services
    .AddDataProtection()
    .PersistKeysToFileSystem(new DirectoryInfo("<location>"));
```

If you wish, you can set the `<location>` on the configuration file, like this:

```
{
  "DataProtectionSettings": {
    "Location": "<location>"
  }
}
```

Here, `<location>` refers to the path where the data file will be stored.

Data protection providers is a big topic and one that is outside the scope of this book. For more information, please consult `https://docs.microsoft.com/en-us/aspnet/core/security/data-protection/`.

So, we've seen how we can protect arbitrary data, and let's now see how we can protect static files.

Protecting static files

There is no way to protect static files on ASP.NET Core. It goes without saying, however, that that doesn't mean you can't do it. Essentially, you have the following two options:

- Keeping the files that you want to serve outside the `wwwroot` folder and using a controller action to retrieve them; this action should enforce any security mechanism you want
- Using a middleware component to check access to your files and optionally restrict access to them

We will see each process in the next sections.

Using an action to retrieve files

So, you want to use an action method to retrieve a file. Either decorate this action method with an `[Authorize]` attribute or check for fine-grained access inside it (`IAuthorizationService.AuthorizeAsync`). Have a look at the following code:

```
private static readonly IContentTypeProvider _contentTypeProvider =
    new FileExtensionContentTypeProvider();

[Authorize]
[HttpGet]
public IActionResult DownloadFile(string filename)
{
    var path = Path.GetDirectoryName(filename);

    //uncomment this if fine-grained access is not required
    if (this._authSvc.AuthorizeAsync(this.User, path, "Download"))
    {
        _contentTypeProvider.TryGetContentType("filename",
         out var contentType);
```

```
            var realFilePath = Path.Combine("ProtectedPath", filename);

            return this.File(realFilePath, contentType);
        }

        return this.Challenge();
    }
```

This will only allow GET requests by authenticated users, and the download policy is checked for the path of the file to retrieve. Then, the requested file is combined with a ProtectedPath in order to get the real filename. An instance of FileExtensionContentTypeProvider is used to infer the content type for the file based on its extension.

Using middleware to enforce security

You know about the ASP.NET Core/**Open Web Interface for .NET (OWIN)** pipeline from Chapter 1, *Getting Started with ASP.NET Core*. Each middleware component in it can affect the others, even by preventing their execution. This other option will intercept any file. Let's add a configuration class and an extension method, as follows:

```
public class ProtectedPathOptions
{
    public PathString Path { get; set; }
    public string PolicyName { get; set; }
}

public static IApplicationBuilder UseProtectedPaths(
    this IApplicationBuilder app, params ProtectedPathOptions []
options)
{
    foreach (var option in options ??
    Enumerable.Empty<ProtectedPathOptions>())
    {
        app.UseMiddleware<ProtectedPathsMiddleware>(option);
    }

    return app;
}
```

Next, the code for the actual middleware component needs to be added quite early in the pipeline (Configure method), like this:

```
public class ProtectedPathsMiddleware
{
```

```
    private readonly RequestDelegate _next;
    private readonly ProtectedPathOptions _options;

    public ProtectedPathsMiddleware(RequestDelegate next,
    ProtectedPathOptions options)
    {
        this._next = next;
        this._options = options;
    }

    public async Task InvokeAsync(HttpContext context)
    {
        using (context.RequestServices.CreateScope())
        {
            var authSvc = context.RequestServices.GetRequiredService
            <IAuthorizationService>();

            if (context.Request.Path.StartsWithSegments
            (this._options.Path))
            {
                var result = await authSvc.AuthorizeAsync(
                    context.User,
                    context.Request.Path,
                    this._options.PolicyName);

                if (!result.Succeeded)
                {
                    await context.ChallengeAsync();
                    return;
                }
            }
        }

        await this._next.Invoke(context);
    }
}
```

This middleware goes through all registered path protection options and checks whether the policy they specify is satisfied by the request path. If not, they challenge the response, effecting redirection to the login page.

To activate this, you need to add this middleware to the pipeline, in the `Configure` method, like this:

```
app.UseProtectedPaths(new ProtectedPathOptions { Path = "/A/Path",
PolicyName = "APolicy" });
```

If, by any chance, you need to lock down your app—meaning bring it offline—you can do so by adding an `app_offline.htm` file to the root of your app (not the `wwwroot` folder!). If this file exists, it will be served, and any other requests will be ignored. This is an easy way to temporarily disable access to your site, without actually changing anything.

We've seen how we can apply authorization policies for static files. In the next section, we see an explanation of what the GDPR is.

Learning about the GDPR

The **European Union** (**EU**) adopted the GDPR in 2018. Although this is mostly for European countries, all sites that are available there should also comply with it. I won't go into the technical aspects of this regulation, but essentially, it ensures that users grant permission for others to access their personal data and are free to revoke this access, and therefore have them destroy this information at any time they like. This can impact applications in many ways, even forcing the adoption of specific requirements. At the very least, for all applications that use cookies for tracking personal information, they are forced to warn users and get their consent.

Read more about the GDPR here: `https://gdpr-info.eu/`

Required cookies

The default ASP.NET Core templates, as of version 3.x, include support for getting user's approval for using cookies. The `CookieOptions` class, used to supply cookie data such as expiration, now has a new property, `IsEssential`, depending on an application's cookie policy, as dictated by its `CookiePolicy` instance's `CheckConsentNeeded` property. This is actually a function, and if it returns `true` but the user has not explicitly granted permission, some things will not work: `TempData` and `Session` cookies won't work.

The actual consent is achieved by setting a client cookie (who could be able to tell?), through the `ITrackingConsentFeature` feature, as illustrated in the following code snippet:

```
HttpContext.Features.Get<ITrackingConsentFeature>().GrantConsent();
```

Or, should we wish to deny this consent, we would run the following code:

```
HttpContext.Features.Get<ITrackingConsentFeature>().WithdrawConsent();
```

At any point, we can check the current state of the grant by running the following code:

```
var feature = HttpContext.Features.Get<ITrackingConsentFeature>();
var canTrack = feature.CanTrack;
var hasConsent = feature.HasConsent;
var isConsentNeeded = feature.IsConsentNeeded;
```

The properties' meanings are as follows:

- `CanTrack`: Whether consent has been given or it is not required
- `HasConsent`: Whether consent has been given
- `IsConsentNeeded`: Whether the application has demanded consent for cookies

The configuration should be done in the `ConfigureServices` method, as illustrated in the following code snippet:

```
services
    .Configure<CookiePolicyOptions>(options =>
    {
        options.CheckConsentNeeded = (context) => true;
        options.MinimumSameSitePolicy = SameSiteMode.None;
        options.HttpOnly = HttpOnlyPolicy.Always;
        options.Secure = CookieSecurePolicy.SameAsRequest;
    });
```

As you can see, `CheckConsentNeeded` is a delegate that takes as its sole parameter an `HttpContext` instance and returns a Boolean value; this way, you can decide on a case-by-case basis what to do.

`MinimumSameSitePolicy`, `HttpOnly`, and `Secure` behave exactly the same as in the `CookieOptions` class, used in setting individual cookies' options.

After the configuration, we need to enforce this by adding the middleware to the pipeline; this goes in the `Configure` method, like this:

```
app.UseCookiePolicy();
```

Personal data

Another thing that we already talked about is that, when using the Identity authentication provider, you should mark any personal properties that you add to the user model with the `[PersonalData]` attribute. This is a hint for you that these properties will need to be supplied to the user, should they ask for that, and, likewise, deleted together with the rest of the user data if the user asks you to.

Keep in mind the GDPR is a requirement in Europe and, generally speaking, is something that is expected all around the world, so this is definitely something that you should be prepared for.

Now, another aspect of security, related to model binding.

Binding security

A whole different subject now. We know that ASP.NET Core automatically binds submitted values to model classes, but what would happen if we hijacked a request and asked ASP.NET to bind a different user or role than the one we have? For example, consider if we have a method that updates the user profile using the following model:

```
public class User
{
    public string Id { get; set; }
    public bool IsAdmin { get; set; }
    //rest of the properties go here
}
```

If this model is committed to the database, it is easy to see that if we pass a value of IsAdmin=true, then we would become administrators instantly! To prevent this situation, we should do either of the following:

- Move out sensitive properties from the public model, the one that is retrieved from the data sent by the user
- Apply [BindNever] attributes to these sensitive properties, like this:

```
[BindNever]
public bool IsAdmin { get; set; }
```

In the latter case, we need to populate these properties ourselves, using the right logic.

> As a rule of thumb, never use as the MVC model the domain classes that you use in your **object-relational mapping (O/RM)**; it is better to have a clear distinction between the two and map them yourself (even if with the help of a tool such as AutoMapper), taking care of sensitive properties.

Be careful with the properties that you are binding because you do not want users to have access to everything. Review your model and binding rules carefully.

Summary

This chapter talked about the many aspects of security. Here, we learned how to make our application more secure and resilient to attacks.

We understood the use of authorization attributes to protect sensitive resources of your application. It's better to use policies than actual named claims or roles because it's so much easier to change a policy configuration, and you can do pretty much everything.

Then, we saw how to use identity for authentication rather than rolling out your own mechanism. If your requirements so allow it, use social logins, as this is probably widely accepted since most people use social networking apps.

Be careful with binding sensitive data to your model; prevent it from happening automatically and use different models for MVC and the actual data storage. We saw that we always HTML-encode data that comes from a database, to prevent the possibility that a malicious user has inserted JavaScript into it.

We saw that we need to be wary of static files as they are not protected by default. It is preferable to retrieve the files.

Finally, in the last part of the chapter, we understood that we should consider moving the entirety of your site to HTTPS, as it significantly reduces the chances of eavesdropping on your data.

This was quite an extensive topic that covered many aspects of security. If you stick to these recommendations, your app will be somewhat safer, but this is not enough. Always follow the security recommendation rules for the APIs you use, and make sure you know what their implications are.

In the next chapter, we shall see how we can extract information as to what is happening
inside ASP.NET Core

Questions

So, by the end of this chapter, you should know the answers to the following questions:

1. What attribute can we use to mark a method or controller so that it can only be called through HTTPS?
2. What is the difference between role-based and policy-based authorization?
3. What is the purpose of CORS?
4. What is the purpose of HSTS?
5. What is the challenge stage of the authentication process?
6. Why should we take care when binding requests to model classes?
7. What is the sliding expiration of a cookie?

Section 3: Advanced Topics

3

This section will cover advanced topics, looking at proven techniques to improve code performance.

This section has the following chapters:

12
Logging, Tracing, and Diagnostics

Logging, tracing, and metrics are essential features of any non-trivial application, for the following reasons:

- **Logging** tells us what the system is doing, what it is about to do, the errors it encounters, and so on.
- **Tracing** is about collecting transactional information about journeys and how they flow in a distributed system.
- **Metrics** involves getting information in real time about what is happening and possibly producing alerts from it.

In this chapter, we will have a look at some of the options we have at hand, from the simplest to the most complex.

We will cover the following topics in this chapter:

- Introducing the .NET Core Common Logging framework
- Writing custom logging middleware
- Using tracing and diagnostics
- Using performance (event) counters for obtaining metrics
- Using telemetry with Microsoft Azure AppInsights, **Amazon Web Services** (**AWS**) CloudWatch, and New Relic
- Performing ASP.NET Core health checks

Technical requirements

In order to implement the examples introduced in this chapter, you will need the .NET Core 3 **software development kit** (**SDK**) and some form of text editor. Of course, Visual Studio 2019 (any edition) meets all the requirements, but you can also use Visual Studio Code, for example.

For using Azure, AWS, or New Relic, you will need working accounts with these providers.

The source code can be retrieved from GitHub here: `https://github.com/ PacktPublishing/Modern-Web-Development-with-ASP.NET-Core-3-Second-Edition`.

Introducing the .NET Core Common Logging framework

Logging is an integral part of .NET Core, which provides several abstractions to support it; needless to say, it is fully pluggable and extensible. The infrastructure classes, interfaces, abstract base classes, enumerations, and so on are contained in the `Microsoft.Extensions.Logging.Abstractions` NuGet package and the built-in implementations are contained in the `Microsoft.Extensions.Logging` package. When you log a message, it is routed to all registered logging providers.

Here, we will see the following:

- Using logging services
- Defining log levels
- Using logging providers
- Filtering logs
- Writing custom log providers
- Using **dependency injection** (**DI**) with the log providers
- Using logging attributes

We will study each of these in the coming sections.

Using logging services

We register the logging services by calling `AddLogging` in the `ConfigureServices` method. This is actually done by other methods, such as `AddMvc`, so there is usually no need to call it manually—except, of course, if we are not using **Model-View-Controller** (**MVC**). There is no harm in doing so, though. Manually, it can be done as follows:

```
services.AddLogging();
```

In order to log into .NET Core, you need an instance of the `ILogger` (or `ILogger<T>`) interface. You normally inject one into your class—controller, view component, tag helper, and middleware—using the DI framework, which fully supports it. This is illustrated in the following code snippet:

```
public class HomeController : Controller
{
    private readonly ILogger<HomeController> _logger;

    public HomeController(ILogger<HomeController> logger)
    {
        this._logger = logger;
    }
}
```

But you can also request an instance of the interface from the `ILoggerFactory` method, as follows:

```
var logger1 = loggerFactory.CreateLogger<MyClass>();
//or
var logger2 = loggerFactory.CreateLogger("MyClass");
```

The category name is taken from the full type name of the generic class parameter.

The `ILogger` interface only offers three methods, plus a number of extension methods. The core methods are listed here:

- `BeginScope`: Starts a block to which all logs made inside it are related
- `IsEnabled`: Checks whether a given log level is enabled to be logged
- `Log`: Writes a log message to a specific log level, with an event ID and optional formatter

Defining log levels

Log levels are defined in the `LogLevel` enumeration, as follows:

Level	Numeric value	Purpose
Trace	0	Logs that contain the most detailed messages. These messages may contain sensitive application data.
Debug	1	Logs that are used for interactive investigation during development. These logs should primarily contain information useful for debugging and have no long-term value.
Information	2	Logs that track the general flow of the application. These logs should have long-term value.
Warning	3	Logs that highlight an abnormal or unexpected event in the application flow, but do not otherwise cause the application execution to stop.
Error	4	Logs that highlight when the current flow of execution is stopped due to a failure. These should indicate a failure in the current activity, not an application-wide failure.
Critical	5	Logs that describe an unrecoverable application or system crash, or a catastrophic failure that requires immediate attention.
None	6	Specifies that a logging category should not write any messages.

As you can see, these log levels have ascending numeric values, starting with the most verbose and potentially uninteresting (except for debugging purposes) and ending in the most severe. The logging framework is designed so that we can filter out levels below a given one, so as to avoid unnecessary clutter in the logging. To check whether a given level is enabled, we use `IsEnabled`.

The `Log` generic method is usually the most interesting one, and it takes the following parameters:

- `logLevel` (`LogLevel`): The desired log level
- `eventId` (`EventId`): An event ID
- `state` (`TState`): The state to log
- `exception` (`Exception`): An exception to log
- `formatter` (`Func<TState, Exception, string>`): A formatting function based on the state and the possible exception

Each log entry has the following information:

- Log level
- Timestamp
- Category
- State of exception
- Event ID
- Scope name (if called from inside a scope)

When we request a logger instance from `ILoggerFactory`, which is normally done automatically by declaring an `ILogger<T>` instance in the constructor of a class, the `T` parameter is the category name; it is the same as the fully qualified type name.

By far the most common message kind that we want to log is strings (or exceptions), so there are a few extension methods that do just that, as follows:

- `LogTrace`
- `LogDebug`
- `LogInformation`
- `LogWarning`
- `LogError`
- `LogCritical`

As you can see, all of these methods are bound to a specific log level, and each has three overloads for taking a combination of these parameters, as follows:

- `message` (`string`): A message to log, with optional parameter placeholders (for example, `{0}`, `{1}`, and so on)
- `parameters` (`params object []`): The optional parameters for the message to log
- `eventId` (`EventId`): A correlation ID
- `exception` (`Exception`): An exception to log, if there is one

Every one of the three overloads takes `message` plus its optional `parameters`, another one takes `eventId`, and the other takes `exception`.

What is the event ID used for?, I hear you ask. Well, it is a correlation ID, an identifier that is possibly unique among requests and which correlates several logging messages together so that someone analyzing them can find out whether they are related. Event IDs are essentially a number plus an optional name. If not supplied, they are not used.

A scope merely includes the given scope name in all the logging messages until the scope is ended. As `BeginScope` returns an `IDisposable` instance, calling its `Dispose` method ends the scope.

Using logging providers

A logging provider is a class that implements the `ILoggerProvider` interface. Logging providers need to be registered with the logging framework so that they can be used. Normally, this is done by either the `ILoggerFactory.AddProvider` method or an extension method supplied by the provider.

Microsoft ships .NET Core with the following providers:

Provider	NuGet package	Purpose
Azure App Service	`Microsoft.Extensions.Logging.AzureAppServices`	Logs to Azure Blob storage or to the filesystem
Console	`Microsoft.Extensions.Logging.Console`	Logs to the console
Debug	`Microsoft.Extensions.Logging.Debug`	Logs using `Debug.WriteLine`
EventLog	`Microsoft.Extensions.Logging.EventLog`	Logs to the Windows EventLog
EventSource	`Microsoft.Extensions.Logging.EventSource`	Logs to **Event Tracing for Windows** (ETW)
TraceSource	`Microsoft.Extensions.Logging.TraceSource`	Logs using `TraceSource`

Normally, we register these providers in the `Startup` class of ASP.NET Core during its bootstrap, but we can also do it earlier, in the `Program` class; this has the benefit of capturing some early events that may be raised before `Startup` comes along. For that, we need to add an extra step to the `IHostBuilder` call, as illustrated in the following code snippet:

```
Host
    .CreateDefaultBuilder(args)
    .ConfigureLogging(builder =>
```

```
{
    builder
        .AddConsole()
        .AddDebug();
})
//rest goes here
```

From ASP.NET Core 2 onward, the configuration of the logging mechanism is done earlier, in the `ConfigureServices` method, when we register the logging providers with the DI framework, as illustrated in the following code snippet:

```
services
    .AddLogging(options =>
    {
        options
            .AddConsole()
            .AddDebug();
    });
```

 Azure App Service logging has, of course, much more to it than the other built-in providers. For a good introduction to it, outside the scope of this book, please have a look at `https://blogs.msdn.microsoft.com/webdev/2017/04/26/asp-net-core-logging`.

There are several other providers for .NET Core out there, including the following:

Provider	NuGet package	Source
AWS	`AWS.Logger.AspNetCore`	`https://github.com/aws/aws-logging-dotnet`
Elmah.io	`Elmah.Io.Extensions.Logging`	`https://github.com/elmahio/Elmah.Io.Extensions.Logging`
Log4Net	`log4net`	`https://github.com/apache/logging-log4net`
Loggr	`Loggr.Extensions.Logging`	`https://github.com/imobile3/Loggr.Extensions.Logging`
NLog	`NLog`	`https://github.com/NLog`
Serilog	`Serilog`	`https://github.com/serilog/serilog`

Of these packages, `Serilog` can do structured logging, something else besides just strings.

Filtering logs

We can restrict (filter) logging based on the following criteria:

- Log level
- Category name

This means that, for a specific provider, we can log events of all levels above or equal to a given one, for categories starting with a particular name.

Since ASP.NET Core 2, we can configure default global filters, per category and log level; the lambda expression lets us return a Boolean value to denote whether or not the log should be processed, as illustrated in the following code snippet:

```
services
    .AddLogging(options =>
    {
        options.AddFilter((category, logLevel) => logLevel >=
        LogLevel.Warning);
    });
```

Or, just filter by category, as in this example, where the lambda just takes the category name:

```
services
    .AddLogging(options =>
    {
        options.AddFilter("Microsoft", LogLevel.Warning);
    });
```

If we want to filter the logging output for a specific provider, we add it as a generic template method to `AddFilter`, as follows:

```
services
    .AddLogging(options =>
    {
        options.AddFilter<ConsoleLoggerProvider>("Microsoft",
        LogLevel.Warning);
        //or, with a lambda
        options.AddFilter<ConsoleLoggerProvider>((categoryName,
         logLevel) => true);
    });
```

This can also be done per provider, category, and log level, like this:

```
services
    .AddLogging(options =>
```

```
    {
        options.AddFilter<ConsoleLoggerProvider>("System", logLevel =>
        logLevel >= LogLevel.Warning);
        //same as this
        options.AddFilter((provider, category, logLevel) =>
        {
            //you get the picture
        });
    });
```

Additionally, providers can be configured in the Program class, as part of the host building process, as illustrated in the following code snippet:

```
Host
    .CreateDefaultBuilder(args)
    .ConfigureLogging((hostingContext, builder) =>
    {
        builder.AddConfiguration(hostingContext.Configuration.
        GetSection("Logging"));
        builder.AddConsole(LogLevel.Warning);
        builder.AddDebug();
    })
    //rest goes here
```

Writing custom log providers

A provider that does not come out of the box—that is, is not included in ASP.NET Core—is one that writes to a file. A (somewhat simple) file logging provider could look like this:

```
public sealed class FileLoggerProvider : ILoggerProvider
{
    private readonly Func<string, LogLevel, bool> _func;

    public FileLoggerProvider(Func<string, LogLevel, bool> func)
    {
        this._func = func;
    }

    public FileLoggerProvider(LogLevel minimumLogLevel) :
        this((category, logLevel) => logLevel >= minimumLogLevel)
    {
    }

    public ILogger CreateLogger(string categoryName)
    {
```

```
            return new FileLogger(categoryName, this._func);
    }

    public void Dispose()
    {
    }
}

public sealed class FileLogger : ILogger
{
    private readonly string _categoryName;
    private readonly Func<string, LogLevel, bool> _func;

    public FileLogger(string categoryName, Func<string, LogLevel,
     bool> func)
    {
        this._categoryName = categoryName;
        this._func = func;
    }

    public IDisposable BeginScope<TState>(TState state)
    {
        return new EmptyDisposable();
    }

    public bool IsEnabled(LogLevel logLevel)
    {
        return this._func(this._categoryName, logLevel);
    }

    public void Log<TState>(
        LogLevel logLevel,
        EventId eventId,
        TState state,
        Exception exception,
        Func<TState, Exception, string> formatter)
        {
            if (this.IsEnabled(logLevel))
            {
                var now = DateTime.UtcNow;
                var today = now.ToString("yyyy-MM-dd");
                var fileName = $"{this._categoryName}_{today}.log";
                var message = formatter(state, exception);

                File.AppendAllText(fileName, $"{message}\n");
            }
    }
}
```

```
internal sealed class EmptyDisposable : IDisposable
{
    public void Dispose() { }
}

public static class LoggerFactoryExtensions
{
    public static ILoggerFactory AddFile(this ILoggerFactory
    loggerFactory,
        Func<string, LogLevel, bool> func)
    {
        loggerFactory.AddProvider(new FileLoggerProvider(func));
        return loggerFactory;
    }

    public static ILoggerFactory AddFile(this ILoggerFactory
    loggerFactory, LogLevel minimumLogLevel)
    {
        return AddFile(loggerFactory, (category, logLevel) => logLevel
>=
        minimumLogLevel);
    }

    public static ILoggingBuilder AddFile(this ILoggingBuilder
    loggingBuilder,
        Func<string, LogLevel, bool> func)
    {
        return loggingBuilder.AddProvider(new
FileLoggerProvider(func));
    }

    public static ILoggingBuilder AddFile(this ILoggingBuilder
    loggingBuilder, LogLevel minimumLogLevel)
    {
        return AddFile(loggingBuilder, (category, logLevel) =>
        logLevel >= minimumLogLevel);
    }
}
```

This example is composed of the following:

- A logger factory class, `FileLoggerFactory`, that is responsible for creating actual loggers
- The `FileLogger` class, which logs to a file

- A helper class, `EmptyDisposable`, that is used to mock scopes
- Some extension methods in the `LoggerFactoryExtensions` class, to make registering the file provider easier, either through an `ILoggerFactory` instance or an `ILoggingBuilder` instance.

The `FileLoggerFactory` class needs to take a single parameter that is the minimum log level to accept, which is then passed along to any created logger. The file to be created has a name in the format `{categoryName}-{yyyy-MM-dd}.log`, where `categoryName` is the value passed to the `CreateLogger` method and `yyyy-MM-dd` is the current date. Simple, don't you think?

Using DI with the log providers

As we've seen, we can inject into our classes either a logger or the logger factory itself. Passing the logger is by far the most common scenario, but we can also pass the logger factory if we want to do some additional configuration, such as register a new logging provider.

 Be warned: you cannot inject an `ILogger` instance, only an `ILogger<T>` instance, where `T` is an actual type—class or struct, abstract or concrete; it doesn't matter. Since ASP.NET Core 2, you do not need to call `AddLogging` explicitly in your `ConfigureServices` method, as the logging services are automatically registered.

Using logging attributes

An interesting use of the filter mechanism explained in Chapter 7, *Implementing Razor Pages*, is to add logging through filter attributes. Depending on where we want to add this logging, we could use resource, result, or action filters, but I'm going to give an example involving action filters, as these have the ability to inspect the model that is going to be passed to the action method and also the result of its invocation.

The following code block shows an attribute that, when applied to a class or a method, will cause a log message to be issued:

```
[AttributeUsage(AttributeTargets.Method | AttributeTargets.Class,
AllowMultiple = true,
    Inherited = true)]
public sealed class LoggerAttribute : ActionFilterAttribute
```

```
{
    public LoggerAttribute(string logMessage)
    {
        this.LogMessage = logMessage;
    }

    public string LogMessage { get; }
    public LogLevel LogLevel { get; set; } = LogLevel.Information;

    private EventId _eventId;

    private string GetLogMessage(ModelStateDictionary modelState)
    {
        var logMessage = this.LogMessage;

        foreach (var key in modelState.Keys)
        {
            logMessage = logMessage.Replace("{" + key + "}",
            modelState[key].RawValue?.ToString());
        }

        return logMessage;
    }

    private ILogger GetLogger(HttpContext context,
    ControllerActionDescriptor action)
    {
        var logger = context
            .RequestServices
            .GetService(typeof(ILogger<>)
            .MakeGenericType(action.ControllerTypeInfo.
            UnderlyingSystemType)) as ILogger;
            return logger;
    }

    public override void OnActionExecuted(ActionExecutedContext
context)
    {
        var cad = context.ActionDescriptor as
ControllerActionDescriptor;
        var logMessage = this.GetLogMessage(context.ModelState);
        var logger = this.GetLogger(context.HttpContext, cad);
        var duration = TimeSpan.FromMilliseconds(Environment.
        TickCount - this._eventId.Id);

        logger.Log(this.LogLevel, this._eventId,
        $"After {cad.ControllerName}.{cad.ActionName} with
        {logMessage} and result
```

```
{context.HttpContext.Response.StatusCode}
        in {duration}", null, (state, ex) => state.ToString());

        base.OnActionExecuted(context);
    }

    public override void OnActionExecuting(ActionExecutingContext
context)
    {
        var cad = context.ActionDescriptor as
ControllerActionDescriptor;
        var logMessage = this.GetLogMessage(context.ModelState);
        var logger = this.GetLogger(context.HttpContext, cad);

        this._eventId = new EventId(Environment.TickCount, $"{cad.
        ControllerName}.{cad.ActionName}");

        logger.Log(this.LogLevel, this._eventId, $"Before {cad.
        ControllerName}.{cad.ActionName} with {logMessage}", null,
        (state, ex) => state.ToString());

        base.OnActionExecuting(context);
    }
}
```

This example depicts an attribute that can be applied to methods or classes. It inherits from `ActionFilterAttribute`, which means that it is a filter (see Chapter 10, *Understanding Filters*, for a refresher on filters). What this means is that before the action execution (`OnActionExecuting`) and after it (`OnActionExecuted`), this attribute performs some action. In this case, it retrieves a logger for the current controller from the DI (please adapt this if you are not using MVC) and it logs a message to it. This attribute needs to take a `logMessage` parameter from its constructor. This parameter can take model names enclosed in brackets (for example, `{email}`) that will then be replaced in the logging message. It uses as the event ID the number of milliseconds that have elapsed since the system restarted (`Environment.TickCount`), and, as the event name, a combination of controller and action names; this event ID is reused in the pre-events and post-events. A message is logged with the log level provided before and after each action method is called. Here is an example declaration:

```
[Logger("Method called with {email}", LogLevel =
LogLevel.Information)]
public IActionResult AddToMailingList(string email) { ... }
```

This may be handy if we wish to add custom logging transparently to some action methods to log out model values.

Now, we will see another, more advanced way to log all requests.

Writing custom logging middleware

We've seen in the previous section how we can write custom attributes to perform actions before and after a controller action, and, in Chapter 1, *Getting Started with ASP.NET Core,* how we can write middleware. Now, a simple middleware class to log all requests can be written as follows:

```
public class LoggingMiddleware
{
    private readonly RequestDelegate _next;
    private readonly ILoggerFactory _loggerFactory;

    public LoggingMiddleware(RequestDelegate next, ILoggerFactory
    loggerFactory)
    {
        this._next = next;
        this._loggerFactory = loggerFactory;
    }

    public async Task InvokeAsync(HttpContext context)
    {
        var logger =
this._loggerFactory.CreateLogger<LoggingMiddleware>
        ();
        using (logger.BeginScope<LoggingMiddleware>(this))
        {
            logger.LogInformation("Before request");
            await this._next.Invoke(context);
            logger.LogInformation("After request");
        }
    }
}
```

Notice that the category of the logger is set to the LoggingMiddleware type's full name, and we are starting a scope for each invocation, which is here just as an example. The way to register this middleware is by calling UseMiddleware in Configure, like this:

```
app.UseMiddleware<LoggingMiddleware>();
```

This adds our middleware to the pipeline, but we must be sure to add it before anything else that we wish to monitor, or else we won't be able to capture it.

And this completes this short section on writing middleware for logging. Now, let's have a look at some tools.

Using tracing and diagnostics

We have mentioned the diagnostics functionality of ASP.NET Core in `Chapter 5`, *Views*. Diagnostics is comparable to logging, but it has a number of advantages, listed as follows:

- Tracing operates on a higher level, capturing a whole journey, not just a moment in time.
- It can do structured logging—that is, it can call methods in the trace loggers that take parameters, not just strings.
- It's easy to plug in new adapters, merely by adding an attribute to a class; even classes in referenced assemblies can be used.

Please refer to `Chapter 5`, *Views*, for a more in-depth explanation. Here, we will cover a Microsoft package, `Microsoft.AspNetCore.MiddlewareAnalysis`. When it is used, it traces all middleware components that execute on the pipeline, through the diagnostics feature. It is configured by a simple call to `AddMiddlewareAnalysis`, as follows:

```
services.AddMiddlewareAnalysis();
```

Then, we register a listener for some new events, as follows:

- `Microsoft.AspNetCore.MiddlewareAnalysis.MiddlewareStarting`: Called when the middleware is starting
- `Microsoft.AspNetCore.MiddlewareAnalysis.MiddlewareFinished`: Called when the middleware has finished
- `Microsoft.AspNetCore.MiddlewareAnalysis.MiddlewareExceptio n`: Called whenever an exception occurs while the middleware is executed

Here is how to register the diagnostic source listener:

```
public void Configure(
    IApplicationBuilder app,
    IWebHostEnvironment env,
    DiagnosticListener diagnosticListener)
```

```
{
    var listener = new TraceDiagnosticListener();
    diagnosticListener.SubscribeWithAdapter(listener);

    //rest goes here
}
```

The `TraceDiagnosticListener` class has methods that will be automatically wired to these events, as illustrated in the following code block:

```
public class TraceDiagnosticListener
{
    [DiagnosticName("Microsoft.AspNetCore.MiddlewareAnalysis.
    MiddlewareStarting")]
    public virtual void OnMiddlewareStarting(HttpContext
    httpContext, string name)
    {
        //called when the middleware is starting
    }

    [DiagnosticName("Microsoft.AspNetCore.MiddlewareAnalysis.
    MiddlewareException")]
    public virtual void OnMiddlewareException(Exception exception,
     string name)
    {
        //called when there is an exception while processing
        //a middleware component
    }

    [DiagnosticName("Microsoft.AspNetCore.MiddlewareAnalysis.
    MiddlewareFinished")]
    public virtual void OnMiddlewareFinished(HttpContext
     httpContext, string name)
    {
        //called when the middleware execution finishes
    }
}
```

Note that this is called for both middleware classes (refer to Chapter 1, *Getting Started with ASP.NET Core*) or for middleware that is added to the pipeline as a custom delegate. The code is shown in the following snippet:

```
app.Properties["analysis.NextMiddlewareName"] = "MyCustomMiddleware";
app.Use(async (context, next) =>
{
    //do something
    await next();
});
```

Notice the line where we set the `analysis.NextMiddlewareName` property—because this middleware does not have a name, it is an anonymous delegate; the property is used for the `name` parameter of each of the `TraceDiagnosticListener` class's methods.

If you want to visually analyze all this activity, you can add another Microsoft package, `Microsoft.AspNetCore.Diagnostics.Elm`. **ELM** stands for **Error Logging Middleware** and is added in the usual way—first, by registering services (`ConfigureServices` method), like this:

```
services.AddElm();
```

Then, add the middleware to the pipeline (`Configure`), like this:

```
app.UseElmPage();
app.UseElmCapture();
```

You may want to add these just for development, by checking the current environment and adding this middleware conditionally. After you do, when you access `/elm`, you will get a nice trace of what is going on, as illustrated in the following screenshot:

You can see all the events that take place when a request is processed. All of these come from the diagnostic feature.

There's another final step: you must enable synchronous **input/output (I/O)** because ELM uses it. In the `Program` class, add the following content to the `ConfigureWebHostDefaults` method:

```
.ConfigureWebHostDefaults(builder =>
{
    builder.UseKestrel(options =>
    {
        options.AllowSynchronousIO = true;
    });
    builder.UseStartup<Startup>();
});
```

If you want to set the **Uniform Resource Locator** (**URL**) that ELM uses, or filter the results, you can certainly do so, like this:

```
services.Configure<ElmOptions>(options =>
{
    options.Path = "/_Elm";
    options.Filter = (name, logLevel) =>
    {
        return logLevel > LogLevel.Information;
    };
});
```

This small code fragment sets the configuration for ELM, as follows:

- The request path is set to `/_Elm` (must start with a `/`).
- Only events with a log level higher than `Information` are shown.

We will now learn about a very important feature that has existed since the initial days of Windows and is now available to .NET Core: event counters.

Using performance (event) counters for obtaining metrics

Performance (event) counters have existed since the beginning of Windows but they have not been implemented in the other operating systems in the same way, which makes them not cross-platform. The idea is that applications emit lightweight, unobtrusive code that is picked up by the operating system and can be used to monitor the application in real time, as it is working, or to generate dump files for post-mortem analysis.

.NET Core 3.0 started supporting event counters to its full extent by introducing the `dotnet-trace`, `dotnet-dump`, and `dotnet-counters` cross-platform global tools. We will see what these do in the following sections.

Included counters

An event counter is a class that emits a value for a named counter. .NET includes the following counters, grouped into two providers:

- `System.Runtime (default)`
- `Microsoft.AspNetCore.Hosting`

The available counters in each provider are shown as follows:

System.Runtime	
cpu-usage	Amount of time the process has utilized the **central processing unit (CPU)** (ms) (mean)
working-set	Amount of working set used by the process (MB) (mean)
gc-heap-size	Total heap size reported by the **garbage collector (GC)** (MB) (mean)
gen-0-gc-count	Number of Generation 0 GCs/second (sum)
gen-1-gc-count	Number of Generation 1 GCs/second (sum)
gen-2-gc-count	Number of Generation 2 GCs/second (sum)
time-in-gc	% time in GC since the last GC (mean)
gen-0-size	Generation 0 heap size (mean)
gen-1-size	Generation 1 heap size (mean)
gen-2-size	Generation 2 heap size (mean)
loh-size	**Large object heap (LOH)** heap size (mean)
alloc-rate	Allocation rate (sum)
assembly-count	Number of assemblies loaded (mean)

`exception-count`	Number of exceptions/second (sum)
`threadpool-thread-count`	Number of `ThreadPool` threads (mean)
`monitor-lock-contention-count`	Monitor lock contention count
`threadpool-queue-length`	`ThreadPool` work items' queue length (mean)
`threadpool-completed-items-count`	`ThreadPool` completed work items' count
`active-timer-count`	Active timers' count
Microsoft.AspNetCore.Hosting	
`requests-per-second`	Request rate (mean)
`total-requests`	Total number of requests (sum)
`current-requests`	The current number of requests (sum)
`failed-requests`	Failed number of requests (sum)

The `System.Runtime` provider contains counters that are independent of the kind of application—web, console, service, or whatnot. `Microsoft.AspNetCore.Hosting`, of course, only contains web-specific counters.

As you can imagine, by monitoring these counters, we can get a good insight as to what is going on inside our ASP.NET Core apps, from a system perspective. In the next sections, we will see how to do this.

Custom counters

We can write code for creating our own counters. Here is an example:

```
[EventSource(Name = SourceName)]
public sealed class LogElapsedUrlEventSource : EventSource
{
    private readonly EventCounter _counter;

    public static readonly LogElapsedUrlEventSource Instance = new
LogElapsedUrlEventSource();

    private const int SourceId = 1;
    private const string SourceName = "LogElapsedUrl";

    private LogElapsedUrlEventSource() : base(EventSourceSettings.
    EtwSelfDescribingEventFormat)
    {
        this._counter = new EventCounter(SourceName, this);
    }

    [Event(SourceId, Message = "Elapsed Time for URL {0}: {1}",
     Level = EventLevel.Informational)]
```

```
public void LogElapsed(string url, float time)
{
    this.WriteEvent(SourceId, url, time);
    this._counter.WriteMetric(time);
}
}
```

You need to add the `System.Diagnostics.PerformanceCounter` NuGet package in order to be able to compile this.

This sample code logs the time that it took to open an arbitrary URL. It takes a URL as a parameter and `time` as a floating-point value. It essentially is a singleton because it has a private constructor, and should only be accessed by its public static `Instance` field. The `LogElapsed` method writes to both the underlying `EventCounter` instance (which takes any number of arguments) and to the base `EventSource` class (which only takes the numeric value). In the end, for the performance counter, what is used is the numeric value.

To use this sample, we do this:

```
LogElapsedUrlEventSource.Instance.LogElapsed("http://google.com",
0.1F);
```

This references the single instance of our newly created event source and logs a value of `0.1` for the `http://google.com` URL. It will be written to the event counter underneath.

Performance monitoring

There is a free tool for Windows called **PerfView** (`https://github.com/microsoft/perfview`) that can be used to visualize performance counters, but, unfortunately, it is not cross-platform. Instead, we need to go with another solution. Let's install the `dotnet-counters` global tool. For that, run the following command:

```
dotnet tool install -g dotnet-counters
```

After the `dotnet-counters` tool is installed (globally, as per this command), we can now use it to monitor existing applications. First, let's see those that can be monitored (running .NET Core apps), as follows:

```
dotnet-counters ps
```

This will give a list of process IDs of running .NET Core apps, regardless of what they are. After you have found the one you're interested in, you feed it to the tool, like this:

```
dotnet-counters monitor -p 3527
```

If you don't specify a provider name after the process ID, it will default to `System.Runtime`. You should get something like this:

```
Press p to pause, r to resume, q to quit.
    Status: Running

[System.Runtime]
    # of Assemblies Loaded                          143
    % Time in GC (since last GC)                      0
    Allocation Rate (Bytes / sec)                 8,168
    CPU Usage (%)                                     0
    Exceptions / sec                                  0
    GC Heap Size (MB)                                 6
    Gen 0 GC / sec                                    0
    Gen 0 Size (B)                                    0
    Gen 1 GC / sec                                    0
    Gen 1 Size (B)                                    0
    Gen 2 GC / sec                                    0
    Gen 2 Size (B)                                    0
    LOH Size (B)                                      0
    Monitor Lock Contention Count / sec              0
    Number of Active Timers                           1
    ThreadPool Completed Work Items / sec             1
    ThreadPool Queue Length                           0
    ThreadPool Threads Count                          1
    Working Set (MB)                                 91
```

So, for example, if you want to monitor our sample counter, you would run this code:

```
dotnet-counters monitor -p 3527 LogElapsedUrl
```

The `dotnet-counters` tool will update continuously until you exit it (*Ctrl + C*).

For additional information on `dotnet-counters` and real-time performance monitoring of .NET Core apps, please refer to `https://github.com/dotnet/diagnostics/blob/master/documentation/dotnet-couunters-instructions.md`. The documentation is available at `https://docs.microsoft.com/dotnet/core/diagnostics/dotnet-counters`.

So, here, we've seen how to monitor events in real time in the console. Now, let's see how we can collect them in a file.

Tracing

Another tool that was introduced with .NET Core 3 is `dotnet-trace`. It is similar to `dotnet-counter` but, instead of outputting the current event counter values to the console, it writes them to a trace file. This has the advantage that it can be read at a later time so as to extract runtime information from it, including its association with meaningful events (contextual information). It can also run in the background and does not require someone to be watching the console.

To install this trace, use the following command:

```
dotnet tool install -g dotnet-trace
```

Similar to `dotnet-counters`, `dotnet-trace` can detect the .NET Core processes that are running on the system, and it also needs to be attached to a process, as follows:

```
dotnet-trace collect -p 3527
```

Now, after the process ID, the `dotnet-trace` command can take the name of a **trace profile**. By default, there is a trace profile defined that includes a number of event counters, but you can also define your own. The providers included are the following ones:

- **Microsoft-Windows-DotNETRuntime** (default)
- **Microsoft-DotNETCore-SampleProfiler**

 I won't go into the details of creating trace profiles, as this is a complex topic.

To create a trace file for the `Microsoft-Windows-DotNETRuntime` profile, we run the following command:

```
dotnet-trace collect -p 3527 --providers Microsoft-Windows-
DotNETRuntime
```

This will result in something like this:

```
Provider Name                          Keywords           Level        Enabled By
Microsoft-Windows-DotNETRuntime        0xFFFFFFFFFFFFFFFF  Verbose(5)   --providers

Process          : /usr/local/share/dotnet/dotnet
Output File      : /Users/dcuser/trace.nettrace

[00:00:00:18]   Recording trace 5.2535    (MB)
Press <Enter> or <Ctrl+C> to exit...
```

Besides profiles, which include a number of items of information other than performance counters, you can just request individual performance counter providers by specifying a provider name as the trace profile, like this:

```
dotnet-trace collect -p 3527 --providers
System.Runtime:0:1:EventCounterIntervalSec=1
```

In this case, `dotnet-trace` will output the performance counter values for all the counters belonging to the `System.Runtime` provider every second.

Trace files have the `trace.nettrace` name and are, by default, created in the same folder where the `dotnet-trace` command was run. To see these files, we have a couple of options.

On Windows systems, we can use Visual Studio, as shown in the following screenshot:

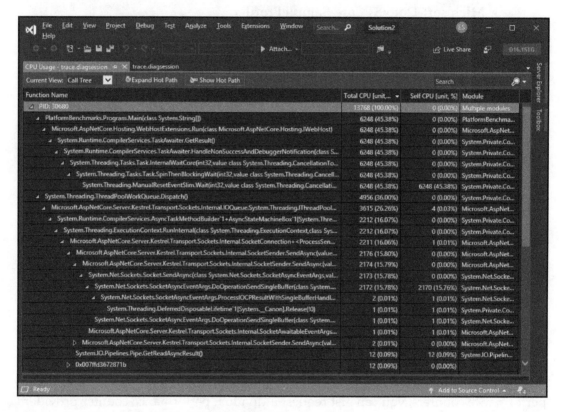

For PerfView, we can use the following:

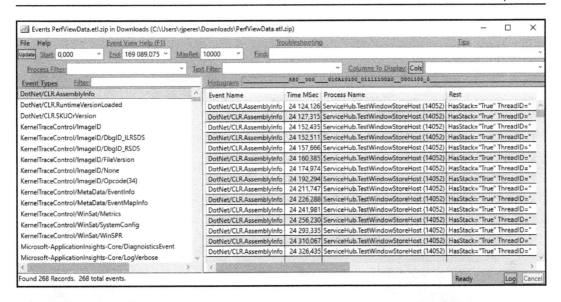

For non-Windows systems that support .NET Core (Linux and macOS), there is, for the time being, no native solution for reading trace files, but a possible alternative is the free **Speedscope** site (`http://speedscope.app`). In order to use it, however, we must tell `dotnet-trace` to generate the trace file in the appropriate format, by running the following code:

```
dotnet-trace collect -p 3527 --providers Microsoft-Windows-
DotNETRuntime --format speedscope
```

Or, if we have a file in the `.nettrace` format, we can convert it afterward so that we can pass it to the Speedscope app. To do this, you would need to run the following code:

```
dotnet-trace convert trace.nettrace --format speedscope
```

The output file will then be called `trace.speedscope.json` instead, as shown in the following screenshot:

For additional information on `dotnet-trace` and the tracing of .NET Core apps, please refer to `https://github.com/dotnet/diagnostics/blob/master/documentation/dotnet-trace-instructions.md`. The documentation is available at `https://docs.microsoft.com/dotnet/core/diagnostics/dotnet-trace`.

We will now look at another tool, but this time, one for more advanced users.

Trace dumps

The third tool that was made available with .NET Core 3 is `dotnet-dump`. This one is more for advanced users, as it requires an in-depth knowledge of **IL** (which stands for **Intermediate Language**), .NET's own assembly. In a nutshell, it can collect a memory dump of a running .NET Core process and write it to disk so that it can be analyzed offline. This may help discover how the application is behaving in terms of memory usage.

`dotnet-dump` only works on Windows and Linux, not macOS, for generating dumps.

To install it, run the following command:

```
dotnet tool install -g dotnet-dump
```

Unlike the previous tools, it cannot list the running processes, so, if you need this capability, you will need to rely on `dotnet-counters` or `dotnet-trace`. Once you locate the one you want, you ask for it to create a dump of the processes' current running state, as follows:

```
dotnet-dump collect -p 3527
```

The dump file will be created on the same folder and will be named `core_YYYYMMDD_hhmmss`.

After you produce a dump file, you can also use `dotnet-dump` to analyze it, like this:

```
dotnet-dump analyze core_20191103_234821
```

This will start an interactive shell (in operating systems that support it) that allows the dump to be explored and **Son of Strike (SOS)** commands to be run (`https://docs.microsoft.com/dotnet/core/diagnostics/dotnet-dump#analyze-sos-commands`).

 `dotnet-dump` only allows dumps to be analyzed on Linux. For additional information on `dotnet-dump`, please refer to `https://github.com/dotnet/diagnostics/blob/master/documentation/dotnet-dump-instructions.md`. The documentation is available at `https://docs.microsoft.com/dotnet/core/diagnostics/dotnet-dump`.

Let's now leave the console and explore some of the options we have for remote monitoring of our apps.

Using telemetry

Telemetry consists of transparently collecting usage data from software over the internet. It can be very helpful in the sense that all your applications are monitored centrally, and telemetry packages usually supply handy tools, such as rich user interfaces for selecting exactly what we want to see, or creating alarms. There are a few alternatives, and we will only touch on a few of the most popular ones in the following sections.

Using trace identifiers

ASP.NET Core provides an `IHttpRequestIdentifierFeature` feature that generates a unique ID per each request. This ID may help you correlate events that happen in the context of a request. Here are three ways to get this ID:

```
//using the TraceIdentifier property in ASP.NET Core 2.x
var id1 = this.HttpContext.TraceIdentifier;

//accessing the feature in earlier versions of ASP.NET Core
var id2 =
this.HttpContext.Features.Get<IHttpRequestIdentifierFeature>().TraceId
entifier;

//another way
var id3 = Activity.Current.Id;
```

A trace identifier is just an opaque reference—such as `0HL8VHQLUJ7CM:00000001`—that is guaranteed to be unique among requests. Interestingly, this implements the **Trace Context World Wide Web Consortium (W3C)** specification (`https://www.w3.org/TR/trace-context`), which means that ASP.NET Core 3 honors the `Request-Id` HTTP header. This is the value that is mapped to these properties.

Make sure you enable the standard W3C format using the following lines, right in the beginning of the app, maybe in `Main` or in `Startup`:

```
Activity.DefaultIdFormat = ActivityIdFormat.W3C;
Activity.ForceDefaultIdFormat = true;
```

Now, whenever you issue an HTTP request to some microservice, make sure you include this trace identifier. For example, if you are using `HttpClient`, you can use `DelegatingHandler` for this purpose, as illustrated in the following code block:

```
public class TraceIdentifierMessageHandler : DelegatingHandler
{
    private readonly IHttpContextAccessor _httpContextAccessor;

    public TraceIdentifierMessageHandler(IHttpContextAccessor
    httpContextAccessor)
    {
        this._httpContextAccessor = httpContextAccessor;
    }

    protected override Task<HttpResponseMessage> SendAsync(
        HttpRequestMessage request, CancellationToken
```

```
cancellationToken)
    {
        var httpContext = this._httpContextAccessor.HttpContext;
        request.Headers.Add("Request-Id",
httpContext.TraceIdentifier);
        request.Headers.Add("X-SessionId", httpContext.Session.Id);
        return base.SendAsync(request, cancellationToken);
    }
}
```

A delegating handler is called to handle the sending of a message, and, in this case, it is used to set a header—Request-Id. It gets this header from the context, which is obtained from the IHttpContextAccessor service, injected into the constructor.

We register one or many HttpClient instances, one for each microservice that we will be calling in the ConfigureServices method, as follows:

```
//this is required for the TraceIdentifierMessageHandler
services.AddHttpContextAccessor();

services
    .AddHttpClient("<service1>", options =>
    {
        options.BaseAddress = new Uri("<url1>");
    })
    .AddHttpMessageHandler<TraceIdentifierMessageHandler>();
```

Of course, you will need to replace <service1> and <url1> with the appropriate values.

When you want to obtain an instance of HttpClient to send messages to this microservice, inject an IHttpClientFactory instance and request the name under which you registered your client, as illustrated in the following code block:

```
public class HomeController : Controller
{
    private readonly IHttpClientFactory _clientFactory;

    public HomeController(IHttpClientFactory clientFactory)
    {
        this._clientFactory = clientFactory;
    }

    public async Task<IActionResult> Index()
    {
        var client = clientFactory.CreateClient("<service1>");
        var result = await client.GetAsync("GetData");
```

```
            //do something with the response

            return this.Ok();
        }
    }
```

Using this approach, we can ensure that we are keeping the same trace identifier on all requests, there's creating a context. This is very important to maintain the state and is used by the logging frameworks that I'm going to present next.

Azure Application Insights

When you create an ASP.NET project using Visual Studio, you are presented with the option to add support for **Application Insights** (**AI**). AI is an Azure service that lets you monitor your web application for availability, performance, and usage, including errors. When you add support for AI to your web app, you can go to the AI console and monitor the behavior of your application in real time, see how it behaved recently, and even get notified in case something unusual happens.

We won't cover AI in full here, but will just give you an overview of how to use it in your ASP.NET Core projects.

The following screenshot shows a typical combined view, displaying response and page load times:

Before you can use AI, you need to have a working Azure account (`https://portal.azure.com`) and you need to create an AI resource.

You can create one from inside Visual Studio, as shown in the following screenshot:

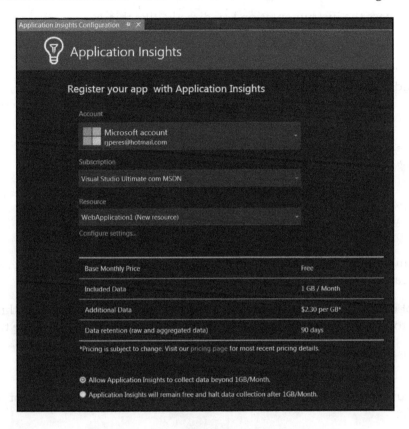

For detailed instructions, please consult `https://github.com/Microsoft/ApplicationInsights-aspnetcore/wiki/Getting-Started-with-Application-Insights-for-ASP.NET-Core`. AI relies on the `Microsoft.ApplicationInsights.AspNetCore` NuGet package, and you will need to add a configuration setting with the instrumentation key that is provided to you in the AI console, once you create an AI resource. If you use a **JavaScript Object Notation (JSON)** configuration file, you will need something like this:

```
{
    "ApplicationInsights": {
        "InstrumentationKey": "11111111-2222-3333-4444-555555555555"
    }
}
```

In any case, you will need to register the AI services directly from your configuration, like this:

```
services.AddApplicationInsightsTelemetry(this.Configuration);
```

Or, you can pass the instrumentation key directly, like this:

```
services.AddApplicationInsightsTelemetry(
    instrumentationKey: "11111111-2222-3333-4444-555555555555");
```

For more advanced options, you can pass in an instance of `ApplicationInsightsServiceOptions`, as illustrated in the following code snippet:

```
services.AddApplicationInsightsTelemetry(new
ApplicationInsightsServiceOptions
{
    InstrumentationKey = "11111111-2222-3333-4444-555555555555",
    DeveloperMode = true,
    EnableDebugLogger = true
});
```

When running in development mode, it is often useful to use the developer mode of AI as you can see results immediately (not in batches).

You do not need to enable exceptions and request telemetry explicitly; as this is done for you automatically, and the code for `_ViewImports.cshtml` looks like this:

```
@using Microsoft.ApplicationInsights.AspNetCore
@inject JavaScriptSnippet snippet
```

In the layout view (probably `_Layout.cshtml`), we must render the script with this line of code:

```
@Html.Raw(snippet.FullScript)
```

This explained how to enable the AI functionality, but the next topic will show how to send actual events to it.

Sending custom events

You can send custom data using the `TelemetryClient` **application programming interface (API)**. Essentially, you build an instance of `TelemetryClient`, as follows:

```
var client = new TelemetryClient();
client.InstrumentationKey =
this.Configuration["ApplicationInsights:InstrumentationKey"];
```

You have the following methods, taken from the documentation (`https://docs.microsoft.com/azure/application-insights/app-insights-api-custom-events-metrics`):

- `TrackPageView`: Pages
- `TrackEvent`: User actions and custom events
- `TrackMetric`: Performance measurements
- `TrackException`: Exceptions
- `TrackRequest`: Frequency and duration of server requests for performance analysis
- `TrackTrace`: Diagnostic log messages
- `TrackDependency`: Duration and frequency of calls to external components that your app depends on

You can call one of its `Track` methods mentioned in the preceding list. For now, let's begin with `TrackEvent`, as follows:

```
client.TrackEvent("Product added to basket");
```

You can also call a specific metric for a single value, like this:

```
client.TrackMetric("TotalCost", 100.0);
```

You can request information, like this:

```
var now = DateTimeOffset.Now;
var timer = Stopwatch.StartNew();
//issue call
client.TrackRequest("Searching for product", now, timer.Elapsed, "OK",
true);
```

To send an exception, execute the following code:

```
client.TrackException(ex);
```

To send a dependency (any called code that is not our own) elapsed time (similar to request tracking), execute the following code:

```
var success = false;
var startTime = DateTime.UtcNow;
var timer = Stopwatch.StartNew();
var id = Guid.NewGuid();

try
{
    success = orderService.ProcessOrder();
}
finally
{
    timer.Stop();
    telemetry.TrackDependency("Order Service", $"Order id {id}",
startTime, timer.Elapsed, success);
}
```

To send a custom trace message, execute the following code:

```
client.TrackTrace("Processing order", SeverityLevel.Warning, new
Dictionary<string,string> { {"Order", id} });
```

For a page view, execute the following code:

```
client.TrackPageView("ShoppingBag");
```

You can also group together several related events inside a scope, as follows:

```
using (var operation =
telemetry.StartOperation<RequestTelemetry>("Order Processing"))
{
    //one or more of Track* methods
}
```

Because AI batches data to send, at any point you can force this to be flushed to Azure by running the following command:

```
client.Flush();
```

All of these events will be made available in the AI console, as shown in the following screenshot:

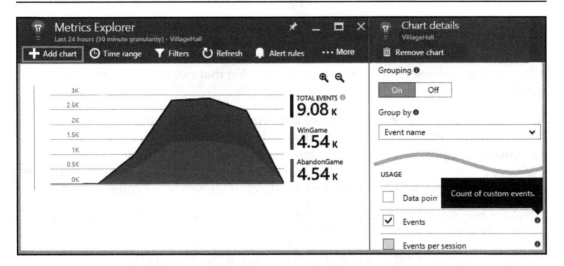

The AppInsights dashboard can display a different visualization of events (for example, grouping the events by name), as can be seen in the following screenshot:

AI can track distributed calls by using the trace identifier that was discussed earlier.

In the next section, I will present the other major cloud provider's log service: AWS CloudWatch.

AWS CloudWatch

AWS CloudWatch is an AWS application and infrastructure monitoring service. It allows you to write semi-structured content to a log that can then be queried and monitored online.

In order to write to it from a .NET Core app, you need to add a reference to the `AWSSDK.Core` and `AWSSDK.CloudWatch` NuGet packages. There is no need to add custom logging frameworks; the built-in logging will do. Register its services in `ConfigureServices` using the application configuration—this is required so that we can inject the services. This can be done by running the following code:

```
services.AddDefaultAWSOptions(this.Configuration.GetAWSOptions());
services.AddAWSService<IAmazonCloudWatch>();
```

The `GetAWSOptions` extension returns the required entries from the configuration—possibly made available in the `appsettings.json` file. These should look something like the following:

```
{
    "AWS": {
        "Profile": "local-profile",
        "Region": "eu-west-1"
    }
}
```

You will, of course, replace `local-profile` and `eu-west-1` for, respectively, the name of the profile you have in your AWS configuration file and the name of the region you want to use, which should be the closest region to where you are located.

You will also need to enable logging to the console. Add the `Microsoft.Extensions.Logging.Console` NuGet package, if you don't already have it, and run this code:

```
services.AddLogging(options =>
{
    options.AddConsole();
});
```

Once the AWS service is registered, as soon as you log in to the console, you will be logging in to AWS CloudWatch as well.

Here is a sample AWS CloudWatch log from the AWS site:

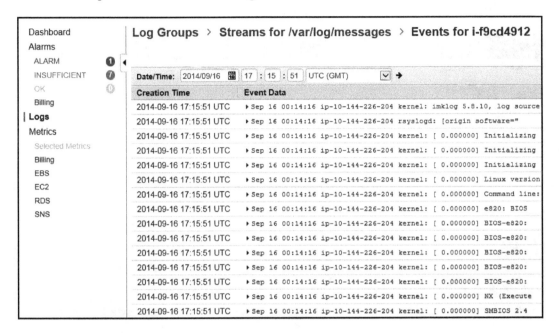

In the next section, I will talk about a very popular commercial tool for real-time monitoring of web applications that can be applied to any site, even those hosted on the cloud.

New Relic

New Relic is a software analytics product for application performance monitoring of web apps. It delivers real-time data regarding the behavior of your web application, such as the number of simultaneous users, memory usage, and errors. You will need to install the New Relic agent on your deployment machine, be this Windows or Linux.

Please follow the instructions available at `https://docs.newrelic.com/docs/agents/net-agent/installation/introduction-net-agent-install` to set up the New Relic agent on your platform of choice.

After it is installed, New Relic intercepts and instruments your .NET Core calls on your machine and adds telemetry to it. New Relic can also be installed on Docker, which makes it perfect for self-contained, automated deployments.

All of the resulting calls are then made available on the New Relic console, as can be seen in the following screenshot from the New Relic site:

Mind you, New Relic is extremely powerful, and I wouldn't even dare to go through it as this would require a book on its own. Please do take a look at the New Relic site and see whether it suits your needs.

Next, we will have a look at a functionality that is new to ASP.NET Core for monitoring the state of the services inside an application.

Performing health checking

Microsoft has been working on a health checking framework called `Microsoft.AspNetCore.Diagnostics.HealthChecks`, and released it as part of ASP.NET Core 2.2. It provides a standard and pluggable way to check the state of services on which your app depends. This is not a feature of ASP.NET itself, but since any complex web app normally has external dependencies, this may come in handy for checking their statuses before taking any action.

After adding the core NuGet package, you will need to add the ones for the checks that you're interested in, such as those for SQL Server. We register those in the `ConfigureServices` method, as follows:

```
services
    .AddHealthChecks()
    .AddCheck("Web Check", new WebHealthCheck("http://
    google.com"), HealthStatus.Unhealthy)
    .AddCheck("Sample Lambda", () => HealthCheckResult.Healthy
    ("All is well!"))
    .AddDbContextCheck<MyDbContext>("My Context"); //check
                                    //a database through EF Core
```

In this example, we are registering three checks, as follows:

- A custom check class, `WebHealthCheck`, that implements the `IHealthCheck` interface
- A lambda-based check
- A check that uses an **Entity Framework (EF)** Core context to check a database for access

For the EF Core check, you'll need to add a reference to the `.EntityFrameworkCore` NuGet package of `Microsoft.Extensions.Diagnostics.HealthChecks`.

The `WebHealthCheck` class looks like this:

```
public class WebHealthCheck : IHealthCheck
{
    public WebHealthCheck(string url)
    {
        if (string.IsNullOrWhiteSpace(url))
        {
            throw new ArgumentNullException(nameof(url));
        }

        this.Url = url;
    }

    public string Url { get; }

    public async Task<HealthCheckResult> CheckHealthAsync(
        HealthCheckContext context,
        CancellationToken cancellationToken =
default(CancellationToken))
    {
        var client = new HttpClient();
```

```
        var response = await client.GetAsync(this.Url);

        if (response.StatusCode < HttpStatusCode.BadRequest)
        {
            return HealthCheckResult.Healthy("The URL is up and
running");
        }

        return HealthCheckResult.Unhealthy("The URL is inaccessible");
    }
}
```

This class issues an HTTP request for the provided URL and returns Healthy or Unhealthy, depending on the HTTP response status code.

On Configure, we register an endpoint for the monitoring of these checks, as follows:

```
app.UseRouting();
app.UseEndpoints(endpoints =>
{
    endpoints
        .MapHealthChecks("/health")
        .RequireHost("localhost")
        .RequireAuthorization();
});
```

Notice the call to MapHealthChecks, with the endpoint name of /health.

We can then have an instance of IHealthCheckService injected into our classes and see whether everything is OK, like this:

```
var timedTokenSource = new
CancellationTokenSource(TimeSpan.FromSeconds(3));
var checkResult = await
_healthCheck.CheckHealthAsync(timedTokenSource.Token);

if (checkResult.CheckStatus != CheckStatus.Healthy)
{
    //Houston, we have a problem!
}
```

This code waits for, at most, 3 seconds while checking the status of all the registered health checks. The result can be one of the following:

- Unknown: The status is unknown, possibly due to a timeout.
- Unhealthy: At least one of the services is not OK.

- `Healthy`: Everything seems to be OK.
- `Warning`: Everything is OK, but with a number of warnings.

Now, the health checking framework enables an endpoint from which you can find the global state of all the check; as we've seen before, we set it as `/health`. If we access it using the browser, we get one of these values.

If, however, we want to have detailed information of all the checks that were executed, and their state, we can modify the endpoint's registration code to something like this:

```
endpoints
    .MapHealthChecks("/health", new HealthCheckOptions
    {
    ResponseWriter = async (context, report) =>
    {
    var result = JsonSerializer.Serialize(new
    {
    Status = report.Status.ToString(),
    Checks = report.Entries.Select(e => new
    {
    Check = e.Key,
    Status = e.Value.Status.ToString()
    })
    });
    context.Response.ContentType = MediaTypeNames.Application.Json;
    await context.Response.WriteAsync(result);
    }
    });
```

This way, we are sending a JSON response with all the individual checks' statuses, besides the global status, as can be seen in the following code snippet:

```
{"Status":"Healthy","Checks":[{"Check":"Web
Check","Status":"Healthy"},{"Check":"Sample
Lambda","Status":"Healthy"},{"Check":"My
Context","Status":"Healthy"}]}
```

In this chapter, we've looked at the new health checking feature of ASP.NET Core. It is a pluggable system that allows you to write your own health checks and check them from a centralized endpoint. It is a valuable asset for checking the state of your web application, and I hope it comes in useful!

Summary

This chapter began with Common Logging, which is a must-have in .NET Core. The infrastructure, although limited, does not support structured logging out of the box—for example, it is built-in, pluggable, and DI-friendly. Use it for the most Common Logging uses. Please explore all the logging providers available to see whether there is one that meets your requirements. Special hosting providers, such as Azure or AWS, offer their own packages, which you should leverage for the best results.

Next, we saw that diagnostic tracing offers the advantage that you can call methods with discrete parameters, which is an advantage as it can lead to more meaningful logs. You can use it to see exactly what middleware is being executed and how much time each step takes.

The other options shown, adding middleware or action filters, are also probably worth exploring, especially action filters.

Then, we saw that telemetry is essential for enterprise applications working 24/7 because it gives you an overview of how things behave during long periods of time, and you can set alerts to respond to emergency situations.

Finally, we also had a look at the different logging and diagnostic options available in ASP.NET Core, helping us to sort issues.

In the next chapter, we will see how we can perform unit tests for all the features discussed in the previous chapters.

Questions

You should now be able to answer these questions:

1. What are event counters?
2. What is the benefit of telemetry?
3. How can we filter logging?
4. What are health checks?
5. How is middleware useful in logging?
6. What is ELM?
7. What are the benefits of diagnostics over Common Logging?

13
Understanding How Testing Works

In previous chapters, we looked at how to build things in ASP.NET Core. We are aware that we should be testing our applications before we consider them done. What happens is that applications evolve and stuff that used to work at one point in time may no longer work now. So, to ensure that these applications do not fail on us, we set up tests that can run automatically and check whether everything is still working as it should.

We will cover the following topics in this chapter:

- Unit testing principles
- Using xUnit, NUnit, and MSTest
- Mocking objects
- Assertions
- User interface tests
- Working on integration tests

In this chapter, we will have a look at two approaches for executing these tests and how they help us ensure that we write well-integrated code.

Technical requirements

In order to implement the examples introduced in this chapter, you will need the .NET Core 3 SDK and a text editor. Of course, Visual Studio 2019 (any edition) meets all the requirements, but you can also use Visual Studio Code, for example.

The source code can be retrieved from GitHub at `https://github.com/ PacktPublishing/Modern-Web-Development-with-ASP.NET-Core-3-Second-Edition`.

Getting started with unit tests

Unit tests are not new. Essentially, a unit test is designed to test a feature of your system in isolation to prove that it is working as it should. The **F.I.R.S.T principles of unit testing** state that unit tests should be the following:

- **Fast**: They should execute fast, meaning they shouldn't carry out any complex or lengthy operations.
- **Isolated/independent**: A unit test should not depend on other systems and should provide results independent of any specific context.
- **Repeatable**: A unit test should yield the same result whenever it executes if nothing is changed on the implementation.
- **Self-validating**: They should be self-sufficient—that is, they should not require any manual inspection or analysis.
- **Thorough/timely**: They should cover all the important stuff, even if not required for 100% of the code.

In a nutshell, a unit test should run fast so that we don't have to wait a long time for the results, and should be coded so that the essential features are tested and do not depend on external variables. Also, unit tests should not produce any side effects and it should be possible to repeat them and get the same results all the time.

Some people even advocate starting to implement unit tests before the actual code. This has the benefit of making the code testable—after all, it was designed with testing in mind, and once we have implemented it, we already have the unit tests to go along with it. This is called **Test-Driven Development** (**TDD**). While I am not a die-hard defender of TDD, I see the advantages of it.

Development using TDD usually goes in a cycle known as **red-green-refactor**, which means that tests are first red (meaning, they fail), then they are green (they pass), and only then, when everything is working properly, do we need to refactor the code to improve it. You can read more about TDD at `https://technologyconversations.com/2014/09/30/test-driven-development-tdd`.

We usually rely on unit test frameworks to help us perform these tests and get their results. There are several of these frameworks for .NET Core, including the following:

- **MSTest**: This is Microsoft's own test framework; it is open source and made available at `https://github.com/Microsoft/testfx`.
- **xUnit**: A popular framework that is even used by Microsoft, available at `https://xunit.github.io`.
- **NUnit**: One of the oldest unit test frameworks, ported from Java's **JUnit**, available at `http://nunit.org`.

These are all open source and their features are similar. You can find a good comparison of the three frameworks at `https://xunit.github.io/docs/comparisons.html`.

If you prefer to start your projects from the console instead of Visual Studio, `dotnet` has templates for MSTest, NUnit, and xUnit—just pick one:

```
dotnet new mstest
dotnet new xunit
dotnet new nunit
```

Let's now get our hands on the code.

Writing unit tests

Here, we will see how we can use some of the most popular unit test frameworks with .NET Core. This won't be an in-depth coverage of the frameworks, just the basics to get you started.

Unit tests are first-class citizens in .NET Core and have their own project types. Essentially, a unit test project uses the `Microsoft.NET.Sdk` SDK, but must reference `Microsoft.NET.Test.Sdk`. The `dotnet` tool knows about these projects and has special options for them, as we will see.

First, we need to create a unit test project using one of the supported frameworks.

Unit test frameworks

There are a number of unit test frameworks out there, but I picked the ones that are most often used, including by Microsoft.

MSTest

MSTest is Microsoft's own test framework, recently made open source. To use MSTest, you need to add a reference to the following NuGet packages:

- `MSTest.TestFramework`

- `MSTest.TestAdapter`

- `Microsoft.NET.Test.Sdk`

The first reference is for the framework itself and the second is the one that allows Visual Studio to interact with MSTest; yes, all of these frameworks integrate nicely with Visual Studio!

Visual Studio offers a template project for MSTest projects, but you can also create one using `dotnet`:

```
dotnet new mstest
```

Add a reference to your your web app project and create a class called `ControllerTests` with the following content:

```
[TestClass]
public class ControllerTests
{
    [TestMethod]
    public void CanExecuteIndex()
    {
        var controller = new HomeController();
        var result = controller.Index();

        Assert.IsNotNull(result);
        Assert.IsInstanceOfType(result, typeof(ViewResult));
    }
}
```

This is a simple unit test that will check that the result of invoking the `Index` method on the `HomeController` class is not `null`.

Notice the `[TestMethod]` attribute in the `CanExecuteIndex` method; it is an indication that this method contains a unit test and it is captured by the **Test Explorer** feature of Visual Studio:

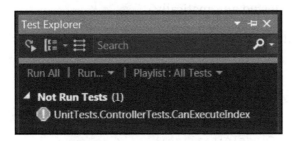

Visual Studio will be able to find any test method, provided that the following is true:

- It is declared in a non-abstract class.
- The class is decorated with a `[TestClass]` attribute.
- It is public.
- It has either the `[TestMethod]` or `[DataRow]` attributes (more on this in a moment).

From here, you can run or debug your tests; try placing a breakpoint inside the `CanExecuteIndex` method and debugging the tests. It is called automatically by Visual Studio and it considers whether the test passes if no exception is thrown. Controllers are usually good candidates for unit testing, but you should also unit test your services and business objects as well. Remember, focus on the most critical classes first and then, if you have the resources, time, and developers, proceed to the less critical code.

Besides `[TestMethod]`, you can also decorate your unit test methods with one or more `[DataRow]` attributes. This allows you to pass arbitrary values for parameters and return values for your method to be supplied automatically by the unit test framework:

```
[TestClass]
public class CalculatorTest
{
    [DataTestMethod]
    [DataRow(1, 2, 3)]
    [DataRow(1, 1, 2)]
    public void Calculate(int a, int b, int c)
    {
        Assert.AreEqual(c, a + b);
```

```
    }
}
```

In this example, we can see that we are providing two sets of values—1, 2, and 3, and 1, 1, and 2. These are tested automatically.

If you want to execute code before or after any tests in the same class, you can apply the following:

```
[TestClass]
public class MyTests
{
    [ClassInitialize]
    public void ClassInitialize()
    {
        //runs before all the tests in the class
    }

    [ClassCleanuç]
    public void ClassCleanup()
    {
        //runs after all the tests in the class
    }
}
```

Alternatively, for running code just before and after each test, apply the following:

```
[TestInitialize]
public void Initialize()
{
    //runs before each test
}

[TestCleanup]
public void Cleanup()
{
    //runs after each test
}
```

If you want to ignore a specific test method, apply the following:

```
[Ignore("Not implemented yet")]
public void SomeTest()
{
    //will be ignored
}
```

The `Assert` class offers a number of useful utility methods to be used in unit tests:

- `AreEqual`: The items to compare are identical.
- `AreNotEqual`: The items to compare are not identical.
- `AreNotSame`: The items to compare have not got the same reference.
- `AreSame`: The items to compare have the same reference.
- `Equals`: The items are equal.
- `Fail`: The assertion failed.
- `Inconclusive`: The assertion was inconclusive.
- `IsFalse`: The condition is expected to be false.
- `IsInstanceOfType`: The instance is expected to be of a given type.
- `IsNotInstanceOfType`: The instance is not expected to be of a given type.

> Please refer to the MSTest documentation at `https://docs.microsoft.com/en-us/visualstudio/test/using-microsoft-visualstudio-testtools-unittesting-members-in-unit-tests?view=vs-2019` for more information.

Next, we have NUnit.

NUnit

NUnit is one of the oldest unit test frameworks. To use it in your code, you need to add the following NuGet packages as references:

- `nunit`

- `NUnit3TestAdapter`

- `Microsoft.NET.Test.Sdk`

Again, the first one is the framework itself and the second is the integration with Visual Studio. To create an NUnit project, besides using the Visual Studio template, you can create one with `dotnet`:

```
dotnet new nunit
```

Add a reference to your web app project and add a class such as this one to a file called `ControllerTests.cs`:

```
[TestFixture]
public class ControllerTests
{
    [Test]
    public void CanExecuteIndex()
    {
        var controller = new HomeController();
        var result = controller.Index();

        Assert.AreNotEqual(null, result);
    }
}
```

Visual Studio is able to automatically find unit tests, provided the following is true:

- They are declared in a non-abstract class.
- The class is decorated with a `[TestFixture]` attribute.
- They are public and non-abstract.
- They have either the `[Test]` or `[TestCase]` attributes.

`[TestCase]` allows us to pass multiple arguments automatically, as well as an expected return value (which is optional):

```
public class CalculatorTest
{
    [TestCase(1, 1, ExpectedResult = 2)]
    public int Add(int x, int y)
    {
        return x + y;
    }
}
```

Notice that in this example, we don't even need to specify an assertion—one is inferred automatically if you specify `ExpectedResult`.

Now, if you want something to run before any tests in your code, you need to have the following in your code:

```
[SetUpFixture]
public class InitializeTests
{
    [OneTimeSetUp]
    public void SetUpOnce()
```

```
    {
        //run before all tests have started
    }

    [OneTimeTearDown]
    public void TearDownOnce()
    {
        //run after all tests have finished
    }
}
```

The names of the class and methods are irrelevant, but the class needs to be public and have a public parameterless constructor, and the methods also need to be public and non-abstract (can be static or instance). Notice the attributes on both the class and the SetUp (runs before) and TearDown (runs after) methods. Not all of them need to be provided, just one.

Likewise, if you wish to have code run before each test, you need to have a method marked as follows:

```
[SetUp]
public void BeforeTest()
{
    //runs before every test
}
```

The difference between the two is that the method marked as [SetUp] runs before every test, while [OneTimeSetUp] and [OneTimeTearDown] only run once for each test sequence (all the tests).

If you wish to ignore a test for some reason, such as if it is failing or not yet complete, you can mark it with another attribute:

```
[Ignored("Not implemented yet")]
public void TestSomething()
{
    //will be ignored
}
```

As in other frameworks, there is a class called Assert that contains some helper methods:

- IsFalse: The given condition is false.
- IsInstanceOf: The passed instance is an instance of a given type.

- `IsNaN`: The passed expression is not a number.
- `IsNotAssignableFrom`: The passed instance is not assignable from a given type.
- `IsNotEmpty`: The collection is not empty.
- `IsNotInstanceOf`: The passed instance is not an instance of the given type.
- `IsNotNull`: The instance is not `null`.
- `IsNull`: The instance is `null`.
- `IsTrue`: The condition is true.

 For more information, please consult the NUnit documentation at `https://github.com/nunit/docs/wiki/NUnit-Documentation`.

Next is xUnit.

xUnit

In order to use xUnit, you need to add a couple of NuGet packages:

- `xunit`
- `xunit.runner.visualstudio`
- `Microsoft.NET.Test.Sdk`

The first is the framework itself and the other two are required for Visual Studio integration. Visual Studio 2019 even provides xUnit test project templates, which is even better!

Let's create a unit test project; because we will be targeting ASP.NET Core features and .NET Core apps, we need to create a unit test project that also targets .NET Core apps—`netcoreapp3.0`. As mentioned, you can do this through Visual Studio or by using the `dotnet` tool to create a template project:

```
dotnet new xunit
```

In this project, we add a reference to our web app and we create a class. Let's call it `ControllerTests`. In this class, we add the following code:

```
public class ControllerTests
{
    [Fact]
    public void CanExecuteIndex()
    {
        var controller = new HomeController();
        var result = controller.Index();

        Assert.NotNull(result);
    }
}
```

This is a very simple test. We are creating a `HomeController` instance, executing its `Index` method, and checking that no exception is thrown (implicit, otherwise the test would fail) and that its result is not `null`.

 Unlike other frameworks, with xUnit, you do not need to decorate a class that contains unit tests.

Visual Studio discovers unit tests automatically—it shows them in the **Test Explorer** window—provided the following is true:

- They are declared in a non-abstract class.
- They are public.
- They have either the `[Fact]` or `[Theory]` attributes.

`[Theory]` is even more interesting as you can supply parameters to your test method and xUnit will take care of calling it with them! See for yourself:

```
[Theory]
[InlineData(1, 2, 3)]
[InlineData(0, 10, 10)]
public void Add(int x, int y, int z)
{
    Assert.Equals(x + y, z);
}
```

This example is a bit simple, but I think you get the picture! `[InlineData]` should have as many parameters as the method it is declared on. As we have two `[InlineData]` attributes, we have two datasets, so the method will be called twice—once for each of the values in one of the `[InlineData]` attributes.

Alternatively, if you want to test an action method model, you could have the following:

```
var controller = new ShoppingController();
var result = controller.ShoppingBag();
var viewResult = Assert.IsType<ViewResult>(result);
var model = Assert.IsType<ShoppingBag>(viewResult.ViewData.Model);
```

You can have as many test methods as you like and you can run one or more from the Visual Studio **Test Explorer** window. Each of your methods should be responsible for testing one feature, so make sure you don't forget that! Normally, unit tests are set up according to **Arrange-Act-Assert** (**AAA**), meaning first we set up (arrange) our objects, then we call some code on them (act), and then we check its results (assert). Do keep this mnemonic in mind!

If the class where you have the unit tests implements `IDisposable`, its `Dispose` method will be called automatically at the end of all the tests. Also, the constructor of the class will be run, of course, so it needs to be public and have no parameters.

If you have your test class implement `IClassFixture<T>`, xUnit will expect it to contain a public constructor that takes an instance of `T` (which must, therefore, be a public and instantiable type) and it will pass an instance of it to all unit test classes that implement the same interface:

```
public class MyTests : IClassFixture<SharedData>
{
    private readonly SharedData _data;

    public MyTests(SharedData data)
    {
        this._data = data;
    }
}
```

Finally, if you wish to ignore a unit test, just set the `Skip` property on the `[Fact]` or `[Theory]` attributes:

```
[Fact(Skip = "Not implemented yet")]
public void TestSomething()
{
    //will be ignored
}
```

There are several utility methods in the xUnit `Assert` class that will throw an exception if a condition is not met:

- `All`: All the items in the collection match a given condition.
- `Collection`: All the items in the collection match all of the given conditions.
- `Contains`: The collection contains a given item.
- `DoesNotContain`: The collection does not contain a given item.
- `DoesNotMatch`: The string does not match a given regular expression.
- `Empty`: The collection is empty.
- `EndsWith`: The string ends with some content.
- `Equal`: Two collections are equal (contain exactly the same elements).
- `Equals`: Two items are equal.
- `False`: The expression is false.
- `InRange`: A comparable value is in a range.
- `IsAssignableFrom`: An object is assignable from a given type.
- `IsNotType`: An object is not of a given type.
- `IsType`: An object is of a given type.
- `Matches`: A string matches a given regular expression.
- `NotEmpty`: A collection is not empty.
- `NotEqual`: Two objects are not equal.
- `NotInRange`: A comparable value is not in range.
- `NotNull`: The value is not `null`.
- `NotSame`: Two references are not the same object.
- `NotStrictEqual`: Verifies that two objects are not equal using the default comparer (`Object.Equals`).
- `Null`: Checks that a value is null.

- `ProperSubset`: Verifies that a set is a proper subset (is contained) of another set.
- `ProperSuperset`: Verifies that a set is a proper superset of (contains) another set.
- `PropertyChanged`/`PropertyChangedAsync`: Verifies that a property was changed.
- `Raises`/`RaisesAsync`: Verifies that an action raises an event.
- `RaisesAny`/`RaisesAnyAsync`: Verifies that an action raises one of the given events.
- `Same`: Two references point to the same object.
- `Single`: The collection contains one—and only one—item.
- `StartsWith`: Verifies that a string starts with another string.
- `StrictEqual`: Verifies whether two objects are equal using the default comparer (`Object.Equals`).
- `Subset`: Verifies that a set is a subset (is contained) of another set.
- `Superset`: Verifies that a set is a superset (contains) of another set.
- `Throws`/`ThrowsAsync`: Verifies that an action throws an exception.
- `ThrowsAny`/`ThrowsAnyAsync`: Verifies that an action throws one of the given exceptions.
- `True`: The expression is true.

Essentially, all of these methods are variations of `True`; you want to assert whether a condition is true. Do not have lots of assertions in your unit test method; make sure only the essentials are tested—for example, check whether a method returns a non-empty or non-null collection in a test and have other test checks for the correctness of the values returned. If you want to test different scenarios or return values, create another unit test.

 For more information, please consult the xUnit documentation at `https://xunit.net/#documentation`.

Let's now see how we can prepare a unit test using xUnit.

Test setup

The examples in this chapter will all use xUnit as the unit test framework.

Injecting dependencies

It may not always be simple; for example, the class you wish to test may contain dependencies. By far the best way to inject dependencies into your controller is through its controller. Here is an example of a controller that carries out logging:

```
ILogger<HomeController> logger = ...;
var controller = new HomeController(logger);
```

Fortunately, the RequestServices property of HttpContext is itself settable, meaning you can build your own instance with the services that you want. Check the following code:

```
var services = new ServiceCollection();
services.AddSingleton<IMyService>(new MyServiceImplementation());

var serviceProvider = services.BuildServiceProvider();

controller.HttpContext.RequestServices = serviceProvider;
```

If your code depends on the current user being authenticated or possessing certain claims, you need to set up an HttpContext object, which you can do like this:

```
controller.ControllerContext = new ControllerContext
{
    HttpContext = new DefaultHttpContext
    {
        User = new ClaimsPrincipal(new ClaimsIdentity(new Claim[]
        {
            new Claim(ClaimTypes.Name, "username")
        }))
    }
};
```

This way, inside your controller, the `HttpContext` and `User` properties will be initialized properly. In the `DefaultHttpContext` class's constructor, you can also pass along a collection of features (the `HttpContext.Features` collection):

```
var features = new FeatureCollection();
features.Set<IMyFeature>(new MyFeatureImplementation());

var ctx = new DefaultHttpContext(features);
```

By using a custom features collection, you can inject values for lots of features, such as the following:

- `Sessions: ISessionFeature`
- `Cookies: IRequestCookiesFeature, IResponseCookiesFeature`
- `Request: IHttpRequestFeature`
- `Response: IResponseCookiesFeature`
- `Connections: IHttpConnectionFeature`
- `Form: IFormFeature`

Either by providing your own implementation in the features collection or by assigning values to the existing one, you can inject values for your tests so as to simulate real-life scenarios. For example, suppose your controller needs a specific cookie:

```
var cookies = new RequestCookieCollection(new Dictionary<string,
string> { { "username", "dummy" } });

var features = new FeatureCollection();
features.Set<IRequestCookiesFeature>(new
RequestCookiesFeature(cookies));

var context = new DefaultHttpContext(features);
```

`RequestCookieCollection` used to be public, but now it's internal, which means that to mock cookies, we need to implement them ourselves. Here is the simplest implementation:

```
class RequestCookieCollection : IRequestCookieCollection
{
    private readonly Dictionary<string, string> _cookies;

    public RequestCookieCollection(Dictionary<string, string> cookies)
    {
        this._cookies = cookies;
    }
```

```
public string this[string key] => _cookies[key];

public int Count => _cookies.Count;

public ICollection<string> Keys => _cookies.Keys;

public bool ContainsKey(string key)
{
    return _cookies.ContainsKey(key);
}

public IEnumerator<KeyValuePair<string, string>> GetEnumerator()
{
    return _cookies.GetEnumerator();
}

public bool TryGetValue(string key, out string value)
{
    return _cookies.TryGetValue(key, out value);
}

IEnumerator IEnumerable.GetEnumerator()
{
    return this.GetEnumerator();
}
}
```

Now, you should note that you cannot change the `HttpContext` object on `ControllerBase`—it is read-only. However, it turns out that it actually comes from the `ControllerContext` property, which is itself settable. Here is a full example:

```
var request = new Dictionary<string, StringValues>
{
    { "email", "rjperes@hotmail.com" },
    { "name", "Ricardo Peres" }
};

var formCollection = new FormCollection(request);
var form = new FormFeature(formCollection);
var features = new FeatureCollection();
features.Set<IFormFeature>(form);

var context = new DefaultHttpContext(features);

var controller = new HomeController();
controller.ControllerContext = new ControllerContext { HttpContext =
context };
```

This example allows us to set the contents of the form request so that they can be accessed in a unit test from inside a controller, as follows:

```
var email = this.Request.Form["email"];
```

To do that, we had to create a form collection (`IFormCollection`) and a feature (`IFormFeature`), build up an HTTP context (`HttpContext`) using this feature, assign a controller context (`ControllerContext`) with the HTTP context, and assign it to the controller that we want to test (`HomeController`). This way, all of its internal properties—`HttpContext` and `Request`—will have the dummy values that we passed as the request.

One of the challenges of dependencies is that because we are executing a limited subset of our system, it may not be easy to get proper functioning objects; we may need to replace them with substitutes. We will now see how we can resolve this.

Mocking

Mocks, fakes, and stubs are similar concepts that essentially mean that an object is substituted for another one that mimics its behavior. Why would we do that? Well, because we are testing our code in isolation and we are assuming that third-party code works as advertised, we do not care about it, so we can just replace these other dependencies with dummies.

 For a comparison of these terms, please refer to `https://blog.`
`pragmatists.com/test-doubles-fakes-mocks-and-stubs-`
`1a7491dfa3da`.

We use mocking frameworks for this purpose, and there are a few available for .NET Core as well, such as the following:

- **Moq**: `https://github.com/moq/moq4`
- **NSubstitute**: `http://nsubstitute.github.io`
- **FakeItEasy**: `https://fakeiteasy.github.io`

Let's pick **Moq**. In order to use it, add the `Moq` NuGet package to your project. Then, when you need to mimic the functionality of a given type, you can create a mock of it and set up its behavior, as shown:

```
//create the mock
var mock = new Mock<ILogger<HomeController>>();
//setup an implementation for the Log method
```

```
mock.Setup(x => x.Log(LogLevel.Critical, new EventId(), "", null,
null));

//get the mock
ILogger<HomeController> logger = mock.Object;
//call the mocked method with some parameters
logger.Log(LogLevel.Critical, new EventId(2), "Hello, Moq!", null,
null);
```

You set up a method by passing an expression consisting of a method or property call with appropriate parameter types, regardless of its actual value. You can pass the mocked object as a dependency of your services or controllers, run your tests, and then make sure that the mocked method was called:

```
mock.Verify(x => x.Log(LogLevel.Critical, new EventId(), "", null,
null));
```

It is also possible to set up a response object—for example, if we are mocking HttpContext:

```
var mock = new Mock<HttpContext>();
mock.Setup(x => x.User).Returns(new ClaimsPrincipal(new
ClaimsIdentity(new[] { new
    Claim(ClaimTypes.Name, "username"), new Claim(ClaimTypes
    .Role, "Admin") }, "Cookies")));

var context = mock.Object;
var user = context.User;

Assert.NotNull(user);
Assert.True(user.Identity.IsAuthenticated);
Assert.True(user.HasClaim(ClaimTypes.Name, "username"));
```

Here, you can see that we are supplying the return value for a call to the User property and we are returning a pre-built ClaimsPrincipal object with all the bells and whistles.

Of course, there's so much more to Moq, but I think this should be enough to get you started.

Assertions

Your unit test will fail if an exception is thrown. So, you can either roll out your own exception-throwing code or you can rely on one of the assertion methods, which actually throw exceptions themselves, provided by your unit test framework; all of them offer similar methods.

 For more complex scenarios, it may be useful to use an assertion library. `FluentAssertions` is one such library that happens to work nicely with .NET Core. Get it from NuGet as `FluentAssertions` and from GitHub at `https://github.com/fluentassertions/fluentassertions`.

With the code, you can have assertions such as the following:

```
int x = GetResult();
x
    .Should()
        .BeGreaterOrEqualTo(100)
    .And
        .BeLessOrEqualTo(1000)
    .And
        .NotBe(150);
```

As you can see, you can combine lots of expressions related to the same object type; numeric values have comparisons, strings have matches, and more. You can also throw in property change detection as well:

```
svc.ShouldRaisePropertyChangeFor(x => x.SomeProperty);
```

Also, execution time can be added:

```
svc
    .ExecutionTimeOf(s => s.LengthyMethod())
    .ShouldNotExceed(500.Milliseconds());
```

 There's a lot more to it, so I advise you to have a look at the documentation, available at `http://fluentassertions.com`.

Next, we have the user interface.

User interface

The unit tests we've seen so far are for testing APIs, such as business methods, and logic. However, it is also possible to test the user interface. Let's see how using **Selenium** helps with this. Selenium is a portable software testing framework for web applications of which there is a .NET port of `Selenium.WebDriver`. As well as this, we will need the following:

- `Selenium.Chrome.WebDriver`: For Chrome
- `Selenium.Firefox.WebDriver`: For Firefox
- `Selenium.WebDriver.MicrosoftWebDriver`: For Internet Explorer and Edge

We start by creating a driver:

```
using (var driver = (IWebDriver) new
ChromeDriver(Environment.CurrentDirectory))
{
    //...
}
```

Notice the `Environment.CurrentDirectory` parameter; this specifies the path where the driver can find the `chromedriver.exe` file—`geckodriver.exe` for Firefox or `MicrosoftWebDriver.exe` in the case of Internet Explorer/Edge (for Windows, of course!). These executables are added automatically by the NuGet packages. Also, if you don't dispose of the driver, the window will remain open after the unit test finishes. You can also call `Quit` at any time to close the browser.

Now, we can navigate to any page:

```
driver
    .Navigate()
    .GoToUrl("http://www.google.com");
```

We can find an element from its name:

```
var elm = driver.FindElement(By.Name("q"));
```

Besides the name, we can also search by the following parameters:

- ID: `By.Id`
- CSS class: `By.ClassName`
- CSS selector: `By.CssSelector`
- Tag name: `By.TagName`

- Link text: `By.LinkText`
- Partial link text: `By.PartialLinkText`
- XPath: `By.XPath`

Once we find an element, we can access its properties:

```
var attr = elm.GetAttribute("class");
var css = elm.GetCssValue("display");
var prop = elm.GetProperty("enabled");
```

We can also send keystrokes:

```
elm.SendKeys("asp.net");
```

Instead of keystrokes, we can also click on the following:

```
var btn = driver.FindElement(By.Name("btnK"));
btn.Click();
```

As we know, page loading can take some time, so we can configure the default time to wait for it to load, probably before we do `GoToUrl`:

```
var timeouts = driver.Manage().Timeouts();
timeouts.ImplicitWait = TimeSpan.FromSeconds(1);
timeouts.PageLoad = TimeSpan.FromSeconds(5);
```

`ImplicitWait` is just the time that Selenium waits before searching for an element; I'm sure you can guess what `PageLoad` does.

If we need to wait for a period of time, such as until an AJAX request finishes, we can do this:

```
var waitForElement = new WebDriverWait(driver,
TimeSpan.FromSeconds(5));
var logo =
waitForElement.Until(ExpectedConditions.ElementIsVisible(By.Id("hplogo
")));
```

The condition passed to `ExpectedConditions` can be one of the following:

- `AlertIsPresent`
- `AlertState`
- `ElementExists`
- `ElementIsVisible`
- `ElementSelectionStateToBe`

- ElementToBeClickable
- ElementToBeSelected
- FrameToBeAvailableAndSwitchToIt
- InvisibilityOfElementLocated
- InvisibilityOfElementWithText
- PresenceOfAllElementsLocatedBy
- StalenessOf
- TextToBePresentInElement
- TextToBePresentInElementLocated
- TextToBePresentInElementValue
- TitleContains
- TitleIs
- UrlContains
- UrlMatches
- UrlToBe
- VisibilityOfAllElementsLocatedBy

As you can see, there is a wealth of conditions that you can use. If the condition is not met before the timer expires, then the value returned by Until is null.

Hopefully, with this, you will be able to write unit tests that can check the user interface aspects of your sites. Of course, they need to point to a live environment, so in this case, the tests won't be self-contained. When we talk about integration tests, we will see how to overcome this.

 For more information about Selenium, please refer to https://selenium.dev.

This is as much as we'll cover about the user interface. Let's see now how we can run tests from the command line.

Using the command line

The `dotnet` command-line tool is the Swiss army knife of .NET Core development and, as such, it has full support for running unit tests. If you are in the project folder where you have your unit tests, just run `dotnet test` and off you go:

```
C:\Users\Projects\MyApp\UnitTests>dotnet test
Build started, please wait...
Build completed.

Test run for
C:\Users\Projects\MyApp\UnitTests\bin\Debug\netcoreapp3.0\UnitTests.dl
l(.NETCoreApp,Version=v3.0)

Microsoft (R) Test Execution Command Line Tool Version 16.3.0
Copyright (c) Microsoft Corporation. All rights reserved.

Starting test execution, please wait...
[xUnit.net 00:00:00.3769248] Discovering: UnitTests
[xUnit.net 00:00:00.4364853] Discovered: UnitTests
[xUnit.net 00:00:00.4720996] Starting: UnitTests
[xUnit.net 00:00:00.5778764] Finished: UnitTests

Total tests: 10. Passed: 10. Failed: 0. Skipped: 0.
Test Run Successful.
Test execution time: 1,0031 Seconds
```

Since the project is set up to use xUnit (the `xunit.runner.visualstudio` package), `dotnet` is happy to use it automatically.

If you wish to see all the tests that are defined, run `dotnet test --list-tests` instead:

```
Test run for
C:\Users\Projects\MyApp\UnitTests\bin\Debug\netcoreapp3.0\UnitTests.dl
l(.NETCoreApp,Version=v3.0)

Microsoft (R) Test Execution Command Line Tool Version 16.3.0
Copyright (c) Microsoft Corporation. All rights reserved.

The following Tests are available:

    CanExecuteIndex
    Add(1, 2, 3)
    Add(0, 10, 10)
```

Let's now look at some of the limitations of unit tests.

Limitations of unit tests

As useful as unit tests are, keep in mind that they are essentially used for regression testing and that they have some limitations:

- They generally do not cover user interfaces, although some frameworks exist that can do so (at the time of writing, there aren't any for .NET Core).
- You cannot test some ASP.NET features, such as filters or views.
- External systems are mocked, so you only have a limited view of a small part of the system.

We saw previously how we can perform tests over the user interface. In the next section, we will see how we can overcome the last two limitations.

Working on integration tests

Here, we will not just think of an **integration test** as a test that executes a test method with some input parameters and asserts the result or whether or not it throws an exception, but also as something that executes real code. An integration test tests different modules of code together, not just a single one.

As part of ASP.NET Core, Microsoft has made the `Microsoft.AspNetCore.Mvc.Testing` NuGet package available. Essentially, it lets us host a web application so that we can execute tests over it as we would in a real-life server, taking out, of course, performance and scalability issues.

In your unit test project, create a class such as this (again, we're using xUnit):

```
public class IntegrationTests :
IClassFixture<WebApplicationFactory<Startup>>
{
    private readonly WebApplicationFactory<Startup> _factory;

    public IntegrationTests(WebApplicationFactory<Startup> factory)
    {
        this._factory = factory;
    }

    [Theory]
    [InlineData("/")]
```

```
public async Task CanCallHome(string url)
{
    //Arrange
    var client = this._factory.CreateClient();

    //Act
    var response = await client.GetAsync(url);

    //Assert
    response.EnsureSuccessStatusCode();

    var content = await response.Content.ReadAsStringAsync();

    Assert.Contains("Welcome", content);
}
}
```

So, what do we have here? If you remember from the *xUnit* section, we have a unit test class where we are injecting `WebApplicationFactory` using the same `Startup` class that is used for the proper app. We then issue a request for a URL, which is injected as inline data. After we get the response, we validate its status code (`EnsureSuccessStatusCode` checks that we don't have 4xx or 5xx) and we actually have a look at the returned contents. Mind you, here, we do not work with `IActionResults` or similar, but with HTTP responses. Because `WebApplicationFactory` uses conventions, it knows where to load the configuration files and assemblies from.

The advantage of this approach is that we are really testing our controllers (and all their services) in a web-like scenario, meaning filters will be run, authentication will be checked, the configuration will be loaded as usual, and all that jazz. This plays nicely with unit tests, as you can see from this example.

 Notice that in this example, the unit test method is asynchronous; this is supported by xUnit and the other unit test frameworks.

You will notice that we are reading the response as a string (`response.Content.ReadAsStringAsync`). This means that we get the response as plain HTML, which may or may not be what we want. We can use libraries such as **AngleSharp** to parse this HTML and build a DOM from it. Then, you can query it using methods similar to those that you have on the browser. AngleSharp is available as a NuGet package.

A final word—you may want to tweak the `WebApplicationFactory` class to add some additional configuration or behavior. It's just a matter of inheriting from it and overriding its virtual methods. For example, suppose you want to disable all of the background services registered on the dependency injection framework:

```
class MyCustomWebApplicationFactory : WebApplicationFactory<Startup>
{
 protected override IHostBuilder CreateHostBuilder()
  {
  return base
  .CreateHostBuilder()
  .ConfigureServices(services =>
  {
  services.RemoveAll<IHostedService>();
  });
  }
}
```

As you can see, after we run the base class's `CreateHostBuilder` parameter, we are removing all registered instances of `IHostBuilder`. We could also change the start up class to a different one or perform any other kind of customization. It's just a matter of specifying this class instead of `WebApplicationFactory<Startup>` on `IClassFixture<T>`.

We've seen how to use unit test frameworks to actually perform integration tests. Be aware that, of course, doing this in an automated way will cause your tests to run for longer and possibly have side effects, something that goes against the philosophy of unit tests.

Summary

You definitely should carry out unit tests for your apps. Whether you follow TDD strictly or not, they can be very useful, especially for regression tests. Most continuous integration tools out there fully support running unit tests. Just don't try to cover everything; focus on the critical parts of your app and, if time allows, then proceed to the other parts. It is unreasonable to think that we will have 100% coverage in most projects, so we need to make decisions. Mocking frameworks play an essential role here as they allow us to simulate third-party services nicely.

Automated integration tests, as we saw here, allow us to test features that aren't available in unit tests, and these cover other parts of our needs.

This chapter covered ways to test our apps, either part of them in isolation or the system as a whole. Unit tests are useful as they can ensure that our application still works the way it is supposed to, even though we are making changes to it.

In the next chapter, we will talk about client-side development with ASP.NET Core.

Questions

So, by the end of this chapter, you should know the answers to the following questions:

1. What are the more popular unit test frameworks?
2. What is the benefit of mocking?
3. What is the difference between unit and integration testing?
4. What is TDD?
5. What are some limitations of unit tests?
6. How can we pass data automatically to unit tests?
7. What does *red-green-refactor* mean?

Client-Side Development

14

Although this book is about ASP.NET Core—a server-side development framework, nowadays, pretty much nothing can be achieved without client-side technologies. Fortunately, ASP.NET Core also includes a number of **application programming interfaces** (**APIs**) and libraries that can help us use third-party, client-side libraries to build modern apps. These apps include **single-page applications** (**SPAs**), which provide a much more user-friendly experience to that offered by old-school sites that need navigating from one page to another. There is also TypeScript, a superset of JavaScript, that can be used to build strongly typed, object-oriented code very similar to what you would write with C#.

Visual Studio also includes some features that make our life easier, and ASP.NET Core introduced interoperability with Node.js, something that wasn't possible earlier, including built-in package managers for **Node package manager** (**npm**). This includes the ability to run npm scripts from .NET code, for example.

We will cover the following topics in this chapter:

- Introducing client-side development
- Using **Library Manager** (**LibMan**)
- Using Node.js
- Using TypeScript

Technical requirements

In order to implement the examples introduced in this chapter, you will need the .NET Core 3 **software development kit** (**SDK**) and some form of text editor. Of course, Visual Studio 2019 (any edition) meets all the requirements, but you can also use Visual Studio Code, for example.

The source code can be retrieved from GitHub here: `https://github.com/PacktPublishing/Modern-Web-Development-with-ASP.NET-Core-3-Second-Edition`.

Introducing client-side development

Client-side development is the counterpart to server-side development. In modern web applications, one cannot exist without the other. Although this book is primarily about ASP.NET Core, a server-side technology, chances are we will be working with JavaScript or **Cascading Style Sheets** (**CSS**). Visual Studio (and Visual Studio Code, too) includes some features that make our life easier, and ASP.NET Core introduced interoperability with Node.js, something that wasn't possible earlier, including built-in package managers (`https://docs.microsoft.com/en-us/visualstudio/javascript/npm-package-management`).

Let's see how it functions in the following sections.

Using LibMan

LibMan is a new open source tool by Microsoft for managing client-side libraries. It consists of a Visual Studio extension and a command-line tool. Both read information from a `libman.json` configuration file. A sample file looks like this:

```
{
  "version": "1.0",
  "defaultProvider": "cdnjs",
  "libraries": [{
    "library": "jquery@3.4.1",
    "destination": "wwwroot/lib"
  },
  {
    "library": "jquery-validation-unobtrusive@3.2.11",
    "destination": "wwwroot/lib"
  }]
}
```

As you can see from the preceding code snippet, in the file, we specify one or more libraries (in this case, jQuery and `jQuery Validation Unobtrusive`) in specific versions, and, for each, we tell the library where to install it (`wwwroot/lib` for both). From inside Visual Studio (for Windows only—Mac does not have support for LibMan), we even have code completion for libraries and their versions, as can be seen in the following screenshot:

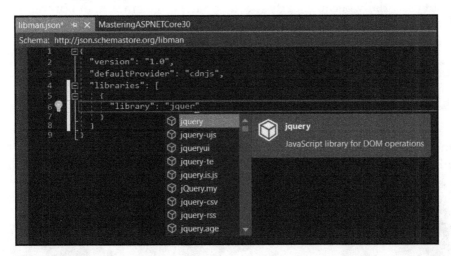

Then, we can use the command-line tool to retrieve these libraries and install them as configured. The command-line tool is a `dotnet` global tool, which first needs to be installed by running the following command:

```
dotnet tool install -g microsoft.web.librarymanager.cli
```

After that, from the folder containing the `libman.json` file, all we need to do is to restore all configured libraries, as follows:

```
libman restore
```

 For additional information, please consult the Microsoft official documentation at `https://devblogs.microsoft.com/aspnet/library-manager-client-side-content-manager-for-web-apps` and the GitHub project page at `https://github.com/aspnet/LibraryManager`.

Having learned about the new package manager, used to retrieve client-side libraries, it's now time to talk about Node.js, the server-side JavaScript engine, and see how we can interact with it from .NET Core.

Using Node.js

Most of you will be familiar with **Node.js** by now—it is essentially JavaScript on the server side. It is an open source project that, at least for now, uses Chrome's V8 JavaScript engine to run JavaScript out of the context of a browser. It has become extremely popular, arguably due to its use of the JavaScript language (some may not agree), but essentially because of its speed and the huge amount of libraries made available through npm—currently, more than 550,000.

 You can find more information about Node.js and npm on their respective sites, `https://nodejs.org` and `https://www.npmjs.com`, and about the Visual Studio support for npm here: `https://docs.microsoft.com/en-us/visualstudio/javascript/npm-package-management`

You can install the Node.js support for Visual Studio through the VS installer tool, but you will also need to have Node.js itself installed, which you can get from `https://nodejs.org`. You get Visual Studio templates for creating Node.js projects, as illustrated in the following screenshot:

You can also add Node.js files to an ASP.NET Core project, but there is no obvious npm explorer in Visual Studio until you add a `package.json` file and reference some package. The `npm` node appears under the **Dependencies** project, as illustrated in the following screenshot:

Node.js files are kept in a `node_modules` folder outside `wwwroot`; this is because these files are usually not meant to be served to the browser. You need to explicitly restore the packages before you can use them.

The next section explains how we can call Node.js code from inside .NET Core code.

Calling Node from .NET Core

Steve Sanderson, of Knockout.js (`http://knockoutjs.com/`) fame, started a pet project called `NodeServices` a few years ago. It was made available as `Microsoft.AspNetCore.NodeServices` a few years ago from NuGet, and it is now part of the ASP.NET Core ecosystem. In a nutshell, it allows us to call Node.js code from ASP.NET Core. Just think about it—we get all the benefits of both ASP.NET Core and Node.js (and npm) at the same time!

In order to use `NodeServices`, we need to register its services in `ConfigureServices`, like this:

```
services.AddNodeServices();
```

After this, we can inject an instance of `INodeServices` into our components, controllers, view components, tag helpers, middleware classes, and more. This interface exposes a single method, `InvokeAsync`, which we can use to invoke one of the modules that we have installed locally. One example might be this:

```
var result = await nodeServices.InvokeAsync<int>("Algebra.js", 10,
20);
```

The `Algebra.js` file would then need to export a default module—something along these lines:

```
module.exports = function(callback, a, b) {
  var result = a + b;
  callback(null, result);
};
```

`NodeServices` expects the default export to return a function that takes a callback, implicitly passed by `InvokeAsync`, and any number of parameters. Make a note of this: these parameters should be of primitive types, but you can pass along a **JavaScript Object Notation (JSON)**-formatted object and have your Node.js code convert it. You can do pretty much whatever you want from your Node.js code, including referencing other modules. At the end of the default `export` instance, you call the implicit callback function with an optional error parameter and the value to return to .NET Core; if you pass an error, the .NET code will raise an exception.

There is another way to call Node.js code, which is often useful—this is to run an npm script. This is explained in the next section.

Serving SPA files

A partial replacement of `NodeServices` exists in the `Microsoft.AspNetCore.SpaServices.Extensions` NuGet package. Notice that WebPack middleware is no longer included in ASP.NET Core. We must use a development server and start an npm script so that we can serve files for SPA projects, as follows:

```
app.UseStaticFiles();
app.UseSpaStaticFiles();
```

```
app.UseRouting();
app.UseEndpoints(endpoints =>
{
    endpoints.MapDefaultControllerRoute();
});

app.UseSpa(spa =>
{
    spa.Options.SourcePath = "ClientApp";

    if (env.IsDevelopment())
    {
        spa.UseReactDevelopmentServer(npmScript: "start");
    }
});
```

Notice that `UseSpaStaticFiles` must go before `UseEndpoints`, and `UseSpa` must go after `UseEndpoints`. `UseReactDevelopmentServer` is really not specific to React; it is used to start a Node script in process. For the `start` script, you need to register it as a script under `package.json`—something like this:

```
"scripts": { "start": "webpack-dev-server --config
webpack.development.js --hot --inline",
```

If you need to proxy requests (forward requests to a running server), we must instead have the following:

```
// Ensure that you start your server manually
spa.UseProxyToSpaDevelopmentServer("http://localhost:8088");
```

Let's not forget to register the required services in `ConfigureServices` first, by executing the following code:

```
services.AddSpaStaticFiles(configuration =>
{
    configuration.RootPath = "ClientApp/build";
});
```

The configuration in the `.csproj` file depends on the type of project being created; each file/project will have slightly different settings. Let's see what types of projects (templates)can be created.

Using SPA templates

Microsoft has made available templates for a number of popular JavaScript SPA frameworks, as follows:

Template	Framework	Moniker
`Microsoft.AspNetCore.SpaTemplates`	Aurelia	`aurelia`
	Knockout.js	`knockout`
	Vue.js	`vue`
`Microsoft.DotNet.Web.Spa.ProjectTemplates`	Angular	`angular`
	React.js	`react`
	React.js + Redux	`reactredux`

You can see the full list of templates at `https://dotnetnew.azurewebsites.net`. To install the templates, use the following code:

```
dotnet new -i Microsoft.AspNetCore.SpaTemplates
dotnet new -i Microsoft.DotNet.Web.Spa.ProjectTemplates
```

You will get all of the listed templates. Then, for example, run the following code:

```
mkdir AngularProject
cd AngularProject
dotnet new angular
dotnet restore
npm install
```

As a result, you will get a nice project skeleton using Angular, waiting to be completed!

To update all the local templates to the more recent versions, just run the following command:

```
dotnet new --update-apply
```

After this, let's move on to understanding how this works with TypeScript.

Using TypeScript

TypeScript is a JavaScript object-oriented superset. It is an open source language developed by Microsoft that offers features that exist in other non-scripted, object-oriented languages, such as modules, classes, interfaces, strong typing, templates, different visibility levels, and method overloading.

By coding in TypeScript, you get all the benefits of these languages but, after the code is transpiled (cross-language compiled), you still get your daddy's JavaScript, although a modern version of it, which you can use in both the client and the server side (Node.js). See more about TypeScript at `https://www.typescriptlang.org` and obtain it from GitHub at `https://github.com/Microsoft/TypeScript`. Alternatively, if you want to play with it a bit first, you should try the TypeScript Playground: `http://www.typescriptlang.org/play`

Visual Studio has two extensions, **TypeScript Build for Microsoft Visual Studio** and **TypeScript for Microsoft Visual Studio**, both installable with the **TypeScript SDK** (`https://marketplace.visualstudio.com/items?itemName=TypeScriptTeam.typescript-331-vs2017`), which can be used to assist you in creating TypeScript code and turning it into JavaScript. You add a TypeScript file to your project by clicking **Add New Item** | **Visual C#** | **ASP.NET Core** | **Web** | **Scripts** | **TypeScript File**. As you add TypeScript content and save the file, Visual Studio automatically transpiles it to a corresponding JavaScript file. Remember that you do not use the TypeScript (`.ts`) files directly, but the JavaScript ones (`.js`), as illustrated in the following screenshot:

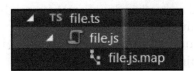

It is also possible to create a TypeScript project on its own, but only for targeting Node.js; it would be pointless to have a TypeScript project for the web outside the scope of an ASP.NET project.

You can create a Node.js console application TypeScript project from Visual Studio using the default templates, as illustrated in the following screenshot:

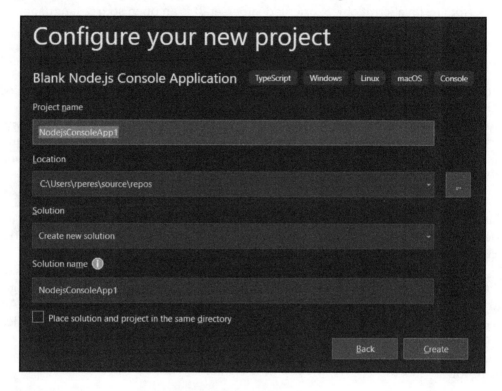

TypeScript is recommended over plain JavaScript for medium-scale and large-scale projects because it makes things easier to organize, with proper support for types—interfaces, classes, enumerations, and so on. Also, in general, it helps prevent errors because of strong typing and more strict checking.

If you just want to compile TypeScript files on a **Microsoft Build** (**MSBuild**) project, all it takes is to add the Microsoft.TypeScript.MSBuild NuGet package and configure the .csproj file accordingly, as per this example:

```
<PropertyGroup>
    <TypeScriptToolsVersion>3.7<TypeScriptToolsVersion>
</PropertyGroup>

<PropertyGroup Condition="'$(Configuration)' == 'Debug'">
    <TypeScriptRemoveComments>false</TypeScriptRemoveComments>
    <TypeScriptSourceMap>true</TypeScriptSourceMap>
</PropertyGroup>
```

```
<PropertyGroup Condition="'$(Configuration)' == 'Release'">
    <TypeScriptRemoveComments>true</TypeScriptRemoveComments>
    <TypeScriptSourceMap>false</TypeScriptSourceMap>
</PropertyGroup>
<Import
Project="$(MSBuildExtensionsPath32)\Microsoft\VisualStudio\v$(VisualSt
udioVersion)\TypeScript\
Microsoft.TypeScript.targets"
Condition="Exists('$(MSBuildExtensionsPath32)\Microsoft\VisualStudio\v
$(VisualStudioVersion)\
TypeScript\Microsoft.TypeScript.targets')" />
```

In this example, we start by defining the target TypeScript version (3.7). Another option is to skip it or to set it to Latest. Then, we have two configurations, one for Debug and another for Release. The difference between the two is optimizations—one removes comments and does not create source maps (Release), and the other does the opposite (Debug). For a list of all the options, refer to https://www.typescriptlang.org/docs/handbook/compiler-options-in-msbuild.html.

Summary

You've seen that Node.js and npm are getting more and more important, even for those of us using ASP.NET and ASP.NET Core, because of its rich wealth of packages. Some of the tools that we've talked about in this chapter rely on it. Because you can now invoke Node.js from ASP.NET Core, you can benefit from its many available packages and thriving community. Even if you are not much of a JavaScript person, I truly advise you to try to get into it.

Make sure you use TypeScript for any medium-to-large projects—anything that is bigger than a single JavaScript file—because it has lots of advantages and can help you be more productive, much faster.

In this chapter, we covered some of the client-side technologies for which Visual Studio offers first-class support. We did not go into great detail, as this is a huge topic and one that seems to be changing very fast, but I left some clues for you, dear reader, to explore and find out more for yourself.

Questions

So, by the end of this chapter, you should know the answers to the following questions:

1. What are the benefits of TypeScript?
2. Does JavaScript only run on browsers?
3. What are SPAs?
4. What is the purpose of LibMan?
5. Are the templates for dotnet SPA frameworks hardcoded?
6. How can we run JavaScript code from .NET Core?
7. Name a few SPA frameworks that have dotnet templates.

15
Improving Performance and Scalability

This chapter talks about the different optimizations that we can apply to ASP.NET Core applications so that they perform faster and are able to handle more simultaneous connections. The two concepts that we will be looking at—performance and scalability—are different and, in fact, to some degree, they conflict with each other. You must apply the right level of optimization to find the sweet spot.

After reading this chapter, you should be able to apply techniques, first to understand what is going wrong or what can be improved in your application, and second, how you can improve it. We will look at some of the available techniques in the forthcoming sections.

We will cover the following topics in this chapter:

- Profiling—how to gain insights into what your application is doing
- Hosting choices and tweaking your host for the best performance
- Bundling and minimization
- Using asynchronous actions
- Caching
- Compressing responses

Technical requirements

In order to implement the examples introduced in this chapter, you will need the .NET Core 3 SDK and a text editor. Of course, Visual Studio 2019 (any edition) meets all the requirements, but you can also use Visual Studio Code, for example.

The source code can be retrieved from GitHub at `https://github.com/PacktPublishing/Modern-Web-Development-with-ASP.NET-Core-3-Second-Edition`.

Getting started

As Lord Kelvin once famously said, *If you cannot measure it, you cannot improve it*. With that in mind, we need to measure our application to see where its problems are. There are some applications, known as **profilers**, that can give us the means to do this. Let's have a look at some of the choices that we have.

MiniProfiler

One open source profiler is **MiniProfiler**, available from `http://miniprofiler.com/dotnet/AspDotNetCore` and from NuGet as `MiniProfiler.AspNetCore.Mvc`. There are also other packages, such as `Microsoft.EntityFrameworkCore.SqlServer`, for the Entity Framework Core SQL Server provider, and `Microsoft.EntityFrameworkCore.Sqlite for SQLite`, which you should add as well.

The following screenshot shows the console, with details regarding the request and the database calls:

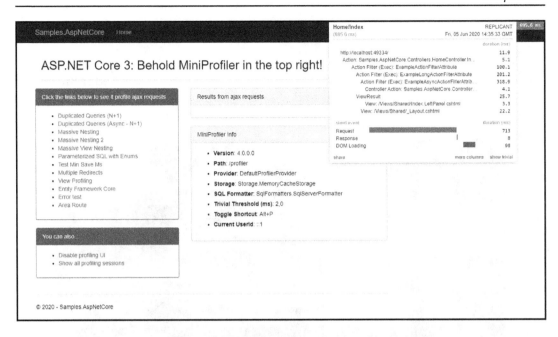

This screen shows some metrics after a page was loaded, including the response time, the time it took the DOM to load, and how long the action method took to execute. To use MiniProfiler, you need to register its services (`ConfigureServices`):

```
services
    .AddMiniProfiler()
    .AddEntityFramework();
```

Add the middleware component (`Configure`):

```
app.UseMiniProfiler()
```

Then, add the client-side JavaScript code:

```
<mini-profiler position="@RenderPosition.Right" max-traces="5" color-
scheme="ColorScheme.Auto" />
```

As this is a tag helper, you will need to register it first (`_ViewImports.cshtml`):

```
@addTagHelper *, MiniProfiler.AspNetCore.Mvc
```

There are other options, such as formatting SQL queries and colorization, and so on, so I suggest you have a look at the sample application available on GitHub.

Stackify Prefix

Stackify Prefix is not an open source product, but rather one that is maintained by the well-known **Stackify** (https://stackify.com). It can be downloaded from https://stackify.com/prefix, and at this time, it is not available with NuGet. It offers more features than the other two, so it might be worth taking a look at:

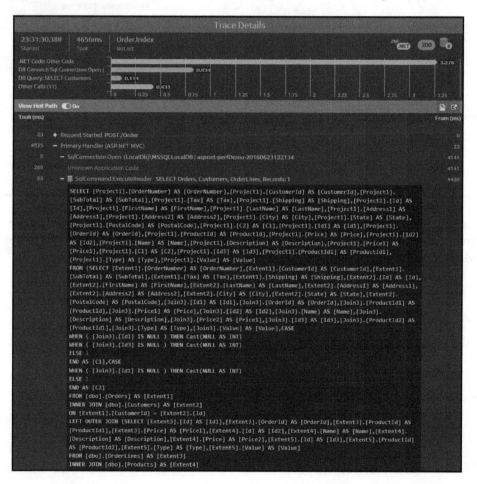

This screenshot shows the result of an invocation of an action method—a POST to order—and it shows a SQL that was executed inside it. We can see how long the .NET code, the database connection, and `SQL SELECT` took to execute.

Let's now look at the hosting options available in ASP.NET Core.

Hosting ASP.NET Core

Hosting is the process that is used to run your ASP.NET Core application. In ASP.NET Core, you have two out-of-the-box hosting choices:

- **Kestrel**: The cross-platform host, which is set by default
- **HTTP.sys (WebListener** in ASP.NET Core pre-2.x): A Windows-only host

If you want your application to run on different platforms, not just on Windows, then Kestrel should be your choice, but if you need to target only Windows, then WebListener/HTTP.sys may offer better performance, as it utilizes native Windows system calls. You have to make this choice. By default, the Visual Studio template (or the ones used by the `dotnet` command) uses Kestrel, which is appropriate for most common scenarios. Let's learn about how we can choose what's best for our purposes.

Choosing the best host

You should compare the two hosts to see how well they behave in stressful situations. Kestrel is the default one and is included in the `Microsoft.AspNetCore.Server.Kestrel` NuGet package. If you want to try HTTP.sys, you need to add a reference to the `Microsoft.AspNetCore.Server.HttpSys` package.

Kestrel is the default host, but if you wish to be explicit about it, it looks like this:

```
public static IHostBuilder CreateWebHostBuilder(string[] args) =>
    Host
        .CreateDefaultBuilder(args)
        .ConfigureWebHostDefaults(builder =>
        {
            builder
                .ConfigureKestrel((KestrelServerOptions options) =>
                {
                    //options go here
                })
                .UseStartup<Startup>();
        });
```

In order to use HTTP.sys in ASP.NET Core 3.x, then you should use the following:

```
public static IHostBuilder CreateWebHostBuilder(string[] args) =>
    Host
        .CreateDefaultBuilder(args)
        .ConfigureWebHostDefaults(builder =>
```

```
    {
        builder
            .UseHttpSys((HttpSysOptions options) =>
            {
                //options go here
            })
            .UseStartup<Startup>();
    });
```

This example shows how to enable the HTTP.sys host and where some of the performance-related settings can be defined.

Configuration tuning

Both hosts, Kestrel and HTTP.sys, support tuning of some of their parameters. Let's look at some of them.

Maximum number of simultaneous connections

For Kestrel, it looks like this:

```
.ConfigureKestrel(options =>
{
    options.Limits.MaxConcurrentConnections = null;
    options.Limits.MaxConcurrentUpgradedConnections = null;
})
```

MaxConcurrentConnections specifies the maximum number of connections that can be accepted. If set to null, there will be no limit, except, of course, system resource exhaustion. MaxConcurrentUpgradedConnections is the maximum number of connections that can be migrated from HTTP or HTTPS to WebSockets (for example). null is the default value, meaning that there is no limit.

An explanation of this code is in order:

- MaxAccepts: This is equivalent to MaxConcurrentConnections. The default is 0, meaning that there is no limit.
- RequestQueueLimit: With this, it is also possible to specify the maximum queued requests in HTTP.sys.

For HTTP.sys, WebListener's replacement in ASP.NET Core 3.x, it is similar:

```
.UseHttpSys(options =>
{
    options.MaxAccepts = 40;
    options.MaxConnections = null;
    options.RequestQueueLimit = 1000;
})
```

This code sets some common performance-related options for the HTTP.sys host, as shown in the following list:

- `MaxAccepts` specifies the maximum number of concurrent accepts.
- `MaxConnections` is the maximum number of concurrent accepts (the default is `null`) to use the machine-global settings from the registry. `-1` means that there are an infinite number of connections.
- `RequestQueueLimit` is the maximum number of requests that can be queued by HTTP.sys. Let's now see how limits work.

Limits

Similar to HTTP.sys, Kestrel also allows the setting of some limits, even a few more than HTTP.sys:

```
.ConfigureKestrel(options =>
{
    options.Limits.MaxRequestBodySize = 30 * 1000 * 1000;
    options.Limits.MaxRequestBufferSize = 1024 * 1024;
    options.Limits.MaxRequestHeaderCount = 100;
    options.Limits.MaxRequestHeadersTotalSize = 32 * 1024;
    options.Limits.MaxRequestLineSize = 8 * 1024;
    options.Limits.MaxResponseBufferSize = 64 * 1024;
    options.Limits.MinRequestBodyDataRate.BytesPerSecond = 240;
    options.Limits.MaxResponseDataRate.BytesPerSecond = 240
})
```

Explaining this code is simple:

- `MaxRequestBodySize`: The maximum allowed size for a request body
- `MaxRequestBufferSize`: The size of the request buffer
- `MaxRequestHeaderCount`: The maximum number of request headers
- `MaxRequestHeadersTotalSize`: The total acceptable size of the request headers

- `MaxRequestLineSize`: The maximum number of lines in the request
- `MaxResponseBufferSize`: The size of the response buffer
- `MinRequestBodyDataRate.BytesPerSecond`: The maximum request throughput
- `MaxResponseDataRate.BytesPerSecond`: The maximum response throughput

Timeouts

Whenever an application is waiting for an external event—waiting for a request to arrive in its entirety, for a form to be submitted, a connection to be established, and so on—it can only wait for a certain period of time; this is so that it does not affect the global functioning of the application. When it elapses, we have a timeout, after which the application either gives up and fails or starts again. Kestrel allows the specification of a number of timeouts:

```
.ConfigureKestrel(options =>
{
    options.Limits.KeepAliveTimeout = TimeSpan.FromMinutes(2);
    options.Limits.RequestHeadersTimeout = TimeSpan.FromSeconds(30);
})
```

As for the two properties being set, here is some information:

- `KeepAliveTimeout` is the client connection timeout in keep-alive connections; 0, the default, means an indefinite time period.
- `RequestHeadersTimeout` is the time to wait for headers to be received; the default is also 0.

For HTTP.sys, the properties are as follows:

- `DrainEntityBody` is the time allowed in keep-alive connections to read all the request bodies.
- `EntityBody` is the maximum time for each individual body to arrive.
- `HeaderWait` is the maximum time to parse all request headers.
- `IdleConnection` is the time before an idle connection is shut down.
- `MinSendBytesPerSecond` is the minimum send rate in bytes per second.
- `RequestQueue` is the time allowed for queued requests to remain in the queue.

Here is a sample code that illustrates these options:

```
.UseHttpSys(options =>
{
    options.Timeouts.DrainEntityBody = TimeSpan.FromSeconds(0);
    options.EntityBody = TimeSpan.FromSeconds(0);
    options.HeaderWait = TimeSpan.FromSeconds(0);
    options.IdleConnection = TimeSpan.FromSeconds(0);
    options.MinSendBytesPerSecond = 0;
    options.RequestQueue = TimeSpan.FromSeconds(0);
})
```

In this section, we explored some of the tweaks available in the ASP.NET Core hosts that can lead to better resource utilization and ultimately lead to better performance and scalability. In the next section, we will look at techniques for improving static resource transmission.

Understanding bundling and minification

Bundling means that several JavaScript or CSS files can be combined in order to minimize the number of requests that the browser sends to the server. Minification is a technique that removes unnecessary blanks from CSS and JavaScript files and changes the function and variable names so that they are smaller. When combined, these two techniques can result in much less data to transmit, which will result in faster load times.

A default project created by Visual Studio performs bundling automatically when the application is run or deployed. The actual process is configured by the `bundleConfig.json` file, which has a structure similar to the following:

```
[
    {
        "outputFileName": "wwwroot/css/site.min.css",
        "inputFiles": [
            "wwwroot/css/site.css"
        ]
    },
    {
        "outputFileName": "wwwroot/js/site.min.js",
        "inputFiles": [
            "wwwroot/js/site.js"
        ],
        "minify": {
            "enabled": true,
```

```
        "renameLocals": true
      },
      "sourceMap": false
    }
  ]
```

We can see two different groups, one for CSS and the other for JavaScript, each resulting in a file (`outputFileName`). Each takes a set of files, which can include wildcards (`inputFiles`), and it is possible to specify whether the result is to be minified (`enabled`), and functions and variables renamed so that they are smaller (`renameLocals`). For JavaScript files, it is possible to automatically generate a source map file (`sourceMap`). You can read about source maps at `https://developer.mozilla.org/en-US/docs/Tools/Debugger/How_to/Use_a_source_map`. Mind you, this behavior is actually not intrinsic to Visual Studio, but rather it is produced by the `Bundler & Minifier` extension by Mads Kristensen, available from the Visual Studio gallery at `https://marketplace.visualstudio.com/items?itemName=MadsKristensen.BundlerMinifier`.

Other options exist, such as adding the `BuildBundlerMinifier` NuGet package, also from Mads Kristensen, which adds a command-line option to `dotnet`, allowing us to perform bundling and minification from the command line at build time. Yet another option is to use Gulp, Grunt, or WebPack, but since these are JavaScript solutions rather than ASP.NET Core ones, I won't discuss them here. For WebPack, Gulp, and Grunt, please refer to `Chapter 14`, *Client-Side Development*.

Next, we will move on to learn how asynchronous actions aid applications.

Using asynchronous actions

Asynchronous calls are a way to increase the scalability of your application. Normally, the thread that handles the request is blocked while it is being processed, meaning that this thread will be unavailable to accept other requests. By using asynchronous actions, another thread from a different pool is assigned the request, and the listening thread is returned to the pool, waiting to receive other requests. Controllers, Razor pages, tag helpers, view components, and middleware classes can perform asynchronously. Whenever you have operations that perform **input/output** (**IO**), always use asynchronous calls, as this can result in much better scalability.

For controllers, just change the signature of the action method to be like the following (note the `async` keyword and the `Task<IActionResult>` return type):

```
public async Task<IActionResult> Index() { ... }
```

In Razor Pages, it is similar (note the `Async` suffix, the `Task<IActionResult>` return type, and the `async` keyword):

```
public async Task<IActionResult> OnGetAsync() { ... }
```

For tag helpers and tag helper components, override the `ProcessAsync` method instead of `Process`:

```
public override async Task ProcessAsync(TagHelperContext context,
TagHelperOutput output) { ... }
```

In view components, implement an `InvokeAsync` method, like this one:

```
public async Task<IViewComponentResult> InvokeAsync(/* any parameters
*/) { ... }
```

Also make sure that you invoke it asynchronously in your views:

```
@await Component.InvokeAsync("MyComponent", /* any parameters */)
```

Finally, in a middleware class, do the following:

```
public async Task Invoke(HttpContext httpContext) { ... }
```

Or, in lambdas, execute the following code:

```
app.Use(async (ctx, next) =>
{
    //async work
    await next();
});
```

Better still, for controller actions, include a `CancellationToken` parameter and pass it along any asynchronous methods that are called inside it. This will make sure that, should the request be canceled by the client (by closing the browser or terminating the call in any other way), all calls will be closed as well:

```
public async Task<IActionResult> Index(CancellationToken token) { ...
}
```

This parameter is the same as the one you'd get from `HttpContext.RequestAborted`, mind you.

That is not all; you should also prefer asynchronous API methods instead of blocking ones, especially those that do I/O, database, or network calls. For example, if you need to issue HTTP calls, always look for asynchronous versions of its methods:

```
var client = new HttpClient();
var response = await client.GetStreamAsync("http://<url>");
```

If you want to pass along the cancellation token, it's slightly more complex, but not much more:

```
var client = new HttpClient();
var request = new HttpRequestMessage(HttpMethod.Get, "<url>");
var response = await client.SendAsync(request, token);
```

Or, should you need to upload potentially large files, always use code like the following (install the `Microsoft.AspNetCore.WebUtilities` NuGet package):

```
app.Use(async (ctx, next) =>
{
    using (var streamReader = new HttpRequestStreamReader
    (ctx.Request.Body, Encoding.UTF8))
    {
        var jsonReader = new JsonTextReader(streamReader);
        var json = await JObject.LoadAsync(jsonReader);
    }
});
```

This has the benefit that you don't block the post while all the payload contents are being read, and in this example, it builds the JSON object asynchronously, too.

With ASP.NET 3, the hosts are now asynchronous all the way, which means that synchronous APIs are disabled by default, and calling them results in exceptions. Should you wish otherwise, you need to change this behavior by turning on a flag on a feature, using a middleware component:

```
var synchronousIOFeature =
HttpContext.Features.Get<IHttpBodyControlFeature>();
synchronousIOFeature.AllowSynchronousIO = true;
```

Or, individually for Kestrel and HTTP.sys, you can do this on the services configuration:

```
//Kestrel
services.Configure<KestrelServerOptions>(options =>
{
    options.AllowSynchronousIO = true;
});
```

```
//HTTP.sys
services.Configure<HttpSysOptions>(options =>
{
    options.AllowSynchronousIO = true;
});

//if using IIS
services.Configure<IISServerOptions>(options =>
{
    options.AllowSynchronousIO = true;
});
```

Here, we've seen how to use asynchronous actions to improve the scalability of our solution. In the next section, we will be looking at a solution to improve performance: caching.

 Keep in mind, however, that asynchronicity is not a panacea for all your problems; it is simply a way to make your application more responsive.

Improving performance with caching

Caching is one of the optimizations that can have a greater impact on the performance of a site. By caching responses and data, you do not have to fetch them again, process them, and send them to the client. Let's look at a couple of ways by which we can achieve this.

Caching data

By caching your data, you do not need to go and retrieve it again and again whenever it is needed. You need to consider a number of aspects:

- How long will it be kept in the cache?
- How can you invalidate the cache if you need to do so?
- Do you need it to be distributed across different machines?
- How much memory will it take? Will it grow forever?

There are usually three ways to specify the cache duration:

- **Absolute**: The cache will expire at a predefined point in time.
- **Relative**: The cache will expire some time after it is created.
- **Sliding**: The cache will expire some time after it is created, but, if accessed, this time will be extended by the same amount.

In-memory cache

The easiest way to achieve caching is by using the built-in implementation of `IMemoryCache`, available in the `Microsoft.Extensions.Caching.Memory` NuGet package (it also comes in the `Microsoft.AspNetCore.All` metapackage). As you can guess, it is a memory-only cache, suitable for single-server apps. In order to use it, you need to register its implementation in `ConfigureServices`:

```
services.AddMemoryCache();
```

After that, you can inject the `IMemoryCache` implementation into any of your classes—controllers, middleware, tag helpers, view components, and more. You have essentially three operations:

- Add an entry to the cache (`CreateEntry` or `Set`).
- Get an entry from the cache (`Get`, `GetOrCreate`, or `TryGetValue`).
- Remove an entry from the cache (`Remove`).

Adding an entry requires you to give it a name, a priority, and a duration. The name can be any object and the duration can either be specified as a relative, sliding expiration, or absolute time. Here's an example:

```
//relative expiration in 30 minutes
cache.Set("key", new MyClass(), TimeSpan.FromMinutes(30));

//absolute expiration for next day
cache.Set("key", new MyClass(), DateTimeOffset.Now.AddDays(1));

//sliding expiration
var entry = cache.CreateEntry("key");
entry.SlidingExpiration = TimeSpan.FromMinutes(30);
entry.Value = new MyClass();
```

You can also combine the two strategies:

```
//keep item in cache as long as it is requested at least once every 5
//minutes
// but refresh it every hour
var options = new MemoryCacheEntryOptions()
    .SetSlidingExpiration(TimeSpan.FromMinutes(5))
    .SetAbsoluteExpiration(TimeSpan.FromHours(1));

var entry = cache.CreateEntry("key");
entry.SetOptions(options);
```

When using the sliding expiration option, it will be renewed whenever the cache item is accessed. Using `Set` will create a new item or replace any existing item with the same key. You can also use `GetOrCreate` to either add one if no item with the given key exists, or to return the existing one as follows:

```
var value = cache.GetOrCreate("key", (entry) =>
{
    entry.AbsoluteExpirationRelativeToNow = TimeSpan.FromMinutes(30);
    return new MyClass();
});
```

The priority controls when an item is evicted from the cache. There are only two ways by which an item can be removed from the cache: manually or when running out of memory. The term *priority* refers to the behavior applied to the item when the machine runs out of memory. The possible values are as follows:

- `High`: Try to keep the item in memory for as long as possible.
- `Low`: It's OK to evict the item from memory when it is necessary.
- `NeverRemove`: Never evict the item from memory unless its duration is reached.
- `Normal`: Use the default algorithm.

It is possible to pass a collection of expiration tokens; this is essentially a way to have cache dependencies. You create a cache dependency in a number of ways, such as from a cancellation token:

```
var cts = new CancellationTokenSource();
var entry = cache.CreateEntry("key");
entry.ExpirationTokens.Add(new CancellationChangeToken(cts.Token));
```

You can also create one from a configuration change:

```
var ccts = new
ConfigurationChangeTokenSource<MyOptions>(this.Configuration);
var entry = cache.CreateEntry("key");
entry.ExpirationTokens.Add(ccts.GetChangeToken());
```

You can even create one from a change in a file (or directory):

```
var fileInfo = new FileInfo(@"C:\Some\File.txt");
var fileProvider = new PhysicalFileProvider(fileInfo.DirectoryName);
var entry = cache.CreateEntry("key");
entry.ExpirationTokens.Add(fileProvider.Watch(fileInfo.Name));
```

And if you want to combine many, so that the cache item expires when any of the change tokens do, you can use CompositeChangeToken:

```
var entry = cache.CreateEntry("key");
entry.ExpirationTokens.Add(new CompositeChangeToken(new
List<IChangeToken> {
    /* one */,
    /* two */,
    /* three */
}));
```

You can also register a callback that will be called automatically when an item is evicted from the cache, as follows:

```
var entry = cache.CreateEntry("key");
entry.RegisterPostEvictionCallback((object key, object value,
EvictionReason reason, object state) =>
{
    /* do something */
}, "/* some optional state object */");
```

This can be used as a simple scheduling mechanism: you can add another item with the same callback so that when the item expires, it will add the item again and again. The key and value parameters are obvious; the reason parameter will tell you why the item was evicted, and this can be for one of the following reasons:

- None: No reason is known.
- Removed: The item was explicitly removed.
- Replaced: The item was replaced.

- `Expired`: The expiration time was reached.
- `TokenExpired`: An expiration token was fired.
- `Capacity`: The maximum capacity was reached.

The `state` parameter will contain any arbitrary object, including `null`, that you pass to `RegisterPostEvictionCallback`.

In order to get an item from the cache, two options exist:

```
//return null if it doesn't exist
var value = cache.Get<MyClass>("key");

//return false if the item doesn't exist
var exists = cache.TryGetValue<MyClass>("key", out MyClass value);
```

As for removing, it couldn't be simpler:

```
cache.Remove("key");
```

This removes the named cache item from the cache permanently.

> A side note: it is not possible to iterate through the items in the cache from the `IMemoryCache` instance, but you can count them by downcasting to `MemoryCache` and using its `Count` property.

Distributed cache

ASP.NET Core ships with two distributed cache providers:

- **Redis:** Available as a NuGet package at `Microsoft.Extensions.Caching.Redis`
- **SQL Server:** Available from `Microsoft.Extensions.Caching.SqlServer`

The core functionality is made available through the `IDistributedCache` interface. You need to register one of these implementations in `ConfigureServices`. For Redis, use the following command:

```
services.AddDistributedRedisCache(options =>
{
    options.Configuration = "serverName";
    options.InstanceName = "InstanceName";
});
```

For SQL Server, use the following command:

```
services.AddDistributedSqlServerCache(options =>
{
    options.ConnectionString = @"<Connection String>";
    options.SchemaName = "dbo";
    options.TableName = "CacheTable";
});
```

Once you have done that, you will be able to inject an `IDistributedCache` instance, which offers four operations:

- Add or remove an item (`Set`, `SetAsync`)
- Retrieve an item (`Get`, `GetAsync`)
- Refresh an item (`Refresh`, `RefreshAsync`)
- Remove an item (`Remove`, `RemoveAsync`)

As you can see, it is similar to `IMemoryCache`, but it is not quite the same—for one thing, it offers asynchronous and synchronous versions for all operations. In addition, it does not feature all of the options that exist for an in-memory cache, such as priorities, expiration callbacks, and expiration tokens. But the most important difference is that all items need to be stored as byte arrays, meaning that you have to serialize any objects that you want to store in the cache beforehand. A special case is strings, where there are extension methods that work directly with strings.

So, in order to add an item, you need to do the following:

```
using (var stream = new MemoryStream())
{
    var formatter = new BinaryFormatter();
    formatter.Serialize(stream, new MyClass());

    cache.Set("key", formatter.ToArray(), new
DistributedCacheEntryOptions
    {
        //pick only one of these
        //absolute expiration
        AbsoluteExpiration = DateTimeOffset.Now.AddDays(1),
        //relative expiration
        AbsoluteExpirationRelativeToNow = TimeSpan.FromMinutes(60),
        //sliding expiration
        SlidingExpiration = TimeSpan.FromMinutes(60)
    });
}
```

As you can see, it does support absolute, relative, and sliding expiration. If you want to use strings, it's simpler:

```
cache.SetString("key", str, options);
```

To retrieve an item, you also need to deserialize it afterward:

```
var bytes = cache.Get("key");
using (var stream = new MemoryStream(bytes))
{
    var formatter = new BinaryFormatter();
    var data = formatter.Deserialize(stream) as MyClass;
}
```

And for strings, you use the following code:

```
var data = cache.GetString("key");
```

Refreshing is easy; if the item uses sliding expiration, then it is renewed:

```
cache.Refresh("key");
```

The same goes for removing:

```
cache.Remove("key");
```

The asynchronous versions are identical, except that they end with the `Async` suffix and return a `Task` object, which you can then await.

As you may know, `BinaryFormatter` is only available from .NET Core 2.0 onward, so, for versions of .NET Core prior to that, you need to come up with your own serialization mechanism. A good one might be `MessagePack`, available from NuGet.

 Both distributed caches and in-memory caches have their pros and cons. A distributed cache is obviously better when we have a cluster of machines, but it also has a higher latency—the time it takes to get results from the server to the client. In-memory caches are much faster, but they take up memory on the machine on which it is running.

In this section, we've discussed the alternatives to caching data, whether in memory or in a remote server. The next section explains how to cache the result of the execution of action methods.

Caching action results

By the means of caching action results, you instruct the browser, after the first execution, to keep the supplied result for a period of time. This can result in dramatic performance improvement; as no code needs to be run, the response comes directly from the browser's cache. The process is specified in an RFC at `https://tools.ietf.org/html/rfc7234#section-5.2`. We can apply caching to action methods by applying the `[ResponseCache]` attribute to either the controller or the action method. It can take some of the following parameters:

- `Duration` (`int`): The cache duration in seconds; it is mapped to the `max-age` value in the `Cache-control` header
- `Location` (`ResponseCacheLocation`): Where to store the cache (one of `Any`, `Client`, or `None`)
- `NoStore` (`bool`): Do not cache the response
- `VaryByHeader` (`string`): A header that will make the cache vary—for example, `Accept-Language` causes a response to be cached for each requested language (see `https://www.w3.org/International/questions/qa-accept-lang-locales`)
- `VaryByQueryKeys` (`string[]`): Any number of query string keys that will make the cache vary
- `CacheProfileName` (`string`): The name of a cache profile; more on this in a moment

The cache locations have the following meanings:

- `Any`: Cached on the client and in any proxies; sets the `Cache-control` header to `public`
- `Client`: Cached on the client only; `Cache-control` is set to `private`
- `None`: Nothing is cached; `Cache-control` and `Pragma` are both set to `no-cache`

But before we can use it, we need to register the required services in `ConfigureServices`:

```
services.AddResponseCaching();
```

It is possible to configure some options by passing a delegate:

```
services.AddResponseCaching(options =>
{
    options.MaximumBodySize = 64 * 1024 * 1024;
```

```
    options.SizeLimit = 100 * 1024 * 1024;
    options.UseCaseInsensitivePaths = false;
});
```

The available options are as follows:

- `MaximumBodySize` (`int`): The maximum cacheable response; the default is 64 KB
- `SizeLimit` (`int`): Maximum size of all the cached responses; the default is 100 MB
- `UseCaseInsensitivePaths` (`bool`): Whether or not paths should be taken as case sensitive; the default is `false`

To make this work, as well as registering the services, we need to add the response-caching middleware (the `Configure` method):

```
app.UseResponseCaching();
```

Rather than passing duration, location, and other parameters, it is better to use **cache profiles**. Cache profiles are defined when we register the MVC services by adding entries such as this:

```
services
    .AddMvc(options =>
    {
        options.CacheProfiles.Add("Public5MinutesVaryByLanguage",
         new CacheProfile
        {
            Duration = 5 * 60,
            Location = ResponseCacheLocation.Any,
            VaryByHeader = "Accept-Language"
        });
    });
```

Here, we are registering some options for a cache profile named `Public5MinutesVaryByLanguage`, which are as follows:

- `Duration` (`int`): The duration, in seconds, of the cached item
- `Location` (`ResponseCacheLocation`): Where to store the cached item; it can either be on the server or on the client (the browser)
- `VaryByHeader` (`string`): An optional request header to have the cache vary upon; in this example, we are changing the cache by the browser's language

If you wish, you could load the configuration from a configuration file. Say you have this structure:

```
{
  "CacheProfiles": {
    "Public5MinutesVaryByLanguage": {
      "Duration": 300,
      "Location": "Any",
      "VaryByHeader" : "Accept-Language"
    }
  }
}
```

You could load it using the configuration API, in `ConfigureServices`:

```
services
    .Configure<Dictionary<string, CacheProfile>>(this.Configuration.
     GetSection("CacheProfiles"))
    .AddMvc(options =>
    {
        var cacheProfiles = this.Configuration.GetSection<Dictionary
        <string, CacheProfile>();
        foreach (var keyValuePair in cacheProfiles)
        {
            options.CacheProfiles.Add(keyValuePair);
        }
    });
```

Using cache profiles allows us to have a centralized location where we can change the profile settings that will be used across all the applications. It's as simple as the following:

```
[ResponseCache(CacheProfileName = "Public5MinutesVaryByLanguage")]
public IActionResult Index() { ... }
```

Response caching also depends on an HTTP.sys setting, which is enabled by default. It is called `EnableResponseCaching`:

```
.UseHttpSys(options =>
{
    options.EnableResponseCaching = true;
})
```

This enables response caching for the HTTP.sys host. Bear in mind that without this, the [ResponseCache] attribute won't work. This is required for sending the appropriate caching response headers.

In this section, we've seen how to cache responses from action methods. Let's now see how we can cache view markup.

Caching views

By using the included tag helpers, <cache> and <distributed-cache>, you will be able to cache parts of your views. As you can infer from their names, <cache> requires a registered instance of IMemoryCache, and <distributed-cache> requires IDistributedCache. I have already talked about these two tag helpers in Chapter 9, *Reusable Components*, so I won't go over them again. We will only look at two examples. This one is for in-memory caching:

```
<cache expires-sliding="TimeSpan.FromMinutes(30)">
    ...
</cache>
```

This one is for distributed caching:

```
<distributed-cache name="redis" expires-
sliding="TimeSpan.FromMinutes(30)">
    ...
</distributed-cache>
```

Anything placed inside <distributed-cache> will be stored in the named distributed cache (in this example, redis) for a period of time (30 minutes) from the first time the view is rendered, and on subsequent occasions, it will directly come from there, without any additional processing.

Do not forget that you need to register an instance of either IMemoryCache or IDistributedCache. These tag helpers, unfortunately, cannot take cache profiles.

Caching is a must-have for any real-life web application, but it must be considered carefully because it may put memory pressure on your system. In the next two sections, we will learn how to optimize responses.

Compressing responses

Response compression is available from the
`Microsoft.AspNetCore.ResponseCompression` package. Essentially, for
browsers that support it, it can compress the response before sending it through the
wire, thereby minimizing the amount of data that will be sent, at the expense of
consuming some time compressing it.

If a browser supports response compression, it should send an `Accept-Encoding:
gzip, deflate` header. Let's see how:

1. We first need to register the response compression services in
   `ConfigureServices`:

   ```
   services.AddResponseCompression();
   ```

2. A more elaborate version allows you to specify the actual compression
   provider (`GzipCompressionProvider` is the one included) and the
   compressible file types:

   ```
   services.AddResponseCompression(options =>
   {
       options.EnableForHttps = true;
       options.Providers.Add<GzipCompressionProvider>();
       options.MimeTypes = ResponseCompressionDefaults.
       MimeTypes.Concat(new[] { "image/svg+xml" });
   });

   services.Configure<GzipCompressionProviderOptions>(options
   =>
   {
       options.Level = CompressionLevel.Fastest;
   });
   ```

   The only option for `GzipCompressionProviderOptions` is the
   compression level, of which there are three options:

   - `NoCompression`: No compression—this is the default
   - `Fastest`: The fastest compression method, which may result
     in bigger responses
   - `Optimal`: The compression method that offers the best
     compression, but potentially takes more time

You can see that you can also configure the file types to compress. As a note, the following content types are automatically compressed:

- `text/plain`
- `text/css`
- `application/javascript`
- `text/html`
- `application/xml`
- `text/xml`
- `application/json`
- `text/json`

3. Finally, you need to add the response compression middleware to the `Configure` method:

```
app.UseResponseCompression();
```

Now, whenever a response is one of the configured mime types, it will be automatically compressed and the response headers will include a `Content-Encoding: gzip` header.

Note that you can roll out your own compression implementation by implementing the `ICompressionProvider` interface and registering it in the `AddResponseCompression` method overload that takes a lambda. Besides GZip, Microsoft also has a **Brotli**-based implementation (`BrotliCompressionProvider` and `BrotliCompressionProviderOptions` classes). Brotli is an open source compression algorithm that is supported by several browsers and provides better compression than GZip.

 The Deflate compression method is not supported in ASP.NET Core 2.x,—only GZip. Read about Deflate at its RFC (`https://tools.ietf.org/html/rfc1951`) and about GZip at `https://tools.ietf.org/html/rfc1952`. Read about Brotli in RFC 7932 (`https://tools.ietf.org/html/rfc7932`) and see the list of supported browsers at `https://www.caniuse.com/#feat=brotli`.

Compression can greatly improve the latency of the response at the cost of some extra processing on the server, and now that we've looked at it, let's see how we can improve the response time by using buffering.

Buffering responses

The final technique we will be covering here is response buffering. Normally, a web server streams a response, meaning that it sends a response as soon as it has its chunks. Another option is to get all these chunks, combine them, and send them at once: this is called *buffering*.

Buffering offers some advantages: it can result in better performance and offer the ability to change the contents (including headers) before they are sent to the client.

Microsoft offers buffering capabilities through the `Microsoft.AspNetCore.Buffering` NuGet package. Using it is simple—for example, you can use it in a middleware lambda:

```
app.UseResponseBuffering();

app.Run(async (ctx) =>
{
    ctx.Response.ContentType = "text/html";
    await ctx.Response.WriteAsync("Hello, World!");

    ctx.Response.Headers.Clear();
    ctx.Response.Body.SetLength(0);

    ctx.Response.ContentType = "text/plain";
    await ctx.Response.WriteAsync("Hello, buffered World!");
});
```

In this example, we are first registering the response buffering middleware (essentially wrapping the response stream), and then, on the middleware lambda, you can see that we can write to the client, clear the response by setting its length to 0, and then write again. This wouldn't be possible without response buffering.

If you want to disable it, you can do so through its feature, `IHttpBufferingFeature`:

```
var feature = ctx.Features.Get<IHttpBufferingFeature>();
feature.DisableResponseBuffering();
```

In this section, we learned about buffering, its advantages, and how to enable it, and with this, we conclude the chapter.

Summary

In this chapter, we learned that using response caching in action methods and views is essential, but it must be used judiciously because you do not want your content to become outdated. Cache profiles are preferred for action methods, as they provide a centralized location, which makes it easier to make changes. You can have as many profiles as you need.

Distributed caching can help if you need to share data among a cluster of servers, but be warned that transmitting data over the wire can take some time, even if, trivially, it is faster than retrieving it from a database, for example. It can also take a lot of memory, and so can cause other unforeseeable problems.

Then, we saw that bundling and minification are also quite handy because they can greatly reduce the amount of data to be transmitted, which can be even more important for mobile browsers.

Asynchronous operations should also be your first choice; some modern APIs don't even allow you to have any other choices. This can greatly improve the scalability of your app.

Lastly, we saw that we need to use a profiler to identify the bottlenecks. Stackify Prefix is a very good choice.

The choice of host greatly depends on deployment needs—if it is non-Windows, then we have no choice other than Kestrel. On both Kestrel and HTTP.sys, there are a great number of parameters that you can tweak to your needs, but be warned that playing with these can result in poor performance.

In this chapter, we looked at some ways by which we can improve the performance and scalability of an application. This is not an exhaustive list, and there is a lot that can be done in the code, especially when it comes to fetching data. Use your best judgment and experiment with things before applying them in production.

In the next chapter, we will be covering real-time communication.

Questions

SO, by the end of the chapter, you should know the answers to the following questions:

1. What are the two hosts available to ASP.NET Core 3?
2. What are the two kinds of cache that are available?
3. What is the benefit of compressing a response?
4. What is the purpose of caching a response?
5. Do asynchronous actions improve performance?
6. What is bundling?
7. What are profilers good for?

16
Real-Time Communication

In this chapter, we will learn about Microsoft **SignalR**, which is a library
for doing real-time communication between the client and the server. It allows the
server to call the client of its own initiative, not as a result of a request. It builds on
well-known technologies such as **AJAX**, **WebSockets**, and **server-sent events**, but in a
transparent manner. You do not need to know what it's using—it basically just works,
regardless of the browser you have. It also supports quite a lot of browsers, including
mobile phones. Let's explore this technology and see what it has to offer—essentially,
the following:

- Setting up SignalR
- Sending messages from the client to the server
- Broadcasting messages from the server to all/some clients
- Sending messages from outside a hub

After reading this chapter, you will learn how to communicate in real time from the
server to clients connected to a page, whether they are on a PC or a mobile device.

Technical requirements

To implement the examples introduced in this chapter, you will need the .NET Core 3
SDK and a text editor. Of course, Visual Studio 2019 (any edition) meets all of the
requirements, but you can also use Visual Studio Code, for example.

The source code can be retrieved from GitHub here: `https://github.com/`
`PacktPublishing/Modern-Web-Development-with-ASP.NET-Core-3-Second-Edition`.

Setting up SignalR

Before starting to use SignalR, several things need to be sorted out first, namely, installing libraries locally.

Perform the following steps to begin this setup:

1. First, install the `Microsoft.AspNetCore.SignalR` NuGet package.
2. You also need a JavaScript library that is made available through **npm** (short for **node package manager**) as `@microsoft/signalr`.
3. Once you install it, you need to copy the JavaScript file, either the minimized or the debug version to some folder under `wwwroot`, as it needs to be retrieved by the browser.
4. The file containing the SignalR library is called `signalr.js` or `signalr.min.js` (for the minimized version) and it is available under `node_modules/@aspnet/signalr/dist/browser`.
5. You will also require the `@aspnet/signalr-protocol-msgpack` package for using `MessagePack` serialization (more on this in a moment) if you wish to use it, but it's not strictly needed.

Unlike previous pre-Core versions, SignalR does not need any other library, such as **jQuery**, but it can happily coexist with it. Just add a reference to the `signalr.js` file before using the code.

For npm, add a `package.json` file similar to this one:

```
{
  "name": "chapter16",
  "version": "1.0.0",
  "description": "",
  "main": "",
  "scripts": {
  },
  "author": "",
  "license": "ISC",
  "dependencies": {
    "@microsoft/signalr": "^3.1.4",
    "@aspnet/signalr-protocol-msgpack": "^1.1.0",
    "msgpack5": "^4.2.1"
  }
}
```

npm files are stored inside the `node_modules` folder but need to be copied to some location inside `wwwroot`, from where they can be made publicly available, for example, served to the browser. A good way to copy the files from the `node_modules` folder into your app is to leverage the **MSBuild** build system. Open your `.csproj` file and add the following lines:

```
<ItemGroup>
    <SignalRFiles Include="node_modules/@microsoft/signalr
    /dist/browser/*.js" />
    <SignalRMessagePackFiles
        Include="node_modules/@aspnet/signalr-protocol-msgpack
        /dist/browser/*.js" />
    <MessagePackFiles Include="node_modules/msgpack5/dist/*.js" />
</ItemGroup>

<Target Name="CopyFiles" AfterTargets="Build">
    <Copy SourceFiles="@(SignalRFiles)"
        DestinationFolder="$(MSBuildProjectDirectory)\wwwroot\lib
        \signalr" />
    <Copy SourceFiles="@(SignalRMessagePackFiles)"
        DestinationFolder="$(MSBuildProjectDirectory)\wwwroot\lib
        \signalr" />
    <Copy SourceFiles="@(MessagePackFiles)"
DestinationFolder="$(MSBuildProjectDirectory)\wwwroot\lib\msgpack5" />
</Target>
```

This will copy the required JavaScript files from their npm-provided directory into a folder inside `wwwroot`, suitable for inclusion on a web page. Another option is to use Libman, described in `Chapter 14`, *Client-Side Development*, in a section of its own. Do have a look! And do not forget that because you are serving static files, you must add the appropriate middleware in the `Configure` method:

```
app.UseStaticFiles();
```

We shall begin with the core concepts of SignalR and move from there.

Learning core concepts

The appeal of SignalR comes from the fact that it hides different techniques for handling (near) real-time communication over the web. These are the following:

- **Server-sent events** (see `https://developer.mozilla.org/en-US/docs/Web/API/Server-sent_events`)
- **WebSockets** (see `https://developer.mozilla.org/en-US/docs/Glossary/WebSockets`)
- **Long polling** (see `https://en.wikipedia.org/wiki/Push_technology#Long_polling`)

Each has its own strengths and weaknesses, but with SignalR, you don't really need to care about that because SignalR automatically picks up the best one for you.

So, what is it about? Essentially, with SignalR, you can do two things:

- Have a client application (such as a web page) send a message to the server and have it routed to all (or some) parties also connected to the same web app
- Have the server take the initiative to send a message to all (or some) connected parties

Messages can be plain strings or have some structure. We don't need to care about it; SignalR takes care of the serialization for us. When the server sends a message to the connected clients, it raises an event and gives them a chance to do something with the received message.

SignalR can group connected clients into groups and can require authentication. The core concept is that of a **hub**: clients gather around a hub and send and receive messages from it. A hub is identified by a URL.

You create an HTTP connection to a URL, create a hub connection from it, add event listeners to the hub connection (system events such as close and hub messages), then start receiving from it, and possibly start sending messages as well.

After setting up SignalR, we will see now how a hub is hosted.

Hosting a hub

A **hub** is a concept that SignalR uses for clients to come together in a well-known location. From the client side, it is identified as a URL, such as `http://<servername>/chat`. On the server, it is a class that inherits from `Hub` and must be registered with the ASP.NET Core pipeline. Here's a simple example of a chat hub:

```
public class ChatHub : Hub
{
    public async Task Send(string message)
    {
        await this.Clients.All.SendAsync("message",
this.Context.User.
            Identity.Name, message);
    }
}
```

The `Send` message is meant to be callable by JavaScript only. This `Send` method is asynchronous and so we must register this hub in a well-known endpoint, in the `Configure` method, where we register the endpoints:

```
app.UseEndpoints(endpoints =>
{
    endpoints.MapHub<ChatHub>("chat");
});
```

You can pick any name you want—you don't need to be restrained by the hub class name.

And you can also register its services, in the `ConfigureServices` method, as follows:

```
services.AddSignalR();
```

The `Hub` class exposes two virtual methods, `OnConnectedAsync` and `OnDisconnectedAsync`, which are fired whenever a client connects or disconnects. `OnDisconnectedAsync` takes `Exception` as its parameter, which will only be not null if an error occurred when disconnecting.

To call a `hub` instance, we must first initialize the SignalR framework from JavaScript, and for that, we need to reference the `~/lib/signalr/signalr.js` file (for development) or `~/lib/signalr/signalr.min.js` (for production). The actual code goes like this:

```
var logger = new signalR.ConsoleLogger(signalR.LogLevel.Information);
var httpConnection = new signalR.HttpConnection('/chat', { logger:
logger });
```

Here, we are calling an endpoint named `chat` on the same host from where the request is being served. Now, in terms of the communication between the client and the server itself, we need to `start` it:

```
var connection = new signalR.HubConnection(httpConnection, logger);

connection
    .start()
    .catch((error) => {
        console.log('Error creating the connection to the chat hub');
});
```

As you can see, the `start` method returns a promise to which you can also chain a `catch` method call to catch any exceptions while connecting.

We can detect that a connection was unexpectedly closed by hooking to the `onclose` event:

```
connection.onclose((error) => {
    console.log('Chat connection closed');
});
```

After the connection succeeds, you hook to your custom events, (`"message"`):

```
connection.on('message', (user, message) => {
    console.log(`Message from ${user}: ${message}`);
});
```

The call to `on` with the name of an event, (`"message"`), should match the name of the event that is called on the hub, in the `SendAsync` method. It should also take the same number (and type) of parameters.

I'm also using `arrow` functions, a feature of modern JavaScript (you can find out more by reading this article: `https://developer.mozilla.org/en-US/docs/Web/JavaScript/Reference/Functions/Arrow_functions`). This is just syntax, and it can be achieved with anonymous functions.

As a remark, you can pass additional query string parameters that may later be caught in the hub. There is another way to do this, using `HubConnectionBuilder`:

```
var connection = new signalR.HubConnectionBuilder()
    .configureLogging(signalR.LogLevel.Information)
    .withUrl('/chat?key=value')
    .build();
```

It is sometimes useful, as there are not many ways to pass data from the client to a hub other than, of course, calling its methods. The way to retrieve these values is shown in the following code:

```
var value =
this.Context.GetHttpContext().Request.Query["key"].SingleOrDefault();
```

Now, we can start sending messages:

```
function send(message) {
    connection.invoke('Send', message);
}
```

Essentially, this method asynchronously calls the `Send` method of the `ChatHub` class, and any response will be received by the `'message'` listener, which we registered previously (see `hub.on('message')`).

In a nutshell, the flow is as follows:

1. A connection is created on the client side (`signalR.HubConnection`) using a hub address (`signalR.HttpConnection`), which must be mapped to a .NET class inheriting from `Hub`.
2. An event handler is added for some event (`connection.on()`).
3. The connection is started (`start()`).
4. Clients send messages to the hub (`connection.invoke()`), using the name of a method declared on the `Hub` class.
5. The method on the `Hub` class broadcasts a message to all/some of the connected clients.
6. When a client receives the message, it raises an event to all subscribers of that event name (the same as declared in `connection.on()`).

The client can call any method on the Hub class, and this, in turn, can raise any other event on the client.

But first things first, let's see how we can define the protocol between the client and the server so that the two can talk.

Choosing communication protocols

SignalR needs to have clients and the server talking the same language—a protocol. It supports the following communication protocols (or message transports, if you like):

- **WebSockets**: In browsers that support it, this is probably the most performant one because it is binary-, not text-, based. Read more about WebSockets here: https://developer.mozilla.org/en-US/docs/Web/API/WebSockets_API.
- **Server-sent events**: This is another HTTP standard; it allows the client to continuously poll the server, giving the impression that the server is communicating directly to it; see https://developer.mozilla.org/en-US/docs/Web/API/Server-sent_events.
- **AJAX long polling**: Also known as **AJAX Comet**, it is a technique by which the client keeps an AJAX request alive, possibly for a long time, until the server provides an answer, which is when it returns and issues another long request.

Usually, signalR determines the best protocol to use, but you can force one from the client:

```
var connection = new signalR.HubConnectionBuilder()
  .configureLogging(signalR.LogLevel.Information)
  .withUrl('/chat', { skipNegotiation: false, transport: signalR.
  TransportType.ServerSentEvents })
```

This can be retrieved from the server as well, but in general, it is recommended to leave it open to all protocols:

```
app.UseEndpoints(endpoints =>
{
    endpoints.MapHub<ChatHub>("chat", opt =>
    {
        opt.Transports = HttpTransportType.ServerSentEvents;
    });
});
```

Forcing one protocol may be required in operating systems where, for example, WebSockets is not supported, such as Windows 7. Or it may be because a router or firewall might not allow some protocol, such as WebSockets. The client side and server side configuration must match, that is, if the server does not have a specific protocol enabled, setting it on the client side won't work. If you don't restrict transport, SignalR will try all of them and choose the one that works best automatically. You may need to choose a specific protocol if you have some sort of restriction, such as protocol incompatibility between client and server. If you do, don't forget to also skip negotiation, as it will save some time.

 Do not restrict the transport types unless you have a very good reason for doing so, such as browser or operating system incompatibilities.

We've seen how to configure a connection, so let's see now how to reconnect automatically in case of a failure.

Automatic reconnection

You can either catch the `close` event and respond to it or have SignalR automatically reconnect when the connection is dropped accidentally (these things happen on the internet, you know!). For that, call the `withAutomaticReconnect` extension method on the client code:

```
var connection = new signalR.HubConnectionBuilder()
    .withAutomaticReconnect()
    .withUrl('/chat')
    .build();
```

This method can be called without parameters or with an array of numeric values that represent the time, in milliseconds, to wait before each attempt to reconnect. The default value is `[0, 2000, 10000, 30000, null]`, which means that first, it will try immediately, then it will wait two seconds, then one second, then three seconds, then it will stop trying (`null`). A third option is with a function that takes a few parameters and returns the next delay, as this example shows:

```
var connection = new signalR.HubConnectionBuilder()
    .withAutomaticReconnect({
        nextRetryDelayInMilliseconds: (retryContext) => {
            //previousRetryCount (Number)
            //retryReason (Error)
            return 2 * retryContext.elapsedMilliseconds;
        })
    .build();
```

In this example, we return an object that takes a lambda function that takes as its parameters the previous return count, the retry reason (an exception), and the elapsed time since the last retry and expects you to return the next delay or null if it's to cancel reconnection.

When automatic reconnection is used, some events are raised:

```
connection.onreconnecting((error) => {
    //a reconnect attempt is being made
});

connection.onreconnected((connectionid) => {
    //successful reconnection
});
```

These events are self-explanatory:

- `onreconnecting` is raised when SignalR is trying to reconnect as the consequence of an error, which is passed as its sole parameter to the callback
- `onreconnected` is raised after a successful reconnection and the new connection ID is passed to the callback

Messages sent to and from a hub need to be serialized, and that is the subject of the next topic.

Message serialization

Out of the box, SignalR sends messages in plaintext JSON, but there is an alternative, which is `MessagePack`. It is a compressed format that can provide a better performance, especially for bigger payloads.

As mentioned earlier, we will need to install the `@aspnet/signalr-protocol-msgpack` npm package and the `Microsoft.AspNetCore.SignalR.Protocols.MessagePack` NuGet package.

An example, where we can specify the `MessagePack` protocol, would be as follows:

```
var connection = new signalR.HubConnectionBuilder()
    .withUrl('/chat')
    .withHubProtocol(new signalR.protocols.msgpack.
    MessagePackHubProtocol())
    .build();
```

If you chose to use `MessagePack`, you also need to add support for it when you register SignalR services:

```
services
    .AddSignalR()
    .AddMessagePackProtocol();
```

Now that we've seen how we can start a conversation, let's look at the SignalR context, where we can get information from the current SignalR session.

Exploring the SignalR context

The SignalR context helps us to understand where we are and who is making the request. It is made available through the `Context` property of the `Hub` class. In it, you will find the following properties:

- `Connection` (`HubConnectionContext`): This is low-level connection information; you can get a reference to the current `HttpContext` from it (`GetHttpContext()`) as well as metadata stuff (`Metadata`) and it is possible to terminate the connection (`Abort()`).
- `ConnectionId` (`string`): This is the one and only connection ID that uniquely identifies a client on this hub.
- `User` (`ClaimsPrincipal`): This is the current user (useful if using authentication) and all of its claims.

The `Context` property is available when any of the `hub` methods is called, including `OnConnectedAsync` and `OnDisconnectedAsync`. Do not forget that for a context, a user is always identified by its `ConnectionId`; only if you use authentication will it also be associated with a username (`User.Identity.Name`).

And if we need to pass arbitrary parameters to the hub? Up next!

Using the query string

Any query string parameters passed on the URL (for example, `"/chat?key=value"`) can be accessed on the server side through the `Query` collection of `Request`:

```
var value = Context.GetHttpContext().Request.
Query["key"].SingleOrDefault();
```

Now, let's find out to what entities a message can be sent out to.

Knowing the message targets

A SignalR message can be sent to any of the following:

- **All**: All connected clients will receive it
- **Group**: Only clients in a certain group will receive it; groups are identified by a name
- **Group Except**: All clients in a certain group except certain clients, identified by their connection IDs
- **Client**: Only a specific client, identified by its connection ID

Clients are identified by a connection ID, that can be obtained from the `Context` property of the `Hub` class:

```
var connectionId = this.Context.ConnectionId;
```

Users can be added to any number of groups (and removed as well, of course):

```
await this.Groups.AddAsync(this.Context.ConnectionId, "MyFriends");
await this.Groups.RemoveAsync(this.Connection.ConnectionId,
"MyExFriends");
```

To send a message to a group, replace the `All` property by a `Group` call:

```
await this.Clients.Group("MyFriends").InvokeAsync("Send", message);
```

Or, similarly, to a specific client use the following:

```
await
this.Clients.Client(this.Context.ConnectionId).InvokeAsync("Send",
message);
```

Groups are maintained internally by SignalR, but, of course, nothing prevents you from having your own helper structures. This is how:

- To send messages to all connected clients (to the hub), you do this:

  ```
  await this.Clients.All.SendAsync("message", message);
  ```

- To send messages to just a specific client, identified by its connection ID, use the following:

  ```
  await
  this.Clients.Client("<connectionid>").SendAsync("message",
  message);
  ```

- To a named group, we can use this:

  ```
  await this.Clients.Group("MyFriends").SendAsync("message",
  message);
  ```

- Or simply to groups, the following can be used:

  ```
  await this.Clients.Groups("MyFriends",
  "MyExFriends").SendAsync("message", message);
  ```

- To all members of a group except one or two connection IDs, we use the following:

  ```
  await this.Clients.GroupExcept("MyFriends", "<connid1>",
  "<connid2>").SendAsync("message", message);
  ```

What if we need to communicate to the hub from outside the web app? Well, that is the subject of the next section.

Communicating from the outside

As you can imagine, it is possible to communicate with a hub, meaning to send messages to a hub. There are two possibilities:

- From the same web application
- From a different application

Let's study each of these.

Communication from the same web application

It is possible to send messages into a hub from the outside of SignalR. This does not mean accessing an instance of, for example, the ChatHub class, but only its connected clients. You can do this by injecting an instance of IHubContext<ChatHub> using the built-in dependency injection framework, shown as follows:

```
public class ChatController : Controller
{
    private readonly IHubContext<ChatHub> _context;

    public ChatController(IHubContext<ChatHub> context)
    {
        this._context = context;
    }

    [HttpGet("Send/{message}")]
    public async Task<IActionResult> Send(string message)
    {
        await this._context.Clients.All.SendAsync("message", this
        .User.Identity.Name, message);
    }
}
```

As you can see, you are responsible for sending all of the parameters to the clients. It is also, of course, possible to send to a group or directly to a client.

Imagine you want to send a recurring message to all clients; you could write code like this in your `Configure` method (or from somewhere where you have a reference to the service provider):

```
public class TimerHub : Hub
{
    public async Task Notify()
    {
        await this.Clients.All.SendAsync("notify");
    }
}

//in Configure
TimerCallback callback = (x) =>
{
    var hub =
app.ApplicationServices.GetService<IHubContext<TimerHub>>();
    hub.Clients.All.SendAsync("notify");
};

var timer = new Timer(callback);
timer.Change(
    dueTime: TimeSpan.FromSeconds(0),
    period: TimeSpan.FromSeconds(1));
```

The preceding code shows a registration for `timerHub` and a `notify` event. When the event is raised, a message is written to the console. If an error occurs when starting the subscription, the error is also logged.

`Timer` will fire every second and broadcast the current time to a hypothetical `TimerHub` class. This `TimerHub` class needs to be registered as an endpoint:

```
app.UseEndpoints(endpoints =>
{
    endpoints.MapHub<TimerHub>("timer");
});
```

It also needs to be registered on the client side:

```
var notificationConnection = new signalR.HubConnectionBuilder()
    .withUrl('/timer')
    .withAutomaticReconnect()
    .configureLogging(signalR.LogLevel.Information)
    .build();
```

```
notificationConnection.on('notify', () => {
    console.log('notification received!');
});

notificationConnection
    .start()
    .catch((error) => {
        console.log(`Error starting the timer hub: ${error}`);
    });
```

Next, let's see how communication happens from a different application

Communicating from a different application

This is a different approach: we need to instantiate a client proxy that connects to the server hosting the SignalR hub. We need the `Microsoft.AspNet.SignalR.Client` NuGet package for this. `HubConnectionBuilder` is used to instantiate `HubConnection`, as can be seen in the following example:

```
var desiredProtocols = HttpTransportType.WebSockets |
HttpTransportType.LongPolling |
    HttpTransportType.ServerSentEvents;

var connection = new HubConnectionBuilder()
    .WithUrl("https://<servername>:5000/chat?key=value", options =>
    {
        options.Transports = desiredProtocols;
    })
    .WithAutomaticReconnect()
    .ConfigureLogging(logging =>
    {
        logging.SetMinimumLevel(LogLevel.Information);
        logging.AddConsole();
    })
    .AddMessagePackProtocol()
    .Build();

connection.On<string>("message", (msg) =>
{
    //do something with the message
});

connection.Closed += (error) =>
{
    //do something with the error
};
```

```
await connection.StartAsync();
await connection.SendAsync("message", message);
```

This example does several things:

- Defines the acceptable communication protocols (WebSockets, long polling, and server-sent events)
- Registers two event handlers (`Closed` and `On("message")`)
- Creates a connection, with reconnection, logging set to `Information` and to the console, using the `MessagePack` protocol, and passing a query string value of `"key"="value"`
- Starts the connection asynchronously
- Invokes the `Send` method on the hub, passing it a string message

This code can be called from any place that has HTTP access to the server hosting the SignalR hub. Notice the setting of the desired protocols and the `WithAutomaticReconnect` and `AddMessagePackProtocol` extension methods. The `AddConsole` extension method comes from the `Microsoft.Extensions.Logging.Console` NuGet package.

We've seen how to send messages to a SignalR hub from the outside of the app hosting it. The following topic explains how authentication works with SignalR.

Using user authentication

SignalR uses the same user authentication mechanism as the encapsulating web app, which means if a user is authenticated to the app, it is authenticated to SignalR. It is possible to send a JWT token upon each request too, and it's done like this:

```
var connection = new signalR.HubConnectionBuilder()
    .withUrl('/chat', { accessTokenFactory: () => '<token>' })
    .build();
```

Notice the `accessTokenFactory` argument; here, we are passing a lambda (it could be a function) that returns a JWT token. On the client code, if you are calling SignalR from an outside app, you need to do this:

```
var connection = new HubConnectionBuilder()
    .WithUrl("http://<servername>/chat", options =>
    {
        options.AccessTokenProvider = () =>
Task.FromResult("<token>");
    })
    .Build();
```

Where SignalR is concerned, the identity of users is dictated by their connection ID. So, depending on your requirements, you may need to build a mapping between this and the user IDs that your app uses.

So, we've seen how to enable authentication; let's see now how we can log the workings of SignalR.

Logging

Logging can help us to diagnose failures and know what is happening in the system in real time. We can enable detailed logging for SignalR in either configuration or through code. For the first option, add the last two lines to your `appsettings.json` file (for "`Microsoft.AspNetCore.SignalR`" and "`Microsoft.AspNetCore.Http.Connections`"):

```
{
    "Logging": {
        "LogLevel": {
            "Default": "Debug",
            "System": "Information",
            "Microsoft": "Information",
            "Microsoft.AspNetCore.SignalR": "Trace",
            "Microsoft.AspNetCore.Http.Connections": "Trace"
        }
    }
}
```

To the latter, add the configuration to the bootstrap code:

```
public static IHostBuilder CreateHostBuilder(string[] args) =>
    Host.CreateDefaultBuilder(args)
        .ConfigureWebHostDefaults(builder =>
```

```
        {
             builder
                .ConfigureLogging(logging =>
                {
                    logging.AddFilter("Microsoft.AspNetCore.SignalR",
                    LogLevel.Trace);
                    logging.AddFilter("Microsoft.AspNetCore.Http.
                    Connections", LogLevel.Trace);
                })
                .UseStartup<Startup>();
        });
```

Mind you, this is just for enabling the flags that make the code output the debugging information. Trace is the most verbose level, so it will output pretty much everything, including low-level network calls. To actually log, you need to add loggers, like the console, for server-side code, or your own custom provider (mind you, this is just a sample):

```
.ConfigureLogging(logging => {
    logging.AddFilter("Microsoft.AspNetCore.SignalR", LogLevel.Trace)
    logging.AddFilter("Microsoft.AspNetCore.Http.Connections",
    LogLevel.Trace);

    logging.AddConsole();
    logging.AddProvider(new MyCustomLoggingProvider());
})
```

For the client side, you need to register a custom function that takes two parameters:

```
function myLog(logLevel, message) {
    //do something
}

var connection = new signalR.HubConnectionBuilder()
    .configureLogging({ log: myLog })
    .withUrl('/chat')
    .build();
```

The first parameter, logLevel, is a number that represents one of the possible log levels:

- signalR.LogLevel.Critical (**5**)
- signalR.LogLevel.Error (**4**)
- signalR.LogLevel.Warning (**3**)
- signalR.LogLevel.Information (**2**)

- `signalR.LogLevel.Debug` **(1)**
- `signalR.LogLevel.Trace` **(0)**: everything, including network messages

The second parameter, `message`, is the textual message that describes the event.

In this section, we've seen how to enable logging in both the client and the server side, with different levels of granularity.

Summary

In this chapter, we saw that we can use SignalR to perform the kind of tasks that we used AJAX for—calling server-side code and getting responses asynchronously. The advantage is that you can use it for having the server reach out to connected clients on its own when it needs to broadcast some information.

SignalR is a very powerful technology because it essentially adapts to whatever your server and client support. It makes server-to-client communication a breeze. Although the current version is not release-quality, it is stable enough for you to use in your projects.

Some advanced aspects of SignalR, such as streaming or clustering, haven't been discussed, as these are more for a dedicated book.

We are reaching the end of this book, so, in the next chapter, we will have a look into some of the APIs that weren't covered in previous chapters.

Questions

You should now be able to answer these questions:

1. What are the two serialization formatters supported by SignalR?
2. What transports does SignalR support?
3. What are the benefits of the `MessagePack` protocol?
4. To which targets can we send messages?
5. Why would we restrict the transport to be used by SignalR?
6. Can we send messages to SignalR from outside the web application where it is hosted?
7. Can we use authentication with SignalR?

17
Introducing Blazor

This chapter will introduce Blazor, a new technology that made its debut in .NET Core 3. It is meant for building **user interface (UI)** applications that run on the browser using the same languages and **application programming interfaces (APIs)** that you would use on the server. This chapter will not be an in-depth guide to Blazor as that would potentially take a whole book, but it should be more than enough to get you started. Here, you will learn about the following:

- The different hosting models
- How components are created
- The life cycle of a component
- How binding works
- How to interact with JavaScript
- How to secure Blazor pages
- How to perform unit tests over Blazor components

Technical requirements

In order to implement the examples introduced in this chapter, you will need the .NET Core 3 **software development kit (SDK)** and some form of text editor. Of course, Visual Studio 2019 (any edition) meets all the requirements, but you can also use Visual Studio Code, for example.

You should have previously read Chapter 16, *Real-Time Communication*, for an understanding of SignalR.

The source code can be retrieved from GitHub at: `https://github.com/PacktPublishing/Modern-Web-Development-with-ASP.NET-Core-3-Second-Edition`.

Getting started with Blazor

Blazor is a whole new technology that was created by **Steve Sanderson,** the same guy who created **KnockoutJS** and **Node services**. It was meant to be a framework for allowing .NET Core to be used for creating UIs for the client-side web along with the server side. The way to do this was that .NET would be compiled into **WebAssembly,** a language that can be run on the browser, on the same interpreter that runs JavaScript. This allows you to write your UI components in Razor and your event-handling code in .NET, and also to reuse code that is written in .NET on both the server side and the client side. In a nutshell, the advantages of using Blazor are the following:

- You can use a good old strongly typed language such as C# (or any other supported by .NET Core) to build your web UI.
- Leverage the rich APIs exposed by the .NET Core framework and all of the available libraries.
- Reuse code between the different layers (client side and server side).

As with all ASP.NET Core elements, Blazor is available as source code from GitHub, at: `https://github.com/aspnet/AspNetCore/tree/master/src/Components`.

We'll start by exploring the available hosting models.

Hosting models

There are two basic hosting models in Blazor, as follows:

- **WebAssembly**: The .NET Core code is compiled into a web assembly and executed on the client, by the browser, by the same virtual machine that executes the JavaScript code, inside a **sandbox**. This means that all referenced assemblies need to be sent to the client, which poses challenges in terms of download size and security as the code can be disassembled on the client side. Because of the sandbox, there are some limits to what the application can do, such as opening sockets to arbitrary hosts.
- **Server**: The .NET Core code runs on the server and the generated code is transported to the client through SignalR. Since all code runs on the server, there are virtually no limits to what it can do.

The WebAssembly mode was the latest to be released to .NET Core but was the one that actually gained most people's attention. The reason is that it runs purely on the client side, in standards-compatible browsers. The following screenshot shows how this appears:

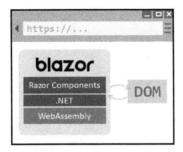

When using the WebAssembly hosting model, everything needs to be downloaded to the client. The process is the following:

1. Some JavaScript is loaded that executes a .NET emulator.
2. The project assembly and all of the referenced .NET **dynamic-link libraries (DLLs)** are loaded to the client.
3. The UI is updated.

The client can then disconnect from the server, as there is no more need for a permanent connection.

Keep in mind that because applications deployed using the WebAssembly hosting model run on the client browser, in a sandbox, this means that it may not be able to open arbitrary sockets to any host, which prevents it from running **Entity Framework (EF)** Core, for example. Only connections to the originating host are allowed.

With the Server model, Blazor does the following:

1. Renders some markup and some JavaScript
2. Uses SignalR to send events to the server
3. Processes them as per the .NET code in our app
4. Sends the response to the client
5. Updates the UI

Because only SignalR is used, there are no postbacks and no AJAX calls (unless, of course, SignalR falls back to AJAX, it normally uses WebSockets, where available). For all purposes, a Blazor app is just a **single-page application** (**SPA**). The following screenshot shows Blazor's Server hosting model:

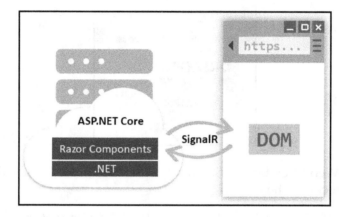

Image taken from https://docs.microsoft.com/en-us/aspnet/core/blazor

In the Server mode, Blazor needs a connection to a server, but on the WebAssembly mode, it works on the client side alone, after all the assemblies are downloaded to the client. In this case, it operates in a standalone manner in the browser without the need for a server, as you can see in the following screenshot:

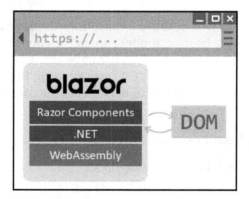

Image taken from https://docs.microsoft.com/en-us/aspnet/core/blazor

Essentially, the main advantage of Blazor is that .NET is used as the language to update the UI and perform any business logic, instead of JavaScript, and this is for both the client side and the server side. The process by which Blazor gets input from the UI, goes to the server, and then back to the UI is called a **circuit**.

Implementing Blazor

Depending on how you are hosting Blazor—through Server or WebAssembly models—the implementation is quite different. Visual Studio has support for creating Blazor Server or WebAssembly projects, as can be seen in the following screenshot:

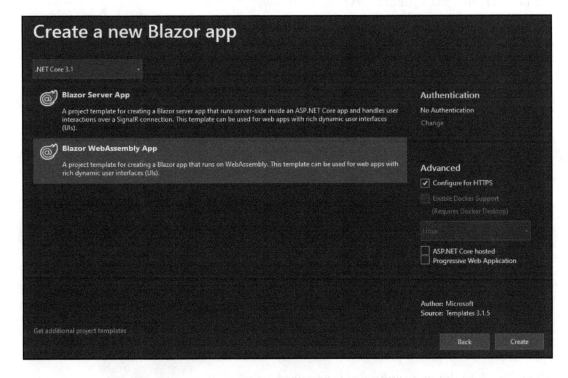

Next, let's see how this works, in the sections ahead.

Implementing Blazor Server

Blazor Server also has the `dotnet` tool, which can be used as follows:

```
dotnet new blazorserver
```

This will create a sample Blazor project in Server mode that communicates to a **representational state transfer** (**REST**) web API. This will be the same as if generating a Blazor project from Visual Studio and checking the **ASP.NET Core hosted** checkbox. If you have a look at the generated project, you will notice that, first, Blazor services need to be registered to the **dependency injection** (**DI**) framework, in ConfigureServices, as follows:

```
services.AddServerSideBlazor();
```

Here, you can also specify other options related to the SignalR service that Blazor's Server model inherently uses, as illustrated in the following code snippet:

```
services
    .AddServerSideBlazor()
    .AddHubOptions(options =>
    {
        //options go here
    });
```

I won't go into the details here, as they are exactly the same options that are described in Chapter 16, *Real-Time Communication*.

It is also necessary to register endpoints for the Blazor SignalR hubs, in Configure, so that ASP.NET Core knows how to process requests, as follows:

```
app.UseEndpoints(endpoints =>
{
    endpoints.MapBlazorHub();
    endpoints.MapFallbackToPage("/_Host");
});
```

The fallback to the page endpoint is required, as we will see.

 It is perfectly possible to mix **Model-View-Controller** (**MVC**), Razor Pages, and Blazor on the same project.

The browser must load a JavaScript file that includes all the logic to call SignalR and do all the **Document Object Model** (**DOM**) manipulations after the responses are received, as follows:

```
<script src="_framework/blazor.server.js"></script>
```

If we want, we can configure some aspects of SignalR. In that case, we need to tell Blazor not to automatically load the defaults, by setting `autostart` to `false` and calling the `Blazor.start` function explicitly, as illustrated in the following code snippet:

```
<script src="_framework/blazor.server.js" autostart="false"></script>
<script>
    Blazor.start({
        configureSignalR: function (builder) {
            builder.configureLogging("information");
        }
    });
</script>
```

The options we can set here are the same as described in Chapter 16, *Real-Time Communication*. There is another reason for preventing the automatic loading, which is to detect whether or not the browser supports Blazor WebAssembly (remember that it runs in the browser). If it doesn't, we can fall back gracefully.

A simple test could be this:

```
<script>
if (typeof(WebAssembly) === 'object' && typeof(WebAssembly.
instantiate) === 'function') {
    //the browser supports WebAssembly
    Blazor.start();
} else {
    location.href = 'BlazorNotSupported.html';
}
</script>
```

Implementing Blazor WebAssembly

For Blazor WebAssembly, the `dotnet` tool can be used to generate a basic project from a template, as follows:

```
dotnet new blazorwasm
```

A sample project is created that only has a client-side part and no server-side code. If you look at the code, you will see that it is quite different from what we have seen so far as there is no `Startup` class, but there is a `Program` one. This class essentially registers a root component named `app`. This component is then referenced in the `index.html` file located inside the `wwwroot` folder. There are no controllers whatsoever, only Blazor components, which we will talk about later on.

The browser must load two JavaScript files and run some code, as follows:

```
<script src="_framework/blazor.webassembly.js"></script>
<script>
//some code here
</script>
<script src="_framework/wasm/dotnet.3.2.0.js" defer=""
integrity="sha256-mPoqx7XczFHBWk3gRNn0hc9ekG1OvkKY4XiKRY5Mj5U="
crossorigin="anonymous"></script>
```

The first file instantiates the .NET Core emulator and the second loads the actual .NET Core JavaScript code. Notice the version number in the second file—it matches the .NET Core version we are loading. Then, it loads all the assemblies, as follows:

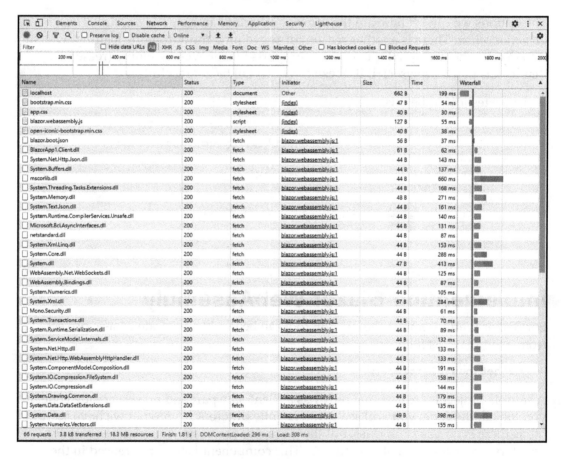

Let's now compare the two hosting models.

Comparing Server and WebAssembly

The Server and WebAssembly models are quite different, for the following reasons:

- The WebAssembly model requires that all code be downloaded to the client; this may cause some performance impact but, of course, can benefit from caching.
- WebAssembly requires a browser that can render `webassembly`, which most modern browsers do; it does not require .NET Core to be installed in the client machines, mind you.
- WebAssembly can work in a disconnected mode—other than, of course, downloading the application—whereas the Server mode cannot.

 See `https://caniuse.com/#feat=wasm` for browser support for WebAssembly.

Everything that we will talk about next will apply to both Server and WebAssembly unless explicitly stated otherwise.

Next, we will see the building blocks of Blazor, starting with pages.

Pages

Pages are special kinds of Blazor components that can be accessed directly by the browser (this is not quite true, but we can think of it like that). They have the `.razor` extension and, by convention, should be placed in a folder called `Pages` under the root folder of our app (or in a folder underneath it). The first line of the file should have a `@page` directive (similarly to Razor Pages)—something like this:

```
@page "/Home"
```

This may seem unnecessary, but this should contain the route that the page accepts, which is likely the same name of the file, without the `.razor` extension, but doesn't have to be so. If a page does not have a `@page` directive, it cannot be accessed by Blazor directly. We'll talk more about this when we discuss routing later on in the chapter.

All Blazor components (and a page is a component) must implement an `IComponent` interface, of which `ComponentBase` is the most obvious, already implemented choice. You do not need to declare this inheritance; it is done by default—all Blazor components implicitly inherit from `ComponentBase`. Pages are compiled to .NET classes, so you can always reference the type for a page by applying the `typeof` operator to the name of the file of which you want to obtain the type, as illustrated in the following code snippet:

```
@code
{
    var mainAppType = typeof(App);   //App comes from the App.razor
file
}
```

A page normally has markup, but it can also have other Blazor components that are declared as markup. We will now talk about the syntax of pages.

Razor syntax

The syntax is exactly the same as the one you would use in a Razor view, with some minor changes, detailed as follows:

- `@page`: Used for Blazor pages (not components)
- `@code`: For code blocks instead of `@functions`, which doesn't work here
- `@namespace`: For setting the namespace of the generated .NET class
- `@attribute`: For adding additional attributes that will be added to the generated class
- `@attributes`: For rendering a dictionary of key values as **HyperText Markup Language** (**HTML**) attributes in a tag
- `@typeparam`: For declaring generic/template components
- `@`: Syntax for .NET event handlers (`@onclick`, for example), not to be confused with JavaScript events

Additionally, it is to be noted that tag helpers do not work and Blazor components are to be declared as markup.

Other than this, all the other keywords and features of Razor pages also work inside Blazor pages, including @inject, @inherits, and @implements. It also has IntelliSense, which provides code completion, as illustrated in the following screenshot:

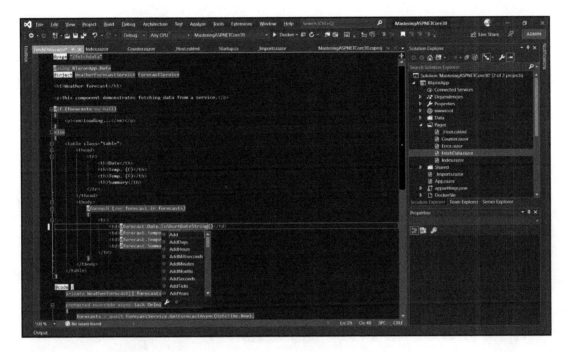

We'll carry on with the Blazor page construction, with class-related stuff.

Namespace imports

We need to import all namespaces for all types that we will be using in our Blazor pages, by adding @using declarations: if we don't add them, our types will not be found and therefore will not be usable. If we do not wish to do that on every page, we can add all @using declarations we want in a file named _Imports.razor that should be placed at the root of the web application, and it will automatically be loaded. The Blazor template already provides with some of the most common namespaces.

Partial classes

Because Blazor files are compiled to classes, you can also split the generated class into multiple files. For example, for a file called `SimpleComponent.razor`, we can also create a partial class called `SimpleComponent.razor.cs`, as follows:

```
public partial class SimpleComponent : ComponentBase
{
}
```

Provided the namespace and the class name are the same and you use the `partial` keyword, you can spawn classes across multiple files.

Pages as code

Pages do not have to be written as `.razor` files, with markup and code; they can just be implemented as .NET classes. All it takes is for them to implement `IComponent` (or inherit from `ComponentBase`). Instead of the `@page` directive, they need to have `[Route]` attributes, and instead of `@layout`, they can have a `[Layout]` attribute, which is what a Blazor page is turned into. The code can be seen in the following snippet:

```
[Route("/")]
[Layout(typeof(MainLayout))]
public partial class Index : ComponentBase
{
}
```

Blazor looks for page/component classes on the Bootstrap assembly and checks them for `[Route]` attributes when deciding to route. Just don't forget that Blazor pages/components need to have a public parameterless constructor.

Pages as components

Remember, a page is a component. So, if you want, you can include a page perfectly inside another page or component. Just include it as you would any other component, like this:

```
<MyPage />
```

Next, we will see how to add some structure to pages by means of page layouts.

Page layouts

Page layouts work in a similar way for Blazor as they do for Razor Pages and views. A Blazor page normally has a layout, and a layout needs to declare where to render the contents of its pages through a `@Body` declaration, as illustrated in the following code snippet:

```
@inherits LayoutComponentBase

<div>This is a layout</div>
<div>Body goes here:</div>
@Body
```

However, Blazor layouts do not support multiple sections, only a single one (the body).

Layouts are declared on the route (see next section), on the `_Imports.razor` file—a way to apply a layout for multiple pages—like this:

```
@layout MyLayout
```

Or, they are declared in the code file for the component, using the `[Layout]` attribute, as follows:

```
[Layout(typeof(MainLayout))]
```

Normally, a layout should inherit from `LayoutComponentBase`, but it is necessary to declare this; otherwise, being a component, it would inherit from `ComponentBase`. `LayoutComponentBase` has the advantage that it defines a `Body` property for the content, which you can render wherever you want. The layout is normally defined from the route (we will see this in a moment), but it also possible to define the layout for a specific page by applying a `@layout` directive, as follows:

```
@layout MyLayout
@page "/Home"
```

Finally, as with Razor layouts, Blazor layouts can be nested too, meaning that a layout can have a layout itself.

For the next subject, we jump from pages into global routing.

Routing

For the default Blazor projects—those generated by Visual Studio or the `dotnet` tool—you will notice that there is no entry page, no `index.html`, no controller, and no default Razor page. Because of that, when you access your app through your browser, you will end up on the fallback page, the one that I mentioned in the *Implement*ing Blazor Server section. If you look at this page, you will notice that it is essentially a simple Razor page with a `<component>` tag helper —one that was just introduced in .NET Core 3. This tag helper is rendering the `App` component, and if you look inside of the `App.razor` file, you will find some weird markup—something like this:

```
<Router AppAssembly="@typeof(Program).Assembly">
    <Found Context="routeData">
        <RouteView RouteData="@routeData" DefaultLayout=
        "@typeof(MainLayout)" />
    </Found>
    <NotFound>
        <LayoutView Layout="@typeof(MainLayout)">
            <p>Sorry, there's nothing at this address.</p>
        </LayoutView>
    </NotFound>
</Router>
```

This file is actually the main Blazor app, even though it merely does routing. In essence, it defines two possible routes, as follows:

- A `found` route (we'll see what that means next)
- A `not found` route

If you look at the `Router` root, it defines an `AppAssembly` attribute that points to the startup assembly; if you want, you can specify an additional `AdditionalAssemblies` attribute with a list of additional assemblies (Razor class libraries) containing additional Blazor components to load.

For the `found` route, what happens is the following:

1. Blazor finds a page that matches the request of **Uniform Resource Locator (URL)**, by looking at the `@page` directives.
2. A page layout is defined for it (in this case, `MainLayout`).
3. A view is instantiated, which is actually an instance of a class called `RouteView`, which is passed to all the route parameters (the `@routeData`).

So, in essence, we never actually directly access a Blazor page (`.razor`), but instead, we hit a fallback page, which, when it detects that the requested page (or one that answers to that URL) exists, displays it.

As for the `not found` route, the following applies:

1. A `LayoutView` is instantiated with a layout of `MainLayout`.
2. Default content is set with an error message.

It is, of course, possible to mimic the same behavior as for the `found` route—that is, to also display a specific page when the requested one is not found. Just add that page as a `<SomePage />` Blazor component.

In the next sections, we will talk about page routes and how to map and enforce route parameters.

Page routes

A page can accept many different routes, as shown in the following code snippet:

```
@page "/Home"
@page "/"
@page "/My"
```

When trying to find the right page from the request URL, Blazor does not look at the page's name (the one that ends with `.razor`), but instead, it looks at the directive or directives.

Route constraints

If you remember when we discussed routing in `Chapter 3`, *Routing*, we also talked about route constraints. If the page expects some parameter, you need to list it here as well, as follows:

```
@page "/Product/{id}"
```

But you also specify the type of this parameter so that if the supplied requested URL does not match with the expected URL, the request will fail. These are route constraints, and, if you recall, the syntax is as follows:

```
@page "/Product/{id:int}"
```

The out-of-the-box constraints are listed here:

- `bool`
- `datetime`
- `decimal`
- `double`
- `float`
- `guid`
- `int`
- `long`

Keep in mind that some of these, such as `float` and `datetime`, are culture-specific, so care must be taken to supply values that are valid according to the culture that the application is using. For example, if the application is using any variety of English, the numeric decimal separator is `.`, whereas if Portuguese is being used, it is `,`. Please refer to Chapter 13, *Understanding How Testing Works* for more information on route constraints.

A catch-all route

A catch-all route is one that is always met. It must be something like this:

```
@page "/{**path}"
```

Here, `path` does not serve any purpose; it is used just to indicate anything after the `/`.

Parameter binding from route

If you have a route with a parameter and you declare a parameter by the same name (case-insensitive), it is automatically bound to the route parameter's value, like this:

```
@page "/Search/{product}"

@code
{
    [Parameter]
    public string Product { get; set; }
}
```

Page navigation

Page navigation in Blazor is achieved through the `NavigationManager` service, which is normally obtained from DI (see the *DI* section). This service exposes as its main method the `NavigateTo` method that can take a relative URL, a Blazor route, and an optional parameter to force the loading of the page, as illustrated in the following code snippet:

```
[Inject]
public NavigationManager NavigationManager { get; set; }

@code
{
    void GoToPage(int page)
    {
        NavigationManager.NavigateTo($"Page/{page}", forceLoad:
false);
    }
}
```

Don't forget that the routes do not end with `.razor`!

Normally, we don't need to force the loading of the page; this means that content is loaded asynchronously by Blazor, using SignalR (when using the Server hosting model), and the URL is added to the history of the browser, but the browser does not load any new pages. If we do force it, then a full page load occurs.

The `NavigationManager` class exposes two properties, as follows:

- `BaseUri` (`string`): The absolute base **Uniform Resource Identifier (URI)** for the Blazor app
- `Uri` (`string`): The absolute URI for the current page

And also, the `LocationChanged` (`EventHandler<LocationChangedEventArgs>`) event is raised whenever we request to navigate to a new page by calling the `NavigateTo` method, with the `forceLoad` parameter set to `false`.

Then, there is the `<NavLink>` component. This component renders a link to a page for the provided content with a CSS `:active` class, depending on whether this link matches the current URL. It acts exactly like an `<a>` element, but it has the following additional property:

- `Match` (`Match`): How the link should be considered—with the prefix (`Prefix`), which is the default, or as a whole (`All`)

The `Match` property determines whether or not the link that is passed is perceived as active or not. For example, consider that the current URL is `http://somehost/someother` and the `href` property is `/someother/page/`. If the `Match` property is set to `Prefix`, then it will show as active, but if it is set to `All`, then it won't. The code can be seen in the following snippet:

```
<NavLink href="/someother/page" Match="All">
Jump to some other page
</NavLink>
```

There's nothing much about `<NavLink>`; it just exists to help us render the current page as active.

Building components

A component is just a file with the `.razor` extension and conforming to the Blazor syntax that does not have the `@page` directive, and therefore cannot be directly accessed. However, it can be included in other Blazor files, pages, or components.

All components implicitly inherit from `ComponentBase`, but you can modify this to other classes through the `@inherits` directive. Including a component is as easy as just declaring it as markup inside your file. For example, if your component is called `SimpleComponent.razor`, you would declare it as follows:

```
<SimpleComponent />
```

And that's it, but there is a new way to embed a Blazor component, which we will see next.

The <component> tag helper

There is a new tag helper, `<component>`, that allows us to embed a Blazor component in the middle of a Razor view. It was also covered in Chapter 9, *Reusable Components*, in the *Tag helpers* section, but for completeness, I will show an example here:

```
<component type="typeof(SomeComponent)" render-
mode="ServerPrerendered" param-Text="Hello, World"/>
```

If you remember, `SomeComponent` is just some `.razor` file that has a `Text` property.

A second option to render a component is through code, by using the `RenderComponentAsync` method from within a Razor Page or view, as illustrated in the following code snippet:

```
@(await Html.RenderComponentAsync<SomeComponent>(RenderMode.Static,
new { Text = "Hello, World" }))
```

The second parameter to `RenderComponentAsync` is optional, and it should be an anonymous object with properties named (and typed) after the properties that the component to render expects.

Blazor component properties

Blazor component properties are declared in the code as public properties and decorated with the `[Parameter]` attribute, as illustrated in the following code snippet:

```
@code
{
    [Parameter]
    public string Text { get; set; } = "Initial value";
}
```

Then, values can be set either using the markup or with the tag helper syntax, as illustrated in the following code snippet:

```
<!-- in a .razor file -->
<SomeComponent Text="Hello, World" />

<!-- in a .cshtml file -->
<component type="typeof(SomeComponent)" param-Text="Hello, World" />
```

Notice the `param-XXX` format of the attribute.

> Properties are case-insensitive—for example, `Text` is identical to `text`.

Properties are not parsed from string values; if the property is not a number, Boolean, or string, we must pass an actual object. For example, for a `TimeSpan` property, you must pass an actual `TimeSpan` object, as follows:

```
@code
{
    public class Clock : ComponentBase
    {
        [Parameter]
        public TimeSpan Time { get; set; }
    }
}

<Clock Time="@DateTime.Now.TimeOfDay" />
```

Or, you must pass a variable of the appropriate time, as follows:

```
@code
{
    TimeSpan now = DateTime.Now.TimeOfDay;
}

<Clock Time="@now" />
```

Attempting to pass a string will result in an error, as, unlike with Web Forms, no parsing will occur.

Cascading properties

A cascading property is always injected from the parent component into a child component. Cascading properties are parameters that do not need to be provided values explicitly, as they are set automatically by the framework from the containing component. They can be of any kind, including complex types. Imagine you have this:

```
<CascadingValue Value="Something">
    <ProfileComponent />
</CascadingValue>
```

Anything you put inside `<CascadingValue>` will receive the `Value` set, no matter how nested (components inside other components receive it too). Receiving properties are declared as follows—for example, inside the hypothetical `ProfileComponent` instance:

```
[CascadingParameter]
private string Text { get; set; } = "<not set>";
```

Notice that these parameters/properties should be set as `private` because there is no point in setting their values manually.

A cascaded property can, of course, be changed on a child component after the initial value is set, but it does not *cascade* back to the originator. The best way to achieve this is by declaring an event on the child component and hooking it from the parent component.

A parent locates the child cascaded parameters automatically by their matching type, but if you have multiple cascaded parameters of the same type, you may need to tell the framework which one maps to which one by setting a name, as follows:

```
<CascadingValue Name="FirstName" Value="Ricardo">
    <ProfileComponent />
</CascadingValue>
```

Their declaration should also appear, inside `ProfileComponent`, as follows:

```
[CascadingParameter(Name = "FirstName")]
private string FirstName { get; set; }

[CascadingParameter(Name = "LastName")]
private string LastName { get; set; }
```

You can also nest multiple `<CascadingValue>` components as follows, and all their values will be passed along to any child components:

```
<CascadingValue Name="FirstName" Value="Ricardo">
    <CascadingValue Name"LastName" Value="Peres">
        <ProfileComponent />
    </CascadingValue>
</CascadingValue>
```

If the cascaded property's value never changes, you may as well declare it as read-only; this has performance benefits, as Blazor does not have to hook to it and potentially update the UI whenever it changes. The code for this can be seen in the following snippet:

```
[CascadingParameter(Name = "FirstName", IsFixed = true)]
private string FirstName { get; set; }
```

This is achieved through `IsFixed`, which defaults to `false`.

Catch-all properties

If you supply values for parameters that do not exist, you get an exception at compile time unless you declare a catch-all property, one that will capture the values for any parameters that do not match existing parameters, shown as follows:

```
[Parameter(CaptureUnmatchedValues = true)]
public Dictionary<string, object> Attributes { get; set; } = new
Dictionary<string, object>();
```

With this approach, you can pass any number of parameters, and if they don't find a matching parameter, they just end up in InputAttributes. Also, you can pass all attributes to a component or HTML element. Each dictionary element is flattened and translated into a key-value pair by using the @attributes keyword, as follows:

```
<input @attributes="@Attributes" />
```

This is a generic way to pass any number of properties and not have to worry about defining properties for each of them.

Child content properties

Some components can have markup set inside of them, including other components; this is called child content. Here is an example of this:

```
<ContainerComponent>
<p>This is the child content's markup</p>
</ContainerComponent>
```

This content can be captured in a property for later use, as follows:

```
[Parameter]
public RenderFragment ChildContent { get; set; }
```

This property must be called ChildContent. The content of it will be the rendered markup, including that of any components that are declared inside the parent component. Now, in your component, you can output (or not, if you prefer) the child content wherever you want to, as illustrated in the following code snippet:

```
<pre>
<!-- child content goes here -->
@ChildContent
</pre>
```

Components with generic parameters

It is possible to declare generic (or templated) components—that is, components with generic parameters. This has the advantage of making your component exactly suit the type you want. For that, we declare the generic template parameter with the `@typeparam` declaration, and then declare one or more fields or properties as generic and having the same template parameter, as follows:

```
//MyComponent
@typeparam TItem

@code
{
    [Parameter]
    public IEnumerable<TItem> Items { get; set; }
}
```

One way to use this component is to declare a value for a generic property and let Blazor infer the generic parameter type, as illustrated in the following code snippet:

```
@code
{
    var strings = new [] { "A", "B", "C" };
}

<MyComponent Items="strings" />
```

Another way is to set the `TItem` property if the type cannot be inferred or we want to enforce a specific one, as follows:

```
@code
{
    var strings = new [] { "A", "B", "C" };
}

<MyComponent Items="strings" TItem="IComparable" />
```

Using this approach, the `Items` property will be prototyped as `IEnumerable<IComparable>`. Because arrays of strings are also arrays of `IComparables`, the types match.

 As of now, it is not possible to define constrained generic types.

Lists of components

When rendering lists of components whose content may change (adding, removing, or modifying an item of the list), it is important to tell Blazor what identifies each item of the list, to prevent unwanted behavior such as Blazor not knowing what to update. For this purpose, there is the @key attribute that should be applied to each list item, with a unique value, which may be a complex object. Let's see an example. Imagine you have a list that is bound to a list of orders, as follows:

```
@code
{
    foreach (var order in Orders)
    {
        <Order
            @key="order.Id"
            Product="order.Product"
            Customer="order.Customer"
            Date="order.Date" />
    }
}
```

Here, we are both passing to a hypothetical Order component the data it needs—Product, Customer, Date—and setting as its key the order ID, which means each component will have a unique identifier.

Locating components

Components have an implicit class associated with them, and this class is located in a namespace that matches the folder where they are located. For example, if SomeComponent.razor is located in a folder called Components under the root folder of the web app, we need to add a @using declaration before we can include it, as follows:

```
@using MyProject.Components
```

Components located in the same folder where they are used or in the Shared folder are automatically found, without the need for @using directives.

Rendering modes

A component can be rendered in one of three modes (RenderMode), which must be specified as follows:

- Static: Statically renders the Blazor component with any parameters that it takes when the page is loaded. This is the fastest option, but the component cannot raise events, which makes it impractical for any advanced use; however, this is the default.
- Server: Renders a page on the server and then sends it to the client only after the page is loaded; this is the slowest option and cannot use any parameters.
- ServerPrerendered: This is a trade-off between the two other modes; Blazor pre-renders the page and sends the component when the page loads, but then it is made interactive. It does not support parameters either.

The render mode is relevant when we talk about interacting with the DOM and raising events, which we will cover in a moment.

The component life cycle

Each component (and let's not forget that pages and page layouts are also components) goes through a life cycle, on which some virtual methods are called. These are, in order, the following:

1. SetParametersAsync: When parameters from the query string are set and any properties that require binding are bound; if you override this method, make sure you call the base implementation.
2. OnInitialized/OnInitializedAsync: When the component is being initialized, giving a chance to change/set properties for other components or DOM elements.
3. OnParametersSet/OnParametersSetAsync: When the component was initialized and all parameters from the component's parent have been set.
4. OnAfterRender/OnAfterRenderAsync: When the component has been rendered.

As you can see, some of these virtual methods have both a synchronous and an asynchronous version. It's better to override the asynchronous version.

The `OnAfterRender/OnAfterRenderAsync` method takes a `firstRender` parameter that indicates whether it's the first time that the component is about to render. This may be useful for you to do some sort of initialization.

There is also a `ShouldRender` method that deserves a mention. As you can imagine, this is called when Blazor needs to decide whether or not the component needs to update its UI; it takes no parameters and returns a Boolean. It's up to you to implement its logic. The `StateHasChanged` method always causes `ShouldRender` to be called, but the first time the component is being rendered (`OnAfterRender/OnAfterRenderAsync` being called with the `firstRender` parameter set to `true`) it is always so, regardless of what `ShouldRender` returns.

If a component implements `IDisposable`, its `Dispose` method is called at the end of its life cycle— for example, when it is removed from the UI, or when the connection is closed. But we must tell that to Blazor explicitly, as follows:

```
@implements IDisposable

@code
{
    public void Dispose()
    {
        //dispose the component
        //this method will be called automatically by the framework
    }
}
```

From the preceding code snippet, we can see that the method will automatically be called by the framework.

Reusing components in different projects

Blazor components can be reused across projects if they are created in a Razor class library project. This is a special project that can be created by Visual Studio or by using dotnet's `razorclasslib` template. This is described in Chapter 9, *Reusable Components*, but essentially, this is nothing more than a project file with the SDK set to `Microsoft.NET.Sdk.Razor`, as illustrated in the following code snippet:

```
<Project Sdk="Microsoft.NET.Sdk.Razor">
    ...
</Project>
```

Any `.razor` file contained in it can be accessed from another project that references that one; it's just a matter of adding an `@using` statement for the right namespace (take into account the root namespace for the project, plus any folders where the `.razor` file may be nested).

Accessing the HTTP context

Should you ever need to access the HTTP context from inside a component (or page, for that matter), all you have to do is inject the `IHttpContextAccessor` service into your class, like this:

```
@code
{
    [Inject]
    public IHttpContextAccessor HttpContextAccessor { get; set; }

    HttpContext HttpContext => HttpContextAccessor.HttpContext;
}
```

Refer to the *DI* section for more information on this.

Sample components

Let's consider the following component:

```
@using System
@using System.Timers

@implements IDisposable

@code
{
    private System.Timers.Timer _timer;

    [Parameter]
    public TimeSpan Delay { get; set; }

    [Parameter]
    public Action OnElapsed { get; set; }

    [Parameter]
    public bool Repeat { get; set; }

    protected override void OnParametersSet()
```

```
        {
            this._timer = new System.Timers.
            Timer(this.Delay.TotalMilliseconds);
            this._timer.Elapsed += this.OnTimerElapsed;
            this._timer.Enabled = true;

            base.OnParametersSet();
        }

        private void OnTimerElapsed(object sender, ElapsedEventArgs e)
        {
            this.OnElapsed?.Invoke();

            if (!this.Repeat)
            {
                this._timer.Elapsed -= this.OnTimerElapsed;
                this._timer.Enabled = false;
            }
        }

        void IDisposable.Dispose()
        {
            if (this._timer != null)
            {
                this._timer.Dispose();
                this._timer = null;
            }
        }
    }
```

This is a timer component—it fires after a certain amount of time. It exposes the following properties:

- `Delay` (`TimeSpan`): The time after which the timer fires.
- `OnElapsed` (`Action`): The callback to call when the timer fires.
- `Repeat` (`bool`): Whether or not to repeat the callback; the default is `false`.

We can see that the component exposes three parameters and implements the `IDisposable` interface privately. It overrides the `OnParametersSet` method because when it is called by the infrastructure, the properties will have already been set; it is a good time to make use of them—in this case, to instantiate the internal timer with the value of the `Delay` parameter. When the timer fires for the first time, the component decides whether or not to continue raising events, depending on whether or not the `Repeat` parameter is set. When the component is disposed of, it also disposes of the internal timer.

We can use this component as follows:

```
<Timer Delay="@TimeSpan.FromSeconds(20)" OnElapsed="OnTick"
Repeat="true" />

@code
{
    void OnTick()
    {
        //timer fired
    }
}
```

Let's now see another component, which only renders content for users having a certain role, as follows:

```
@code
{
    [Inject]
    public IHttpContextAccessor HttpContextAccessor { get; set; }

    HttpContext HttpContext => HttpContextAccessor.HttpContext;
    ClaimsPrincipal User => HttpContext.User;

    [Parameter]
    public string Roles { get; set; } = "";

    [Parameter]
    public RenderFragment ChildContent { get; set; }
}
@if (string.IsNullOrWhitespace(Roles) || Roles.Split(",").Any(role =>
User.IsInRole(role)))
{
    @ChildContent
}
```

This example injects the `IHttpContextAccessor` service, from which we then extract current `HttpContext`, and, from it, the current `User`. We have a `Roles` property and `ChildContent`. The `ChildContent` is only rendered if the current user is a member of any of the roles supplied in the `Roles` property or if it is empty.

As you can see, it's easy to build useful and reusable components! Now, let's see how we can work with forms—a very common need when we talk about the web.

Working with forms

Blazor has support for working with forms that are tied to models. There are a few components that know how to bind to properties of given types and display them accordingly as HTML DOM elements and a form component that takes care of binding to a model and validating it.

Form editing

For validating a model and allowing its edition, the component to use is `EditForm`. Its usage is shown in the following code snippet:

```
<EditForm
    Model="@model"
    OnSubmit="@OnSubmit"
    OnInvalidSubmit="@OnInvalidSubmit"
    OnValidSubmit="@OnValidSubmit">
    ...
    <button>Submit</button>
</EditForm>

@code
{
    var model = new Order(); //some model class
}
```

The `EditForm` component exposes two properties, as follows:

- `Model` (`object`): A **POCO** (short for **Plain Old Common Language Runtime (CLR) Object**) that contains the properties to bind to the form components; it is generally the only property that is needed.
- `EditContext` (`EditContext`): A form context; generally, it is not supplied explicitly—one is generated for us by the `EditForm` component.

And it also exposes three events, listed as follows:

- `OnInvalidSubmit` (`EventCallback<EditContext>`): Raised when the form was trying to submit but there were validation errors
- `OnSubmit` (`EventCallback<EditContext>`): Raised when the form was submitted explicitly, with no automatic validation
- `OnValidSubmit` (`EventCallback<EditContext>`): Raised when the form was submitted with success, with no validation errors

---

[636]

As you can see, `EditForm` expects `Model` (mandatory) and possibly one or more event handlers for the `OnSubmit`, `OnInvalidSubmit`, or `OnValidSubmit` events. Inside of it, there must be some HTML element that causes submission, such as a `button` or `input` with `type="submit"`—this is what actually will trigger the form submission. Mind you, the actual submission will be the action associated with either the `OnSubmit` or `OnValidSubmit` handlers.

Form context

The form context is an instance of `EditContext` and is exposed by a cascading property of the same name as the `EditForm` class. The context exposes the following properties and events:

- `Model` (`object`): The model
- `OnFieldChanged` (`EventHandler<FieldChangedEventArgs>`): An event that is raised when a field changes
- `OnValidationRequested` (`EventHandler<ValidationRequestedEventArgs>`): An event that raises when validation is requested
- `OnValidationStateChanged` (`EventHandler<ValidationStateChangedEventArgs>`): An event that raises when the validation state changes

The context also exposes a few methods that can be used either to force validation, check if the model has changed, or to get the validation errors, of which the most relevant are the following:

- `GetValidationMessages`: Gets all the validation messages or just for some field
- `IsModified`: Checks if the value for a given model property has changed
- `MarkAsUnmodified`: Marks a specific model property as not modified
- `NotifyFieldChanged`: Raises an event notifying about a field property change
- `NotifyValidationStateChanged`: Raises an event notifying about a validation state change
- `Validate`: Checks the current model values for validity according to the validation API in use

There are also some events too, listed as follows:

- `OnFieldChanged`: A model field value has changed.
- `OnValidationRequested`: Validation has been requested.
- `OnValidationStateChanged`: The validation state has changed.

The form context is available from either `EditForm` or from any form component located inside of it.

Form components

The form components included with Blazor are listed as follows:

- `InputText`: Renders `input` with `type="text"`
- `InputTextArea`: Renders `textarea`
- `InputSelect`: Renders `select`
- `InputNumber` (for `int`, `long`, `float`, `double`, or `decimal`): Renders `input` with `type="number"`
- `InputCheckbox`: Renders `input` with `type="checkbox"`
- `InputDate` (for `DateTime` and `DateTimeOffset`): Renders `input` with `type="date"`

These are really just convenient helpers that save us from writing some HTML. These should be placed inside `EditForm` and bound to the properties of the model. An example of this is shown in the following code snippet:

```
<EditForm Model="@model">
    <InputSelect @bind-Value="@model.Color">
        <option></option>
        <option>Red</option>
        <option>Green</option>
        <option>Blue</option>
    </InputSelect>
</EditForm>
```

In this example, `InputSelect` has a few options and is bound to the `Color` property of the model, which is probably one of these options.

Form validation

As of now, the only available validator is `DataAnnotationsValidator`, which uses the **Data Annotations API**. In order to have validation on your form, you need to declare a validator inside `EditForm`, like this:

```
<EditForm Model="@model">
    <DataAnnotationsValidator />
    . . .
</EditForm>
```

If you supply a handler for the `EditForm` instance's `OnSubmit` event, you will have to force the validation yourself by calling `EditContext.Validate()`, which will, in turn, trigger the Data Annotations API validation, or you can do it yourself.

And, should you wish to display a summary of the validation errors, you might as well include a `ValidationSummary` component, as follows:

```
<EditForm Model="@model">
    <DataAnnotationsValidator />
    <ValidationSummary Model="@model" />
    . . .
</EditForm>
```

Convenient as it is, there is not much you can do to customize how the error messages appear, other than tweaking the **Cascading Style Sheets** (**CSS**) classes in the generated markup. Of course, you can also handle the `OnInvalidSubmit` event on `EditForm` yourself and add your own messages for the invalid data, without using the `ValidationSummary` component.

Next, working with DOM elements!

Working with DOM elements

In this section, we will learn how to work with DOM elements: accessing them, binding to properties, adding events and handlers, and so on.

Two-way binding

One way to set a property to an element's value is to declare it in the element's attribute, like this:

```
<input type="text" name="name" value="@Name" />
```

The named element will receive the value of the `Name` property, but it will not *bind* the element to that property. However, the following property will bind:

```
<input type="text" name="name" @bind="Name" />
```

Notice the usage of the `@bind` keyword. It is used to tie the element to the passed property or field. By default, it hooks to the element's `value` attribute, because this is the usual one for DOM form elements (`input`, `select`, `textarea`). This is really two-way binding: when the value of the element's value changes, the value of the property also changes!

If we wish to bind to other properties of a component, we just specify its name after `bind-`, as follows:

```
<MyComponent @bind-Text="Name" />
```

If we need to specify a format for a property that you wish to bind to, there is a special syntax for that, illustrated in the following code snippet:

```
<input type="text" @bind="StartDate" @bind:format="yyyy-MM-dd" />
```

This example binds an input field to a property called `StartDate` using a specific format. The date will show according to that format.

Finally, we can specify an alternative event to bind to, as follows:

```
<input type="text" name="name" @bind-value="Name" @bind-
value:event="oninput" />
```

The default event for DOM form events is `onchange`, but other candidates are `oninput` or `onblur`. For custom events of your own components, you will have to specify your own event.

Event handling

You can also respond to events raised by the elements, as follows:

```
<button @onclick="OnButtonClick">Click Me</button>
@code
{
    void OnButtonClick(MouseEventArgs e)
    {
        //button was clicked!
    }
}
```

Other than adding a function to handle an event, we can also do it inline, which results in somewhat ugly code, as can be seen in the following snippet:

```
<button @onclick="(evt) => Console.WriteLine("Clicked")>Click
Me</button>
```

For preventing the default behavior of an event, there is a special keyword, shown in the following code snippet:

```
<button @onsubmit:preventDefault>Click me</button>
```

This can be made conditional too by using a Boolean property or a field (as in this example), as follows:

```
<button @onsubmit:preventDefault="_preventDefault">Click me</button>
```

And there is another one for stopping the propagation of an event, shown in the following code snippet:

```
<button @onclick:stopPropagation>Click me</button>
```

It also allows a conditional operator, shown in the following code snippet:

```
<button @onclick:stopPropagation="_stopPropagation">Click me</button>
```

It is possible to expose our own event handlers as parameters of components as well, by running the following code:

```
[Parameter]
public EventCallback<ChangeEventArgs> OnChange { get; set; }
```

There are two options declaring custom event handlers, as follows:

- `EventCallback<T>`: A strongly typed event handler; requires a delegate matching it
- `EventCallback`: A delegate that takes an `object` parameter

This will seem very similar to Web Forms to those who have used it! From the handler, we can do pretty much anything we want, such as accessing the values of properties and other components, calling back the server, and so on.

Blazor has classes for all events that can be raised by the browser DOM. Each of these contains information relevant to the event that occurred, as shown in the following table:

Type	Argument Class	DOM Events
Clipboard	`ClipboardEventArgs`	`oncut, oncopy, onpaste`
Drag and Drop	`DragEventArgs`	`ondrag, ondragstart, ondragenter,` `ondragleave, ondragover, ondrop, ondragend`
Error	`ErrorEventArgs`	`onerror`
General Purpose	`EventArgs`	`onactivate, onbeforeactivate,` `onbeforedeactivate, ondeactivate,` `onended, onfullscreenchange,` `onfullscreenerror, onloadeddata,` `onloadedmetadata, onpointerlockchange,` `onpointerlockerror, onreadystatechange,` `onscroll` `onbeforecut, onbeforecopy, onbeforepaste` `oninvalid, onreset, onselect,` `onselectionchange, onselectstart,` `onsubmit` `oncanplay, oncanplaythrough, oncuechange,` `ondurationchange, onemptied, onpause,` `onplay, onplaying, onratechange, onseeked,` `onseeking, onstalled, onstop, onsuspend,` `ontimeupdate, onvolumechange, onwaiting`
Focus	`FocusEventArgs`	`onfocus, onblur, onfocusin, onfocusout`
Input	`ChangeEventArgs`	`onchange, oninput`
Keyboard	`KeyboardEventArgs`	`onkeydown, onkeypress, onkeyup`

Mouse	MouseEventArgs	`onclick, oncontextmenu, ondblclick, onmousedown, onmouseup, onmouseover, onmousemove, onmouseout`
Mouse Pointer	PointerEventArgs	`onpointerdown, onpointerup, onpointercancel, onpointermove, onpointerover, onpointerout, onpointerenter, onpointerleave, ongotpointercapture, onlostpointercapture`
Mouse Wheel	WheelEventArgs	`onwheel, onmousewheel`
Progress	ProgressEventArgs	`onabort, onload, onloadend, onloadstart, onprogress, ontimeout`
Touch	TouchEventArgs	`ontouchstart, ontouchend, ontouchmove, ontouchenter, ontouchleave, ontouchcancel`

All of these classes inherit from `EventArgs`: for your event classes, consider inheriting too, and also adding the `EventArgs` suffix is considered a good practice too.

Referencing elements

An element or a custom component can be associated with a field or a property. This way, you can access its public API programmatically. The way to achieve this is by adding a `@ref` attribute to it that points to an appropriately typed field or property, as illustrated in the following code snippet:

```
<MyComponent @ref="_cmp" />

@code
{
    MyComponent _cmp;
}
```

If we are talking about a generic DOM element, the field or property must be typed as `ElementReference`. You can also declare parameter properties of this type and pass properties from one component to another; this way, you can pass DOM element references around. By the way, `ElementReference` does not expose any property or method other than `Id`. The only way to interact with the element it refers to is through JavaScript interoperability (there are no properties or methods that you can invoke on this object).

Be warned, though: `ElementReferences` are only set when the `OnAfterRender/OnAfterRenderAsync` methods are called; before that, they are just `null`.

Updating the state

After you've made changes to a component's properties or to properties bound to a component or DOM element, you need to tell Blazor to update the UI: for that, we have the `StateHasChanged` method. When it is called, Blazor will re-render the component, which can be the whole page or just a child component.

Moving on, let's now see how Blazor supports DI.

DI

Blazor, of course, has rich support for DI. As you know, this improves the reusability, isolation, and testability of our code. Service registration is done, as usual, in the `ConfigureServices` method of the `Startup` class (for the Server model) or in the `WebAssemblyHostBuilder.Services` collection of the `Program` class (for WebAssembly).

Injecting services

Blazor can use any services registered on the DI framework. These can be retrieved through a `@inject` directive on a `.razor` file, which works in exactly the same way as in a Razor view, as shown in the following code snippet:

```
@inject IJSRuntime JSRuntime
```

Or, on the code (a `@code` block or a partial class), you can also decorate a property with an `[Inject]` attribute to have it populated from the DI, as in this code snippet:

```
@code
{
    [Inject]
    IJSRuntime JSRuntime { get; set; }
}
```

In this case, properties can have any visibility (for example, public, private, or protected).

One thing that you must not forget is that, if you use partial classes for your pages, you cannot have dependencies injected on the constructor. Blazor demands a public parameterless constructor for its pages and components.

Registered services

Some services are already pre-registered for us, as follows:

- IJSRuntime: For a JavaScript interoperability check (Scoped for Server, Singleton for WebAssembly).
- NavigationManager: For navigation and routing (Scoped for Server, Singleton for WebAssembly).
- AuthenticationStateProvider: For authentication (Scoped).
- IAuthorizationService: For authorization (Singleton)—this is not specific to Blazor, of course.

You can access them by using either the @inject or the [Inject] approaches.

Scoped lifetime

There is a difference in the Scoped lifetime: in the Server hosting model, it maps to the current connection (that is, it lasts until the connection is dropped or the browser refreshes), whereas in WebAssembly, it is identical to Singleton.

Next, we will move on to understanding how to work with JavaScript.

JavaScript interoperability

Since Blazor runs on the browser, there are situations where we may need to execute a browser-native functionality. For that, there is no way to avoid JavaScript! There are two ways in which JavaScript and Blazor (.NET) can interoperate, as follows:

- .NET calls JavaScript functions.
- JavaScript calls .NET methods.

Calling JavaScript functions from .NET

Blazor can call any JavaScript function that is present on the hosting web page. It does this through the IJSRuntime object, which is automatically made available through the DI framework when you register Blazor.

For example, on the .razor file, add this code:

```
@inject IJSRuntime JSRuntime;

function add(a, b) { return a + b; }

@code
{
    var result = await JSRuntime.InvokeAsync<int>("add", 1, 1);
}
```

IJSRuntime allows you to invoke any function by its name, passing an arbitrary number of parameters and receiving a strongly typed result, by calling InvokeAsync. If a JavaScript function does not return anything, it can be called through InvokeVoidAsync, like this:

```
await JSRuntime.InvokeVoidAsync("alert", "Hello, World!");
```

Let's now see how we can do the opposite—that is, calling .NET code from JavaScript!

Calling .NET methods from JavaScript

From a web page, JavaScript can call methods on a Blazor component provided they are public, static, and decorated with the [JSInvokable] attribute, as illustrated in the following code snippet:

```
[JSInvokable]
public static int Calculate(int a, int b) { return a + b; }
```

The syntax to call an instance function (such as the one shown in the preceding code snippet) is this, synchronously:

```
var result = DotNet.invokeMethod('Blazor', 'Calculate', 1, 2);
```

Or, if you wish to do things asynchronously, execute the following code:

```
[JSInvokable]
public static async Task<int> CalculateAsync(int a, int b) { return a
+ b; }
```

```
DotNet
    .invokeMethodAsync('Blazor', 'CalculateAsync', 1, 2)
    .then((result) => {
        console.log(`Result: ${result}`);
    });
```

Here, `Blazor` is the name of my Blazor project/app; it does not have to be this.

If we need to call instance methods on some class, we need to wrap it inside of a `DotNetObjectReference` object and return it to JavaScript, as follows:

```
public class Calculator
{
    [JSInvokable]
    public int Calculate(int a, int b) { return a + b; }
}

var calc = DotNetObjectReference.Create(new Calculator());
await JSRuntime.InvokeVoidAsync("calculate", calc);
```

Then, on the JavaScript side, call `invokeMethod` or `invokeMethodAsync` to call public instance methods on the received object, like this:

```
function calculate(calc) {
    var result = calc.invokeMethod('Calculate', 1, 2);
}
```

So, in the previous code snippet, we are creating a .NET object of the `Calculator` type, through `DotNetObjectReference.Create`, and we are storing a reference to it in a local variable. This variable is then passed to a JavaScript function, by means of `JSRuntime.InvokeVoidAsync`, and inside this function (`calculate`), we finally use `invokeMethod` to call the .NET `Calculate` method with some parameters. A rather convoluted— but necessary—way!

Next, we will see how to maintain the state.

Maintaining state

In terms of state management, there are a few options, listed as follows:

- Using the DI-managed objects to keep the state
- Using the ASP.NET Core session (only for the Server hosting model)

- Using the state kept in HTML elements
- Saving the state on the browser

For the DI option, this should be simple: if we inject a container service that has either a `Singleton` or a `Scoped` lifetime, any data saved to it will live up to the boundaries of that lifetime. Session storage has also been described in Chapter 4, *Controllers and Actions*. Saving data in HTML elements is straightforward, and, as there are no postbacks and no need to repopulate the form elements, this is much easier to achieve than with traditional web programming.

Saving the state on the browser using `localStorage` or `sessionStorage` is a different subject. One approach is to use JavaScript interoperability to directly invoke methods in these browser objects—cumbersome, but possible. Let's say that we expose a simple set of functions, like this:

```
window.stateManager = {
    save: (key, value) => window.localStorage.setItem(key, value),
    load: (key) => window.localStorage.getItem(key),
    clear: () => window.localStorage.clear(),
    remove: (key) => window.localStorage.removeItem(key)
};
```

We can then call these functions using JavaScript interoperability very easily, as we've seen earlier, like this:

```
var value = await JSRuntime.InvokeAsync<string>("stateManager.load",
"key");
```

But there are some problems, listed as follows:

- We need to wrap the JavaScript calls ourselves.
- Any complex types need to be serialized to JSON previously.
- No data protection.

Another alternative is to use a third-party library to do the job for us. Microsoft has a NuGet library currently in preview called `Microsoft.AspNetCore.ProtectedBrowserStorage`, which not only provides access to the browser storage facilities but does so in a secure way, by leveraging the **Data Protection API**. This means that if you look at the values stored using the browser tools, you won't be able to make much out of them, as they are encrypted. Microsoft does warn that this library is still not ready for production use, but eventually, it will get there, so I'm going to show you how to use it.

So, after you add a reference to the
`Microsoft.AspNetCore.ProtectedBrowserStorage` preview NuGet package,
you need to make sure a script file is loaded to your browser every time you are
going to use it; just add the following code to the `_Host.cshtml` file, for example:

```
<script src="_content/Microsoft.AspNetCore.ProtectedBrowserStorage/
    protectedBrowserStorage.js"></script>
```

Now, you need to register some services to the DI framework (`ConfigureServices`),
as follows:

```
services.AddProtectedBrowserStorage();
```

And hey presto—you now have two additional services registered,
`ProtectedSessionStorage` (for the `sessionStorage` DOM object) and
`ProtectedLocalStorage` (for `localStorage`), both with the same public API,
which essentially offers three methods, as follows:

- `ValueTask SetAsync(string key, object value)`: Saves a value to
  the store
- `ValueTask<T> GetAsync<T>(string key)`: Retrieves a value from the
  store
- `ValueTask DeleteAsync(string key)`: Deletes a key from the store

When setting a complex value (a POCO class), it is first serialized to JSON. You can
now inject your desired service into your Blazor page or component and start using it
to persist data on the client side, in a safe manner.

> For more information about `sessionStorage` and `localStorage`,
> please see `https://developer.mozilla.org/en-US/docs/Web/API/`
> `Window/sessionStorage` and `https://developer.mozilla.org/en-`
> `US/docs/Web/API/Window/localStorage`.

The next section explains the recommended approach for making HTTP calls from a
Blazor app.

Making HTTP calls

One typical need in Blazor apps is to make HTTP calls. Think of AJAX-style
(`XMLHttpRequest` or `fetch`) operations, which are the bread and butter of SPAs. For
that, we need an HTTP client, and the most convenient one is `HttpClient`.

We first need to register the services for it in the `ConfigureServices` method (for the Server hosting model), as follows:

```
services.AddHttpClient();
```

Then, we can inject the `IHttpClientFactory` service in our Blazor app, and from it build `HttpClient`, as illustrated in the following code snippet:

```
[Inject]
public IHttpClientFactory HttpClientFactory { get; set; }

HttpClient HttpClient => HttpClientFactory.CreateClient();
```

There are different overloads to `AddHttpClient`, for when we need to configure a named client with specific settings—default headers, timeouts—and then create that client in `CreateClient`, but I won't go through that here.

`HttpClient` can send `POST`, `GET`, `PUT`, `DELETE`, and `PATCH` requests, but you will need to provide the content such as text, which means you probably will need to serialize some classes to JSON, as it is the most common format nowadays. One alternative you might consider is the `Microsoft.AspNetCore.Blazor.HttpClient` preview NuGet package that takes care of this, but of course it is still not in the final version, which means that it may still contain bugs or its API may change in the future, so be warned. This package exposes extension methods over `HttpClient` that already allow you to `POST`, `GET`, `PUT`, `DELETE`, and `PATCH` any content that will be serialized internally to JSON.

To serialize to JSON, the best approach is to use the new `System.Text.Json` NuGet package, a lightweight and more performant approach to JSON.NET (`Newtonsoft.Json`), by executing the following code:

```
var json = JsonSerializer.Serialize(item);
var content = new StringContent(json, Encoding.UTF8,
"application/json");
var response = await HttpClient.PostAsync(relativeUrl, content);
```

It couldn't be easier than this: we serialize some payload to JSON, then we create a string content message with it, and we post it to some URL asynchronously.

Applying security

Here, we will see how we can enforce security rules in a Blazor app. In this context, we will we cover authentication and authorization, the two main topics of security, and also briefly talk about **Cross-Origin Resource Sharing (CORS)**.

Requesting authorization

Blazor uses the same authentication mechanism as ASP.NET Core—that is, based on cookies: if we are authenticated to ASP.NET Core, then we are authenticated to Blazor. As for authorization, Blazor resources (pages) are protected by applying an [Authorize] attribute, with or without properties (roles or policies—policies are more generic). Attributes can be applied to a page either by applying an @attribute directive on a .razor file or on a .cs code-behind file, like this:

```
@attribute [Authorize(Roles = "Admin")]
```

 Mind you, it is pointless to apply [Authorize] attributes to components—they only make sense in pages.

If we want to enforce authorization rules, we must modify the App.razor file and use AuthorizeRouteView, as follows:

```
<Router AppAssembly="@typeof(Program).Assembly">
    <Found Context="routeData">
        <AuthorizeRouteView RouteData="@routeData" DefaultLayout
        ="@typeof(MainLayout)" />
    </Found>
    <NotFound>
        <LayoutView Layout="@typeof(MainLayout)">
            <p>Sorry, there's nothing at this address.</p>
        </LayoutView>
    </NotFound>
</Router>
```

If you compare this route definition with the previous one, you will notice that the only difference is that we swapped `RouteView` for `AuthorizeRouteView`. When using an `AuthorizeRouteView` component we can then use an `AuthorizeView` component, in our pages and components to selectively display the following states:

- `Authorized`: Content is displayed when the user is authenticated and authorized.
- `Authorizing`: For the WebAssembly model only, this content is displayed when the Blazor app is authorizing using an external endpoint.
- `NotAuthorized`: Content is displayed when the user is not authorized.

For example, have a look at the following code snippet:

```
<AuthorizeView>
    <Authorized>
        <p>Welcome, authenticated user!</p>
    </Authorized>
    <NotAuthorized>
        <p>You are not authorized to view this page!</p>
    </NotAuthorized>
</AuthorizeView>
```

The `AuthorizeView` component can also take the following as properties:

- `Roles`: A comma-separated list of roles to check for membership
- `Policy`: The name of a policy to check for authorization
- `Resource`: An optional resource

If none of these properties is supplied, it just means it requires an authenticated user.

The component uses the `IAuthorizationService.AuthorizeAsync` method as the source of truth for the `IAuthorizationService` security check being injected automatically by the DI framework.

Getting the current user

We can check the identity of the current user programmatically in one of three ways:

- By injecting `AuthenticationStateProvider` and checking its authentication state, as illustrated in the following code snippet:

```
@inject AuthenticationStateProvider
AuthenticationStateProvider
```

```
@code
{
    var authState = await AuthenticationStateProvider
    .GetAuthenticationStateAsync();
    var user = authState.User;

    if (user.Identity.IsAuthenticated)
    {
        //authenticated
    }
}
```

- By using the `<CascadingAuthenticationState>` cascading value component to inject an authentication state task as a cascaded parameter, as illustrated in the following code snippet:

```
<CascadingAuthenticationState>
    <Router AppAssembly="@typeof(Program).Assembly">
        <Found Context="routeData">
            <AuthorizeRouteView RouteData="@routeData"
             DefaultLayout="@typeof(MainLayout)" />
        </Found>
        <NotFound>
            <LayoutView Layout="@typeof(MainLayout)">
                <p>Sorry, there's nothing at this address.</p>
            </LayoutView>
        </NotFound>
    </Router>
</CascadingAuthenticationState>
```

- By injecting the `IHttpContextAccessor` service, extracting the current `HttpContext`, and from it, the current `User`, as illustrated in the following code snippet:

```
@code
{
    [Inject]
    public IHttpContextAccessor HttpContextAccessor { get;
set; }

    HttpContext HttpContext =>
HttpContextAccessor.HttpContext;
    ClaimsPrincipal User => HttpContext.User;
}
```

There's no problem with wrapping the whole `<Router>`; all we get is a cascaded parameter called `AuthenticationStateTask` in all of the apps, as illustrated in the following code snippet:

```
[CascadingParameter]
private Task<AuthenticationState> AuthenticationStateTask { get; set;
}

@code
{
    var authState = await AuthenticationStateTask;
    var user = authState.User;

    if (user.Identity.IsAuthenticated)
    {
        //authenticated
    }
}
```

The three approaches are very similar. The `AuthenticationState` type only exposes a `User` property that is of the `ClaimsPrincipal` type; this provides access to all the claims supplied by the authentication process.

Checking permissions explicitly

Once we get hold of `ClaimsPrincipal`, we can evaluate whether it matches a given policy by leveraging `IAuthorizationService`, which is available from the DI library, as follows:

```
@inject IAuthorizationService AuthorizationService

@code
{
    async Task<bool> IsAuthorized(ClaimsPrincipal user, string
     policyName, object resource = null)
    {
        var result = await AuthorizationService.AuthorizeAsync(
            user: user,
            policyName: policyName,
            resource: resource);

        return result.Succeeded;
    }
}
```

If you remember from `Chapter 11`, *Security*, the registered authorization handler will then be triggered and return the appropriate result.

Or, if we just need to check whether the current user belongs to a certain role, we just need to call `IsInRole`, as follows:

```
var isInRole = user.IsInRole(roleName);
```

Remember that roles are generally mapped to claims.

CORS

It is recommended that you disable CORS on the endpoints that you wish to make available to Blazor only, by adding the CORS middleware and applying the `[DisableCors]` attribute to the controllers, or by creating a proper policy. Please refer to `Chapter 11`, *Security* for more information.

Let's now see how we can unit test Blazor components.

Unit testing

We can use the unit test concepts and frameworks that we've seen in `Chapter 13`, *Understanding How Testing Works*, but Microsoft (again, with Steve Sanderson) has also been working on something to make our lives easier if we're dealing with Blazor.

Steve has a project, available on GitHub at `https://github.com/SteveSandersonMS/BlazorUnitTestingPrototype`, which contains a prototype of a unit testing framework that can be used to easily test Blazor components. It's called `Microsoft.AspNetCore.Components.Testing` and, unfortunately, it is still unavailable on NuGet, but you can clone the code and use it directly. Then, you can write code like this:

```
var host = new TestHost();

//Counter is a Blazor component
var component = host.AddComponent<Counter>();

//count is a named element inside Counter
var count = component.Find("#count");
Assert.NotNull(count);

var button = component.Find("button");
```

```
Assert.NotNull(button);

button.Click();
```

As you can see, it's very easy to use. Let's hope Steve and Microsoft make it available on NuGet soon for us to be able to use it more easily.

Summary

In this chapter, we've seen Blazor, the new and cool technology that Microsoft made available with .NET Core 3.0. It is still at its very early stages, and much can be expected of it in terms of features, community adoption, and libraries.

It is advisable to split work into components and to use page layouts, as is usual for Razor Pages and views.

In this chapter, we saw that we need to keep complex logic on the server. Remember that when the WebAssembly hosting model comes, all assemblies will need to be sent to the client, and thus will need to be kept small and with the most minimal logic possible.

Think about security from the start, and define policies and roles for the key parts of your app that you want to keep secure.

It is important to enforce route constraints, as they will keep your code more resilient and fault-tolerant. The next chapter will have a few new topics included in this version of ASP.NET Core.

You can see more examples for the Server hosting model of Blazor from Microsoft at `https://github.com/aspnet/AspNetCore.Docs/tree/master/aspnetcore/blazor/common/samples/3.x/BlazorServerSample` and also from the Blazor workshop (also from Microsoft) at `https://github.com/dotnet-presentations/blazor-workshop`.

Questions

You should now be able to answer these questions:

1. What is the difference between a page and a component?
2. What is the difference between the Server and WebAssembly hosting models?
3. Can we use tag helpers in Blazor pages?
4. Is it possible to access the containing web page from inside Blazor?
5. Does Blazor support DI?
6. Do Blazor page layouts support regions?
7. What is the difference between the different rendering modes of a component?

18
gRPC and Other Topics

In this chapter, we will cover some of the topics that didn't fit in earlier chapters of this book. This is because although they are important, there was no ideal location for them in previous chapters or they would require a mini-chapter of their own.

Some of these topics are quite important—namely, **Google Remote Procedure Call (gRPC)**, a new technology for cross-platform, cross-technology, strong-typed messaging. gRPC integrates well with the new ASP.NET Core endpoint routing system, which allows ASP.NET Core to serve pretty much any protocol you can think of. We will also cover the best practices for using **Entity Framework (EF)** Core with ASP.NET Core. Static files are also important because we can't live without them.

Essentially, the topics we will cover in this chapter include the following:

- Areas
- Static files
- Application lifetime events
- Conventions
- Embedded resources
- Hosting extensions
- URL rewriting
- Background services
- Using EF Core
- Understanding the gRPC framework
- Using HTTP client factories

Let's see what they are all about.

Technical requirements

In order to implement the examples introduced in this chapter, you will need the .NET Core 3 SDK and a text editor. Of course, Visual Studio 2019 (any edition) meets all of the requirements, but you can also use Visual Studio Code, for example.

The source code for this chapter can be retrieved from GitHub at `https://github.com/PacktPublishing/Modern-Web-Development-with-ASP.NET-Core-3-Second-Edition`.

Using areas for organizing code

An area is a feature that physically separates your app's content in a logical way. For example, you can have an area for administration and another area for the other stuff. This is particularly useful in big projects. Each area has its own controllers and views, which were discussed in `Chapter 3`, *Routing*.

In order to use areas, we need to create an `Areas` folder in our app at the same level as `Controllers` and `Views`. Underneath it, we will create a specific area folder—for example, `Admin`—and inside that, we need a structure similar to the one we have in the root—that is, with the `Controllers` and `Views` folders:

The use of areas in code

Controllers are created in the same way, but we need to add an `[Area]` attribute:

```
[Area("Admin")]
public class ManageController : Controller
{
}
```

 It is OK to have multiple controllers with the same name, provided they are in different namespaces (of course) and are in different areas.

The views for this controller will automatically be located in the `Areas/Admin/Views/Manage` folder; this is because the built-in **view location expander** (which you can read about in `Chapter 5, Views`) already looks at the folders under `Areas`. What we need to do is register a route for the area before the default route (or any bespoke one) in the `Configure` method:

```
app.UseEndpoints(endpoints =>
{
    endpoints.MapControllerRoute(
        name: "areas",
        pattern: "{area:exists}/{controller=Home}/{action=Index}");

    endpoints.MapAreaControllerRoute(
        name: "default",
        areaName: "Personal",
        pattern: "{area=Personal}/{controller=Home}/{action=Index}
        /{id?}");
});
```

The call to `MapControllerRoute` just makes sure that any path with a specified area that exists is accepted, and the call to `MapAreaControllerRoute` registers an explicit area named `Personal`, which is not really needed as the first call will cover it.

Routes now have an additional built-in template token—`[area]`—which you can use in your routes in pretty much the same way as `[controller]` and `[action]`:

```
[Route("[area]/[controller]/[action]")]
```

Let's see how we can reference areas in the built-in tag helpers.

Tag and HTML helpers

The included tag helpers (such as `<a>`, `<form>`, and more) recognize the `asp-area` attribute, which can be used to generate the correct URL to a controller under a specific area:

```
<a asp-controller="Manage" asp-action="Index" asp-
area="Admin">Administration</a>
```

However, this is not the case with HTML helpers, where you need to provide the route's `area` parameter explicitly:

```
@Html.ActionLink(
    linkText: "Administration",
    actionName: "Index",
    controllerName: "Manage",
    routeValues: new { area = "Admin" } )
```

This code produces a hyperlink that references, aside from the controller and action, the area where the controller is located—something such as `/Admin/Manage/Index`.

Let's now move on from areas to static files. We can't live without them, as we are about to find out!

Working with static files and folders

ASP.NET Core can serve static files—images, stylesheets, JavaScript scripts, and text—and it even respects filesystem folders. This is useful because they are extremely important as not all content is generated on the fly. Let's first focus on their configuration.

Configuration

The default template in Visual Studio includes the `Microsoft.AspNetCore.StaticFiles` NuGet package, which is also included in the `Microsoft.AspNetCore.All` metapackage. Also, the code to initialize the host—Kestrel or HTTP.sys—defines the root folder of the application as the root folder for serving static files (such as HTML, JavaScript, CSS, and images), as returned by `Directory`.

This is `.GetCurrentDirectory()`, but you can change that in the `Program` class, where the host is initialized, by using `UseContentRoot`:

```
public static IHostBuilder CreateHostBuilder(string[] args)
{
    Host.CreateDefaultBuilder(args)
        .ConfigureWebHostDefaults(webBuilder =>
        {
            webBuilder
                .UseContentRoot("<some path>")
                .UseStartup<Startup>();
        });
}
```

Mind you, there are actually two folders involved here:

- The root folder where the web application is hosted
- The root folder from which files are served

We will explore this further in a moment.

Allowing directory browsing

Directory browsing for the filesystem can be enabled for the whole app; it's just a matter of calling `UseDirectoryBrowser` without any parameters (in `Configure`):

```
app.UseDirectoryBrowser();
```

 Beware—if you do this instead of running the default action of the default controller, you will end up with a file listing the files on the root folder!

However, you may want to expose your root folder under a virtual path:

```
app.UseDirectoryBrowser("/files");
```

Notice the leading forward slash (/) character, which is required. Also, note that if you don't include support for static files—which we will cover next—you won't be able to download any of them and an HTTP `404 Error` message will be returned instead. This is *not* a physical location, but rather just the path where ASP.NET Core will show the files that are in the `wwwroot` folder.

Digging into this a little further, it is possible to specify what files are to be returned and how to render them; this is done through an overload of `UseDirectoryBrowser`, which takes a `DirectoryBrowserOptions` parameter. This class has the following properties:

- `RequestPath` (`string`): The virtual path.
- `FileProvider` (`IFileProvider`): A file provider from which to obtain the directory contents. The default is `null`, in which case `PhysicalFileProvider` will be used.

An example of configuring a root directory is as follows:

```
app.UseDirectoryBrowser(new DirectoryBrowserOptions
{
    RequestPath = "/resources",
    FileProvider = new
EmbeddedFileProvider(Assembly.GetEntryAssembly())
});
```

This very simple example exposes all of the current app's assembly-embedded resources under the `/resources` virtual path.

 You can serve multiple directory browsers with different options.

You can retrieve the folder where the ASP.NET Core application is installed by looking at `IWebHostEnvironment.ContentRootPath`. The default root directory (`wwwroot`) is available as `IWebHostEnvironment.WebRootPath`. It's OK to just use `Path.GetFullPath("wwwroot")`, which will get the full path to the `wwwroot` folder.

Serving static files

In order to serve (allow the download of) static files, we need to call `UseStaticFiles`:

```
app.UseStaticFiles();
```

Again, it is possible to set the virtual root to some arbitrary folder, as we saw in the previous section:

```
app.UseStaticFiles("/files");
```

However, you need to do more to actually be able to serve files.

There is another overload of `UseStaticFiles` that takes a `StaticFileOptions` parameter. It has the following properties:

- `DefaultContentType` (`string`): The default content type for unknown files. The default is `null`.
- `ServeUnknownFileTypes` (`bool`): Whether or not to serve files with unknown MIME types. The default is `false`.
- `ContentTypeProvider` (`IContentTypeProvider`): Used to get the MIME type for a given extension.
- `FileProvider` (`IFileProvider`): The file provider used to retrieve the file's content; by default, this is `null`, which means that `PhysicalFileProvider` is used.
- `OnPrepareResponse` (`Action<StaticFileResponseContext>`): A handler that can be used to intercept the response, such as setting default headers or plainly rejecting it.
- `RequestPath` (`string`): The virtual base path.

It is important that you use this overload if you are specifying a virtual path:

```
app.UseStaticFiles(new StaticFileOptions
{
    RequestPath = "/files",
    FileProvider = new
PhysicalFileProvider(Path.GetFullPath("wwwroot"))
});
```

For embedded files, use the following:

```
app.UseStaticFiles(new StaticFileOptions
{
    RequestPath = "/resources",
    FileProvider = new
EmbeddedFileProvider(Assembly.GetEntryAssembly())
});
```

You can have multiple calls to `UseStaticFiles`, as long as they have different `RequestPath` parameters.

For files, it is important to set the content (**MIME**) type; this is inferred from the file's extension and we can choose whether to allow the download of unknown file types (those without registered MIME types for their extension), as follows:

```
app.UseStaticFiles(new StaticFileOptions
{
    DefaultContentType = "text/plain",
    ServeUnknownFileTypes = true
});
```

Here, we are allowing the download of any files with unknown extensions and serving them with the `text/plain` content type. If `ServeUnknownFileTypes` is not set to `true` and you try to download a file like this, you will receive an HTTP `404 Error` message.

However, there is a class that knows about the common file extensions—`FileExtensionContentTypeProvider`—and it implements `IContentTypeProvider`, which means we can assign it to the `ContentTypeProvider` property of `StaticFileOptions`:

```
var provider = new FileExtensionContentTypeProvider();
provider.Mappings[".text"] = "text/plain";

app.UseStaticFiles(new StaticFileOptions
{
    ContentTypeProvider = provider,
    DefaultContentType = "text/plain",
    ServeUnknownFileTypes = true
});
```

As you can see, we are adding a new extension (`.text`) and its associated MIME type (`text/plain`) to the built-in list. If you are curious, you can iterate over it to see what it contains or start from scratch by calling `Clear`. The extensions need to have a `.` character and they are case-insensitive.

As with directory browsing, we can specify `IFileProvider`, which will be used to retrieve the actual file content, by setting the `FileProvider` property.

If we want to set a custom header for all the files or implement security, which is conspicuously absent from static file handling, we can use something along these lines:

```
app.UseStaticFiles(new StaticFileOptions
{
    OnPrepareResponse = ctx =>
    {
    ctx.Context.Response.Headers.Add("X-SENDER", "ASP.NET Core");
    };
});
```

Of course, we can also return an HTTP error code, redirect, or any other kind of operation.

Serving default documents

If we enable directory browsing, we may as well serve a default document, if it exists. For that, we need to add some middleware by calling `UseDefaultFiles` (always before `UseStaticFiles`):

```
app.UseDefaultFiles();
app.UseStaticFiles();
```

Needless to say, the default documents can be configured by passing an instance of `DefaultFilesOptions`. This class contains the following:

- `DefaultFileNames` (`IList<string>`): The ordered list of default files to serve
- `RequestPath` (`string`): The virtual path
- `FileProvider` (`IFileProvider`): The file provider from which to obtain the files list, which is `null` by default

In case you are interested, the default filenames are as follows:

- `default.htm`
- `default.html`
- `index.htm`
- `index.html`

An example of configuring a single default document is as follows:

```
app.UseDefaultFiles(new DefaultFilesOptions
{
    DefaultFileNames = new [] { "document.html" };
});
```

If a file called `document.html` exists in any browsable folder, it will be served and the folder's content will not be listed.

Applying security

As I mentioned earlier, security is absent from static file handling, but we can implement our own mechanism by using the `OnPrepareResponse` handler of `StaticFileOptions` as the basis, as follows:

```
app.UseStaticFiles(new StaticFileOptions
{
    OnPrepareResponse = ctx =>
    {
        //check if access should be granted for the current user and
file
        if (!AccessIsGranted(ctx.File, ctx.Context.User))
        {
            ctx.Context.Response.StatusCode = (int) HttpStatusCode.
            Forbidden;
            ctx.Context.Abort();
        }
    };
});
```

If you want to serve files from outside the `wwwroot` folder, pass a custom `IFileProvider` property—perhaps an instance of `PhysicalFileProvider` that is set to use a different root.

File providers

ASP.NET Core includes the following file providers, which are implementations of `IFileProvider`:

- `PhysicalFileProvider`: Looks up physical files on the filesystem
- `EmbeddedFileProvider`: Used to access files embedded in assemblies and is case-sensitive

- `ManifestEmbeddedFileProvider`: Uses a manifest compiled in the assembly to reconstruct the original paths of the embedded files when they were embedded into the assembly
- `CompositeFileProvider`: Combines multiple file providers
- `NullFileProvider`: Always returns `null`

A file provider (the `IFileProvider` implementation) is responsible for the following:

- Returning the list of files for a given folder (`GetDirectoryContents`)
- Returning information for a named file inside a folder (`GetFileInfo`)
- Getting a notification when a file mask (files inside folders) changes (`Watch`)

How exactly this is implemented is up to the provider and may even only occur virtually.

As you can see, there are two providers that work with embedded files. The difference between the two is that `ManifestEmbeddedFileProvider` respects the structure of the filesystem with full fidelity at the time the assembly got to build and allows us to properly enumerate **directories**. It is also preferred over `EmbeddedFileProvider`.

Let's now move on from physical files to application events.

Application lifetime events

ASP.NET Core exposes events for the whole application life cycle. You can hook up to these events to be notified of when they are about to happen. These events are called by the host with the use of the application (`IHostLifetime`), which was explained in Chapter 1, *Getting Started with ASP.NET Core*. The entry point to this is the `IHostApplicationLifetime` interface, which you can get from the dependency injection framework. It exposes the following properties:

- `ApplicationStarted` (`CancellationToken`): Raised when the host is fully started and is ready to wait for requests.
- `ApplicationStopping` (`CancellationToken`): Raised when the application is about to stop in what is known as a graceful shutdown. Some requests may still be in process.
- `ApplicationStopped` (`CancellationToken`): Raised when the application is fully stopped.

Each of these is a `CancellationToken` property, which means that it can be passed along any methods that take this kind of parameter, but, more interestingly, it means that we can add our own handlers to it:

```
public void Configure(IApplicationBuilder app, IWebHostEnvironment
env, IHostApplicationLifetime events)
{
    events.ApplicationStopping.Register(
        callback: state =>
        {
            //application is stopping
        },
        state: "some state");

    events.ApplicationStarted.Register(state =>
    {
        //application started
        var appParameter = state as IApplicationBuilder;
    }, app);
}
```

The `state` parameter is optional; if not supplied, the `callback` parameter does not take any parameters.

There are numerous ways to cause a graceful shutdown—one of them is by calling the `IHostApplicationLifetime` interface's `StopApplication` method, while another is by adding an `app_offline.htm` file. If this type of file is present, the app stops responding and just returns its contents with each request.

Finally, you should hook up to application events as soon as possible, either in the `Configure` method (as just shown) or during the application bootstrap process:

```
public static IHostBuilder CreateHostBuilder(string[] args) =>
    Host
        .CreateDefaultBuilder(args)
        .ConfigureWebHostDefaults(builder =>
        {
            builder.Configure(builder =>
            {
                var events = builder.ApplicationServices.
                GetRequiredService<IHostApplicationLifetime>();
                //hook to events here
            });
            builder.UseStartup<Startup>();
        });
```

If you want to have events at the start or end of a request, you're better off using a filter. You can read about filters in `Chapter 10`, *Understanding Filters*.

That's all for application events. Now, let's move on to assembly-embedded resources.

Working with embedded resources

Since the original versions of .NET, it has been possible to embed content within the assembly, including binary files. The reason for this is simple—it minimizes the number of files to distribute as they are included within the application binary. For that, we can use Visual Studio to set the **Build Action** property in the property explorer of Visual Studio:

Then, to retrieve an embedded resource, you will need an instance of either
`EmbeddedFileProvider` (discussed previously) or
`ManifestEmbeddedFileProvider`. These classes belong to the
`Microsoft.Extensions.FileProviders.Embedded` package and implement the
`IFileProvider` interface, meaning they can be used in any API that expects
`IFileProvider`. You can initialize each of them by passing it an assembly, as
follows:

```
var embeddedProvider = new ManifestEmbeddedFileProvider
(Assembly.GetEntryAssembly());
```

An optional base namespace can also be passed:

```
var embeddedProvider = new ManifestEmbeddedFileProvider
(Assembly.GetEntryAssembly(), "My.Assembly");
```

This base namespace is the one specified in the project's properties:

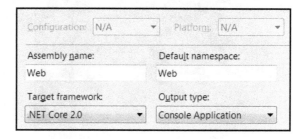

The difference between `EmbeddedFileProvider` and
`ManifestEmbeddedFileProvider` is that the latter needs to have the original file
path stored in the assembly, and you need to add this (in bold) to the `.csproj` file:

```
<PropertyGroup>
    <TargetFramework>netcoreapp3.1</TargetFramework>
    <GenerateEmbeddedFilesManifest>true</GenerateEmbeddedFilesManifest>
</PropertyGroup>
```

Just stick to `EmbeddedFileProvider` and don't worry too much about this.

It is up to you to know what is inside an embedded resource; for example, this could
be text or binary content. You should know that ASP.NET Core 3 also allows the
inclusion of static content from Razor class libraries, which might prove a better
solution. This was discussed in Chapter 9, *Reusable Components*.

The next section talks about the built-in infrastructure mechanisms for loading classes
automatically and for running background tasks.

Hosting extensions

We are now going to talk about a mechanism to automatically load classes from other assemblies and another one for spawning background threads automatically. The first is used by .NET to automatically register certain extensions (namely for Azure and Application Insights), and the second is for performing work in the background, without getting in the way of the web app. Let's start with hosting code from external assemblies.

Hosting startup

There is an interface, `IHostingStartup`, that exposes a single method:

```
public class CustomHostingStartup : IHostingStartup
{
 public void Configure(IWebHostBuilder builder)
 {
 }
}
```

This can be used at the host start up time to inject additional behavior into the host. `IWebHostBuilder` is exactly the same instance that is used in the `Program.Main` method. So, how is this class loaded? This is done in one of two ways:

- By adding a `[HostingStartup]` attribute at the assembly level. We can specify one or more `IHostingStartup`-implemented classes that should be loaded automatically from the application's assembly.
- By setting a value to the `ASPNETCORE_HOSTINGSTARTUPASSEMBLIES` environment variables, which can be a semicolon-separated list of assembly names and/or fully qualified type names. For each assembly name, the hosting framework will detect any `[HostingStartup]` attributes, and for the type names, if they implement `IHostingStartup`, they will be loaded automatically.

This is a great mechanism for loading classes, such as plugins, and in fact, this is how some Microsoft packages actually work, such as Application Insights.

Let's now see how we can run tasks in the background.

Hosting background services

The `IHostedService` interface defines a contract for a background task. By implementing this interface in a concrete class, we can spawn workers in the background of our app and we don't interfere with it. These services have the life cycle of the ASP.NET app.

There is a special template in Visual Studio for creating a worker service:

This is a special kind of project that you can't use for serving web content. If you are curious, it uses the following declaration:

```
<Project Sdk="Microsoft.NET.Sdk.Worker">
```

ASP.NET Core offers a convenience class, `BackgroundService`, from which you can inherit, instead of implementing `IHostedService`:

```
public class BackgroundHostedService : BackgroundService
{
    protected override Task ExecuteAsync(CancellationToken
    cancellationToken)
    {
        while (!cancellationToken.IsCancellationRequested)
        {
            //do something

            Task.Delay(1000, cancellationToken);
```

```
            }

        return Task.CompletedTask;
    }
}
```

`ExecuteAsync` is, of course, called automatically when the hosted service starts. It takes a `CancellationToken` parameter, which can be used to know when the hosted service has been canceled. Inside it, we generally execute a loop that runs forever (until `cancellationToken` is canceled). Here, we are waiting for 1,000 milliseconds, but the time you want to delay between loops is up to you and your requirements.

Hosted services need to be registered in the dependency injection framework in the early stage of bootstrapping—namely, in the `Program` class—for a **Worker Service** project:

```
public static IHostBuilder CreateHostBuilder(string [] args) =>
    Host
        .CreateDefaultBuilder(args)
        .ConfigureServices(services =>
        {
            services.AddHostedService<BackgroundHostedService>();
        });
```

However, they can also be used in a web application; in this case, it's all just a matter of registering our background service class as a singleton instance of `IHostedService` in `ConfigureServices`:

```
services.AddSingleton<IHostedService, BackgroundHostedService>();
```

Hosted services can have services injected into them through their constructor, just like any other service that is built from the dependency injection container. They have the same life cycle as the ASP.NET Core app and, even though they are registered in the dependency injection container (as transient instances), they are not really meant to be retrieved manually. Should you need to do so, please consider registering as singletons and having some registered service to pass data to and from.

The next topic is about ASP.NET Core model conventions, which can be used for default behaviors.

ASP.NET Core model conventions

ASP.NET Core has support for conventions, which are classes that implement well-known interfaces and can be registered to the application to modify certain aspects of it. The convention interfaces are as follows:

- `IApplicationModelConvention`: This provides access to application-wide conventions, allowing you to iterate over each of the following levels—that is, the controller model, action model, and parameter model.
- `IControllerModelConvention`: These are conventions that are specific to a controller, but also allow you to evaluate lower levels (the action model).
- `IActionModelConvention`: This lets you make changes to action-level conventions, as well as to any parameters of the actions (the parameter model).
- `IParameterModelConvention`: This is specific to parameters only.
- `IPageRouteModelConvention`: This lets us customize the default routes to Razor Pages (ASP.NET Core 2.x).
- `IPageApplicationModelConvention`: This allows the customization of Razor models.

From the highest to the lowest scope, we have the application, then the controller, then the action, and finally, the parameter.

Non-Razor conventions are registered through the `Conventions` collection of `MvcOptions`:

```
services
    .AddMvc(options =>
    {
        options.Conventions.Add(new CustomConvention());
    });
```

So, this goes for `IApplicationModelConvention`, `IControllerModelConvention`, `IActionModelConvention`, and `IParameterModelConvention`. The Razor conventions are configured on a similar collection in `RazorPagesOptions`:

```
services
    .AddMvc()
    .AddRazorPagesOptions(options =>
    {
        options.Conventions.Add(new CustomRazorConvention());
    });
```

It is also possible to apply custom conventions by having a custom attribute implement one of the convention interfaces and applying it at the correct level:

- `IControllerModelConvention`: The controller class
- `IActionModelConvention`: The action method
- `IParameterModelConvention`: The action method parameter

So, what can we do with custom conventions? Some examples are as follows:

- Register new controllers and add attributes to existing ones dynamically
- Set a route prefix for all or some controllers dynamically
- Define authorization for action methods dynamically
- Set the default location for parameters in action methods dynamically

If we want to add a new controller to the list of registered ones, we would do something like this:

```
public class CustomApplicationModelConvention :
IApplicationModelConvention
{
    public void Apply(ApplicationModel application)
    {
        application.Controllers.Add(new ControllerModel
        (typeof(MyController),
            new List<object> { { new AuthorizeAttribute() } }));
    }
}
```

To add a global filter, we can do the following:

```
application.Filters.Add(new CustomFilter());
```

If we want to have a `[Route]` attribute to all controllers with a certain prefix (`Prefix`), we would do the following:

```
foreach (var applicationController in application.Controllers)
{
    foreach (var applicationControllerSelector in
    applicationController.Selectors)
    {
        applicationControllerSelector.AttributeRouteModel =
            new AttributeRouteModel(new RouteAttribute("Prefix"));
    }
}
```

This could also go in an `IActionModelConvention` implementation but serves to show that you can apply conventions at all levels from `IApplicationModelConvention`.

Now, to add an `[Authorize]` attribute to certain action methods, ending in `Auth`, we do the following:

```
foreach (var controllerModel in application.Controllers)
{
    foreach (var actionModel in controllerModel.Actions)
    {
        if (actionModel.ActionName.EndsWith("Auth"))
        {
            var policy = new AuthorizationPolicyBuilder()
                .RequireAuthenticatedUser()
                .Build();
            actionModel.Filters.Add(new AuthorizeFilter(policy));
        }
    }
}
```

Finally, we can set the source for parameters to be the service provider whenever their name ends in `Svc`:

```
foreach (var controllerModel in application.Controllers)
{
    foreach (var actionModel in controllerModel.Actions)
    {
        foreach (var parameterModel in actionModel.Parameters)
        {
            if (parameterModel.ParameterName.EndsWith("Svc"))
            {
                if (parameterModel.BindingInfo == null)
                {
                    parameterModel.BindingInfo = new BindingInfo();
                }
                parameterModel.BindingInfo.BindingSource =
                BindingSource.Services;
            }
        }
    }
}
```

For Razor Pages, it is somewhat different as there is no relationship between the two convention interfaces; that is, they are used for totally different purposes. Two examples are as follows:

- Setting all the page model properties to be automatically bound to the service provider
- Setting the root of all the pages

For the first example, we need an `IPageApplicationModelConvention` implementation:

```
public class CustomPageApplicationModelConvention :
IPageApplicationModelConvention
{
    public void Apply(PageApplicationModel model)
    {
        foreach (var property in model.HandlerProperties)
        {
            if (property.BindingInfo == null)
            {
                property.BindingInfo = new BindingInfo();
            }
            property.BindingInfo.BindingSource =
BindingSource.Services;
        }
    }
}
```

What this does is it automatically sets the dependency injection as the binding source for any properties in a page model class; this would be the same as setting a `[FromServices]` attribute on them.

For setting a custom route prefix, an `IPageRouteModelConvention` implementation is used:

```
public class CustomPageRouteModelConvention :
IPageRouteModelConvention
{
    public void Apply(PageRouteModel model)
    {
        foreach (var selector in model.Selectors)
        {
            if (selector.AttributeRouteModel == null)
            {
                selector.AttributeRouteModel = new
AttributeRouteModel(new
```

```
            RouteAttribute("Foo"));
    }
    else
    {
        selector.AttributeRouteModel = AttributeRouteModel
            .CombineAttributeRouteModel(selector.
                AttributeRouteModel,
                new AttributeRouteModel(new RouteAttribute
                ("Foo")));
    }
    }
  }
}
```

Here, what we are doing is setting the [Route] attribute for all the Razor pages to start with Foo.

Next, we will see how to modify incoming requests.

Applying URL rewriting

As convenient as MVC routing is, there are, however, times when we need to present different URLs to the public, or vice versa—be able to accept a URL that the public knows about. This is where URL rewriting comes in.

URL rewriting is not new; it's been around since ASP.NET Web Forms, natively, and in a more advanced way, through the **IIS URL Rewrite** module (see https://www.iis.net/downloads/microsoft/url-rewrite). ASP.NET Core offers similar functionality through the Microsoft.AspNetCore.Rewrite package. Let's see how it works.

Essentially, URL rewriting is a feature by which you can turn request URLs into something different based on a set of preconfigured rules. Microsoft suggests some situations where this may come in handy:

- Providing unchanging URLs for resources that need to be changed, temporarily or permanently
- Splitting request across apps
- Reorganizing URL fragments
- Optimizing URLs for **Search Engine Optimization (SEO)**
- Creating user-friendly URLs

- Redirecting insecure requests to secure endpoints
- Preventing image (or other assets) hotlinking (someone referencing your assets from a different site)

The `Microsoft.AspNetCore.Rewrite` package can be configured through code, but it can also accept an IIS Rewrite Module configuration file (`https://docs.microsoft.com/en-us/iis/extensions/url-rewrite-module/creating-rewrite-rules-for-the-url-rewrite-module`). Since, after all, ASP.NET Core is cross-platform, Apache's `mod_rewrite` configuration (`http://httpd.apache.org/docs/current/mod/mod_rewrite.html`) is also supported, alongside IIS.

URL rewriting is different from URL redirect—in the latter, the server sends a `3xx` status code upon receiving a request that should be redirected, and it's up to the client to follow that request. In URL rewriting, the request is processed immediately by the server without another round-trip, but the application sees it differently, according to the rewrite rules. `Microsoft.AspNetCore.Rewrite` supports both situations.

To start with, there is the `RewriteOptions` class, which is used to define all the rules. There are a couple of extension methods for it:

- `AddRedirect`: Adds a URL redirect rule with an optional status code (`3xx`)
- `AddRewrite`: Adds a URL rewrite rule
- `Add(Action<RewriteContext>)`: Adds a delegate that can be used to produce a rewrite or redirect rule on the fly
- `Add(IRule)`: Adds an implementation of `IRule`, which defines a runtime rule, in a way that is similar to the `Action<RewriteContext>` delegate

Then, there are two extension methods that are specific to Apache and IIS:

- `AddApacheModRewrite`: Reads from a `mod_rewrite` configuration file
- `AddIISUrlRewrite`: Reads from an IIS URL Rewrite module configuration file

These two methods either take a file provider (`IFileProvider`) and a path or a `TextReader` instance that is already pointing to an open file.

Finally, there are two methods for forcing HTTPS:

- `AddRedirectToHttps`: Tells the client to ask for the same request, but this time using the HTTPS protocol instead of HTTP.
- `AddRedirectToHttpsPermanent`: This is analogous to the previous method, except it sends a `301 Moved Permanently` message instead of `302 Found`.

These methods will force a redirect to HTTPS if the request was for HTTP for any resource on the server. Let's look at URL redirection next!

URL redirection

First, let's look at an example of URL redirection. This example uses the `RewriteOptions` class:

```
services.Configure<RewriteOptions>(options =>
{
    options.AddRedirect("redirect-rule/(.*)", "redirected/$1",
    StatusCodes.Status307TemporaryRedirect);
});
```

The first parameter is a regular expression that should match the request and in it, we can specify captures (inside parentheses). The second parameter is the redirection URL; notice how we can make use of the captures defined in the first parameter. The third parameter is optional and if it is not used, it defaults to `302 Found`.

 Read about HTTP redirection in the HTTP specification at `https://www.w3.org/Protocols/rfc2616/rfc2616-sec10.html#sec10.3`.

URL rewriting

Next, we see what an internal URL rewrite is. An example of `AddRewrite` could be the following:

```
options.AddRewrite(@"^rewrite-rule/(\d+)/(\d+)",
"rewritten?var1=$1&var2=$2", skipRemainingRules: true);
```

Here, we are instructing `Microsoft.AspNetCore.Rewrite` to turn any path components after `rewrite-rule` that are made up of digits (this also uses regular expressions) into query string parameters. If a match for the first parameter is found, the third parameter (`skipRemainingRules`) instructs the rewriting middleware to stop processing any other rules and just use this one. The default for the `skipRemainingRules` parameter is `false`.

Runtime evaluation

The extensions that take `Action<RewriteContext>` or `IRule` actually do the same thing—the first action just wraps the passed delegate in `DelegateRule`, a specific implementation of `IRule`. This interface merely defines a single method:

```
void ApplyRule(RewriteContext context)
```

`RewriteContext` offers a couple of properties from which you can access the context and set the response:

- `HttpContext` (`HttpContext`): The current HTTP context.
- `StaticFileProvider` (`IFileProvider`): The current file provider to use to check for the existence of static files and folders.
- `Logger` (`ILogger`): A logger.
- `Result` (`RuleResult`): The rule evaluation result, which must be set. The default is `ContinueRules`, which instructs the middleware to continue processing other requests, and the other possible values are `EndResponse` (which does what you would expect) and `SkipRemainingRules`, which holds off on processing other rules and just applies the current one.

To use `IRule` or a delegate, we use one of the following:

```
.Add(new RedirectImageRule("jpg", "png"));
```

We can also use the following:

```
.Add((ctx) =>
{
    ctx.HttpContext.Response.Redirect("/temporary_offline",
     permanent: true);
    ctx.Result = RuleResult.EndResponse;
});
```

The `RedirectImageRule` rule looks something like this:

```
public sealed class RedirectImageRule : IRule
{
    private readonly string _sourceExtension;
    private readonly string _targetExtension;

    public RedirectImageRule(string sourceExtension, string
    targetExtension)
    {
        if (string.IsNullOrWhiteSpace(sourceExtension))
        {
            throw new ArgumentNullException(nameof(sourceExtension));
        }

        if (string.IsNullOrWhiteSpace(targetExtension))
        {
            throw new ArgumentNullException(nameof(targetExtension));
        }

        if (string.Equals(sourceExtension, targetExtension,
            StringComparison.InvariantCultureIgnoreCase))
        {
            throw new ArgumentException("Invalid target extension.",
            nameof(targetExtension));
        }

        this._sourceExtension = sourceExtension;
        this._targetExtension = targetExtension;
    }

    public void ApplyRule(RewriteContext context)
    {
        var request = context.HttpContext.Request;
        var response = context.HttpContext.Response;

        if (request.Path.Value.EndsWith(this._sourceExtension,
        StringComparison.OrdinalIgnoreCase))
        {
            var url = Regex.Replace(request.Path, $@"^(.*)\.
            {this._sourceExtension}$",
                $@"$1\.{this._targetExtension}");
            response.StatusCode =
StatusCodes.Status301MovedPermanently;
            context.Result = RuleResult.EndResponse;

            if (!request.QueryString.HasValue)
            {
```

```
        response.Headers[HeaderNames.Location] = url;
      }
      else
      {
        response.Headers[HeaderNames.Location] = url + "?" +
        request.QueryString;
      }
    }
  }
}
```

This class turns any request for a specific image extension into another. The delegate is purposely very simple as it merely redirects to a local endpoint, ending the request processing.

Redirecting to HTTPS

The extensions that redirect to HTTPS, if the current request was HTTP, are straightforward. The only options are to send a 301 Moved Permanently message instead of 301 Found or to specify a custom HTTPS port:

```
.AddRedirectToHttps(sslPort: 4430);
```

Next, we move on to platform-specific rewriting.

Platform-specific

AddIISUrlRewrite and AddApacheModRewrite have identical signatures—they both can take a file provider and a path or a stream to an existing file. Here is an example of the latter:

```
using (var iisUrlRewriteStreamReader =
File.OpenText("IISUrlRewrite.xml"))
{
    var options = new RewriteOptions()
        .AddIISUrlRewrite(iisUrlRewriteStreamReader)
}
```

 I have not covered the format of the **IIS Rewrite module** or the mod_rewrite configuration files. Please refer to its documentation for more information.

Next, we will see how to enforce URL rewriting.

Enforcing URL rewriting

In the `Configure` method, we must add a call to `UseRewriter`. If we don't pass a parameter, it will use the `RewriteOptions` action that was previously configured in the dependency injection, but we can also pass an instance of it here:

```
var options = new RewriteOptions()
    .AddRedirectToHttps();

app.UseRewriter(options);
```

Let's now see some practical advice on how to use EF Core with ASP.NET Core.

Using EF Core

EF Core is a popular **Object-Relational Mapper (ORM)** for retrieving and updating data. ASP.NET Core has good support for it, as you can imagine, as both are Microsoft tools. This section will present some common uses of EF Core with ASP.NET Core.

Make sure you first install the latest `dotnet-ef` global tool:

```
dotnet tool install --global dotnet-ef
```

Next, let's look at how to register contexts.

Registering DbContext

First, we can register a `DbContext` instance to the dependency injection framework:

```
services.AddDbContext<MyDbContext>(options =>
{
    options.UseSqlServer(this.Configuration.GetConnectionString
    ("<connection string name>"));
});
```

As you can see in this example, we have to set the provider and its connection string; otherwise, the context is pretty much useless. By default, the context will be registered as a scoped instance, which is generally what we want because it will be destroyed at the end of the request. After it is registered, it can be injected anywhere we want, such as in a controller. If you remember from Chapter 2, *Configuration*, GetConnectionString is an extension method that retrieves a connection string from the configuration from a well-known location—("ConnectionStrings:<named connection>").

Your DbContext-derived class must have a special public constructor, taking a parameter of the DbContextOptions type or DbContextOptions<T>, where T is the type of the context (in this case, MyDbContext):

```
public class OrdersContext : DbContext
{
    public OrdersContext(DbContextOptions options) : base(options) { }
}
```

Having this constructor is mandatory but you can have other constructors, even a parameterless one.

Using asynchronous methods

Whenever possible, use the asynchronous versions of the methods available (AddAsync, FindAsync, ToListAsync, and SaveAsync). This will improve the scalability of your app. Also, if you wish to pass data to a view, which has no chance of being modified, use the AsNoTracking extension method on the result query:

```
return this.View(await this.context.Products.AsNoTracking()
.ToListAsync());
```

This ensures that any records returned from the data source after they are instantiated are not added to the change tracker, which makes the operation faster and takes up less memory.

> Do have a look at Microsoft's documentation for asynchronous programming at https://docs.microsoft.com/en-us/dotnet/csharp/programming-guide/concepts/async.

Eager loading

When returning entities that have lazy associations, fetch them eagerly if you're sure that they will be used. This will minimize the number of database calls:

```
var productsWithOrders = await this.context.Products.Include(x =>
x.Orders).ToListAsync();
```

This is particularly important if you are returning data from a web API because once the entities are sent, they lose their connection to the database and therefore, it is no longer possible to load lazy data from it.

Pay attention, however—eager loading often results in INNER JOINs or LEFT JOINs being issued, which may increase the number of results that are returned.

Initializing a database

This is probably one of the tasks that needs to be done as soon as the app starts. The best way to do this is upon application bootstrap:

```
public static class HostExtensions
{
    public static IHost CreateDbIfNotExists(IHost host)
    {
        using (var scope = host.Services.CreateScope())
        {
            var services = scope.ServiceProvider;
            var logger =
services.GetRequiredService<ILogger<Program>>();

            try
            {
                var context = services.GetRequiredService
                <OrdersContext>();
                var created = context.Database.EnsureCreated();
                logger.LogInformation("DB created successfully:
                {created}.", created);
            }
            catch (Exception ex)
            {
                logger.LogError(ex, "An error occurred while
                 creating the DB.");
            }
        }
```

```
            return host;
        }
    }
```

This code creates a scope and requests `DbContext` from inside it; this way, we are certain that it will be disposed of properly at the end of the scope, thereby freeing up all resources. The `EnsureCreated` method will return `false` if the database already existed and `true` if it was created.

Just enqueue a call to this method when building the generic host:

```
public static void Main(string [] args)
{
    CreateHostBuilder(args)
        .Build()
        .CreateDbIfNotExists()
        .Run();
}
```

If you instead need to migrate a database to the latest migration version, just replace the call to `EnsureCreated` with `Migrate`:

```
context.Database.Migrate();
```

Without any parameters, it will migrate the database to the latest migration version. If your migration assembly is different than the application one, you must do this when registering the context:

```
services.AddDbContext<OrdersContext>(options =>
{
    //set options, like, connection string and provider to use
    options.MigrationsAssembly("MyMigrationAssembly");
});
```

This example declares `MyMigrationAssembly` to be the assembly that contains all of the migration code.

Showing migration errors and running migrations

When running in development mode, it is common to have a developer exception page that shows the error that occurred, with its stack trace and additional information. While this is useful, it does not include errors that may arise from database mismatches, such as missing migrations. Fortunately, ASP.NET Core includes a middleware component that captures those errors and presents a friendly error page to highlight them.

In order to use this database error page, we need to add a reference to the `Microsoft.AspNetCore.Diagnostics.EntityFrameworkCore` NuGet package. Then, add the middleware to the pipeline in the `Configure` method with the following call:

```
app.UseDatabaseErrorPage();
```

This would normally only be enabled for the development environment, and it can go together with `UseDeveloperExceptionPage` or other error handlers that you may have.

Now, you may also want to trigger the application of the latest migrations, probably to solve a related error; this middleware also allows you to do that. It makes an endpoint at `"/ApplyDatabaseMigrations"` available just for this purpose. You need to post a fully qualified name type of a context using a field name of `context`. The following is an example:

```
POST /ApplyDatabaseMigrations HTTP/1.1

context=Orders.OrderContext,Orders
```

This example uses a hypothetical context named `Orders.OrderContext` in the `Orders` assembly.

If, for any reason, you need to modify the endpoint, you can do so as follows:

```
app.UseDatabaseErrorPage(new DatabaseErrorPageOptions {
MigrationsEndPointPath = "/Migrate" });
```

This will use `"/Migrate"` instead of the default path.

Integrating an EF context with an HTTP context

Sometimes, you may need to get some information from the HTTP context when initializing the EF context. Why? Well, for example, this might be needed to get user-specific information from the request or the request domain, which can be used to select the connection string, in the case of multitenant scenarios.

In this case, the best approach is to get hold of the application service provider from the HTTP context, and the only way we can do this is by injecting the IHttpContextAccessor service into the constructor of DbContext:

```
public class OrdersContext : DbContext
{
    public class OrdersContext(DbContextOptions options,
    IHttpContextAccessor httpContextAccessor) :
        base(options)
    {
        this.HttpContextAccessor = httpContextAccessor;
    }

    protected IHttpContextAccessor HttpContextAccessor { get; }

    //rest goes here
}
```

Do not forget that we need to register our DbContext class by a call to AddDbContext. After we have IHttpContextAccessor, we can use it in OnConfiguring to get the current user:

```
protected override void OnConfiguring(DbContextOptionsBuilder builder)
{
    var httpContext = this.HttpContextAccessor.HttpContext;
    var userService = httpContext.RequestServices.GetService
    <IUserService>();

    var user = httpContext.User.Identity.Name;
    var host = httpContext.Request.Host.Host;

    var connectionString = userService.GetConnectionStringForUser
    (userService);
    //var connectionString = userService
    //.GetConnectionStringForDomain(host);

    builder.UseSqlServer(connectionString);
```

```
        base.OnConfiguring(builder);
    }
```

In this example, we are retrieving the user and the host from the current request. Then, we are using an imaginary service—`IUserService`—to retrieve the connection string for that user (`GetConnectionStringForUser`) or host (`GetConnectionStringForDomain`), which we then use. This is made possible because of the injected `IHttpContextAccessor` class, which needs to be registered by a call to `AddHttpContextAccessor` in `Startup.ConfigureServices`.

 Some people may object that this ties `DbContext` to ASP.NET Core. Although this is true, for the scope of this book, it makes total sense to do that.

Let's now see a more complex example of how we can build a fully functional REST service using EF Core.

Building a REST service

Here is a full example of a REST service that uses EF Core as the underlying API for data access. It features operations for retrieving, creating, updating, and deleting entities and is suitable for use as either a web API or in an AJAX-style web application:

```
[ApiController]
[Route("api/[controller]")]
public class BlogController : ControllerBase
{
    private readonly BlogContext _context;

    public BlogController(BlogContext context)
    {
        this._context = context;
    }

    [HttpGet("{id?}")]
    public async Task<ActionResult<Blog>> Get(int? id = null)
    {
        if (id == null)
        {
            return this.Ok(await this._context.Blogs.AsNoTracking()
            .ToListAsync());
        }
```

```
            else
            {
                var blog = await this._context.Blogs.FindAsync(id);

                if (blog == null)
                {
                    return this.NotFound();
                }
                else
                {
                    return this.Ok(blog);
                }
            }
        }

[HttpPut("{id}")]
public async Task<ActionResult<Blog>> Put(int id, [FromBody]
 Blog blog)
{
    if (id != blog.Id)
    {
        return this.BadRequest();
    }

    if (this.ModelState.IsValid)
    {
        this._context.Entry(blog).State = EntityState.Modified;
        try
        {
            await this._context.SaveChangesAsync();
        }
        catch (DbUpdateConcurrencyException)
        {
            return this.Conflict();
        }
        return this.Ok(blog);
    }
    else
    {
        return this.UnprocessableEntity();
    }
}

[HttpDelete("{id}")]
public async Task<IActionResult> Delete(int id)
{
    var blog = await this._context.Blogs.FindAsync(id);
```

```
            if (blog == null)
            {
                return this.NotFound();
            }

            this._context.Blogs.Remove(blog);
            await this._context.SaveChangesAsync();
            return this.Accepted();
        }

        [HttpPost]
        public async Task<ActionResult<Blog>> Post([FromBody] Blog blog)
        {
            if (blog.Id != 0)
            {
                return this.BadRequest();
            }

            if (this.ModelState.IsValid)
            {
                this._context.Blogs.Add(blog);
                await this._context.SaveChangesAsync();
                return this.CreatedAtAction(nameof(Post), blog);
            }
            else
            {
                return this.UnprocessableEntity();
            }
        }
    }
}
```

As you can see, this controller has several action methods—one for each HTTP verb (GET, POST, PUT, and DELETE). Here is how it works:

- The controller takes an instance of the DbContext-derived class in its constructor, which comes from the dependency injection framework.
- All methods are asynchronous.
- All methods follow conventions and their names match the HTTP verb they accept.
- All methods describe what they are returning in their signature.
- All calls to the DbContext-derived class are asynchronous.

- The `Get` method takes an optional `id` parameter, which, if supplied, issues a query for a single instance from that primary key. If this is not found, a `404 Not Found` result is returned; otherwise, a `200 OK` result is returned. If no ID is passed, then all entities are returned but are not tracked as they are not meant to be modified.
- The `Put` method takes an ID and an entity read from the body of the request; if the ID does not match the one that is read from the request, a `501 Bad Request` error is returned. The entity is then validated and, if considered invalid, a `422 Unprocessable Entity` result is returned. Otherwise, an attempt to mark it as modified and save it is done, but if the optimistic concurrency check fails, a `409 Conflict` result is returned. If all goes well, a `200 OK` result is returned
- The `Post` method takes an entity that is read from the body of the request. If this entity already possesses an ID, a `501 Bad Request` result is returned; otherwise, it tries to validate it. If it fails, `422 Unprocessable Entity` is returned. Otherwise, the entity is added to the context and saved, and a `201 Created` result is returned
- Finally, the `Delete` method takes the ID of the entity to delete and tries to load an entity from it; if one cannot be found, it returns a `404 Not Found` result. Otherwise, it marks the entity as deleted and saves the changes, returning a `202 Accepted` result.

That's it! This can serve as a general-purpose recipe for building a REST service using EF Core.

You can read more about API controllers and REST in `Chapter 8`, *API Controllers*.

Understanding the gRPC framework

gRPC is a relatively new framework for **Remote Procedure Calls** (RPC) that has bindings to .NET Core. Put simply, it allows structured, high-performance, type-safe communication between a client and a server in multiple languages (including C#, Java, JavaScript, C++, Python, Dart, and PHP). ASP.NET Core 3 includes an implementation of gRPC.

gRPC was created by **Google** but is now open source and uses modern standards, such as HTTP/2 for data transmission and **Protocol Buffers** for the serialization of content. This section does not aim to provide in-depth coverage of gRPC, but it should be enough to get you started!

First, in order to use it with ASP.NET Core, we need the NuGet `Grpc.AspNetCore` metapackage. Both Visual Studio and the `dotnet` tool can create a template project for gRPC:

```
dotnet new grpc
```

You can have a look at the generated code before we get started.

Interface definition

We first need to define an interface definition in gRPC's own definition language, from which stubs can be generated in the programming language we're interested in (in our case, C#). This includes the methods and types that will be sent back and forth. Here is an example of one such definition (`Greet.proto`):

```proto
syntax = "proto3";

option csharp_namespace = "Greet";

package Greet;

enum Ok
{
    No = 0;
    Yes = 1;
}

service Greeter
{
    rpc SayHello (HelloRequest) returns (HelloReply);
}

message HelloRequest
{
    string name = 1;
}

message HelloReply
```

```
{
    string message = 1;
    Ok ok = 2;
}
```

We can see a few things here:

- A C# namespace definition—Greet, in this case—that matches the package definition, which will be used for the generated code. We will look at this further in a moment.
- An enumeration—Ok—with two possible values. Notice how each of them must have a unique numeric value set.
- A service, or interface, definition—Greeter—with a single method of the RPC type—SayHello—taking a message as a parameter (HelloRequest) and returning a message as a response (HelloReply).
- Two message definitions—HelloRequest and HelloReply—each with some fields and assigned a unique number.

Each field in a message will be one of the following types (in parentheses is their corresponding .NET type):

- A message type
- An enumeration type
- double: double
- float: float
- int32, sint32, and sfixed32: int
- int64, sint64, and sfixed64: long
- uint32 and fixed32: uint
- uint64 and fixed64: ulong
- bool: bool
- string: string (up to 2^{32} UTF-8 characters)
- bytes: byte[] (up to 2^{32} bytes)

It is possible to include definitions from other files, too:

```
import "Protos\common.proto";
```

After we have an interface definition file that describes the services that we want to call, we must compile it so as to produce the source code for the language that we're interested in. As of now, we need to add the file manually to our `.csproj` file with an entry such as this for the server side:

```
<ItemGroup>
    <Protobuf Include="Protos\greet.proto" GrpcServices="Server" />
</ItemGroup>
```

The following entry is required for the client side:

```
<ItemGroup>
    <Protobuf Include="Protos\greet.proto" GrpcServices="Client" />
</ItemGroup>
```

The difference between the client- and server-side generated source code is in terms of what we want to do with it. Is the code meant to be used on an ASP.NET Core web app to host a service or is it for a client app that wishes to connect to it?

Messaging kinds

Imagine we have a **ping-pong** service that sends **pings** and receives **pongs**. gRPC defines four types of messaging:

- **Unary RPC**: The client sends a request to the server and gets a response back:

  ```
  rpc Ping(PingRequest) returns (PongResponse);
  ```

- **Server-streaming RPCs**: The client sends a request to the server and gets a stream from which it can read messages until there are no more messages:

  ```
  rpc LotsOfPongs(PingRequest) returns (stream PongResponse);
  ```

- **Client-streaming RPCs**: The client writes a sequence of messages to the server in a continuous stream:

  ```
  rpc LotsOfPings(stream PingRequest) returns (PongResponse);
  ```

- **Bidirectional-streaming RPCs**: Both sides send a sequence of messages using independent read-write streams:

  ```
  rpc BidiPingPong(stream PingRequest) returns (stream PongResponse);
  ```

Keep in mind that a full description of all of these messaging types is beyond the scope of this chapter, but you can find more information on the gRPC site at `https://grpc.io/docs/guides/concepts`.

Its declaration would be as follows:

```
syntax = "proto3";

option csharp_namespace = "PingPong";

package PingPong;

message PingRequest
{
    string name = 1;
};

message PongResponse
{
    string message = 1;
    Ok ok = 2;
};

enum Ok
{
    No = 0;
    Yes = 1;
};

service PingPongService
{
    rpc Ping(PingRequest) returns (PongResponse);

    rpc LotsOfPongs(PingRequest) returns (stream PongResponse);

    rpc LotsOfPings(stream PingRequest) returns (PongResponse);

    rpc BidiPingPong(stream PingRequest) returns (stream
PongResponse);
};
```

Next, we will see how to host a service.

Hosting a service

In the `Startup` class's `ConfigureServices` method, we must register the services needed for gRPC:

```
services.AddGrpc();
```

It is possible to configure some options for the endpoint, but let's leave this for now. Then, we need to create an endpoint for the gRPC service (or services) that we wish to expose:

```
app.UseEndpoints(endpoints =>
{
    endpoints.MapGrpcService<PingPongService>();
});
```

The `PingPongService` class is what we need to implement; it is the core of the service for which we specified the interface definition. We can implement it as follows:

```
public class PingPongService :
PingPong.PingPongService.PingPongServiceBase
{
    private readonly ILogger<PingPongService> _logger;

    public PingPongService(ILogger<PingPongService> logger)
    {
        this._logger = logger;
    }

    public async override Task<PongResponse> Ping(PingRequest request,
    ServerCallContext context)
    {
        this._logger.LogInformation("Ping received");

        return new PongResponse
        {
            Message = "Pong " + request.Name,
            Ok = Ok.Yes
        };
    }
}
```

You can see that the base class that we are inheriting from `PingPong.PingPongBase` defines the methods defined in the interface definition file as an abstract, so we need to implement them—hence the `override` keyword.

When you start coding this in Visual Studio, you will notice something weird—you do not have IntelliSense for some of the types (namely, the `PingPong` namespace and the `PingPong.PingPongBase` type). This is because they are generated at compile time from the definitions on the `PingPong.proto` file and therefore, the .NET equivalents are not yet available.

We can see that the `using` declaration directly matches `csharp_namespace` on the `.proto` file, and the `PingPong` static class (that's what it is!) comes from the name of the service on that file. `PingPongBase` was generated from the compiler because we set the `Server` option in the `.csproj` file.

We can see that the dependency injection works in pretty much the same way as we are used to. In this example, we are injecting a logger through the constructor. Actually, by default, a gRPC service is instantiated by the dependency injection framework as a transient, but we can register it manually to have a different lifetime (normally, with a singleton):

```
services.AddSingleton<PingPongService>();
```

Let's now see what is in the request context.

Request context

In the implementation of a gRPC method, the last parameter is always `ServerCallContext`. This allows us to get a lot of useful information from the server where we are running and the client that issued the request. For once, we can get hold of `HttpContext` for the current request by calling the `GetHttpContext` extension method, and from there, we can access all the properties and methods that we are familiar with. We also have the following:

- `Host` (`string`): The name of the host that was called
- `Method` (`string`): The name of the method that was called (the current one)
- `Peer` (`string`): The address of the client, in URI format
- `RequestHeaders` (`Metadata`): All the headers sent by the client
- `ResponseTrailers` (`Metadata`): All the headers that will be sent back to the client
- `Status` (`Status`): The status to send to the client when the operation finishes, which is normally set automatically

- UserState (IDictionary<object, object>): Data that can be used to pass information between interceptors (discussed shortly)
- WriteOptions (WriteOptions): A set of flags that can be used to tweak some aspects of the response (such as compression and response buffering)

The Metadata class is nothing more than a dictionary of keys and values and Status just holds together a status code (integer) and a detail (string).

Now, how can we intercept a message?

Interceptors

An interceptor can be used to perform operations before, after, or instead of a gRPC method. An interceptor must inherit from a base class, appropriately called Interceptor, which offers virtual methods for each of the messaging kinds. The following is a simple example:

```
public class LogInterceptor : Interceptor
{
    private readonly ILogger<LogInterceptor> _logger;

    public LogInterceptor(ILogger<LogInterceptor> logger)
    {
        this._logger = logger;
    }

    public override AsyncUnaryCall<TResponse> AsyncUnaryCall<TRequest,
    TResponse>(
        TRequest request,
        ClientInterceptorContext<TRequest, TResponse> context,
        AsyncUnaryCallContinuation<TRequest, TResponse> continuation)
    {
        this._logger.LogInformation("AsyncUnaryCall called");
        return base.AsyncUnaryCall(request, context, continuation);
    }

    public override TResponse BlockingUnaryCall<TRequest, TResponse>(
        TRequest request,
        ClientInterceptorContext<TRequest, TResponse> context,
        BlockingUnaryCallContinuation<TRequest, TResponse>
continuation)
    {
        this._logger.LogInformation("BlockingUnaryCall called");
        return base.BlockingUnaryCall(request, context, continuation);
    }
```

```
public override Task<TResponse> UnaryServerHandler<TRequest,
TResponse>(
    TRequest request,
    ServerCallContext context,
    UnaryServerMethod<TRequest, TResponse> continuation)
{
    this._logger.LogInformation("UnaryServerHandler called");
    return base.UnaryServerHandler(request, context,
continuation);
    }
}
```

This just logs when a request of the unary RPC type is received and when the response is about to be sent. We do not need to override any methods, just the ones that we're interested in. Each messaging type has a blocking and an async version, depending on how the request was issued. If we wish to return our own response, we just return whatever we want from it, rather than calling the base implementation. Because all of these methods are generic, we need to use reflection to find out what the exact parameters (request and response) are. Also, notice the presence of the `ServerCallContext` parameter in all the methods.

Interceptors are registered either by instance or type when the gRPC services are added to the dependency injection framework from a type:

```
services.AddGrpc(options =>
{
    options.Interceptors.Add<LogInterceptor>();
});
```

With an instance, we have the following:

```
services.AddGrpc(options =>
{
    options.Interceptors.Add(new LogInterceptor());
});
```

After this, let's check the listening options.

Listening options

When running in development mode, you may either need to listen on a different port or disable encrypted connections (TLS). You can do so in the `Program` class as follows:

```
Host
    .CreateDefaultBuilder(args)
    .ConfigureWebHostDefaults(builder =>
    {
        builder.ConfigureKestrel(options =>
        {
            options.ListenLocalhost(5000, o => o.Protocols =
            HttpProtocols.Http2);
        });
        builder.UseStartup<Startup>();
    });
```

This will have Kestrel listen on port `5000` with `HTTP/2` and without TLS.

Using HTTP client factories

We live in a world of microservices and, in the .NET world, these microservices are quite often invoked using APIs, such as `HttpClient`. The problem with `HttpClient` is that it is often misused because, even though it implements `IDisposable`, it is really not meant to be disposed of after each usage, but rather should be reused. It is thread-safe and you should have a single instance of it per application.

Disposing of it circumvents the original purpose of the class and, because the contained native socket is not immediately disposed of, if you instantiate and dispose of many `HttpClient` APIs in this way, you may end up exhausting your system's resources.

.NET Core 2.1 introduced `HttpClient` factories for creating and maintaining pools of pre-configured `HttpClient` APIs. The idea is simple—register a named client with a base URL and possibly some options (such as headers and a timeout) and inject them whenever needed. When it is no longer needed, it is returned to the pool but kept alive; then, after some time, it is recycled.

Let's look at an example. Suppose we want to register a call to a microservice that needs to take a specific authorization as a header. We would add something like the following to the `ConfigureServices` method:

```
services.AddHttpClient("service1", client =>
{
    client.BaseAddress = new Uri("http://uri1");
    client.DefaultRequestHeaders.Add("Authorization",
      "Bearer <access token>");
    client.Timeout = TimeSpan.FromSeconds(30);
});
```

The only mandatory setting is `BaseAddress`, but here I am also setting `Timeout` and a header (`"Authorization"`), for completeness. `<access token>`, obviously, should be replaced with an actual token.

If we need to use an instance of `HttpClient`, we inject `IHttpClientFactory` using the dependency injection and create a named client from it:

```
public class HomeController : Controller
{
    private readonly IHttpClientFactory _httpClientFactory;

    public HomeController(IHttpClientFactory httpClientFactory)
    {
        this._httpClientFactory = httpClientFactory;
    }

    public async Task<IActionResult> Index()
    {
        var client = this._httpClientFactory.CreateClient("service1");
        var result = await client.GetAsync("Process");
         //URL relative to the base address

        //do something with the result

        return this.View();
    }
}
```

The name passed to `CreateClient` must be the same name that was registered with `AddHttpClient`. Notice that we didn't dispose of the created client; this is not necessary.

When registering `HttpClient`, there is an overload of `AddHttpClient`, which also receives a parameter of the `IServiceProvider` type, which you can use to obtain services from the dependency injection framework:

```
services.AddHttpClient("service1", (serviceProvider, client) =>
{
    var configuration = serviceProvider.GetRequiredService
    <IConfiguration>();
    var url = configuration["Services:Service1:Url"];
    client.BaseAddress = new Uri(url);
});
```

In this example, I am retrieving the `IConfiguration` instance from the DI and obtaining a URL for the `service1` microservice, which I am using to set as the base address of `HttpClient`.

Another example is what if you need to pass information to `HttpClient` coming from the current user or the current context? In that case, the only way is to use a custom `DelegatingHandler` instance and leverage the `IHttpContextAccessor` service that we have mentioned quite a few times before. Some sample code, starting with `DelegatingHandler`, is as follows:

```
public class UserIdHandler : DelegatingHandler
{
    public UserIdHandler(IHttpContextAccessor httpContextAccessor)
    {
        this.HttpContext = httpContextAccessor.HttpContext;
    }

    protected HttpContext HttpContext { get; }

    protected override Task<HttpResponseMessage>
    SendAsync(HttpRequestMessage request,
        CancellationToken cancellationToken)
    {
        request.Headers.Add("UserId", this.HttpContext.User.
        Identity.Name);

        return base.SendAsync(request, cancellationToken);
    }
}
```

This class receives on its constructor an instance of `IHttpContextAccessor`, which is a service that can be used to obtain the current `HttpContext` class. On the `SendAsync` override, it adds a header with the content of the current username.

The `HttpClient` instance's factory registration, in this case, is done like this:

```
services
    .AddHttpClient("service1", client =>
    {
        client.BaseAddress = new Uri("http://uri1");
    })
    .AddHttpMessageHandler<UserIdHandler>();
```

The only difference is the call to `AddHttpMessageHandler` with the generic parameter of the class we just created.

As I mentioned in the beginning, the `HttpClient` instances returned by `IHttpClientFactory` are pooled and, after some time, they are recycled. What this actually means is that the internal `HttpMessageHandler` class that holds the native socket is kept alive and the socket is kept open for a period of time for performance reasons, after which it is disposed of and the socket is closed. When `HttpClient` is requested again, the socket is opened once more. It is possible to tune the period of time for which `HttpClient` is kept alive through the `SetHandlerLifetime` method:

```
services
    .AddHttpClient("service1", client =>
    {
        client.BaseAddress = new Uri("http://uri1");
    })
    .SetHandlerLifetime(TimeSpan.FromMinutes(5));
```

The default time is 3 minutes. Leaving it open for too long is not recommended because you may end up wasting resources if you do not need to send requests, and you may not detect changes in DNS configuration, such as the target host address changing. This needs to be chosen according to the use of the microservice. If it is used very frequently for a period of time, you may want to increase this. If you are unsure, just leave it as it is.

We have another option to use `HttpClient` with a client factory that consists of strongly typed clients. Essentially, this is just a class that takes `HttpClient` in its constructor and exposes some methods to retrieve data that comes from `HttpClient`. Let's imagine that we want to retrieve weather information from a city anywhere in the world.

Rather than implementing a method ourselves, we can use an existing one, such as **OpenWeatherMap** (`https://openweathermap.org`). OpenWeatherMap makes available a free REST API for developers that returns quite a lot of useful information in real time. In order to use this API, we need to write some classes to model the data that it sends:

```
public class OpenWeatherCoordinates
{
    public float lon { get; set; }
    public float lat { get; set; }
}

public class OpenWeatherWeather
{
    public int id { get; set; }
    public string main { get; set; }
    public string description { get; set; }
    public string icon { get; set; }
}

public class OpenWeatherMain
{
    public float temp { get; set; }
    public int pressure { get; set; }
    public int humidity { get; set; }
    public float temp_min { get; set; }
    public float temp_max { get; set; }
}

public class OpenWeatherData
{
    public OpenWeatherCoordinates coord { get; set; }
    public OpenWeatherWeather [] weather { get; set; }
    public string @base { get; set; }
    public OpenWeatherMain main { get; set; }
    public int visibility { get; set; }
    public OpenWeatherWind wind { get; set; }
    public OpenWeatherClouds clouds { get; set; }
    public OpenWeatherSys sys { get; set; }
    public int dt { get; set; }
    public int id { get; set; }
    public string name { get; set; }
    public int cod { get; set; }
}

public class OpenWeatherSys
{
```

```
    public int type { get; set; }
    public int id { get; set; }
    public float message { get; set; }
    public string country { get; set; }
    public int sunrise { get; set; }
    public int sunset { get; set; }
}

public class OpenWeatherClouds
{
    public int all { get; set; }
}

public class OpenWeatherWind
{
    public float wind { get; set; }
    public int deg { get; set; }
}
```

 Don't bother with all of these properties; they are required to fully map the information returned by OpenWeatherMap, but you can safely ignore most of it!

As for the service itself, we can represent it as follows:

```
public interface IOpenWeatherMap
{
    Task<OpenWeatherData> GetByCity(int id);
}
```

A possible implementation using `HttpClient` is the following:

```
public class OpenWeatherMap : IOpenWeatherMap
{
    //this is for sample data only
    //get your own developer key from https://openweathermap.org/
    private const string _key = "439d4b804bc8187953eb36d2a8c26a02";

    private readonly HttpClient _client;

    public OpenWeatherMap(HttpClient client)
    {
        this._client = client;
    }

    public async Task<OpenWeatherData> GetByCity(int id)
    {
```

```
        var response = await this._client.GetStringAsync($"/data/2.5
        /weather?id=${id}&appid=${_key}");

        var data =
JsonSerializer.Deserialize<OpenWeatherData>(response);

        return data;
    }
}
```

The only issue here is that you must change the key for your own use. This one is only used for sample purposes; you need to register with OpenWeatherMap and get your own key from `https://openweathermap.org/appid`.

 You can download the list of city codes from `http://bulk.openweathermap.org/sample/city.list.json.gz`.

Now, all we need to do is register this contract and its implementation in `ConfigureServices`:

```
services.AddHttpClient<IOpenWeatherMap,
OpenWeatherMap>("OpenWeatherMap", client =>
{
    client.BaseAddress = new
Uri("https://samples.openweathermap.org");
});
```

After this, you will be able to inject `IOpenWeatherMap` using dependency injection.

In this section, we learned how to use HTTP client factories to preprepare `HttpClient` instances for calling microservices. This has several advantages over creating instances on the fly and it is definitely something worth using.

Summary

In this chapter, we saw that if you want to serve some files on a filesystem, always specify a virtual path for it so as not to interfere with your controllers.

Using areas is a handy way to structure your content. They are particularly useful in big ASP.NET Core projects.

We also learned that to combine the usage of static files, directory browsing, and default documents, you can just call `UseFileServer`. You should also beware of unwanted file downloads, as it's not easy to apply security to them.

Then, we saw that resource files can be quite useful as we do not need to distribute the files separately from the assembly, and can use the same versioning as the rest of the code. They are definitely worth considering.

In the next section, we saw that we should use URL rewriting if we do not wish to expose the inner structure of our site, to comply with an externally defined URL, and to use hosted services to spawn background services automatically and have them linked to the application's lifetime.

EF Core is a useful tool, but it has a few gotchas when used in a web environment. Make sure you avoid lazy loading when returning data from a web API, use its asynchronous methods, and do not track changes to entities that you aren't going to modify.

Then, we introduced gRPC, which offers a high-performance framework for distributed programming that is language-agnostic and can, therefore, be very useful for putting disparate systems in communication.

Finally, we saw that `HTTPClient` factories can improve the readability and scalability of code that needs to call multiple microservices by registering the configuration needed for each in a central location and allowing the injection of clients through a dependency injection.

This chapter concludes our tour of the ASP.NET Core APIs. We looked at some of the less-used features that nevertheless play an important role in ASP.NET Core. In the next chapter, we will cover the different options we have regarding application deployment.

Questions

You should now be able to answer these questions:

1. What is gRPC?
2. What is the purpose of URL rewriting?
3. What are background services useful for?
4. What is the purpose of areas?
5. What are conventions useful for?
6. How can we execute code from a referenced assembly automatically?
7. Can we load files from inside assemblies?

19
Application Deployment

After reading the previous chapters and once you have implemented your application and tested it, and you are happy with it, it's time to deploy it. This will make it available to the outside world, or at least part of it!

In this chapter, we will see how we do that and explore some of the options available by covering the following topics:

- Deploying manually and compiling real-time changes
- Deploying using Visual Studio
- Deploying to IIS
- Deploying to NGINX
- Deploying to Azure
- Deploying to **Amazon Web Services** (**AWS**)
- Deploying to Docker
- Deploying as a Windows service

Technical requirements

To implement the examples introduced in this chapter, you will need the .NET Core 3 SDK and a text editor. Of course, Visual Studio 2019 (any edition) meets all of the requirements, but you can also use Visual Studio Code, for example.

If you will be deploying to the cloud (Azure or AWS), you will need a usable account on your provider of choice.

Deploying the application manually

To deploy the application manually, the `dotnet` command-line tool offers the `publish` command. In a nutshell, what it does is pack everything together, get all of the required dependencies from the project file, build the application and any dependent projects, and then copy all output to a target folder. It offers lots of options, but the most usual ones are probably the following:

hey are running from the user interface. Let's see how:

- `-c | --configuration`: This defines the build configuration. The default value is **Debug** and the other common option is **Release**, but of course, you can create other Visual Studio profiles.
- `-r | --runtime`: This publishes the application for a given runtime, in the case of self-contained deployments; the default is to use whatever runtime is available on the target machine. See the description in the *Self-contained deployments and runtimes* section.
- `-f | --framework`: This sets the target framework. See the following list in *Setting the target framework* section.
- `-o | --output`: This sets the path of the target output folder.
- `-h | --help`: This displays usage information.
- `-v | --verbosity`: This sets the build verbosity level—from level one of `q[uiet]` (no output), to `m[inimal]`, `n[ormal]`, `d[etailed]`, and `diag[nostic]` (highest level). The default is `n[ormal]`.
- `--force`: This forces all dependencies to be resolved even if the last restore was successful; it effectively deletes all output files and tries to retrieve them again.
- `--self-contained`: This publishes the .NET Core runtime together with your application so that it doesn't need to be installed on the target machine.

 For more information, please use the `help` command.

The following is an example of the `dotnet publish` command:

```
dotnet publish MyApplication -c Release -o /Output
```

It is worth mentioning that you can also pass parameters to MSBuild, by making use of the p flag:

```
dotnet publish /p:Foo=Bar
```

> Do not forget that the target environment is defined by the ASPNETCORE_ENVIRONMENT environment variable, so you may want to set it before calling dotnet publish.

See the next section for the list of supported target frameworks.

Setting the target framework

When you target a framework in an app or library, you're specifying the set of APIs that you'd like to make available to the app or library. If you target one of the .NET Standards, you are making it available on a wider set of platforms, for example, Linux will not have the full .NET Framework, but it will have .NET Standard. This framework is specified in the project file, but you can override it for a particular publication.

The monikers to use for the framework command are as follows:

Target framework	Name
.NET Standard	netstandard1.0 netstandard1.1 netstandard1.2 netstandard1.3 netstandard1.4 netstandard1.5 netstandard1.6 netstandard2.0 netstandard2.1
.NET Core	netcoreapp1.0 netcoreapp1.1 netcoreapp2.0 netcoreapp3.0 netcoreapp3.1 LTS

An example setting the framework could be as follows:

```
dotnet publish MyApplication -c Release -o /Output -f netcoreapp3.0
```

 For your information, I have only listed the most useful ones; you can find the full (and updated) list at: https://docs.microsoft. com/en-us/dotnet/standard/frameworks.

Let's now see the supported runtimes.

Self-contained deployments and runtimes

If you specify a target **runtime** for your app, you are also setting the default of **self-contained** to **true**. What this means is that the publish package will include everything it needs to run. This has some advantages and some disadvantages.

Here are its advantages:

- You have full control over the version of .NET that your app will run on.
- You can be assured that the target server will be able to run your app, as you are providing the runtime.

Here are the disadvantages:

- The size of the deployment package will be larger, as it includes the runtime; if you deploy many different apps with their own runtimes, this is likely to take lots of disk space.
- You need to specify the target platforms beforehand.

The names to use with the **runtime** command are composed of the following:

- A target operating system moniker
- A version
- An architecture

The examples for these include `ubuntu.14.04-x64`, `win7-x64`, and `osx.10.12-x64`. For a full list and the general specifications, please refer to `https://docs.microsoft.com/en-us/dotnet/core/rid-catalog`.

> You may want to have a look at `https://docs.microsoft.com/en-us/aspnet/core/publishing` and `https://docs.microsoft.com/en-us/dotnet/core/deploying` for a more in-depth introduction to deploying ASP.NET Core applications.

And finally, the next topic is monitoring the changes to the application and rebuilding them in real time.

Real-time rebuilding

A `dotnet` command that offers a functionality by which it can monitor, in real time, any changes to the code and automatically builds it in case it changes is `dotnet watch`. You can read all about it at: `https://docs.microsoft.com/en-us/aspnet/core/tutorials/dotnet-watch`.

In a nutshell, to use this, you need to add the `Microsoft.DotNet.Watcher.Tools` package to your project in the `.csproj` file:

```
<ItemGroup>
    <PackageReference Include="Microsoft.DotNet.Watcher.Tools"
Version="2.0.2" />
</ItemGroup>
```

After this, instead of issuing a `dotnet run` command, you would instead run `dotnet watch`:

```
dotnet watch run
```

That is enough with the command line; let's move on to Visual Studio.

Deploying with Visual Studio

Most of the time (for me, at least) we use Visual Studio for all of our development and publishing work. All of the options for `dotnet publish` are available in Visual Studio as well. We need to create a publish profile, which we can do by right-clicking the project in Visual Studio and clicking **Publish**, as shown in the following screenshot:

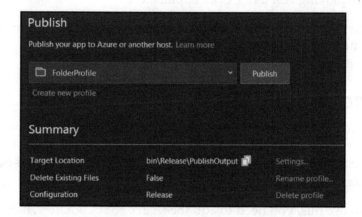

After this, we need to select a publish method from the choices of **File System**, **FTP**, **Web Deploy**, or **Web Deploy Package** (more on these two later).

Regardless of the `publish` method, we can configure the common publishing options by clicking on **Settings**, as shown here:

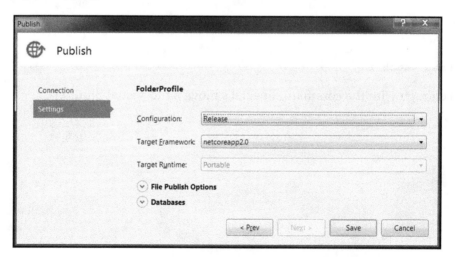

For a more in-depth guide, please refer to `https://docs.microsoft.com/en-us/aspnet/core/publishing/web-publishing-vs`.

Visual Studio publish profiles are stored in the `Properties\PublishProfiles` folder:

This section was about deployment with Visual Studio, but if the application is deployed to IIS, we can use it to deploy as well. Let's see how.

Deploying through IIS

Probably the most common server for the application deployment will be **Internet Information Server** (**IIS**). It actually happens that IIS merely acts as a **reverse proxy**, directing HTTP/HTTPS traffic to the .NET Core host. IIS hosting supports Windows 7 and above. It requires the **ASP.NET Core Module**, installed by default with Visual Studio 2019 and the .NET Core SDK.

Why would you use IIS rather than just Kestrel or HTTP.sys? IIS offers some more options to you, such as the following:

- **Authentication**: You can easily set up Windows authentication, for example.
- **Logging**: You can configure IIS to produce logs for all accesses.
- **Custom response**: IIS can serve different pages per HTTP response code.
- **Security**: You can set up HTTPS for your site, and it's easy to configure SSL certificates—IIS Manager even generates dummy ones.
- **Management**: It provides easy management, even from remote servers, using the **IIS Manager** tool.

You should have IIS/IIS Manager installed on the target machine and, in your host creating code, add support for IIS hosting. ASP.NET Core 3.x already does this by default, so no change is required.

You can use Visual Studio to automatically create the website for you at run time or publishing time, or you can do it yourself; the only two things that you need to keep in mind are the following:

- The application pool should not use a .NET CLR version (**no managed code**).
- The `AspNetCoreModule` module should be enabled.

If you remember, two of the publish methods were **Web Deploy** and **Web Deploy Package**. **Web Deploy** makes use of the **Web Deployment Agent Service** (**MsDepSvc**) Windows service that is installable through the Web Deployment Tool (`https://www.iis.net/downloads/microsoft/web-deploy`). If it is running, you can have Visual Studio directly connect to a remote (or local) site and install the web project there if you select the **Web Deploy** method, as shown here:

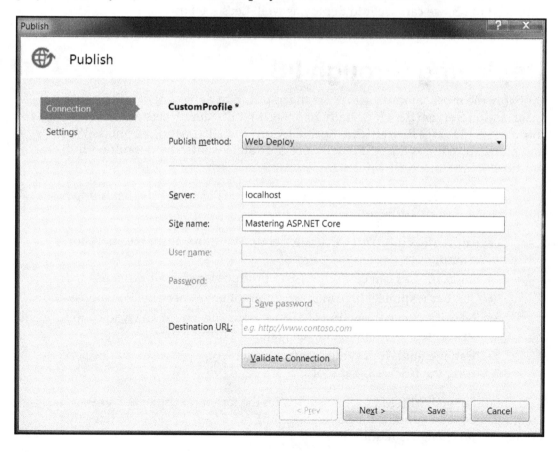

The **Web Deploy Package**, on the other hand, produces a `.zip` file containing a package that you can deploy through the IIS Manager console; just right-click on any site and select **Deploy | Import Server or Site Package...**:

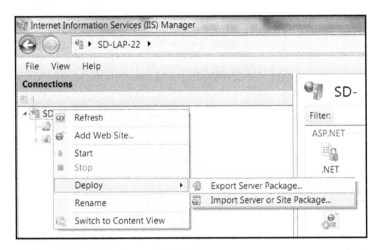

You may have noticed the `Web.config` file that is produced by `dotnet publish` (or the Visual Studio publish wizard). It is not used by ASP.NET Core but rather by the `AspNetCoreModule` module. It is only required if you wish to host your app behind IIS. You can tweak some settings, such as enabling output logging to a file:

```xml
<?xml version="1.0" encoding="utf-8"?>
<configuration>
  <system.webServer>
    <aspNetCore
      processPath="dotnet"
      arguments=".\MyApplication.dll"
      stdoutLogEnabled="true"
      stdoutLogFile=".\logs\stdout.log" />
  </system.webServer>
</configuration>
```

Here, I changed the `stdoutLogEnabled` and `stdoutLogFile` attributes; this should be pretty easy to understand.

 Once again, for the full documentation, please refer to `https://docs.microsoft.com/en-us/aspnet/core/publishing/iis`.

Ler's see now how to use NGINX for proxying requests to ASP.NET Core.

Deploying with NGINX

NGINX is a very popular reverse-proxy server for the Unix and Linux family of operating systems. Like IIS, it offers interesting features that are not provided out of the box by the ASP.NET Core hosts, such as caching requests, serving files straight from the filesystem, SSL termination, and others. You can configure it to forward requests to an ASP.NET Core application that is running standalone. This application needs to be modified to acknowledge forwarded headers as in the following:

```
app.UseForwardedHeaders(new ForwardedHeadersOptions
{
    ForwardedHeaders =
        ForwardedHeaders.XForwardedFor |
        ForwardedHeaders.XForwardedProto |
        ForwardedHeaders.XForwardedHost
});
```

What this code does is extract information from the headers, **X-Forwarded-For** (requesting the client IP and possibly the port), **X-Forwarded-Proto** (the requesting protocol), and **X-Forwarded-Host** (the requesting host), and sets it in the appropriate properties of the `HttpContext.Connection` property. This is because NGINX strips off this request information and stores it in these headers, so ASP.NET Core needs this, and that you can find it where you normally expect it.

We also need to configure NGINX to forward requests to ASP.NET Core (`/etc/nginx/sites-available/default`):

```
server
{
  listen 80;
  server_name server.com *.server.com;
  location /
  {
    proxy_pass http://localhost:5000;
    proxy_http_version 1.1;
    proxy_set_header Upgrade $http_upgrade;
    proxy_set_header Connection keep-alive;
    proxy_set_header Host $host;
    proxy_set_header X-Forwarded-For $proxy_add_x_forwarded_for;
    proxy_set_header X-Forwarded-Proto $scheme;
    proxy_cache_bypass $http_upgrade;
  }
}
```

This code sets up NGINX to listen to port `80` and to forward requests to `localhost` on port `5000`. The HTTP version is set to `1.1` and some additional headers (see the preceding .NET code). The server name is set to `server.com` but also accepts anything below `server.com`.

Read all about NGINX at: `https://docs.microsoft.com/en-us/aspnet/core/publishing/linuxproduction`.

Deploying to Azure

Microsoft Azure is also a very strong candidate for hosting your app. To publish to Azure, right-click on your project and select publish:

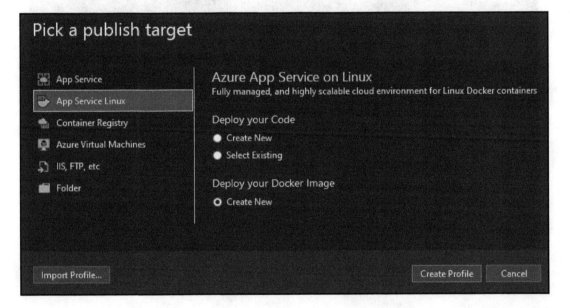

When creating a publish profile, select **Azure App Service** as the publish target:

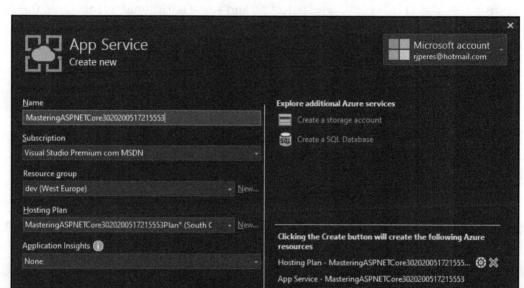

You will need to select all of the appropriate settings: **Subscription**, **Resource Group**, **App Service Plan**, and so on.

 Of course, you need to have a working Azure subscription. There is no need for resource groups or app service plans—these can be created from inside the Visual Studio publish wizard.

If you need more information, navigate to `https://docs.microsoft.com/en-us/aspnet/core/tutorials/publish-to-azure-webapp-using-vs`.

Deploying to AWS

AWS is the Amazon competitor to Microsoft Azure. It is a cloud provider that offers very similar features to Azure. Visual Studio can interact with it through the **AWS Toolkit for Visual Studio**, available for free from here: `https://marketplace.visualstudio.com/items?itemName=AmazonWebServices.AWSToolkitforVisualStudio2017`. You will, of course, need to have a working account with AWS.

We will see how we can deploy an ASP.NET Core app to AWS Elastic Beanstalk, Amazon's easy-to-use hosting and scaling service for web apps:

1. To deploy to Elastic Beanstalk, we must first create an environment using the AWS Elastic Beanstalk Console (`https://console.aws.amazon.com/ elasticbeanstalk`).

2. Then, we need to ZIP all our apps' contents, minus any third-party NuGet packages or binary outputs, and upload them to AWS. Luckily, AWS Toolkit for Visual Studio does all of this for us! Just right-click on the project in Solution Explorer and select **Publish to AWS Elastic Beanstalk**:

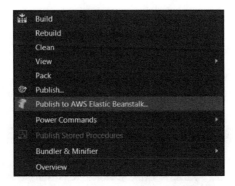

3. Then, you can specify all aspects of the deployment or just stick with the defaults, as shown here:

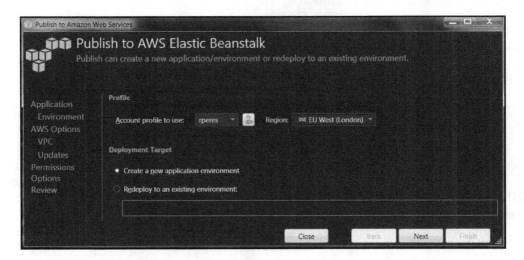

This was a very basic introduction to deployment to AWS. Next up, we have Docker.

Deploying with Docker

Docker offers an excellent option when it comes to creating and destroying containers very quickly, with the same exact contents. This way, you can be pretty sure that things will work as you expect them to!

Docker support comes built in for ASP.NET Core projects. When you create one, you get a **Dockerfile** in your project. It will contain something like this:

```
FROM mcr.microsoft.com/dotnet/core/aspnet:3.1
ARG source
WORKDIR /app
EXPOSE 80
COPY ${source:-obj/Docker/publish} .
ENTRYPOINT ["dotnet", "MyApplication.dll"]
```

Notice an extra solution folder called `docker-compose`. Docker Compose is the tool used to define and run multi-container Docker applications and you can read about it at: `https://docs.docker.com/compose`. In this folder, you will find three files:

- `docker-compose.ci.build.yml`: A Docker Compose file to be used for **Continuous Integration (CI)**
- `docker-compose.yml`: A base Docker Compose file used to define the collection of images to be built and run
- `docker-compose.override.yml`: An override to `docker-compose.yml` for the development environment

You can create files similar to `docker-compose.override.yml` for other environments.

The toolbar will add extra options for Docker:

You can run and even debug your app using Docker; it is transparent. Visual Studio 2019 introduced excellent support for containers. In the following screenshot, you can see the defined environment:

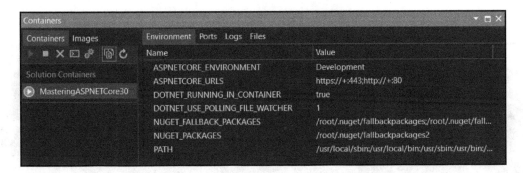

Here is the filesystem:

The following screenshot shows the execution logs:

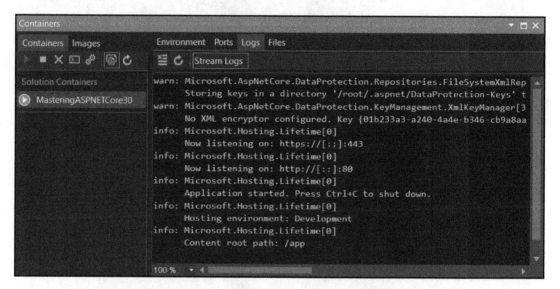

Even if you have multiple Docker projects in your solution, you will be able to jump seamlessly from one to the other while debugging, which is pretty cool! When building your project, you just need to make sure that Docker is running beforehand and the Docker image (`mcr.microsoft.com/dotnet/core/aspnet:3.1`) is available locally.

 Docker images for ASP.NET Core are listed at `https://hub.docker.com/_/microsoft-dotnet-core-aspnet`.
As of now, running under Docker requires **Docker For Windows** (`https://www.docker.com/docker-windows`).

For more information, jump to `https://docs.microsoft.com/en-us/aspnet/core/publishing/docker` and `https://docs.microsoft.com/en-us/aspnet/core/publishing/visual-studio-tools-for-docker`.

Docker is an invaluable tool for modern development and is at the root of cloud development, so I strongly suggest you have a look. But since we have to live with other setups, let's now see how we can deploy our app as a Windows service.

Deploying as a Windows service

A different alternative for deploying our apps is to host the ASP.NET Core app as a Windows service. Of course, this is inherently not portable as Windows services are only available, well, on Windows (Windows Docker containers do exist, of course). Anyway, sometimes, especially for simple apps/APIs, this is the best option because you can easily start and stop the service as you like, and easily see whether they are running from the user interface. Let's see how:

1. Start by adding the `Microsoft.AspNetCore.Hosting.WindowsServices` and `Microsoft.Extensions.Hosting.WindowsServices` NuGet packages.

2. Then, modify your `Program` class like this:

```
Host
    .CreateDefaultBuilder(args)
    .UseWindowsService()
    .ConfigureWebHostDefaults(builder =>
    {
        builder.UseStartup<Startup>();
    });
```

3. Then, use `dotnet publish` to deploy your app to a folder on your machine and then register and start the service with Windows:

```
sc create MyService binPath="C:\Svc\AspNetCoreService.exe"
sc start MyService
```

In summary, this will do the following:

- Set `WindowsServiceLifetime` as `IHostLifetime` of your app.
- Set the current directory as `AppContext.BaseDirectory`.
- Enable logging to the EventLog with the application name as the event source name.

The page at `https://docs.microsoft.com/en-us/aspnet/core/hosting/windows-service` contains all of this information and more; make sure you read it.

Summary

This chapter will help you to get a good understanding of the different hosting options available and how to use them. In particular, Azure, AWS, and Docker can be quite useful; both Azure and AWS fully support Docker, so make sure you consider all of them as part of your deployment strategy!

Even if it's convenient to use Visual Studio to deploy your apps, it is useful that you know how to do so using the command line, which is essentially what Visual Studio does.

Most of the time, we Windows developers will be deploying to IIS; so, you should learn how to use the Web Deployment Tools service and user interface. You can distribute the web deployment packages as `.zip` files quite easily. For users of other operating systems, NGINX is a popular option, with a vast community of users.

Docker is the new (cool) kid on the block; it provides unprecedented easiness in creating containers, which you can then just pick and deploy to Azure, AWS, or other cloud providers or just run on your local infrastructure.

A Windows service sometimes is useful for simple things; you can just start and stop it whenever you want and you don't need to care much about it. I don't expect you to be making much use of them, but it's nice to know that this option is available.

And this concludes this book. I hope you have enjoyed it—I certainly enjoyed writing it! Please let me and Packt know your thoughts about it and what could be improved in any future editions! Many thanks for your company!

Questions

So, by the end of this chapter, you should know the following:

1. What are the advantages of using IIS for exposing your app to the outside?
2. Why would you host your web app as a Windows service?
3. What is the advantage of using Docker?
4. What is a self-contained deployment?
5. Is it possible to detect changes and recompile the code automatically at runtime?
6. Can we deploy using the command line or do we need Visual Studio?
7. To what cloud providers can you deploy from inside Visual Studio?

20
Appendix A: The dotnet Tool

The dotnet Tool

The `dotnet` tool is the Swiss Army knife of .NET Core development. It can be used for a lot of things, from running and creating new projects, to building them, adding NuGet references, running unit tests—you name it. It is installed with the .NET Core **software development kit (SDK)**. Here, we will see some of the most useful commands that it has to offer.

By default, `dotnet` always operates with the latest .NET Core version it can find. You can list all of the installed versions through the `--info` argument, as follows:

```
dotnet --info
```

Build

This tool can be used to build a project or a whole solution. The command used for the build is `build`, and the most typical arguments are the following ones:

- `<solution | project>`: Builds a specific project or solution; if none is specified, it tries to find a single one in the current folder
- `-c <configuration>`: One of the configuration values, such as **Debug**, **Release**, and many others
- `-r <runtime>`: One of the supported runtime configurations, if you wish to target a specific one; for a list of the possible values, see Chapter 19, *Application Deployment*

- `-f <framework>`: One of the supported frameworks; for a list of the possible values, see Chapter 19, *Application Deployment*
- `-o <folder>`: The destination output directory; if not specified, it defaults to the current folder

In addition, the `clean` command cleans all previous builds, and it takes the same parameters, except the solution or project.

Creating projects from templates

It is sometimes useful to create projects from templates, even without using Visual Studio. The command for this is `new`, and typical arguments are the following ones:

- `-l`: Lists the available templates
- `<template> -name <name>`: Creates a project from a template with a given name; if no name is specified, it defaults to the current folder name
- `<template> -lang <lang>`: Creates a project from a template from a given language; supported languages are **C#**, **F#**, and **Visual Basic** (**VB**), **C#** being the default if not specified
- `-o <folder>`: The destination output directory; if not specified, it defaults to the current folder
- `--update-apply`: Updates the local templates

Unit testing

`dotnet` can list and run unit test projects by using the `test` command. The most common arguments are the following ones:

- `-t`: Lists tests
- `--filter <expression>`: Only executes tests that match the given expression; see https://aka.ms/vstest-filtering for the supported syntax
- `-d <logfile>`: Enables logging to a file
- `-r <folder>`: The folder in which to place the results
- `--blame`: Generates a file (`Sequence.xml`) that describes the run sequence, so as to isolate problems that caused the test host to crash

- `<solution | project>`: Builds a specific project or solution; if none is specified, it tries to find a single one in the current folder
- `-c <configuration>`: One of the configuration values, such as **Debug,** **Release**, and many others
- `-r <runtime>`: One of the supported runtime configurations, if you wish to target a specific one; for a list the possible values, see `Chapter 19`, *Application Deployment*
- `-f <framework>`: One of the supported frameworks; for a list of the possible values, see `Chapter 19`, *Application Deployment*
- `-o <folder>`: The destination output directory; if not specified, it defaults to the current folder

Managing package references

The `dotnet` tool can be used to add or remove references to NuGet packages or other projects to a project file. The command is either `add` or `remove`, and some common arguments are the following ones:

- `<project> package <nugetref>`: Add or remove a NuGet reference to a project; cannot be combined with `reference`
- `<project> reference <projectref>`: Add or remove a project reference to a project; the project reference must either be absolute or relative to the project where it is to be added; cannot be combined with `package`

Run

The tool can run a project, optionally restoring dependencies and building it first. By default, it builds the project with the default settings (profile, framework, and runtime) and restores all dependencies. The command is `run`, and typical arguments (which can be combined) are the following ones:

- `-p <project>`: The path to the project to run; if it is not supplied, it tries to find a single project or solution in the current folder
- `--launch-profile <profile>`: Runs a profile from `launchSettings.json`
- `--interactive`: Allows interactivity, such as asking for authentication or user input

- `--no-restore`: Does not restore dependencies (NuGet packages) before building
- `--no-dependencies`: Does not restore dependent project dependencies, only the target project
- `--force`: Forces dependencies to be resolved, even if the last restore failed
- `--no-build`: Does not build the project prior to running it; assumes that a version is already built
- `-v <verbosity>`: Sets the logging verbosity level for the output (**quiet**, **minimal**, **normal**, **detailed**, and **diagnostic**)
- `-c <configuration>`: One of the configuration values, such as **Debug**, **Release**, and many others
- `-r <runtime>`: One of the supported runtime configurations, if you wish to target a specific one; for a list of the possible values, see Chapter 19, *Application Deployment*
- `-f <framework>`: One of the supported frameworks; for a list of the possible values, see Chapter 19, *Application Deployment*

Publish

For publishing, the command is `publish`, and typical arguments are the following ones:

- `--manifest <manifest>`: The path to a manifest file that contains the list of packages to be excluded from the `publish` command
- `--self-contained`: Will publish the app as self-contained—that is, so that it does not need the .NET Core runtime installed on a target machine; cannot be combined with `--no-self-contained`
- `--no-self-contained`: Will publish the app so that it does require the .NET Core runtime installed on the target machine; cannot be combined with `--self-contained`; this is the default
- `--interactive`: Allows interactivity, such as asking for authentication or user input
- `--no-restore`: Does not restore dependencies (NuGet packages) before building
- `--no-dependencies`: Does not restore dependent project dependencies, only the target project
- `--force`: Forces dependencies to be resolved, even if the last restore failed

- `--no-build`: Does not build the project prior to running it; assumes that a version is already built
- `-v <verbosity>`: Sets the logging verbosity level for the output (**quiet**, **minimal**, **normal**, **detailed**, and **diagnostic**)
- `-o <folder>`: The destination output directory; if not specified, it defaults to the current folder
- `-c <configuration>`: One of the configuration values, such as **Debug**, **Release**, and many others
- `-r <runtime>`: One of the supported runtime configurations, if you wish to target a specific one; for a list of the possible values, see `Chapter 19`, *Application Deployment*
- `-f <framework>`: One of the supported frameworks; for a list of the possible values, see `Chapter 19`, *Application Deployment*

NuGet

There are several commands available for producing and publishing NuGet packages. First, we can pack a project as a NuGet package. This is achieved through the `pack` command, and typical arguments are the following ones:

- `<project | solution>`: Project or solution to pack
- `--include-symbols`: Includes packages with debug symbols
- `--include-source`: Includes `.pdb` and source files
- `--no-build`: Does not build the project prior to running it; assumes that a version is already built
- `-v <verbosity>`: Sets the logging verbosity level for the output (**quiet**, **minimal**, **normal**, **detailed**, and **diagnostic**)
- `--interactive`: Allows interactivity, such as asking for authentication or user input
- `--no-restore`: Does not restore dependencies (NuGet packages) before building
- `--no-dependencies`: Does not restore dependent project dependencies, only the target project
- `--force`: Forces dependencies to be resolved, even if the last restore failed
- `-o <folder>`: The destination output directory; if not specified, it defaults to the current folder

- `-c <configuration>`: One of the configuration values, such as **Debug**, **Release**, and many others
- `-r <runtime>`: One of the supported runtime configurations, if you wish to target a specific one; for a list of the possible values, see Chapter 19, *Application Deployment*
- `-f <framework>`: One of the supported frameworks; for a list of the possible values, see Chapter 19, *Application Deployment*

Once you have the NuGet file (`.nupkg`), you can publish it to a NuGet repository or remove an existing version. This is achieved through the `nuget` command, and these are the most common arguments:

- `push <package> -s <url> -k <apikey>`: Pushes a package with a specific version to a source server using an NuGet **application programming interface** (**API**) key
- `--skip-duplicate`: Ignores if the package and version already exists on the server
- `delete <package> -s <url> -k <apikey>`: Deletes a package with a specific version from a NuGet repository
- `locals -l`: Lists the local NuGet cache locations
- `locals -c <all | http-cache | global-packages | temp>`: Clears one of the specified NuGet caches; `all` clears all of them

Global tools

.NET Core has global tools that can be used as extensions to the `dotnet` tool; for example, user secrets and **Entity Framework** (**EF**) Core are global tools that are accessed and installed through `dotnet` itself. The command is `tool`, and some of the most common arguments are the following ones:

- `install <tool>`: Installs a tool; obviously incompatible with `uninstall` or `update`
- `uninstall <tool>`: Uninstalls a tool; cannot be used with `install` or `update`
- `update <tool>`: Updates a tool to the latest version; cannot be used with `install` or uninstall
- `-g`: Installs/uninstalls/updates the tool globally; if not specified, it operates on the local folder

- `--version <version>`: Installs a specific version; only for `install`
- `list`: Lists the installed tools
- `restore`: Restores the tools specified in a manifest file; cannot be used with `-g`
- `--tool-manifest <manifest>`: The path to a manifest file
- `--configfile <file>`: Specifies the path to a NuGet configuration file
- `--add-source <location>`: Adds an additional package source; `<location>` can be a NuGet repository **Uniform Resource Locator (URL)** or a local folder

Tools can either be installed globally in a default, operating system-specific location that is added to the path or locally, in a `bin` folder. Tools are installed from NuGet repositories.

User secrets

`dotnet` can be used to manage user secrets too. The command is `user-secrets`, and the most used arguments are the following ones:

- `-p <project>`: The path to the project to run; if it is not supplied, it tries to find a single project or solution in the current folder
- `-c <configuration>`: One of the configuration values, such as **Debug**, **Release**, and many others
- `clear`: Clears the user secrets
- `init`: Initializes the user secrets database
- `list`: Lists the current keys
- `remove <key>`: Removes a secret key
- `set <key> <value>`: Sets a key value
- `--id <id>`: The user secret's ID to use; it is normally specified on the `.csproj` file

File watcher

The `dotnet` tool, through the `watch` extension, can be used to run a command while monitoring the files under a folder. It is useful for detecting changes to files and reacting immediately to them. Any command can be run through `watch`, and the **Microsoft Build (MSBuild)** `.csproj` syntax supports specifying exclusions to extensions or files that need not be monitored. The command is `watch`, and any other commands that you would pass to `dotnet` can be passed after it, such as, for example, the following:

```
dotnet watch test
```

By default, `watch` tracks all file extensions; if you wish to exclude and include only certain ones, you can specify them on a `.csproj` file, using global patterns, as follows:

```
<ItemGroup>
    <Watch Include="**\*.js"
Exclude="node_modules\**\*;**\*.js.map;obj\**\*;bin\**\*" />
</ItemGroup>
```

This monitors all `.js` files except any files under `node_modules`, `obj`, or `bin`, and any files ending with `.js.map`. It is also possible to specify on a file-by-file basis which files should not be monitored on a project file. It goes like this:

```
<ItemGroup>
    <Compile Include="File.cs" Watch="false" />
    <EmbeddedResource Include="Resource.resx" Watch="false" />
    <ProjectReference Include="..\ClassLibrary\ClassLibrary.csproj"
Watch="false" />
</ItemGroup>
```

In this example, we can see that we turned off monitoring for a single file, an embedded resource, and a whole project reference.

EF Core

The way to have EF Core interact with a database is also through `dotnet`—specifically, the `ef` tool. Here are a few useful commands:

- `database drop`: Drops the target database
- `database drop -f`: Forces the drop operation without confirmation

- `database drop --dry-run`: Shows what would be dropped, but does not actually do it
- `database update <0 | migration>`: Updates the target database to a specific migration; if none (or 0) is specified, it defaults to the latest
- `-c <context>`: The context type name or fully qualified type name; if not specified, it must be the only context on the target project
- `-p <project>`: The project to use for the context
- `-s <startupproject>`: The startup project to use
- `--no-build`: Does not build the project prior to running it; assumes that a version is already built
- `--configuration <configuration>`: One of the configuration values, such as **Debug**, **Release**, and many others
- `-r <runtime>`: One of the supported runtime configurations, if you wish to target a specific one; for a list the possible values, see `Chapter 19`, *Application Deployment*
- `-f <framework>`: One of the supported frameworks; for a list of the possible values, see `Chapter 19`, *Application Deployment*
- `migrations add <migration>`: Creates a new migration with a given name
- `migrations add <migration> -o <folder>`: The destination output directory; if not specified, it defaults to **Migrations**
- `migrations list`: Lists the existing migrations
- `migrations remove`: Removes the latest migration
- `migrations script <0 | from> <to>`: Generates a **Structured Query Language** (**SQL**) script with the changes from the source migration (which, if not specified, defaults to the initial one) to the target one (if not specified, is the last)
- `dbcontext list`: Lists the available contexts on the target project
- `dbcontext info`: Shows info about a specific context; requires the -c parameter

- `dbcontext scaffold <connection> <provider>`: Generates **Plain Old Common Language Runtime (CLR) Object (POCO)** classes for a specific connection string and provider
- `--schema <schema>`: The schema name for which to generate POCO classes; multiple ones can be supplied; if none, all schemas are included
- `--table <table>`: The table name for which to generate POCO classes; multiple ones can be supplied; if none, all tables are selected
- `--use-database-names`: Instead of using C#-like names, use the names as they are in the database
- `-d`: Uses attributes to configure the model generated from `scaffold`
- `--context-dir <path>`: The path on which to place the generated context

Assessments

Chapter 1

1. **What are the benefits of dependency injection?**

   It allows better separation of the interface and the actual implementation and lets us change the implementation at any time. It also recursively injects all required dependencies.

2. **What are environments?**

   A named set of startup values.

3. **What does MVC mean?**

   Easy peasy: model-view-controller!

4. **What are the supported lifetimes in the built-in dependency injection container?**

   `Transient` (a new instance is created every time), `Scoped` (a new instance is created on each HTTP request and always returned), and `Singleton` (a single instance is created).

5. **What is the difference between .NET Core and .NET Standard?**

   .NET Standard is just a standard set of APIs that is implemented by .NET and .NET Core, among others.

6. **What is a metapackage?**

   A set of packages, as defined by Microsoft. It contains all the packages that you will typically need for a simple ASP.NET Core project.

7. **What is OWIN?**

   OWIN stands for **Open Web Interface for .NET**, and you can read about it at `http://owin.org`. Essentially, it's a specification for decoupling a web application from a particular server, like IIS.

Chapter 2

1. **What is the root interface for retrieving configuration values?**

   It's `IConfiguration`. It's where `IConfigurationRoot` and `IConfigurationSection` inherit from.

2. **What are the built-in file-based configuration providers in .NET Core?**

   JSON, XML, and INI.

3. **Is it possible to bind configurations to POCO classes out of the box?**

   Yes, but we need to add the `Microsoft.Extensions.Configuration.Binder` NuGet package.

4. **What is the difference between the `IOptions<T>` and `IOptionsSnapshot<T>` interfaces?**

   `IOptionsSnapshot<T>` gets updated whenever the underlying configuration changes (if we configured it for that), but `IOptions<T>` always retains the original configured value.

5. **Do we need to register the configuration object explicitly in the dependency injection container?**

   No. As of ASP.NET Core 2.0, `IConfiguration` is injected automatically.

6. **How can we have optional configuration files?**

   When registering a file-based configuration file, set the `optional` parameter to `true`.

7. **Is it possible to get notifications whenever a configuration changes?**

   Yes. We need to get a reload token and then register in it a change callback delegate.

Chapter 3

1. **What are the special route tokens?**

   [controller], [action], and [area].

2. **How can we prevent a route from being selected depending on the request's HTTP verb?**

   Apply one of the [HttpPost], [HttpGet], [HttpPut], or other HTTP attributes to its action method.

3. **How can we prevent a route from being selected unless the request uses HTTPS?**

   Apply the [RequireHttps] attribute to the route's action method.

4. **How can we serve different views depending on the HTTP error code that occurred?**

   One way is to use either UseStatusCodePagesWithRedirects or UseStatusCodePagesWithReExecute inside the Configure method of the Startup class, create an action method on a controller that responds to the specific error code (for example, /error/401) by adding an [HttpGet("error/401")] attribute to it.

5. **How can we prevent methods in controllers from being called?**

   The best way is to apply a [NonAction] attribute to the methods that we want to hide.

6. **How can we force a route value to be of a particular type (for example, a number)?**

   Add the number validation token—for example, [HttpGet("{id:number}")].

7. **What is a route handler?**

   It's the implementation of the IRouter interface that actually processes the request. For MVC, it is normally the MvcRouteHandler class, which is added to the pipeline by the UseMvc extension method.

Chapter 4

1. **What is the default validation provider for the model state?**

   It is the Data Annotations API.

2. **What is an action?**

   A method that can be called on a controller in response to an HTTP request.

3. **What is globalization and how does it differ from localization?**

   Globalization means your application will support multiple cultures. Localization is the process of making your application work and react accordingly to a specific culture.

4. **What is temporary data used for?**

   Temporary data is used to persist data between two subsequent requests for the same client, like a micro-session.

5. **What is a cache good for?**

   A cache is useful for data that either takes a long time to produce or to retrieve. We store such data in the cache and can quickly access it.

6. **What is a session?**

   A session is a group of user interactions with a website that takes place within a given time frame. Each interaction is associated with the session by means of session ID.

7. **What are the benefits of a controller inheriting from the** `Controller` **base class?**

   The `Controller` class offers some useful methods that are not present in `ControllerBase`, such as methods to return views (`View`).

Chapter 5

1. **What is the base class for a view?**

   It's RazorPage<T>, where the T generic type is dynamic by default.

2. **How can you inject services into a view?**

   Either by using the @inject declaration on a .cshtml file or by inheriting from the RazorPage<T> class and using constructor injection.

3. **What is a view location expander?**

   It's a component that can be used to tell ASP.NET Core where to look for the physical .cshtml files.

4. **What is a view layout?**

   It is similar to master pages in ASP.NET Classic. Essentially, it defines the layout, or structure, that different pages can use.

5. **What are partial views?**

   Partial views are similar to web user controls (.ascx files) in ASP.NET Classic. They are files containing reusable markup and possibly code that is meant to be reused across different views.

6. **What functionality can replace partial views?**

   View components.

7. **What does the special file _ViewStart.cshtml do?**

   Whatever code, @using, or @inject declarations you put in it is executed before the actual view.

Chapter 6

1. **What is the default validation provider?**

   It's the data annotations validator.

2. **What do we call the methods that are used to render HTML fields?**

   HTML helpers.

3. **What is model metadata?**

   It's the code that describes what a model's properties are, such as their display name, whether or not they are required, what validation should they use, and so on.

4. **Does ASP.NET Core support client-side validation?**

   Yes, it does.

5. **What is the base interface that can be bound to an uploaded file?**

   `IFormFile`.

6. **What is unobtrusive validation?**

   It's the process by which adding a couple of JavaScript libraries automatically sets up validation, based on some conventions.

7. **How can we perform server-side validation?**

   By leveraging the `[Remote]` attribute and implementing a validation action method on a controller.

Chapter 7

1. **What attribute can we use to mark a method or controller so that it can only be called through HTTPS?**

   `[RequireHttps]`.

2. **What is the difference between role-based and policy-based authorization?**

   Policy-based authorization is more powerful; it can use both roles or any other custom requirement that you can think of.

3. **What is the purpose of CORS?**

   CORS is a mechanism by which servers can tell the browsers to bypass their normal security restrictions and allow the loading of static resources (normally scripts) from different sources (servers).

4. **What is the purpose of HSTS?**

   It is a web policy for telling the browsers that they should only interact with a server through HTTPS. It is specified in RFC 6797.

5. **What is the challenge stage of the authentication process?**

   The challenge is when the server asks the client for valid credentials.

6. **Why should we take care when binding requests to model classes?**

   We do not want sensitive information that should not be provided by the client to be bound to the model.

7. **What is the sliding expiration of a cookie?**

   It means that on each request, the cookie is renewed for the same amount of time that it was initially set to.

Chapter 8

1. **What is OData?**

   OData is an open protocol for exposing and consuming queryable RESTful data models.

2. **What is content negotiation?**

   It is a process by which the client and the server agree on the type of content that is to be returned.

3. **Why is it not suitable to use cookies for authentication in web APIs?**

   Because usually the client for these APIs will not be a web browser, and therefore may not have the capacity to store cookies.

4. **What are the different ways by which we can ask for a specific version of our API?**

   The query string or an HTTP header.

5. **What is the purpose of conventions in regard to action methods?**

   A convention allows us to define the return type and HTTP status code that is returned from each action method, and any exceptions that may arise.

6. **What are problem details?**

   A way to return error information in a standard way. Problem details are defined in RFC 7807.

7. **What is REST?**

   An architectural style for defining web services, designed for interoperability, that relies on HTTP verbs, URLs, and headers.

Chapter 9

1. **How can we load partial views from a different assembly?**

   By using embedded resources, or better, Razor class libraries.

2. **What are the two ways to render partial views?**

   One is to use the `Html.PartialAsync` method and the other is to use the `<partial>` tag helper.

3. **What is the difference between tag helpers and tag helper components?**

   Tag helpers render a component instead of a custom or an HTML tag, and a tag helper component allows us to intercept and possibly modify all HTML tags before they are rendered.

4. **How can we restrict what is displayed on a view depending on the environment?**

   By using the `<environment>` tag helper.

5. **What is the difference between Razor class libraries and class libraries?**

   Razor class libraries allow us to make static resources available to web projects very easily, whereas class libraries are only about code.

6. **What are embedded resources?**

   Static files (images, text, and others) that are included inside assemblies and can be retrieved from them.

7. **What are the two syntaxes for executing view components?**

   One is the code syntax—`Component.InvokeAsync("mycomponent", new { arg1 = "...", arg2 = 123 })`—and the other is markup—`<mycomponent arg1="..." arg2="123"/>`.

Chapter 10

1. **What are the two interfaces that are used to control authorization to a resource?**

   `IAuthorizationFilter` and `IAsyncAuthorizationFilter`.

2. **Why are there two versions of each kind of filter?**

   There is always an asynchronous version, which should probably be preferred.

3. **How can we apply a filter by specifying its type on an action method?**

   Either through the `ServiceFilterAttribute` or `TypeFilterAttribute`.

4. **How can we apply an ordering to the application of filters?**

   When applying a filter using attributes, we can use the `Order` property.

5. **What are the different levels to which we can apply filters?**

   Global, controller, and action method.

6. **How can we pass context from one filter to others?**

   Using the `HttpContext.Items` collection.

7. **How can filters make use of dependency injection?**

   The `[ServiceFilter]` can obtain filters from DI depending on their type.

Chapter 11

1. **Do Razor Pages use code-behind?**

   Yes, they can, but it is not mandatory. The code-behind class must inherit from `PageModel` and be located together with the `.cshtml` file.

2. **What is the purpose of the Page Model?**

   It is where the handlers for the different HTTP verbs (`GET`, `POST`, and so on) are implemented.

3. **What are page handlers?**

   They are the code that processes the requests inside a `PageModel` class.

4. **How can we restrict a Razor Page from being called by anonymous users?**

   We add a convention using the `AllowAnonymousToPage` extension method when configuring Razor Page options with the `AddRazorPagesOptions` method, following `AddMvc`.

5. **What are the two ways by which we can inject services into a Razor Page?**

   One way is to use constructor injection on the `PageModel` class and the other is by using the `@inject` directive on the `.cshtml` file.

6. **Do Razor Pages use page layouts?**

   Yes—just make sure you keep them separated from the other view layouts.

7. **Where are Razor Pages served by default?**

   The `Pages` folder.

Chapter 12

1. **What are event counters?**

   Lightweight code that is emitted by the applications and picked up by the operating system.

2. **What is the benefit of telemetry?**

   To centralize the storing of logs and events and monitor applications from a single dashboard.

3. **How can we filter logging?**

   By category name or log level.

4. **What are health checks?**

   They indicate how well our application or dependencies (for example, databases, external services, and so on) are.

5. **How is middleware useful in logging?**

   It can sit in the middle of the request and log before and after the request is processed.

6. **What is ELM?**

   Error logging middleware—it is used to view events raised during the processing of a request.

7. **What are the benefits of diagnostics over common logging?**

   Diagnostics offers strong typed events and integration with ELM for the easy viewing of events.

Chapter 13

1. **What are the more popular unit test frameworks?**

   NUnit, xUnit, and MSTest.

2. **What is the benefit of mocking?**

   Substituting dependencies.

3. **What is the difference between unit and integration testing?**

   A unit test should be fast, not have any side effects, and should only test a specific operation, whereas an integration test works on a much bigger scale.

4. **What is TDD?**

   Test-driven development: a methodology that advocates starting with the unit tests.

5. **What are the limitations of unit tests?**

   They usually do not test aspects such as user interfaces or database operations.

6. **How can we pass data automatically to unit tests?**

   All of the studied unit test frameworks allow the passing of data from attributes to test methods.

7. **What does red-green-refactor mean?**

   It's a practice of TDD where we start by writing the tests, which initially fail (red), then we make them pass (green), and only then should we worry about refactoring the code so as to make it more efficient.

Chapter 14

1. **What are the benefits of TypeScript?**

    It has strong typing and is a full object-oriented programming model.

2. **Does JavaScript only run on browsers?**

    No—it can also run on the server side.

3. **What are SPAs?**

    Single-page applications, applications based on JavaScript that call server-side functionality through AJAX-style calls.

4. **What is the purpose of Library Manager?**

    To install client-side libraries in local projects.

5. **Are the templates for dotnet SPA frameworks hardcoded?**

    No—they are available as NuGet packages, and can be installed and updated.

6. **How can we run JavaScript code from .NET Core?**

    NodeServices provides this functionality.

7. **Name a few SPA frameworks that have dotnet templates.**

    Vue, React, Angular, Aurelia, and Knockout.

Chapter 15

1. **What are the two hosts available to ASP.NET Core 3?**

    Kestrel and HTTP.sys.

2. **What are the two kinds of cache that are available?**

    In-memory and distributed.

3. **What is the benefit of compressing a response?**

   Minimizing the latency of the response.

4. **What is the purpose of caching a response?**

   Avoiding the need to request and send responses.

5. **Do asynchronous actions improve performance?**

   No, but they improve scalability.

6. **What is bundling?**

   Bundling is the combining of multiple files in a single response.

7. **What are profilers good for?**

   They can show us what parts of our code are taking the most time to execute.

Chapter 16

1. **What are the two serialization formatters supported by SignalR?**

   JSON and Message Pack.

2. **What transports does SignalR support?**

   AJAX long polling, WebSockets, and server-sent events.

3. **What are the benefits of the Message Pack protocol?**

   Message Pack is more compact, thereby resulting in lower latency.

4. **Which targets can we send messages to?**

   Single recipient, all users, or groups of users.

5. **Why would we restrict the transport to be used by SignalR?**

   Some transports might not be supported or might be restricted—for example, WebSockets.

6. **Can we send messages to SignalR from outside the web application where it is hosted?**

    Yes.

7. **Can we use authentication with SignalR?**

    Yes.

Chapter 17

1. **What is the difference between a page and a component?**

    The only difference between the two is that pages can be directly accessed from the browser.

2. **What is the difference between the Server and WebAssembly hosting models?**

    The Server model relies on SignalR to communicate to and from the server, whereas WebAssembly lives only on the client that is being compiled to `webassembly`, hence the name. WebAssembly can work while disconnected.

3. **Can we use tag helpers in Blazor pages?**

    No, we can't (in `.razor` files).

4. **Is it possible to access the containing web page from inside Blazor?**

    Yes, it is, using JavaScript interoperability.

5. **Does Blazor support dependency injection?**

    Yes, it does, but not constructor injection.

6. **Do Blazor page layouts support regions?**

   Yes, but only a single region—body.

7. **What is the difference between the different rendering modes of a component?**

   The difference lies in performance and capacities: `Static` is fastest, but does not support server events, `Server` is the slowest and cannot take parameters, and `ServerPrerendered` is a tradeoff between the two—a part of the component is prerendered, but the actual interaction only starts when the page fully loads.

Chapter 18

1. **What is gRPC?**

   gRPC is Google Remote Procedure Call, a cross-platform technology for implementing web services that are agnostic regarding the technology.

2. **What is the purpose of URL rewriting?**

   Presenting user-friendly URLs that will be translated to something meaningful to the application.

3. **What are background services useful for?**

   Running tasks on the background.

4. **What is the purpose of areas?**

   Physically and conceptually separating parts of the application.

5. **What are conventions good for?**

   Automatically enforcing defaults.

6. **How can we execute code from a referenced assembly automatically?**

   By adding a `[HostingStartup]` attribute to a library and by including it in the `ASPNETCORE_HOSTINGSTARTUPASSEMBLIES` environment variable.

7. **Can we load files from inside assemblies?**

   Yes—either as embedded resources or from Razor class libraries.

Chapter 19

1. **What are the advantages of using IIS for exposing your app to the outside?**

   You can add logging and Windows authentication, for example.

2. **Why would you host your web app as a Windows Service?**

   It makes it easier to start and stop and to see whether the service is running.

3. **What is the advantage of using Docker?**

   You can accurately control the dependencies and the running environment.

4. **What is a self-contained deployment?**

   It is a deployment that does not require .NET Core to be installed on the target machine.

5. **Is it possible to detect changes and recompile the code automatically at runtime?**

   Yes—we just need to run the `dotnet watch` command.

6. **Can we deploy using the command line or do we need Visual Studio?**

   We can use both the command line (`dotnet`) or Visual Studio.

7. **To what cloud providers can you deploy from inside Visual Studio?**

   Azure and AWS are two examples.

Other Books You May Enjoy

If you enjoyed this book, you may be interested in these other books by Packt:

C# 8 and .NET Core 3 Projects Using Azure - Second Edition
Paul Michaels, Dirk Strauss, Et al

ISBN: 978-1-78961-208-0

- Understand how to incorporate the Entity Framework Core 3 to build ASP.NET Core MVC applications
- Create a real-time chat application using Azure's SignalR service
- Gain hands-on experience of working with Cosmos DB
- Develop an Azure Function and interface it with an Azure Logic App
- Explore user authentication with Identity Server and OAuth2
- Understand how to use Azure Cognitive Services to add advanced functionalities with minimal code
- Get to grips with running a .NET Core application with Kubernetes

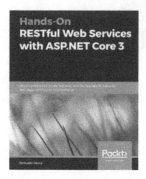

Hands-On RESTful Web Services with ASP.NET Core 3
Samuele Resca

ISBN: 978-1-78953-761-1

- Gain a comprehensive working knowledge of ASP.NET Core
- Integrate third-party tools and frameworks to build maintainable and efficient services
- Implement patterns using dependency injection to reduce boilerplate code and improve flexibility
- Use ASP.NET Core's out-of-the-box tools to test your applications
- Use Docker to run your ASP.NET Core web service in an isolated and self-contained environment
- Secure your information using HTTPS and token-based authentication
- Integrate multiple web services using resiliency patterns and messaging techniques

Leave a review - let other readers know what you think

Please share your thoughts on this book with others by leaving a review on the site that you bought it from. If you purchased the book from Amazon, please leave us an honest review on this book's Amazon page. This is vital so that other potential readers can see and use your unbiased opinion to make purchasing decisions, we can understand what our customers think about our products, and our authors can see your feedback on the title that they have worked with Packt to create. It will only take a few minutes of your time, but is valuable to other potential customers, our authors, and Packt. Thank you!

Index